PANJABI

A Comprehensive Grammar

Panjabi: A Comprehensive Grammar is a complete reference guide to Panjabi grammar.

It presents a fresh, accessible and thorough description of the language, concentrating on the real patterns of use in modern Panjabi. The book moves from the script and sound through morphology and word classes to a detailed analysis of sentence structures and semantic features.

The volume is organised to promote a thorough understanding of Panjabi grammar. It offers a stimulating analysis of the complexities of the language, and provides full and clear explanations. Throughout, the emphasis is on Panjabi as used by present-day native speakers.

An extensive index and numbered paragraphs provide readers with easy access to the information they require.

Features include:

- detailed treatment of the common grammatical structures and parts of speech
- extensive exemplification
- particular attention to areas of confusion and difficulty
- Gurmukhi script and transliteration and provided throughout
- additional chapter on the Shahmukhi script.

Panjabi: A Comprehensive Grammar is an essential reference source for the learner and user of Panjabi. With clear and simple explanations it will remain the standard reference work for years to come for learners and linguists alike. A Workbook and Reader to accompany this Grammar can be downloaded from https://www.routledge.com/products/9781138793866.

Mangat Rai Bhardwaj is a native speaker of Panjabi with a Ph.D. in linguistics from the University of Manchester. He has taught Panjabi, Hindi-Urdu, English and translation and interpreting in colleges and worked as a freelance translator and interpreter.

Routledge Comprehensive Grammars

Comprehensive Grammars are available for the following languages:

Bengali
Burmese
Cantonese
Catalan
Chinese
Danish
Dutch
Greek
Indonesian
Japanese
Kazakh
Korean
Modern Welsh
Modern Written Arabic
Polish
Slovene
Swedish
Ukrainian

Panjabi

A Comprehensive Grammar

Mangat Rai Bhardwaj

Routledge
Taylor & Francis Group
LONDON AND NEW YORK

First published 2016
by Routledge
2 Park Square, Milton Park, Abingdon, Oxon OX14 4RN

and by Routledge
711 Third Avenue, New York, NY 10017

Routledge is an imprint of the Taylor & Francis Group, an informa business

Publisher's Note
This book has been prepared from camera-ready copy provided by the author.

British Library Cataloguing in Publication Data
A catalogue record for this book is available from the British Library

Library of Congress Cataloging in Publication Data
Names: Bhardwaj, Mangat Rai, 1946- author.
Title: Panjabi : a comprehensive grammar / Mangat Rai Bhardwaj.
Description: Milton Park, Abingdon, Oxon ; New York, NY : Routledge, [2016] | Series: Routledge Comprehensive Grammars | Includes bibliographical references and index.
Identifiers: LCCN 2015042069| ISBN 9781138793859 (hardback : alk. paper) | ISBN 9781138793866 (pbk. : alk. paper) | ISBN 9781315760803 (ebook)
Subjects: LCSH: Panjabi language--Grammar. | Panjabi language--Spoken Panjabi. | Panjabi language--Textbooks for foreign speakers--English.
Classification: LCC PK2633 .B396 2016 | DDC 491.4/282421--dc23
LC record available at http://lccn.loc.gov/2015042069

ISBN: 978-1-138-79385-9 (hbk)
ISBN: 978-1-138-79386-6 (pbk)
ISBN: 978-1-315-76080-3 (ebk)

Designed, illustrated and typeset in Times, Arial and LokLipi
by Mangat Rai Bhardwaj

MIX
Paper from responsible sources
FSC® C013056

Printed and bound in Great Britain by
TJ International Ltd, Padstow, Cornwall

श्रीशब्दब्रह्मणे नमः

ਜੇਤਾ ਸਬਦੁ ਸੁਰਤਿ ਧੁਨਿ ਤੇਤੀ ਜੇਤਾ ਰੂਪੁ ਕਾਇਆ ਤੇਰੀ।

- Guru Nanak Dev

Our little systems have their day;
They have their day and cease to be:
They are but broken lights of thee,
And thou, O Lord, art more than they.

- Alfred Tennyson

Table of Contents

Part III: Grammar and Meaning

Part IV: Appendices, Glossary and Indexes

Preface

While anybody is welcome to use/read this book, I had two types of users in mind – (i) fairly advanced learners of the language and (ii) students and professionals in the field of theoretical and "applied" linguistics (such as speech therapy, translation theory, language teaching, first and second language acquisition theory, psycholinguistics etc.) *in this order of priority*. I regard as "fairly advanced" learners those who have successfully gone through my *Colloquial Panjabi* and *Colloquial Panjabi 2* (or similar courses) if they learnt Panjabi as a second/foreign language. A grammar book such as this one is not a primary language learning tool. It is meant to be a *reference* grammar to be used by the fairly advanced learners of a language to *rationally understand and consolidate* their existing competence in order to take it further. If Panjabi is their mother tongue, I regard them as fairly advanced learners/users if they are interested in learning more about the structure of their language for various reasons – for example, studying the language of the holy Sikh scripture after obtaining a better knowledge of the grammatical structure of modern Panjabi, or teaching Panjabi linguistics at the postgraduate level, or teaching Panjabi as a foreign language. So the complexity of the language as used in real life is faced head-on, and not avoided, in this book. Many salient grammatical features of Panjabi, ignored by the past grammarians, are dealt with for the first time in this book. Most chapters of this book have a section "For teachers and other more advanced users" which gives, in an outline form, some more technical information about the phonological and grammatical structural features of Panjabi. It has been one of the principles of good language pedagogy since remote antiquity that teachers should know much more than they are supposed to teach and should be able to answer the learners' "why" questions in addition to teaching them "how" skills in language comprehension and production. These sections can be skipped by the users not interested in them. (They do not become any *less* advanced by doing so!) However, I am sure that if they get addicted to such technicalities, they will start enjoying them. All such technicalities are fully explained and no previous knowledge of linguistics is assumed. But I must also add that even at other places (especially in the later chapters), this book presents ideas which will challenge many of the pre-conceived notions of many people and jolt them out of their Eurocentric prejudices into fresh thinking about the grammatical structures of other languages. I hope that any serious advanced learners of Panjabi (and other North Indian languages) will welcome them.

Having been an advanced learner of Hindi-Urdu and English as my second and third language respectively, and having been trained as a theoretical linguist, I believe that I understand fairly well what these two types of users of grammar books such as this one generally look for. As my mother tongue, Panjabi is "in my blood" and I have "the native speaker's intuitions" about what the various constructions of the language *really mean* or *tend to mean* in different contexts and situations. I can both *judge* the Panjabi constructions *from outside* as well as *participate* in the process of their genesis and *feel them from inside*.

Grammar books can be placed on a continuum, with the pedagogical ones at the one end and the theoretical ones at the other and the descriptive ones in the middle (Leech 2006: 2). I would like to regard this book as a descriptive grammar looking both ways. Having presented pedagogical grammar of Panjabi (albeit in an outline form) in my books mentioned above, I believe that the fairly advanced learners of Panjabi should be able to move on to a descriptive reference grammar. But no grammar (not even a pedagogical one) can be one hundred percent theory-neutral. The writer of a book such as this one has to make a choice from the traditionally accepted views and terminology and her/his own theoretical views (if she/he *explicitly* holds any). The choice is nearly always some sort of subjective compromise.

I think that it would be appropriate for me to mention my own academic and theoretical background and professional experience here and how I came to develop the views underlying this book. I was trained as a theoretical linguist but I never practised academic linguistics. So I never felt obliged or pressurised to toe the line of any linguist or school of linguistics. All my working life, I worked as a teacher of Panjabi, Hindi-Urdu and English. For about four years (1982–86), I worked as a researcher (or "applied linguist") on the European Science Foundation Project on Second Language Acquisition by Adult Immigrants. The experience of my interaction with my European colleagues on this project with "universalistic" persuasions and commitments helped me clearly define and consolidate my own thinking as a linguist and learn something extremely valuable – how *not* to analyse and study a language.

Apart from teaching Panjabi, Hindi-Urdu and English, I also taught translation and interpreting in two colleges in the UK. More significantly, I also work as a freelance translator and interpreter in all sorts of situations including civil and criminal courts in the UK.

In linguistics, I am strongly sceptical of "language universals". A search for these "universals" has been a hallmark of Western thinking from Plato onwards, dominated by the dualism of being and experience, what something really is (or its true being) hidden behind "mere appearances" through which it manifests itself. When European scholars (mostly missionaries, civil servants or army officers) wrote grammars of the languages of the people subjected to European rule, they endeavoured to fit by violence the varieties found in other languages (or "mere appearances") into the European categories arbitrarily and imperialistically regarded as "language-independent rational and logical categories" existing in some Platonic heaven and imperfectly represented in the languages spoken by the people who were weak enough to become subjected to European rule. This practice has not stopped. Even now some linguists are creating ambitious "language-independent" frameworks of semantic categories (especially spatio-temporal ones) and syntactic frameworks with universalistic ambitions and pretensions. They create their webs of "universal" categories on the basis of the study of a few European languages (mainly English) and then impose them upon other languages with the help of superficial translational equivalences, or by setting up *convenient Euro-centred* "abstract levels", "deep structures", "logical forms", "underlying forms" (which I love to abbreviate as UFOs!) etc. The latest theoretically respectable attempt, the so-called Chomskyan Revolution in linguistics in the second half of the last century, is essentially a crystallisation of this tradition (with the difference that these "universal" categories now reside in a separate "language organ" or "language module" within the human brain, and not in a Platonic heaven). If we learn any lesson from the fate of such grand theoretical frameworks, it is this: a framework that attempts to accommodate *all* languages ends up by accommodating *no* language. Sands of the history of modern linguistics are littered with the broken remains of many such Ozymandiases!

The first article of my grammarian's faith is that each language developed its present form in order to satisfy its speakers' socio-cultural needs, and not to fit into a linguist's ready-made theoretical framework.

For several years, I carefully studied the grammars of Panjabi and Hindi-Urdu written from the 18th century onwards including some written by modern linguists. I took most of their analyses with a pinch of salt. Luckily, "taking with a pinch of salt" is an idiomatic expression, and no physical salt is involved; otherwise I would have swallowed a kilogram of salt (NaCl) by now! There were glaring counter-examples to the "tenses" of Panjabi and Hindi-Urdu they set up. John Beames, an English magistrate in Calcutta, was the first to challenge this practice of setting up "tenses" for North Indian languages in his monumental three-volume *A Comparative Grammar of the Modern Aryan Languages of India* (1872–79), but his challenge was simply ignored. Kali Charan Bahl (1964, 1969) also expressed serious doubts about analysing the Panjabi "tense" system in this way, but did not present his own detailed analysis.

A careful study of the Panjabi TMA (Tense Mood Aspect) system and how the Panjabi verb-forms evolved over centuries from Pāṇini onwards (discussed in Chapter 2) has convinced me that fitting the Panjabi TMA system into the "universal" European categories is the greatest injustice to Panjabi. A study of the view of time in Indian culture and philosophy, as it developed over the past two thousand years, has also convinced me about the hollowness of the claim that the armchair semantic categories based on European languages are universal. William Haas, my first teacher of linguistics in Manchester, UK, was never tired of emphasising the need for asking the right questions. "If you ask wrong questions, you get confusing answers," he always said. His Goethean way of looking at living things

(Haas 1957) was infectious. My Ph.D. research supervisor N.E. Collinge always encouraged me to ask honest and searching questions, study the ancient Indian linguists and develop my own independent views. I am deeply indebted to both these teachers of mine, as every page of this book shows. A careful study of the past grammars of Panjabi and Hindi-Urdu has convinced me that the European scholars who started this tradition (Beames being a notable exception) started with wrong questions and expectations. A major part of this book is devoted to correcting their mistake.

This grammar book deals with the meaning potential of various types of constructions in Panjabi. Panjabi, like any other language, has some unique features which, I believe, can be of interest to advanced learners of the language as well as to linguists working on a wide variety of languages, especially Indian languages with which Panjabi shares these features. I have highlighted them in the book. During my teaching career, I have frequently met highly motivated and critical learners of Panjabi and Hindi-Urdu. It is my moral duty to present to them what I *honestly* believe are the structural features of Panjabi. I have made no attempt to fit Panjabi forcibly into any theoretical framework, formal or functional or traditional, especially the one about which I have serious doubts. I paint a picture of Panjabi grammar "warts and all" as I see it from my own highly flexible (and frankly *pragmatic*) standpoint, keeping in view my first commitment to writing a pedagogical grammar for language learners. In this book, I have included the results of my own research as well. So it is necessary for me to mention in Chapter 2 my own theoretical views regarding language and linguistics which are shared by the scholars whose views I mention with approval in the book. But this book cannot go into all the technical details useful for professional linguists. If they wish to pursue the subject, they can modify them for themselves. I have full faith in the intellectual competence of *all* the users of this book, linguists and well as advanced learners who wish to explore the language in some depth.

Though Panjabi has certain features (**serial verb constructions**, among others) not found in English and other major European languages, it is nevertheless an Indo-European language. So we can expect Panjabi to share some *structural* features with these languages. A linguist working on Panjabi can benefit from the insights of the linguists working on European languages. I have found two monumental grammars of

English – *A Comprehensive Grammar of the English Language* (Quirk *et al.* 1985) and *The Cambridge Grammar of the English Language* (Huddleston and Pullum 2002) extremely helpful. I learnt some analytical concepts and techniques from the authors of these grammars. But I have always been on my guard against what I call the *Platonising* habit of the past grammarians of Indian languages – regarding categories like **tense, passive voice** etc. as well-defined "language-independent" categories existing in some Platonic heaven and incarnating themselves in different languages.

It will be ethnocentric to assume that Panjabi is not rich enough a language to enable a team of dedicated linguists to produce a grammar of around 2000 pages (similar to the two English grammars mentioned above). But, working within my own limitations, I am painfully aware that I am leaving out more than I am including in the book. There are inevitably a number of loose ends and a less than adequate treatment of some important topics. I can only hope that some future grammarian will take the task further from where I leave.

In the field of linguistics, I always welcome good ideals from everywhere. Apart from the scholars (ancient and modern) mentioned in Chapter 2, I was also deeply influenced by the British linguists Firth and Halliday, particularly by the latter's view of "language as a social semiotic" (Halliday 1978). But I seriously followed only Firth in a paradoxical manner. In his life Firth did not follow anybody. So a real follower of Firth does not follow anybody, not even Firth!

When I started planning this book, I knew that I would be ploughing a lone furrow. I feel envious of the authors of the other grammar books who acknowledge the help they received from other scholars in their fields working in various universities. I have not been so lucky. Over the past forty years (since I decided to enter the field of linguistics) I tried to contact all the Panjabi linguists I had heard of. I received help and encouragement from only one of them – Kali Charan Bahl from the University of Chicago. I am profoundly grateful to him for this. The rest did me a great favour by reinforcing my spirit of fierce independence! Rabindranath Tagore wrote in Bengali in 1905 *Jodi tor đak shune keu na ashe tôbe êkla chôlo re* – "If no one responds to your call, then go your own way alone."

I have made minimum possible use of any published texts for my data. Most of the examples I analyse are actually used by me or I have actually heard them from native speakers, with the proper stressing of words and intonation, in all sorts of situations. I have also taken some examples from Panjabi nursery rhymes, folk songs and published poetry. I have always been guided by the 5th–6th century Indian linguist Bhartṛhari's dictum that a grammarian should deal with a language used in लोकव्यवहार *lokavyavahāra* '(social) activities of the people'. The modern linguist whose thinking is closest to Bhatṛhari's is Daniel Everett (2013).

The most inspiring source of data for me are the words, phrases and sentences, along with all their prosodic features, of the stories and nursery rhymes I heard in my childhood (repeatedly, as all children do) from my illiterate mother. They are still fresh in my memory. Panjabi is *literally* my mother tongue! And I present this book as a tribute to my mother's departed soul!

The only linguist who always personally inspired and helped me is my friend Narinder Singh. As with all my past writings, he read every word of this book and offered constructive suggestions. My wife Usha has martyred herself for more than four decades in putting up with all my antics resulting from my chronic absent-mindedness, which becomes a lot worse when I am in the process of writing something. No words can fully express my gratitude for Narinder and Usha.

This book is the outcome of more than four decades of careful observation and analysis of the working of my mother tongue in all sorts of real life situations and of meditation upon the creative use of the language in Panjabi literature from the 15th century onwards, anonymous Panjabi folk songs, folk tales and nursery rhymes and the priceless gems of grammatical and semantic creativity I heard from children struggling to acquire Panjabi as their first language.

It would be ungrateful for me to pretend that I have entirely rejected the good work done by the past Panjabi grammarians, especially those mentioned in Chapter 1. I studied these scholars painstakingly and benefited enormously from them, but I tried my best to avoid (what I think are) their mistakes. I offer no apologies for learning from the practices and the ideas of ancient Indian linguists. As linguists, they were more perceptive, creative and dedicated than many modern ones, and we should be proud of them.

Many speakers of the Western (Pakistani) dialects of Panjabi would have loved the inclusion of Shahmukhi script (used for writing Panjabi in Pakistan) and the coverage of these dialects in the book. Both Shahmukhi and these dialects are certainly worthy of serious study, but two factors prevented me from doing this – (i) I could not increase the size of the book beyond its present one by bringing in the dialects which are best excluded from a book like this, because this is not a book on Panjabi dialectology; (ii) my own limited means and resources did not allow me to spend a few months doing field work in Pakistan. In East Punjab, a lot of work on the Eastern Panjabi dialects – their specific phonological and grammatical features, typical vocabulary, idioms and usage – has been or is being done in the universities and privately by individuals. But no similar work on the Western dialects of Panjabi done recently by their native speakers in Pakistan has come to my attention. The little work recently done on some of these dialects by Punjabi University Patiala for its *Linguistic Atlas of the Punjab* (1973) is not detailed enough. This book deals with what may be called Modern Standard Panjabi. Many grammars of Modern Standard Arabic (e.g., Ryding (2005) and Alhawary (2011)) have been published. But none of them includes any regional dialects of Arabic such as Egyptian, Iraqi, Lebanese, Algerian, Moroccan, Tunisian and others. Similarly, no recent grammar of Modern Standard Hindi (e.g., Bahl (1967), Kachru (1980) and Agnihotri (2007)) deals with the regional varieties of Hindi such as Rajasthani, Braj Bhasha, Awadhi, Bhojpuri, Maithili and others. So it would be unfair to expect this book to cover all the regional dialects of Panjabi and to compare Panjabi with its sister languages such as Hindi-Urdu. I have made it very clear in Chapter 1 which dialects of Panjabi I deal with. But I have pointed out at some places how some significant features of this variety of Panjabi differ from their equivalents in the Western dialects and in the sister language Hindi-Urdu.

The problem of the size again prevented me from including Shahmukhi. Moreover, Panjabi has some rules of grammar involving the Panjabi sounds for which Shahmukhi has no characters. I hope that the phonetic transcript used throughout this book will help those who do not read Gurmukhi. Also, I use a number of diagrams in the book to make my analysis clearer. Some of these diagrams (e.g., in Chapters 4 and 13) have directional arrows. Inclusion of the right to left Shahmukhi in these diagrams would have complicated them unnecessarily without adding any clarity to them. The professional drawing program I used for creating these diagrams does not accept any Arabic Unicode text. So I could not have included any Shahmukhi text in them even if I had wanted to. Some essential information about Shahmukhi is given in Chapter 18, where the Gurmukhi and the Shahmukhi systems are compared.

I must also express my gratitude to Samantha Vale Noya, the series editor, for her support, encouragement and constructive suggestions regarding the contents, design and layout of the book, which I decided to do myself at home, using my own PC. Ruth Berry, the production editor, and an anonymous copy editor gave useful suggestions which helped me enormously in giving a profesional touch to my amateurish attempt.

While the publication of this book gives me immense satisfaction, I will not claim that it is free from any flaws or that it offers an exhaustive treatment of the subject. I will be grateful to any reader/user/reviewer who offers any constructive suggestions for the improvement of the book.

Introductory Note

How to use this book

Language learners

This book is primarily meant to be used as a *reference* grammar by the learners of Panjabi at the *intermediate* and *advanced* levels. It will give you a *comprehensive in-depth* knowledge of the phonological system, (Gurmukhi) writing system and grammatical structures of Panjabi. There is a *free* multimedia complementary (or *complimentary*) *Workbook and Reader* downloadable from the publisher's website. Details can be found at the back of the cover of this book. This *Workbook* will give you plenty of practice materials (audio-recorded as well as printed) to practise and refine your linguistic skills in Panjabi.

Read and try to digest the information given in each chapter and appendix of this grammar book even if you find it challenging and different from what you expect from a grammar book as a result of your experience with the grammars of European languages. Although Panjabi is an Indo-European language, it is different from European languages in some significant ways. This complexity *is* there in Punjabi and cannot be ignored or wished away by any serious and responsible teacher and learner of this language at an advanced level. Learning a foreign language at an advanced level is a challenging task requiring a lot of patience and hard work. But everything is explained in depth and with examples and no previous knowledge of linguistics is assumed. There is also a Glossary of technical terms to help the users.

The theoretical framework of Panjabi grammar developed by me for my books *Colloquial Panjabi* (1995/2012) and *Colloquial Punjabi 2* (2013) is elaborated and presented in greater detail and depth in this book. Each chapter heading indicates the subject it deals with. The general Subject Index lists all the details of these subjects, topics and sub-topics. A separate Index of Grammatical Words is also there to help the learner locate the pages dealing with each of these words. The technical terms of grammar and the abbreviations used in the book are briefly explained in the Glossary of Technical Terms and Abbreviations, where the numbers of the chapters dealing with these terms and concepts in full detail are given. Learners are advised to use both the Indexes and the Glossary.

The *Workbook,* which presents, briefly analyses and comments on some longer Panjabi texts used in *real life*, will demonstrate that *all* the technical details very carefully included in the system set up for Panjabi in this book (such as the **phases of the verb**, **synthetic case forms, serial verb constructions**, role of flexible **word order**, **particles** and **intonation** in creating **cohesion** in text and discourse), completely overlooked by the past Panjabi grammarians, are needed for an explanation of the phonetic, phonological, grammatical and semantic structure of this language.

Linguists

Since not much is known to theoretical and "applied" linguists about Panjabi, which is a major world language, this book may be of interest to them. Panjabi, like Bengali, has some unique and interesting features. But, living in the shadow of their big sister Hindi-Urdu, they do not attract as much attention as they deserve.

My theoretical and philosophical views are described in Chapter 2. My approach is eclectic and pragmatic. I have borrowed ideas from a number of linguists, including ancient Indian linguists. But I have tried to create (what I think is) a *suitable* theoretical framework for Panjabi, instead of fitting it into an existing one. *I believe that while every language shares a few features with some other languages, it is ultimately unique and its individuality should be respected.* The "one size fits all" ideal, however desirable theoretically, does not suit a book of this type. For the benefit of those who do not know the Panjabi (Gurmukhi) script, every Panjabi word and sentence used in this book is also given in the phonetic transcription originally developed in the 19th century for Sanskrit.

Notational and Typographical Conventions

`	Low tone, e.g., **[kòṛā]** [[kòɽɑ]
´	High tone, e.g., **[kóṛā]** [kóɽɑ]
ˈ	Stressed syllable, e.g., **[ˈkoṛā]** [ˈkoɽɑ]
.	Syllable boundary, e.g., **[ko.ṛā]** [ko.ɽɑ]
˜	Nasalised vowel, e.g, **[kā̃]** [kɑ̃]
→	"becomes"
*	Ungrammatical or unacceptable expression
(?)	Expression which sounds odd
Ø	Zero realisation of a linguistic element
≺	Anaphoric (backward-looking) expression
≻	Cataphoric (forward-looking) expression

Body text	Serif font
English translation	'Serif font within single quotes'
Quoted words	"Serif font within double quotes"
Emphasised words	*Serif font italic*
Words with extra emphasis	***Serif font bold italic***

Transliteration of Sanskrit words	*Serif font italic with additions, e.g., aṣṭādhyāyī*
Technical terms of grammar (where highlighted)	**Serif font bold**
Relational syntactic terms	SERIF FONT ALL CAPITALS, e.g., SUBJECT, PREDICATOR, OBJECT, ADJUNCT
Section headings	**Sans Serif font bold**
Panjabi phonetic transcription	**Sans Serif font bold with additions, e.g., g^{h}āḷā**
Pronunciation of Panjabi words	**[Sans Serif font in square brackets] e.g., [kahā̀ṇī]**
IPA transcription	[IPA Serif font in square brackets] e.g., [pɐɲdʒɑbi]
Abbreviations used in glosses	Sans Serif font small size
Panjabi words	Gurmukhi font ਗੁਰਮੁਖੀ Shahmukhi font شاہ مُکھی
Sanskrit and Hindi words	Devanagari font देवनागरी

Abbreviations

The following abbreviations are used in the grammar chapters, especially to write the glosses underneath the examples to save space. The grammatical terms and concepts these abbreviations stand for are briefly explained in the Glossary and in detail in the chapter where each concept or term is introduced for the first time. Refer to the Glossary first, as this gives the chapter number where the grammatical concept is dealt with in detail. The Subject Index shows all the pages dealing with the concept or subject.

Adj	Adjective	Def	Definite
ADJCT	Adjunct	Deff1	Derived free form 1
AdjPh	Adjective phrase	Deff2	Derived free form 2
AdPh	Additive phase of the verb	Dem	Demonstrative pronoun
Adv	Adverb	Det	Determiner
AdvP	Adverb phrase	Dir	Direct form
Agt	Agentive post-postion ने **ne**	Expr	Experiencer
Aux	Auxiliary verb	Fem	Feminine gender
COMP(O)	Object comple-ment	Ger	Gerund
COMP(S)	Subject complement	GR	Goal of result
ConjP	Conjunctive participle	ImmAgt	Immediate agent
Co-or	Co-ordinator	ImP	Imperfect participle
Cop	Copula	Imper(P)	Plain imperative

Imper(S)	Suggestive imperative	Pnt	Patient
Inst	Instrumental case form	PotP	Potential participle
IntAgt	Intermediate agent	PP	Postpositional phrase
IntiAgt	Initiator (agent)	Pron	Pronoun
Loc	Locative case form	Rel	Relative clause
Mas	Maculine gender	SA	Substratum of activity
Neu	Neuter verb agreement	Sg	Singular number
NFC	Non-finite clause	SR	Substratum of result
NomC	Nominal subor-dinate clause	SUB	Subject
NP	Noun phrase	Subo	Subordiantor
OBJ	Object	SubPh	Subtractive phase of the verb
Obl	Oblique form	V	Verb
P	Postposition	V-caus	Causative verb
Part	Participle	V-intr	Intransitive verb
Per	Person	VP	Verb phrase
PerP	Perfect participle	V-tr	Transitive verb
Pl	Plural number		

Part I
General Introduction

Chapter 1

Panjabi Language, Scripts and Grammar: A Spatio-temporal Perspective

Preview of the chapter

This chapter gives very brief information about the history of Panjabi and the geographical location of the "Panjabi-speaking areas" where the majority of the people speak it as their first language. The Panjabi dialect areas covered in this book are also shown in the maps given below. Some important Panjabi grammars written since 1812 are also briefly reviewed.

According to the latest information available from Ethnologue (in *Wikipedia*) Panjabi stands 10th among the 6700+ languages of the world if we take into account the number of its speakers of Indian and Pakistani origin (about 102 million or 1.44% of the population of the world). Additionally, speakers of this language are found in almost every inhabited part of the globe. There is a joke that "Panjabis and potatoes are found in every part of the world!" Until a few years ago, the largest chunk of the immigrant population (0.5%) in the UK spoke Panjabi. Now they have been overtaken by the speakers of Polish (1%). Among the speakers of the non-official languages in Canada, the largest group (1.3%) are speakers of Panjabi.

1.1 Panjabi – a very brief history

Panjabi is a member of the Indic branch of the large Indo-European family. The following partial family tree shows Panjabi's immediate cousin and sister languages relevant to what is discussed below.

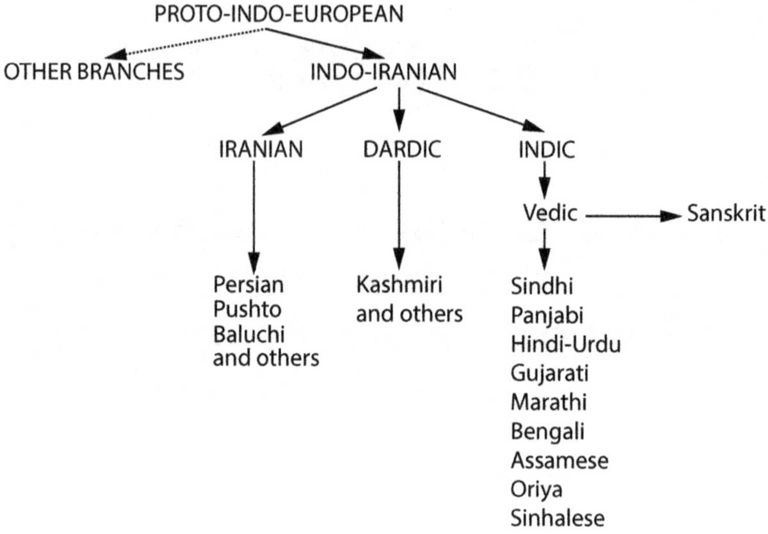

Figure 1.1 A partial family tree of Panjabi and related languages

Figure 1.1 above and Figure 1.4 on p.7 also show some of Panjabi's cousins of the Iranian and Dardic branches. The oldest recorded language of the Indic branch is Vedic, the language of the Hindu religious books the *Vedas*. The theory of the Aryan invasion of India around 1000 BC is now fully discredited and rejected by historians (Feuerstein, Kak and Frawley 2005, Kazanas 2015). The *Vedas* contain references to the river Sarasvati, which is called a "mighty river". This river (now known as Ghaggar) dried up around 1900 BC because of tectonic changes. So the time of the *Vedas* has to be pushed back at least a thousand years, if not more. The area where Vedic was spoken was known as Saptasindhu (or the land of seven rivers – now known as Indus, Jhelum, Chenab, Ravi, Beas, Satluj and Ghaggar). The great linguist Pāṇini wrote a grammar of later Vedic and since then this language has been known as Sanskrit ('refined speech'). For many centuries following this, Sanskrit was a language of great literature and books on science, mathematics, politics, philosophy, medicine, surgery and other branches of learning. There still are writers in India who write in Sanskrit. The modern Indic languages are descendants of the language whose "refined" form is Sanskrit. So we have to refer to Sanskrit in order to know the past history of these languages.

Vedic and Sanskrit are collectively known as Old Indic. The Old Indic period is believed to have lasted until 500 BC. The Earlier Middle

Indic period (500 BC–500 AD) is the period of various regional Prākrit languages, the oldest and best known of which is Pāli, the language of Buddhist literature. Later Prākrits include Māgadhī, Ardhamāgadhī, Mahārāṣṭrī, Śaurasenī and Paiśachī.

The Later Middle Indic period from 500 AD to 1000 AD is the period of Apabhraṁśa languages. The regional Prākrits evolved further towards becoming the modern Indic languages. No extensive samples of Śaurasenī and Paiśachī Apabhraṁśa languages have come down to us. The 11th century Muslim poet Addahmāṇ (Abdul Rahman), who lived in Multan (West Punjab), is the last major Apabhraṁśa poet or the first major Panjabi poet (depending on how you look upon his language – it is impossible to draw a precise historical boundary between Middle and Modern Indic.)

Modern Panjabi is believed to have passed through four phases – the First Phase (1000–1400 AD), the Second Phase (1400–1700 AD), the Third Phase (1700–1850 AD) and the Fourth Phase (1850 AD to the present) (Padam: 1954). Fariduddin Ganjshakar (1173–1266) is regarded as a major writer of the First Phase. He is more popularly known as Baba Farid. His poetry is included in the Sikh holy book *Srī Gurū Granth Sāhib*. But the authorship of this poetry is disputed. Its language clearly belongs to the Second Phase. Farid lived close to Multan where Addahmāṇ lived a century earlier. But Farid's language is so different from Addahmāṇ's that it does not appear to belong to the 12th–13th century. Many scholars, therefore, argue that the poetry attributed to Fariduddin Ganjshakar was actually authored by the 11th successor of his mission, whose name was Ibrahim Farid. He is also known as Farid Sani (Farid the Second), who died in 1552 in Sirhind (East Punjab). His disciples were spread all over the Punjab and Delhi region. He was greatly respected for his scholarship and saintly character. His language is Lahandi (see below), but there are definite influences of Eastern Panjabi on his language. Guru Nanak Dev, the first Guru of the Sikh faith, once met him. So it is possible that Farid II handed over some of his writings to the Guru. Another possibility is that each generation of Farid I's followers kept altering his poetry to make it intelligible to the common people. So for our purpose the first major Panjabi writer is Guru Nanak Dev (1469–1539). Guru Nanak Dev's language is considerably influenced by Sadhu Bhasha or Sant Bhasha, a variety of Hindi used by the Hindu saints in North India. He probably deliberately chose this influence because he wanted to reach more people in the Hindi-speaking areas as well, where he travelled extensively. But its roots lie in the variety of Panjabi which was spoken in the area marked as "Panjabi merging into Lahandi" in Figures 1.4 and 1.5 on p.7. The Apabhraṁśa elements are also quite prominent in his language.

1.2 The "Panjabi-speaking" areas

"Panjabi" means the language of the geographical region known as Panjab or Punjab. This Persian word means 'a land of five rivers' (Jhelum, Chenab, Ravi, Beas and Satluj). The name of the region was well-established by the 14th century because it is mentioned in the travelogue of the Moroccan traveller Ibn Batuta, who visited India in the 14th century. But Panjabi is still spoken all over the older Saptasindhu area and beyond. The following maps show the areas where the majority of the population "officially" speaks Panjabi as their first language.

Figure 1.2 An overview of the Panjabi-speaking areas in India and Pakistan

Figure 1.5 also shows the principal towns and cities in the areas where the Panjabi dialects studied in this book (Majhi, Doabi, Puwadhi and Malwai) are spoken.

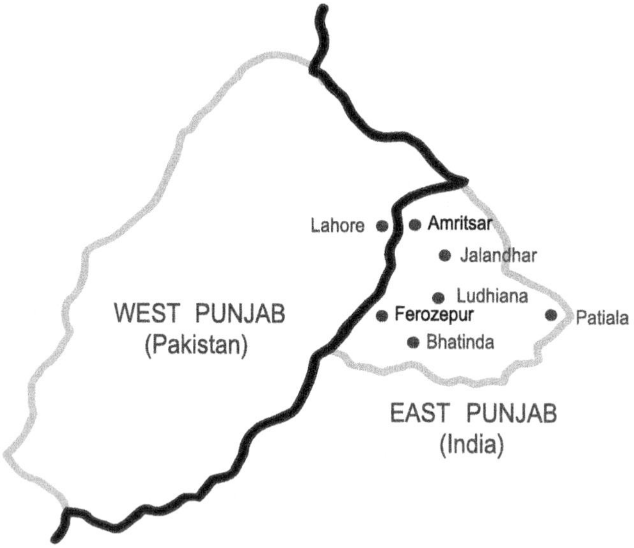

Figure 1.3 Detailed map of the Panjabi-speaking areas in India and Pakistan

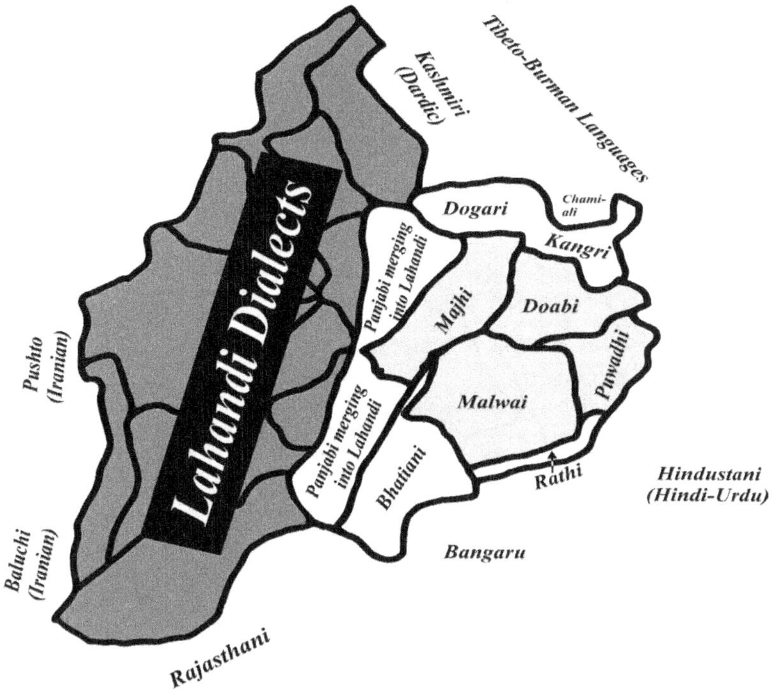

Figure 1.4 Areas where Eastern Panjabi and Western Panjabi (Lahandi) dialects are spoken

It should be noted that the *Vedas* were composed in the Saptasindhu area. Pāṇini was a native of this area and there is a tradition that he based his Sanskrit grammar on the language he spoke as his mother tongue. Even today, Panjabi, especially the Western variety (Lahandi) is grammatically the most conservative of the modern Indic languages and is grammatically closest to Sanskrit. Some scholars quite justifiably regard Vedic as the earliest recorded form of Panjabi.

The exact number of the Panjabi dialects is, and will always remain, a matter of controversy. But what is not controversial is that the Panjabi dialects can be divided into two major groups, Eastern Panjabi and Western Panjabi (or Lahandi) as shown in Figure 1.4. This map also shows the neighbouring areas where non-Indic languages of the Iranian and Dardic families are spoken. Figure 1.5 below shows the principal town or towns in each dialect area. The areas shaded in this map are the areas whose dialects are covered in this book.

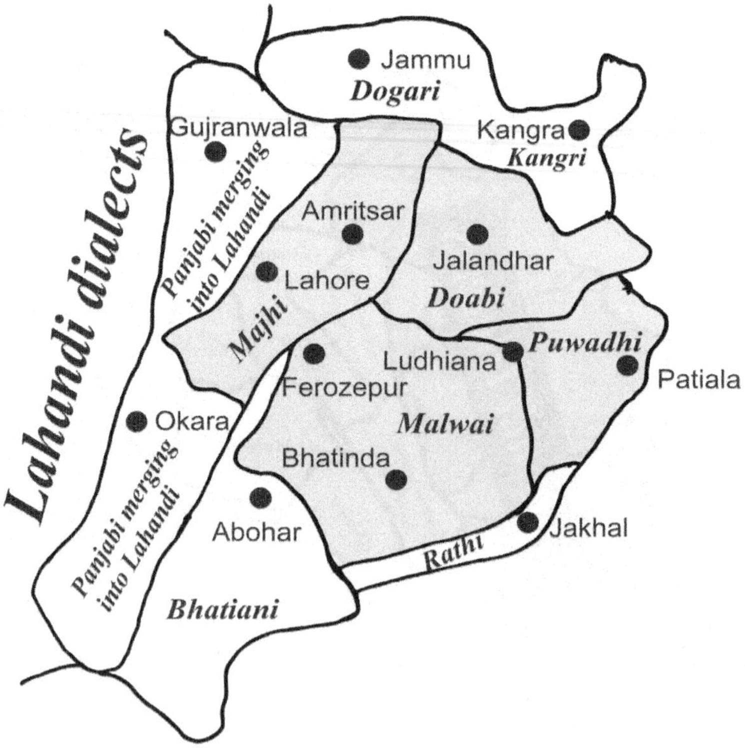

Figure 1.5 Areas (shaded) of Eastern Panjabi dialects dealt with in this book

A *disclaimer* is made here – that these maps are intended to give a *very rough*, and not cartographically accurate, pictures of the geographical location of these areas and that the language boundaries shown here are approximate and are *not political boundaries*. These maps are based on Sir George Grierson's monumental *The Linguistic Survey of India* (1894–1927) (Vol. VIII Part 1 and Vol. IX Part 1).

Most Indian (especially Panjabi) scholars do not agree with Grierson, in regarding Lahandi as a separate language. (He used the name Lahanda, which was corrected by Indian linguists because Lahanda is a masculine word and a language is feminine in Panjabi.) Whether the language spoken in an area is a dialect of a language or an independent language is rarely a purely linguistic question because questions of politics and cultural and religious identity etc. are invariably involved in this part of the world. But the reason given by Grierson can be easily rejected. Grierson says:

> I explained that the whole Panjab was the meeting ground of two distinct forms of speech, *viz.*, the old Outer language strongly influenced by Dardic, if not actually Dardic, which expanded from the Indus Valley eastwards, and the old Midland language, the parent of modern Western Hindī, which expanded from the Jamna Valley westwards. In the Panjab these overlapped. In the Eastern Panjab the wave of Dardic with old Lahandā had nearly exhausted itself, and the old Western Hindī had the mastery, the resultant language being Pañjābī, while in the Western Panjab the old Western Hindī had nearly exhausted itself, the resultant language being modern Lahandā. It is impossible to draw any clear dividing line between Pañjabī and Lahandā...
>
> (Vol 1, 1916: 608)

Grierson adds that

> ... It thus happens that, although in India we continually see two neighbouring languages gradually merging into each other, nowhere is the process so gradual as in the case of Pañjābī and Lahandā.
>
> (*ibid.*)

So he had to admit that "I have been guided mainly by vocabulary." (*ibid.*).

But he does not give any sample of the "vocabulary" in order to support his argument. His admission that "It is impossible to draw any clear dividing line between Pañjābī and Lahandā..." is significant. Jodh Singh, a Panjabi scholar and native speaker of Lahandī, says, "A speaker of Lahandī reading every single word in Mr Grierson's Kashmiri

Dictionary finds no proof of his claim... If we exclude the Arabic and Persian words from that dictionary, at least I cannot understand anything, and I am a speaker of Lahandī... If we compare [Lahandī with] Panjabi, we find that eighty or ninety percent of the words are shared by them. A speaker of Lahandī speaking to a speaker of Panjabi feels that the main difference between the languages is that of style" (1959: iii. Translated from Panjabi).

In the absence of any supporting evidence, Grierson's view must be regarded as pure speculation. Lahandi is an Indic language, which is neither Dardic nor strongly influenced by Dardic. Being "guided mainly by vocabulary" is an outdated and questionable "philological" practice which no modern linguist can take seriously. About 60% of Modern English vocabulary comes from Latin and French and less than 30% of it is of native Germanic origin. So a person "guided mainly by vocabulary" and ignorant of the history of English might conclude that English is a Romance language like French, Italian and Spanish. The actual DNA (using a slightly inexact analogy about a language) of a language is judged from its verb system and case-marking, particularly that of pronouns. Languages borrow vocabulary (mainly nouns, adjectives and adverbs) from other languages. Careful speakers can maintain the original grammatical markers on the borrowed words for some time before the native tendencies get an upper hand. Grammatical markers of TMA (Tense Mood Aspect) categories on the verb, auxiliary verbs and pronouns and their inflections are seldom borrowed. A careful study of Lahandi grammar can trace back almost all such grammatical features to Sanskrit. This cannot be attempted in this book. Some hints can be found in Duni Chandra (1959), Sekhon (1961) and Padam (1954).

But, taking a clue from Grierson, we can *speculate* better that Lahandi and Eastern Panjabi may be descendants of different and neighbouring Apabhraṁśas. Paiśāchī Apabhraṁśa was spoken in what is now the Lahandi area, and Śaurasenī Apabhraṁśa was spoken in the modern Western Hindi area. In the area of modern East Panjabi Śaurasenī "merged into" Paiśāchī. Paiśāchī means the speech of the Piśācha people. This derogative name (meaning 'eaters of raw flesh') was probably given to these people because they did not observe the food taboos and some other customs of the orthodox Brahmins of the Ganga-Yamuna plains.

The linguists who prepared the *Linguistic Atlas of the Punjab* (1973) carefully studied the dialects of Panjabi spoken at more than twenty places in the Panjabi/Lahandi-speaking areas and beyond. They got a Panjabi folk tale (the story of the Panjabi saint Pūran Bhagat) translated into the dialects spoken at these places, including the Lahandi dialects spoken in Rawalpindi, Dhudial, Talagang, Mianwali, Sargodha, Jhang and Shujabad. These translations and the speech of the people from these areas confirm Jodh Singh's views given above. Grammatically, Eastern Panjabi is a lot closer to Lahandi than, for example, to the neighbouring Indic language Hindi-Urdu. Some Sanskrit case markers on nouns and pronouns and some Sanskrit markers on the verb such as those for TMA (Tense Mood Aspect) and passive voice are better preserved in Lahandi and (to a smaller extent) in Eastern Panjabi than in the other modern Indic languages. Some of these features are discussed in the following chapters. The main difference between Eastern Panjabi and Lahandi is that the latter has preserved the breathy voiced consonants which Eastern Panjabi has lost. (See Chapter 3.)

Interactions between and mixing of the speakers of Eastern Panjabi and Lahandi have been going on for centuries. A lot of fine Panjabi literature was written in Lahandi, such as the writings of Farid Ganjshakar (or probably of Ibrahim Farid), Sultan Bahu, Mian Muhammad Bakhsh, Khwaja Ghulam Farid and others. The language used by Guru Nanak Dev, Shah Husain and some other Panjabi poets is heavily influenced by Lahandi. Guru Arjan Dev (the fifth Guru of the Sikh faith, a speaker of Eastern Panjabi) wrote in pure Lahandi as well. Some of the prominent modern writers who wrote in Eastern Panjabi were native speakers of Lahandi. Two relatively recent examples of the migration of the speakers from one area to the other can be given. Towards the close of the 19th century, with the spreading of a canal network in West Punjab, thousands of farmers from East Punjab bought farms in West Punjab. The partition of India in 1947 brought tens of thousands of Hindu and Sikh refugees from West Punjab to East Punjab.

As pointed out earlier, the issue of dividing Panjabi into dialects and whether the western dialects are the dialects of Panjabi or belong to a separate Lahandi language is not a purely linguistic question. Political, social and emotive issues are also involved. Most native speakers of both the eastern and the western dialects of Panjabi believe that they speak the same language. We have already quoted Jodh Singh (a native speaker of Lahandi) above. Duni Chandra (1959), another native speaker of Lahandi, believed the same. Both were fine linguists. The fact that they wrote in Panjabi, and not in English, is no disqualification. Their intuitions should be respected more than the supposedly "objective" views of the non-native linguists. *All* linguists (including the author of this book) have their theoretical biases, various other prejudices and even personal likes and dislikes. Pure "objectivity" claimed by/for linguists is highly exaggerated. There can be no guarantee that the linguists who worked on Panjabi dialects later should be more reliable and free from any personal prejudices and political or ideological motivation. We can disagree with Grierson's view that Lahandi is a separate language and still agree with his division of Panjabi/Lahandi into regional dialects. There is no controversy anywhere regarding the Panjabi dialects dealt with in this book. (See Figures 1.4 and 1.5). This should be enough for our purpose. However, readers interested in knowing more are referred to Masica (1993) and the linguists mentioned therein.

This book deals with the four eastern dialects of Panjabi – Majhi, Doabi, Malwai and Puwadhi. They are very similar and are collectively known as ਕੇਂਦਰੀ ਪੰਜਾਬੀ **kendrī panjābī** or 'Central Panjabi'. This variety of Panjabi has now become the dominant variety used in Panjabi literature and newspapers and on radio and TV inside and outside the Panjabi-speaking areas. The term ਟਕਸਾਲੀ ਪੰਜਾਬੀ **ṭaksālī panjābī** 'standard Panjabi' is avoided here because that would imply that the other dialects are non-standard or sub-standard. All the speakers of the other dialects including Lahandi understand this variety and *vice versa.*

1.3 The Panjabi scripts

For historical reasons, since the closing decades of the 19th century, the communal harmony in the Panjabi-speaking area has been severely disturbed by the division of the Panjabi-speaking people on religious grounds. Each religious group chose a language and a script as a part of its identity: Sikhs chose Panjabi in the Gurmukhi script, Muslims chose Urdu in the Perso-Arabic script and Hindus chose Hindi in the Devanagari script, notwithstanding the fact that they all spoke Panjabi. Most Hindus in East Punjab have now accepted Panjabi and Gurmukhi, and some major Panjabi writers are Hindus. But the situation has not changed in West Punjab (Pakistan). While India has recognised twenty-three official languages, Pakistan's "national" language is Urdu spoken by about 5% of its population that migrated from India in 1947. While it makes sense to use only one script (the Perso-Arabic script) for all the languages spoken in Pakistan, giving no official status to Panjabi spoken by the largest chunk of the population is a different matter.

1.3.1 Shahmukhi

Shahmukhi (the name given recently to the Perso-Arabic script when used for writing Panjabi in Pakistan), because of its Arabic origin, appeals to the religious sentiments of the Panjabi-speaking Muslims, and Gurmukhi appeals to Sikh sentiments because it is used in their holy book *Srī Gurū Granth Sāhib*. An unbiased historical and structural analysis of both these scripts is given below to dispel certain myths that either of the scripts is "better" than the other for writing Panjabi, especially the myth that Gurmukhi was created by Guru Angad Dev, the second Guru of the Sikh faith. Another myth that Panjabi (written in Gurmukhi) is a "phonetic" language in which "you write as you speak and speak as you write" is the subject of Chapters 3 and 4.

Chapter 18 deals with some salient features of Shahmukhi in some detail, but a very brief introduction can be included here. The name Shahmukhi was coined on the analogy of Gurmukhi. The Arabic script designed for a Semitic language was used for writing the Indo-European language Persian. The speakers of Persian could not pronounce some Arabic sounds. So they pronounced two distinct Arabic sounds as [t], three Arabic sounds as [s], four Arabic sounds as [z] and two Arabic sounds as [h]. They added four letters for the Persian sounds not found in Arabic. With the establishment of Muslim rule in India, the ruling class chose the Persianised version of the Arabic script for writing the language spoken in and around Delhi, which they called by different names. But the name Urdu (the Turkish name for an army camp) ultimately prevailed. They added three letters for the retroflex sounds. For writing the aspirated sounds, they started combining ھ with a letter. They did not create any letter for the retroflex nasal sound [ɳ], ostensibly because this sound was not significant in their variety of Urdu. But, as argued in Chapter 18, the *real* reason was different. Leaving Urdu aside, [ɳ] is a prominent and very significant Panjabi sound and Shahmukhi has no letter for it. None of the half a dozen digital Urdu fonts created in India and Pakistan has a symbol for this sound. Hundreds of Arabic and Persian words used in Urdu and Panjabi have their original spelling but Indian pronunciation. The result is that the Shahmukhi script has four letters for [z], three letters for [s], two letters for [t], two letters for [h] and no letters for [ŋ]. Some writers use the Unicode symbol 0768 ݨ for [ŋ], but this is not a standard practice. Most Panjabi writers writing in Shahmukhi are carrying on without any letter for this sound. Another symbol for this sound is given and discussed below. Leaving short vowels unmarked in writing is an ancient Arabic practice carried on in Persian, Urdu and Shahmukhi writing. So, on the whole, Shahmukhi is 100% Urdu script with the Urdu writing conventions carried on *in toto* into the writing of Panjabi, even where the pronunciation of the words shared by the two languages is different in Panjabi. No attempt has been made to standardise the spellings of Panjabi words in Shahmukhi. A dictionary of standardised spellings of Panjabi words in Gurmukhi known as **ਪੰਜਾਬੀ ਸ਼ਬਦ-ਰੂਪ ਤੇ ਸ਼ਬਦ-ਜੋੜ ਕੋਸ਼ panjābī śabad-rūp te śabad-joṛ kośh** (A dictionary of the forms and spellings of Panjabi words) was published in 1988. No comparable dictionary has been published for Panjabi written in Shahmukhi.

A comparison with the Sindhi script is made in Chapter 18, where it is mentioned that when the script based on the Arabic script was created for Sindhi by Sir Richard Francis Burton (with the help of Sindhi scholars), in the 19th century, special letters were provided for *all* the specific Sindhi sounds as well as for the sounds in the words borrowed from Arabic and Persian. This script has sixty-nine characters: thirty-seven consonants, ten independent vowels, nine vowel signs, three miscellaneous signs and ten digits. The Shahmukhi script, too, needs a similar overhaul.

1.3.2 Gurmukhi

The (mis)interpretatation of the name Gurmukhi by some Sikh scholars (and the list includes some respected names) and the popular belief that Guru Angad Dev (the second Guru of the Sikh faith) "invented" this script has done great disservice to the script by putting off many Muslims and Hindus. The traditional interpretation 'from the Guru's mouth' does not make any sense because a script is not related to the mouth. Many serious Sikh scholars (e.g. Padam 1954 and Sidhu 2004) argue that the name Gurmukhi comes from the Panjabi word **ਗੁਰਮੁਖ gurmukʰ** (meaning 'guru-oriented' or 'pious' and now used mostly for a devout Sikh). So Gurmukhi was the script used by Gurmukh (pious) Sikhs even when the Perso-Arabic script was fashionable in the area. Even the word **ਗੁਰਮੁਖ**

gurmuk^h is older than Sikhism and is found in the writings of the ascetic Hindu saints (known as the Siddhs or Naths) who predate Guru Nanak Dev (1469–1539), the first Guru of the Sikh faith (Sidhu 2004). Guru Angad Dev did not "invent" this script. His original name was Lehna and he lived with Guru Nanak Dev for several years before he assumed Guruship in 1539. All the traditional thirty-five letters and other symbols used in Gurmukhi already existed (G.B. Singh 1950). They are mentioned by Guru Nanak Dev in a hymn in *Srī Gurū Granth Sāhib* p. 432), probably written many years before he met Lehna, who became Guru Angad Dev later. He uses the names of the letters which are still used today (but also see Chapter 3). The Guru's earliest biography written around 1634 (published in Kirpal Singh 1969) says that the priest of his village taught him this alphabet when he was seven years old (i.e., in 1476). Gurmukhi belongs to the north-western branch of the Brahmi family. Brahmi was well-established in India by 500 BC, and modern Indian scholars claim that it developed from the Indus valley script and is not Semitic in origin. Some scripts of this family like Landa, Sharda, Bhatt Achhari and Siddh Matrika were in use in the Punjab and its neighbouring areas. In Guru Nanak Dev's times, two types of scripts were in use in the area where he was born – ਪਟੀ **paṭī** or ਪੈਂਤੀ **paintī** (with thirty-five letters) and ਬਾਵਨ ਅਖਰੀ **bāvan ak^{h}arī** (with fifty-two letters, used for writing Sanskrit). A consonant letter in a script of the Brahmi family represents the syllable consisting of consonant+**a**. The Sanskrit word for this is *akṣara*, which was pronounced as ਅਖਰ **ak^{h}ar** or ਅਛਰ **ac^{h}ar** in Guru Nanak Dev's times. The modern pronunciation is ਅੱਖਰ **akk^{h}ar**. What Guru Angad Dev did (most probably under Guru Nanak Dev's guidance) was the refinement and standardisation of the script and Panjabi spelling for writing Guru Nanak Dev's writings. It is also believed that he wrote primers for the teaching and propagation of this script. The name Gurmukhi was probably given later to the script. The earlier script that Gurmukhi comes closest to is Siddh Matrika.

Guru Nanak Dev knew the Perso-Arabic script (and Persian and Arabic languages) well. But he favoured a Brahmi-based script apparently for three reasons. The Perso-Arabic script has a baggage of consonant symbols not needed for Panjabi. (For the same reason he did not choose ਬਾਵਨ ਅਖਰੀ **bāvan ak^{h}arī**.) The grammatical importance and correct pronunciation of short vowels (particularly at the end of some nouns and verbs) is extremely important for the correct interpretation of his poetry (Sahib Singh 1935, Randhir Singh 1954, Harkirat Singh 2011, Bhardwaj 2013). Leaving out short vowels in writing in the Perso-Arabic script is an ancient tradition, and he probably feared that later generations might do the same to his writings if he wrote in the Perso-Arabic script. This has been done frequently in transliterating Gurbani into the script now known as Shahmukhi. Last (or perhaps first) of all, he was a thoroughgoing nationalist. He fearlessly described in great detail how the Muslim invader Babur overran the Punjab area with fire and sword (*Srī Gurū Granth Sāhib* p. 360). He was extremely critical of the Indians who blindly imitated their Muslim rulers' language, mannerisms and customs. (*SGGS,* pp. 470, 472, 663, 1191). His love for the native Indian traditions extended to the scripts of Indian origin. But he was not against borrowing words from other languages. He also wrote a hymn in Persian as spoken in his times.

> Although the Sikh Gurus were nationalists to the core and did not like Panjabis speaking foreign languages and wearing foreign clothes, they borrowed extensively from other languages to enrich Panjabi with synonyms, antonyms and homonyms. According to one estimate at least 6% Arabic and Persian words are in Gurbani.
>
> (Sidhu 2004: 64)

But the main reason why he rejected the Persian script must have been linguistic: he found it *inadequate* for writing the language he was using. The Perso-Arabic (Urdu) script does not have symbols for three important Panjabi sounds represented by the Gurmukhi letters **ਙ [ṅ]** [ŋ], **ਞ [ñ]** [ɲ], and **ਣ [ṇ]** [ɳ]. **ਙ [ṅ]** [ŋ] and **ਞ [ñ]** [ɲ] have since then become quite marginal as *independent* consonants. (See section 3.1 in Chapter 3.) But **ਣ [ṇ]** [ɳ] is still one of the most important consonant sounds in Panjabi. Examples of **ਙ [ṅ]** [ŋ] and **ਞ [ñ]** [ɲ] used as independent consonants by Guru Nanak Dev are given below. The page references are to *Srī Gurū Granth Sāhib* (*SGGS*).

ਅੰਙਣੜੇ (580), ਰੰਙਣਿ (722), ਸਿੰਙੀ (886, 907), ਪਿਙਾਣਾ (902), ਮੁੰਞੀ (19), ਵੰਞਣੁ (56), ਸਿਞਾਣੀਐ (58), ਸਿਞਾਪੈ (243)

ਣ [ṇ] [ɳ] is still an important independent consonant in Panjabi for which the Perso-Arabic script (Shahmukhi) has no agreed symbol. A symbol shown in Figure 1.6 was created by a Pakistani writer Jameel Pal in the last decade of the 20th century.

Kirpal Singh Pannu adopted this symbol and created two more. He recently published (free on the Web) a Shahmukhi transliteration of *SGGS*. He created a special Shahmukhi font for this purpose. His transliteration of the words ਰੰਙਣਿ and ਵੰਞਣੁ (on pages 722 and 56 respectively of *SGGS*), breaks the Shahmukhi writing conventions and the words with these symbols will be unrecognisable to a normal reader of Shahmukhi. The words cannot be typed except in Pannu's own special font (not available to this author).

Figure 1.6 Three new Shahmukhi characters used by Pannu

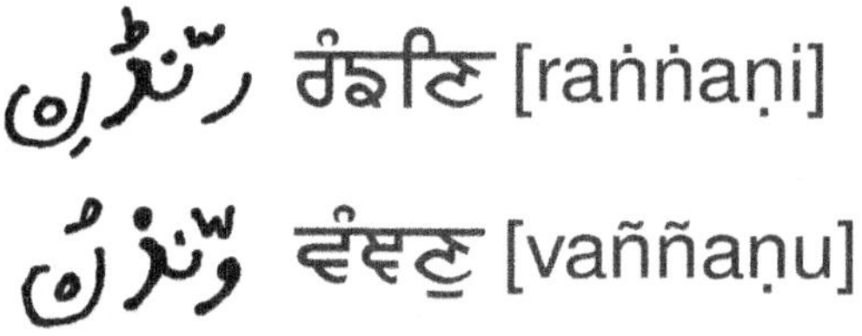

Figure 1.7 Shahmukhi transliteration of two old Panjabi word used by Guru Nanak Dev

The whole book is full of such examples (involving ਙ **[ṅ]** [ŋ], ਞ **[ñ]** [ɲ] and ਣ **[ṇ]** [ɳ]). But the value of his innovation is dubious. As a Sikh, he could not misrepresent his Guru's writing. But the idiosyncratic font and the devices he employed for this purpose will be unintelligible to the target readers. Instead of doing this, he could have borrowed the three symbols (ڱ , ڃ and ڻ respectively) from the well-planned and carefully designed Arabic-based Sindhi script (based on a sound phonological analysis of this Indic language) and included them in his font and typed Guru Nanak Dev's words as shown below. Panjabi and Sindhi are neighbouring languages which share many grammatical features as well.

رّڱِڻ ਰੰਙਣਿ [raṅṅaṇi]

وّڃُڻ ਵੰਞਣੁ [vaññaṇu]

Figure 1.8 Transliteration of Guru Nanak Dev's words in the Sindhi script

Thanks to Guru Nanak Dev's choice of Gurmukhi, modern linguists have a good knowledge about the pronunciation and grammar of Old Panjabi, which would have been lost in the Perso-Arabic script.

Another myth regarding Gurmukhi is also prevalent – that in Panjabi written in Gurmukhi, "you speak as you write and write as you speak." This claim may have been true *to some extent* before the development of tones in Panjabi (Chapter 4), but now this myth is so seriously misleading for learners of language and for linguists studying the phonology of the language that a whole chapter is needed to explode it.

No Panjabi grammar or dictionary published from 1812 onwards used the Perso-Arabic script (now called Shahmukhi) for writing Panjabi. They used either Gurmukhi or phonetic transcription for this. The first text books written by Shardha Ram Phillauri for teaching Panjabi to British civil servants – ਸਿੱਖਾਂ ਦੇ ਰਾਜ ਦੀ ਵਿਥਿਆ **sikk^{h}ā̃ de rāj dī vik^{h}iā** (1866) and ਪੰਜਾਬੀ ਬਾਤ ਚੀਤ **panjabā bāt cīt** (1868) – were in Gurmukhi. Beharee Lal was the first Indian scholar to publish a grammar of Panjabi in 1867, and he, too, used Gurmukhi. For the last two centuries, Panjabi and Gurmukhi have been intimately associated with each other. No serious learner of Panjabi can do without Gurmukhi. Educational institutions in East Punjab have spent billions of rupees to create Panjabi dictionaries and encyclopaedias of idioms, proverbs and folklore in Gurmukhi. ਗੁਰੁਸ਼ਬਦ ਰਤਨਾਕਰ ਮਹਾਨ ਕੋਸ਼ **guruśabad ratnākar mahān koś**, an encyclopaedia of Sikhism by Kahn Singh Nabha (a mine of information about Panjabi history and culture as well) is in Gurmukhi. A number of Panjabi scholars have published grammars of modern and old Panjabi and histories of the language in Gurmukhi. No comparable work has been done in the Pakistani Punjab, where Panjabi is written in Shahmukhi. Instead, the Pakistani government has banned the use of Panjabi in the provincial legislative assembly in favour of its "national" language Urdu.

This unbiased analysis of the historical and political situations concerning the two scripts is not intended to give the impression that either script is better than the other for writing Panjabi *for normal day-to-day use*. Notwithstanding any religious or political considerations, there is no escaping the fact that Gurmukhi was tailor-made for Panjabi (and is used for writing Panjabi only) and Shahmukhi is a variety of the Arabic script imported from outside via Persian and then altered and adjusted for Indian languages.

This book assumes that the *learner* has learnt Panjabi through Gurmukhi (through *Colloquial Panjabi, Colloquial Panjabi 2* or similar courses, all of which use Gurmukhi). For the benefit of those who cannot read Gurmukhi (such as linguists using this book and those Panjabis who do not read Gurmukhi), all the Panjabi examples are provided in phonetic transcription as well (and also in IPA where appropriate). Bringing in Shahmukhi would have increased the size (and price) of the book without adding to its usefulness.

All the classical Panjabi literature originally written in the Perso-Arabic script (by Farid, Shah Husain, Bulleh Shah, Waris Shah, Sultan Bahu, Hashim and others) is now available in Gurmukhi as well. Those who are interested in the modern Pakistani Panjabi literature can learn this script (Shahmukhi) from several websites. Or they can learn the script from *Colloquial Urdu* or any other book that teaches Urdu. Shahmukhi is useful for reading the modern Panjabi literature written in Pakistan. But if you wish to study Panjabi grammar in depth and make use of the books about the history and socio-cultural background of the language from a historical perspective (such as the writings of Duni Chandra, Piara Singh Padam, Sant Singh Sekhon, Kahn Singh Nabha, Sahib Singh, Harkirat Singh, Gurbachan Singh Sidhu and others), you have to learn Gurmukhi.

1.4 Panjabi grammar

The first full-fledged Panjabi grammar was published by the Rev. William Carey in 1812. He wrote the book for his fellow missionaries with the explicitly stated purpose of converting Indians to Christianity. Then other missionaries, army officers and civil servants also published utilitarian grammars of Panjabi for the benefit of their colleagues. It would be pointless to list all of them here. It would also be unfair to expect their analyses of the language to be scholarly. But there is one important exception. John Beames, an English magistrate in Calcutta, published his three-volume *A Comparative Grammar of the Modern Aryan Languages of India* (1872–79) in which he analysed the major modern Indic languages (including Panjabi) as a serious linguist. It may be said that he used his legal expertise painstakingly to analyse the structure of these languages (also taking into account the historical development of these languages) and tried to do justice to these languages on the basis of the evidence he found. The Rev. S.H. Kellogg's *A Grammar of the Hindi Language* is one of the books he criticised. But the irony of history is that Kellogg's elegant-looking framework of "tenses" in Hindi proved to be highly influential and was imitated by several later Hindi and Panjabi grammarians (e.g., the Rev. E.P. Newton (1898) and Duni Chandra (1964)), some of whom had no utilitarian motives, often without acknowledging Kellogg as the originator of the framework. Beames's perfectly justified objection to Kelloggs's practice of choosing some verb forms or sequences of verb forms as "tenses" and ignoring others, was simply ignored.

Other attempts to set up Panjabi "tenses" on non-Kelloggian lines were also made. In 1888, Major Henry Court published an English translation of Phillauri's ਸਿੱਖਾਂ ਦੇ ਰਾਜ ਦੀ ਵਿਖਿਆ **sikkʰã de rāj dī vikʰiā** and added *A Short Gurmukhi Grammar* to it. Court first sets up two "moods" – Imperative and Indicative. Various Panjabi "tenses" are accommodated in the latter. One of these "tenses" is quite oddly named "future past". T. Grahame Bailey published *Panjabi Grammar: A Brief Grammar of Panjabi as Spoken in the Wazirabad District* in 1904. In 1912, he published (in collaboration with T. Cummings) *Panjabi Manual and Grammar: A Guide to the Colloquial Panjabi.* This book has been reprinted several times and is still available. In his lifetime, Bailey enjoyed the reputation of being able to "speak Panjabi and Urdu better than the native speakers". He uses his own "tense" system for Panjabi, and, like all other European scholars of Panjabi before him, simply ignores the complicated verb sequences found in the language. The Panjabi tense system presented in Jawahir Singh's *A Guide to Panjabi* (1930), designed for teaching Panjabi to English officers, followed Court with a few minor changes. Another Panjabi grammar meant for the non-native speakers is N.I. Tolstaya's *The Panjabi Language: A Descriptive Grammar*, which was originally written for the Russian learner of Panjabi. The English translation of this thin volume of eighty pages was published in 1981.

From the beginning of the 20th century some Sikh and Hindu scholars started feeling seriously the need for teaching Panjabi to their younger generation. In the state schools, Urdu was the medium of instruction and Panjabi was taught in only some of them as an optional subject. The first major (and voluminous) work on Panjabi grammar was published by Ram Singh in 1924, called ਵੱਡਾ ਪੰਜਾਬੀ ਵਿਆਕਰਣ **vaḍḍā panjābī viākaraṇ**. This book remains unmatched in the detailed coverage of all the aspects of the language. Two or three years later, some Panjabi scholars formed a ਵਿਆਕਰਣ ਸੁਧਾਰਕ ਕਮੇਟੀ *Viākaraṇ Sudhārak Kameṭī* (Grammar Reform Committee), which held several meetings and discussed Panjabi grammar in order to "reform" it. After one of these meetings came the final verdict, "After a discussion lasting full three days, the Committee has decided that the Panjabi verbs have three major tenses which can be further subdivided into nine, *and no more*" (Karam Singh 1929: 196. Translated from Panjabi and emphasis added). This "tense system" of Panjabi described and used in Karam Singh's ਨਵੀਨ ਪੰਜਾਬੀ ਵਿਆਕਰਣ, ਭਾਗ 3 **navīn panjābī viākaraṇ, b^{h}āg 3** was literally "designed by a committee". An account the historical development of Panjabi and its grammar is found in Duni Chandra's ਪੰਜਾਬੀ ਭਾਸ਼ਾ ਦਾ ਵਿਕਾਸ **panjābī b^{h}āśā dā vikās** (1959) and ਪੰਜਾਬੀ ਭਾਸ਼ਾ ਦਾ ਵਿਆਕਰਣ **panjābī b^{h}āśā dā viākaraṇ** (1964), in which he follows the Kelloggian tense system with a few minor modifications. More recently, Boota Singh Brar published ਪੰਜਾਬੀ ਵਿਆਕਰਨ ਸਿਧਾਂਤ ਅਤੇ ਵਿਹਾਰ **panjābī viākaran sid^{h}ānt ate vihār** (2008) on more modern lines. Ram Singh, Karam Singh, Duni Chandra and Boota Singh Brar wrote their books in Panjabi.

15th–17th century Panjabi is one of the languages used in the Sikh holy book *Srī Gurū Granth Sāhib*. Sahib Singh's ਗੁਰਬਾਣੀ ਵਿਆਕਰਣ **gurbāṇī viākaraṇ** (1939) and Harkirat Singh's ਗੁਰਬਾਣੀ ਦੀ ਭਾਸ਼ਾ ਤੇ ਵਿਆਕਰਨ **gurbāṇī dī b^{h}āśā te viākaran** (2011) deal with this old variety of Panjabi. These books are indispensable for any grammarian of *modern* Panjabi as well. With the loss of word-final short (lax) vowels, some verb forms have become homophonous but continue to behave in their old ways. They can be (and actually have been) a trap for the unwary grammarian, as Chapter 11 shows.

Some academic linguists who are native speakers of Panjabi also published grammars of Panjabi in English. The first of these books is H.S. Gill's (written in collaboration with his mentor H.A. Gleason) *A Reference Grammar of Punjabi* (1961/1969). Kali Charan Bahl wrote a thin volume of fewer than one hundred pages, *A Grammatical Sketch of Panjabi* (1964). Gill and Gleason's book was was re-published in India in

1969. This book strictly follows the American Structuralist tradition. This book is important as a pioneering work in this field done by two academic linguists. But a volume of just 160 pages without an index is hardly a "reference" grammar by modern standards.

The most significant Panjabi grammar recently written by a native speaker academic linguist is Tej K. Bhatia's *Punjabi: A Cognitive-Descriptive Grammar* (1993). This book was published in the series *Lingua Descriptive Studies*, started in 1977, whose aim was to produce grammars of individual languages for cross-language comparison. This book is authoritative, very detailed and *very technical* as well. It is meant exclusively for theoretical linguists and not for language learners. So Bhatia's book and this book (published by the same publisher) are not meant to compete with but complement each other. Users of this book who want more information can go to Bhatia's book. But it must be made clear to readers that the theoretical views underlying the analyses of Panjabi presented in the two books differ in some important respects.

For teachers and other more advanced users

This chapter is based on the author's own research as well as information gathered from many other sources. Interested readers are referred to:

(Duni) Chandra (1959)

(Sir George) Grierson (1894–1927)

(Piara Singh) Padam (1954)

(Sant Singh) Sekhon (1961)

(Gurbachan Singh) Sidhu (2004)

Linguistic Atlas of the Punjab (1973)

and the numerous works cited by Chandra, Padam and Sidhu.

Masica (1993) also deals briefly with Panjabi and mentions some other writings on the subject.

Chapter 2

Language as a Social Semiotic or Cultural Tool

> Our language can be regarded as an ancient city: a maze of little streets and squares, of old and new houses, of houses with extensions from various periods, and all this surrounded by a multitude of new suburbs with straight and regular streets and uniform houses.
>
> - Ludwig Wittgenstein (2009 (1953): 11[e])

> Language is a labyrinth of paths. You approach from *one* side and know your way about; you approach the same place from another side and no longer know your way about.
>
> - Ludwig Wittgenstein (*ibid.* 88[e])

This chapter gives in an outline form the author's theoretical views regarding language and grammar. The title of this chapter sums up these views.

The standard European way of conceptualising and symbolising the world for the purpose of speaking a language (or "thinking for speaking" (Slobin 1987)), is just *one* of the many actual and possible ways of doing this and is certainly not "universal" despite the fact that many (but not all) conservative and old-fashioned European and American linguists and their followers elsewhere still hold this view. New research on non-European languages (especially the so-called "exotic" languages) is rapidly changing this old-fashioned view. It may actually turn out that the European view is a *minority* view. Panjabi is an Indo-European language like the majority of European languages. But it conceptualises the world (especially the spatio-temporal constituency of situations) in radically different ways, resulting in grammatical features which were thoroughly misunderstood, twisted and often ignored by past grammarians with Euro-centred biases and prejudices. A serious advanced learner of Panjabi must learn to approach the language with a right mindset free from any Euro-centred prejudices.

This chapter is a bit philosophical and theoretical in orientation. Those not interested in this may move on to Chapter 3 (and come back to this chapter later on, if they wish). Some of the important ideas presented below will also be briefly discussed in the following chapters.

For teachers and other more advanced users

Briefly, the theoretical views underlying this book involve a rejection of the Platonic-Cartesian tradition that has dominated European thinking about language for centuries. Basically, this classical approach separates the realm of the supposedly "universal" categories of meaning (in actual practice, categories of European languages and culture imposed upon other languages and cultures) from the realm of linguistic forms in different languages. It views the world standing "out there" nicely categorised (according to European categories, of course) which different languages present in different ways. For centuries, this linguistic philosophy has plagued the analyses of non-European languages made by European scholars and by the non-European scholars who uncritically followed them. The views underlying this book are more akin to those of ancient Indian linguists and the philosophers of the Phenomenological movement in European philosophy that originated in the first half of the 20th century. Most philosophers in the Phenomenological tradition consciously and explicitly rejected the Platonic-Cartesian dualistic tradition. They insisted on dealing with *phenomena*, taking appearances seriously instead of trying to go behind them in search of the pure Platonic categories they "imperfectly reveal". Many ancient Indian philosophers of different schools practised their own varieties of phenomenology, and many modern Indian philosophers do the same (Chattopadhyaya, Embree and Mohanty 1992). The phenomenological point of view is that language should be studied as a *phenomenon* in real world situations of culture and context.

> In such original works language is nothing like an instrument just 'putting into words' what has already been thought in the author's mind. On the contrary,

> here language is the medium in which thinking comes into expression – in which thinking forms itself into expressed thought. When we approach it dynamically, we see that the language in which thinking comes into expression gives form to *what* is thought, and does not take what is already thought and simply does it in words. Yet at the same time this does not mean that what is thought is only the product of the words which express it. Gadamer says that 'a thought first attains determinate existence in being formulated in words,'...
>
> (Bortoft 2012: 114)

What the world is "really like" before being represented in a given language should be a non-issue for linguists but it had plagued studies of language in the West for centuries. Ancient Indian linguists holding phenomenological views, like the 5th–6th century Indian linguist Bhartṛhari, always insisted that grammar should deal with the world as it manifests itself in language, not with the world as "it really is" (if it is possible to know this at all.)

> Since the universe which is a bundle of powers is always there in all its aspects, some power or other is intended to be conveyed in a particular context.
>
> (*Vākyapadīya* III.7.2)

> There is no cognition in the world in which word does not figure. All knowledge, as it were, is intertwined with the word.
>
> (*Vākyapadīya* I.110)

> Words are based on cognitions which do not reveal the full reality and so present things in another form, not determined by their real form.
>
> (*Vākyapadīya* III.3.4)

> It is through the word that the object is established.
>
> (*Vākyapadīya* I.115)

This book is not an attempt to fit Panjabi into any pre-existing theoretical *syntactic framework* with "universalistic" ambitions and pretensions. The theoretical *approaches* (not "language-independent" theoretical frameworks) which inspire this work – Cognitive Grammar (Taylor 2002, Croft and Cruse 2004, Langacker 2008, and others), Usage-based approach (Tomasello 2005, Bybee 2010, Evans 2014, and others), Construction Grammar (Goldberg 1995, Croft 2001, and others), Language as Social Semiotic (Halliday 1978), Thinking for Speaking (Slobin 1987, 1996) – all come from the *Functionalist* stable, their common denominator being what Evans (2014) pithily calls "language-as-use" stance as opposed to the "language-as-instinct" stance taken by the Rationalist tradition represented by Noam Chomsky and his followers.

The structure of a language, for us, is the way it is because it has adapted to the needs of language users in their socio-cultural activities or what Bhartṛhari called लोकव्यवहार *lokavyavahāra* or 'the (social) activities of the people'. This being the case, a language cannot be anything other than a self-organising complex adaptive system (Larsen-Freeman and Cameron 2008), in which *structuration* is always going on and *structures* are simply temporary islands of relative stability in a sea of constant change. Indian linguists used the term प्रवाहनिरन्तरता *pravāhanirantaratā* 'stream-like continuity' for the continuity in languages. They never regarded a language as an abstract mathematical system. These structures cannot be fully explained exclusively in terms of their constituents, which is the central dogma in what are known as the "structuralist" approaches of various flavours. Moreover, a purely *synchronic* approach advocated by the structuralist camp (considering the *present* state of the system only) is not enough. *Diachronic* considerations (taking into account historical development of the structures) are necessary – if the information is available. The results of evolutionary and adaptive processes can be found everywhere in the system, with the different components of the system evolving in different ways and at different rates, so that Wittgenstein's first observation quoted at the start of this chapter is true of every living language. The grammatical system of a living language does not obey, synchronically or diachronically, any "logic" other than the one internal to itself.

Pāṇini (*circa* 7th–6th century BC), the author of the formidable and algebraically formalised Sanskrit grammar, takes this into account. A modern Indian linguist observes:

> He knows that he is not building a logical system where consistency is to be prized. He is rather discovering a system underlying the facts of language which strangely enough turns out to be of a heterogeneous nature and not amenable to explanation in terms of its units. Language is a system where elements are drawn from various sources and forged into a system by forces of time, space and numerous currents and cross currents of human behaviour. This frees him from the responsibility of stretching linguistic facts to conform to the Procrustean framework of thought in our terms of linguistic units alone. The prime task of a linguist, according to him, is to seek an explanation in terms of total human behaviour.
>
> J.D. Singh (1971: 263)

One of the rules (VIII.2.83) in Pāṇini's grammar is "In an answer to a salutation, but not when the other person has a low social status, the last vowel of the sentence becomes *pluta* (extra long) and gets the acute (high-falling) tonal accent." It is difficult to find a more ancient and better example of a grammarian taking "total human behaviour" into consideration. More recent examples of such an explanation come from Everett (2013), who presents the formula "Cognition + Culture + Communication = Language", and that "every society's values have helped mold a language to its needs over hundreds or even thousands of years" (p. 35).

"Total human behaviour" includes not only social interaction but also the conceptualisation and symbolisation of the reality, and language is the chief instrument for this. So language can aptly be described as a "cultural tool" (the sub-title of Everett's book mentioned above). It might be argued that the social interaction and the conceptualisation functions of language are logically independent of each other, so that one can take place without the other, but this is not the case in the total human behaviour in real life. So our approach to the "labyrinth of paths" of Panjabi grammar can be characterised as Cognitive Functionalism. This is not to claim that approaching "the same place from another side" (of "formalistic language universals") is not possible or cannot be fruitful but that is *not* the gate we have chosen for our enterprise.

While the modern scholars mentioned in this chapter should be credited for developing their views independently, a person familiar with the Indian grammatical tradition cannot help feeling that "there is nothing new under the sun". There is a strange similarity between the views of Bhartṛhari and those of modern Cognitive Grammarians and Usage-based theorists. Studying form-meaning pairings is not a new idea either. Patañjali (4th century BC) wrote his *Mahābhāṣya* ('great commentary') on Pāṇini's Sanskrit grammar. This commentary is in the form of a dialogue between two persons. One of them asks, "On what premises then does the great teacher Pāṇini proceed to write up his grammar?" The answer he gets is, "(On the assumption that) the relationship between linguistic elements and their meanings is continuous" (सिद्धे शब्दार्थसम्बन्धे *siddhe śabadārthasambandhe*). The Sanskrit word *siddha* also means 'accomplished', 'firmly established', 'enduring' etc. A close study of Pāṇini's Sanskrit grammar (regarded as the greatest grammar ever written for any language in the world and "one of the greatest monuments of human intelligence" by Bloomfield 1933) shows that Patañjali's characterisation of Pāṇini's methodology is perfectly correct. Pāṇini started neither with disembodied meanings nor with empty forms to which meanings are attached. He started with form-meaning pairings. In Sanskrit, as in any other natural language, there is no one-to-one correspondence of form and meaning, and he honestly presented the situation as he found it. It is interesting to know how the American Sanskritist W.D. Whitney (a dyed-in-the-wool dualist) brutally attacked Pāṇini for not proceeding dualistically "after our manner" and for following "the vastly more difficult and dangerous method" of working with form-meaning pairings. Whitney's damning verdict on Pāṇini's methodology is, "Anything more crude or unphilosophical than this could not well be imagined" (Whitney 1972 (1893): 165). Whitney's reaction is not surprising. He was an old-fashioned staunch adherent to the traditional Aristotelian philosophical view of categories (including grammatical categories) according to which categories are abstract containers with things either inside or outside the category and all the inside members sharing the same features. Pāṇini, who predated Aristotle by a few centuries, lived and worked in a very different intellectual milieu and his methodology *as a linguist* is perfectly refined and philosophical by his own standards (and also by the standards of many modern linguists mentioned above).

This is not to deny some cross-linguistic similarities (since all human beings share their biology and many socio-cultural needs), but imagining "language universals" *a priori* on the basis of some hypothesised Universal Grammar (UG) or Core Grammar built as a "a language organ" or "language module" inside the human brain or "language instinct" and then imposing these "abstract universals" (features of European languages in actual practice) on all human languages "at a deeper and abstract" level is a practice mostly discredited among serious linguists now. Some linguists are rejecting the very existence of "language universals" (Evans and Levinson 2009, Everett 2013, Evans 2014) and are even proclaiming that "Universal grammar is dead" (Tomasello 2009).

Practitioners of Construction Grammars in various flavours, linguists holding the Usage-based views and many others have started rejecting this dualistic practice of separating meaning and form and are insisting on studying form-meaning pairings.

As Cognitive Grammarians of all shades and persuasions agree, the role of conceptual metaphors is extremely significant not only in everyday language but also in the evolution and development of grammar. The process of some "content" words and constructions becoming "grammatical words" is known as *grammaticalisation* (or *grammaticisation*) (Bybee, Perkins and Paglicua 1994). A well-known example is the English *be going to* used to express the meaning of future time, as in *I am going to see him soon*, where a forward movement in space is metaphorically viewed as a forward movement in time. As we will see Chapter 8, the Panjabi postposition ਕੋਲ਼ **koḷ** 'near' is also used to express the meaning of transferable possession. Grammaticalisation leads to the phonetic abrasion of the word or construction. Many speakers of English now pronounce *going to* as *gonna* and most speakers of Panjabi in their fluent speech pronounce ਕੋਲ਼ **koḷ** as ਕੋ **ko**. But the cross-linguistic semantic similarity between the notions of possession and location was known to linguists decades before the concepts of metaphor and grammaticalisation came into modern linguistics (Allen 1964, Lyons 1967).

Evolutionary changes in a living language take place slowly over centuries, and different sub-systems evolve differently and at different speeds, so that at any particular time the first Wittgenstein quote given above aptly characterises any living language. An honest presentation of Panjabi grammar in the following chapters from our cognitive-functional perspective demonstrates this. In this book, we have not *defined* the word classes we have dealt with so far in any precise way. We have *characterised* each word class in three ways, taking a hint from Huddleston and Pullum (2005). The variety of forms and functions within each class is presented with an effort to make sense of the variety. The picture of Panjabi grammar is painted in the "warts and all" fashion in this book. As in English and most other living languages, it is very often not possible to assign a word or construction *in isolation* to any word class. This depends on how it is *used*. In Chapter 10 we deal with the Panjabi **copular-existential verb** or **copula** (the equivalent of the English *be*), but it is not possible to say whether it is unambiguously a **verb** or an **adverb of time** in some constructions. This may appear strange, but this *is* the case. Unfortunately, detailed and reliable samples of ancestor Prākrit languages of Panjabi (intervening between Sanskrit and modern Panjabi; see Chapter 1) are not available. But this copular-existential verb or copula has had an interesting history since Sanskrit as outlined below.

But the chapters dealing with the Panjabi **verb phrase** are going to present something not attested in any major Indo-European language outside the Indian sub-continent – the **serial verb constructions**. Such constructions are found in genetically unrelated and geographically non-contiguous languages in many parts of the world (Aikhenvald and Dixon 2006). Cultural factors – how the Indian view of time developed over the past three thousand years – seems to be responsible for this non-Indo-European development in the North Indian languages.

Our commitment to "Language as a Social Semiotic" or "Language as a Cultural Tool" view of language for an analysis of syntax entails commitment to (i) studying the grammatical *resources* of a language within the *context of culture* and (ii) studying the actual *use* of these resources within the *context of situation*. For practical reasons, a strict adherence to these principles is not always possible, but an attempt is made wherever possible throughout this book.

Let us look at two seemingly unrelated features of Panjabi.

1. Panjabi has the same word ਕੱਲ੍ਹ **kall^h** for both 'yesterday' and 'tomorrow', ਪਰਸੋਂ **parsõ** for both 'day before yesterday' and 'day after tomorrow' and so on, as shown in the following diagram.

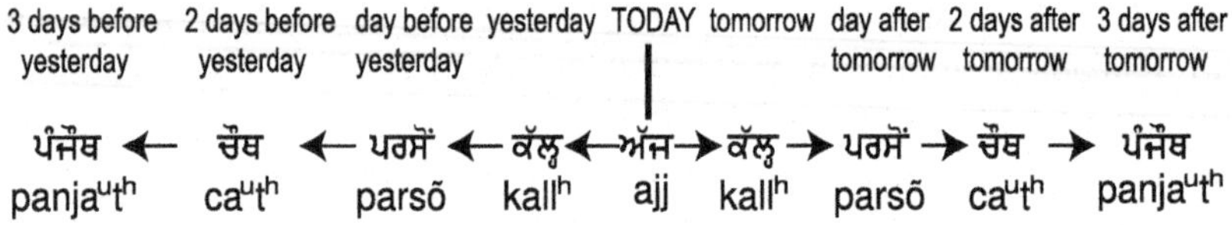

Figure 2.1 An overview of how Panjabi (and other Indian languages) symbolise time

What seems to matter is the *distance* from today, not whether the day lies in the past or the future.

2. What in English and most European languages is regarded as a single action is divided into component parts in Panjabi as in

ਮੈਂ	ਸੁੱਤਾ	ਪਿਆ	ਸੀ	ਤੇ	ਕੋਈ	ਮੇਰਾ	ਕੰਬਲ
mã^i	**suttā**	**piā**	**sī**	**te**	**koī**	**merā**	**kambaḷ**
I	slept	fallen	was	and	someone	my	blanket

ਲਾਹ	ਕੇ	ਲੈ	ਗਿਆ
lāh	**ke**	**la^i**	**giā**
having removed		having taken	gone

'I was sleeping and someone took away my blanket'

ਕਿਤਾਬ ਲੈ ਆਓ
kitāb la^i āo
book having taken come
'Bring the book'

It would be irresponsible to dismiss these features as "arbitrariness of the sign" or "superficial surface structure features". This is the way the temporal aspect of the world reveals itself as a *phenomenon* in Panjabi.

It was observed more than half a century ago by Cassirer (1955: 217ff) (who took his examples from African languages and did not mention any Indian language in his book) that in such languages

> Involuntarily, language transposes the structural relations of time into relations of space... As in the intuition of space, everything is here reduced to the simple distinction of near and far. The only essential difference that is grasped and clearly expressed is that between "now" and "not now" – between immediate present and which lies "outside it"... For this form of primary temporal intuition, the whole consciousness and its contents falls, as it were, into two spheres: a bright sphere illuminated by the light of the "present," and another, dark sphere... It produces abundant *gradations of time*, all encompassed in a unitary temporal order in which every moment has its specific position... The simple distinction of separate points in time must be transformed into a concept of mutual dynamic dependence between them, time as a form of pure intuition must be permeated with the function of causal judgement... The unity of action literally breaks into bits. At this stage language can represent an action only by dissecting it into all its particulars and rendering each one separately... Hence the whole of an action cannot be apprehended either in thought or language unless the consciousness literally "actualizes" it in all its details, thrusting each of it, one after another, into the light of the now.

Centuries earlier, Bhartṛhari made a similar interesting observation.

> What is called an action is a collection of parts produced in a sequence and mentally conceived as one and identical with the parts which are subordinate to it.
>
> (*Vākyapadīya* III.8.1)

> Verbs express things in that condition (i.e., having sequence), nouns on the other hand, operate as though suppressing this sequence.
>
> (*Vākyapadīya* III.8.29)

No better description of the semantics of a **serial verb** (discussed in Chapter 13) has ever been given. It should be mentioned here that Bhartṛhari was dealing with Sanskrit, in which serial verb constructions do not figure prominently, but they had appeared in the Middle Indic Parākrit-Apabhraṁśa language he spoke as his mother tongue, and the Indian view of time mentioned below had become an integral part of the Indian culture. So he probably projected this view into his analysis of the semantics of the Sanskrit verb.

This is the Indian philosophy of time, which we will call "spatialisation of time" and "atomisation of time". This philosophy is the basis of the well-known Buddhist doctrine of momentariness – dividing time into a succession of atomic moments and viewing only the present moment as real. But it was not invented by the Buddha or any other known thinker. It appears to be non-Aryan and popular in origin and became dominant as a part of the evolution of Indian culture (Thomas 1951: 165). It evolved over centuries in the post-Vedic North Indian culture and languages. The North Indian word **kal** (or **kall**^{h} in Panjabi, meaning both 'yesterday' and 'tomorrow') comes from the Sanskrit *kāle* 'in time', implying that 'today' is not 'in time'. The Buddha asked his followers to "seize the moment" and to get "instantaneous illumination" (Eliade 1958: 185). This view is shared by many non-Buddhistic philosophers as well. Patañjali's Yoga philosophy recommends "meditation on the instant and succession of instants in order to attain knowledge born of discernment" (Pannikkar 1976: 32). The Indian astronomers and mathematicians also adopted this view of time. (Stcherbatsky 1923: 41). It can be found in the non-Buddhistic religious books – the Shaiva book *Vāyavīya Saṁhitā* (9th or 10th century) and the Vaishnava book *Bhāgavata Purāṇa* (12th century). (Dasgupta 1922: 164).

A social semiotic is

> ... a system of meanings that constitute the 'reality' of the culture. This is the higher level system to which language is related; the semantic system of a language is a realisation of this social semiotic. There are many other forms of its symbolic realisation besides language; but language is unique in having its own semantic stratum.
>
> (Halliday 1978:123)

But how is the story relevant for Panjabi grammar? The examples of **serial verb constructions** given above are interesting in themselves. *But the more interesting part of the story is that tense as a grammatical category almost completely disappeared from Panjabi.* Language as a symbolic system or a part of its culture could not remain unaffected by this developing view of time.

Tense as a grammatical category indicates the time of an event etc. in relation to the moment of speaking. It divides the time notionally into **present** (at the moment of speaking), **past** (earlier than the moment of speaking) and **future** (later than the moment of speaking). What is significant here is that tense involves *situation-external* perspective, viewing time as moving from past to future. **Aspect**, on the other hand, adopts a *situation-internal* perspective and distinguishes the status of an event as completed, in progress, potential etc. With the above-mentioned view of time (involving the adoption of situation-internal perspective) gaining prominence in Indian culture over centuries, **tense** as a grammatical category was bound to become less and less important in the grammars of Indian languages with **aspect** gaining prominence.

The Panjabi **copula ਹੈ haⁱ** comes from the Sanskrit verb root √*as*. The grammatical behaviour of √*as* was idiosyncratic even in Pāṇini's times. It belonged to the second (or *ad* class) of roots and was conjugated in the *sārvadhātuka* or "general" tenses only (Pāṇini III.4.113–114). Another Sanskrit root √*bhū* was the substitute of √*as* in *ārdhadhātuka* or "special" tenses. The relevant rule given by Pāṇini is *asterbhūḥ* (II.4.52). This peculiarity of the root √*as* in Pāṇini's Sanskrit is ominous. In the Middle Indic languages, all the roots except √*as* were regularised and made to behave like the roots of the first (or √*bhū*) class. *Thus √as was considered to be outside the system of the Middle Indic verb.* It went on becoming more and more marginalised as time passed. The Panjabi verb ਹੋ **ho** comes from √*bhū*. In modern Panjabi, no verb except ਹੈ **haⁱ** is inflected for **tense**. But even this is sometimes doubtful. In some constructions, it is even difficult to decide whether ਹੈ **haⁱ** is a verb or an adverb of time. All other Panjabi verbs (including ਹੋ **ho**) have **aspectual adjectival** and **nominal** forms only. But ਹੈ **haⁱ**, on the other hand, has no aspectual form. The presence of ਹੈ **haⁱ** is not obligatory in a Panjabi clause. Even when it is there, it does not become a part of the verb cluster or serial verb and does not affect the **valency** of the serial verb and a mono-clausal interpretation is the right one. (See Chapter 13.)

The reason why ਹੈ **haⁱ** suffered this fate seems to be that its meaning ('pure existence') is not that of a proper verb mentioned by Bhartṛhari: "a collection of parts produced in a sequence and mentally conceived as one". All other verbs are treated in Panjabi grammar as 'becoming' verbs, but √*as* ਹੈ **haⁱ** conveys the meaning 'being' only, and *hence it is not a verb at all.*

Systems and sub-systems within a language change slowly and at different rates over time. So if the Panjabi ਹੈ **ha'** behaves differently and inconsistently in different structures, this should not surprise us. At any given time, a language is *poly*sytemic, rather than *mono*systemic. In this book, Panjabi is treated as such.

In this book, the *grammatical* meaning of a **serial verb construction** is analysed in Bhartṛharian terms. This probably applies to such constructions in many other genetically unrelated and geographically non-contiguous languages as well. An interesting example from Pirahã given by Everett in his iconoclastic and provocative book *Language The Cultural Tool* (2013: 132) is worth mentioning here. The Pirahã equivalent of

That smells good.

is literally

It pleases me, the smoke, which hits my nose, as I pass by your fire.

Other examples abound in the study of serial verb constructions in more than a dozen languages presented in Aikhenvald and Dixon (2006: 182). In Tariana,

I managed to return passing over and up away (from here), up until that place.

is literally

I return–I arrive–I pass–I go up–I go.

Their Tariana consultant remarked to the researchers about the use of several verbs in a mono-clausal serial verb construction, "It is not like Portuguese, we just cannot say it with one verb." The temporal aspect of the world as a phenomenon reveals itself in different ways in Portuguese and Tariana. It will be interesting to interpret this in the light of Cassirer's observations mentioned above. The concerted efforts of generations of passionately committed Eurocentric linguists and philosophers have not been able to exorcise and lay at rest the spirit of Benjamin Lee Whorf! By the way, Whorf simply (and unknowingly) repeated the vital truth uttered centuries earlier by the proto-Whorfian linguist Bhartṛhari (Iyer 1969). The grammar of a language (as a cultural tool) will symbolically picture the world and its spatio-temporal processes as the rest of the culture of its speakers does. It follows its own "logical categories", and not the the allegedly "universal" and "language-independent" categories dreamt up by an armchair linguist, however "logical" or "elegant" they may appear.

The number of such possible clusters in Indian languages is staggeringly large, as will be argued in Chapter 13. Construction Grammarians have shown that the abstract *skeleton* of a construction (the English ditransitive construction, for example) is meaningful (i.e., has meaning potential) in itself (Goldberg 1995). But there should be no "learnability" problem for a speaker of Panjabi (or of any other language with serial verb constructions). If they can learn the meanings of thousands of words in different contexts, they should have no problem learning the meaning potential of two hundred or so abstract skeletons of constructions as well.

Panjabi has an additional complication of the so-called "split ergativity" (also unjustifiably and derogatively called "(merely) morphological" ergativity or "pseudo-ergativity"). But the usage-based or form-meaning pairing approach adopted in this book emphatically denies that anything is "split" or "(merely) morphological" or "pseudo" about Panjabi ergativity. It fits perfectly well into the inner semantic logic of verb agreement and case marking in Panjabi grammar. This is the way some aspects of the world manifest themselves in Panjabi. Another complication arises from the fact that some members of the verb cluster are grammaticalised "auxiliary" versions of some lexical verbs. Different auxiliary verbs are at different stages of grammaticalisation. All such features have meaning potential in the ever evolving system of Panjabi grammar.

These and many other types of *phenomena* in Panjabi and other languages simply *exist*, having come into existence as a result of the evolutionary and ongoing inner dynamics of the system. In dealing with them, it is unnecessary to bring in *essences* dwelling in some Platonic heaven. In 1924, the Panjabi grammarian Ram Singh identified about a dozen "passive" structures in Panjabi, as if each was an imperfect incarnation of the Platonic category "passive voice". The term "peculiar passives" has been used for some constructions in Hindi (Davison 1981). Such constructions exist in Panjabi as well. Describing the variety of ergativity in Panjabi and Hindi as "split" or "merely morphological" or a "superficial surface structure phenomenon" and the variety found in the Australian language Dyirbal as "true" and so on smacks of Platonism

– that the true and perfect essences of **passive voice** or **ergativity** exist Platonistically and manifest themselves imperfectly in Panjabi. This approach is firmly rejected in this book. For us, linguistic forms, structures and constructions simply *exist* as *phenomena* and should be dealt with as such. If they happen to have some similarity with those in other languages, this should be noted and investigated. So our approach may be described as *phenomenological existentialism*. Sartre's famous dictum "Existence precedes essence" is adopted throughout our analysis of Panjabi grammar.

Coming back to **serial verb constructions** (dealt with in detail in Chapter 13), which are a characteristic feature of Panjabi and other Indian languages, it may turn out that the languages with such constructions in the world outnumber the ones without them. This will open a fertile field for future linguists. Aikhenvald and Dixon (2006) have made a *very* good start. Similar technical analyses of Indian languages are also needed.

But, as was pointed out in the Preface, this book is *primarily* intended as a pedagogical descriptive grammar, and not a research monograph. So no attempt has been made to fit Panjabi into any theoretical framework or to go into very technical details. It is hoped that linguists interested in a wide variety languages (and especially the features shared by Indian languages, such as the woefully neglected **serial verb constructions**) will find the book useful. But they will need to interpret the analysed examples for their purpose. This chapter has been included to make it clear what they can expect from the book.

Part II
Phonetics, Phonology and Script

Chapter 3

Panjabi Sounds and Script

Preview of the chapter

Panjabi is claimed to be a "phonetic language". This claim is then explained as "In Panjabi, you write exactly as you speak and speak exactly as you write." But this claim is wrong on two counts – (i) A *language* must not be confused with the *script* used for writing it; no *language* is "phonetic"; only a *writing system* may be so in the sense that there is "one to one correspondence" between its symbols and the phonemes (distinctive sounds) of the language it is used for, and (ii) the Panjabi writing system is not perfectly "phonetic" even in this sense. In this chapter we study only the native Panjabi script known as Gurmukhi used for writing Panjabi in India and by the Panjabi people of Indian origin living outside India. In Pakistan, Panjabi is written in a modified form of the Arabic script known as Shahmukhi. For reasons of space, and also for reasons mentioned in the Preface and Chapter 18, Shahmukhi is not included in the main body of this book.

3.1 The Panjabi "alphabet"

The native Panjabi script, also known as Gurmukhi, belongs to the north-western group of the scripts of the Brahmi family. It is thus related to all the major indigenous modern Indian scripts such as Devanagari, Bangla, Gujarati, Tamil, Telugu, Kannada and Malyalam as well as to the Thai and Tibetan scripts. The writing system underlying all these scripts is neither purely alphabetic like the Latin alphabet nor purely syllabic in the sense of having a separate symbol for every possible syllable in the language. It is a nice synthesis of the two, known as an *alpha-syllabic* system (Matthews 2007: 16), as the rest of this chapter will demonstrate.

The present form of the Panjabi writing system is believed to have been finalised in the first half of the 16th century by Guru Angad Dev, the second guru of the Sikh faith, to write the sacred compositions of his faith and Panjabi as it was spoken at that time by making use of and refining and systematising the existing writing conventions used in and around the Panjabi-speaking areas. The result is an extremely simple and logical writing system ideally suitable for writing Panjabi. Almost all the letters and symbols of the system already existed in the regional scripts of the Brahmi family (G.B. Singh 1950). The earlier forms of these regional varieties were well-established in India by the 5th century BC. Some modern scholars argue that the original Brahmi script developed from the Indus Valley script and does not have a Semitic origin.

However, some changes have taken place in the pronunciation of Panjabi since then. Some of the earlier writing conventions have been discarded and some new ones developed. Certain changes have taken place in the older *phonological* system (the underlying system governing the actual pronunciation) on which the Gurmukhi script was based. While this chapter deals with this *basic* phonological system, these changes are dealt with in the next chapter. But still, a *systematic* relation exists between this basic system and the slightly modified but still the same older writing system and the new *phonetic* changes in pronunciation. So a proper understanding of this system is necessary in order to understand the Panjabi **tones**, which make Panjabi unique among the major languages of the Indian sub-continent.

3.2 The phonetic transcription

The phonetic transcript is used throughout this book for the benefit of those (including the users of Shahmukhi) who do not read Gurmukhi. In other words, this book does not "force" the Panjabi script on any reader. This transcription system is the one developed in the 19th century for transcribing Sanskrit. But three changes have been made: (i) when two letters are used to represent one distinct sound, the second letter has been superscripted to make it clear that the composite symbol represents one sound, and not a sequence of two sounds, (ii) **ḷ** and **ṛ** are used differently in this book, and (iii) new symbols have been added for the sounds borrowed from Arabic, Persian and English. The Sanskrit sounds represented by **ḷ** and **ṛ** do not exist in Panjabi and the Panjabi sounds they are used for here do not exist in Sanskrit. Also, Sanskrit words are transcribed using a different font in this book. So there should be no confusion. The IPA symbols used in the charts, diagrams and elsewhere in the book are there for the benefit of linguists interested in the phonetic technicalities. But they are not explained; it is assumed that these scholars know these symbols well.

The Panjabi phonological system and the Gurmukhi letters for representing it are given in the following chart. Gurmukhi originally had the first thirty-five letters given in the chart. So it is still known as ਪੈਂਤੀ **pa'ntī** 'thirty-five'. The remaining seven letters were added later.

Some of the symbols in the chart are put in shaded boxes. They had or have developed certain phonetic peculiarities which affect their pronunciation and/or spelling of the words in which they occur. We shall deal with these peculiarities later in this chapter and the next.

PANJABI (GURMUKHI) SCRIPT AND TRANSCRIPTION

Vowel Bearers

ੳ	ਅ	ੲ

Older Fraicatives

ਸ s [s]	ਹ h [ɦ]

Consonant Square

	Voiceless Unaspirate	Voiceless Aspirate	Voiced Unaspirate	Voiced Aspirate	Nasal
Velar	ਕ k [k]	ਖ k^{h} [k^{h}]	ਗ g [g]	ਘ g^{h} [g^{ɦ}]	ਙ ṅ [ŋ]
Palatal	ਚ c [ʧ]	ਛ c^{h} [ʧ^{h}]	ਜ j [ʤ]	ਝ j^{h} [ʤ^{ɦ}]	ਞ ñ [ɲ]
Retroflex	ਟ ṭ [ʈ]	ਠ ṭ^{h} [ʈ^{h}]	ਡ ḍ [ɖ]	ਢ ḍ^{h} [ɖ^{ɦ}]	ਣ ṇ [ɳ]
Dental	ਤ t [t]	ਥ t^{h} [t^{h}]	ਦ d [d]	ਧ d^{h} [d^{ɦ}]	ਨ n [n]
Bilabial	ਪ p [p]	ਫ p^{h} [p^{h}]	ਬ b [b]	ਭ b^{h} [b^{ɦ}]	ਮ m [m]

Frictionless Continuants

ਯ y [j]	ਰ r [r]	ਲ l [l]	ਵ v [v]	ੜ ṛ [ɽ]

New Fricatives

ਸ਼ ś [ʃ]	ਖ਼ x [x]	ਗ਼ ɣ [ɣ]	ਜ਼ z [z]	ਫ਼ f [f]

More Recent Additions

ਲ਼ ḷ [ɭ]	ਕ਼ q [q]

Figure 3.1 Gurmukhi "alphabet" and phonetic transcription

ਙ, ਞ, ਣ, ੜ and the more recently added ਲ਼ do not occur word-initially (except in their names!). ਙ and ਞ do not occur (or occur extremely rarely) as *independent* nasal consonants. (For those who are more deeply interested, the only commonly used words in which they occur are ਲੰਙਾ 'lame', ਕੰਞਣ 'bracelet', ਵਾਂਙ 'in the manner of', ਜੰਞ 'marriage party' and ਅੰਞਾਣਾ, 'ignorant' or 'child'.)

3.3 Names of the letters

A chart of the Panjabi letters is given below with the name of each letter shown in the Panjabi script itself and in phonetic transcription. Since the *sound* or *pronunciation* of each character is more important than its *name*, this chart can be ignored by readers not interested in Gurmukhi. The names of the consonant letters have a pattern except in the case of ਟ, whose older name has become homophonous to a taboo word in the language. For the pronunciation of the names of the voiced aspirate letters, read the next chapter. It is notable that the group of the letters in each of the rows from 2–5 has a name. Each name consists of the first letter of the group *plus* the word ਵਰਗ **varag** 'group'. Consonants in each group are **homorganic**. It will become clear later in this chapter why they are treated as special in the Panjabi spelling conventions.

	ੳ ਊੜਾ ūṛā	ਅ ਐੜਾ a'ṛā	ੲ ਈੜੀ īṛī	ਸ ਸੱਸਾ sassā	ਹ ਹਾਹਾ hāhā
ਕਵਰਗ kavarg	ਕ ਕੱਕਾ kakkā	ਖ ਖੱਖਾ k^hakk^{h}ā	ਗ ਗੱਗਾ gaggā	ਘ ਘੱਗਾ g^haggā	ਙ ਙੰਙਾ ṅaṅṅā
ਚਵਰਗ cavarg	ਚ ਚੱਚਾ caccā	ਛ ਛੱਛਾ c^hacc^{h}ā	ਜ ਜੱਜਾ jajjā	ਝ ਝੱਜਾ j^hajjā	ਞ ਞੰਈਆ ñaīyā
ਟਵਰਗ ṭavarg	ਟ ਟੈਂਕਾ ṭā'kā	ਠ ਠੱਠਾ $ṭ^h$aṭṭ^{h}ā	ਡ ਡੱਡਾ ḍaḍḍā	ਢ ਢੱਡਾ $ḍ^h$aḍḍā	ਣ ਣਾਣਾ ṇāṇā
ਤਵਰਗ tavarg	ਤ ਤੱਤਾ tattā	ਥ ਥੱਥਾ t^hatt^{h}ā	ਦ ਦੱਦਾ daddā	ਧ ਧੱਦਾ d^haddā	ਨ ਨੰਨਾ nannā
ਪਵਰਗ pavarg	ਪ ਪੱਪਾ pappā	ਫ ਫੱਫਾ p^happ^{h}ā	ਬ ਬੱਬਾ babbā	ਭ ਭੱਬਾ b^habbā	ਮ ਮੱਮਾ mammā
	ਯ ਯੱਈਆ yaīā	ਰ ਰਾਰਾ rārā	ਲ ਲੱਲਾ lallā	ਵ ਵੱਵਾ vavvā	ੜ ੜਾੜਾ ṛāṛā
	ਸ਼	ਖ਼	ਗ਼	ਜ਼	ਫ਼

Figure 3.2 Names of the Gurmukhi letters

Letters in the other rows are not treated as belonging to a special group. As will be pointed out later, letters in the last group are recent additions, so they do not have any established names. Generally, the words ਬਿੰਦੀ ਵਾਲ਼ਾ **bindī vāḷā** 'with a dot' is added to the name of the older letter to which a dot is added. For example, ਸ਼ is called ਬਿੰਦੀ ਵਾਲ਼ਾ ਸੱਸਾ **bindī vāḷā sassā** ('ਸ with a dot') For two more recent additions, see the chart on page 42.

3.4 Panjabi pronunciation

We shall first discuss the Panjabi consonants inside the Consonant Square. All these consonants are basically **stop** consonants. The flow of the outgoing breath is *stopped in the mouth*. In the case of the **nasal** consonants, however, it goes on escaping through the nose. Each row in the chart represents a **place of articulation** and each column a **manner of articulation**. Each consonant's unique identity is determined by its place in the grid. The Panjabi ਡ **ḍ** sound, for example, is a **voiced unaspirate retroflex** stop. These technical terms are explained below.

3.4.1 Panjabi stop consonants

A. Place of articulation

Velar	The outgoing breath is stopped by the back of the tongue touching the soft palate as for the English *k* and *g* sounds.
Palatal	The front part of the tongue touches the hard palate behind the gum ridge as for the English *ch* in *church*. The Panjabi **palatal** stop consonants are released with a friction-like sound like the English **palatal** consonants. So they are also known as **affricates**.
Retroflex	The underside of the curled tongue touches the hard palate behind the gum ridge. English has no equivalent sounds.
Dental	The tip of the tongue touches the upper teeth as for the Italian and French *t* and *d*.
Bilabial	The upper and the lower lip join to stop the flow of air.

All the five consonants in a row are known as **homorganic** consonants because the same organs of speech are involved in the articulation of all of them.

B. Manner of articulation

Voiceless	The vocal chords in the throat do not vibrate.
Voiced	Vocal chords in the throat vibrate and create a buzzing sound.
Unaspirate	The outgoing flow of breath is strictly controlled and the consonant is released with little or no puff of air.
Aspirate	The flow of air is very strong and the consonant is released with a strong puff of air. It should be noted that the English voiceless *k* and *p* in most positions are lightly aspirated. The Panjabi voiceless stops are either completely unaspirated or strongly aspirated. The English-like light aspiration will not work in Panjabi.
Nasal	The flow of air stopped in the mouth goes on escaping through the nose. All the nasal consonants of Panjabi are ***voiced***.

Some modern phoneticians object to the term **voiced aspirate**, arguing that true voicing and aspiration are not involved in the production of these consonants. They suggest the use of the term **breathy voiced**. Leaving aside the merit of their argument, the term **voiced aspirate** makes a lot of sense in Panjabi phonology. In the dialects of Panjabi dealt with in this book, the voiced aspirate consonants have lost their aspiration in all positions and voicing in some positions.

Panjabi ਣ **ṇ**, though included in this part of the chart (as per tradition), is, strictly speaking, not a **stop** consonant. It is a **flap** consonant, articulated by rapidly flapping the underside of the curled tongue against the part of the palate behind the gum ridge. All the flap consonants in Panjabi are **lax** because the muscles of the tongue are lax for the articulation of these consonants. The non-lax consonants are sometimes called **tense**. As we shall see below, Panjabi has three lax vowels as well. The importance of this distinction and the phonetic behaviour of these lax sounds is described later in this chapter and the next chapter.

3.4.2 Panjabi continuant consonants

While the flow of the outgoing breath is *stopped* in the mouth for the **stop** consonants, it is only *obstructed* in one way or the other but not completely stopped for the articulation of the continuants. If it goes out with a frictional sound, the consonant is called a **fricative**. If no frictional sound is produced, the consonant is known as a **frictionless continuant**. Panjabi originally had only two fricatives – **ਸ s** and **ਹ h**. Five more were added with the words borrowed from Arabic, Persian and English. One of these **fricatives (ਸ਼ ś)** has an extremely interesting history. They are described in the following chart. As you can see, the Panjabi letters for these sounds have been created by adding a dot beneath the letter for closest-sounding Panjabi consonant. These letters were created towards the close of the 19th century but came into general use in the twenties and thirties of the 20th century. Many speakers of Panjabi pronounce them like the closest-sounding Panjabi consonants (a dot has been added to those symbols to create letters for these new sounds) and many writers who do not know the Urdu script (in which the original Arabic and Persian spellings are preserved) are often not sure where these letters should be used.

3.4.2.1 Fricatives

ਸ s	It sounds like the voiceless English *s* in *sink*.
ਹ h [ɦ]	You can pronounce it like the English voiceless *h* sound. But it is actually a **voiced aspirate** or **breathy voiced** fricative with friction created in the throat and not in the mouth. It simply adds a breathy voiced effect to the neighbouring vowels and consonants. Historically, breathy voice has been the cause of the generation of tones in Panjabi. The interesting mischief it has been causing in the Panjabi pronunciation and spelling for the last five centuries is discussed in the next chapter.
ਸ਼ ś	It sounds like *sh* in the English word *ship*. This sound existed in Panjabi's ancestor language Sanskrit but disappeared later for some centuries. With the borrowing of words from Arabic and Persian with this sound, it re-emerged in Panjabi speech. But the letter **ਸ਼** was added much later towards the close of the 19th century. Some speakers of Panjabi use **ਸ s** in its place in their speech.

	In some dialects, ਸ਼ **ś** and ਛ **c^h** are merging, resulting in a sound which is more like **ś** than **c^h**. In Panjabi writing, this often results in the use of ਸ਼ where ਛ should be used. For example ਛੋਲੇ 'chickpeas' is often written as ਸ਼ੋਲੇ.
ਖ਼ **x**	It is pronounced somewhat in the manner of the voiceless ਕ **k**, but the tongue only approaches the soft palate without touching it. It is pronounced with a light friction.
ਗ਼ **ɣ**	It is the voiced counterpart of ਖ਼ **x**.
ਜ਼ **z**	It sounds like the voiced English *z* in *zinc*. It is the voiced counterpart of ਸ **s**.
ਫ਼ **f**	It sounds like the voiceless *f* sound in the English word *find*. But the Panjabi sound is a bilabial fricative unlike the labio-dental English *f*. Some speakers pronounce **p^h** as **f** in some positions. But the reverse is more common.

3.4.2.2 Frictionless continuants

All these consonants are ***voiced***.

ਯ **y**	It sounds like the English *y* sound in *year*. But also see the next chapter.
ਰ **r**	It is generally pronounced as a lightly trilled sound as in the Scottish pronunciation. But in some positions, it becomes a single tap or even an approximant as in the London variety of English. But it sounds very different from the American variety.
ਲ **l**	It sounds like the English *l* in *light* (but not in *bull*).
ਵ **v**	It sounds like a cross between the English *v* and *w*. The lips are not rounded as for *w*. But it also lacks the slight friction heard in the pronunciation of *v*. But you can pronounce it either like the English *v* or *w*. Also see the next chapter.

ੜ ṛ	This is not a frictionless continuant but a **flap** sound like ਣ **ṇ.** You can regard it as a flapped version of ਡ **ḍ** or a non-nasal version of ਣ **ṇ**.

3.4.3 More recent additions

Two more letters were added, quite controversially, to the Panjabi alphabet in the middle of 20th century. They are

ਲ਼ ḷ	This is a **retroflex flap** version of ਲ **l**. It is a native Panjabi sound and has been there in some dialects of the language probably for many centuries. But only less than half of the Panjabi-speaking people use it in their speech. Most of those who use it are not in favour of having a separate letter ਲ਼ for this sound.
ਕ਼ q	This voiceless stop is articulated further back than ਕ **k** in the mouth. The tongue touches the uvula and hence it is called the **voiceless uvular stop**. It occurs in the speech of only a few extremely careful speakers, who pronounce it in some words borrowed from Arabic and Persian. We are not using this letter in this book and will use ਕ **k** in its place.

But the use of these two letters (especially ਕ਼) is regarded as unnecessarily pedantic by most writers.

3.5 Vowel bearer letters

The three letters ੳ, ਅ and ੲ do not stand for any sounds. So no sounds are associated with them in the diagram. Their place in the Gurmukhi writing system is discussed later on in this chapter.

The system of the Panjabi vowels is best discussed with the help of the following topological map showing which part of the tongue is raised to what height in order to change the shape of the resonance chamber in the mouth to achieve a distinct acoustic quality for the sound of each vowel.

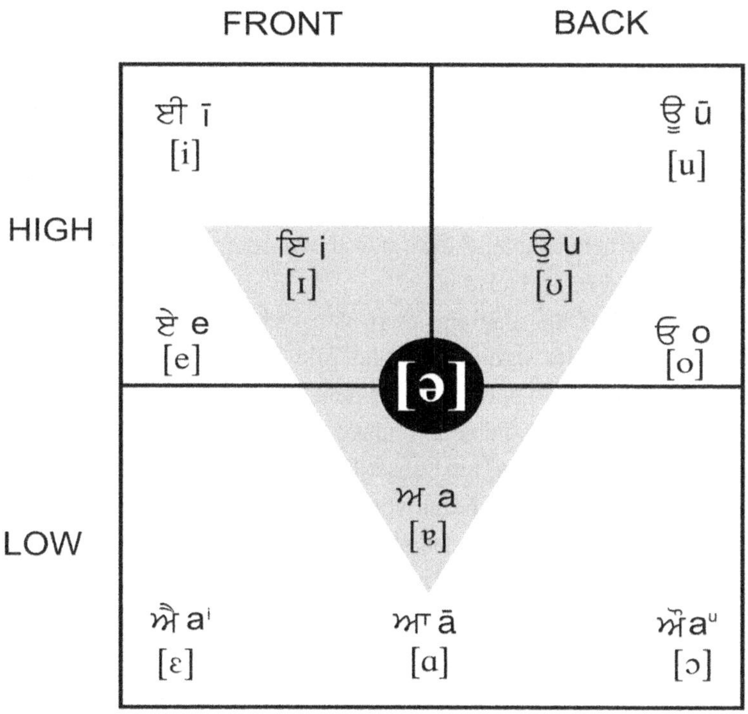

Figure 3.3 Panjabi vowels

The Panjabi vowels can first be divided into two groups – **high** and **low**. The High vowels can be further divided into **front** and **back** vowels. You can see that the **high front** vowels are written by adding vowel symbols to the **vowel bearer** letter ੲ, the **high back** vowels are written by adding vowels symbols to the vowel bearer letter ੳ, and the **low** vowels (irrespective of their front or back position) are written by adding vowel symbols to the vowel bearer letter ਅ. The vowel symbol for **a** is *invisible*. As we shall see later, it would be wrong to say that it "has no symbol".

Cross-cutting this main division, three vowels (one in each group) are grouped together. Traditionally, they are known as **short** vowels. Even in the traditional phonetic transcription used here, in which length is indicated by a bar sign above a vowel symbol, **a** looks like a shorter version of **ā, i** a shorter version of **ī** and **u** a shorter version of **ū.** But this is not the whole story. Of course, they are *quantitatively* shorter, but they are also *qualitatively* different. Taking into account the position of the tongue, they are also more **centralised** than the other vowels, which are contrastively know as **peripheral** vowels. They are also known as **lax** vowels because the muscles of the tongue are relatively more lax for their articulation. So the other vowels are also contrastively known as the **tense** vowels. Since such "short-long" pairs among the remaining four vowels do not exist, a bar sign is unnecessary there. It is important to keep these distinctions in mind because they have phonetic consequences to be discussed in the next chapter. As we saw above, some Panjabi consonants (ਣ **ṇ**, ਰ **r**, ੜ **ṛ** and ਲ਼ **ḷ**) are also lax.

In the centre of the diagram, there is a white [ə] symbol against a black background. Its significance and role in the system of Panjabi pronunciation will be explained in the next chapter. For the time being, regard it as a nice design element to make the diagram look beautiful!

In this map, ਐ **a**^{i} and ਔ **a**^{u} are transcribed by composite symbols. These vowels were diphthongs or gliding vowels in Panjabi some centuries ago and are still so in some dialects. ਐ **a**^{i} is a quick glide from **a** to **i** and ਔ **a**^{u} a quick glide from **a** to **u**. In this glide, the starting vowel is considerably stronger than the target vowel. But in most dialects they are pure non-gliding low vowels now. This historical information is important because it explains some Gurmukhi spelling rules to be dealt with in the later chapters.

For the articulation of the back vowels and ਔ **a**^{u}, ਊ **ū**, ਉ **u** and ਓ **o**, lips are generally rounded. But for the low back vowel ਔ **a**^{u} some speakers only slightly round their lips and others do not round them at all. In some Western dialects, ਔ **a**^{u} does not exist and ਓ **o** is used in its place. In other words, these dialects have only nine distinct vowels.

These vowels can either be **oral** (pronounced through the mouth only) or **nasalised** (pronounced through the mouth and the nose at the same time (as many French vowels are). In our transcription, a nasalised vowel is marked with a squiggle, as **ã**, **ā̃**, **u**, **ū̃**, **ĩ**, **ī̃**, **ã**^{i}, **ã**^{u}, for example.

3.6 Panjabi vowel symbols

The Panjabi (Gurmukhi) script is sometimes said to be a syllabic writing system as opposed to the alphabetic writing systems used for the European languages. But it would be more appropriate to call the Panjabi writing system semi-syllabic because it has some characteristics of an alphabetic system as well. Some linguists use the term alpha-asyllabic for the Indian writing systems. Quite significantly, the Panjabi word for a letter of the alphabet is ਅੱਖਰ **akk^{h}ar**, which comes from the Sanskrit word *akṣara* 'syllable'. In most cases, a consonant letter in Gurmukhi does not stand for a consonant sound but for the syllable **consonant+a**. This is why the symbol for the Panjabi vowel ਅ **a** is regarded as invisible. The Panjabi name for this invisible vowel symbol is ਮੁਕਤਾ **muktā** 'liberated' because its pure liberated soul is free from all earthly blackness! The symbols for the Panjabi vowels are:

a	**ā**	**i**	**ī**	**u**	**ū**	**e**	**a^i**	**o**	**a^u**
Invisible	ਾ	ਿ	ੀ	ੁ	ੂ	ੇ	ੈ	ੋ	ੌ

A vowel in Panjabi can be either **oral** (the air going out from the mouth only) or **nasalised** (the air going out from the mouth and the nose at the same time).

If you are interested in the names of the *visible* vowel symbols of Panjabi, here they are:

ਾ	ਿ	ੀ	ੁ	ੂ	ੇ	ੈ
ਕੰਨਾ	ਸਿਹਾਰੀ	ਬਿਹਾਰੀ	ਔਂਕੜ	ਦੁਲੈਂਕੜ	ਲਾਂ	ਦੁਲਾਂ
kannā	**sihārī**	**bihārī**	**a^{u}nkaṛ**	**dula^{i}nkaṛ**	**lā̃**	**dulā̃**

ੋ	ੌ
ਹੋੜਾ	ਕਨੌੜਾ
hoṛā	**kana^{u}ṛā**

This is an example of how these symbols are added to the consonant letter ਸ:

ਸ	ਸਾ	ਸਿ	ਸੀ	ਸੁ	ਸੂ	ਸੇ	ਸੈ	ਸੋ	ਸੌ
sa	**sā**	**si**	**sī**	**su**	**sū**	**se**	**sa^i**	**so**	**sa^u**

They are added to the vowel bearer letters as shown below. (Also see the Vowel Diagram on page 49.)

ਅ	ਆ	ਇ	ਈ	ਉ	ਊ	ਏ	ਐ	ਓ	ਔ
a	**ā**	**i**	**ī**	**u**	**ū**	**e**	**a^i**	**o**	**a^u**

You can see that ਾ and ੀ are placed *after* the consonant letter. ਿ is placed *before* the consonant letter, ੁ and ੂ come *beneath* the letter, and ੇ, ੈ, ੋ and ੌ come *above* the letter. (For typographical reasons, the symbol for the vowel **o**, when added to the vowel bearer letter ੳ looks like ਓ).

This is how a consonant letter and a vowel symbol are combined in the *most basic* type of syllable in Panjabi, which is **CV** (**consonant+vowel** sounds). There are quite a few deviations from this most basic type of syllable, and they are described and discussed below. The structure of a syllable in Panjabi, on the whole, is quite simple. There are no complicated syllable-initial and/or syllable-final consonant clusters. The Gurmukhi script, which, as we said earlier, was tailor-made for Panjabi, reflects this simplicity. This script does not have a large number of mutilated consonant letters as, for example, its sister scripts Devanagari (now used for writing Sanskrit, Hindi, Marathi and Nepali), Gujarati and Bengali have. A Gurmukhi consonant letter can stand either for Consonant+**a** sequence or for a lone consonant. It is not mutilated in the latter case. A vowel by itself can constitute a **syllable**. In that case the vowel symbol is added to one of the vowel bearer letters, as shown in the vowel map given above.

The Gurmukhi writing system is based on the following principles which are best applied in this order:

(1) **CV** sequences (or basic syllables)
(2) Nasalised vowels
(3) Homorganic nasal consonants
(4) Long (or geminated) consonants

3.6.1 CV sequences (or basic syllables)

Start dividing the word into consonants (**C**s) and vowels (**V**s), starting from the left. Then find **CV** sequences. An example is

amarjīt

a	**m**	**a**	**r**	**j**	**ī**	**t**
V	C	V	C	C	V	C
V	CV		C	CV		C
a	**ma**		**r**	**jī**		**t**

A **V** at the beginning stands alone. If there are two or more **C**s next to each other, the rightmost goes with the **V** and the other stands alone. A **C** or a **V** the end of a word (and not attached to a **C**) also stands alone. In the Panjabi script,

(a) A **CV** sequence is represented by a consonant letter *plus* a vowel symbol;
(b) A lone **C** sound is represented by a consonant letter;
(c) A lone **V** sound is represented by a vowel bearer letter *plus* a vowel symbol.

As pointed out above, the symbol for the vowel **a** is *invisible*. But this symbol has to be added to the vowel bearer letter ਅ if need arises. The example analysed above is written in Panjabi like this:

amarjīt

a	**m**	**a**	**r**	**j**	**ī**	**t**		
C	C	V	C	C	V	C		
C	CV		C	CV		C		
a	**ma**		**r**	**jī**		**t**		
ਅ	ਮ		ਰ	ਜੀ		ਤ	= ਅਮਰਜੀਤ	a name

In this example, ਮ represents **m** plus invisible **a**, but ਰ and ਤ stand for lone consonants. The invisible symbol for the lone vowel **a** is added to vowel bearer letter ਅ.

A careful study of the following examples will make the application of these rules clear.

sipāhī
si + pā + hī
ਸਿ + ਪਾ + ਹੀ = ਸਿਪਾਹੀ 'soldier'

bijalī
bi + ja + lī
ਬਿ + ਜ + ਲੀ = ਬਿਜਲੀ 'electricity'

umar

u	**m**	**a**	**r**		
V	C	V	C		
V	CV		C		
ਉ	ਮ		ਰ	= ਉਮਰ	'age'

juāī					
j u	**ā**	**ī**			
C V	V	V			
CV	V	V			
ਜੁ	ਆ	ਈ	=	ਜੁਆਈ	'son-in-law'

3.6.2 Nasalised vowels

In the Panjabi script a nasalised vowel is represented by the addition of one of the following symbols:

ੰ	or	ਂ
(Called Tippi **ṭippī**)		(Called Bindi **bindī**)

In some Panjabi grammar books you will find a list of rules determining which of the two to choose. But there is only one simple rule: Always use Bindi with

ਾ ੀ ੇ ੈ ੋ ੌ ਓ

and Tippi everywhere else. In other words, do not use the Tippi where it can touch the vowel marker or a part of the letter.

gā̃			
g	**ā̃**		
C	V		
	(Nasalised V)		
C	V		
ਗਾ	ਂ		
CV			
ਗਾਂ	=	ਗਾਂ	'cow'

kã^{i}cī						
k	**ã^{i}**	**c**	**ī**			
C	V	C	V			
	(Nasalised V)					
C	V	C	V			
ਕ	ੈਂ	ਚ	ੀ			
CV		CV				
ਕੈਂ		ਚੀ		=	ਕੈਂਚੀ	'scissors'

gũd				
g	**ũ**	**d**		
C	V	C		
	(Nasalised V)			
C	V	C		
ਗ	ੂੰ	ਦ		
CV		C		
ਗੂੰ		ਦ	=	ਗੂੰਦ 'glue'

3.6.3 Homorganic nasals

Homorganic means "produced by the same speech organs" or having the same place of articulation. It was pointed out that within the Consonant Square on page 42 above, all the consonants in a group or row are homorganic. For example, **t**, **t^h**, **d**, **d^h** and **n** are homorganic because they are all produced by the same organs – the tip of the tongue touching the teeth. Similarly, **k**, **k^h**, **g**, **g^h** and **ṅ** are also homorganic. For the production of all these five consonants, the back of the tongue touches the soft palate. The front of the tongue touches the hard palate for the five homorganic consonants **c**, **c^h**, **j**, **j^h** and **ñ.**

In each of the five groups in the Consonant Square, there is a nasal consonant. Thus, we have five nasal consonants in Panjabi – **ṅ**, **ñ**, **ṇ**, **n** and **m**

Clusters involving a nasal and a homorganic non-nasal or oral consonant are found probably in all languages, including English and Panjabi. In English, the nasal consonant sound immediately before **k** in the word 'sink' **[siṅk]** [sɪŋk] is homorganic to the oral consonant **k**. Like **k**, this **ṅ** is pronounced by touching the soft palate with the back of the tongue. Similarly, the nasal consonant in the word 'inch' **[iñc]** [ɪɲʧ] is homorganic to the oral consonant **c** [ʧ]. (Both are produced by touching the hard palate with the front part of the tongue.)

Since **ṅ** and **ñ** in Panjabi nearly always occur in such clusters as nasal sounds homorganic to the following non-nasal or oral consonants, and rarely as independent nasal consonants (as **ṇ**, **n** and **m** can in words like **pāṇī, nakk** and **kamm** respectively), the use of the phonetic symbols **ṅ** and **ñ** has been unnecessary. (But also see page 42). We have used **n** where **ṅ** and **ñ** could have been used. But if you pronounce words fluently and effortlessly, you will always pronounce, for example, the word **manjā** as **[mañjā]** [mɐɲdʒɑ]. In anticipation of the **j** sound, the front part of your tongue will go the hard palate, and pronounce the nasal consonant preceding **j** as **ñ** [ɲ] even though it is transcribed as **n**. After all, you most probably do pronounce 'sink' as **[siṅk]** [siŋk]. In anticipation of **k**, the back of the tongue goes to the soft palate and you pronounce the letter **n** as **[ṅ]** [ŋ] in the process.

In the Panjabi script, a **homorganic nasal consonant** is represented by a Tippi or a Bindi.

Since **ṅ** and **ñ** almost always occur only as homorganic nasals in the types of clusters mentioned above, and almost never as independent sounds, they are nearly always represented by a Tippi or a Bindi. This means that you may never in your life use the letters ਙ and ਞ. Many users of Gurmukhi are unable to say how these letters sound in isolation or even which is which!

uṇgaḷī

u	**ṅ**	**g**	**a**	**ḷ**	**ī**
V	C	C	V	C	V
	(Homorganic Nasal C)				
V	C	CV		CV	
ਉ	ਂ	ਗ		ਲ਼ੀ	
V	CCV	CV			
ਉ	ਂਗ	ਲ਼ੀ		= ਉਂਗਲ਼ੀ 'finger'	

You generally use a Tippi ੰ with ੁ, the symbol for the lax vowel sound **u**. But only the Bindi ਂ can be used with the vowel bearer letter ੳ.

mañjā

m	**a**	**ñ**	**j**	**ā**
C	V	C	C	V
		(Homorganic Nasal C)		
CV		C	CV	
ਮ		ੰ	ਜਾ	
CV		CCV		
ਮ		ੰਜਾ	=	ਮੰਜਾ 'cot'

kaṇḍā

k	**a**	**ṇ**	**ḍ**	**ā**		
C	V	C	C	V		
	(Homorganic Nasal C)					
CV	C	CV				
ਕ		ੰ	ਡਾ			
CV		CCV				
ਕ		ੰਡਾ			= ਕੰਡਾ	'thorn'

bandā

b	**a**	**n**	**d**	**ā**		
C	V	C	C	V		
	(Homorganic Nasal C)					
CV		C	CV			
ਬ		ੰ	ਦਾ			
CV		CCV				
ਬ		ੰਦਾ			= ਬੰਦਾ	'man'

It is notable that in such a word, the first syllable has a lax vowel (**a, i** or **u**). The syllable boundary lies between the homorganic nasal consonant (represented by the Bindi or the Tippi) and the following oral consonant. The two syllables of **bandā** are **ban.dā**. A syllable ending with a consonant sound is known as a **closed syllable** and the one ending with a vowel sound is known as an **open syllable**. The word **bandā** has a closed syllable followed by an open syllable.

3.6.4 Long consonants

A **long** (or double or **geminate**) **consonant** is one which is prolonged. They are not commonly found in English. The following words need to be studied carefully.

ਗਦਾ **gadā**	'mace'	ਗੱਦਾ **gaddā**	'cushion'
ਪਤਾ **patā**	'address'	ਪੱਤਾ **pattā**	'leaf'
ਪਿਤਾ **pitā**	'father'	ਪਿੱਤਾ **pittā**	'physique'
ਗਿਲਾ **gilā**	'complaint'	ਗਿੱਲਾ **gillā**	'wet'
ਲੁਕ **luk**	'to hide'	ਲੁੱਕ **lukk**	'coal tar'
ਦੁਖ **duk^h**	'to ache'	ਦੁੱਖ **dukk^h**	'pain'

Read below about the use of the symbol ˘.

In our transcription, a long aspirated consonant has only one ^{h}. For example, the long **t^{h}** consonant in **patt^{h}ar** 'stone' is transcribed as **tt^{h}**, and not as **t^{h}t^{h}**, which not only looks odd but is also technically wrong, because the strong breath symbolised by ^{h} comes out only at the end of the comparatively longer "hold" phase of the consonant.

In the Panjabi script, the length of a long consonant (other than that of a nasal) is represented by the symbol

ੱ

(Called ਅੱਧਕ Addhak)

The word Addhak means 'excessive'. The name explains itself.

In the case of a **long nasal consonant**, however, the first half is regarded as a **nasal consonant homorganic** to the second half and is therefore represented by a Tippi or a Bindi (as the following examples show).

kuttā						
k	**u**	**tt**	**ā**			
C	V	C	V			
		(Long C)				
C	V	C	V			
ਕ	ੁ	ੱਤ	ਾ			
CV		CV				
ਕੁ		ੱਤਾ		=	ਕੁੱਤਾ	'dog'

vacc^{h}ā						
v	**a**	**cc^{h}**	**ā**			
C	V	C	V			
		(Long C)				
C	V	C	V			
ਵ		ੱਛ	ਾ			
CV		CV				
ਵ		ੱਛਾ		=	ਵੱਛਾ	'calf'

A **long oral consonant** is represented by an Addhak placed before it (on the preceding letter). But a **long nasal consonant** is represented by a Tippi or a Bindi.

lammā

l	**a**	**mm**	**ā**			
C	V	C	V			
		(Long Nasal C)				
CV		C				
ਲ		ੰਮ	ਾ	=	ਲੰਮਾ	'long'

unnī

u	**nn**	**ī**			
V	C	V			
	(Long Nasal C)				
V	C	V			
ਉ	ਂਨ	ੀ	=	ਉਂਨੀ	'nineteen'

kinnī

k	**I**	**nn**	**ī**			
C	V	C	V			
		(Long Nasal C)				
CV						
ਕਿ		ੰਨ	ੀ	=	ਕਿੰਨੀ	'how much'

The first syllable of such a word has a **lax** vowel. The syllable boundary lies in the middle of the long (or double or geminate) consonant. So the first syllable is a closed one. Only a **tense** consonant can be geminated in Panjabi. This means that the lax consonants ਣ **ṇ**, ੜ **ṛ** and ਲ਼ **ḷ** do not geminate. Also, they do not occur in word-initial position in the language. In other words no Panjabi word can start with any of these three consonants.

3.7 Subscript characters

We have covered all the letters and symbols of the Panjabi script except the following **subscript** symbols (which are put beneath the letters, or literally "in the foot of a letter", as speakers of Panjabi say):

੍ਹ ੍ਰ ੍ਵ

Of the three symbols ੍ਹ is very commonly used. The other two are going out of fashion and their use is debatable among Panjabi scholars.

3.7.1 Subscript ੍ਹ

This symbol is a variant of the letter ਹ but is not pronounced as **h** or $^{\mathbf{h}}$. In old Panjabi, it used to represent breathy voice after some voiced sounds (nasal consonants and **r**, **l**, **v**, **ṛ** and **ḷ**). For example

ਣ੍ਹ	was pronounced as **ṇh** or **ṇ**$^{\mathbf{h}}$	as in	ਕਣ੍ਹਾ **kaṇhā** 'long-legged spider'
ਨ੍ਹ	was pronounced as **nh** or **n**$^{\mathbf{h}}$	as in	ਬੰਨ੍ਹ **bannh** 'to bind'
ਮ੍ਹ	was pronounced as **mh** or **mh**	as in	ਥੰਮ੍ਹ **thammh** 'pillar'
ਰ੍ਹ	was pronounced as **rh** or **r**$^{\mathbf{h}}$	as in	ਵਰ੍ਹ **varh** 'to rain'
ਲ੍ਹ	was pronounced as **lh** or **l**$^{\mathbf{h}}$	as in	ਕੱਲ੍ਹ **kallh** 'yesterday/ tomorrow'
ਲ਼	was pronounced as **ḷh** or **ḷ**$^{\mathbf{h}}$	as in	ਸਲ਼੍ਹਾ **saḷhā** 'locusts'
ਵ੍ਹ	was pronounced as **vh** or **v**$^{\mathbf{h}}$	as in	ਰਵ੍ਹੇ **ravhe** 'may stay'
ੜ੍ਹ	was pronounced as **ṛh** or **ṛ**$^{\mathbf{h}}$	as in	ਪੜ੍ਹ **paṛh** 'to read'

and so on. This pronunciation has been preserved in some Western Panjabi dialects. Most modern speakers of Panjabi do not pronounce this symbol but use a tone in the word having this symbol. We shall deal with this symbol and tone in the next chapter.

3.7.2 Subscript ੍ਰ

When the second consonant in a CCV cluster is **r**, this **r** is written as ੍ਰ in the Panjabi script. Examples are

prem

p	**r**	**e**	**m**		
C	C	V	C		
CCV			C		
ਪ੍ਰੇ			ਮ	=	ਪ੍ਰੇਮ 'love', a name

prītam

p	**r**	**ī**	**t**	**a**	**m**		
C	C	V	C	V	C		
CCV			CV		C		
ਪ੍ਰੀ			ਤ		ਮ	=	ਪ੍ਰੀਤਮ 'sweetheart', a name

But many writers have started using the full ਰ in most such words and use the subscript ੍ਰ in names only and in a few "learned words". The Sikh greeting **sat srī akāl,** is written as ਸਤਿ ਸ੍ਰੀ ਅਕਾਲ . The first word of this greeting has older spelling. But it is now pronounced as **sat,** and not as **sati**.

3.7.3 Subscript ੍ਵ

The use of this symbol is also going out of fashion. But some old-fashioned writers are still using it. It is used exactly like the Subscript ੍ਰ, i.e., when the second consonant in a **CCV** cluster is **v**. Examples are

svar
s v a r
C C V C
CCV C
ਸ੍ਵ ਰ = ਸ੍ਵਰ 'sound, vowel'

sva^{i}-jīvanī

s	**v**	**a^{i}**	**j**	**ī**	**v**	**a**	**n**	**ī**
C	C	V	C	V	C	V	C	V
CCV			CV		CV		CV	
ਸ੍ਵੈ			ਜੀ		ਵ		ਨੀ	

ਸ੍ਵੈ-ਜੀਵਨੀ
'self-biography' (i.e., autobiography)

ਸ੍ਵਰ has retained its old spelling. But everywhere else, most writers have started using a full ਵ. The most common modern spelling of **sva^{i}-jīvanī** is ਸਵੈ-ਜੀਵਨੀ.

See Appendix 1 for how the words with the subscript letters are entered in Panjabi dictionaries.

The **CCV** sequences with **r** or **v** as the second **C** are the only **consonant clusters** found syllable-initially in the modern Panjabi dialect dealt with in this book. A consonant cluster is found *within* a syllable. There are no syllable-final consonant clusters in Panjabi (like the **[ks]** cluster in the English word *marks*). A **consonant cluster** is different from a **consonant sequence**, where the consonants occur across a syllable boundary. In the word ਖਟਰਸ **k^{h}aṭras** 'sour taste', **ṭ** and **r** occur in a consonant sequence with the intervening syllable boundary, as ਖਟ.ਰਸ **k^{h}aṭ.ras**.

So the word is not written as ***ਪਦ੍ਮ**. (When a * is added to a word or expression, it means that the expression does not occur in the language or is unacceptable to the native users of the language.) The eminent Panjabi poet Dhani Ram Chatrik (1876–1954) (who, as a printer, standardised the shapes of the modern Gurmukhi letters) pronounced his name as **cā.trik** and accordingly spelt it as **ਚਾਤ੍ਰਿਕ**.

In Panjabi, there are no restrictions on which consonants can occur in **consonant sequences**.

Summing up and looking ahead

This chapter describes the salient phonological features of Panjabi in relation to the Panjabi (Gurmukhi) writing system. This system does not look like a repertoire of haphazardly arranged letters but an extremely logical system based on an in-depth analysis of the Indic languages going back nearly three thousand years. Gurmukhi is a script of the Brahmi family, whose design is based on more than two thousand years of phonetic analysis of the Indic languages. Such a systematic relation between the spoken and written forms of the language, or between pronunciation and spelling, does not exist between Panjabi and Shahmukhi, which was borrowed from Arabic and then adapted for Panjabi. The overall spirit of the Gurmukhi system has remained unchanged since the first preserved writings in Gurmukhi appeared in the 16th century. But some major changes have taken place in the pronunciation of Panjabi, resulting in making Panjabi a tone language, and thus unique among the major Indian languages. Within the Indo-European family of languages (to which Panjabi belongs), lexical tone is an extremely rare phenomenon. Norwegian, Swedish and Serbo-Croat are the only other major Indo-European languages with tones. There is some evidence that these changes in Panjabi pronunciation started almost imperceptibly (as all the linguistic changes do!) some time before the 16th century and are still going on. The evolutionary effects of these changes on Panjabi pronunciation and spelling are discussed in the next chapter.

For teachers and other more advanced users

As stated in the Preface and Chapter 1, this section is meant for those who wish to delve more deeply into the phonological and grammatical structure of the language. You can skip it. But you can return to it later on at any time if you wish. Theoretical linguists may also find these sections interesting and informative.

3.8 Panjabi vowel and consonant diagram and chart

The Panjabi vowel and consonant diagram and chart are given below for the benefit of linguists without any comments except that the uvular ਕ਼ **q** is not included among the Panjabi consonants because hardly any speaker of Panjabi uses it. Exactly how the vowels (especially the centralised lax ones) are pronounced differs from dialect to dialect, person to person and context to context.

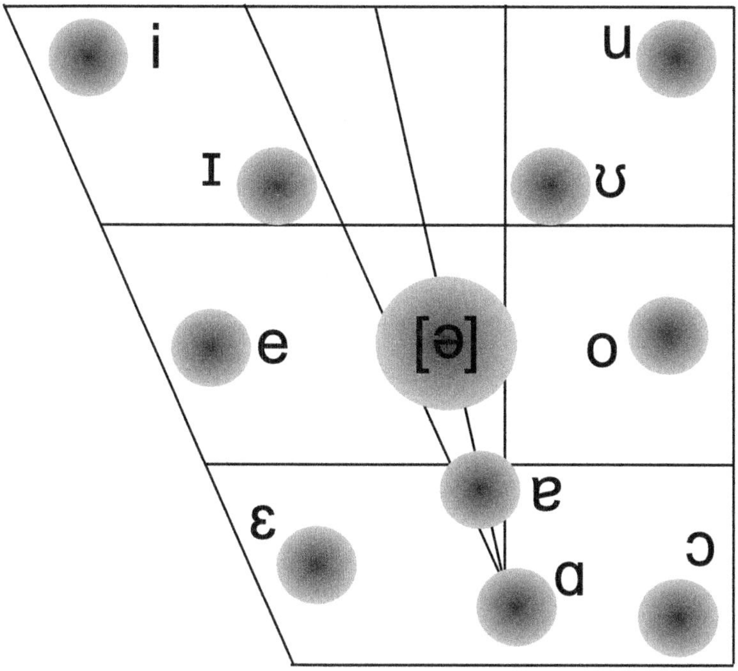

Figure 3.4 Panjabi vowel diagram IPA style

	Bilabial		Dental		Retroflex		Palatal		Velar		Glottal	
	Voice-less	Voiced	Voice-less	Voiced	Voice-less	Voiced	Voice-less	Voiced	Voice-less	Voiced	Voice-less	Voiced
Plosive	p p^{h}	b $b^{ɦ}$	t t^{h}	d $d^{ɦ}$	ʈ $ʈ^{h}$	ɖ $ɖ^{ɦ}$			k k^{h}	g $g^{ɦ}$		
Affricate							ʧ $ʧ^{h}$	ʤ $ʤ^{ɦ}$				
Nasal		m		n		ɳ (flap)		ɲ		ŋ		
Trill/tap/flap				r (trill/tap)		ɽ (flap)						
Fricative	(f)		s	(z)			ʃ		(x)	(ɣ)		ɦ
Lateral approxi-nant				l		ɭ (flap)						
Semi Vowel		w						j				

Note: The 'voiced aspirated' (breathy voiced) $b^{ɦ}$, $d^{ɦ}$, $ɖ^{ɦ}$, $ʤ^{ɦ}$ and $g^{ɦ}$ have disappeared from the Eastern Panjabi dialects; f, z, x and ɣ are used in words borrowed from other languages. The breathy voiced ɦ is not pronounced in many positions. The loss of these consonants has given rise to the Panjabi tones.

Figure 3.5 Panjabi consonants chart IPA style

3.9 There are more things in Panjabi...

Among the major languages of the Indian sub-continent, Panjabi has a unique phonetic and phonological character. Its major feature, the Panjabi tones, is dealt with in the next chapter. But some less known and unique features of the system, known as the "Panjabi Accent" often colour the speech of the speakers of Panjabi when they speak other languages.

The pronunciation of some words with a short (lax) vowel in spelling is notable. Words now spelt as ਗਿਆਨ and ਸੁਆਦ/ਸਵਾਦ are actually pronounced as **[gyā.ān]** [gja.an] and **[svā.ād]** [swa.ad] respectively. A century ago, the spellings were ਗ੍ਯਾਨ and ਸ੍ਵਾਦ respectively, which represent the pronunciation more closely. (The truncated form ਯ of ਯ is a typographical equivalent of a subscript form.) Earlier still, this word was spelt differently, with ਯ written as a subscript character ੵ (as in ਗੵਾਨੁ) in the Sikh holy book completed in 1604. This word has always had two syllables, and not three as the modern spelling indicates. The pronunciation has not changed over the last five centuries, but spellings have. (Also see the next chapter.)

The Sanskrit/Hindi word ਵੀਰੇਂਦ੍ਰ **vīrendra** is pronounced as ਵਰਿੰਦਰ **varindar** by most speakers of Panjabi. Several features of the Panjabi phonological system are involved in this change. We shall look at them in the next chapter.

We have to stop here because syllable stress is involved in the explanation, and we are going to discuss it in the next chapter.

Chapter 4

Tone and Related Phenomena in Panjabi

Preview of the chapter

Among the major languages of the Indian sub-continent, Panjabi is distinct in the sense that it is a "tone language" (or more properly a "pitch accent language"). But the Panjabi (Gurmukhi) script historically developed before this phenomenon appeared in Panjabi. This chapter analyses the phonetics of Panjabi tones or pitch accents (variation of pitch at the level of the word) and their relation to the Panjabi script. In Panjabi you do not "speak exactly as you write" or "write exactly as you speak" but the relation is fairly systematic. Panjabi also has sentence intonation (variation of pitch at the level of the sentence). The two types of pitch variations interact with each other fairly systematically so that there is no confusion.

4.1 Panjabi as a "tone language"

Ever since the Rev T. Grahame Bailey first "discovered tones in Panjabi" in 1914, "Panjabi is a tone language" has been a sort of received wisdom among Panjabi scholars and linguists in general. But over a century since then, we have come to know a lot about hundreds of tone languages in the world. So Bailey's claim that Panjabi is a tone language should be examined critically in the light of this knowledge.

Tone, defined as lexical pitch or the use of pitch variation to differentiate the meaning of words, is a very rare phenomenon in the Indo-

European languages. Notable major examples are Norwegian, Swedish, Serbo-Croat and Panjabi. Even these languages are best described as **pitch accent languages** rather than true **tone languages**. In a true **tone language** like Chinese, Vietnamese, Thai or Igbo, relative pitch contrast or pitch variation is associated with *every* word or all the syllables in each word. This is clearly not the case with Panjabi. Not more than 20% of the vocabulary of Panjabi is tonal in this sense. Even in such a word, only *one* syllable (the **stressed** or the **accented** one) has contrastive pitch level or pitch variation. So Panjabi is really a pitch accent language like its Indo-European cousins mentioned above. But since the term **tone** is well-established in the usage of Panjabi scholars and linguists, we will use it in the rest of the book in the sense of **pitch accent**.

The following analysis of Panjabi tones applies to the Eastern variety of Panjabi. In this variety, the older **voiced aspirated** (or **breathy voiced**) consonants have disappeared and given rise to the tones. Western Panjabi (Lahanda) has retained these consonants. Some pitch variation is also associated with the words having these consonants. But a detailed discussion is beyond the scope of this book because it does not deal with these dialects. (See Chapter 1.)

4.2 Pitch accent or tone in Panjabi

The definition of **pitch** relevant to our purpose is "the auditory property of a sound that is conditioned by its higher or lower frequency of the vibration of vocal cords relative to other sounds". **Accent** means the prominence given in speech to a word or syllable relative to other words or syllables. When pitch is involved in accent, the relevant word or syllable is said to receive **pitch accent**. Pitch may or may not be involved (or significantly involved in the sense of changing the lexical meaning of a word) in the process of accentuation. The articulatory and auditory/acoustic correlates of accent or stress (used interchangeably in this book) may differ from language to language. In Panjabi, a stressed or accented syllable is articulated more energetically and sounds a bit louder and more prominent (than the unstressed ones). The vowel sounds in the unstressed syllables *tend to* become lax and move towards the centre of vowel space (the shaded area in the diagram on page 49). Often, an unstressed vowel sounds like the vowel [ə] in the diagram. This IPA (International Phonetic Alphabet) symbol represents a completely **central** and **unstressed** vowel known as **schwa** (ਸ਼੍ਵਾ **śvā**). Look at the following visual representation of the pronunciation of three Panjabi words having the same consonant and vowel sounds but different pitch accents.

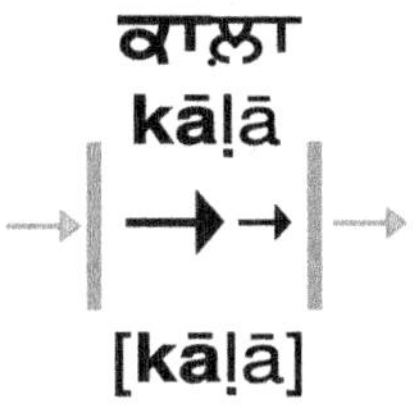

ਕਾਲ਼ਾ **kāḷā**

[kɑɭɑ] 'black'

Figure 4.1 Accent or stress without tonal contour

The first syllable (represented by the thicker arrow) has stress or accent, but not a pitch accent. So this word has **stress without tone**. The pitch is the same as that of the neighbouring words (represented by grey arrows) *unless there is pitch variation because of* **intonation**. (See below for intonation.)

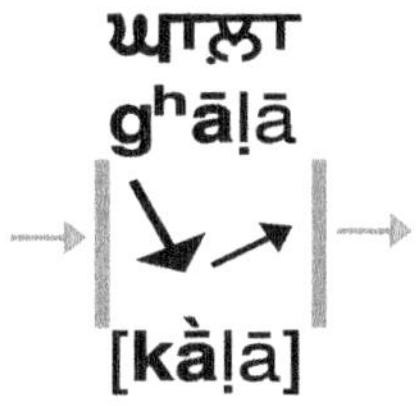

ਘਾਲ਼ਾ **gʰāḷā**

[kā̀ḷā] [kɑ̀ɭɑ] 'fraud'

Figure 4.2 Accent or stress with the pitch contour of a low tone

On the stressed syllable, the pitch falls *rapidly* from a *higher level* than that of the preceding word or syllable and then rises comparatively *less rapidly* to the level of the following word or syllable. We will call this type of pitch accent the **low tone**. There is some constriction in the throat which affects the voice quality. So this tone is accompanied by a **constricted phonation** or constricted voice quality. It is also notable that the **breathy voiced** (or **voiced aspirate**) consonant (ਘ **gʰ** in this particular example) is replaced by the **voiceless unaspirate** consonant ਕ **k**.

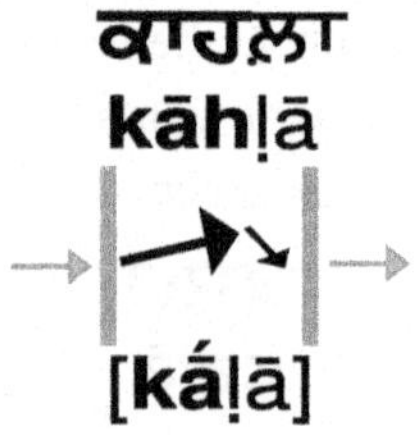

ਕਾਹਲਾ **kāhḷā**
[káḷā] [káɭɑ] 'impatient'

Figure 4.3 Accent or stress with the pitch contour of a high tone

The pitch rises on the stressed syllable and then falls. The rise is *more gradual* relative to the rather *abrupt* fall on the following syllable.

To sum up, ਕਾਲਾ **kāḷā** 'black' has stress without tone, ਘਾਲਾ **g^hāḷā** 'fraud' has a low tone (*plus* constricted phonation) and ਕਾਹਲਾ **kāhḷā** 'impatient' has a high tone.

In our transcription, the low tone is marked by ` and the high tone by ´ *on* the vowel symbol of the tone bearing syllable, which is always the *stressed syllable* in Panjabi. A word in Panjabi can be without a tone, but if it has one, it must be on the stressed syllable, where the fall or the rise of pitch is really significant. What happens subsequently is predictable. If it is necessary to mark a **toneless stressed syllable**, it will be marked in the standard IPA manner by a vertical mark placed *before* the syllable as in **['ko.ṛā]** ['ko.ɽɑ]. The dot marking the syllable boundary will be omitted if it is clear where this boundary lies.

It is notable that the Panjabi tones can be heard in whispered speech as well, though pitch variation is impossible in a whisper. The reason for this is that the low tone is accompanied by a special voice quality known as constricted phonation. This constriction can be heard in a whisper as well. Also, the length of the vowel bearing a low tone *increases* slightly. The high tone, on the other hand, slightly *decreases* the length of the vowel. Instrumental analysis shows this very clearly. But this discussion is beyond the scope of this book. It is clear that vowel length and the constriction phenomenon are as much a part of the Panjabi tones as pitch variation is.

4.3 Tone and the voiced aspirated (breathy voiced) stop consonants in Panjabi

It appears that the Panjabi tones first started in the words containing one of the five **voiced aspirated** or **breathy voiced** consonants or ਹ **h** (which is also breathy voiced in Panjabi). Subsequently, they spread to some other words in the speech of some people, but still more than 90% of the tonal words in the language are those which had (and still have in the Panjabi spelling) the breathy voiced consonants.

4.3.1 Voiced aspirated (breathy voiced) stops and tones

In an old Panjabi word and in Panjabi writing, a **voiced aspirate** consonant can occur either before or after the stressed vowel. If it occurs *before* the stressed vowel, it can occur either at the beginning or in the middle of the word. And if occurs *after* the stressed vowel, it can occur either in the middle of the word or at the end. Below, we explore all these possibilities (dealing with the **stop** consonants first).

(a) Word-initially

The rule is

Voiced Aspirate → Voiceless Unaspirate + Low Tone

In such a word, the **voiced aspirated** consonant must necessarily come *before* the stressed vowel. In other words, the consonant in the fourth column of the Consonant Square in the chart on page 42 is replaced by the one in the first column and the vowel gets the low tone. The consonant loses both its **voice** and **aspiration**. Examples are

ਘੋੜਾ **g^h^oṛā → [kòṛā]** 'horse'
ਘਟਾ **g^h^aṭā → [kàṭā]** 'dark clouds'
ਘਟਾ **g^h^a'ṭā → [kaṭà]** 'to make less'
ਭਗਵਾਨ **b^h^ag'vān → [pagvàn]** 'God'

(b) Word-medially before the stressed vowel

Voiced Aspirate → Voiced Unaspirate + Low Tone

The consonant loses its **aspiration** but not **voice**.

ਖੰਘਾਰ **k^{h}an'g^{h}ār → [k^{h}angàr]** 'phlegm'
ਸੁਧਾਰ **su'd^{h}ār → [sudàr]** 'reform'
ਗੰਭੀਰ **gam'b^{h}īr → [gambī̀r]** 'serious'

(c) Word-medially after the stressed vowel

Voiced Aspirate → Voiced Unaspirate + High Tone

The consonant loses its **aspiration** but not **voice**.

ਕੰਘੀ **kang^{h}ī → [kángī]** 'comb'
ਸਾਧੂ **sād^{h}ū → [sā́dū]** 'hermit'
ਲੋਭੀ **lob^{h}ī → [lóbī]** 'greedy'

(d) Word-finally

Voiced Aspirate → Voiced Unaspirate + High Tone

The consonant loses its **aspiration** but not **voice**.

ਸੰਘ **sang^{h} → [sáng]** 'throat'
ਮੱਝ **majj^{h} → [májj]** 'buffalo'
ਜੀਭ **jīb^{h} → [jī́b]** 'tongue'

4.4 ਹ h and the Panjabi tones

Before we move any further, we have to understand a few facts about the Panjabi ਹ **h** and its less than harmonious relation with the Panjabi tones. The **phonation** (what happens in the throat in the production of a sound) of ਹ **h** is **breathy voiced**. The IPA symbol for this type of ਹ **h** sound is [ɦ]. This type of phonation is a combination of voice and aspiration. You may have realised by now that the real historical agent in the generation of the Panjabi tones is the **breathy voiced phonation**. The nature of the Panjabi ਹ **h** is different from that of the English **h**, which is **voiceless**. While the stop consonants in the fourth column of the Consonant Square on page 42 have both **phonation** and **articulation** (what happens in the mouth), ਹ **h** consists of breathy voiced phonation only. Some millennia ago, it originated in an ancestor language of Panjabi when some **breathy voiced** consonants lost their **articulation** in some positions. Panjabi's ancestor language Sanskrit had both the voiceless and the breathy voiced varieties of **h**. (Some languages, such as Russian, have *no* variety of **h**!)

The Panjabi ਹ **h** simply adds (or *used to* add) the breathy voiced effect to the accompanying consonant and/or vowel(s). Tone affected the other consonants' breathy voiced phonation only, not their articulation. But since ਹ **h** has no articulation to preserve, it can do one of the following three things:

1. stubbornly resist the **tone**; or
2. co-exist with the **tone**; or
3. gracefully give way to the **tone** and make an exit.

All the three possibilities are attested in modern Panjabi – to different degrees in different dialects, in the speech of different communities within a dialect area, in different generations within the same family, and even in different stages in the life of an individual speaker!

4.4.1 Subscript ਹ h (੍ਹ)

In Panjabi script, ਹ can occur both in its full form and the subscript form as ੍ਹ. As was pointed out in Chapter 3, before the development of tones in Panjabi, the sound represented by the subscript ੍ਹ used to add a breathy voice to the preceding consonant. (These consonants are listed in **3.7.1**.) Now the subscript ੍ਹ is *never* pronounced and the word is always tonal. But the pronunciation of the full ਹ often depends upon its position in the word and also differs in different dialects.

(a) Before the stressed vowel

੍ਹ → **Ø + Low Tone**

The symbol Ø means the disappearance of the **breathy voiced phonation** represented by ੍ਹ.

ਪੜ੍ਹਾਈ **pa'ṛhāī** → **[paṛȁī]** 'education'
ਨਲ੍ਹਾ **na'ḷhā** → **[naḷȁ]** 'to give a bath/shower'
ਸਲ੍ਹਾਬਾ **sa'lhābā** → **[salȁbā]** 'dampness'

(b) After the stressed vowel

੍ਹ → **Ø + High Tone**

ਚੜ੍ਹ **caṛh** → **[cáṛ]** 'to climb'

ਵਰ੍ਹਾ **varhā** → **[várā]** 'year'

ਥੰਮ੍ਹ **tʰammh** → **[tʰámm]** 'pillar'

4.4.2 Full ਹ h

The sound represented by the 'full' ਹ has proved fairly stable in some positions over the centuries, but tone has started breaking into these words as well – **low tone** if ਹ **h** occurs *before* the **stressed vowel** and **high tone** if it occurs *after* the **stressed vowel**. The sound ਹ **h** can co-exist with the **low tone** but never with the **high tone**.

(a) Word-initial

No change

The 'No change' rule applies to the speech of most educated speakers. But **low tone** has started appearing in such words in some dialects, particularly in the speech of the younger generation.

ਹਦਵਾਣਾ **had'vāṇā** 'watermelon'

ਹਾਸਾ **hāsā** 'laughter'

ਹੀਰਾ **hīrā** 'diamond'

(b) Inside a word before the stressed vowel

No change

ਠਹਾਕਾ **ṭʰa'hākā** 'loud laughter'

ਕਹਾਣੀ **ka'hāṇī** 'story'

ਨਿਹੰਗ **ni'hang** 'member of a Sikh sect'

You can often hear ਕਹਾਣੀ **kahāṇī** pronounced as **[kahā̀ṇī]** or even as **[kā̀ṇī]** in which case it is homophonous to ਘਾਣੀ **gʰāṇī [kā̀ṇī]** 'mud'. You may also hear ਨਿਹੰਗ **nihang** pronounced as **[nihàng]** or **[niàng]** or **[nìng]** in different areas.

(c) Inside a word after the stressed vowel

No change

ਪੈਹਾ **'paⁱhā** 'footpath'
ਲਹੂ **'lahū** 'blood'
ਚੂਹਾ **'cūhā** 'rat'

But **high tone** has started appearing in such words. For example, the pronunciation **[cū́ā]** of ਚੂਹਾ **cūhā** is quite common.

(d) Word final

ਹ → Ø + High Tone

ਸਾਹ **sāh [sā́]** 'breath'
ਵੀਹ **vīh [vī́h]** 'twenty'
ਲੂਹ **lūh [lū́h]** 'to scorch'

(e) Words like ਕਹਿਣਾ kahiṇā [káⁱṇā] [kɛ́ɳɑ]

The information given in **(e)** and **(f)** below may sound too technical to some readers. They can skip it if they are not interested in such phonetic technicalities.

We have chosen to transcribe the Panjabi vowel ਐ as **aⁱ** and ਔ as **aᵘ**, not only because these vowels are **diphthongs** or vowel **glides** in some Panjabi dialects, but also for another reason which we wish to make clear now. The second superscripted member of each pair shows that the second member in the diphthong is considerably weaker in articulation than the first member. In words like

ਕਹਿਣਾ **'kahiṇā [káⁱṇā]** [kɛ́ɳɑ] 'to say'
ਰਹਿ **rahi [ráⁱ]** [rɛ́] 'to stay'
ਪਹਿਲਾ **'pahilā [páⁱlā]** [pɛ́lɑ] 'first'
ਲਹਿਰਾਂ **'lahirā̃ [láⁱrā̃]** [lɛ́rɑ̃] 'waves'

the ਹ **h** sound comes *after* the stressed vowel. So according to the rules given above, ਹ **h** should disappear and the word should get a high tone. But the story does not end here. Where could the widowed **short/lax** vowel **i** of the second syllable in the older pronunciation go? In the new pronunciation of the word, after the loss of **h** and of its syllable, the combination of **a** and **i** became a single gliding vowel or diphthong with a high tone. After some time, and in many dialects, the gliding vowel **aⁱ** became a pure non-gliding vowel represented by the IPA symbol [ɛ].

Sometimes, this matching of spelling and pronunciation is extended to words which do not fit into this story. Some words borrowed from other languages have now got the vowel **a**^{i}. In Panjabi (and Hindi-Urdu as well) the vowel **a** when followed by **h** in these words is pronounced as **a**^{i} or [ɛ]. Because of the presence of **h**, they developed a tonal pronunciation in Panjabi. So the spelling rule was applied *in reverse* to them. Their Panjabi spellings do not correspond exactly to their original spellings. Examples are

ਸ਼ਹਿਰ **śahir [śá^{i}r]** 'city'
ਮਹਿਲ **mahil [má^{i}l]** 'palace'

In their Persian pronunciation, these words are without the **[i]** vowel sound and should be transliterated in Panjabi as ਸ਼ਹਰ and ਮਹਲ respectively.

In some words with high tone from which ਹ **h** has disappeared and which lie outside the scope of this rule (because they have **[e]** in their pronunciation), there is discrepancy between spelling and pronunciation. The most commonly used among them are

ਮਿਹਨਤ **mihnat [ménat]** 'hard work'
ਮਿਹਰ **mihar [mér]** 'benevolence, mercy'
ਸਿਹਤ **sihat [sét]** 'health'

But many writers use ੇ in them and write them as ਮੇਹਨਤ, ਮੇਹਰ and ਸੇਹਤ.

(f) Words like ਬਹੁਤਾ bahutā [bá^{u}tā] [bɔ́tɑ]

ਬਹੁਤਾ **bahutā [bá^{u}tā]** [bɔ́tɑ] 'too much, excessive'
ਸਹੁਰਾ **sahurā [sá^{u}rā]** [sɔ́rɑ] 'father-in-law'
ਪਹੁ **pahu [pá^{u}]** [pɔ́] 'dawn'
ਸਹੁੰ **sahũ [sá̃^{u}]** [sɔ̃́] 'oath'
ਪਹੁੰਚ **pahũc [pá̃c^{h}]** [pɔ̃́ʧ] 'approach'

The story is very similar to the one given above, with the only difference being that the widowed **short/lax** vowel **u** of the second syllable joined with **[a]** to make the diphthong **[a^{u}]**, which later became the pure non-gliding vowel represented by the IPA symbol [ɔ].

Pronunciation has changed but the older spellings continue. A similar example from English is the spelling and pronunciation of the word *knowledge.*

4.5 Intonation in Panjabi

We have analysed in some detail above the Panjabi **tone** or variation of pitch at the level of the *word.* Let us call it the *word-level* melodic contour or word-level melody. But *sentence-level, clause-level* and *phrase-level* melodic contours also occur in Panjabi (as in English, as well as in Punjabi's cousins Norwegian, Swedish and Serbo-Croat, which have tone in the form of pitch accent).

The study of **intonation** is a vast subject and various theoretical approaches have been, and are still being, developed to analyse tonal contours in different languages. Our *pragmatic* view is that cutting a tonal contour is like cutting a potato: your method depends on what you wish to do with the result. There is no single "true" or "best" method or approach. For learners of Panjabi, who also need to know how the **tonal** and the **intonational** contours interact and affect each other, the *holistic* or the *whole contour* approach is the best. Avoiding any irrelevant details or intricacies, the system of Panjabi intonation is quite similar to that of English (for our purpose).

4.5.1 Major intonation contours in Panjabi

The following major intonation contours are used in Panjabi. The name of each contour is given after the *direction* which it takes from the **nucleus** or the **nuclear syllable** in the sentence or clause or phrase and how it ends. This syllable is the stressed syllable (printed in **bold letters** in these examples) of the *most significant* word.

The representation of **intonation** in the following diagrams is considerably *simplified* to mark the *general direction* of the tonal contour and to make the phenomenon intelligible. Words with **tonal pitch** are avoided.

1. Falling intonation

This type of intonation is generally used with statements or open questions (also known as **k-questions**, because all the question words in Panjabi start with the sound **k**), just as all the question words or **wh-** words in English have **w** and **h** in them). This contour can be graphically represented as

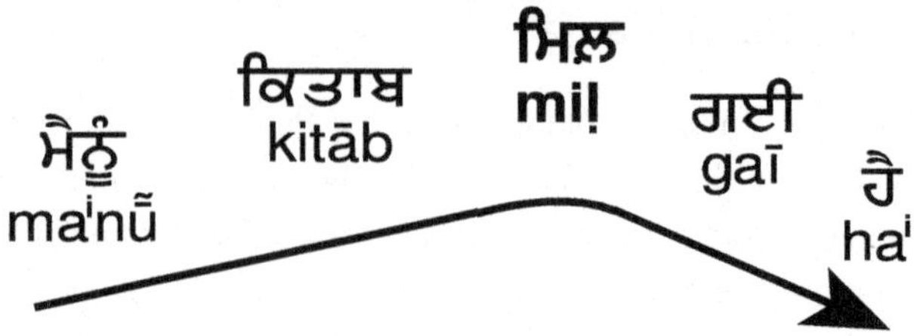

ਮੈਨੂੰ ਕਿਤਾਬ ਮਿਲ਼ ਗਈ ਹੈ

'I ***have received*** the book.'

Figure 4.4 Falling intonation contour 1

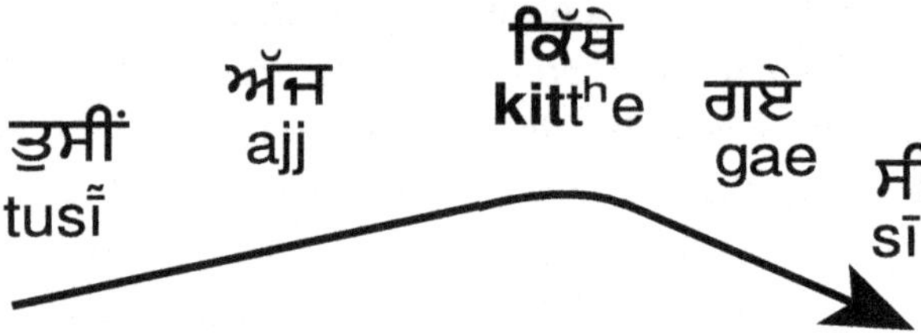

ਤੁਸੀਂ ਅੱਜ ਕਿੱਥੇ ਗਏ ਸੀ?

'***Where*** did you go today?'

Figure 4.5 Falling intonation contour 2

2. Rising intonation

This type of intonation is used for **open questions** (or **yes-no questions**). But it is also commonly used for **k-questions** when the speaker wants to sound more polite and less demanding.

ਤੁਸੀਂ ਅੱਜ ਸਕੂਲ ਗਏ ਸੀ?

'Did you go to the ***school*** today?'

Figure 4.6 Rising intonation contour 1

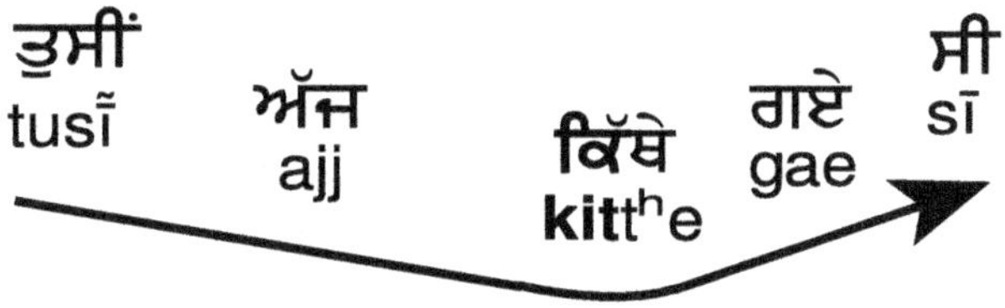

ਤੁਸੀਂ ਅੱਜ ਕਿੱਥੇ ਗਏ ਸੀ?

'***Where*** did you go today?'

Figure 4.7 Rising intonation contour 2

3. Level intonation

Instead of going up or down at the end, the contour halts at the midpoint, indicating that the speaker has not finished and is going to continue after the slight pause.

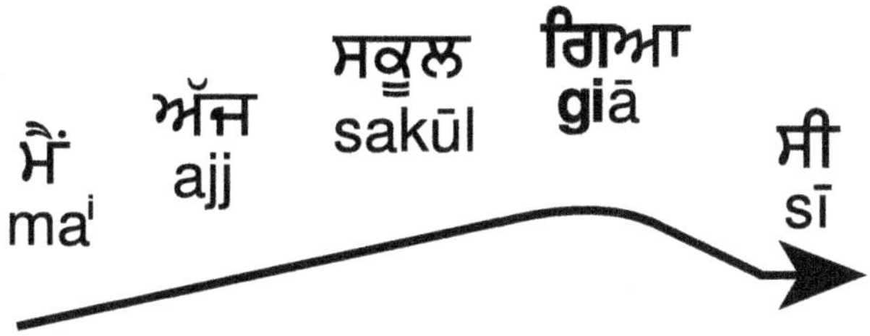

ਮੈਂ ਸਕੂਲ ਗਿਆ ਸੀ...

'I ***did go*** to the school, (but...)'

Figure 4.8 Level intonation contour

Like the other intonation contours in the language, this contour is *complete* in the sense that it has its boundaries. But it can also be regarded as an *incompletion* contour because the speaker gives the impression that she/he has not finished yet and is going to add something. We shall see later (in **4.5.2** below and also in Chapter 16) that variation in word order is combined with this contour to achieve various "stylistic effects".

4. Falling-rising intonation 1

This intonation contour is a variation of the **level intonation contour**. It is also an *incompletion* contour. The contour falls and rises to indicate some *implication* associated with the word having the **nuclear syllable**.

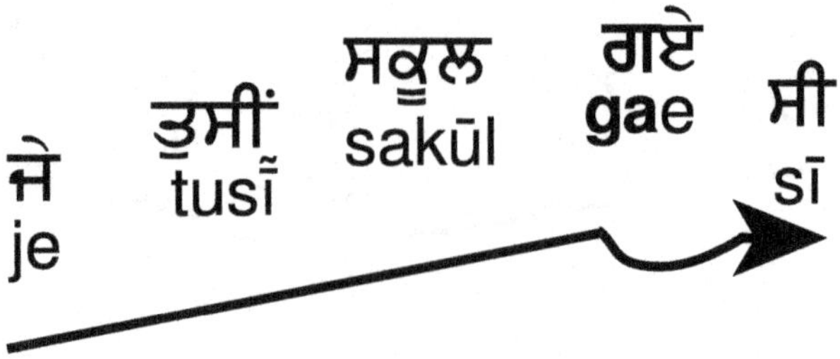

ਜੇ ਤੁਸੀਂ ਸਕੂਲ ਗਏ ਸੀ, ...
'If you ***went*** to school, ...
(I doubt whether you went there).

Figure 4.9 Falling-rising intonation contour 1

5. Falling-rising intonation 2

When the pitch falls at the end of what could have been an *implicational* intonation contour instead of staying level, the contour can be regarded as expressing a *taunting meaning*.

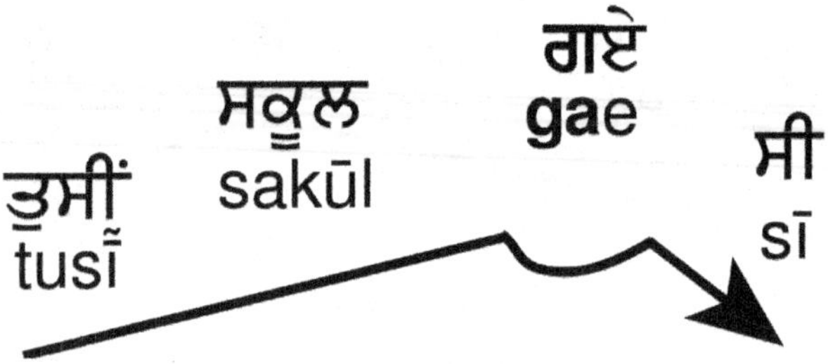

ਤੁਸੀਂ ਸਕੂਲ ਗਏ ਸੀ! ...
'You ***went*** to school!'
(What a preposterous idea!)

Figure 4.10 Falling-rising intonation contour 2

4.5.2 Mixing of intonation contours within a sentence

A clause boundary and intonation contour boundary tend to coincide in Panjabi. But this tendency is often overridden to create "stylistic effects" involving the manipulation of word order within a clause. This is a subject for Chapter 16. But an example can be given here. The sentence

> ਮੇਰੇ ਪੁੱਤਰ ਨੇ ਅੱਠ ਮੈਡਲ ਜਿੱਤੇ
> **mere puttar ne aṭṭ^h ma^{i}ḍal jitte**
> my son AGT eight medals won
> 'My son won eight medals'

can rephrased as

> ਮੇਰੇ ਪੁੱਤਰ ਨੇ ਜਿੱਤੇ ॥ ਅੱਠ ਮੈਡਲ
> **mere puttar ne jitte ॥ aṭṭ^h ma^{i}ḍal**

to highlight and emphasise "eight medals". The symbol || represents the intonation contour boundary within a clause. This can be graphically represented as

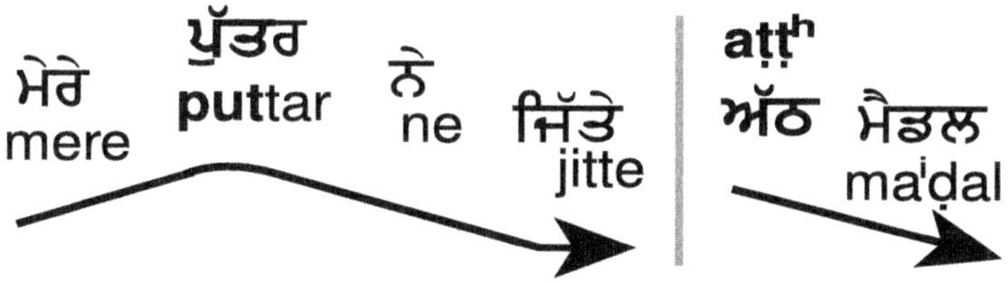

Figure 4.11 Mixed intonation contours

4.6 Interaction of the tonal and the intonational pitches

Tones or **pitch accents** in Panjabi are a fairly recent phenomenon and appeared after the writing system was well established. **Intonation** is more basic (and historically *older*) in Panjabi, and the **tone** is simply a perturbation in the **intonational contour**. In the following examples the Panjabi words ਕਾਲ਼ਾ **kāḷā** [kɑɭɑ] 'black', ਘਾਲ਼ਾ **g^{h}āḷā** [kɑ̀ɭɑ] 'fraud' and ਕਾਹਲ਼ਾ **kāhḷā** [kɑ́ɭɑ] 'impatient' are used in the sentence frame

> ਪੈ ਗਿਆ ____?
> **pa^i giā̃ ____ ?**
> [pɛ gɪɑ ____?]

All three words have the same consonants and vowels. They differ in their **tones** only, as is clearly shown in the IPA transcription.

Here is diagrammatic representation of the toneless ਕਾਲ਼ਾ **kāḷā** [kɑɭɑ]. There is no perturbation in the rising intonation contour. The rest of the contour is shown as a grey line.

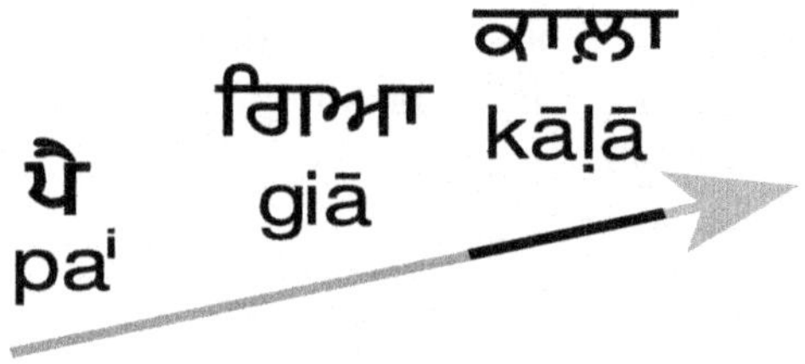

ਪੈ ਗਿਆ ਕਾਲ਼ਾ?

pa^{i} giā kāḷā?

'Has it turned black?'

Figure 4.12 Toneless word in a rising intonation contour

Now the **low tone** word ਘਾਲ਼ਾ **g^{h}aḷā** [kàɭɑ] in the same intonational contour.

ਪੈ ਗਿਆ ਘਾਲ਼ਾ?

pa^{i} giā g^{h}āḷā?

'Has a fraud taken place?

Figure 4.13 Low tone word in a rising intonation contour

The **tonal** pitch contour superimposes itself on the intonational pitch contour. The same thing happens with the other **tone** on the word ਕਾਹਲ਼ਾ **kāhḷā** [káɭɑ].

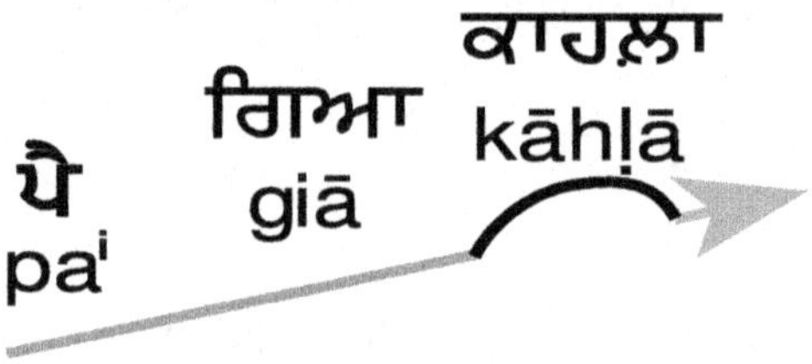

ਪੈ ਗਿਆ ਕਾਹਲ਼ਾ?

pa^{i} giā kāhḷā?

'Has he become impatient?'

Figure 4.14 High tone word in a rising intonation contour

The system works smoothly mainly because the speakers recognise the tone words and *also* because the **tonal** falls and rises are steeper and more abrupt than the **intonational** ones. Moreover, the **constricted phonation** associated with the low tone is also there.

4.7 Homophonous and homographic words in Panjabi

Homophonous words are the words that differ in spelling but have the same pronunciation. Examples from English are 'week' and 'weak'. **Homographic** words have the same spelling but different pronunciations. Examples are 'row' (line) and 'row' (fierce quarrel). With the major changes in Panjabi pronunciation as a result of the arrival of the tones but only a few minor changes in the spelling conventions, you should expect to meet both types of words in the language. The claim that "In Panjabi you speak exactly as you write and write exactly as you speak" is a little bit exaggerated!

1. Homophonous words

Try applying the rules given above to see how the following words will be pronounced with tones. They are **causative forms** of two different verbs. Causative forms are the subject of Chapter 9. Here we can simply mention that the **causative suffix -ā** or **-vā** is added to the **stem**. This suffix is **stressed**. As a result, the vowel in the stem becomes short or lax.

> ਝਾੜ+ਵਾ → ਝੜਵਾ
>
> **j^{h}āṛ+vā → j^{h}aṛ'vā [caṛvà]**
>
> 'to get dusted'

Since the **breathy voiced** or **voiced aspirate j^{h}** occurs before the stressed vowel **ā**, it becomes **voiceless unaspirate c** and the stressed **ā** get the **low tone**. The resulting pronunciation is **[caṛvà]**. The final **vā** in a **causative** form is stressed, and vowel of the stem becomes unstressed, lax and shortened **a**.

Now look at

> ਚਾੜ੍ਹ+ਵਾ → ਚੜ੍ਹਵਾ
>
> **cāṛh+vā → caṛh'vā [caṛvà]**
>
> 'to get raised/taken up'

The **h** sound (written in the subscript form in Panjabi) occurs before the stressed vowel **ā**. So the vowel gets the **low tone**. The result is **[caṛvā̀]**. The vowel of the stem becomes lax and shortened **a**. Two different words spelt as ਝੜਵਾ and ਚੜ੍ਹਵਾ have the same pronunciation. This is not accidental as in the case of *week* and *weak*, but a perfectly rule-governed phenomenon. If someone tells you

darīā̃ [caṛvā̀ dio]
'carpets' ________

You will need to clarify whether he is asking you to get the carpets dusted or taken up (unless the request comes in Gurmukhi *writing*!)

2. Homographic words

The spellings of these two words are the same. But each is pronounced differently.

ਵਰ੍ਹਾ 'varhā [várā]
'year'

The vowel of the first syllable is stressed and **h** come *after* this vowel. So the stressed vowel gets the **high tone**.

But in the causative form of ਵਰ੍ਹ **varh** 'to rain', the final **ā** is stressed. So **h** comes before this vowel and the word gets a **low tone**.

ਵਰ੍ਹਾ va'rhā [varā̀]
'to make the rain fall'

as in the Punjabi nursery rhyme ਰੱਬਾ ਰੱਬਾ ਮੀਂਹ ਵਰ੍ਹਾ **rabbā rabbā mī̃h varhā** 'O God, O God, make the rain fall.'

Examples of some other homographic pairs are ਘਟਾ **'gʰaṭā [kàṭā]** 'dark clouds' and ਘਟਾ **gʰa'ṭā [kaṭā̀]** 'to make less', and ਝਟਕਾ **jʰaṭkā [càṭkā]** 'jerk' and ਝਟਕਾ **jʰaṭ'kā [caṭkā̀]** 'to behead with one blow of the weapon'.

As was discussed in Chapter 1, a language is always changing, and the grammar of a language (such as presented in this book) is a still snapshot of an ongoing action. Each linguistic element (morpheme, word, grammatical category, phrase etc. – we call them **constructions**) stored in the **lexicon** of a community joins two poles – the **phonetic** pole (dealing with pronunciation) and the **semantic** pole (dealing with the meaning). At each pole lie bundles of potentialities, phonetic potentialities and semantic potentialities, only some of which are realised when constructions are actually used in speech. Chapters 3 and 4 of this book deal with the phonetic pole, the rest of the book deals with the semantic pole. So far we have dealt with some changes taking place at the phonetic pole.

For teachers and other more advanced users

An exhaustive study of the phonological features of Panjabi will need a separate full length book. What has been presented in this part of the present book is just a preliminary sketch.

4.8 When did the tones appear in Panjabi?

There some evidence that tones first appeared in the types of words mentioned above in section **4.4** in the 15th century or earlier. But details cannot be discussed here. See Bhardwaj (2013) and Harkirat Singh (2011).

4.9 Monosyllabic words in Panjabi?

It was pointed out above that the **tonal** pitch falls or rises on the **stressed syllable** and comes back to the normal level in the following **unstressed syllable**. Now the question arises: What about the **monosyllabic** (with only one syllable) words like ਸਾਹ **'sāh [sá̄]** and ਘਾਹ **'gʰāh [kā̀]** 'grass'? Where does the pitch come to the normal level? The answer is that if *in actual speech* such a word is followed by a toneless syllable, the pitch comes to the normal level in that syllable. If there is no **toneless syllable**, the speaker *creates* one. A word in the citation form (spoken as an example) is a one-word sentence. If the word has a **tense** vowel, it is prolonged or **geminated**, so that it gets two syllables. In the citation form, these words are pronounced as **[sá̄.a]** and **[kā̀.a]** respectively. But such prolongation of the vowels is not needed in ਸਾਹ ਖਿੱਚੋ **sāh kʰicco** 'breathe in' and ਘਾਹ ਤੇ ਬੈਠੋ **gʰāh te baᴵṭʰo** 'sit on the grass' because in the sentence the tonal syllable is followed by a non-tonal one where the tonal pitch can come to a normal level. If the word has a **lax** vowel (which cannot be geminated) and ends in a consonant, as in ਚੜ੍ਹ **caṛh [cáṛ]**, the **schwa** vowel is added at the end, so that the last consonant makes the second **CV** syllable with an extremely short version of the vowel schwa. (This is known as the **vocalic release**.) Thus ਚੜ੍ਹ **carhʰ** is pronounced as [cə́ṛᵊ].

Again, this does not happen if there is a following toneless syllable in actual speech.

In *most* Panjabi words (excluding some grammatical words, to be discussed in the following chapters), the **penultimate** (second from the back) syllable is stressed, so that there is one syllable after the stressed one *whether or not the word has a tone*. Whether Panjabi developed this feature because of the tones or already had it and the tones found it handy is a chicken and egg question!

4.10 Strong stress in Panjabi

The symbol ਅੱਧਕ (ੱ) **add^{h}ak**, showing **gemination** or doubling of consonants, is not used in the Sikh holy book (completed in 1604). In most cases in Panjabi, consonant gemination results from a strong stress. Harkirt Singh (2011) concludes that stress was not a prominent feature of Panjabi speech in the 16th century. Though the doubling of consonants even at that time cannot be ruled out, it was not an important feature of the language. This symbol first appeared in Panjabi writing in the 18th century. There are several consequences of strong stress. But two need mentioning here.

4.10.1 Weakening and centring of the unstressed vowels

Vowels in the unstressed syllables tend to become weak, lax and centred. The worst affected **vowels** are the ones in **pre-stress** syllables. Often they move towards the centre of the vowel space (the shaded area) and very often are reduced to schwa. If the word starts with ਅ **a**, the vowel often disappears altogether. **i** and **u** often become **non-syllabic y** and **v** respectively.

Examples are

ਵੀਰੇਂਦ੍ਰ → ਵਰਿੰਦਰ
vīrendra **varindar**
[vi'rendrə] [və'rindər]

Panjabi does not allow word-final [drə]. So it becomes [dər]. The penultimate syllable [rin] is stressed. The vowel in the pre-stress [vi] syllable is weakened and centred to become [ə].

ਅਖੰਡ → ਖੰਡ
ak^{h}aṇḍ **k^{h}aṇḍ**
[ɐ'khɐɳɖ] ['khɐɳ.ɖ^ə]

ਅਖੰਡ **ak^{h}aṇḍ** means 'unbroken'. A reading of the Sikh holy book continuously for about seventy-two hours by different priests in turn is called ਅਖੰਡ ਪਾਠ **ak^{h}aṇḍ pāṭ^h** 'unbroken reading'. But many speakers of Panjabi pronounce it as ਖੰਡ ਪਾਠ **k^{h}aṇḍ pāṭ^h**, which means the exact opposite, much to the annoyance of Sikh priests and educated Sikhs. Now look at

ਆਰਾਮ → ਅਰਾਮ → ਰਾਮ
ārām **arām** **rām**
[ɑ'ram] [ə'rɑ.ɑm] ['rɑ.ɑm] 'rest'

The tense vowel of the second syllable is geminated to create another unstressed syllable. The pre-stress vowel is either reduced to [ə] or is completely dropped.

An extreme case is the pronunciation of ਇਤਿਹਾਸ **itihās** 'history' as **[atyàs]** [ə.tjɑ̀.ɑs] or even as **[tyà.ās]** [tjɑ̀.ɑs]. **h** disappeared and gave the **low tone** to the **stressed syllable**, whose **tense** vowel was geminated. The vowel at the beginning of the word first became [ə] and was then dropped. The vowel **[i]** after **[t]** became non-syllabic (consonant) **[y]**. Now **[tyà.ās]** [tjɑ̀.ɑs] has only two syllables with penultimate stress, which is the general pattern in Panjabi. In the speech of some people, particularly uneducated ones in some areas, you can often hear ਹਦਵਾਣਾ **hadvāṇā** 'watermelon' pronounced as **dvā.ṇā** [dwɑ̀.ɳɑ].

Even tense **[ī]** and **[ū]** often become **non-syllabic** and **geminated** consonants **[y]** and **[v]** in ਭਾਈਆ **b^{h}āiā [pàiā]** [pɑ̀j.jɑ] 'old man' and ਪਊਆ **paūā [pav.vā]** [pɐw.wɑ] 'one quart of liquid'. This is excellent stuff for academic phonologists to theorise about. The Panjabi alphabet has symbols for the semi-vowels ਯ and ਵ corresponding to the *lax* vowels **[i]** and **[u]** respectively. But it has no symbols for the semi-vowels derived from the *tense* **[ī]** and **[ū]**.

4.10.2 Preference for closed syllables

A very recent tendency in Panjabi speech is turning syllables with **tense vowels** into **closed syllables** by geminating the following consonant.

The spelling “Punjabi” of the name of this language appears to have been given by someone from the North of England where the vowel pronounced as [ʌ] in Southern English is pronounced as [ʊ], so that “shut up” was (and still is) pronounced as [ʃʊt ʊp]. That person stressed the word on the first syllable and pronounced it as [pʊn]. But many English writers used the spelling “Panjabi” as well. The Panjabi stress rules place the stress on the penultimate syllable [ʤɑ]. In most other North Indian languages such as Hindi-Urdu, a syllable with a long vowel is normally an ***open syllable***. But a recent tendency in Panjabi pronunciation is to turn even such open syllables into closed ones by geminating the consonant of the following syllable and grabbing half of the consonant *if the consonant is a* ***tense*** *one and can be* ***geminated***. The name of the language is most commonly pronounced by its speakers as [pəɲˈʤɑb.bi], and not as [pəɲˈʤɑ.bi], and *never* as [ˈpʊɲ.ʤɑbɪ]. The spelling of the name of a language should be based on the pronunciation of its speakers, and not on the 18th century *mis*pronunciation of an English person probably from Yorkshire, England. **ਨੀਲਾ nīlā** ‘blue’ with a tense **l** is generally pronounced as **[nīl.lā]** but the lax **ḷ** in **ਪੀਲ਼ਾ pīḷā** ‘yellow’ cannot be geminated. The most common Panjabi pronunciation of the Urdu word **ਖ਼ਾਲੀ xālī** ‘empty’ is **k^hāl.lī**. The stressed syllable with the tense vowel [ɑ] thus becomes a closed one. The Arabic/Persian sound [x] becomes [k^h], as in the speech of most speakers of Panjabi who are not careful.

Tones, strong stress, weakening and centring of unstressed vowels and preference for closed syllables are together known as the “Panjabi accent” which colours the speech of the speakers of this language when they speak other languages. Hearing the Panjabi-speaking Pakistanis speak their “national language” Urdu (mother tongue of less than 5% of its total population who migrated from India in 1947) with an overwhelmingly Panjabi accent is linguistically an interesting and amusing experience!

Tones and strong stress developed together in Panjabi. A more interesting question is “Did Panjabi develop **tones** because **breathy voiced phonation** became incompatible with strong stress?” A great deal of research in phonology and human anatomy and physiology is needed to answer this question.

Part III
Grammar and Meaning

Chapter 5

Panjabi Grammar in Outline

Preview of the chapter

This chapter presents a very brief outline of Panjabi grammar and introduces *most* of the important technical terms used in the book. Like any other intellectual discipline, grammar has its own technical terminology. Utmost care has been taken here to follow what is known as the *Principle of Parsimony* or *Occam's Razor* – the principle that we should not use more entities (and categories) than the minimum needed. Many of the unnecessary categories used in the older Panjabi grammars have been shaved off.

A grammar book without its own technical terminology is like a chemistry book without chemical formulas or a physics book without equations. But all the technical terms introduced in this chapter are fully explained with lots of examples in the following chapters. Some of the technical information given below may be new for many users of this book. So it is repeated in some places.

5.1 Introduction

After dealing with Sanskrit phonology in the first chapter of his monumental Sanskrit grammar *Aṣṭādhyāyī*, Pāṇini starts the grammar part in the second chapter with a metarule समर्थः पदविधिः *samarthaḥ padavidhiḥ,* that the subsequent rules apply to *samartha* or "syntactically competent" words. We do the same in this book. In the Indian linguistic tradition, a sentence is regarded as a group of *samartha* words – समर्थपदसमूहो वाक्यम् *samarthapadasamūho vākyam*. The word *samartha* is a combination of *sam* ('together') and *artha* ('wealth', 'intention', 'meaning' etc.). So a *samartha* word in Panjabi is mostly an inflected word playing a syntactic role in the company of other *samartha* words in the sentence. While *samartha* words make a sentence, it is the word's role in the sentence that endows it with *sāmarthya* or *samartha*-hood. It is mutual or dialectical causation, as in a living body. The grammatical structure of Panjabi has historically evolved to become very different from that of Sanskrit and our style of presentation is also going to be very different. But Pāṇini's great insight is followed throughout the book. We will sometimes use the term **clause** instead of **sentence** when we discuss the *structure of a simple sentence* with only one **nuclear verb** or **verb phrase**. The reason will be made clear later. We also introduce the main technical terms used in the book.

We should first of all differentiate the **inflection** from the **derivation** of a **lexeme**. A lexeme is an *abstract* dictionary unit which assumes different grammatical or inflected forms. For the sake of convenience, the abstract lexeme is represented by one of its inflected forms (usually the most common one). For example, the Panjabi lexeme ਵੱਡਾ **vaḍḍā** 'large', 'great' can assume the forms ਵੱਡਾ **vaḍḍā**, ਵੱਡੀ **vaḍḍī**, ਵੱਡੇ **vaḍḍe** or ਵੱਡੀਆਂ **vaḍḍīā̃**, depending on its position and role in the clause. The affixes used for creating these forms are known as **inflectional affixes**. But we can also *derive* other lexemes from ਵੱਡਾ **vaḍḍā** by adding other types of affixes known as **derivational affixes**. For example, we can form lexemes like ਵਡਿਆਈ **vaḍiāi** 'praise', ਵਡੱਪਣ **vaḍappaṇ** 'greatness' and ਵਡੇਰਾ **vaḍerā** 'ancestor'. We can also create a **compound lexeme** by combining it with other lexemes, such as ਵਡਭਾਗਾ **vaḍbʰāgā** 'fortunate', ਵਡਮੁੱਲਾ **vaḍmullā** 'very valuable' and ਵੱਡ-ਅਕਾਰੀ **vaḍḍ-akārī** 'large sized'. If these derived lexemes are used in a sentence, they must assume the correct **inflectional** forms. This grammar deals mostly with inflectional forms. A study of the formation of the inflectional forms of lexemes is known as **inflectional morphology**. **Derivational morphology** is the province of the dictionary writer, but it is touched briefly in Chapter 17.

As any grammarian or language teacher knows, dealing with the **inflectional morphology** of a language can be a nightmare, and each grammarian finds their own solution to the problem. A language is a self-organising dynamical system or a complex adaptive system in which *structuration processes* are always going on and *structures* are simply temporary islands of relative stability. A study of the history of a living language, if known, is always a fascinating subject. Within the systems and structures in a language, there are sub-systems and sub-structures with their own irregular patterns of organisation. At any given time, a language is *polysytemic* rather than *monosystemic*. A rather too familiar example is the conjugation system of the English verb. The currently productive process of creating the past tense and the past participle forms is by adding the suffix *-ed* to the base form, as in *bake, baked, baked*. But the historical relic *take, took, taken* is still there as an irregular verb. The comparative and superlative forms of the adjective *sad* formed according to the currently productive process are *sadder* and *saddest* respectively. But *bad* continues to have *worse* and *worst*. We can say that if *take* were not an irregular verb, it "*could have*" been conjugated as *take, *taked, *taked*. Similarly, we can say that *bad* "*could have*" **badder* and **baddest* as its comparative and superlative forms respectively. A language teacher often has to say, "This is the currently productive rule. But, for historical reasons, it does not apply to such and such cases. But it *could have* applied." Sure enough, many historical irregularities *are* regularised. Nobody now uses *kine* as a plural form of *cow* or *wrought* as a past tense form of *work*. Many people have started using *mouses* as a plural form of a computer *mouse*. In the presentation of the rules of Panjabi grammar in this book, we have to resort to the use of "*could have*" in many places.

This should handle *most* of the problems of irregularity in grammar and a grammarian should honestly and realistically aim at just this. But a few problems resulting from historical relics defy all solutions and have to be accepted as such. A well-known example from English grammar is the ***were*-subjunctive** in *If **I were** you, I would resign my job* and the **mandative subjunctive** in *We demand that **he resign** his job*. In these examples, the usual rules of the agreement of the verb with the subject of the clause do not apply. Such historical relics are found in Panjabi as well (and probably in all languages). Developing new trends may also create some anomalies or irregularities.

5.2 Word classes or "parts of speech" in Panjabi

The lexemes of Panjabi can be divided into word classes or "parts of speech" to study their role in the grammar of the languages. A living and constantly evolving language is never a well-defined and internally consistent logical structure. So each "part of speech" has to be *characterised* (the use of the word "*defined*" would not be appropriate) in more than one mutually complementary way. The traditional **notional** or **semantic** way of doing this was not wrong but imprecise and insufficient. For example, defining the **noun** class as referring to persons, places, things and abstract entities is not basically wrong, but defining an abstract entity is a problem. So the language-specific **formal** characteristics (such as inflection, controlling the **agreement** of the **verb**) and **functional** role (such as being an ARGUMENT of a PREDICATOR) also have to be taken into consideration. For the purpose of this book, we set up the following word classes:

1 Noun	ਮੁੰਡਾ ਆਇਆ *muṇḍā* āiā
	'The *boy* came'
2 Verb	ਮੁੰਡਾ ਆਇਆ muṇḍā *āiā*
	'The boy *came*'
	ਮੁੰਡਾ ਹੁਸ਼ਿਆਰ ਹੈ muṇḍā huśiār *ha*[i]
	'The boy *is* intelligent'
	(Copular-existential verb)
3 Adjective	ਮੁੰਡਾ ਹੁਸ਼ਿਆਰ ਹੈ muṇḍā *huśiār* ha[i]
	'The boy is *intelligent*'
	ਉਹ ਮੁੰਡਾ ਹੁਸ਼ਿਆਰ ਹੈ *uh* muṇḍā huśiār ha[i]
	'*That* boy is intelligent'
	(Determiner)
4 Adverb	ਮੁੰਡਾ ਛੇਤੀ ਆਇਆ muṇḍā *c*[h]*etī* āiā
	'The boy came *quickly*'
	ਮੁੰਡਾ ਤਾਂ ਛੇਤੀ ਹੀ ਆਇਆ muṇḍā *tā̃* c[h]etī *hī* āiā
	'*As for* the boy, he *certainly* came quickly'
	(Particles)
5 Postposition	ਮੁੰਡਾ ਕਮਰੇ ਵਿਚ ਹੈ muṇḍā kamre *vic* ha[i]
	'The boy is *in* the room'
6 Co-ordinator	ਮੁੰਡਾ ਅਤੇ ਕੁੜੀ ਆਏ muṇḍā *ate* kuṛī āe
	'The boy *and* the girl came'
7 Subordinator	ਮੈਨੂੰ ਪਤਾ ਸੀ ਕਿ ਮੁੰਡਾ ਆਏਗਾ
	ma[i]nū̃ patā sī *ki* muṇḍā āegā
	'I knew *that* the boy would come'

The examples given above are very simple. The following chapters will deal with these word classes in detail. It is notable that the effect of use of the **particles** in Panjabi can be only partially captured in the English translation because English has no equivalent word class. **Particles** are what we call a **discourse-related** category, and they always work in combination with appropriate sentence **stress** and **intonation**. This is discussed in later chapters. There are reasons for classifying the **copular-existential verb** (or **copula**) ਹੈ **ha**[l] as a special type of verb in spite of its markedly different grammatical behaviour. Similarly, the **determiner** ਉਹ **uh**, is best classified as a special type of **adjective** and a **pronoun** is regarded as a special type of **noun**. The **particles** ਹੀ **hī**, ਵੀ **vī** and ਤਾਂ **tā̃** are best regarded as special members of the word class **adverb**. The nuances they contribute to the organisation of the text cannot be easily expressed in English translation. (Chapters 7 and 16 deal with them in some detail.) But the grammatical behaviour of the **co-ordinators** and **subordinators** (traditionally regarded as **conjunctions**) is so different that they have to be regarded as different word classes. A number of Panjabi verbs function as **explicator auxiliaries** (dealt with in Chapter 10). Morphologically and syntactically, Panjabi **adjectives** behave very much, but not exactly, like the **nouns**. This has been the case in North Indian languages for centuries. But such indeterminacies are to be expected. All this is discussed in detail in later chapters.

We have not clearly defined the grammatical terms introduced in this chapter. But we will do this with examples as they come up in the following chapters.

5.3 The concept of the "phrase"

A **phrase** is a grammatical unit which may consist of one or more than one word and which acts as one of the classes of constituents into which a sentence can be divided. For example, there can be one or more **VP (verb phrase)**, **NP (noun phrase)**, **AdjP (adjective phrase)**, **PP (postpositional phrase)** and **AdvP (adverb phrase)** in a sentence. A phrase may consist of a HEAD only, or it may also have one or more DEPENDENTS from its own or different word classes. The HEAD of a **PP**, for example, is always a **postposition**. But its DEPENDENTS may be **nouns**, **pronouns** or **NPs** and even other **PPs**.

5.4 Canonical finite clause patterns in Panjabi

*This section and section **5.5** below are extremely important for an understanding of the grammatical structure of Panjabi. So readers and users are advised to read them very carefully and digest the information presented in them.*

A **clause** is "Any syntactic unit whose structure is, or is seen as reduced from, that of a sentence. Thus, in particular, one which includes a verb and the elements that accompany it" (Matthews 2007: 58). Using the "divide and conquer" strategy (which is not the monopoly of politicians!) we will start this study of Panjabi grammar with the **canonical clause.**

The concept of **canonical clause** is borrowed from Huddleston and Pullum (2005) and is *adapted* here for Panjabi as **canonical finite clause**. A Panjabi canonical finite clause is syntactically the most basic one and is a **declarative**, **positive**, non-**co-ordinate**, **main clause** whose **VP** (**verb phrase**) is not a **serial verb** or a verb in the **subtractive phase** (discussed in Chapters 13 and 9 respectively), and which has not undergone any of the **discourse-related** processes described in Chapter 16. The term **finite** *as applicable to Panjabi* is defined below. A canonical finite clause has no ADJUNCTS or **non-finite clauses** or **subordinate clauses** embedded in it. (All these technical details are explained below and in later chapters.)

We can set up four **canonical finite clause** patterns in Panjabi. They are discussed in detail and with examples in the following sections.

Pattern 1

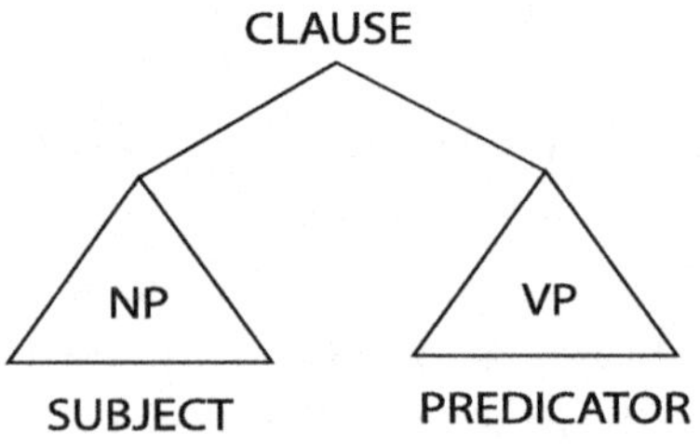

Figure 5.1 Panjabi canonical finite clause pattern 1

Pattern 2

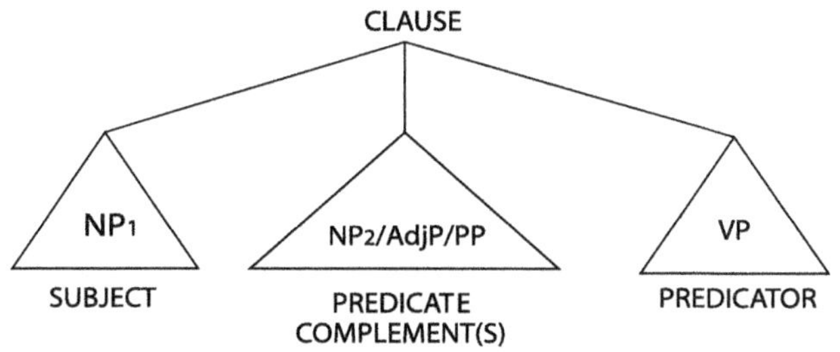

Figure 5.2 Panjabi canonical finite clause pattern 2

Pattern 3

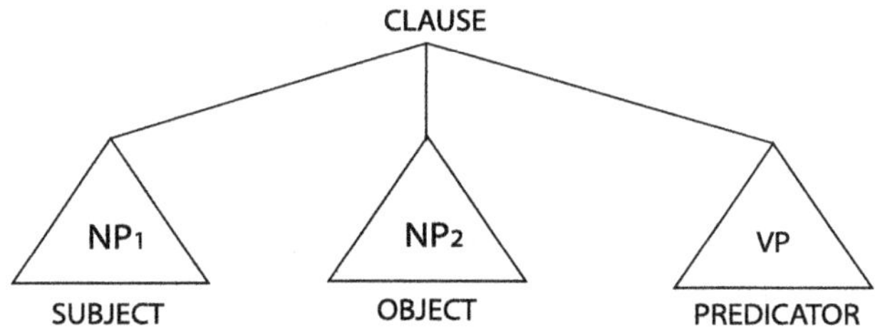

Figure 5.3 Panjabi canonical finite clause pattern 3

Pattern 4

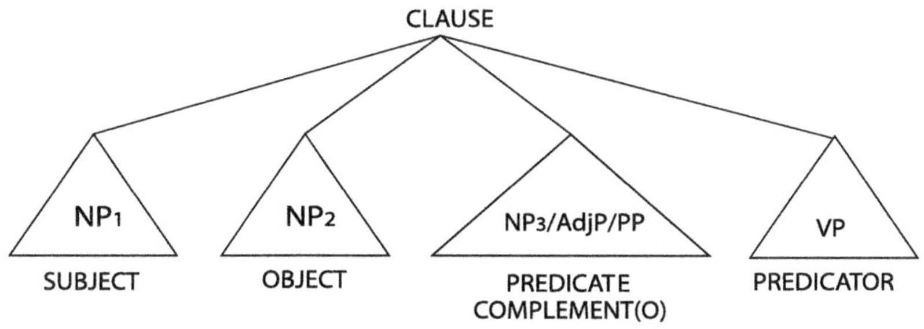

Figure 5.4 Panjabi canonical finite clause pattern 4

5.5 Formal, functional, semantic and discourse-related categories

A lot of confusion in grammar can be avoided by separating the grammatical categories into the following classes:

1. Formal and functional categories

The categories **VP (verb phrase)**, **NP (noun phrase)**, **AdjP (adjective phrase**) and **PP (postpositional phrase**) (included in these diagrams), and **AdvP (adverb phrase**) are **non-relational formal** categories. In the diagrams, they appear within triangles. A **noun phrase**, for example, is a phrase (a group of words) whose HEAD is most often a noun. Similarly, a **verb phrase** is a phrase headed by a **verb**. On the other hand, PREDICATOR, SUBJECT, OBJECT, PREDICATE COMPLEMENT(S) or COMP(S) and PREDICATE COMPLEMENT(O) or COMP(O) are **relational** or **functional** categories. In this book, they appear in ALL CAPITAL letters. A PREDICATOR is the hub of a clause. In Panjabi, a PREDICATOR is always instantiated by a **VP**. The SUBJECT or OBJECT of a clause is typically an **NP**, but, as we see in later chapters, a **PP** or a **non-finite clause** or an **embedded finite clause** may also play this role.

2. Semantic categories

Semantics (the study of meaning) in concerned with the linguistic representation of the "outside world" or a language user's "encyclopaedic" knowledge of the world. This part of a language user's knowledge can never be codified because it is governed not by any definite rules but by tendencies. This knowledge always remains in a state of flux and often differs in different contexts. Categories like **agent, patient, experiencer, causer/causing agent, instrument** and numerous others are among the **semantic** categories we have to make use of in analysing constructions in a language. All that we can do is choose the ones which best serve our purpose of saying or interpreting something. It should be kept in mind that there need not be any consistent one-to-one relationship between the syntactic and the semantic categories language-internally or cross-linguistically. For example, an **experiencer** can be the SUBJECT of a clause in English and the PREDICATE COMPLEMENT(S) in Panjabi. The Panjabi equivalent of the English *I have a headache* is

(1)	ਮੈਨੂੰ	ਸਿਰਪੀੜ	ਹੈ
	ma^{i}nū̃	**sirpīṛ**	**ha^{i}**
	me-to	headache	is
	Expcr	SUB	PRED

For all practical purposes, *headache* is the SUBJECT of the clause. The English translation should not misguide us. English and Panjabi present the "same" (?) situation in different ways, neither of which is more "natural" or "logical".

3. Discourse-related categories

The order of words and phrases in a Panjabi clause is considerably more flexible than in English. But this does not mean that "you can put anything anywhere in a Panjabi clause". The general tendency in Panjabi is that of the **SOV** (SUBJECT OBJECT VERB) word order. But two other interacting tendencies also work: (i) The information **given** in the context tends to precede the **new** information and (ii) the pragmatically more **salient** information tends to precede the less salient. We call the latter process **fronting.** In (1) above, a human being is pragmatically more salient than headache and is **fronted**. So the PREDICATE COMPLEMENT(S) precedes the SUBJECT. **Intonation** (discussed in Chapter 4) and some words known as **particles** are also often involved. (See Chapter 16.)

5.6 More examples of the four canonical clauses

1. Canonical clause pattern 1

(2)	ਬੱਚਾ	ਹੱਸਿਆ
	baccā	**hassiā**
	child	laughed
	SUBJ	PRED

The PREDICATOR is an **intransitive verb** with the **noun** *the child* in the **structural** or **syntactic** role of the SUBJECT in the clause. **Semantically** (as regards meaning), the child is the **agent**. The reason for making this distinction has been explained in section **5.5** above. Later chapters will also make it clear why the **syntactic** and the **semantic** roles should be kept separate.

2. Canonical clause pattern 2

(3)	ਬੱਚਾ	ਬੀਮਾਰ	ਹੈ
	baccā	**bīmār**	**ha^{i}**
	The child	ill	is
	SUBJ	COMP(S)	PRED
	'The child is ill'		

The COMPLEMENT(S) or COMP(S) says something about the SUBJECT. Both the SUBJECT and the SUBJECT COMPLEMENT(S) are needed to **complete** the meaning of the clause whose PREDICATOR is ਹੈ **ha^{i}** *is*.

Another example is

(4)	ਇਹ ਬੱਚਾ	ਮੁੰਡਾ	ਹੈ
	ih baccā	**muṇḍā**	**ha^{i}**
	This child	boy	is
	SUBJ	COMP(S)	PRED
	'This child is a boy'		

3. Canonical clause pattern 3

(5)	ਬੱਚੇ ਨੇ	ਦੁੱਧ	ਪੀਤਾ
	bacce ne	**dudd^{h}**	**pītā**
	The child	milk	drank
	SUBJ	OBJ	PRED
	'This drank milk'		

ਪੀ **pī** is a transitive verb PREDICATOR with the **agent** SUBJECT ਬੱਚਾ **baccā** and **patient** OBJECT ਦੁੱਧ **dudd^{h}** as COMPLEMENTS.

4. Canonical clause pattern 4

(6)	ਠੰਢ ਨੇ	ਬੱਚਾ	ਬੀਮਾਰ	ਕੀਤਾ
	t^{h}aṇḍ^{h} ne	**baccā**	**bīmār**	**kītā**
	The cold	child	ill	did
	SUBJ	OBJ	COMP(O)	PRED
	'The cold made the child ill'			

ਬੀਮਾਰ **bīmār** completes the meaning of the clause by saying something about the OBJECT ਬੱਚਾ **baccā**. So it is OBJECT COMPLEMENT or

COMP(O). Later chapters explain why some words change their form and some COMPLEMENTS get a **postposition**. (7) below exemplifies the same clause pattern.

(7)	ਮੈਂ	ਉਹਨੂੰ	ਸਿਆਣਾ	ਸਮਝਦਾ	ਹਾਂ
	mãi	**uhnũ**	**siāṇā**	**samajʰdā**	**hã**
	I	him	wise	consider	
	SUBJ	OBJ	COMP(O)	PRED	
	'I consider him wise'				

5.7 Complements and adjuncts

The **verb phrase (VP)** (called PREDICATOR as a **functional** category) is the hub of the clause. SUBJECT, OBJECT, PREDICATE COMPLEMENT(S) and PREDICATE COMPLEMENT(O) are called COMPLEMENTS because they are obligatory components needed to *complete* the meaning of the **VP** or the PREDICATOR. But other components known as ADJUNCTS can be *adjoined* to provide additional meaning. For example, one could say

(8)	ਮੈਨੂੰ	ਸਵੇਰ	ਤੋਂ	ਸਿਰਪੀੜ	ਹੈ
	maiṅnũ	**saver**	**tõ**	**sirpīṛ**	**hai**
	me-to	morning	from	headache	is
	Expcr	ADJCT		SUB	PRED
	'I have had a headache since morning'				

The complements of the PREDICATOR are also known as its **syntactic valency** set. The predicator in Pattern 4 (in 7 above) given above has a **syntactic valency** set consisting of SUBJECT, OBJECT and PREDICATE COMPLEMENT(O). As already explained, the PREDICATE COMPLEMENT(S) is subject-related and PREDICATE COMPLEMENT(O) is object-related. The members of this **syntactic valency** set are said to be **licensed** by the PRDICATOR. **ਸਵੇਰ ਤੋਂ saver tõ** is not syntactically obligatory in (8). It is a syntactically optional ADJUNCT, though it does contribute to the meaning of the sentence. In the Indian linguistic tradition, **syntactic valency** was called *ākāṅkṣā* 'expectancy'. The verb *expects* some COMPLEMENTS in order to express its meaning completely.

It should be added here that each verb-form inside the PREDICATOR (if it is a verb sequence known as **serial verb**, see Chapter 13) has its own

semantic valency set as well as the **syntactic valency** set, which have to be taken into account in interpreting the meaning of the clause or sentence. It must be admitted, however, that semantic categories cannot be clearly defined and their number may run into dozens. Considerable stretching of metaphoric imagination is needed to regard ਠੰਢ **ṭʰaṇḍʰ** 'cold' in (6) as an **agent** or **actor**. At best it can be described as the **initiator** of the state.

5.8 Finite clause in Panjabi

In English, a **finite** clause is one that contains a finite verb marked for **tense**. As we shall see, not every clause in Panjabi has such a *tensed* **verb**. But there is no reason why we should follow English grammar. We define a **finite clause** in Panjabi as a clause which

(i) has the SUBJECT of the verb marked with the post-position ਨੇ **ne**

OR *if* (i) *is not the case*, then

(ii) the verb **agrees** in **person** *and* **number** or **gender** *and* **number** with the SUBJECT.

The use of ਨੇ **ne** or **agreement** to mark the SUBJECT depends on the **form** of the verb – whether the verb is in the **personal** form or the **adjectival** form. Panjabi verbs have **nominal** forms as well, known as **gerund** and **conjunctive participle**. The latter can either be identical to the verb **stem** or have ਕੇ **ke** added to it. The **unmarked** or **subjunctive** form of a Panjabi verb is **personal**. It agrees with the SUBJECT in **person** and **number**. The **adjectival** form **imperfect participle** agrees with the SUBJECT in **gender** and **number**. The **perfect participle** form sometimes does and sometimes does not agree with the SUBJECT, which is then marked with ਨੇ **ne**. Similarly, the **potential participle** either agrees with the SUBJECT or does not. In the latter case, the SUBJECT is marked with ਨੇ **ne**. It should be noted that ਨੇ **ne** is used with the SUBJECT only when the verb does not agree with it. A clause in which the verb does not agree with the SUBJECT is sometimes called an **ergative** clause. In such a clause the verb agrees either with the OBJECT or is in the **neuter** form (homophonous to the **masculine singular** form).

Sometimes ਨੇ **ne** is not added to the SUBJECT **NP** for historical reasons. But it "*could have*" been added. (See Chapter 12.) In some dialects, the use of ਨੇ **ne** in this position has disappeared. But there is evidence that it *was* there. These anomalies do not invalidate our generalisation given above. The logic of a *living* language does not have the *rigor mortis* of philosophical logic.

The Panjabi **copular-existential verb** ਹੈ **ha^i** is a class in itself. A number of Panjabi verbs function as **explicator auxiliaries**. All this is discussed in detail in later chapters. The structure of the **verb phrase** inside the PREDICATOR in a **finite clause** and in **non-finite clauses** is the most complicated (and interestingly challenging) part of Panjabi grammar and needs several chapters for a detailed discussion. These **serial verb constructions** are found in a number of languages genetically unrelated and geographically non-contiguous to Panjabi (Aikhenvald and Dixon 2006). This grammar book is not theoretical. But a brief discussion of how these constructions in Panjabi are similar to and different from the ones found in some other languages will be interesting.

5.9 Noun phrase and other phrases in Panjabi

We study the Panjabi **pronouns** under the **noun phrase**. They are best treated as a special small subset of **nouns**. Some older morphological forms of nouns and pronouns have survived in Panjabi. Most (but not all) nouns and adjectives are inflected for **gender** and **number** and have special forms when followed by a **postposition**. These forms are called **oblique** forms. Many adjectives are not inflected at all. They are called (quite colourfully!) **red adjectives**. The ones which are inflected are known as **black adjectives**. All these technicalities are explained with lots of examples in the following chapters.

Summing up and looking ahead

This is Panjabi grammar in an outline form. We are attempting to present the *system* of Panjabi grammar generating the structures found in the language, not a *list* of the structures, as some past grammarians did. This system is actually a confederation of systems which can be regarded as the United Systems of Panjabi Grammar (or USPG). The systems of Panjabi phonology presented in Chapters 3 and 4 are members of this federation, and some salient features of these systems will feature in the following chapters on Panjabi grammar.

Chapter 6

Noun and Noun Phrase

Preview of the chapter

This chapter deals with the morphology (forms assumed when used in sentences) of Panjabi nouns and pronouns.

6.1 The three-way characterisation of nouns in Panjabi

Noun is the largest class of words in Panjabi. We shall characterise each word class in three ways.

1. *Notionally* or *semantically*, nouns refer to entities (persons, places, things, substances and abstractions of various kinds).

2. *Formally*, a noun in Panjabi must have **gender** (**masculine** or **feminine**) and **number** (**singular** or **plural**). A noun followed by a **postposition** assumes a morphological form known as the **oblique form**. The shape of the **oblique form** depends on the **number**, **gender** and the phonological shape of the noun. Some nouns can have the **synthetic case forms** inherited from Apabhraṃśa and old Panjabi. All this is discussed below.

3. *Functionally*, a noun acts as the HEAD of a **noun phrase** (**NP**) which can function as the SUBJECT or OBJECT or COMPLEMENT or ADJUNCT in a clause.

6.1.1 Classification of nouns in Panjabi

Taking into account the semantic and formal characteristics, the Panjabi nouns belong to three classes.

1. Proper nouns. Important examples of proper nouns are
(i) personal names (e.g. ਮੋਹਨ **mohan**, ਰਣਜੀਤ **raṇjīt** , ਸਿੰਘ **sing^h**)

(ii) place names (e.g. ਲੰਡਨ **laṇḍan**, ਅਫ਼੍ਰੀਕਾ **afrīkā**, ਮੁੰਬਈ **mumbaī**)

(iii) organisation names (e.g. ਕਾਂਗ੍ਰੇਸ **kā̃gres**, ਬਾਰਕਲੇਜ਼ ਬੈਂਕ **bārklez bã'nk**, ਸੋਸ਼ਲਿਸਟ ਪਾਰਟੀ **soślist pārṭī**)

(iv) time names (e.g. ਸੋਮਵਾਰ **somvār** 'Monday', ਦਸੰਬਰ **dasambar** 'December', ਕ੍ਰਿਸਮਸ **krismas** 'Christmas'

2. Common nouns. The names of objects, places and entities which are not proper nouns.

Examples of common nouns are

ਬੰਦਾ **bandā** 'man', ਸ਼ਹਿਰ **śahir** 'city', ਸੰਸਥਾ **sansat^{h}ā** 'organisation', ਦਿਨ **din** 'day'

3. Mass and collective nouns. Examples of such nouns are

ਇੱਜੜ **ijjaṛ** 'flock', ਕਣਕ **kaṇak** 'wheat', ਮਖੀਲ/ਮਖਿਆਲ਼ **mak^{h}īl/mak^{h}iāḷ** 'swarm of bees'

4. Abstract nouns. Examples of such nouns are

ਗੁੱਸਾ **gussā** 'anger', ਖ਼ੁਸ਼ੀ **xuśī** 'happiness', ਝੂਠ **j^{h}ūṭ^h** 'lie', ਸੱਚ **sacc** 'truth', ਕੁੜੱਤਣ **kuṛattaṇ** 'bitterness', ਮਿਠਾਸ **miṭ^{h}ās** 'sweetness'

6.2 Number and gender in Panjabi

6.2.1 Number and gender in common nouns

Each Panjabi **noun** has grammatical **number** (**singular** or **plural**) and gender (**masculine** or **feminine**). How Panjabi *notionally* views a noun as singular or plural may differ from how English does. For example, ਕੈਂਚੀ **kã'cī** 'scissors' and ਪਜਾਮਾ **pajāmā** 'pyjamas' are singular in Panjabi and plural in English. On the other hand, **masculine** foodgrains like

ਮਾਂਹ **mā̃h** 'black lentils', ਚੌਲ **ca^u^ḷ** 'rice' and ਛੋਲੇ **c^h^ole** 'chickpeas' are grammatically **plural** in Panjabi.

ਚਰਨ **caran** 'holy feet' and ਪ੍ਰਾਣ **prāṇ** 'vital breath', 'breath of life' occur in the **masculine plural** form only. ਪ੍ਰਾਣ **prāṇ** is historically related to the Greek word *pnein* 'to breathe'.

Gender is grammatical in Panjabi. Male animate beings are mostly **masculine** and female animate beings are mostly **feminine**. But the sex of an animate being cannot always be easily known or is unimportant. In such cases, gender is arbitrarily assigned. ਕਾਂ **kā̃** 'crow', ਉੱਲੂ **ullū** 'owl', ਮੱਛਰ **macc^h^ar** 'mosquito' and ਬਿੱਛੂ **bicc^h^ū** 'scorpion' are **masculine**, and ਘੁੱਗੀ **g^h^uggī** 'dove', ਗਿਰਝ **girj^h^** 'vulture', ਮੱਖੀ **makk^h^ī** 'fly' and ਮੱਕੜੀ **makkaṛī** 'spider' are feminine. This arbitrariness applies to inanimate objects, parts of the body, food items and places as well. ਬੂਹਾ **būhā** 'door' is masculine, but ਬਾਰੀ **bārī** 'window' is feminine; ਸਿਰ **sir** 'head' is masculine and ਬਾਂਹ **bā̃h** 'arm' is feminine; ਦੁੱਧ **dudd^h^** 'milk' is masculine and ਚਾਹ **cāh** 'tea' is feminine; ਲੰਡਨ **laṇḍan** 'London' is masculine and ਦਿੱਲੀ **dillī** 'Delhi' is feminine... and the list can be a long one. Perhaps Freudian analysis can shed some light on why ਦਾਹੜੀ **dāhṛī** 'beard' and ਮੁੱਛ **mucc^h^** 'moustache', symbols of masculinity since time immemorial, are feminine in Panjabi. ਸਵਾਰੀ **savārī** 'passenger', whether male or female, is feminine, but ਮੁਸਾਫ਼ਿਰ **musāfir** 'traveller' of either sex is masculine.

Most nouns ending in **-ā** are **masculine** and those ending in in **-ī** are **feminine**. ਸਵਾਰੀ **savārī** 'passenger' is feminine probably because of its ending. But this is not a strict rule. ਨਾਈ **nāī** 'barber' and ਜੁਆਈ **juāī** 'son-in-law' are masculine and ਵਾਰਤਾ **vārtā** 'long story' and ਗੰਗਾ **gangā** (the river with this name, older name Ganges) are feminine. Interestingly, ਮਾਲਾ **mālā** 'garland' is feminine but ਮਾਲੀ **mālī** 'male gardener' is masculine. Comparative size sometimes determines gender, as in masculine ਪੀਪਾ **pīpā** 'large can' and feminine ਪੀਪੀ **pīpī** 'small can', **masculine** ਥੈਲਾ **t^h^a^i^ lā** 'large bag' and feminine ਥੈਲੀ **t^h^a^i^lī** 'small bag' and **masculine** ਪਹਾੜ **pahāṛ** 'mountain' and feminine ਪਹਾੜੀ **pahāṛī** 'hill'.

6.2.2 Number and gender in mass and collective nouns

The **number** and **gender** of a **mass noun** or **collective noun** does not depend upon that of constituent entities.

ਮਖੀਲ/ਮਖਿਆਲ਼ **mak^h^īl/mak^h^iāḷ** 'swarm of bees' is masculine, although (ਸ਼ਹਿਦ ਦੀ) ਮੱਖੀ **(śahid dī) makk^h^ī** 'bee' is feminine. ਮੰਢੀਰ 'group of boys' is feminine, although ਮੁੰਡਾ **muṇḍā** 'boy' is masculine. ਦਰਖ਼ਤ **daraxt** 'tree' and ਪੇੜ **peṛ** 'tree' are masculine but ਝਿੜੀ **j^{h}iṛi** 'grove' is feminine. ਵੱਗ **vagg** and ਚੌਣਾ **ca^{u}ṇā** 'herd of cattle', which may contain both male and female animals, are masculine.

Foodgrains are more interesting. **Masculine** foodgrains are always **plural** and **feminine** foodgrains are always **singular**. ਮਾਂਹ **mā̃h** 'black lentils', ਚੌਲ਼ **ca^{u}ḷ** 'rice' and ਛੋਲੇ **c^{h}ole** 'chickpeas' are grammatically **masculine plural**. But ਮੂੰਗੀ **mū̃gī** 'green lentils', ਕਣਕ **kaṇak** 'wheat' and ਰਾਈ **rāī** 'mustard' are grammatically **feminine singular**. To refer to a single grain, for example, we say ਚੌਲ਼ਾਂ ਦਾ ਦਾਣਾ **ca^{u}ḷā̃ dā dāṇā** with ਚੌਲ਼ਾਂ **ca^{u}ḷā̃** in the plural form. But a single grain of wheat is ਕਣਕ ਦਾ ਦਾਣਾ **kaṇak dā dāṇā** with ਕਣਕ **kaṇak** in the singular form.

Two common nouns ਬੰਦਾ **bandā** 'man, person' and ਰੁਪਈਆ **rupaīā** 'rupee' can be used as a collective noun or mass noun, as in

ਸੌ ਬੰਦਾ **sa^{u} bandā** '(a collection of) one hundred men'

ਸੌ ਰੁਪਈਆ **sa^{u} rupaīā** '(a sum of) one hundred rupees'

This starts with one hundred and rises in increments of fifty. To emphasise the *size* of a gathering, rather than the number of the people, you can say (ਇੱਕ) ਹਜ਼ਾਰ ਬੰਦਾ **(ikk) hazār bandā** 'one thousand men' or (ਇੱਕ) ਲੱਖ ਬੰਦਾ **(ikk) lakk^{h} bandā** 'a hundred thousand men', but not, for example, *ਇਕ ਸੌ ਵੀਹ ਬੰਦਾ ***ik sa^{u} vīh bandā** 'one hundred and twenty men'. The same applies to ਰੁਪਈਆ **rupaīā**. But ਇੱਕ ਸੌ ਇੱਕ ਰੁਪਈਆ **ikk sa^{u} ikk rupaīā** or ਇਕੋਤਰ ਸੌ ਰੁਪਈਆ **ikotar sa^{u} rupaīā** 'one hundred and one rupees' can be used when the exact amount is paid formally during a marriage/engagement ceremony. To emphasise the *number*, you can say ਹਜ਼ਾਰ ਬੰਦੇ **hazār bande** 'one thousand men' and ਸੌ ਰੁਪਈਏ **sa^{u} rupaīe**, with the plural forms **bande** ਬੰਦੇ and ਰੁਪਈਏ **rupaīe**. (See **6.3** below for these forms.)

There are no helpful **articles** in Panjabi like the ones in some European languages. In German, for example, you can learn a new noun word along with the **masculine**, **feminine** or **neuter article**, such as *der*, *Wein die*, *Schule das Rathaus*. But in Panjabi, you have to learn whether the noun is masculine or feminine and then "do as the Panjabis do".

6.3 Noun morphology in Panjabi

It is essential to know the gender and number of nouns as this affects the morphological forms they assume and the forms of the pronouns and adjectives associated with them and the forms of verbs which agree with them in number and gender. The morphological forms a Panjabi **noun** assumes as a result of its syntactic role depend on its **(i) number**, **(ii) gender** and **(iii) ending**. These forms include **direct**, **oblique** and **vocative** forms. A noun assumes an **oblique** form when a **postposition** follows it. Postpositions are dealt with in detail in Chapter 8. Here we use a very common postposition ਨੂੰ **nū̃** 'to'. Very often the **direct** and the **oblique** forms are identical. Here we make use of the "*could have*" principle mentioned in Chapter 5. The direct and the oblique forms "*could have*" been different under different conditions. The vocative form (used for addressing) may also be different in each case. In the following tables, some vocative forms may sound rather fanciful. But we are giving the *possible* grammatical forms. The reason why some boxes are shaded is explained later.

1a. **Masculine nouns** ending in **-ā** (ਮੁੰਡਾ **'muṇḍā** 'boy')

	Direct form	Oblique form	Vocative form
Singular	ਮੁੰਡਾ **muṇḍā**	ਮੁੰਡੇ (ਨੂੰ) **muṇḍe (nū̃)**	ਮੁੰਡਿਆ! **muṇḍiā!**
Plural	ਮੁੰਡੇ **muṇḍe**	ਮੁੰਡਿਆਂ (ਨੂੰ) **muṇḍiā̃ (nū̃)**	ਮੁੰਡਿਓ! **muṇḍio!**

These are the forms of the nouns having an *unstressed* final syllable. If the final syllable is stressed, the forms are:

1b. **Masculine nouns** ending in **-ā** (ਭਰਾ **bʰa'rā** 'brother')

	Direct form	Oblique form	Vocative form
Singular	ਭਰਾ **bʰarā**	ਭਰਾ (ਨੂੰ) **bʰarā (nū̃)**	ਭਰਾਵਾ! **bʰarāvā!**
Plural	ਭਰਾ **bʰarā**	ਭਰਾਵਾਂ (ਨੂੰ) **bʰarāvā̃ (nū̃)**	ਭਰਾਵੋ! **bʰarāvo!**

ਪਿਤਾ **pitā** 'father', ਅੱਬਾ **abbā** 'father', ਅੱਲਾ **allā** 'God', ਖ਼ੁਦਾ **xudā** 'God', ਪਰਮਾਤਮਾ **parmātmā** 'God' and ਮਹਾਤਮਾ **mahātmā** 'great soul' have an unstressed final syllable, but they are inflected like those of ਭਰਾ **bʰarā** 'brother', which is stressed on the second syllable. Some Pakistani Panjabi speakers also use the oblique form ਅੱਬੇ **abbe**.

2. Masculine nouns ending in **-ī** (**ਨਾਈ nāī** 'barber')

	Direct form	Oblique form	Vocative form
Singular	ਨਾਈ nāī	ਨਾਈ (ਨੂੰ) nāī (nū̃)	ਨਾਈਆ! nāīā!
Plural	ਨਾਈ nāī	ਨਾਈਆਂ (ਨੂੰ) nāīā̃ (nū̃)	ਨਾਈਓ! nāīo!

3. Masculine nouns ending in **-ū** (**ਬਾਬੂ bābū** 'office worker')

	Direct form	Oblique form	Vocative form
Singular	ਬਾਬੂ bābū	ਬਾਬੂ (ਨੂੰ) bābū (nū̃)	ਬਾਬੂ! bābū! ਬਾਬੂਆ! bābūā!
Plural	ਬਾਬੂ bābū	ਬਾਬੂਆਂ (ਨੂੰ) bābūā̃ (nū̃)	ਬਾਬੂਓ! bābūo!

The case endings added to the masculine nouns ending in -**e** and **-o** are the same as for the ones ending in **-ū**. Examples are the words **ਦਿਓ dio** 'giant', 'ogre'(pronounced as **ਦੇ de** in some dialects) and **ਪਿਓ pio** 'father' (pronounced as **ਪੇ pe** in some dialects).

4. Masculine nouns ending in a consonant (**ਮਰਦ mard** 'man')

	Direct form	Oblique form	Vocative form
Singular	ਮਰਦ mard	ਮਰਦ (ਨੂੰ) mard (nū̃)	ਮਰਦਾ! mardā!
Plural	ਮਰਦ mard	ਮਰਦਾਂ (ਨੂੰ) mardā̃ (nū̃)	ਮਰਦੋ! mardo!

5a. Feminine nouns ending in **-ā** (**ਹਵਾ havā** 'air/wind')

	Direct form	Oblique form	Vocative form
Singular	ਹਵਾ havā	ਹਵਾ (ਨੂੰ) havā (nū̃)	ਹਵਾ! havā! ਹਵਾਏ! havāe!
Plural	ਹਵਾਵਾਂ havāvā̃	ਹਵਾਵਾਂ (ਨੂੰ) havāvā̃ (nū̃)	ਹਵਾਓ! havāo!

5b.   **Feminine nouns** ending in nasalised **-ā̃** (ਗਾਂ **gā̃** 'cow')

	Direct form	Oblique form	Vocative form
Singular	ਗਾਂ **gā̃**	ਗਾਂ (ਨੂੰ) **gā̃ (nū̃)**	ਗਾਏਂ **gā̃ẽ!**
Plural	ਗਾਂਵਾਂ **gā̃vā̃** ਗਾਂਈਆਂ **gā̃īā̃**	ਗਾਂਵਾਂ (ਨੂੰ) **gā̃vā̃ (nū̃)** ਗਾਂਈਆਂ (ਨੂੰ) **gā̃īā̃ (nū̃)**	ਗਾਂਈਓ **gā̃io!**

6.   **Feminine nouns** ending in **-ī** (ਭਾਬੀ **bʰābī** 'brother's wife')

	Direct form	Oblique form	Vocative form
Singular	ਭਾਬੀ **bʰābī**	ਭਾਬੀ (ਨੂੰ) **bʰābī (nū̃)**	ਭਾਬੀ! **bʰābī!** ਭਾਬੀਏ! **bʰābīe!**
Plural	ਭਾਬੀਆਂ **bʰābīā̃**	ਭਾਬੀਆਂ (ਨੂੰ) **bʰābīā̃ (nū̃)**	ਭਾਬੀਓ! **bʰābīo!**

7.   **Feminine nouns** ending in **-ū** (ਬਹੂ **bahū** 'daughter-in-law')

	Direct form	Oblique form	Vocative form
Singular	ਬਹੂ **bahū**	ਬਹੂ (ਨੂੰ) **bahū (nū̃)**	ਬਹੂ! **bahū!**
Plural	ਬਹੂਆਂ **bahūā̃**	ਬਹੂਆਂ (ਨੂੰ) **bahūā̃ (nū̃)**	ਬਹੂਓ! **bahūo!**

8.   **Feminine nouns** ending in **-e** (ਬੇਬੇ **bebe** 'mother', 'older sister')

	Direct form	Oblique form	Vocative form
Singular	ਬੇਬੇ **bebe**	ਬੇਬੇ (ਨੂੰ) **bebe (nū̃)**	ਬੇਬੇ! **bebe!**
Plural	Does not exist	Does not exist	Does not exist

9.   **Feminine nouns** ending in **-o** (ਲੋ **lo** 'light')

	Direct form	Oblique form	Vocative form
Singular	ਲੋ **lo**	ਲੋ (ਨੂੰ) **lo (nū̃)**	ਲੋਏ! **loe!**
Plural	ਲੋਆਂ **loā̃**	ਲੋਆਂ (ਨੂੰ) **loā̃ (nū̃)**	Does not exist

10. Feminine nouns ending in a consonant (ਪੰਜਾਬਣ **panjābaṇ** 'Panjabi woman')

	Direct form	Oblique form	Vocative form
Singular	ਪੰਜਾਬਣ **panjābaṇ**	ਪੰਜਾਬਣ (ਨੂੰ) **panjābaṇ (nū̃)**	ਪੰਜਾਬਣੇ! **panjābaṇe!**
Plural	ਪੰਜਾਬਣਾਂ **panjābaṇā̃**	ਪੰਜਾਬਣਾਂ (ਨੂੰ) **panjābaṇā̃ (nū̃)**	ਪੰਜਾਬਣੋ! **panjābaṇo!**

It is notable that the **oblique** form differs from the corresponding **direct** form only in **masculine nouns**. These forms are shaded in the tables. But there is a definite pattern even here. The only irregularity is in **(1a)** when the masculine noun ends in **-ā** and the final syllable is unstressed.

6.4 Synthetic case forms in Panjabi

Put very simply in relation to Panjabi, the relation of an **NP** to the other constituents in a clause, particularly the **VP**, such as the agent, patient, instrument, location etc. is known as a **case** relation. The linguistic form expressive of this relation involving the noun is known as its **case form.** If the case form is audibly and visibly (in Gurmukhi) a single word, it is known as **synthetic** case form. In Panjabi's ancestor language Sanskrit, a noun had three numbers **singular**, **dual** and **plural** and seven synthetic case forms for each number, thus totalling twenty-one.

Without going into details, examples of some of the Sanskrit case forms of the word *nagar* 'city' are given below. These examples are chosen because descendants of these synthetic case forms are found in Panjabi. The basic **direct form**, which is supposed to go with these morphological changes is also known as the **nominative form** in relation to these forms.

Locative singular	Sanskrit	*nagare* 'in the town'
	Panjabi	ਨਗਰ ਵਿਚ **nagar vich**
Locative plural	Sanskrit	*nagareṣu* 'in the towns'
	Panjabi	ਨਗਰਾਂ ਵਿਚ **nagarā̃ vich**

Instrumental dual	Sanskrit	*nagarābhyām* 'with (two) towns'
	Panjabi	(ਦੋ) ਨਗਰਾਂ ਨਾਲ਼ **(do) nagarā̃ nāḷ**
Ablative singular	Sanskrit	*nagarāt* 'from the town'
	Panjabi	ਨਗਰ ਤੋਂ **nagar tō̃**

As we can see, English and Panjabi have to combine two or more words to express the same meaning. English adds a **preposition** *before* a **noun** or **NP**, and Punjabi adds a **postposition** *after* a noun or NP. The resulting form of the phrase is known as an **analytic case form**. While the **case forms** of the English **nouns** are completely analytic now, and most case relations are also expressed analytically in Panjabi too, some older **synthetic case forms** from the Apabhraṃśa stage have survived in Panjabi, making Panjabi the most conservative among the modern Indic languages. *The use of these forms is more widespread and theoretically more significant than the past Panjabi grammarians have recognised so far.* As we shall see in Chapter 8, synthetic case forms are the basis of most Panjabi postpositions. Below, we take up these forms in an ascending order – from the less widespread to the more widespread.

6.4.1 Instrumental dual "synthetic" case forms

Some body parts such as eyes, ears, hands and feet occur in pairs. When both members of the pair are involved in some activity, the noun is marked with the **instrumental dual case suffix -ਈਂ -ī̃**.

ਅੱਖੀਂ ਦੇਖਿਆ akkʰī̃ dekʰiā
'seen by (both) the eyes'

ਕੰਨੀਂ ਸੁਣਿਆ kannī̃ suṇiā
'heard by (both) the ears'

ਹੱਥੀਂ ਕੀਤਾ ਕੰਮ hattʰī̃ kītā kamm
'work done with (both) the hands'

ਪੈਰੀਂ ਚਲ ਕੇ ਜਾਣਾ pa^{i}rī̃ cal ke jāṇā
'going by walking on (both) the feet'
ਨੰਗੇ ਪੈਰੀਂ nange pa^{i}rī̃
'with (both) bare feet = barefoot'

6.4.2 *Locative plural "synthetic" case forms*

The suffix **-ਈਂ -ī̃** is added to the noun.

ਘਰੀਂ g^{h}arī̃
'in homes'

ਜੜ੍ਹੀਂ ਤੇਲ ਦੇਣਾ jarhī̃ tel deṇā
'put oil into the roots = do great harm'

ਵੇਲਾਂ ਰੁੱਖੀਂ ਚੜ੍ਹੀਆਂ velā̃ rukk^{h}ī̃ caṛhīā̃
'the creepers climbed onto the trees'

ਹੱਡੀਂ ਰਚਿਆ ਇਸ਼ਕ haḍḍī̃ raciā iśk
'love steeped into the bones = deep love'

ਕੰਮੀਂ ਰੁੱਝੀਆਂ ਮਾਂਵਾਂ kammī̃ rujj^{h}īā̃ mā̃vā̃
'mothers busy in activities'

ਅੱਖੀਂ ਘੱਟਾ ਪਾਉਣਾ akk^{h}ī̃ g^{h}aṭṭā pāuṇā
'throw dust into the eyes = deceive'

The last of these examples involves both the eyes. But they are involved as *location*, not as instrument. So it is a **locative plural**, and not an **instrumental dual**, expression in spite of the common -**ਈਂ -ī̃** ending used in both.

6.4.3 *Ablative singular "synthetic" case forms*

The suffix -**ਓਂ -õ** is added to the noun, and very often, to the **nominal** (**gerund**) form of a verb with the meaning 'being afraid', 'staying away', 'hesitating' etc. (metaphorically suggesting an act of separation). Comparison of two entities is also expressed with this form. How this form underlies some postpositions will be discussed in Chapter 8.

ਘਰੋਂ ਜਾਣਾ g^{h}arõ jāṇā
'going from home'

ਕੱਖੋਂ ਹੌਲ਼ਾ **kakkʰõ haᵘḷā**
'lighter than a straw'

ਕੌਡੀਓਂ ਖੋਟਾ **kaᵘḍīõ kʰoṭā**
'less valuable (worse) than a cowrie shell'

ਜਾਣੋਂ ਝਿਜਕਣਾ **jāṇo jʰijkaṇā**
'hesitating from going'

ਜੜ੍ਹੋਂ ਪੁੱਟਣਾ **jaṛhõ puṭṭṇā**
'put out from the roots = uproot'

ਮਰਨੋਂ ਡਰਨਾ **marnõ ḍarnā**
'being afraid of dying'

There is a famous Panjabi folk song

ਮਰਨੋਂ ਨਾ ਡਰਦੇ ਜਿਹੜੇ ਪ੍ਰੇਮ ਦੀ ਨਦੀ ਦੇ ਵਿਚ ਤਰਦੇ
marnõ na ḍarde jihṛe prem dī nadī de vic tarde
'(They) are not afraid of dying – (they) who swim in the river of love'
Lit. 'afraid *from* dying'

6.4.4 Locative singular "synthetic" case forms

The suffix parts **-ਏ -e** is added to the noun.

ਕਿਧਰੇ **kidʰre**
'somewhere'

ਘਰੇ **gʰare**
'at home, in the house'

ਭੁੰਜੇ **bʰunje**
'on the ground'

ਬਾਬਾ ਬਕਾਲ਼ੇ **bābā bakāḷe**
'the spiritual master (is) in Bakala'

ਛਾਂਵੇਂ ਬਹਿਣਾ **cʰā̃vẽ bahiṇā**
'sit in the shade'

ਸਿੱਧੇ ਰਾਹੇ ਪੈਣਾ **siddʰe rāhe pa'ṇā**
'go on the right path'

Most Panjabi **postpositions** are, or have developed from, this "synthetic" case form, as we shall see in Chapter 8. For several centuries, Panjabi has been moving from being a "synthetic" language to an "analytic" one. It seems quite ironic that these postpositions which have helped the process a great deal are themselves "synthetic" forms.

6.5 Pronouns in Panjabi

Panjabi **pronouns** are best treated as a special set of **nouns** rather than a separate class of words. *Notionally* and *formally*, they differ from the nouns in some ways, but it makes considerable sense to group them together *functionally* because they typically form **noun phrases**.

Notionally, a pronoun is said to "stand for" a noun or **NP** or any more specific expression regarded as an entity. So **pronouns** are partly defined by this criterion. Most Panjabi pronouns look backwards (or **anaphorically**) and refer to the elements already known. But sometimes they also look forward (**cataphorically**) to the elements to be mentioned later.

Formally, the Panjabi pronouns are a mixed bag because of their historical origin. The **first person** and the **second person pronouns** come from Sanskrit, in which pronouns had **singular**, **dual** and **plural** forms but were not marked for **gender**. In Panjabi, the **first** and the **second person pronouns** have **singular** and **plural** forms only. The Sanskrit **third person pronouns**, which were marked for **masculine, feminine** and **neuter genders**, did not historically reach Panjabi, and **demonstratives**, marked neither for **number** nor **gender** but for **distance**, have replaced them. Each pronoun in Sanskrit has numerous **case forms**. A **pronoun** in Panjabi has only a **direct** and the **oblique** form when followed by a postposition, which sometimes becomes fused with the **pronoun** but is still recognisable. There are, of course, no vocative forms of **pronouns**.

Functionally, a pronoun acts as **NP** in a clause, sometimes in a slightly different manner from that of a noun, as we shall see later. In this chapter, we deal with the forms only. The postposition ਨੂੰ **nū̃** means 'to' and ਤੋਂ **tõ** means 'from'. ਤੋਂ **tõ** is pronounced and written as ਥੋਂ **tʰõ** when it is added to some pronouns.

6.5.1 Personal pronouns

	Direct form	Oblique form with ਨੂੰ nū̃	Oblique form with ਤੋਂ tõ
First person			
Singular	ਮੈਂ maĩ	ਮੈਨੂੰ maᶦnū̃	ਮੈਥੋਂ maᶦtʰõ
Plural	ਅਸੀਂ asī̃	ਸਾਨੂੰ sānū̃	ਸਾਥੋਂ sātʰõ
		ਅਸਾਂ ਨੂੰ asā̃ nū̃	ਅਸਾਂ ਤੋਂ asā̃ tõ
Second person			
Singular	ਤੂੰ tū̃	ਤੈਨੂੰ taᶦnū̃	ਤੈਥੋਂ taᶦtʰõ
Plural	ਤੁਸੀਂ tusī̃	ਤੁਹਾਨੂੰ tuhānū̃	ਤੁਹਾਥੋਂ tuhātʰõ
		ਤੁਸਾਂ ਨੂੰ tusā̃ nū̃	ਤੁਸਾਂ ਤੋਂ tusā̃ tõ

ਆਪਾਂ **āpā̃** is often used colloquially in place of ਅਸੀਂ **asī̃**, generally in the sense of 'inclusive we' to include the listener. **Singular** ਤੂੰ **tū̃** is used when the relations of the speaker with the addressee are close and intimate or the speaker regards the addresses as socially inferior. The **plural** ਤੁਸੀਂ **tusī̃** is used to show respect even to one addressee. Adjectives and verbs are accordingly marked as **plural** as well. Additionally, to show respect to a woman, **masculine plural** forms are used. Panjabi pronouns are not marked for gender, but many adjectives and verb forms are.

ਤੈਂ **tāᶦ** is used in place of ਤੂੰ **tū̃** in the **ergative** constructions (see Chapter 12) in some dialects and by some speakers of the older generation. But ਤੂੰ **tū̃** is now increasingly replacing ਤੈਂ **tāᶦ**.

The oblique forms ਅਸਾਂ **asā̃** and ਤੁਸਾਂ **tusā̃** are used in some Western dialects only. They are not used in formal written Panjabi. In the past, they were used before the agentive postposition ਨੇ **ne** as well. (See the table above.) Though most of these dialects have stopped using ਨੇ **ne**, the oblique form is still used in those positions, indicating that ਨੇ **ne** was once used in that position. When ਨੇ **ne** is dropped in this way from a "third person singular pronoun" (see below), the forms ਇਸ and ਉਸ, and not ਇਹ and ਉਹ are used. for example, either ਉਹਨੇ ਜਾਣਾ ਹੈ **uhne jāṇā haᶦ** or ਉਸ ਨੇ ਜਾਣਾ ਹੈ **usne jāṇā haᶦ** can be said, but those who drop ਨੇ **ne** always say ਉਸ ਜਾਣਾ ਹੈ , and not *ਉਹ ਜਾਣਾ ਹੈ.

ਨੇ **ne** is not used with ਅਸੀਂ **asī̃** and ਤੁਸੀਂ **tusī̃**. The speakers who use ਨੇ **ne** with the first and second person plural pronouns say ਅਸਾਂ ਨੇ **asā̃ ne** and ਤੁਸਾਂ ਨੇ **tusā̃ ne**. If they drop ਨੇ **ne**, they still use the forms ਅਸਾਂ **asā̃** and ਤੁਸਾਂ

tusā̃. We need not go into the dialectal history of the language to explain why this happens. The use of the agentive postposition ਨੇ **ne** is explained in Chapter 12.

6.5.2 Demonstratives ("*third person pronouns*")

	Direct form	**Oblique form with ਨੂੰ nū̃**	**Oblique form with ਤੋਂ tõ**
Proximal			
Singular	ਇਹ **ih**	ਇਹਨੂੰ **ihnū̃** ਇਸ ਨੂੰ **is nū̃**	ਇਹਤੋਂ **ihtõ** ਇਸ ਤੋਂ **is tõ**
Plural	ਇਹ **ih**	ਇਹਨਾਂ ਨੂੰ **ihnā̃ nū̃**	ਇਹਨਾਂ ਤੋਂ **ihnā̃ tõ**
Distal			
Singular	ਉਹ **uh**	ਉਹਨੂੰ **uhnū̃** ਉਸ ਨੂੰ **us nū̃**	ਉਹਤੋਂ **uhtõ** ਉਸ ਤੋਂ **us tõ**
Plural	ਉਹ **uh**	ਉਹਨਾਂ ਨੂੰ **uhnā̃ nū̃**	ਉਹਨਾਂ ਤੋਂ **uhnā̃ tõ**

ਮੈਥੋਂ **ma^{l}t^{h}õ**, ਸਾਥੋਂ **sāt^{h}õ**, ਤੈਥੋਂ **ta^{l}t^{h}õ** and ਤੁਹਾਥੋਂ **tuhāt^{h}õ** are used in the so-called 'standard dialect' of Punjabi. Many speakers of other dialects use **-tõ** in these forms. But the spelling in the Gurmukhi script, changes in the pronunciation of the constituents and the pronunciation of each of these forms as *one* phonological word are indicative of something more significant – that the constituents are now *glued* together. This process is known as **agglutination**. We shall discuss this in detail in Chapter 11. Some writers use the spellings ਇਨ੍ਹਾਂ and ਉਨ੍ਹਾਂ in place of ਇਹਨਾਂ and ਉਹਨਾਂ. Either way of spelling these forms represents the tonal pronunciation of these forms correctly. (See Chapter 4 on Panjabi tones.)

6.5.3 Possessive adjectives

Since the Panjabi **possessive adjectives** (equivalents of the English *my*, *our*, *your*, *his*, *her*, *its* and *their*) are inflectionally derived from pronouns, they are best mentioned in this chapter. They are all **black adjectives** dealt with in the next chapter.

Pronoun	Direct Form	Possessive Adjective
First Person	ਮੈਂ **mãⁱ** ਅਸੀਂ **asī̃**	ਮੇਰਾ **merā** ਸਾਡਾ **sāḍā**
Second Person	ਤੂੰ **tū̃** ਤੁਸੀਂ **tusī̃**	ਤੇਰਾ **terā** ਤੁਹਾਡਾ **tuhāḍā**
Third Person (Demonstrative)	ਇਹ **ih** (singular) ਇਹ **ih** (plural) ਉਹ **uh** (singular) ਉਹ **uh** (plural)	ਇਹਦਾ **ihdā** ਇਹਨਾਂ ਦਾ **ihnā̃ dā** ਉਹਦਾ **uhdā** ਉਹਨਾਂ ਦਾ **uhnā̃ dā**

6.5.4 Reflexive pronoun

The Panjabi **reflexive pronoun ਆਪ āp** occurs in different forms which have different uses.

1. **For emphasis**

   ਮੈਂ ਇਹ ਕੰਮ ਆਪ ਕੀਤਾ
   mãⁱ ih kamm *āp* kītā
   'I myself did this work'

Here ਖ਼ੁਦ **xud** (borrowed from Persian) can also be used in place of ਆਪ **āp** for emphasis.

2. **In place of ਤੁਸੀਂ tusī̃ for showing extra respect**

   ਆਪ ਇੱਥੇ ਕਦ ਆਏ?
   ***āp* ittʰe kad āe?**
   'When did you come here?'

Often ਜੀ **jī**, the marker of politeness, is added to ਆਪ **āp** to make ਆਪ ਜੀ **āp jī**.

   ਆਪ ਜੀ ਨੂੰ ਬੇਨਤੀ ਹੈ ਕਿ . . .
   ***āp jī* nū̃ bentī haⁱ ki...**
   'It is a request to you that...'

3. **To refer to a third person respectfully**

   ਆਪਦਾ (or *ਆਪ ਜੀ ਦਾ*) ਜਨਮ ਦਿੱਲੀ ਵਿਚ ਹੋਇਆ
   āpdā (or ***āp jī* dā**) **janam dillī vic hoiā**
   'He was born in Delhi'

Adding ਜੀ **jī** to ਆਪ **āp** makes it extra-respectful (so to say).

4. Possessive adjective ਆਪਣਾ āpṇā.

ਆਪਣਾ **āpṇā** is used in place of an ordinary possessive adjective when its antecedent is the SUBJECT of the clause.

> *ਤੁਸੀਂ ਆਪਣਾ ਕੰਮ ਕਰੋ, ਤੇ ਮੈਂ ਆਪਣਾ ਕੰਮ ਕਰਾਂਗਾ*
> **tusī̃ *āpṇā* kamm karo, te mãi *āpṇā* kamm karā̃gā**
> 'You should do *your* work, and I will do *my* work'

The actual grammatical rule is slightly more complicated. But this will do here. Some Panjabi speakers of the younger generation have started using the ordinary possessive adjectives instead of ਆਪਣਾ **āpṇā** in such cases. ਆਪੋ ਆਪਣਾ **āpo āpṇā** is used in the sense of of 'each individual's own' as ਖ਼ਿਆਲ ਆਪੋ ਆਪਣਾ **xiāl āpo āpṇā** 'each individual's own opinion' or

> *ਆਪੋ ਆਪਣਾ ਕੰਮ ਕਰੋ*
> ***āpo āpṇā* kamm karo**
> 'Do your own individual work'

ਆਪੋ ਆਪਣਾ **āpo āpṇā** is a more colloquial version of ਆਪਣਾ ਆਪਣਾ **āpṇā āpṇā**, but is used in writing as well. We will deal with deal with the repetition of words in Appendix 2.

5. ਆਪਣੇ ਆਪ **āpṇe āp**, ਆਪੇ **āpe** and ਆਪੇ ਈ **āpe ī**

This adverb means 'automatically' or 'by oneself/oneselves'.

> *ਪੱਥਰ ਆਪਣੇ ਆਪ ਰੁੜ੍ਹ ਪਿਆ*
> **pattʰar *āpṇe āp* ruṛh piā**
> 'The stone started rolling automatically'

> *ਅਸੀਂ ਆਪਣੇ ਆਪ ਆ ਗਏ*
> **asī̃ *āpṇe āp* gae**
> 'We came by ourselves (uninvited or without anybody's help)'

ਆਪੇ **āpe** is often used in place of ਆਪਣੇ ਆਪ **āpṇe āp**. ਆਪੇ **āpe** started as a combination of ਆਪ **āp** and the emphatic particle ਹੀ **hī** (dealt with later in Chapters 7 and 16). Some speakers add ਹੀ **hī** (pronounced as ਈ **ī**) once again to make it extra-emphatic (like adding ਜੀ **jī** to ਆਪ **āp** to make it extra-respectful.

6.5.5 Other pronouns

ਕੌਣ kaᵘṇ ('Who?')

	Direct form	Oblique form with ਨੂੰ nū̃	Oblique form with ਤੋਂ tõ
Singular	ਕੌਣ kaᵘṇ	ਕਿਹਨੂੰ kihnū̃ ਕਿਸ ਨੂੰ kis nū̃	ਕਿਹਤੋਂ kihtõ ਕਿਸ ਤੋਂ kis tõ
Plural	ਕੌਣ kaᵘṇ	ਕਿਹਨਾਂ ਨੂੰ kihnā̃ nū̃	ਕਿਹਨਾਂ ਤੋਂ kihnā̃ tõ

ਕੋਈ koī ('Any')

	Direct form	Oblique form with ਨੂੰ nū̃	Oblique form with ਤੋਂ tõ
Singular	ਕੋਈ koī	ਕਿਸੇ ਨੂੰ kise nū̃	ਕਿਸੇ ਤੋਂ kise tõ
Plural	ਕੋਈ koī	Does not exist	Does not exist

ਕਿਹੜਾ kihṛā ('Which?' – Masculine)

	Direct form	Oblique form with ਨੂੰ nū̃	Oblique form with ਤੋਂ tõ
Singular	ਕਿਹੜਾ kihṛā	ਕਿਹਨੂੰ kihnū̃ ਕਿਸ ਨੂੰ kis nū̃	ਕਿਹਤੋਂ kihtõ ਕਿਸ ਤੋਂ kis tõ
Plural	ਕਿਹੜੇ kihre	ਕਿਹਨਾਂ ਨੂੰ kihnā̃ nū̃	ਕਿਹਨਾਂ ਤੋਂ kihnā̃ tõ

ਕਿਹੜੀ kihṛī ('Which?' – Feminine)

	Direct form	Oblique form with ਨੂੰ nū̃	Oblique form with ਤੋਂ tõ
Singular	ਕਿਹੜੀ kihṛī	ਕਿਹਨੂੰ kihnū̃ ਕਿਸ ਨੂੰ kis nū̃	ਕਿਹਤੋਂ kihtõ ਕਿਸ ਤੋਂ kis tõ
Plural	ਕਿਹੜੀਆਂ kihrīā̃	ਕਿਹਨਾਂ ਨੂੰ kihnā̃ nū̃ ਕਿਹੜੀਆਂ kihrīā̃ nū̃	ਕਿਹਨਾਂ ਤੋਂ kihnā̃ tõ ਕਿਹੜੀਆਂ ਤੋਂ kihrīā̃ tõ

ਜਿਹੜਾ jihṛā, ਜਿਹੜੀ jihṛī (‘Who’ – Relative Pronouns)

Forms are derived in the same way as those of **ਕਿਹੜਾ kihrā** and **ਕਿਹੜਾ kihṛī** respectively. In the next chapter we deal with these and more **J-words** and **K-words** of Panjabi.

6.5.6 Possessive adjectives and adjectives used as pronouns

We have already mentioned **possessive adjectives** above related to and derived from **personal pronouns**. Many Panjabi adjectives can also be used as pronouns in some contexts. This is discussed in the next chapter.

6.6 Structure of the noun phrase in Panjabi

A phrase is a construction with a HEAD and one or more DEPENDENT elements embedded in it. The head of a **noun phrase** in Panjabi is a **noun** (or **pronoun**) and the DEPENDENT can belong to various word classes and can itself be a phrases or even clause. An example is given below.

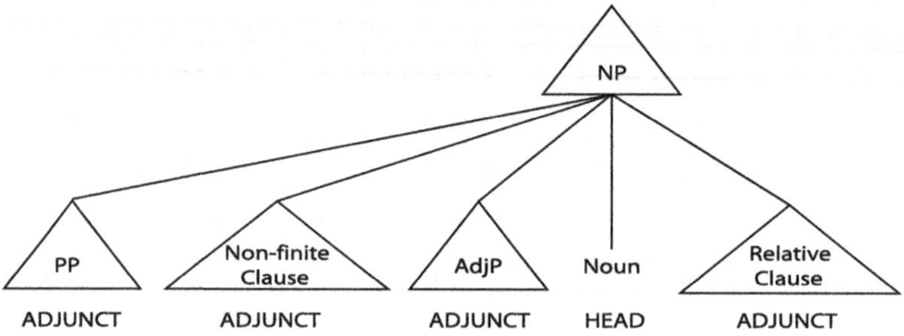

Fig 6.1 Structure of a noun phrase in Panjabi

ਲੋਕਾਂ ਵਿਚ	ਕੰਮ ਕਰਕੇ	ਖ਼ੁਸ਼ ਰਹਿਣ ਵਾਲ਼ਾ	ਉਹ ਬੜਾ ਨੇਕ ਬੰਦਾ
lokā̃ vic	**kamm karke**	**xuś rahiṇ vāḷā**	**uh baṛā nek bandā**
in people	having worked	happy remaining	that very pious man
PP	NFC	AdjP	NP

ਜਿਹਦਾ ਸਭ ਸਨਮਾਨ ਕਰਦੇ ਹਨ

jihdā sab^h sanmān karde han

whom all respect

RelC

This is not the only combination possible in Panjabi. Many other combinations are also possible and do occur in people's speech and writing.

A full finite or non-finite clause may also *replace* an **NP** as the SUBJECT or OBJECT or COMPLEMENT(S) or COMPLEMENT(O) in a clause. When constructions other than an NP play this syntactic role, they will be regarded as playing a **nominal** role. We shall deal with these complications in later chapters.

For teachers and other more advanced users

6.7   Historical perspective

A look at the history of the Panjabi personal pronouns can be of interest to some linguists.

Sanskrit	Old Panjabi (15th–18th centuries)	Modern Panjabi
Nominative Singular अहम् *aham*	ਹਉ **hau**	
Instrumental Singular मया *mayā*	ਮੈ **maⁱ**	ਮੈਂ **mā̃ⁱ**
Nominative Singular त्वम् *tvam*	ਤੂ **tū**	ਤੂੰ **tū̃**
Instrumental Singular त्वया *tvayā*	ਤੈ **taⁱ**	ਤੈਂ **tā̃ⁱ**

In old Panjabi, the forms of the **pronouns** derived from the Sanskrit Instrumental forms were used in the **ergative** constructions for the **agentive** SUBJECT. Their **instrumental** past became semantically irrelevant. ਹਉ **hau** has since disappeared in favour of ਮੈਂ **mā̃ⁱ** and ਤੈ **taⁱ** (ਤੈਂ **tā̃ⁱ**) is giving way to ਤੂੰ **tū̃**. The word ਹਉਮੈ **haumaⁱ** 'extreme egotism' used in the Sikh holy book to refer to what Sikhism regards a sinful state of mind appears to be derived by combining ਹਉ **hau** and ਮੈ **maⁱ**.

The Sanskrit instrumental case suffix *-ena* was added to nouns and third person pronouns only, as in तेन *tena* 'by him' and गजेन *gajena* 'by the elephant'. This *-ena* is the source of the Panjabi agentive postposition ਨੇ **ne** used as the marker of the SUBJECT in the modern Panjabi **ergative** constructions. This explains why ਨੇ **ne** is not used with ਮੈਂ **mã^{i}** and ਤੂੰ **tū̃**. This will be discussed in Chapter 12 as well.

6.8 From a Panjabi folk song

Some lines from a Panjabi folk song having the forms of Panjabi nouns and pronouns dealt with in this chapter are give below. This deeply moving and haunting Western Panjabi song has regional and dialectal variations. Following lines occur in a commonly sung version.

1	ਅਸਾਂ ਨੂੰ ਮਾਣ ਵਤਨਾਂ ਦਾ,	**asā̃ nū̃ māṇ vatnā̃ dā,**
2	ਅਸੀਂ ਹਾਂ ਤੇਰੇ ਯਾਰ ਪਰਦੇਸੀ।	**asī̃ hā̃ tere yār pardesī.**
3	ਅੱਧੀ ਰਾਤੀਂ ਟੁੱਟਣ ਤਾਰੇ -	**add^{h}ī rātī̃ ṭuṭṭaṇ tāre -**
4	ਜੁਦਾਈ ਵਾਲ਼ੇ ਤੀਰ ਕਿਸ ਮਾਰੇ?	**judāī vāḷe tīr kis māre?**
5	ਨਾ ਅਸਾਂ ਮਾਰੇ, ਨਾ ਤੁਸਾਂ ਮਾਰੇ;	**nā asā̃ māre, nā tusā̃ māre;**
6	ਜੁਦਾਈ ਵਾਲ਼ੇ ਤੀਰ ਰੱਬ ਮਾਰੇ।	**judāī vāḷe tīr rabb māre.**

'We are proud of (our) motherland, and we are your bosom friends living in distant lands. Stars burst at midmight. Who shot the arrows of separation? Neither we nor you shot the arrows of separation; God shot the arrows of separation.'

The notable points in these lines are

1. The **oblique** form ਅਸਾਂ **asā̃** is used when the postposition ਨੂੰ **nū̃** follows. This is an **experiencer construction.** (See Chapter 12).
2. The **direct** form ਅਸੀਂ **asī̃** is used without a postposition.
3. ਰਾਤੀਂ **rātī̃** 'at night' is the **locative synthetic** case form of ਰਾਤ **rāt** 'night'.
4. The postposition ਨੇ **ne** is omitted after the subject in this ergative clause with the **perfect participle** verb form. (See Chapter 11). This omission of ਨੇ **ne** is quite common in the Western dialects and in poetry. But the oblique form ਕਿਸ **kis** shows that ਨੇ **ne** is omitted here.
5. The postposition ਨੇ **ne** is omitted, but the oblique forms ਅਸਾਂ **asā̃** and ਤੁਸਾਂ **tusā̃** show this omission.
6. The postposition ਨੇ **ne** is omitted after the subject ਰੱਬ **rabb** 'God' in this ergative clause. Since this singular masculine noun does not end is **-ā**, its direct and oblique forms are homophonous.

Chapter 7

Adjective, Adjective Phrase, Adverb and Adverb Phrase

Preview of the chapter

Panjabi **adjectives** and **adverbs** are the subject of this chapter. Their morphology is described in detail. The fact that multi-word constructions (known as **phrases**) also act as **adjectives** and **adverbs** (especially the latter) is taken into account. Most Panjabi **postpositions** are actually adverbs and can play both roles. However, postpositions are dealt with in detail in Chapter 8.

7.1 The three-way characterisation of adjectives in Panjabi

Traditionally, Indian grammatical tradition did not consider **adjectives** as a class different from **nouns**. Both were regarded as **substantives**. Even in modern Panjabi, adjectives and nouns share some formal and behavioural characteristics. But differences are also there and it makes sense to regard them as different word classes.

1. *Notionally* or *semantically*, **adjectives** characteristically express properties of people, places or concrete and abstract entities (referred to as **nouns** or **pronouns**).

2. *Formally*, most Panjabi adjectives fall into one of two categories – the **black** adjectives (inflected for number, gender and oblique form) and

the **red** adjectives (not inflected in this way). Adjectives can occur in the **attributive** or **predicative** position. But **determiners**, a subset of adjectives, occur in the **attributive** position only.

3. *Functionally*, an adjective acts as the HEAD of an **adjective phrase (AdjP)**.

7.2 Determiners and full adjectives

Determiners are special types of **adjectives** which mark an **NP** as **definite** or **indefinite** in a given context. ਇਕ **ik** (unstressed, as opposed to the stressed numeral ਇੱਕ **ikk**) means 'one of the many' whose identity is definite now. If the number is more than one, ਕੁਝ **kuj**^{h} (ਕੁਛ **kuc**^{h} or ਕੁਸ਼ **kuś** in some dialects) and its variants ਕੁਝ ਕੁਝ **kuj**^{h} **kuj**^{h}, ਕੁਝ ਤਾਂ **kuj**^{h} **tā̃**, ਕੁਝ ਕੁ **kuj**^{h} **ku**, ਕੁਝ ਨਾ ਕੁਝ . . . ਤਾਂ **kuj**^{h} **na kuj**^{h}**... tā̃**, are used. If the identity is still indefinite or the speaker is not interested in establishing the identity, ਕੋਈ **koī** or its variants ਕੋਈ ਕੋਈ **koī koī**, ਕੋਈ ਤਾਂ **koī tā̃**, ਕੋਈ ਵੀ **koī vī**, ਹਰ ਕੋਈ **har koī**, ਕੋਈ ਨਾ ਕੋਈ . . . ਤਾਂ **koī na koī ... tā̃** are used for one as well as more than one. The meanings of these variants are discussed below. After the identity is established, the NP is mentioned without any determiner, or the **demonstrative** ਇਹ **ih** or ਉਹ **uh** is used for emphasis. While it is true to say that "Panjabi has no English-like **articles**", these **determiners** (and their ancestors) have been in use in Panjabi (and its ancestor languages) for many centuries. Most other adjectives can be used attributively as well as predicatively, but the determiners are used attributively only. Examples of these two uses are

Attributive use	ਚਿੱਟਾ ਘੋੜਾ **ciṭṭā g**^{h}**oṛā** 'white horse'
Predicative use	ਘੋੜਾ ਚਿੱਟਾ ਹੈ **g**^{h}**oṛā ciṭṭā ha**^{i} 'The horse is white'
Attributive use	ਇਕ ਘੋੜਾ **ik g**^{h}**oṛā** 'a horse'
Predicative use	*ਘੋੜਾ ਇਕ ਹੈ **g**^{h}**oṛā ik ha**^{i} (?)
Attributive use	ਕੋਈ ਘੋੜਾ **koī g**^{h}**oṛā** 'some horse'
Predicative use	*ਘੋੜਾ ਕੋਈ ਹੈ **g**^{h}**oṛā koī ha**^{i} (?)

7.3 Classification of Panjabi full adjectives

Panjabi adjectives can be classified into the following types:

1. Adjectives of quality are the most numerous among the Panjabi adjectives. They define more precisely the reference of a noun or pronoun. Most of them can be used both attributively and predicatively. Examples are ਚੰਗਾ **cangā** 'good', ਬੁਰਾ **burā** 'bad', ਨਵਾਂ **navā̃** 'new', ਪੁਰਾਣਾ **purāṇā** 'old', ਸੁਹਣਾ **suhṇā** 'beautiful', ਭੱਦਾ **b^haddā** 'ugly', ਚਿੱਟਾ **ciṭṭā** 'white', ਲਾਲ **lāl** 'red', ਕਾਲ਼ਾ **kāḷā** 'black'.

Some of these adjectives have a comparative form, such as ਉਚੇਰਾ **ucerā** 'higher' from ਉੱਚਾ **uccā** 'high', ਵਡੇਰਾ **vaderā** 'greater, bigger' from ਵੱਡਾ **vaḍḍā** 'great, big', ਡੂੰਘੇਰਾ **ḍū̃g^herā** 'deeper' from ਡੂੰਘਾ **ḍū̃g^hā** 'deep', ਛੁਟੇਰਾ **c^huṭerā** 'smaller, younger' from ਛੋਟਾ **c^hoṭā** 'small, young', ਬਹੁਤੇਰਾ **bahuterā** 'a great deal' from ਬਹੁਤ **bahut** 'much'. ਬਹੁਤੇਰਾ **bahuterā** is more commonly written and pronounced as ਬਥੇਰਾ **bat^herā**. These are **synthetic** forms. Comparison can also be expressed analytically with **postpositional phrases** dealt with in the next chapter.

2. Adjectives of quantity indicate the quantity of the reference of a noun/pronoun. These adjectives can be

(a) Definite, such as ਕਿੱਲੋ ਭਰ **killo b^har** 'a kilogram', ਚਾਰ ਗਜ਼ **cār gaz** 'four yards'.

(b) Indefinite, such as ਕੁਝ ਕੁ **kuj^h ku** 'a little bit', ਬਹੁਤ ਸਾਰਾ **bahut sārā** 'quite a lot', ਬਹੁਤ ਕੁਝ **bahut kuj^h** 'quite a lot', ਚੋਖਾ **cok^hā** 'a great deal', ਬਹੁਤਾ **bahutā** 'much', ਥੋੜਾ **t^hoṛā** 'a little', ਥੋੜਾ ਜਿਹਾ **t^hoṛā jihā** 'a little bit', ਰੀਣ ਕੁ **rīṇ ku** 'a little'.

3. Adjectives of number indicate the number or numerical order of the reference of a noun/pronoun. These adjectives can be

(a) Cardinal, such as ਇੱਕ **ikk** 'one', ਦੋ **do** 'two', ਦਸ ਹਜ਼ਾਰ **das hazār** 'ten thousand'.

(b) Ordinal, such as ਪਹਿਲਾ **pahilā** 'first', ਦੂਸਰਾ **dūsarā** 'second', ਦਸ ਹਜ਼ਾਰਵਾਂ **das hazārvā̃** 'ten thousandth'.

(c) Distributive, such as ਇਕ-ਇਕ **ik-ik** 'one by one', ਦੋ-ਦੋ **do-do** 'in pairs', ਦਸ-ਦਸ **das-das** 'in groups of ten'.

3. Demonstrative pronouns can be used as adjectives as well. They are

(a) Proximal, indicating nearness, such as ਇਹ (ਕੁਰਸੀ) **ih (kursī)** 'this (chair)', ਇਹ/ਐਹ (ਬੰਦੇ) **ih/a^{i}h (bande)** 'these (men)'.

(b) Distal, indicating distance, such as ਉਹ (ਕੁਰਸੀ) **uh (kursī)** 'that (chair)', ਉਹ/ਔਹ (ਬੰਦੇ) **uh/a^{u}h (bande)** 'those (men)'.

4. Pronominal adjectives are either the pronouns used as adjectives or are derived from pronouns.

(a) Examples of **non-derived** ones are ਕੀ **kī** 'what?', ਕੌਣ **ka^{u}ṇ** 'who?', ਕਿਹੜਾ? **kihṛā** 'which?'.

(b) The best examples of the **derived** ones are the **possessive adjectives** ਮੇਰਾ **merā** 'my', ਸਾਡਾ **sāḍā** 'our', ਤੇਰਾ **terā** 'your' (singular), ਤੁਹਾਡਾ **tuhāḍā** 'your' (plural), ਇਹਦਾ **ihdā** 'his, her, its' (proximal), ਉਹਦਾ **uhdā** 'his, her, its' (distal), ਕਿਹਦਾ **kihdā** 'whose? (question word), ਜਿਹਦਾ **jihdā** 'whose' (relative adjective).

7.4 "Black" and "red" adjectives

The **black adjectives** are inflected for number and gender and have oblique forms. But the **red adjectives** are invariable. Indian linguists use these "colourful" terms because the North Indian word ਕਾਲ਼ਾ **kāḷā** 'black' is a typical "black" adjective and ਲਾਲ **lāl** 'red' is a typical "red" adjective. It is quite easy to find out the "colour" of an adjective. If it ends in **-ā** in the **masculine singular** form or **-ī** in the **feminine singular** form, it is "black"; otherwise it is "red".

The following tables show the inflectional suffixes which the **direct** and **oblique** forms of the "black" adjectives take. An adjective takes the oblique forms when a **postposition** follows the noun it qualifies, *whether or not the noun itself has an oblique form different from a direct form.*

(a) Direct forms

	Singular	**Plural**
Masculine	-ਆ **-ā** ਕਾਲ਼ਾ ਘੋੜਾ **kāḷā gʰoṛā** 'black horse'	-ਏ **-e** ਕਾਲ਼ੇ ਘੋੜੇ **kāḷe gʰoṛe** 'black horses'
Feminine	-ਈ **-ī** ਕਾਲ਼ੀ ਘੋੜੀ **kāḷī gʰoṛī** 'black mare'	-ਈਆਂ **-īā̃** ਕਾਲ਼ੀਆਂ ਘੋੜੀਆਂ **kāḷīā̃ gʰoṛīā̃** 'black mares'

(b) Oblique forms

	Singular	**Plural**
Masculine	-ਏ **-e** ਕਾਲ਼ੇ ਘੋੜੇ (ਨੂੰ) **kāḷe gʰoṛe (nū̃)** '(to) the black horse'	-ਇਆਂ **-iā̃** ਕਾਲ਼ਿਆਂ ਘੋੜਿਆਂ (ਨੂੰ) **kāḷiā̃ gʰoṛiā̃ (nū̃)** '(to) the black horses'
Feminine	-ਈ **-ī** ਕਾਲ਼ੀ ਘੋੜੀ (ਨੂੰ) **kāḷī gʰoṛī (nū̃)** '(to) the black mares'	-ਈਆਂ **-īā̃** ਕਾਲ਼ੀਆਂ ਘੋੜੀਆਂ (ਨੂੰ) **kāḷīā̃ gʰoṛīā̃ (nū̃)** '(to) the black mares'

As with nouns, only the **masculine direct** forms differ from the **oblique** forms. If the adjective in the above tables is ਲਾਲ **lāl** 'red', it will not change whatever inflectional changes may take place because of **number**, **gender** and **oblique** form in the **noun** it qualifies.

7.4.1 Perfect participles ending in -iā used as adjectives

When a **perfect participle** (see Chapter 11) ending **-iā** (in the masculine singular form) is used as an adjective, it behaves like a **black adjective** but *with one minor difference* in the **masculine singular oblique** form. The direct and oblique forms of ਟੁੱਟਿਆ **ṭuṭṭiā** 'broken' are given below.

(a) Direct forms

	Singular	Plural
Masculine	ਟੁੱਟਿਆ ਪੱਖਾ **ṭuṭṭiā pakkʰā** 'broken fan'	ਟੁੱਟੇ ਪੱਖੇ **ṭuṭṭe pakkʰe** 'broken fans'
Feminine	ਟੁੱਟੀ ਕਲਮ **ṭuṭṭī kalam** 'broken pen'	ਟੁੱਟੀਆਂ ਕਲਮਾਂ **ṭuṭṭīā̃ kalmā̃** 'broken pens'

(b) Oblique forms

	Singular	Plural
Masculine	ਟੁੱਟੇ ਪੱਖੇ (ਨੂੰ) **ṭuṭṭe pakkʰe (nū̃)** '(to) the broken fan'	ਟੁੱਟੇ ਪੱਖਿਆਂ (ਨੂੰ) **ṭuṭṭe pakkʰiā̃ (nū̃)** ਟੁੱਟਿਆਂ ਪੱਖਿਆਂ (ਨੂੰ) **ṭuṭṭiā̃ pakkʰiā̃ (nū̃)** '(to) the broken fans'
Feminine	ਟੁੱਟੀ ਕਲਮ (ਨੂੰ) **ṭuṭṭī kalam (nū̃)** '(to) the broken pen'	ਟੁੱਟੀਆਂ ਕਲਮਾਂ (ਨੂੰ) **ṭuṭṭīā̃ kalmā̃ (nū̃)** '(to) the broken pens'

The notable difference is that both ਟੁੱਟੇ **ṭuṭṭe** and ਟੁੱਟਿਆਂ **ṭuṭṭiā̃** are used by different speakers as **masculine plural oblique** forms, with either **-e** or **-iā̃** suffix.

7.4.2 Adjectives ending in -īā

The two similar-sounding endings **-iā** and **-īā** should not be confused. Two very commonly used adjectives ਵਧੀਆ **vad^{h}īā** 'superior' and ਘਟੀਆ **g^{h}aṭīā** 'inferior' and some comparatively less commonly used adjectives like ਦੁਖੀਆ **duk^{h}īā** 'anguished', ਸੁਖੀਆ **suk^{h}īā** 'happy' and ਰਸੀਆ **rasīā** 'fond of' have **-ā** at the end, but they behave like **red adjectives** and are not inflected. For example, you have ਵਧੀਆ ਘੋੜਾ **vad^{h}īā g^{h}oṛā** 'superior horse', ਵਧੀਆ ਘੋੜੀਆਂ **vad^{h}īā g^{h}oṛīā̃** 'superior mares', ਵਧੀਆ ਘੋੜਿਆਂ ਨੂੰ **vad^{h}īā g^{h}oṛiā̃ nū̃** 'to the superior horses'.

The endings of the direct forms of the **black adjectives** are added to many **verb** forms as well. They are given in the square below. Some teachers of Panjabi use the term **Magic Square** for it and ask the learners to memorise them.

	Singular	Plural
Masculine	-ਆ **-ā**	-ਏ **-e**
Feminine	-ਈ **-ī**	-ਈਆਂ **-īā̃**

If the noun has a synthetic case form, the black adjective simply takes the **oblique** form, but not the synthetic form of the noun. The synthetic form of the noun is regarded as having a **postposition** built into it. Examples are ਮੇਰਾ ਘਰ **merā g^{h}ar** 'my house' and ਮੇਰੇ ਘਰੋਂ **mere g^{h}arõ** 'from my house', not *ਮੇਰਿਓਂ ਘਰੋਂ ***meriõ g^{h}arõ**. The synthetic form ਮੇਰੇ ਘਰੋਂ **mere g^{h}arõ** is regarded as an equivalent of the **analytic form** ਮੇਰੇ ਘਰ ਤੋਂ **mere g^{h}ar tõ**. In this example, the **masculine noun** ਘਰ **g^{h}ar** does not have a different **oblique** form because it does not end in **-ਆ -ā** (see Chapter 6), but the **black adjective** ਮੇਰਾ **merā** assumes the **oblique** form ਮੇਰੇ **mere**.

7.5 Adjectives used as pronouns

The words, phrases and constructions of a natural language acquire their meaning potential and behaviour potential gradually over centuries from the social interactions of its speakers. So some words function as more than one "part of speech" while keeping their meaning potential more or less intact. The English word *who* functions as a **question word** in *Who did this?*, as a **subordinator** in *I know who did this* and as a **relative pronoun** in *I know the man who did this.*

In the following sentence

> **ਇਹਨਾਂ ਅੰਬਾਂ ਵਿਚੋਂ ਪੱਕੇ ਕੱਢ ਲਓ ਅਤੇ ਕੱਚੇ ਉੱਥੇ ਰਹਿਣ ਦਿਓ**
> **ihnā̃ ambā̃ vicõ *pakke* kaḍḍʰ lao ate *kacce* uttʰe rahiṇ dio**
>
> 'From these mangoes, take out the *ripe* ones and leave the *unripe* ones there'

the adjectives ਪੱਕੇ **pakke** and ਕੱਚੇ **kacce** refer to the ripe mangoes and unripe mangoes respectively. Since these **adjectives** characterise the mangoes mentioned earlier, there is no need to mention them again. So these **adjectives** function as **pronouns** because they "stand for" **NP**s. Their English counterparts cannot function as **pronouns** and need the pro-form *ones* to act as a **noun**.

7.6 Adverbs in Panjabi

As a category, the **adverb** has existed in the Western grammatical tradition since antiquity. But many modern linguists who insist on clear and watertight categories doubt the viability of this word class. Some call it a "dustbin" category into which words or expressions which do not fit into any other easily defined word class are dumped. But natural languages being what they are, and keeping in mind that they are always evolving and are in a state of flux, we should expect just this.

Traditionally, an **adverb** is a word class whose most characteristic role is traditionally that of modifying a **verb** or **verb phrase**: e.g. *badly* in *He wrote it badly*, where (in different accounts) it modifies either the verb *wrote* or the phrase *wrote it*. But in actual practice, "In the grammar of English and many similar languages, an adverb is effectively a word that modifies anything other than a noun" (Matthews 2007: 10). The best thing for learners of Panjabi is to keep in mind "modifies anything other than a noun" and learn important Panjabi adverbs classified below. The word class of **particles** (with three members ਵੀ **vī**, ਹੀ **hī** and ਤਾਂ **tā̃**), dealt with later in this chapter and also in Chapter 16, can be regarded as a special subclass of **adverbs.**

7.6.1 Classification of Panjabi adverbs

The classification of Panjabi adverbs traditionally made in educational books (e.g. Duggal 2011) should be fine for our purpose. Duggal classifies Panjabi adverbs into eight classes.

1. Adverbs of time, which indicate the time of the action of a **verb**. Examples are

ਉਦੋਂ **udõ** 'then', ਜਦੋਂ/ਜਦ **jadõ/jad** 'when', ਕਦੋਂ/ਕਦ **kadõ/kad** 'when?', ਕਦੀ **kadī** 'at some time', ਹੁਣ **huṇ** 'now', ਕੱਲ੍ਹ **kallʰ** 'yesterday' or 'tomorrow', ਪਰਸੋਂ **parsõ** 'day before yesterday' or 'day after tomorrow', ਸਵੇਰੇ **savere** 'in the morning', ਦੁਪਹਿਰੇ **dupahire** 'at midday', ਕੁਵੇਲੇ **kuvele** 'at a wrong time', ਸੁਵੇਲੇ **suvele** 'at the right time', ਕਦੀ ਕਦਾਈਂ **kadī kadāī̃** 'occasionally', ਫਿਰ **pʰir** 'again', ਹਮੇਸ਼ਾ **hameśā** 'always', ਸਦਾ **sadā** 'always', ਘੜੀ ਮੁੜੀ **gʰaṛī muṛī** 'again and again'.

Some adverbs of time started as **adjective phrases** (adjective+noun), but are now single words, clearly because they have been used together a great deal. Examples are ਓਦਣ **odaṇ** (ਉਸ ਦਿਨ **din** 'that day'), ਜਿੱਦਣ **jiddaṇ** (ਜਿਸ ਦਿਨ **jis din** 'on what day', ਓਸੇਲੇ **osele** (ਉਸ ਵੇਲੇ **us vele** 'at that moment'), ਕੇਰਾਂ **kerā̃** (ਇਕ ਵੇਰਾਂ **ik verā̃** 'once').

2. Adverbs of place, which indicate the place of the action of a **verb**. Examples are

ਉੱਤੇ **utte** 'above', 'over', ਉੱਪਰ **uppar** 'above', 'over', ਹੇਠਾਂ **heṭʰā̃** 'below', 'underneath', ਵਿਚਕਾਰ **vickār** 'in the middle', ਅੰਦਰ **andar** 'inside', ਉਰ੍ਹੇ **urhe** 'on this side', ਪਰ੍ਹੇ **parhe** 'on that side', ਇਧਰ/ਏਧਰ **idʰar/edʰar** 'on this side', ਉਧਰ/ਓਧਰ **udʰar/odʰar** 'on that side', ਇੱਥੇ **ittʰe** 'here', ਓਥੇ **otʰe** 'there', 'that side', ਕਿੱਧਰ **kiddʰar** 'where?', ਕਿੱਥੇ **kittʰe** 'where?', ਜਿੱਥੇ **kittʰe** 'where', ਬਾਹਰ **bāhar** 'outside', ਅੰਦਰ **andar** 'inside', ਨੇੜੇ **neṛe** 'nearby', ਦੂਰ **dūr** 'at a distance', ਵਿਚ **vic** 'inside', ਸੱਜੇ **sajje** 'on the right side', ਖੱਬੇ **kʰabbe** 'on the left side', ਕੋਲ਼ **koḷ** 'near', ਕੋਲ਼ੇ **koḷe** 'near'. As we will see in the next chapter some of these adverbs function as **postpositions** as well.

While the meanings of all these adverbs presuppose an observer's point of view, three special "body in the mind" (the term used by Lakoff and Johnson 1999) adverbs of place need a special mention. They are ਅੱਗੇ **agge** 'in front' (from Sanskrit *agre*), ਗੱਭੇ **gabbʰe** 'in the middle' (from Sanskrit *garbhe* 'in the womb') and ਪਿੱਛੇ **piccʰe** 'behind' (from Sanskrit *pṛṣṭhe* 'at the back'). Their **-e** ending shows that they are locative singular forms of the nouns ਅੱਗਾ **aggā** 'front', ਗੱਭਾ **gabbʰā** 'middle', 'centre' and ਪਿੱਛਾ **piccʰā** 'behind' respectively.

3. Adverbs of manner, which indicate the manner of the action of a **verb**. Examples are

ਇੰਜ **inj** ‘in this way’, ਉਂਜ **unj** ‘in that way’, ਇੱਦਾਂ **iddā̃** ‘in this way’, ਓਦਾਂ **odā̃** ‘in that way’, ਇਸ ਤਰ੍ਹਾਂ/ ਏਤਰ੍ਹਾਂ **is tarhā̃/etrhā̃** ‘in this way’, ਉਸ ਤਰ੍ਹਾਂ/ ਓਤਰ੍ਹਾਂ **us tarhā̃/otrhā̃** ‘in that way’, ਇਵੇਂ **ivẽ** ‘in this way’, ਕਿਵੇਂ **kivẽ** ‘how?’, ਕਿੱਦਾਂ **kiddā̃** ‘how?’, ਜਿਵੇਂ **jivẽ** ‘as if’, ‘in a way that’, ਜਿੱਦਾਂ **jiddā̃** ‘as if’, ‘in that way’, ਹੌਲ਼ੀ **ha^{u}ḷī** ‘slowly’, ਤੇਜ਼ **tez** ‘fast’, ਛੇਤੀ **c^{h}etī** ‘quickly’.

4. Adverbs of quantity, which indicate quantity of the action of a verb and qualify **adjectives** and other **adverbs**.

ਇੰਨਾ **inna** ‘this much’, ਇੰਨਾ ਕੁ **inna ku** ‘about this much’, ਉਂਨਾ **unnā** ‘that much’, ਉਂਨਾ ਕੁ **unnā ku** ‘about that much’, ਜਿੰਨਾ **jinnā** ‘as much’, ਜਿੰਨਾ ਕੁ **jinnā ku** ‘about as much’, ਕਿੰਨਾ **kinnā** ‘how much?’, ਕਿੰਨਾ ਕੁ **kinnā ku** ‘about how much?’, ਸਾਰਾ **sārā** ‘completely’, ਬਹੁਤ ਸਾਰਾ **bahut sārā** ‘very much’, ਰਤਾ ਕੁ **ratā ku** ‘a little bit’, ਮਾੜਾ ਜਿਹਾ **māṛā jihā** ‘a little bit’, ਮਸਾਂ **masā̃** ‘hardly’, ਪੂਰਾ **pūrā** ‘completely’, ਅਧੂਰਾ **ad^{h}ūrā** ‘incompletely’, ਘੱਟ **g^{h}aṭṭ** ‘a little’, ‘less’, ਵੱਧ **vadd^h** ‘a lot’, ‘more’, ਬਹੁਤ **bahut** ‘much’, ‘a lot’, ਕੁਝ **kuj^h** ‘somewhat’, ‘a little’, ਨਿਰਾ **nirā** ‘completely’, ‘perfectly’, ਨਿਰਾ ਪੂਰਾ **nirā purā** ‘perfectly’, ਮਸਾਂ **masā̃** ‘hardly’, ਬਿਲਕੁਲ **bilkul** ‘perfectly’.

5. Adverbs of number, which indicate number or frequency of the action of a **verb.**

ਇਕ-ਇਕ **ik-ik** ‘one by one’, ਇਕਹਿਰਾ **ikahirā** ‘single’, ਦੋ-ਦੋ **do-do** ‘in twos’, ਦੂਹਰਾ **dūhrā** ‘double’, ਕਈ ਵਾਰ **kaī vār** ‘many times’, ਵਾਰ ਵਾਰ **vār vār** ‘again and again’, ਘੜੀ-ਮੁੜੀ **g^{h}aṛī-muṛī** ‘frequently’.

6. Adverbs of affirmation and negation, which indicate the occurrence or non-occurrence of an event or affirmation or negation thereof.

ਹਾਂ **hā̃** ‘yes’, ਆਹੋ **āho** ‘yes’, ਹਾਂ ਜੀ **hā̃ jī** ‘polite yes’, ਜੀ ਹਾਂ **jī hā̃** ‘polite yes’, ਨਹੀਂ **nahī̃** ‘no’, ਨਹੀਂ ਜੀ **nahī̃ jī** ‘polite no’, ਜੀ ਨਹੀਂ **jī nahī̃** ‘polite no’, ਬਹੁਤ ਅੱਛਾ **bahut acc^{h}ā** ‘very well’, ਸਤ ਵਚਨ **sat vacan** ‘respectful agreement’, ਸੱਚੀਂ **saccī̃** ‘really’, ਸੱਚਮੁਚ **sacmuc** ‘really’.

7. Adverbs of cause or effect, which indicate the cause or effect of an event.

ਕਿਉਂਕਿ **kiũki** ‘because’, ਕਿਉਂ ਜੁ **kiũ ju** ‘because’, ਤਾਂ ਜੁ **tā̃ ju** ‘so that’, ਤਾਂ ਕਿ **tā̃ ki** ‘so that’, ਇਸ ਕਰਕੇ **is karke** ‘therefore’, ‘consequently’, ਸੋ **so** ‘therefore’, ਤਾਂ ਹੀ **tā̃ hī** ‘exactly because of this’, ਆਖ਼ਿਰ **āxir** ‘after all’.

These **adverbs** also act as **co-ordinators** and **subordinators**. (See Chapter 15.)

8. Adverbs of emphasis, which we regard as a special subset of **adverbs** and call then **particles**. They are

ਵੀ **vī**, ਹੀ **hī** and ਤਾਂ **tā̃**. They are used for organising the text and giving particular nuances to certain parts of it. It is not easy to translate them and they are dealt with in Chapter 16 as well.

It is important to remember that some of these **adverbs** can also function as other parts of speech, such as **adjectives, postpositions, subordinators** and **question words**. Some **adverbs** ending in **-ā** are inflected like **black adjectives** if they are followed by a **postposition.**

ਉਹ ਮੁੰਡਾ *ਕਿੰਨਾ ਕੁ* ਲੰਮਾ ਸੀ?

uh muṇḍā *kinnā ku* lamma sī?

'About how tall was that boy?'

ਉਹ ਕੁੜੀਆਂ *ਕਿੰਨੀਆਂ ਕੁ* ਲੰਮੀਆਂ ਸਨ?

uh kuṛīā *kinnīā ku* lammīā̃ san?

'About how tall were those girls?'

Of the two words forming this adverb, only ਲੰਮਾ **lamma**, the one that ends in **-ā**, is inflected like a **black adjective**. ਕੁ **ku**, ending in **-u** is not inflected. But in the following examples

ਨਿਰਾ ਪੁਰਾ ਘਟੀਆ ਮਕਾਨ

***nirā purā* g^hāṭīā makān**

'perfectly worthless house'

ਨਿਰੇ ਪੁਰੇ ਘਟੀਆ ਮਕਾਨਾਂ ਵਿਚ

***nire pure* g^haṭīā makānā̃ vic**

'in perfectly worthless houses'

ਨਿਰਾ and ਪੁਰਾ end in **-ā**. So they are inflected like **black adjectives**. As we have seen above, ਘਟੀਆ is not a black adjective even though it ends in **-ā**. (See **7.4.2** on p.131.) ਮਕਾਨ **makān** assumes the plural oblique form ਮਕਾਨਾਂ **makānā̃** which a masculine noun ending in a consonant does. (See Chapter 6.)

But adverbs like ਜ਼ਰਾ ਕੁ **zarā ku**, ਰਤਾ ਕੁ **ratā ku** and ਭੋਰਾ ਕੁ **b^{h}orā ku** (all meaning 'a little bit') behave differently. In

ਜ਼ਰਾ ਕੁ ਖੱਟਾ ਸੰਤਰਾ
zarā ku *k^{h}aṭṭā* santrā
Mas Sg
'a little bit sour orange'

ਜ਼ਰਾ ਕੁ ਖੱਟੇ ਸੰਤਰੇ
zarā ku *k^{h}aṭṭe* santre
Mas Pl
'a little bit sour oranges'

ਜ਼ਰਾ ਕੁ ਖੱਟੀ ਖੁਮਾਨੀ
zarā ku *k^{h}aṭṭī* k^{h}umānī
Fem Sg
'a little bit sour apricot'

ਜ਼ਰਾ ਕੁ ਖੱਟੀਆਂ ਖੁਮਾਨੀਆਂ
zarā ku *k^{h}aṭṭīā̃* k^{h}umānīā̃
Fem Pl
'a little bit sour apricots'

the adjective ਖੱਟਾ **k^{h}aṭṭā**, ending in **-ā** is inflected like a black adjective. But ਜ਼ਰਾ **zarā**, also ending in **-ā** is not inflected. The same would be the case with ਰਤਾ ਕੁ **ratā ku** and ਭੋਰਾ ਕੁ **b^{h}orā ku**. Such irregularities and anomalies are to be expected among the members of the "dustbin category" **adverb.**

7.6.2 Pre-modifier and post-modifier adverbs

While most adverbs modifying adjectives are **pre-modifiers** coming *before* the adjectives/adverbs, some are **post-modifiers**, coming *after* the adjectives/adverbs. The subclass of adverbs known as **particles** are **post-modifiers**, but they can modify or specify the meaning of *any* word or phrase or clause.

1. Ordinary post-modifier adverbs

ਤਕ **tak** (with variants ਤੀਕ **tīk**, ਤੀਕਰ **tīkar**, ਤੀਕਣ **tīkaṇ** and ਤਾਈਂ **tāī̃**), ਕੁ **ku**, ਜਿਹਾ **jihā** and ਸਾਰਾ **sārā** are such adverbs. ਤਕ **tak**, ਕੁ **ku** and ਜਿਹਾ

jihā function as post-modifier adverbs only. But ਸਾਰਾ **sārā** functions as an ordinary adjective/adverb as well.

ਤਕ **tak** 'till, until, up to' modifies adjectives and adverbs of space, time, number and frequency.

> ਹੁਣ ਤਕ
> **huṇ tak**
> 'until now'
>
> ਸੌ ਤਕ
> **sa^{u} tak**
> 'up to one hundred'
>
> ਦਸ ਵਾਰ ਤਕ
> **das vār tak**
> 'up to ten times'
>
> ਕੁਝ ਦੂਰ ਤਕ
> **kuj^{h} dūr tak**
> 'up to some distance'

ਤਕ **tak** also functions as a **postposition**, as we will see in the next chapter. As has been pointed out repeatedly in this book, a lexeme in Punjabi can belong to more than one word class. What is important is how it *functions* in a particular construction.

ਕੁ **ku** further diminutes the sense of the adjective/adverb it qualifies. But ਸਾਰਾ **sārā** has the opposite effect.

> ਕੁਝ ਕੁ
> **kuj^{h} ku**
> 'a little bit, a few'
>
> ਜ਼ਰਾ ਕੁ
> **zarā ku**
> 'a little bit'
>
> ਵੱਡਾ ਸਾਰਾ
> **vaḍḍā sārā**
> 'quite big'

ਮੋਟਾ ਸਾਰਾ
moṭā sārā
'quite fat'

ਜਿਹਾ **jihā** means 'pseudo-' or 'somewhat like'.

ਲਾਲ ਜਿਹਾ
lāl jihā
'reddish/red-looking'

ਭੈੜਾ ਜਿਹਾ
b^{h}a^{i}ṛā jihā
'bad-looking'

2. Particles

The particles ਹੀ **hī**, ਵੀ **vī** and ਤਾਂ **tā̃** are difficult to translate into English and the nuances they impart to the text are best captured by observing them in use. Roughly,

ਹੀ **hī** is known as **exclusive particle** or **emphatic particle**, roughly meaning 'only'.

ਮੈਨੂੰ ਪਾਲਕ *ਹੀ* ਚਾਹੀਦੀ ਹੈ
ma^{i}nū̃ pālak *hī* cāhīdī ha^i
'I want spinach *only*' (and I am not interested in any other vegetable)

Very often, it gets fused with the word it modifies.

ਤੁਸੀਂ *ਹੁਣੇ* ਜਾਓ
tusī̃ *huṇe* jāo
'You (should) go *right now*'

ਹੁਣੇ **huṇe** is ਹੁਣ+ਹੀ **huṇ+hī** ('now'+emphasis).

ਵੀ **vī** is known as **inclusive particle**, roughly meaning 'also'.

ਮੈਨੂੰ ਪਾਲਕ *ਵੀ* ਚਾਹੀਦੀ ਹੈ
ma^{i}nū̃ pālak *vī* cāhīdī ha^i
'I want spinach *also*' (in addition to the other vegetables I am interested in)

The rough meaning of ਤਾਂ **tā̃** is 'as far x' or 'as far as x is concerned'.

> ਮੈਨੂੰ ਤਾਂ ਪਾਲਕ ਚਾਹੀਦੀ ਹੈ
> **ma^{i}nū̃ *tā̃* pālak cāhīdī ha^{i}**
> (*As far as* I am concerned) 'I want spinach' (Whatever other people may be interested in)

All three particles are at work in

> ਅੰਬ ਆਖ਼ਿਰ ਅੰਬ ਹੈ; ਥੋੜਾ ਬਹੁਤ ਖੱਟਾ ਤਾਂ ਹੋਏਗਾ *ਹੀ*
> **amb āxir amb ha^{i}; t^{h}oṛā bahut k^{h}aṭṭā *tā̃* hoegā *hī***
> 'A mango is a mango after all; it will definitely be more or less sour'
> (*As far as* its being sour is concerned, it will *definitely* be so).

> ਬਿਲਕੁਲ ਠੀਕ, ਇਹ ਅੰਬ ਥੋੜਾ ਥੋੜਾ ਖੱਟਾ *ਵੀ* ਹੈ ਤੇ ਥੋੜਾ
> **bilkul ṭ^{h}īk, ih amb t^{h}oṛā t^{h}oṛā k^{h}aṭṭā *vī* ha^{i} te t^{h}oṛā**
> ਥੋੜਾ ਮਿੱਠਾ *ਵੀ*
> **t^{h}oṛā miṭṭ^{h}ā *vī***
> 'Perfectly true, this mango is a little bit sour *as well as* a little bit sweet'

The repetition of ਥੋੜਾ **t^{h}oṛā** 'a bit' emphasises the meaning of the adverb.

7.7 I-words, U-words, J-words and K-words

The English question words like *who*, *where*, *when* and *how* are known as **Wh-words** because they all have 'w' and 'h' in them. For the same reason, the Panjabi question words are known as **K-words** because they all have the ਕ **k** sound in them. Like the English **Wh-words**, the Panjabi **K-words** can be classified into **pronouns**, **adjectives** and **adverbs**. But there is also a big difference in English and Panjabi in this respect. The English **Wh-words** can function as **question words**, **relative pronouns** and **subordinators**. (See Chapter 15.) But in Panjabi, the **K-words** are **question words** only. Most Panjabi **K-words** have associated **J-words** to work as **relative pronouns**. (**Relative pronouns** are dealt with in Chapter 15). The following tables give a list of the Panjabi **K-words** and **J-words**.

Interestingly enough, the **K-words** and **J-words** are phonologically as well as semantically related to the **demonstrative pronouns** (which also function as third person pronouns in Panjabi. The demonstratives beginning with the **front vowels [i], [e] and [a^{i}]** indicate nearness and the ones beginning with the **back vowels [u], [o] and [a^{u}]** indicate distance. This distinction also applies to the words/phrases in which the demonstratives occur. We will use the the terms **I-words** and **U-words** in the table below.

Pronouns

I-word	U-word	K-word	J-word
ਇਹ ih 'he/she/it/this/ these'	**ਉਹ uh** 'he/she/it/that/ those'	**ਕੀ kī** 'what?'	**ਜੋ jo** 'what'
		ਕੌਣ ka^{u}ṇ 'who?'	**ਜੋ jo** 'who'
		ਕਿਹੜਾ kihṛā 'which?'	**ਜਿਹੜਾ jihṛā** 'which'
ਇਹਨੂੰ ihnū̃ 'to him/her/it/ this'	**ਉਹਨੂੰ uhnū̃** 'to him/her/it/ that'	**ਕਿਹਨੂੰ kihnū̃** 'to whom/ what?'	**ਜਿਹਨੂੰ jihnū̃** 'to whom/what'
ਇਹਨਾਂ ਨੂੰ ihnā̃ nū̃ 'to them/these'	**ਉਹਨਾਂ ਨੂੰ uhnā̃ nū̃** 'to them/those'	**ਕਿਹਨਾਂ ਨੂੰ kihnā̃ nū̃** 'to whom/what?'	**ਜਿਹਨਾਂ ਨੂੰ jihnā̃ nū̃** 'to whom/what'
ਇਹਤੋਂ ihtõ 'from him/her/ it/this'	**ਉਹਤੋਂ uhtõ** 'from him/her/ it/that'	**ਕਿਹਤੋਂ kihtõ** 'from whom/ what?'	**ਜਿਹਤੋਂ jihtõ** 'from whom/what'
ਇਸ ਤੋਂ is tõ 'from him/her/ it/this'	**ਉਸ ਤੋਂ us tõ** 'from him/her/ it/that'	**ਕਿਸ ਤੋਂ kis tõ** 'from whom/ what?'	**ਜਿਸ ਤੋਂ jis tõ** 'from whom/what'
ਇਹਨਾਂ ਤੋਂ ihnā̃ tõ 'from them/these'	**ਉਹਨਾਂ ਤੋਂ uhnā̃ tõ** 'from them/ those'	**ਕਿਹਨਾਂ ਤੋਂ kihnā̃ tõ** 'from whom?'	**ਜਿਹਨਾਂ ਤੋਂ jihnā̃ tõ** 'from whom'

Possessive adjectives

I-word	U-word	K-word	J-word
ਇਹਦਾ **ihdā** 'his/her/its'	ਉਹਦਾ **uhdā** 'his/her/its'	ਕਿਹਦਾ **kihdā** 'whose?'	ਜਿਹਦਾ **jihdā** 'whose'
ਇਸ ਦਾ **is dā** 'his/her/its'	ਉਸ ਦਾ **us dā** 'his/her/its'	ਕਿਸ ਦਾ **kis dā** 'whose?'	ਜਿਸ ਦਾ **jis dā** 'whose'
ਇਹਨਾਂ ਦਾ **ihnā̃ dā** 'their'	ਉਹਨਾਂ ਦਾ **uhnā̃ dā** 'their'	ਕਿਹਨਾਂ ਦਾ **kihnā̃ dā** 'whose?'	ਜਿਹਨਾਂ ਦਾ **jihnā̃ dā** 'whose'

Adverbs

I-word	U-word	K-word	J-word
ਇੱਥੇ **ittʰe** 'here'	ਉੱਥੇ **uttʰe** 'there'	ਕਿੱਥੇ **kittʰe** 'where?'	ਜਿੱਥੇ **jittʰe** 'where'
ਇੱਥੋਂ **ittʰõ** 'from here'	ਉੱਥੋਂ **uttʰõ** 'from there'	ਕਿੱਥੋਂ **kittʰõ** 'from where?'	ਜਿੱਥੋਂ **jittʰõ** 'from where'
ਇੱਧਰ **iddʰar** 'here'	ਉੱਧਰ **uddʰar** 'there'	ਕਿੱਧਰ **kiddʰar** 'where?'	ਜਿੱਧਰ **jiddʰar** 'where'
		ਕਦ **kad** 'when?'	ਜਦ **jad** 'when'
	ਉਦੋਂ **udõ** 'then'	ਕਦੋਂ **kadõ** 'when?'	ਜਦੋਂ **jadõ** 'when'
		ਕਿਉਂ **kiũ** 'why?'	ਜਿਉਂ **jiũ** 'why'
ਇਵੇਂ **ivẽ** 'in this way'	ਓਵੇਂ **ovẽ** 'in that way'	ਕਿਵੇਂ **kivẽ** 'how?'	ਜਿਵੇਂ **jivẽ** 'how'
ਇੱਦਾਂ **iddā̃** 'in this way'	ਉੱਦਾਂ **uddā̃** 'in that way'	ਕਿੱਦਾਂ **kiddā̃** 'how?'	ਜਿੱਦਾਂ **jiddā̃** 'how'

The empty boxes in the tables show that the possible form simply does not exist in the language. Some of the forms mentioned above may be described as "just dialectal" or "non-standard" by some speakers. But they are nevertheless widely used and deserve to be included in this book. What is "non-standard" today may become "standard" tomorrow, and *vice versa*.

7.8 Adjective phrase and adverb phrase

The structures of these phrases can be summarised diagrammatically as below. As in all our syntactic diagrams, the triangles indicate the constructions into which other constructions can be embedded.

It is notable that within a phrase, there is a HEAD and there may also be COMPLEMENTS and/or ADJUNCTS.

Adjective phrase

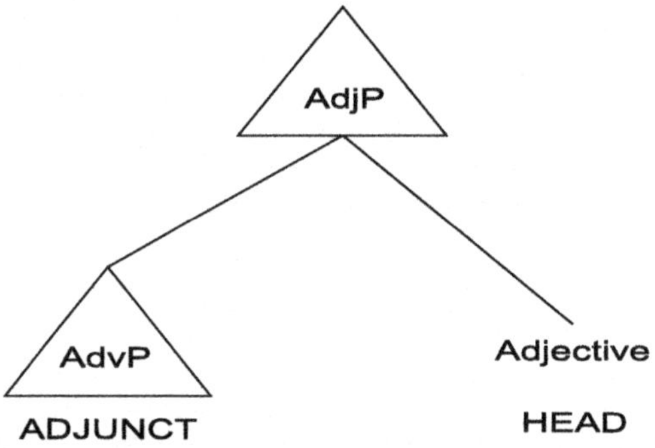

Figure 7.1 Possible detailed structure of an adjective phrase in Panjabi

Adverb phrase

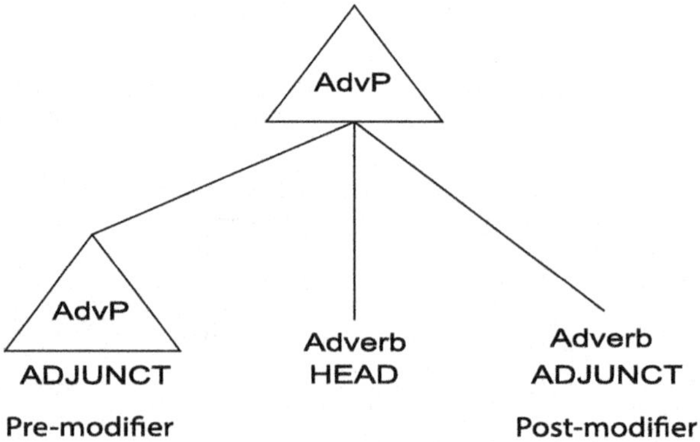

Figure 7.2 Possible detailed structure of an adverb phrase in Panjabi

An **adjective** is the HEAD of an **adjective phrase** (**AdjP**), which may have one or more **adverbs** or **adverb phrases** as ADJUNCT(S). The HEAD of an **adverb phrase** (**AdvP**) is an **adverb**, but the phrase may contain one or more **adverb(s)** as ADJUNCT(S). An adverb in Panjabi can be a single word or may have more than one word. It is treated as an **AdvP** if it is modified by another adverb or an AdvP.

7.9 Other phrases and constructions playing an adjectival or adverbial role

The role of an **adjective** – denoting properties of the persons, places and objects referred to in an **NP** – can also be played by syntactic structures other than adjective phrases. Constructions and phrases such as **postpositional phrases** and **relative clauses** can also play this adjectival role. Likewise, the main role of an adverb phrase – specifying and modifying the meaning of a verb phrase – can also be played by other syntactic constructions such as postpositional phrases, finite and non-finite clause. The syntactic constructions playing this role are collectively known as **adverbials**. We will deal with the various types of adverbials operating in Panjabi grammar in later chapters.

Summing up and looking ahead

There is no watertight boundary separating **adjectives** from **nouns/ pronouns** on the one hand and **adverbs** on the other. How a word is *used* makes it one or the other. The use of the forms given in the tables listing the related **I-words, U-words, K-words** and **J-words** in later chapters is going to demonstrate this.

Chapter 8

Postpositions and Postpositional Phrases

Preview of the chapter

Panjabi **postpositions** are, to a large extent, mirror images of their English counterparts. As the name clearly indicates, they *follow* the NP COMPLEMENTS in the **postpositional phrases** (**PP**s), but, as we shall see, a Panjabi postpositional phrase involving a **compound postposition**, is most often the literal translation of its English equivalent but is "read from the other end".

8.1 The three-way characterisation of postpositions in Panjabi

(i) *Notionally* or *semantically*, a **postposition** is a word or group of words that comes *after* an **NP** and denotes relations in time or space or marks the syntactic or sematic case role of an NP.

(ii) *Formally*, the Panjabi postpositions fall into one of the three groups:

(a) single-word uninflecting postpositions, (b) single-word postpositions inflecting like **black adjectives**, and (c) single word or multi-word post-positions which are or are derived from inflected case forms of nouns. The common characteristic of all the postpositions is that the nouns and adjectives in the NPs in the postpositional phrase have an **oblique** form. As we saw in Chapter 6, an **oblique** form is very often phonetically identical to non-oblique (or **direct**) form.

(iii) *Functionally*, a postposition acts as the HEAD of a **postpositional phrase** (**PP**) with the preceding **NP** as its COMPLEMENT.

8.2 The three classes of postpositions

8.2.1 Single-word uninflecting postpositions

This section deals with the Panjabi postpositions

ਨੇ **ne**, ਨੂੰ **nū̃**, ਤੋਂ **tõ** and ਤਕ **tak**.

(i) ਨੇ **ne**

ਨੇ **ne** (the **agentive** postposition) marks the SUBJECT of an **ergative clause** in which the verb agrees with the OBJECT or is the **neuter form** (homophonous to the **masculine singular** form). We shall deal with this in detail in Chapter 12. Two examples are given below.

> (1) ਕਵੀ   ਨੇ   ਮੰਚ   ਤੇ ਕਵਿਤਾ   ਪੜੀ
> **kavī   *ne*   manc te kavitā   paṛhī**
> SUB   Agt   Fem Sg Fem Sg
> 'The poet read the poem on the stage'

> (2) ਇਸ   ਕੁੜੀ   ਨੇ   ਮੈਚ   ਜਿੱਤਣਾ   ਹੈ
> **is   kuṛī   *ne*   maᶦc   jittṇā haᶦ**
> SUB Fem Sg Agt   OBJ Mas Sg   Neu
> 'This girl is going to win the match'

(ii) ਨੂੰ **nū̃**

ਨੂੰ **nū̃** 'to' mainly indicates *direction*.

> (3) ਅਸੀਂ ਸ਼ਹਿਰ   ਨੂੰ ਜਾ ਰਹੇ   ਹਾਂ
> **asī̃ śahir nū̃ jā rahe hā̃**
> 'We are going *to* the city'

ਨੂੰ **nū̃** has some other uses as well, as we shall see in a later chapter. But one of them can be mentioned here. It is used to make the OBJECT of a clause **definite**.

(4) ਇਸ ਮੁੰਡੇ ਨੂੰ ਮੈਂ ਪਹਿਲਾਂ ਕਦੇ ਨਹੀਂ ਦੇਖਿਆ
is munḍe *nū̃* mã^i pahilā̃ kade nahī̃ dek^{h}iā
OBJ Def VP Neu
'I have never seen this (particular) boy before'

(iii) ਤੋਂ tõ

ਤੋਂ **tõ** (with ਥੋਂ **t^{h}õ** as a variant) originated as an inflected (**ablative**) form of a noun. (See **8.2.3** below.) But it functions as a single-word uninflected postposition now.

(5) ਕੱਲ੍ਹ ਤੋਂ ਕੰਮ ਸ਼ੁਰੂ ਕਰੋ
kall^h *tõ* kamm śurū karo
'Start the work *from* tomorrow'

(6) ਉਹਨੇ ਮੈਥੋਂ ਪੈਸੇ ਲਏ
uhne ma^i*t^{h}õ* pa^{i}se lae
'He got the money *from* me'

(7) ਉਹਤੋਂ ਪੈਸੇ ਲੈ ਲਓ
uh*tõ* pa^{i}se la^i lao
'Take the money *from* him'

But also see section **8.3** below for more information about ਤੋਂ **tõ** because in some respects it still behaves like the **postposition** of that group.

(iv) ਤਕ tak

ਤਕ **tak** 'up to', 'till', 'until' (with variants ਤੀਕ **tīk**, ਤੀਕਰ **tīkar**, ਤੀਕਣ **tīkaṇ**)

(8) ਮੈਂ ਦਿੱਲੀ ਤਕ ਹੀ ਜਾਣਾ ਹੈ
mã^i dillī *tak* hī jāṇā ha^i
'I am going *up to* Delhi only'

(9) ਉਹ ਕੱਲ੍ਹ ਤਕ ਇੱਥੇ ਰਹੇਗਾ
oh kall^h *tak* itt^{h}e rahegā
'He will stay here *till* tomorrow'

Like ਤੋਂ **tõ**, ਤਕ **tak** also behaves like the postpositions discussed in section **8.3** below.

8.2.2 Single-word inflecting postpositions

The major postpositions of this group are

ਦਾ **dā**, ਵਰਗਾ **vargā**, ਜਿਹਾ **jihā**, ਜਿੱਡਾ **jiḍḍā**, ਜਿੰਨਾ **jinnā** and ਵਾਲ਼ਾ **vāḷā**

(i) ਦਾ dā

ਦਾ **dā** (expressing possession) inflects for **number** and **gender** and has **oblique** forms as well.

(10) ਚਾਹ ਦਾ ਕੱਪ
cāh *dā* kapp
'Cup *of* tea'

ਸਕੂਲ ਦੀਆਂ ਕੁੜੀਆਂ
sakūl *dīā̃* kuṛīā̃
'Girls *of* the school'

ਮੁੰਡੇ ਦੇ ਕਮਰੇ ਵਿਚ
munḍe *de* kamre vic
'In the boy*'s* room'

In this sentence, ਮੁੰਡਾ **munḍā** gets the **oblique** form ਮੁੰਡੇ **munḍe** because of the following **postposition** ਦਾ **dā** and ਕਮਰਾ **kamrā** assumes the **oblique** form ਕਮਰੇ **kamre** because of the **postposition** ਵਿਚ **vic**. But the postposition which would otherwise be ਦਾ **dā** also assumed the oblique form ਦੇ **de** because of the following postposition ਵਿਚ **vic**.

(ii) ਵਰਗਾ vargā

ਵਰਗਾ **vargā** ('similar to', '-like') inflects like ਦਾ **dā**.

(11) ਉਹ ਗਧੇ ਵਰਗਾ ਬੰਦਾ ਹੈ
uh gad^he *vargā* bandā ha^i
SUB COMP(S) PRED
'He is an ass-*like* man'

ਗਧੇ **gad^he** is the oblique form of ਗਧਾ **gad^hā** 'ass' because of the postposition ਵਰਗਾ **vargā**. The pronoun SUBJECT ਉਹ **uh** is not within the scope of ਵਰਗਾ **vargā**.

(12) ਇਹ ਉਸ ਗਧੇ ਵਰਗੇ ਬੰਦੇ ਦਾ ਕੰਮ ਹੈ
ih us gad^{h}e *varge* bande dā kamm ha^{i}
SUB (........................COMP(S)....................) PRED
'This is the work of that ass-*like* man'

The COMPLEMENT of the postposition ਦਾ **dā** is the full **NP** ਉਹ ਗਧੇ ਵਰਗਾ ਬੰਦਾ **uh gad^{h}e vargā bandā**. So ਉਹ **uh**, ਗਧਾ **gad^{h}ā**, ਵਰਗਾ **vargā**, and ਬੰਦਾ **bandā** all assume the **oblique forms**.

(iii) ਜਿੱਡਾ jiḍḍā, ਜਿਹਾ jihā and ਜਿੰਨਾ jinnā

Coming to ਜਿੱਡਾ **jiḍḍā** 'of the size of', ਜਿਹਾ **jihā** 'similar to', '-like' and ਜਿੰਨਾ **jinnā** 'similar in quantity to', they are used as shown in the following examples.

(13) ਅਰਸਤੂ *ਜਿੱਡਾ* ਵਿਦਵਾਨ
arastū *jiḍḍā* vidvān
'a scholar *of* Aristotle's calibre'

ਚੰਨ *ਜਿਹਾ* ਮੁੱਖੜਾ
cann *jihā* mukk^{h}ṛā
'moon-*like* face'
(i.e., very beautiful face)

ਸਰੂਆਂ *ਜਿਹੇ* ਜਵਾਨ
sarūā̃ *jihe* javān
'young men *like* cypress trees'
(i.e., very tall young men)

ਹਾਥੀ *ਜਿੰਨਾ* ਜ਼ੋਰ
hāt^{h}ī *jinnā* zor
'power *equal to* (that of) an elephant'

(iv) ਵਾਲ਼ਾ vaḷā

The behaviour of ਵਾਲ਼ਾ **vāḷā**, which has multiple meanings and uses, is similar to the other postpositions of this group.

(14) ਬੱਚਿਆਂ *ਵਾਲ਼ੀਆਂ* ਔਰਤਾਂ
bacciā̃ vāḷiā̃ a^{u}rtā̃
'women *with* children'

ਪੈਸੇ ਵਾਲ਼ਾ ਬੰਦਾ
pa'se *vāḷā* bandā
'the man *possessing* money'

ਪੈਸੇ ਵਾਲ਼ੇ ਬੰਦੇ ਤੋਂ
pa'se *vāḷe* bande tõ
'from the man *possessing* money'

ਤੋਂ **tõ** gives oblique form not only to ਬੰਦਾ **bandā** but also to ਪੈਸਾ **pa'sā** and ਵਾਲ਼ਾ **vāḷā**.

8.2.3 Postpositions derived from the inflected case-forms of nouns, or postpositions with locative meaning

The postpositions of this group are the most interesting ones. They started as, and basically still continue to be, spatial expressions involving **inflected nouns**. But they are moving towards membership of the group dealt with in **8.2.1** above.

The most commonly used postpositions of this group are

ਅੰਦਰ **andar**, ਬਾਹਰ **bahar**, ਉੱਤੇ **utte**, ਹੇਠ **heṭʰ** (or ਹੇਠਾਂ **heṭʰā̃**), ਵਿਚ **vic**, ਨਾਲ਼ **nāḷ**, ਕੋਲ਼ **koḷ**, ਵਿਚਾਲ਼ੇ **vicāḷe**, ਵਿਚਕਾਰ **vickār** and ਵਲ **val**.

The "body in the mind" adverbs (mentioned in Chapter 7) ਅੱਗੇ **agge** 'in front', ਗੱਭੇ **gabbʰe** 'in the middle' and ਪਿੱਛੇ **piccʰe** 'behind' also belong to this group.

ਤੋਂ **tõ** and ਤਕ **tak** originated in this group but have now moved partly (but not completely) to the group considered in **7.2.1** above.

The basic underlying structure of these postpositions is

X ਦਾ Y
'Y of X'

where Y denotes a location, as (15a).

(i) ਅੰਦਰ andar

(15a) ਕਮਰੇ ਦਾ ਅੰਦਰ
kamre *dā andar*
room *of inside*
'the inside of the room'

The postposition ਦਾ **dā** gives the **oblique** form ਕਮਰੇ **kamre** to ਕਮਰਾ **kamrā** (in 15a). The assumption of the status of a postposition by ਅੰਦਰ **andar** in (15b) and (15c) gives the **oblique** form ਦੇ **de** to ਦਾ **dā**, resulting in the **postpositional phrase (PP)** ਕਮਰੇ ਦੇ ਅੰਦਰ **kamre de andar**, which acts as a **nominal expression.**

(15b) ਕਮਰੇ ਦੇ ਅੰਦਰ
kamre *de andar*
'inside the room'

This is now the **emphatic** form. The more commonly used expression is

(15c) ਕਮਰੇ ਅੰਦਰ
kamre *andar*

The phrases (15b) and (15c) can act as **adverbials of place.**

The **genitive** postposition ਦਾ **dā** is added to nouns and **third person pronouns** only. The **first person** and the **second person** pronouns have inflected forms. (See Chapter 6.) So we will have

(15d) ਮੇਰਾ ਅੰਦਰ
merā *andar*
'my inside'

turn into

(15e) ਮੇਰੇ ਅੰਦਰ
mere *andar*
'inside me'

But the syntactic behaviour of each major postposition in this group has a few unique features as well.

(ii) ਉੱਤੇ utte

ਉੱਤੇ utte is clearly the synthetic **locative singular** form as the **-e** ending shows. But there is no word *ਉੱਤ **utt** or *ਉੱਤਾ **uttā** in modern Panjabi whose **locative** form it is. It survives as the fossilised form of a word which has historically disappeared. This is the case with some other postpositions as well. In its spoken form, it is weakened or shortened to 'ਤੇ **te** (which some writers write with and apostrophe). In postpositions phrases, we find it used in three ways, as in

(16a) ਛੱਤ 'ਤੇ
cʰatt *te*
'on the roof' (normal colloquial speech)

(16b) ਛੱਤ ਉੱਤੇ
cʰatt *utte*
'on the roof' (for emphasis in speech, in formal writing)

(16c) ਛੱਤ ਦੇ ਉੱਤੇ
cʰatt *de utte*
'on the roof' (for extra emphasis in speech and in writing)

ਉੱਤੋਂ uttõ 'from above' is the **ablative form** and it is also used in all the three ways.

(17a) ਛੱਤ 'ਤੋਂ
cʰatt *tõ*
'from (above) the roof'

(17b) ਛੱਤ ਉੱਤੋਂ
cʰatt *uttõ*

(17c) ਛੱਤ ਦੇ ਉੱਤੋਂ
cʰatt *de uttõ*

ਉੱਤੋਂ uttõ is also used as a **co-ordinating conjunction** or **co-ordinator** (meaning 'moreover' or 'additionally') to connect a clause referring to something unpleasant or undesirable, something 'from above'.

(18) ਮੈਂ ਪਹਿਲਾਂ ਹੀ ਬੀਮਾਰ ਸਾਂ; ਉੱਤੋਂ ਮੇਰੇ ਸੱਟ ਲਗ ਗਈ
mãĩ pahilā̃ hī bīmār sā̃; *uttõ* mere saṭṭ lag gaī
'I was already ill; *additionally*, I got injured'

Conjunctions are the subject of Chapter 15.

(iii) ਵਿਚ vic

ਵਿਚ **vic** 'in/inside' has the shortened form 'ਚ **c**. In all other respects, it behaves like ਉੱਤੇ **utte**. It, too, occurs in postpositional phrases like ਕਮਰੇ ਵਿਚ **kamre vic** and ਕਮਰੇ ਦੇ ਵਿਚ **kamre de vic** 'inside the room'. ਵਿਚ **vic** is the **locative** form, and the **ablative** form is ਵਿਚੋਂ **vicõ** ('ਚੋਂ **cõ**) 'from inside'. Some writers spell the emphatic form as ਵਿੱਚ.

(iv) ਨਾਲ਼ nāḷ

ਨਾਲ਼ **nāḷ** 'with' has the shortened form 'ਨਾ **nā,** used almost exclusively in colloquial speech. In other respects, it behaves like ਉੱਤੇ **utte**. The **ablative form** is ਨਾਲ਼ੋਂ **nāḷõ**.

(v) ਕੋਲ਼ koḷ

ਕੋਲ਼ **koḷ** 'near' has the shortened form 'ਕੋ **ko**, used exclusively in colloquial speech. In other respects, it behaves like ਉੱਤੇ **utte**. The **ablative form** is ਕੋਲ਼ੋਂ **koḷõ**. In some areas people say ਕੋਲ਼ **koḷ dī** or ਕੋਲ਼ੋਂ ਦੀ **koḷõ dī** instead of ਕੋਲ਼ੋਂ **koḷõ**. This is the case with almost all other forms ending in **-õ** *when they are used non-metaphorically or refer to physical space.*

(vi) ਵਿਚਕਾਰ vickār

ਵਿਚਕਾਰ **vickār** 'in the middle' and ਵਿਚਾਲ਼ੇ **vicāḷe** 'between' behave like ਉੱਤੇ **utte**. Their **ablative forms** are ਵਿਚਕਾਰੋਂ **vickārõ** and ਵਿਚਾਲ਼ਿਓਂ **vicāḷiõ**. ਵਿਚ **vic** and ਵਿਚਾਲ਼ੇ **vicāḷe**, are sometimes combined into ਵਿਚ ਵਿਚਾਲ਼ੇ **vic vicāḷe**, translatable as 'in between'. The **ablative form** of the combination is ਵਿਚ ਵਿਚਾਲ਼ਿਓਂ **vic vicāḷiõ**.

(vii) ਹੇਠ heṭ^h

ਹੇਠ **heṭ^h** 'under/below' (with the variant ਹੇਠਾਂ **heṭ^{h}ā̃**), ਥੱਲੇ **ṭ^{h}alle** 'under/below', ਸਾਹਮਣੇ **sāhmaṇe** 'facing/in front of', ਵਲ **val** 'towards' and ਗੱਭੇ **gabb^{h}e** 'in the middle' are **locative forms**. They behave like ਉੱਤੇ **utte** and their **ablative forms** are ਹੇਠੋਂ **heṭ^{h}õ**, ਸਾਹਮਣਿਓਂ **sāhmaṇiõ** and ਗੱਭਿਓਂ **gabb^{h}iõ** respectively.

It was mentioned in **8.2.1** above that ਤੋਂ **tõ** and ਤਕ **tak** behave partly as single-word **uninflected** postpositions and partly as the postpositions of this group.

(viii) ਤੋਂ tõ

ਤੋਂ tõ (or its variant **ਥੋਂ t^{h}õ**) can follow both the **nominative** and the **genitive** forms of **pronouns**. But **noun+ ਦੇ de** (the equivalent of the genitive form of a pronoun) cannot be the COMPLEMENT of **ਤੋਂ tõ**. Thus you have

(19) **ਮੈਂਥੋਂ ma^{i}tõ** and **ਮੇਰੇ ਤੋਂ mere tõ** 'from me'
ਤੁਹਾਥੋਂ tuhāt^{h}õ and **ਤੁਹਾਡੇ ਤੋਂ tuhāḍe tõ** 'from you'
ਉਹਤੋਂ uhtõ and **ਉਹਦੇ ਤੋਂ uhde tõ** 'from him/her'

But while **ਮੁੰਡੇ ਤੋਂ munḍe tõ** is possible, ***ਮੁੰਡੇ ਦੇ ਤੋਂ *munḍe de tõ** is not.

(ix) ਤਕ tak

ਤਕ tak 'up to', when used with **pronouns**, occurs only with the **genitive form**. With **nouns**, it occurs only with the **nominative form**. Examples are

(20) **ਮੇਰੇ ਤਕ mere tak** but not ***ਮੈਂ ਤਕ *mã^i tak** 'up to me'
ਤੇਰੇ ਤਕ tere tak but not ***ਤੂੰ ਤਕ *tũ tak** 'up to you'
ਉਹਦੇ ਤਕ uhde tak but not ***ਉਹ ਤਕ *uh tak** 'up to him/her'

But the opposite happens with

(21) **ਉਹਨਾਂ ਤਕ uhnā̃ tak** but not ***ਉਹਨਾਂ ਦੇ ਤਕ *uhnā̃ de tak** 'up to them'

ਅਸਾਂ ਤਕ asā̃ tak 'up to us' and **ਤੁਸਾਂ ਤਕ tusā̃ tak** 'up to you' (plural) occur in some varieties of Panjabi with the older oblique forms of **ਅਸੀਂ asī̃** 'we' and **ਤੁਸੀਂ tusī̃** 'you' (plural).

Such irregularities and anomalies simply show that the language is developing, which is one of the defining features of every living language. Historical linguistic changes take place and spread to different parts of a language slowly. This is happening in Panjabi.

We will use the term **compound postposition** for the construction **postposition+locative expression**. The locative expression may be an inflected **noun** (such as **ਦੇ ਘਰੋਂ de g^{h}arõ** or a **noun** followed by a **postposition** such as **ਦੇ ਘਰ ਤੋਂ de g^{h}ar tõ**).This is similar to the English compound preposition exemplified by *in front of*, *on top of* etc.

(x) ਪਿੱਛੇ picc^he, ਗੱਭੇ gabb^he and ਅੱਗੇ agge

These "body in the mind" adverbs/postpositions, meaning 'behind', 'in the middle' and 'in front of' respectively, behave like ਤਕ **tak**. They can act as single postpositions and also be a part of compound postpositions.

>   (22)   ਘਰ ਪਿੱਛੇ g^har picc^he and ਘਰ ਦੇ ਪਿੱਛੇ g^har de picc^he
>   'behind the house'
>
>   ਬੂਹੇ ਅੱਗੇ būhe agge and ਬੂਹੇ ਦੇ ਅੱਗੇ būhe de agge
>   'in front of the door'

But ਗੱਭੇ **gabb^he** mostly (but not invariably) features in a compound postposition as in ਕਮਰੇ ਦੇ ਗੱਭੇ **kamre de gabb^he** 'in the middle of the room'. They are used with pronouns with some restrictions.

>   ਮੇਰੇ ਪਿੱਛੇ **mere picc^he** but not *ਮੈਂ ਪਿੱਛੇ ***mā̃i picc^he** 'behind me'
>   ਤੇਰੇ ਅੱਗੇ **tere agge** but not *ਤੂੰ ਅੱਗੇ ***tū̃ agge** 'in front of you'

8.3   Postpositions/adverbs with ablative meaning

ਦੂਰ **dūr** 'away from', ਪਰੇ **pare** 'removed from' (with variants ਪਰਾਂ **parā̃** and ਪਰ੍ਹਾਂ **parhā̃**) are the frequently used Panjabi **postpositions** or **adverbs** with **ablative** or 'separated from' as their basic meaning. The basic meaning of the postpositions discussed in **8.2.3** above is **locative**. A comparison with the **locative** postposition ਹੇਠ **heṭ^hā̃** 'under/below' will make this clear. We can have

>   (23a)   ਕਮਰੇ   ਹੇਠਾਂ
>   **kamre *heṭ^hā̃***
>   'below the room'
>
>   ਕਮਰੇ   ਦੇ   ਹੇਠਾਂ
>   **kamre *de heṭ^hā̃***
>   'below the room' (emphatic)

ਹੇਠਾਂ **heṭ^hā̃** basically indicates a *location*. The grammatical **ablative** form ਹੇਠੋਂ **heṭ^hõ** means 'from below the room'. We can have both

>   (23b)   ਕਮਰੇ   ਹੇਠੋਂ
>   **kamre *heṭ^hõ***
>   'from below the room'

ਕਮਰੇ ਦੇ ਹੇਠੋਂ
kamre *de heṭʰõ*
'from below the room' (emphatic)

ਦੂਰ **dūr** 'away from' and ਪਰੇ **pare** 'removed from' behave differently. Constructions like (24a) are not possible.

(24a) *ਕਮਰੇ ਦੂਰ
***kamre dūr**
'away from the room'

*ਕਮਰੇ ਦੇ ਦੂਰ
***kamre de dūr**
'below the room'

Rather we have

(24b) ਕਮਰੇ ਤੋਂ ਦੂਰ
kamre *tõ dūr*
'away from the room'

or

ਕਮਰਿਓਂ ਦੂਰ
kamriõ *dūr*

Also

ਕਮਰੇ ਤੋਂ ਦੂਰੋਂ
kamre *tõ dūrõ*
'from a distance away from the room'

is grammatical. So is

(?) ਕਮਰਿਓਂ ਦੂਰੋਂ
(?) kamriõ dūrõ
'from a distance away from the room'

but it is highly unlikely you will come across this.

ਪਰਾਂ **parã̄** 'away' with the grammatical **ablative** form ਪਰਿਓਂ **pariõ** behaves like ਦੂਰ **dūr**.

ਬਾਹਰ **bāhar** 'outside' behaves both like ਹੇਠਾਂ **heṭʰã̄** and ਦੂਰ **dūr**. We can have both ਘਰ ਦੇ ਬਾਹਰ **g^{h}ar de bāhar** and ਘਰ ਤੋਂ ਬਾਹਰ **g^{h}ar tõ bāhar** (or ਘਰੋਂ ਬਾਹਰ **g^{h}arõ bāhar**), both translatable as 'outside the house'. But the construction with ਦੇ **de** focuses on *location* and the one with ਤੋਂ **tõ** focuses on *separation* from the house. This is the case with ਘਰ ਦੇ ਬਾਹਰੋਂ **g^{h}ar de bāhrõ** and ਘਰ ਤੋਂ ਬਾਹਰੋਂ **g^{h}ar tõ bāhrõ** as well, though both translate as 'from outside the house'.

ਪਿੱਛੇ **picc^{h}e** 'behind', ਗੱਭੇ **gabb^{h}e** 'in the middle' and ਅੱਗੇ **agge** 'in front of' also have **ablative forms**.

(25) ਘਰ ਦੇ ਪਿੱਛਿਓਂ **g^{h}ar de picc^{h}iõ**
'from behind the house'

ਮੈਦਾਨ ਦੇ ਗੱਭਿਓਂ **ma^{i}dān de gabb^{h}iõ**
'from the centre of the playground'

ਮੇਰੇ ਅੱਗਿਓਂ **mere aggiõ** 'from my front'
ਅੱਗੋਂ **aggõ** is an alternative form of ਅੱਗਿਓਂ **aggiõ**.

8.4 Metaphorical use of postpositions

ਕੋਲ਼ **koḷ** 'near' is used to express the meaning of **transferable** or alienable possession, as in

(26) ਮੇਰੇ ਕੋਲ਼ ਤਿੰਨ ਕਾਰਾਂ ਹਨ
mere *koḷ* tinn kārā̃ han
'I have three cars'
(*Lit.* 'Three cars are near me')

and

(27) ਇਸ ਬੰਦੇ ਕੋਲ਼ ਬਹੁਤ ਪੈਸਾ ਹੈ
is bande *koḷ* bahut pa^{i}sā ha^i
'This man has a lot of money'
(*Lit.* 'A lot of money is near this man')

Cars and money are transferable possessions expressed *metaphorically* by using ਕੋਲ਼ **koḷ**. These possessions can be transferred to others. So a construction involving the use of *have* in this sense in translated into Panjabi by using this postposition. But there are non-transferable possessions such as *I have three brothers*. They are expressed in Panjabi as

(28) ਮੇਰੇ ਤਿੰਨ ਭਰਾ ਹਨ
mere tinn b^harā han
'I have three brothers'
(*Lit.* 'My three brothers are')

ਤੋਂ **tõ** 'from', ਨਾਲ਼ੋਂ **nāḷõ** 'from closeness' and ਕੋਲ਼ੋਂ **koḷõ** 'from closeness' are used (like the English *than* and *of*) to express comparison. Examples are

(29) ਮੇਰਾ ਪੁੱਤਰ ਮੈਥੋਂ ਵੱਧ ਲੰਮਾ ਹੈ
merā puttar ma^i*t^hõ* vadd^h lamma ha^i
'My son is taller than me'
(*Lit.* 'My son is more tall from me')

(30) ਇਹ ਭਲਵਾਨ ਹੋਰ ਸਭਨਾਂ ਨਾਲ਼ੋਂ ਵੱਧ ਤਕੜਾ ਹੈ
ih b^halvān hor sab^{h}nā̃ nāḷõ vadd^h takṛā ha^i
'This wrestler is stronger than all the rest'
(*Lit.* 'This wrestler is more strong from all the rest')

We saw in Chapter 6 that the **ablative synthetic form** of a **noun** (from which the **ablative postpositions** developed) is also used for this purpose, as by the 17th century poet Sultan Bahu (1621–1691).

(31) ਦਿਲ ਦਰਿਆ *ਸਮੁੰਦਰੋਂ* ਡੂੰਘੇ
dil dariā samundarõ ḍū̃g^{h}e
'Rivers of hearts (are) deeper than the ocean'

This metaphorical use of the **ablative form** for comparison is quite understandable. The entities to be compared are first brought together in imagination because they share a certain trait X and then separated on the basis of their being difference in respect of one of them being "more X" than the other.

The originally **spatial adverb/postposition** ਪਿੱਛਿਓਂ **picc^{h}iõ** or ਪਿੱਛੋਂ **picc^{h}õ** 'from behind' is frequently used as a temporal adverb/postposition as well.

(32) ਪ੍ਰੋਗਰਾਮ ਮੇਰੇ ਜਾਣ *ਪਿੱਛੋਂ* ਖ਼ਤਮ ਹੋਇਆ
progrām mere jāṇ *picc^{h}õ* xatam hoiā
'The program ended after my departure'

ਅੱਗੋਂ **aggõ** is often used to introduce a clause or sentence to express something unexpecxted.

(33) **ਅਸੀਂ ਘਰੋਂ ਨਿਕਲ਼ੇ ਹੀ ਸਾਂ ਕਿ *ਅੱਗੋਂ* ਮੀਂਹ ਸ਼ੁਰੂ ਹੋ ਗਿਆ**
asī̃ g^{h}arõ nikḷe hī sā̃ ki *aggõ* mī̃h śurū ho giā
'We had just come out of the house when the rain started'

8.5 Chained postpositional phrases

The structure of a postpositional phrase in Panjabi, despite the complications mentioned above, is quite simple.

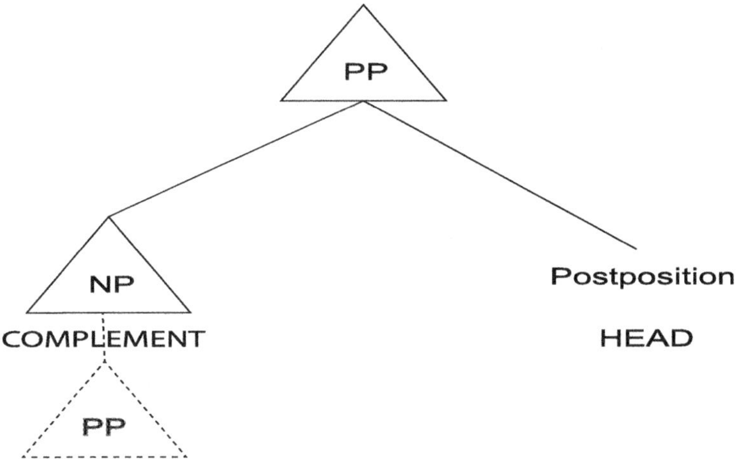

Figure 8.1 Possible detailed structure of a postpositional phrase in Panjabi

The only complication that may arise is that the **NP** *inside* a **PP** phrase may be followed by (or be a COMPLEMENT to) another PP, thus **embedding** a PP (shown by the "ghostly" triangle in the diagram above) within a PP. This is known as **recursion**, which may be repeated several times, thus leading to **chained postpositional phrases** similar to the ones in English

The colour of the uniform of the children in the nursery class of this school

Its Panjabi translation is

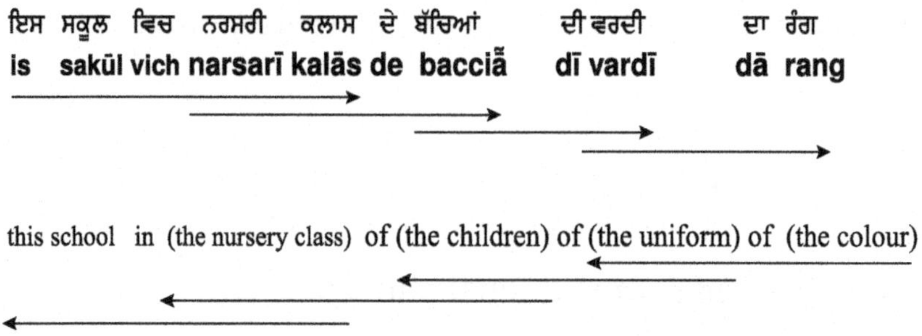

Figure 8.2 Panjabi chained postpositional phrases and English chained prepositional phrases

The reading of this mirror image translation "from the other end" is quite interesting. The only difference is that Panjabi uses no definite article here and its postposition ਦਾ **dā** is inflected for **number** and **gender** and has **oblique** form.

Summing up and looking ahead

With this chapter we conclude our discussion of the structure and functions of the **noun phrase** and its constituents. In spite of some significant differences (especially the ones discussed in this chapter) Panjabi appears as sharing a great many family resemblances with English. But the following chapters dealing with the Panjabi **verb phrase** and its constituents often prove a real challenge to the non-Indian (especially European) learners of Indian languages. So you are advised to proceed slowly and cautiously and try to understand what the Indian concept of time is. You are advised to read Chapter 2 (or read it once again if you have already done this).

Consideration of how a language (as a part of a culture) conceptualises and symbolises the spatio-temporal aspect of the reality is of paramount importance for a grammarian of a language, as Indian linguists like Bhartṛhari said centuries ago and as Western linguists realised (with a few rare exceptions like Sapir and Whorf) only in the last two decades of the last century. Chapters 7 and 8 show that it is impossible to overestimate the importance of such considerations.

For teachers and other more advanced users

8.6 More about the metaphorical use of postpositions

The Western tradition in linguistics, following Aristotle, has traditionally regarded metaphor as a "figure of speech", or *deviation* from normal usage, in which a word or expression normally used for one kind of object or action, etc. is extended to another. It was dealt with not in the discipline of grammar but in rhetoric.

But many modern linguists think differently and study metaphor as a legitimate part of linguistics. For example, the the word *waste* is normally used in connection with *wasting money*. So in the expression *wasting time*, the domain of time is viewed and spoken of in terms of the domain of money. This matching of domains is often systematic, making possible expressions like *saving time*, *utilising time* etc. The domain of war is the source of expressions like *attacking someone's argument* or *defending one's intellectual position* etc.

> A metaphor involves a relationship between a **source domain**, the source literal meaning of the metaphorical expression, and a **target domain**, the domain of experience actually being described by the metaphor. For example, to *waste time* involves comparing TIME (the target domain) to MONEY (the source domain) in the metaphor represented by the Lakoffian formula TIME IS MONEY (Lakoff and Johnson 1980).
>
> (Croft and Cruse 2004: 55)

While Indian linguists have recognised for centuries that grammar is thoroughly metaphorical, it was Lakoff and Johnson's epoch-making book *Metaphors We Live By* (1980) that first accorded a respectable place to metaphor in Western linguistics. Lakoff and Johnson proved that metaphor is not a mere "figure of speech" or "deviation from ordinary language use" but an integral part of everyday language use.

Using SMALL CAPITALS (e.g., TIME IS MONEY, ARGUMENT IS WAR) to write the underlying metaphoric formula is now a standard practice.

As the examples given by Lakoff and Johnson clearly show, metaphor is something extremely common in everyday speech. Interestingly, the word *metaphor* itself is originally a metaphor! The Greek word *metapherein* it comes from means 'to transfer', and this is exactly what a metaphor does – *transfer* the meaning of one semantic domain into another, generally from the more familiar or the more concrete into the less familiar or the more abstract.

Even a large number of grammatical constructions originated as, and can be usefully analysed as, metaphors.

The use of the **spatial postposition ਕੋਲ koḷ** 'near' as the **source domain** to convey the meaning of transferable possession as the **target domain** involves the metaphor TRANSFERABLE POSSESSION IS SPATIAL PROXIMITY. The cross-linguistic use of this spatial metaphor to convey the meaning of possession has been recognised by linguists for quite some time (Allen 1964, Lyons 1967).

Similarly, the use of the spatial postpositions **ਤੋਂ tõ** 'from', **ਨਾਲੋਂ nāḷõ** *'from closeness'* and **ਕੋਲੋਂ koḷõ** *'from closeness'* to make comparison, involves the metaphor COMPARISON IS SEPARATION. Comparison involves first bringing two or more entities together to make the comparison possible and then separating them to make the comparison. This is how Bhartṛhari explained the use of the Sanskrit **ablative** case form to make comparison. In the chapters dealing with the Panjabi verb, we will come across many spatial metaphors involved in the use of *spatial* **auxiliary verbs** like **ਜਾ jā** 'go' and the use of **postpositions** like **ਨੂੰ nū̃** 'to' and **ਤੋਂ tõ** 'from' to mark the participants in the events. The family of metaphors called Location ESM (*Location Event Structure Metaphor*) by Dancygier and Sweetser (2014: 45) is involved. This metaphor is discussed in Chapter 12.

Chapter 9

Verb and Verb Phrase

Preview of the chapter

Chapters 9-13 are the hub of this book because they deal with the **verb phrase** (**VP**), which is the hub of a clause in Panjabi grammar. These chapters will also demonstrate why our *usage-based* methodology of dealing with *form-meaning pairings* and their *meaning potential* is the only sensible way of dealing with the complexity found in Panjabi (and in other North Indian languages, which are very similar to Panjabi in grammatical structure). Great views and insights of the Indian linguists who practised this type of linguistics centuries before some modern Western linguists adopted them in the last two decades of the 20th century are made use of throughout this book.

The morphology of Panjabi verbs is considerably more complicated than that of verbs in English. This means that these morphological forms can express a richer variety of meanings in the constructions they are used in.

9.1 The meaning potential of a verb in the traditional Indian linguistic tradition

According to Bhartṛhari, mentioned several times earlier in the book, a sentence conveys four types of meaning – *kriyā* 'action/event', *kāraka* 'means/accessories' (literally 'do-ers'), *kāla* 'time' and *dik* 'direction'. His views and the technical terms of grammar he uses are fully elaborated, explained and exemplified in this and the later chapters. As already mentioned, he lived in the 5th–6th century when the Later Middle Indic languages were spoken in North India and many grammatical features which characterise modern North Indian languages (including his mother tongue) had appeared. (There is some controversy regarding which part of India he belonged to.) So his ideas are extremely useful for our purpose. Many grammatical structures and semantic features of Panjabi which the Euro-centred linguistic frameworks cannot handle (or handle clumsily at best in spite of the "universalistic" claims of their makers) can be easily explained using Bhartṛhari's ideas.

This chapter (dealing with the **inner inflections** of a verb) shows how each **phase** of a verb indicates the action/event (*kriyā*) as well as the **semantic valency** (*kārka*) or the **nominal accessories** (or **case roles**) involved in the action/event. The meaning expressed by a verb is traditionally regarded as "a particular mode of behaviour on the part of the accessories" (*kārakāṇām pravṛttiviśeṣaḥ*) in the ancient Indian grammatical tradition. The **inner inflections** are closer to the meaning of the roots than the middle and the external inflections. Chapters 10 and 11 will deal with the *kāla* ('time') aspect of the meaning of the verb, and later chapters will show why Bhartṛhari insightfully used the term *dik* ('direction') and not one of the many Sanskrit words for 'space'.

9.2 Verb phrase and main verbs in Panjabi

To avoid any confusion, it should be clarified at the very beginning that the term **verb phrase** or **VP** is *not* used here in the sense it is used in many text books on syntactic theory, i.e., what remains of a clause when the subject **NP** is taken out (or the traditional "predicate" part of the clause without the SUBJECT). In this sense, a **VP** includes most of the clause COMPLEMENTS and ADJUNCTS as well. *As used in this book*, a **verb phrase (VP)** is a phrase containing a **main verb** which may be accompanied by **auxiliary verb(s)** and **particles** and the **negative particle**.

This chapter deals with the **main verb** class. The motley group of different types of **auxiliary verbs** are dealt with in Chapter 10. The unqualified term **verb** used in this chapter means a **main verb**.

1. *Notionally* or *semantically*, verbs are a large class of words which indicate actions, events, processes and states of affairs.

2. *Formally*, the Panjabi verbs undergo the three layers of grammatical inflections dealt with in section **9.3** below.

3. *Functionally*, a verb plays the syntactic role of a PREDICATOR in the clause. (See Chapter 5.)

9.3 Three layers of inflection on verb stems

We differentiate between a **verb root** and a **verb stem** in this book. A verb **root** is an *abstract* theoretical entity posited to explain the structure of the verb forms (known as **stems**) actually used in speech and writing. Various types of grammatical inflections are applied to the root to make workable stems. In Panjabi, the posited abstract root has the same form as the simplest stem (though the situation is considerably more complicated in languages like Sanskrit and Arabic). The following examples should make this clear.

(1)

ਮੁੰਡਾ	ਸੰਗੀਤ	ਸਿੱਖਦਾ	ਹੈ
muṇḍā	**sangīt**	***sikk^{h}dā***	**ha^i**
ImmAgt	Pnt	Verb	
SUBJ	OBJ	PRED	

'The boy is learning music'

(2)

ਉਸਤਾਦ	ਮੁੰਡੇ ਨੂੰ	ਸੰਗੀਤ	ਸਿਖਾਉਂਦਾ	ਹੈ
ustād	**muṇḍe nū̃**	**sangīt**	***sik^{h}āũdā***	**ha^i**
IniAgt	ImmAgt	Pnt	V-cau	
SUBJ	ADJCT	OBJ	PRED	

'The teacher is teaching music to the boy'

(3)

ਮੈਂ	ਉਸਤਾਦ ਤੋਂ	ਮੁੰਡੇ	ਨੂੰ	ਸੰਗੀਤ
mā̃^{i}	**utstād tõ**	**muṇḍe**	**nū̃**	**sangīt**
IniAgt	IntAgt	ImmAgt		Pnt
SUBJ	ADJCT	ADJCT		OBJ

ਸਿਖਵਾਉਂਦਾ	ਹਾਂ
sik^{h}vāũdā	**hā̃**
Vcau	
PRED	

'I get the teacher to teach music to the boy'
'I get music taught to the boy by the teacher'

A **zero suffix** is added to the **transitive root ਸਿੱਖ sikk^h** to make a homophonous stem. We regard it as an **inner inflection** indicating the **semantic valency** of the stem or the **nominal entities** involved in the action denoted by the **verb**. In the case of the basic **transitive phase ਸਿੱਖ sikk^h**, the two **nominal entities** in its **semantic valency set** are the **agent ਮੁੰਡਾ muṇḍā** 'boy' and the **patient ਸੰਗੀਤ sangīt** (music). The next layer is that of the **middle inflection**. The affix -ਦ- **-d-** indicates **imperfective aspect**, or the action ongoing in time. (See Chapter 11.) Then there is the **outer inflection**, the **masculine singular affix** -ਆ **-ā**, showing the **agreement** of the verb with the **agent** SUBJECT. In (2) the suffix of the inner inflection added to the root is -ਆ- **-ā-**. This creates a **causative stem ਸਿਖਾ sik^{h}ā**. The nominal entities involved in the action are the **initiator agent** SUBJECT **ਉਸਤਾਦ utstād** 'teacher', the **immediate agent (recipient) ਮੁੰਡਾ muṇḍā** 'boy' and the **patient** OBJECT **ਸੰਗੀਤ sangīt** 'music'. The **second causative** stem in (3) is derived by the addition of the causative suffix -ਵਾ- **-ā-** to the root. Now the semantic nominal entities are the **initiator agent** SUBJECT **ਮੈਂ mã^i** ('I'), the **intermediate agent ਉਸਤਾਦ utstād** and the **immediate agent (recipient) ਮੁੰਡਾ muṇḍā** and the **patient** OBJECT **ਸੰਗੀਤ sangīt**. The **middle inflections** (showing **aspect**) and the **outer inflections** (showing **agreement**) are the same in (1), (2) and (3).

What is significant in these examples is that *not every entity in the* ***semantic valency set*** *(or the meaning structure) of a clause is* ***syntactically*** *obligatory or is* ***licensed*** *(or "expected") by the* PREDICATOR *or is a* COMPLEMENT *of the* PREDICATOR. *Syntactically*, non-obligatory entities marked with **postpositions** in (2) and (3) are optional ADJUNCTS. The clauses will be perfectly *grammatical* without them, though the meaning conveyed will be different. Without the **immediate agent (recipient)** (boy), (2) could be said about the teacher's profession, and without the **intermediate agent** (the teacher) and the **immediate agent (recipient)** (boy), (3) could mean that the **initiator agent** is running a music school in which he himself does not do any teaching.

The **causative** suffix -ਆ- **-ā-** and -ਵਾ- **-ā-** in such **stems** is always **stressed**. So the first syllable becomes weaker and **ਸਿੱਖ sikk^h** becomes ਸਿਖ- **sik^h-**. The insertion of the nasalised **ũ** in **sik^{h}āũdā** ਸਿਖਾਉਂਦਾ and **sik^{h}vāũdā** ਸਿਖਵਾਉਂਦਾ is dealt with in Chapter 11. In this book, the morphological form obtained by the addition of **inner inflectional suffix** (which may be a **zero suffix**) is called the **phase** of the verb. The form resulting from the addition of the middle and the outer suffix is called the **form** of a verb. This terminological distinction is made to avoid confusion because the situation is more complicated than in English grammar.

ਸਿੱਖ **sikk^h** is a **transitive root**. But there are also **intransitive roots** in Panjabi. The **suffixes** -ਆ- **-ā-** and -ਵਾ- **-vā-** are also added to such **roots**. But the first **additive** stem of an **intransitive** root should be described as **transitive**, and not as **causative**. An additional complication arises from the fact that with some roots the older versions with internal vowel change or some other phonetic change and not involving the addition of -ਆ- **-ā-** and -ਵਾ- **-vā-** have survived. An example is the root ਮਰ **mar** 'to die'. Its second or **transitive phase** is ਮਾਰ **mār**, and the third or **causative phase** is both ਮਰਾ **marā**, and ਮਰਵਾ **marvā**, which are often used interchangeably. But ਮਰਵਾ **marvā** is more common. A subtle difference in meaning is that the **initiating (causing) agent** is more involved in the action denoted by ਮਰਾ **marā**. Examples are

(4)	ਉਹ	ਕੱਲ੍ਹ	ਮਰਿਆ
	uh	**kallh**	**mariā**
	ImAgt		Verb
	SUBJ		PRED

'He died yesterday'

(5)	ਉਹਨੇ	ਸ਼ੇਰ	ਮਾਰਿਆ
	uhne	**śer**	**māriā**
	ImAgt	Pnt	Verb
	SUBJ	OBJ	PRED

'He killed a tiger'

(6a)	ਉਹਨੇ	ਸ਼ਿਕਾਰੀ ਤੋਂ	ਸ਼ੇਰ	ਮਰਾਇਆ
	uhne	**śikārī tõ**	**śer**	**marāiā**
	CausAgt	ImAgt	Pnt	CausV
	SUBJ	ADJCT	OBJ	PRED

'He made a hunter kill a tiger'
'He got a tiger killed by a hunter'

(6b) ਉਹਨੇ ਸ਼ਿਕਾਰੀ ਤੋਂ ਸ਼ੇਰ ਮਰਵਾਇਆ
uhne śikārī tõ śer marvāiā
CausAgt ImAgt Pnt CausV
SUBJ ADJCT OBJ PRED
'He made a hunter kill a tiger'
'He got a tiger killed by a hunter'

The use of ਮਰਾਇਆ **marāiā** in (6a) gives the impression that the **initiating (causing) agent** was there personally directing the operation of the immediate agent ਸ਼ਿਕਾਰੀ **śikārī** 'hunter'. This meaning is not conveyed by (6b). The **immediate agent** is not *syntactically* obligatory in (6a) and (6b).

The stems dealt with so far are **additive phases**, involving the *addition* of agents. *Semantically*, a **causing agent** gets the action performed by an **immediate agent**. But *syntactically*, the **immediate agent** is not an ARGUMENT or COMPLEMENT of the PREDICATOR. It is simply a syntactically non-obligatory ADJUNCT.

This, however, is not the whole story. There are **subtractive phases** as well, involving the *elimination* of any definite **agent** or the **causing agent**. **Elimination** is different from **backgrounding**. The *eliminated* agent *must not* be mentioned, unless it is ਅਸੀਂ **asī̃** 'we'. (See below.) The **backgrounded agent**, on the other hand, can be mentioned as an ADJUNCT postpositional phrase as in (6a and 6b) above. The meaning resulting from the elimination of the immediate agent is some sort of advice or principle applicable outside the situation as well. Or the agent is ਅਸੀਂ **asī̃** 'we' and the clause conveys a boastful meaning. Morphologically, the **subtractive phase** is derived by adding -ਈ- **-ī-** to the corresponding **basic phase** or **additive phase**. For example, the phases of ਸਿੱਖ **sikk^{h}** on the **additive** side are ਸਿਖਾ **sik^{h}ā** and ਸਿਖਵਾ **sik^{h}vā**. The corresponding subtractive phases are ਸਿੱਖੀ **sikk^{h}ī**, ਸਿਖਾਈ **sik^{h}āī** and ਸਿਖਵਾਈ **sik^{h}vāī**, with stress on **-ā-** and **-vā-** . Examples are

(7) ਗੰਦੀ ਭਾਸ਼ਾ ਨਹੀਂ ਸਿੱਖੀਦੀ
gandī b^{h}āśā nahī̃ sikk^{h}īdī
Verb SubPh
SUBJ PRED
'Foul language should not be learnt'

(8) ਬੱਚਿਆਂ ਨੂੰ ਗੰਦੀ ਭਾਸ਼ਾ ਨਹੀਂ ਸਿਖਾਈਦੀ
bacciā̃ nū̃ gandī b^{h}āśā nahī̃ sik^{h}āīdī
Rcpt Pnt Verb SubPh
SUBJ PRED
'Foul language should not be taught to children'

(9) ਬੱਚਿਆਂ ਨੂੰ ਗੰਦੀ ਭਾਸ਼ਾ ਨਹੀਂ ਸਿਖਵਾਈਦੀ
bacciā̃ nū̃ gandī b^{h}āśā nahī̃ sik^{h}vāīdī
Rcpt Pnt Verb SubPh
SUBJ PRED
'Foul language should not be got taught to children'

No particular or definite agent or causing agent is there in the meaning of the expressions. In such a clause with a *boastful* meaning, the **agent** is always ਅਸੀਂ **asī̃** 'we' but it is the **patient** that becomes the SUBJECT of the clause.

(10) ਅਸੀਂ ਖ਼ੂਬ ਮਸਤੀ ਕਰੀਦੀ ਸੀ
asī̃ xūb mastī karīdī sī
ImAgt Pnt Verb
SUBJ PRED
we lot of fun "used to do"
'We used to indulge in a lot of fun'

Now the interesting question is what should be the SUBJECT of the clause when the **agent** of an **intransitive** verb (the only nominal entity in the **semantic valency** set) of ਹੱਸ **hass** 'laugh', for example, is eliminated in this way.

(11) ਬਹੁਤਾ ਹੱਸੀਦਾ ਨਹੀਂ
bahutā hassīdā nahī̃
Verb
SUBJ/PRED
too much laughing not
'One should not laugh too much'

The best we can say is that the action denoted by the verb is both the SUBJECT and the PREDICATOR of the clause.

Constructions involving ਚਾਹੀਦਾ **cāhīdā** (of the root ਚਾਹ **cāh** 'desire') and its variants are an exception. They are dealt with in Chapter 12.

This -ਈ- **-ī-** affix almost certainly comes from the Sanskrit **passive affix** *-ī* - or *-īya-*, and the meaning of the **subtractive phase** of a verb does have some features of **passive voice**. But Panjabi has some other constructions as well which have some "passive" features. We shall examine them in later chapters to see what family resemblances all these "passive" constructions have. We do not regard them as different and partial manifestations of an "abstract" category called "passive voice".

A special feature of the **subtractive phases** is that they can have only the **imperfect participle** form dealt with in detail in Chapter 11. The **basic phase** and the **additive phases** can have any of the verb forms.

A proper understanding of the different **phases** of Panjabi (full) verbs and their **semantic valency** and **syntactic valency** (discussed in later chapters) is extremely important for an understanding of the working of **serial verb constructions (SVC)** in Panjabi, which Panjabi scholars have completely neglected or misanalysed.

It has been argued (Bybee 1985) that the closer an **inflectional suffix** is to the **root**, the more closely it is related to the meaning of the root. This certainly seems true of Panjabi. **Semantic valency** or the nominal entities involved are more significant than the temporal constituency of the situation, which is more significant than **transitivity** indicated by the **agreement** of the verb in **number** *and* **person** or in **number** *and* **gender** with one of the nominal entities or the lack of any such agreement. All these things are discussed in later chapters.

9.4 Classification of main verbs in Panjabi

Verbs in Panjabi can be divided into two broad classes, which we call **Class 1** and **Class 2**. The **Class 1** verbs far outnumber the ones in **Class 2**. Since the days predating Sanskrit, two types of verbs have existed in Indian languages, called *parasmaipada* and *ātmanepada* verbs by Sanskrit grammarians. Basically, the *parasmaipada* verbs are believed to indicate an action done by the agent *for others as well* and the *ātmanepada* verbs indicate an action done *solely for oneself*. But the real difference between the two classes is formal, the **inflectional suffixes** they take. This semantic distinction between the Panjabi **Class 1** (*parasmaipada*) verbs and the **Class 2** (*ātmanepada*) is maintained. It is not immediately apparent in the inflectional suffixes these verbs take, but it comes out clearly, as we shall see, in the choice of **postpositions** in the **causative constructions**. An example can be given here.

There are some verbs like ਖਾ **kʰā** 'eat' ਪੀ **pī** 'drink', ਸਿੱਖ **sikkʰ** 'learn', ਸੁਣ **suṇ** 'hear' etc. whose "benefit" can come only to the agent of the action. The agent can "take" this "benefit" but cannot "give" it to anyone else. So the **explicator auxiliary** ਦੇ **de** 'give' cannot be used with such verbs. The use of the explicator auxiliary ਲੈ **laⁱ** 'take' is fine. We can say

(12) ਚਾਹ ਪੀ ਲੈ
cāh pī laⁱ
tea drink 'take'
'Drink tea (for your benefit)'

But

*ਚਾਹ ਪੀ ਦੇ
***cāh pī de**
tea drink 'give'

does not make any sense.

So these verbs belong to Class 2 (*ātmanepada*). There are some verbs like ਪੜ੍ਹ **paṛʰ** 'read' which belong to *both* the classes. You can read for your own information or you can read aloud for others. The importance of this division of Panjabi verbs into these classes will become clear in the following chapters.

9.5 Further classification of class 1 verbs

Morphologically (and sometimes with associated meaning differences), Panjabi **Class 1** verbs can be divided into the following three groups. Only the **additive phases** of some verbs representing each group will be given here. As we have seen above, you only need to add the -ਈ- **-ī-** affix to the additive phase to derive the corresponding **subtractive phase**. Additive phases of some more verbs are given in Chapter 17.

Group 1

Phase 1 is **intransitive**. **Phase 2** (**transitive**) is derived by adding stressed -ਆ **-ā-**, and **Phase 3** (**causative**) is derived by adding -ਵਾ **-vā-**.

Phase 1	Phase 2	Phase 3
ਉੜ **uṛ** ‘fly’	ਉੜਾ **uṛā**	ਉੜਵਾ **uṛvā**
ਹਟ **haṭ** ‘move aside’	ਹਟਾ **haṭā**	ਹਟਵਾ **haṭvā**
ਚਲ **cal** ‘move’	ਚਲਾ **calā**	ਚਲਵਾ **calvā**
ਚੜ੍ਹ **caṛh** ‘rise’	ਚੜ੍ਹਾ **caṛhā**	ਚੜ੍ਹਵਾ **caṛhvā**
ਜਗ **jag** ‘light up’	ਜਗਾ **jagā**	ਜਗਵਾ **jagvā**
ਜਾਗ **jāg** ‘wake up’	ਜਗਾ **jagā**	ਜਗਵਾ **jagvā**
ਦੁਖ **duk^h** ‘ache’	ਦੁਖਾ **duk^{h}ā**	ਦੁਖਵਾ **duk^{h}vā**
ਭੱਜ **b^{h}ajj** ‘run’	ਭਜਾ **b^{h}ajā**	ਭਜਵਾ **b^{h}ajvā**

Some interesting points are worth noting. **Phase 2** and **Phase 3** of ਜਗ **jag** and ਜਾਗ **jāg** have the same pronunciation and spelling. Since the affixes **-ā** and **-vā** are stressed, the vowel **/ā/** of **/jāg/** is weakened to **/a/** in **Phase 2** and **Phase 3**. Reasons for this have already been discussed in Chapter 4 and need not be repeated here.

Group 2a

Phase 1 is **intransitive**. **Phase 2** is not derived by adding a **suffix**. An older form with internal vowel change or some other phonetic change has survived in modern Panjabi. **Phase 3** has two forms, one derived by adding **-ā** and other by adding **-vā**. They are often used interchangeably but sometimes differ subtly in meaning. See (6a) and (6b) above.

Phase 1	Phase 2	Phase 3
ਬਦਲ **badal** ‘change’	ਬਦਲ **badal**	ਬਦਲਾ **badlā** / ਬਦਲਵਾ **badalvā**
ਤੁਰ **tur** ‘walk’	ਤੋਰ **tor**	ਤੁਰਾ **turā** / ਤੁਰਵਾ **turvā**
ਝੜ **j^{h}aṛ** ‘drop down’	ਝਾੜ **j^{h}āṛ**	ਝੜਾ **j^{h}aṛā** / ਝੜਵਾ **j^{h}aṛvā**
ਮਰ **mar** ‘die’	ਮਾਰ **mār**	ਮਰਾ **marā** / ਮਰਵਾ **marvā**
ਰਹਿ **rahi** ‘stay’	ਰੱਖ **rakk^h**	ਰਖਾ **rak^{h}ā** / ਰਖਵਾ **rak^{h}vā**

ਡਿਗ **ḍig** 'fall down	ਡੇਗ **ḍeg**	ਡਿਗਾ **ḍigā** / ਡਿਗਵਾ **ḍigvā**
ਟੁੱਟ **ṭuṭṭ** 'break by itself'	ਤੋੜ **toṛ**	ਤੁੜਾ **tuṛā** / ਤੁੜਵਾ **tuṛvā**
ਭੱਜ **b^{h}ajj** 'break by itself'	ਭੰਨ **b^{h}ann**	ਭਨਾ **b^{h}anā** / ਭਨਵਾ **b^{h}anvā**
ਜੁੜ **juṛ** 'walk'	ਜੋੜ **joṛ**	ਜੁੜਾ **juṛā** / ਜੁੜਵਾ **jurṛvā** /

It would be interesting to compare the phases of ਭੱਜ **b^{h}ajj** 'break by itself' in this group with those of ਭੱਜ **b^{h}ajj** 'run' in **Group 1**. Another interesting thing to note is that ਚੜ੍ਹਾ **caṛhā** and ਝੜਾ **j^{h}aṛā** differ in spelling and meaning but have the same pronunciation [cɐɽà] with **low tone**. This is the case with ਚੜ੍ਹਵਾ **caṛhā** and ਝੜਵਾ **j^{h}aṛvā** [cɐɽvà] also. This has already been discussed in detail in Chapter 4 and need not be repeated here.

Group 2b

The roots are **transitive. Phase 2** has two forms, one derived by adding **stressed -ā** and other by adding **stressed -vā**. The meaning is causative and the forms are often used interchangeably but sometimes differ subtly in meaning. See (6) above.

Phase 1	**Phase 2**
ਚੀਰ **cīr** 'tear apart'	ਚਿਰਾ **cirā** / ਚਿਰਵਾ **cirvā**
ਢਕ **ḍ^{h}ak** 'cover'	ਢਕਾ **ḍ^{h}akā** / ਢਕਵਾ **ḍ^{h}akvā**
ਪੀਹ **pīh** 'grind'	ਪਿਹਾ **pihā** / ਪਿਸਵਾ **pisvā** ਪਿਸਾ **pisā**
ਚੁੱਕ **cukk** 'lift'	ਚੁਕਾ **cukā** / ਚੁਕਵਾ **cukvā**
ਕੱਟ **kaṭṭ** 'cut'	ਕਟਾ **kaṭā** / ਕਟਵਾ **kaṭvā**
ਠੋਕ **ṭ^{h}ok** 'hammer in'	ਠੁਕਾ **ṭ^{h}ukā** / ਠੁਕਵਾ **ṭ^{h}ukvā**
ਕਰ **kar** 'do'	ਕਰਾ **karā** / ਕਰਵਾ **karvā**
ਚੁੱਕ **cukk** 'lift'	ਚੁਕਾ **cukā** / ਚੁਕਵਾ **cukvā**

When **Phase 2** of these verbs has both the **-ā** and **-vā** forms, there is often a subtle difference in their meanings. There is a Panjabi song, in which a young woman implores her husband to help her lift a heavy pitcher full of water.

(13) ਮਾਹੀਆ, ਘੜਾ ਚੁਕਾ
māhīā, g^{h}aṛā cukā
'O sweetheart, help me pick up the pitcher (of water)'

ਚੁਕਵਾ **cukvā** could never be used here because the helper is being requested to use his own hands (and not, for example, get a servant to help her!). On the other hand, only ਚੁਕਵਾ **cukvā** seems appropriate in

(14)

ਮੈਂ	ਨੌਕਰਾਂ	ਤੋਂ	ਕੂੜਾ	ਚੁਕਵਾਇਆ
mã^{i}	**na^{u}karā̃**	**tõ**	**kūṛā**	**cukvāiā**
CausAgt	ImmAgt		Pnt	CausV
SUB	ADJCT		OBJ	PRED

'I got the rubbish lifted by the servants'

The use of ਚੁਕਾ **cukā** in (14) would imply that the causing agent was *personally* involved in the process (and perhaps helping the servants). But in (14) as it is, he appears to have simply given the orders.

Group 3

The roots are intransitive. **Phase 2** has two forms, the older one involving vowel change or some other phonetic change and the other derived by adding stressed **-ā**. Phase 3 is derived by adding stressed **-vā**.

Phase 1	**Phase 2**	**Phase 3**
ਚੜ੍ਹ **carh** 'rise'	ਚਾੜ੍ਹ **cārh** / ਚੜ੍ਹਾ **carhā**	ਚੜ੍ਹਵਾ **caṛhvā**
ਤਰ **tar** 'swim/float'	ਤਾਰ **tār** / ਤਰਾ **tarā**	ਤਰਵਾ **tarvā**
ਮਿਟ **miṭ** 'disappear'	ਮੇਟ **meṭ** / ਮਿਟਾ **miṭā**	ਮਿਟਵਾ **miṭvā**

The older forms have special meanings. ਚਾੜ੍ਹ **cārh** means 'to force something up' as in the idiom ਗੱਡੀ ਚਾੜ੍ਹਨਾ **gaḍḍī cāṛhnā** 'to force someone into a train (to the next world)'. ਤਾਰ **tāṛ** has a religious meaning 'to save someone from sinking in the ocean of worldliness'. ਮੇਟ **meṭ** is used in the sense of 'to erase the writing of destiny'. The forms derived by adding **-ā** have the ordinary **transitive** meaning. ਚੜ੍ਹ **caṛh** and ਚਾੜ੍ਹ **cāṛh** are pronounced with a **high tone** as [ʧə́ɽ] and [ʧɑ́ɽ] respectively, and ਚੜ੍ਹਵਾ **caṛhvā** is pronounced with a **low tone** as [cəɽvɑ̀]. If **Phase 1** of a verb is toneless, **Phase 2** and **phase 3** are also toneless. But if **Phase 1** has either of the two **tones** (low or high), the other two phases must have only the **low tone** (and *never* the **high tone**). See Chapter 4 for details regarding tonal pronunciation.

9.6 Class 2 verbs

Verbs belonging to this class in Panjabi are far fewer in number than the verbs of **Class 1**. Their meanings involve actions (in the wider sense of the word) such as perceiving, tasting, ingesting, grasping etc. which can be done only for oneself and not for others (or whose benefit can only be "taken" but not "given"). When the **immediate agent** of such a verb is **backgrounded** in a **causative construction** and the **initiator (causative) agent** becomes the SUBJECT of the clause, the **immediate agent** is mentioned (if need be) with the **goal postposition** ਨੂੰ **nū̃** 'to' and not with the **source postposition** ਤੋਂ **tõ** 'from'. Examples are

(15) ਬੱਚੇ ਨੇ ਕਹਾਣੀ ਸੁਣੀ

bacce ne kahāṇī suṇī

ImmAgt Pnt Verb

SUB OBJ PRED

'The child heard the story'

(16) ਮਾਂ ਨੇ ਬੱਚੇ ਨੂੰ ਕਹਾਣੀ ਸੁਣਾਈ

mā̃ ne bacce *nū̃* kahāṇī suṇāī

IniAgt ImmAgt Pnt CausV

SUB ADJCT OBJ PRED

'The mother told the child a story'

Lit. 'The mother caused the child to hear the story'

The **immediate agent** of (15) becomes the syntactically optional ADJUNCT phrase in (16).

The most commonly used **Class 2** verbs in Panjabi are

Phase 1	Phase 2	Phase 3
ਖਾ **k^{h}ā** 'eat'	ਖਿਲਾ **k^{h}iḷā**	ਖਿਲਵਾ **k^{h}iḷvā**
	ਖੁਆ **k^{h}uā̤**	
ਸਿੱਖ **sikk^h** 'learn'	ਸਿਖਾ **sikk^{h}ā**	ਸਿਖਵਾ **sikk^{h}vā**
ਪੀ **pī** 'drink'	ਪਿਲਾ **piḷā̤**	ਪਿਲਵਾ **piḷvā**
	ਪਿਆ **piā**	
ਚੱਟ **caṭṭ** 'lick'	ਚਟਾ **caṭā**	ਚਟਵਾ **caṭvā**
ਚਰ **car** 'graze'	ਚਰਾ **carā**	ਚਰਵਾ **carvā**
ਰੱਜ **rajj** 'be content'	ਰਜਾ **rajā**	ਰਜਵਾ **rajvā**
ਦੇਖ **dek^h** 'see, look'	ਦਿਖਾ **dik^{h}ā**	ਦਿਖਵਾ **dik^{h}vā**
ਵੇਖ **vek^h** 'see, look'	ਵਿਖਾ **vik^{h}ā**	ਵਿਖਵਾ **vik^{h}vā**
ਸੁਣ **suṇ** 'hear, listen'	ਸੁਣਾ **suṇā**	ਸੁਣਵਾ **suṇvā**
ਸਮਝ **samaj^h** 'understand'	ਸਮਝਾ **samaj^{h}ā**	(?) ਸਮਝਵਾ (?) **samaj^{h}vā**

ਦੇਖ **dek^h** and ਸੁਣ **suṇ** can also be used in construction of **experiencer** type (Chapter 12). The verbs ਜਾਣ **jāṇ** 'know' and ਸੋਚ **soc** 'think' should be **Class 2 verbs**. But they do not have **Phase 2** and **Phase 3**.

9.7 Suppletion

There are a few verbs whose **Phase 2** and **Phase 3**, if derived by the productive rules, would produce results that are phonetically unpronounceable by speakers of Panjabi. So phases of different roots are brought in. This is known as **suppletion**. (An example of **suppletion** from English is *went* as the past tense form of *go*.)

Phase 1	Phase 2	Phase 3
ਆ **ā** 'come'	ਮੰਗਾ **mangā** 'send for'	ਮੰਗਵਾ **mangvā** 'get brought'
ਜਾ **jā** 'go'	ਭੇਜ **b^{h}ej** 'send'	ਭਿਜਵਾ **b^{h}ijvā** 'get sent'

ਲੈ **la^{i}** 'take'	ਦੇ **de** 'give'	ਦੁਆ **duā** 'get given'
ਹੋ **ho** 'become'	ਕਰ **kar** 'do/make'	ਕਰਾ **karā** / ਕਰਵਾ **karvā** 'get done/made'

Suppletion makes perfect logical sense in all these cases. For example, *making* someone *take* something is logically the same action as *giving* it to her/him.

It is possible to argue that the formation of **Phase 2** and **Phase 3** involves **derivation**, and not **inflection**. Arguments can be given to support either of the two positions. But regarding the process as **inflection** appears quite *insightful* because the resulting forms are more closely related *formally* and *semantically* than is normally the case with the new lexemes resulting from **derivation**. Anyway, language evolution shows no respect for a grammarian's *either-or* style classification, as is clear from almost every chapter of this book.

Summing up and looking ahead

It is important to remember that the stems formed by adding the affixes mentioned in this chapter are work*able* stems, and not work*ing* stems. **Phase 1** involves adding the **zero** affix to the supposed abstract root, which we can write as **root+Ø**. The **additive phases** are formed with **root+ā** or **root+vā** and the **subtractive phases** are formed by *further* adding **-ī-** to **Phase 1** or **Phase 2** or **Phase 3**. These workable stems must be further inflected as shown in the following chapters.

A **lexical** (or **main** or **nuclear**) **verb** is not always the only member of a **VP** in Panjabi, though it is the principal one imparting its meaning to the group. There may be (and often *are*) other types of verbs known as **auxiliaries** to modify the meaning of the main verb and impart various nuances to the overall meaning of the **VP**. These auxiliaries can be further classified on the basis of their inflectional patterns and function in the VP. Then the Panjabi **copular-existential verb** (the Panjabi equivalent of the English *be*) may also be present, which may be either a **nuclear verb** in the clause or may be appended to the **VP** without becoming its member. The following chapters deal with all these types of **verbs**.

For teachers and other more advanced users

9.8 Where the idea of verb "phases" comes from

The idea of verb **phases** in North Indian languages was first suggested by John Beames in the third volume of his monumental *A Comparative Grammar of the Modern Aryan Languages of India* (1872–1879). We have considerably changed and adapted Beames's ideas to suit the grammatical structure of Panjabi. But Beames's analysis is insightful in its own right and any linguist seriously interested in North Indian languages should read it. Our approach to grammatical analysis is definitely influenced by Beames's in the sense that his approach is not *Platonistic*. Unlike his contemporary grammarians and most later grammarians working on Indian languages, he takes the *actual* linguistic *phenomena* seriously and analyses them honestly rather than start with with some allegedly "universal" grammatical and semantic categories and impose them onto a language on the basis of *superficial* and *convenient* translations (and simply ignoring the facts that do not fit into these categories).

Chapter 10

Auxiliary Verbs and the Copula

Preview of the chapter

This chapter deals with the various types of Panjabi **auxiliary verbs** coming from the different stages in the historical evolution of the language, and thus playing different types of roles. Some of them are really *auxiliary* verbs and some are *not-so-auxiliary* ones doing a part-time "auxiliary" business.

10.1 The redundant category of "tense" in Panjabi grammar

The surest way to misunderstand and misanalyse the grammatical structure of modern North Indian languages including Panjabi is to look for "tenses" in them. The term **tense** is used in two different senses by grammarians – (1) inflectional category whose basic role is to indicate the time of an event *in relation to the moment of speaking* and (2) an inflected form of the **verb** or a group of inflected verb forms conveying a definite combined TMA (Tense Mood Aspect) meaning. **Tense** in sense (1) is almost completely absent in the modern colloquial Eastern variety of Panjabi, and only some traces are left. It is not obligatorily marked in the finite Panjabi clause as is the case in English. In sense (2), the number of the "tense" combinations in Panjabi is staggeringly large and no grammarian can analyse all of them. Joginder Singh Puar (1990) compiled a list of thirty-one "past tense", twenty-nine "present tense" and nineteen "future tense" combinations of verb forms. But this is a futile task. It can be easily shown that he has left out at least as many (if not more) actual and possible combinations. Despite the warning sounded by John Beames (1879: 99) that the number of "tenses" (in this sense) in the modern North Indian languages would be infinite, brave efforts to set up a small number of "tenses" in these languages by grammarians (including some modern linguists) have continued. The reason simply is the Platonistic view that semantic categories like the "present tense", "past tense" and "future tense" exist language-independently and incarnate themselves in various languages. Approximate (and often convenient) English translation is used as evidence for this. Often the grammatical category of "tense" and the (possibly extra-linguistic) notion of "time" are confusingly mixed up. For example, a verb form or a combination of verb forms referring to future *time* in *some* contexts is hastily branded as the "future *tense*" form, without the slightest consideration whether this is its *prototypical* meaning and what it means in many other contexts. Following the tradition used by Kellogg in his Hindi grammar (1875), some combinations were arbitrarily chosen as "tenses" of various types while others were simply ignored. We reject both the Kelloggian and the Puarian approaches.

No search for "tenses" in Panjabi is attempted in this book. The number of the "tenses" (in sense (2) mentioned above) in Panjabi may be staggeringly large, if not "infinite" as Beames suspected. (He was dealing with *all* the major Indic languages of North India.) But the number of **inflections** of **lexical verbs** and **auxiliaries** entering these combinations is quite small. If we know the *meaning potential* of each of these inflections and the auxiliaries, we can have a fairly good idea of what meaning each combination would convey. It is true that the meaning of a clause/sentence comes as an undivided gestalt and is not simply a sum of its parts. Bhartṛhari called this gestalt perception of meaning *akhaṇḍa vākya sphoṭa* (undivided sentence/utterance meaning bursting forth) grasped by our *pratibhā* (intuition), and not as computed by adding the meanings of the components. It is like the gestalt effect of a melody in music, which is more than a sum of the parts. But musical notes and musical scales and their "grammars" *are* studied by musicians and musicologists. The Sanskrit word *vyākaraṇa* for grammar literally means 'differentiation' or 'analysis'. Any serious grammarian knows that both unity in diversity and diversity in unity are equally significant in grammatical anlysis. All that a modern grammarian can do is what past grammarians have always done – differentiate and analyse the component parts and their meaning potential. In the last chapter, we looked at the grammatical meanings conveyed by the inflections resulting in the **phases** of various types of verbs. In this chapter we examine the **auxiliary verbs** and the **copular-existential verb** (or **copula**) of Panjabi.

10.2 Types of auxiliary verbs in Panjabi

As is the case with English and many other languages genetically related and unrelated to Panjabi, the **auxiliary verbs** historically developed from ordinary (lexical) **verbs** through a process known as **grammaticalisation**, the process by which a **lexical** word becomes a **grammatical** word. (Bybee, Perkins and Pagliuca 1994). This process, like all other linguistic changes, is gradual. Two Panjabi **auxiliaries** are quite old and have become **suffixes** now. But others (except two), called **explicator auxiliaries** in this book, work as ordinary verbs as well and started their "auxiliary" business relatively recently. The process of grammaticalisation involves a number of changes in the syntactic and semantic behaviour of the verbs: "... grammaticalization is not just one process, but many processes that occur together." (Bybee 2015: 18).

10.2.1 Older auxiliaries

-ਗਾ **-gā** and ਕੇ **ke** are the older **auxiliaries** in Panjabi. -ਗਾ **-gā** is added as a **suffix** to the **unmarked** (for TMA) form of the verb (called the **subjunctive** form in Chapter 11) and to ਹੈ **ha^{i}** and ਸੀ **sī** to add the meaning of 'definiteness' to the meaning of the verb. ਕੇ **ke** is added to the **conjunctive participle** form to emphasise the 'having done' meaning. The next chapter deals with them in detail.

It would be interesting to look at their history. -ਗਾ **-gā** comes from the Sanskriṭ *gataḥ* 'gone'. With the passage of time (and with phonetic abrasion) this **perfective** form acquired the meaning of definiteness. It is marked for **number** and **gender** like an **adjectival** verb form. Having made this contribution in the past, the Panjabi verb ਜਾ **jā** 'go' has started the **auxiliary** business once again and is moving in the same direction. ਕੇ **ke** comes from the Sanskrit *kṛtvā* 'having done' through the stages *kṛtvā →karia →kari →kai →ke*. The modern form ਕੇ **ke** was written as ਕੈ **ka^{i}**

and pronounced with a diphthong in the 17th century. ਕੇ **ke** is an invariant form and does not inflect. It is added to the **conjunctive participle** form of a verb, but is still written separately (in Gurmukhi) by most writers, as in ਕਰ ਕੇ **kar ke** 'having done'. There is also a **postposition** ਕਰਕੇ **karke** 'because of' which is clearly an extension of the meaning of ਕਰ ਕੇ **kar ke**. The **conjunctive participle** ਕਰ ਕੇ **kar ke** and the **postposition** ਕਰਕੇ **karke** have exactly the same pronunciation.

10.2.2 Explicator auxiliaries

An **explicator auxiliary** modifies or adds to the meaning of a lexical verb. The best analysis of the explicator auxiliaries of Panjabi was done by Kali Charan Bahl in his *A Grammatical Sketch of Punjabi* (1964). Bahl's classification is given below. We disagree with Bahl at one place and make two additions to his list. Bahl classified these **auxiliaries** in pairs on the basis of their semantics.

1. Completion		
cislocative	ਆ **ā**	'come'
translocative	ਜਾ **jā**	'go'
2. Suddenness		
commencement	ਉੱਠ **uṭṭ^h**	'get up'
termination	ਬੈਠ **ba^{i}ṭ^h**	'sit down'
3. Vehemence		
indeliberate	ਪੈ **pa^i**	'be put'
deliberate	ਸੁੱਟ **suṭṭ**	'throw'
	(ਮਾਰ **mār** 'beat down')	
4. Benefaction		
egobenefaction	ਲੈ **la^i**	'take'
allobenefaction	ਦੇ **de**	'give'
5. Precedence		
concern	ਰੱਖ **rakk^h**	'keep'
indifference	ਛੱਡ **c^{h}aḍḍ**	'leave'

6. Inception

involvement	ਚਲ **cal**	'move'
alleviation	ਨਿਕਲ਼ **nikaḷ**	'escape'

7. Process

cessanat	ਚੁਕ **cuk**	'carry, lift' (?)
	(ਹਟ **haṭ**)	'move away'
incessant	ਰਹਿ **rahi**	'stay'

8. Accomplishment

phenomenal	ਹੋ **ho**	'become, happen'
abilitative	ਸਕ **sak**	'be able to'

We will now often use the simpler term **auxiliary** instead of **explicator auxiliary** because ਗਾ **gā** and ਕੇ **ke** (though still written separately) are now best described as **affixes**.

We have added ਮਾਰ **mār** 'beat down' and ਹਟ **haṭ** 'move away' to Bahl's list. But ਚੁਕ **cuk** and ਹਟ **haṭ** do not convey exactly the same meaning. Glossing ਚੁਕ **cuk** as 'carry, lift', as Bahl did, is not correct. This **auxiliary** is not related to the modern Panjabi verb ਚੁੱਕ **cukk** meaning 'carry, lift' either historically or syntactically. The reason is that the auxiliary ਚੁਕ **cuk** (like ਰਹਿ **rahi** 'stay' with opposite meaning) is **intransitive**. As will be pointed out below (and also in Chapter 13), when a **lexical verb** becomes an auxiliary, it retains its original **transitive** or **intransitive** phase. The auxiliary ਚੁਕ **cuk** comes most probably from some reduplicative perfect form like Sanskrit *cakram* 'had passed on' or 'had moved ahead'.

As we saw in the last chapter, a **lexical verb** has one or two **additive phases**, indicating increase in the **semantic valency set** and an equal number of **subtractive phases** indicating decrease in the **valency set** with the elimination of the **agent** of the action from the **syntactic valency set**. But an **auxiliary** has only *one* phase, the original one (the **transitive** or the **intransitive**). Moreover, its meaning is considerably restricted and rather metaphorical. *In fact, a close scrutiny of the meanings of these explicator auxiliaries shows that most of them are metaphorical, indicating some sort of* ***movement*** *or* ***location*** *in space. We will discuss spatial metaphors in Panjabi grammar in Chapter 12.*

A few examples of how an **auxiliary** modifies the meaning of the lexical verb are given below. In the glosses in these examples, the translation of the **auxiliary** is put within single quotation marks. This subject is taken up again in Chapter 13 dealing with **serial verb constructions**.

(1) ਖ਼ਤ ਪੜ੍ਹ ਲੈ
xat paṛh la^{i}
letter read 'take'
'Read the letter (for your own information)'

(2) ਖ਼ਤ ਪੜ੍ਹ ਦੇ
xat paṛh de
letter read 'give'
'Read the letter (aloud for someone else)'

(3) ਖਾਣਾ ਖਾ ਲੈ
k^{h}āṇā k^{h}ā la^{i}
food eat 'take'
'Eat the food (for your own nourishment or satisfaction)

(4) *ਖਾਣਾ ਖਾ ਦੇ
***k^{h}āṇā k^{h}ā de**
food eat 'give'

(4) makes no sense because the benefit of eating can be "taken" but cannot be "given" to anyone else. Sometimes it is not possible to say whether or not a verb has been used as an auxiliary.

(5)

ਰਾਮ	ਮੇਰਾ	ਕੰਮ	ਕਰ	ਗਿਆ
ram	**merā**	**kamm**	**kar**	**giā**
SUB		OBJ		PRED
Ram	my work		having done	'gone'

(6)

ਗਲਾਸ	ਭਰ	ਗਿਆ	ਹੈ
galās	**b^{h}ar**	**giā**	**ha^{i}**
SUB	OBJ	PRED	
glass	having become full	'gone'	is

(7)	ਉਹ	ਕੱਲ੍ਹ	ਮਰ	ਗਿਆ
	uh	**kall^h**	**mar**	**giā**
	SUB		PRED	
	he	yesterday	having died	'gone'

In (5) **ਗਿਆ giā** is a lexical verb with the original meaning indicating that Ram went away after doing my work. In (6) it conveys the translocative meaning of completeness. The filling of the glass is complete, but the glass is still lying there and has not "gone" anywhere. The interpretation of the meaning of **ਗਿਆ giā** in (7) depends on whether the life of the deceased is viewed as having been completed or he is viewed as having literally "gone" to the next world.

The **syntactic valency** of the **VP** as a whole depends on the syntactic valency of the *last* member in the **VP** (as will be shown in later chapters, especially Chapter 13). The **copula** can be *appended* to a **VP**, but it does not become its member. In (5), **ਕਰ kar** 'do' is **transitive** with Ram as the **agent** and **ਕੰਮ kamm** 'work' as the **patient**. But since **ਗਿਆ giā** 'gone' is **intransitive**, the combination **ਕਰ ਗਿਆ kar giā** is **intransitive** and the SUBJECT of the combination is marked like the SUBJECT of an **intransitive verb**. The Panjabi verb **ਲਿਆ liā** 'bring' started as a **ਲੈ ਆ la^i ā** 'take come'. Though **ਲਿਆ liā** has a transitive meaning, its SUBJECT is often still marked like that of an **intransitive** verb. But people are forgetting its origin and have also started marking its SUBJECT like that of a **transitive** verb. Needless to say, there is a subtle difference in meaning in the two usages, as we shall see in detail in Chapter 13.

The lexical verbs **ਆ ā** 'come' and **ਜਾ jā** 'go' have opposite meanings. But they can occur together when **ਜਾ jā** is an auxiliary, as in

(8)	ਉਹ	ਆ	ਗਿਆ	ਹੈ
	uh	**ā**	**giā**	**ha^i**
	SUB		PRED	
	he	having come	'gone'	is

'He has come'

Lit. 'The action of his coming is complete'

We will deal with more combinations after we have discussed the meanings of the middle and the outer inflections.

We have glossed the lexical verb before the auxiliary as a **conjunctive participle** form with the meaning 'having X-ed'. Some Panjabi grammarians, including some modern linguists, who care little for historical and structural considerations have called this form the "root". This is a grave error. The verb forms of *go* in *I go there daily*, *Please go now*, *I wish to go* and *I will go* are homophonous. But for historical, structural and semantic reasons, we have to regard the first as the **present tense** form, the second as the **imperative** form and the last two as **infinitive** forms. The Panjabi **conjunctive participle** form which sounds and looks like a bare stem these days was pronounced and written with the vowel -ਇ **-i** at end, as ਆਇ **āi**, ਜਾਇ **jāi**, ਮਰਿ **mari** etc. until about 400 years ago. They have become homophonous to the basic stem as a result of the loss of word-final -ਇ **-i**. But their grammatical behaviour and meaning shown in our glosses have not changed. Similarly, the **imperative** form of a Panjabi verb, which also sounds and is written like a bare stem, was pronounced and written differently and has become homophonous to the basic stem as a result of historical changes. Since this historical information is available, not making use of it would be wrong.

As a **grammatical word**, an **auxiliary** often becomes phonetically distorted when it follows a full **lexical verb**. This happens in English and many other languages as well. The exact nature of this distortion depends upon the members of the pair. Examples are

(9) ਕਰ ਦਿੱਤਾ
kar dittā
pronounced as ਕਰੱਤਾ [kɐrɐʔttɑ],

(10) ਰੱਖੀ ਹੋਈ
rakkʰī hoī
pronounced as ਰੱਖੀਉਈ [rɐkkʰiui], and

(11) ਕੀਤਾ ਹੋਇਆ
kītā hoiā
pronounced as ਕੀੱਤਾਯਾ [kittɑjɑ]

and

(12) ਜਾਂਦਾ ਹਾਂ
jā̃dā hā̃

pronounced as ਜਾਂਣਾਂ [ʤɑn.nɑ̃] or ਜਾਂਣਾਂ ਯਾਂ [ʤɑn.nɑ̃.jɑ̃] or ਜਾਂਣਾਂ ਵਾਂ [ʤɑn.nɑ̃.wɑ̃] – with [j] or [w] as epenthetic (intruding for making pronunciation easier) semi-vowels.

It should be clear from the examples given above that the meaning of a composite construction involving an explicator auxiliary (analysed in detail as **serial verb constructions** in Chapter 13) is not **compositional**, or a sum of the meanings of the members. They are semi-idiomatic expressions. Some more examples with ਬੋਲ **bol**+explicator auxiliary

(13) ਮੈਂ ਕੁਝ ਗ਼ਲਤ ਬੋਲ ਗਿਆ
mã^{i} kuj^{h} ɣalat bol giā
I something wrong speak 'gone'
'I said something wrong (which I perhaps should not have)'

(14) ਮੈਂ ਕੁਝ ਗ਼ਲਤ ਬੋਲ ਬੈਠਾ
mã^{i} kuj^{h} ɣalat bol ba^{i}ṭā
I something wrong speak 'sat'
'I said something wrong (which I did thoughtlessly and which I now regret)'

(15a) ਉਹ ਇਕਦਮ ਬੋਲ ਪਿਆ
uh ikdam bol piā
He suddenly speak 'fallen'
'He suddenly spoke out (which was quite unexpected)'

A less common version of (15) is

(15b) ਉਹ ਇਕਦਮ ਬੋਲ ਉੱਠਿਆ
uh ikdam bol uṭṭ^{h}iā
He suddenly speak 'risen'

The explicator auxiliaries used in (15a) and (15b) have opposite meanings, but in these expressions, they both convey the meaning of a sudden and unexpected behaviour.

(16) ਮੈਂ ਸੱਚ ਬੋਲ ਦਿੱਤਾ ਹੈ
mã^{i} sacc bol dittā ha^{i}
I truth speak 'given' is
'I have spoken the truth (selflessly and without caring for any consequences for myself')

(17) ਤੁਸੀਂ ਬਹੁਤ ਝੂਠ ਬੋਲ ਲਿਆ ਹੈ
tusī̃ bahut j^{h}ūṭ^{h} bol liā ha^{i}
You a lot untruth spoke 'taken' is
'You have told lots of lies (in order to gain personal benefit)'

10.3 The copular-existential verb (copula) in Panjabi

The Panjabi **copula** shares two important features with its English cousin *be*. Both can function as nuclear verbs in some types of clauses as well as non-nuclear verbs, and both have certain inflectional peculiarities when inflected for **tense**, **person** and **number**.

In Panjabi, the **copula** is the only verb inflected for two **tenses** (traditionally known as **present** and **past**, but we will regard them as **non-remote** and **remote** respectively for reasons to be discussed later. To refer to a future situation, a different Panjabi verb ਹੋ **ho** has to be brought in. If you have read Chapter 2, you know what has been happening to this verb since the time of Sanskrit. The next chapter deals with this subject in detail. But a little bit of relevant information is due here.

In (18a) and (18b) below instantiating **canonical finite clause pattern 2** (Chapter 5), ਹੈ **ha^{i}** and its **remote** (past) tense form ਸੀ **sī** act as **lexical** verb PREDICATORS.

(18a) ਖਾਣਾ ਗਰਮ ਹੈ
k^{h}āṇā garam ha^{i}
SUB COMP(S) PRED
'The food is hot'

(18b) ਖਾਣਾ ਗਰਮ ਸੀ
k^{h}āṇā garam sī
'The food was hot'

(18c) ਖਾਣਾ ਗਰਮ ਹੋਏਗਾ
k^{h}āṇā garam hoegā
'The food will be hot'

While ਹੈ **ha^{i}** is the **non-remote (present) tense** form and ਸੀ **sī** is the **remote (past) tense** form of the Panjabi **copula**, it would be wrong to regard ਹੋਏਗਾ **hoegā** as its **future tense**. There are no *system-internal* reasons for regarding ਹੋਏਗਾ **hoegā** as a future "tense form". The *grammatical* category of "tense" must not be confused with the extralinguistic concept of "time".

10.4 The copula outside the VP

The marking of **tense** in a **finite clause** is *not* obligatory in Panjabi as it is in English. As we pointed out in Chapter 5, our definition of a finite clause in Panjabi is different. But **tensed** ਹੈ **haⁱ** or ਸੀ **sī** or some form of non-tensed ਹੋਏਗਾ **hoegā** can be appended to a **VP** to indicate the time of the situation relative to the time of utterance or some other point in time outside the situation itself.

(19a) ਉਹ ਸਦਾ ਸੱਚ ਬੋਲਦਾ ਰਿਹਾ
uh sadā sacc boldā rihā
SUB OBJ PRED
'He always kept speaking the truth'

The prototypical meaning of the **perfect participle** form ਰਿਹਾ **rihā** is **+completed** as will be argued in Chapter 11. But this is *not* a **past tense** form, as many past grammarians and some modern linguists describe it. The *usual* interpretation of the time of the situation described in (19a) is the past time, unless the context or the **intonation** force some other interpretation. *This often happens.* We can add both ਹੈ **haⁱ** 'is' and ਸੀ **sī** 'was' to (19a). This shows that its meaning is closer to that of the English **past participle** than the **past tense** form

(19b) ਉਹ ਸਦਾ ਸੱਚ ਬੋਲਦਾ ਰਿਹਾ ਹੈ
uh sadā sacc boldā rihā haⁱ
'He has always kept speaking the truth'

to emphasise the present relevance of the situation (as the English translation in the so-called "present perfect continuous tense" shows). To make the situation relevant to some point in time in the past, we can say

(19c) ਉਹ ਸਦਾ ਸੱਚ ਬੋਲਦਾ ਰਿਹਾ ਸੀ
uh sadā sacc boldā rihā sī
'He had always kept speaking the truth'

This is what could be described as the "past perfect continuous tense". Similarly, the situation can be made relevant to some point in the future time ("future perfect continuous tense") in

(19d) ਉਹ ਸਦਾ ਸੱਚ ਬੋਲਦਾ ਰਿਹਾ ਹੋਏਗਾ
uh sadā sacc boldā rihā hoegā
'He will always have kept speaking the truth'

ਹੈ **ha^{i}**, ਸੀ **sī** and ਹੋਏਗਾ **hoegā** certainly contribute the meaning of the sentence, but they are not part of the **VP** and do not affect its **valency** and case marking etc., as the following chapters will also show. They act more like **adverbials**.

The English translations of (19a–19d) simply show how *English* grammatically conceptualises the situation. This is not the "real" or the "underlying", "language-independent" meaning or the "underlying tense". Many traditional Panjabi grammarians and some modern linguists have fallen into this trap and set up for Panjabi the above-mentioned "tenses" picked up from J.C. Nesfield's English grammar first published in 1898 specifically for learners of English in India.

10.5 Other developments in the grammar of the Panjabi copula

In some Panjabi dialects the auxiliary affix -ਗਾ **-gā** is added to ਹੈ **ha^{i}** and ਸੀ **sī** to form ਹੈਗਾ **ha^{i}gā** and ਸੀਗਾ **sīgā** and their **number-gender** variants. Since -ਗਾ **-gā** is a marker of definiteness, ਹੈਗਾ **ha^{i}gā** means 'definitely is' and ਸੀਗਾ **sīgā** means 'definitely was'. These forms occur almost exclusively in colloquial spoken Panjabi.

Of these two, ਸੀਗਾ **sīgā** seems slightly older because -ਗਾ **-gā** is tightly **agglutinated** to it, whereas the association of -ਗਾ **-gā** with ਹੈ **ha^{i}** is looser. Moreover, while ਸੀਗਾ **sīgā** unambiguously refers to a previous or remote situation, ਹੈਗਾ **ha^{i}gā** indicates a 'definite existence but not necessarily in the present time'. The following examples are interesting.

(20a) ਉਹ ਘਰ ਸੀਗਾ
uh g^{h}ar sīgā
SUB PRED
'He was definitely at home'

(21a) ਉਹ ਘਰ ਹੈਗਾ ਸੀ
uh g^{h}ar ha^{i}gā sī
'He was most certainly at home'

The **negative particle** ਨਹੀਂ **nahī̃** can come between ਹੈ **ha^{i}** and ਗਾ **gā** but not between ਸੀ **sī** and ਗਾ **gā**.

Both ਹੈ **ha^{i}** and ਸੀ **sī** are present in (21a) without creating any contradiction because while ਸੀ **sī** unambiguously indicates existence in the past, ਹੈ **ha^{i}** simply refers to bare existence not related to any time, though it is regarded as referring to the present existence unless there is a clear indication that this is not the case.

(22a) ਉਹ ਘਰ ਹੈ ਨਹੀਂ ਗਾ
uh g^{h}ar ha^{i} nahī̃ gā
'He is definitely not at home'

(22b) *ਉਹ ਘਰ ਸੀ ਨਹੀਂ ਗਾ
***uh g^{h}ar ha^{i} nahī̃ gā**

You need to say

(22c) ਉਹ ਘਰ ਨਹੀਂ ਸੀਗਾ
uh g^{h}ar nahī̃ sīgā
'He was definitely not at home'

In a negative sentence with ਹੈ **ha^{i}** (but not ਸੀ **sī**) the main verb ਹੈ **ha^{i}** is often omitted. So it is possible to say

(23a) ਉਹ ਘਰ ਨਹੀਂ (ਹੈ)
uh g^{h}ar nahī̃ (ha^{i})
'He is not at home'

(23b) ਉਹ ਘਰ (ਹੈ) ਨਹੀਂ ਗਾ
uh g^{h}ar (ha^{i}) nahī̃ gā
'He is definitely not at home'

Since such sentences occur almost exclusively in spoken Panjabi, the pronunciation of ਨਹੀਂ **nahī̃** in such utterances is always tonal [nɐ́ĩ].

We shall see in the next chapter that ਗਾ **gā** is marked for **number** and **gender**. So other **number-gender** variants of ਗਾ **gā** (ਗੇ **ge**, ਗੀ **gī**, ਗੀਆਂ **gīā̃**) are also used.

Because of the fact that ਹੈਗਾ **ha^{i}gā** and ਸੀਗਾ **sīgā** occur almost exclusively in spoken Panjabi, past written records do not help us decide when they appeared in the language. These forms are mentioned by Beames in his grammar already mentioned. Beames started his research work in 1866. These forms are not found in the earlier Panjabi literature. But the reason for this may be that they are colloquial expressions.

Interestingly, ਹੈਂਗਾ **haˈngā**, which sounds very similar to ਹੈਗਾ **haˈgā** and also has a very similar meaning, is used in the variety of Hindi-Urdu spoken in some areas in the states of Maharashtra and Telengana in India. Quite understandably, language purists living there hate ਹੈਂਗਾ **haˈngā**, but are unable to stop their children from using it in their Hindi-Urdu speech!

Summing up and looking ahead

The only sensible way of dealing with the syntax of Panjabi is to prepare a suitable grammatical framework for it and not to fit it into any pre-exiting Procrustean bed by cutting or stretching its limbs by violence. A theoretical framework suitable for Panjabi is constructed in the following chapters.

Chapter 11

Tense, Mood and Aspect

Preview of the chapter

This chapter deals with the **middle inflections** denoting the **TMA** (Tense Mood Aspect) or *kāla* aspect or the temporal constituency of the action/event denoted by a **verb phrase** in Panjabi. A note of mild caution is due here. The system presented here is very different from what readers may be used to as a result of their exposure to European languages only or believing in the claims made by those linguists who set up, on the basis of European languages, the grammatical and semantic frameworks with "universalistic" ambitions and pretensions.

11.1 Main constituents of the verb phrase in Panjabi

It will be useful to define **TMA** (Tense Mood Aspect) here. The basic role of **tense** as an **inflectional** category is to indicate the time of a situation (action/event) *in relation to the moment of speaking* (and sometimes to a point in time *outside* the situation). **Tense** takes a *situation-external* perspective. **Aspect**, on the other hand, takes *situation-internal* perspective and marks the situation as completed, incomplete or ongoing, recurring etc. *For our purpose*, **modality** marks a situation as certain, uncertain, possible, desirable, imperative etc. We use the term **modality** to encompass **mood** as well, and the the two terms are used interchangeably here, as by many other grammarians. The three are sometimes inextricably mixed in the meaning of a **middle inflection**. But we have to keep in mind whether the *basic* or **prototypical** meaning of an inflection is **tense**-related, or **aspectual** or **modal**. The following diagrams show in a summary form the Panjabi verbs, their **inflections** and the **prototypical** meaning of each.

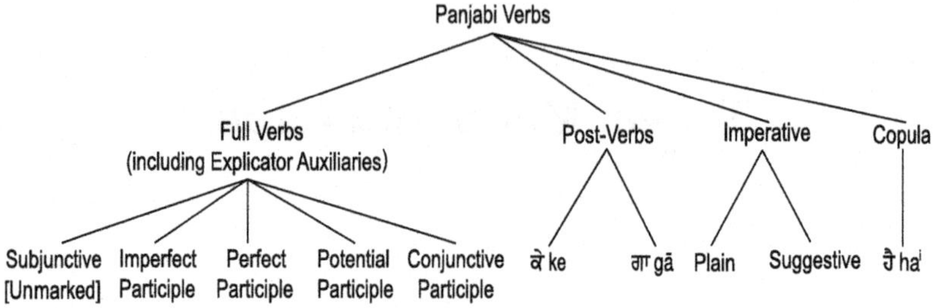

Figure 11.1 Classification of Panjabi verbs

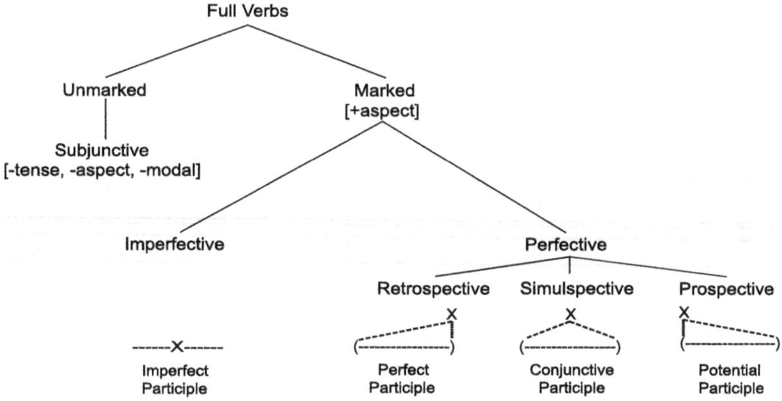

Figure 11.2 Semantic features of full verb-forms

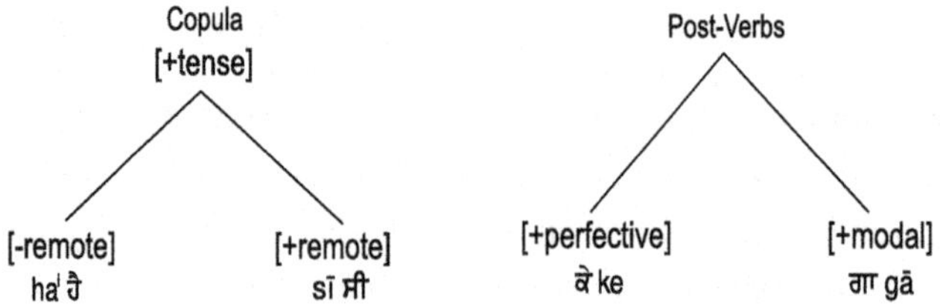

Figure 11.3 Semantic features of the copula and the post-verbs

As was also pointed out in Chapter 9, the Panjabi verbs can be divided into three categories.

(i) Full verbs and (explicator) auxiliaries

These verbs have **personal** (for **person** and **number**) and/or **adjectival** (for **number** and **gender**) **inflections**. While **full verbs** have **additive** and **subtractive phases**, **(explicator) auxiliaries** (most of them being the **full verbs** doing a sort of part-time **auxiliary** job) only have the single **basic phase**. These verbs are not inflected for **tense**. Only the **copula** is inflected for **tense**.

(ii) Post-verbs

ਕੇ **ke** and -ਗਾ **-gā** are **affixes** added to some forms of **full verbs**. ਕੇ **ke** is written separately by most writers, but there is no phonetic "juncture" between the **main verb** and ਕੇ **ke** in spoken Panjabi. ਕੇ **ke** is not inflected. ਗਾ **gā** is inflected for **number** and **gender** like an **adjectival form** and is not written separately in Gurmukhi.

(iii) Copula ਹੈ haⁱ

As pointed out in Chapter 2, this verb has been a class by itself for many centuries ever since the time of Sanskrit (and possibly since earlier) in the Indic languages. It will be dealt with in section **11.2.3** below. It is inflected for **person** and **number**. It is *supposed to* have the **present tense** and the **past tense** forms. But it makes better sense to regard them as **non-remote** and **remote** tenses, as we shall see below. When needed, it can be *appended* to a **verb phrase** without becoming its member.

11.2 Personal inflectional forms of full verbs, (explicator) auxiliaries and the copula

Main verbs and **(explicator) auxiliaries** in Panjabi can have **personal** and **adjectival** inflections. The **copula** has only **personal** forms and -ਗਾ **-gā** has only **adjectival** forms. ਕੇ **ke** and the **conjunctive participle** are uninflected. As pointed out in Chapter 10 and also below, ਕੇ **ke** itself historically developed from the **conjunctive participle** form of the verb ਕਰ **kar** 'do'. This section deals with the personal forms.

11.2.1 The subjunctive (unmarked) form

The name **Subjunctive** seems ideal for this form and is much better than the misleading names like "contingent future", "indefinite future" etc. traditionally used for this "tense" by past Panjabi and Hindi grammarians.

Beames used the name Aorist because, according to him, its semantics is similar to that of the Greek Aorist. But this is not entirely true. We avoid this frightening name and choose **subjunctive** because it conveys the sense of a simple *subjective* (and somewhat indefinitely potential) view of a situation *without* locating it in time (**tense**) or regarding it as completed and incomplete (**aspect**) etc. (for which Panjabi has other verb forms, as we will see).

A **personal inflection** of a verb stem marks **person** and **number**. The nine endings are shown in the following table.

	Singular	**Plural**
First person	-ਆਂ **-ā̃**/-ਵਾਂ **-vā̃** (-ਉਂ **-ū̃**)	-ਈਏ **-īe**
Second person	-ਏਂ **-ẽ** / -ਵੇਂ **-vẽ**	-ਓ **-o** / -ਵੋ **-vo**
Third person	-ਏ **-e** / -ਵੇ **-ve** (-ਊ **-ū**)	-ਣ **-ṇ** / -ਨ **-n**

The choice between the endings with and without -ਵ **-v** is mainly dialectal, but also sometimes phonologically conditioned. Only -ਵਾਂ **-vā̃** is added to a stem ending ਆ **ā**.

The **first person singular** affix -ਉਂ **-ū̃** and the **third person singular** affix -ਊ **-ū** (in the brackets in the table) appear to be more recent developments and their meaning is discussed below in section **11.2.2.** The choice between -ਣ **-ṇ** and -ਨ **-n** is also **phonologically conditioned**. Normally -ਣ **-ṇ** is used except after ਣ **ṇ** , ਰ **r**, ੜ **ṛ** and ਲ਼ **ḷ**.

Forms of two verbs ਕਰ **kar** 'do' and ਜਾ **jā** 'go' are given in the following table.

	Singular	**Plural**
First person	ਕਰਾਂ **karā̃** ਜਾਵਾਂ **jāvā̃**	ਕਰੀਏ **karīe** ਜਾਈਏ **jāīe**
Second person	ਕਰੇਂ **karẽ** ਜਾਏਂ/ਜਾਵੇਂ **jāẽ/jāvẽ**	ਕਰੋ **karo** ਜਾਓ/ਜਾਵੋ **jāo/jāvo**
Third person	ਕਰੇ **kare** ਜਾਏ/ਜਾਵੇ **jāe/jāve**	ਕਰਨ **karan** ਜਾਣ/ਜਾਵਣ **jāṇ/jāvaṇ**

The semantics of this form is the most *unspecified* one. Though it comes from the Sanskrit **present tense**, it does not locate the situation anywhere in time, does not give any aspectual meaning to the verb and does not express any specific modality. So we characterise it as **-tense**, **-aspect** and **-modal**. It conveys the simple *idea* or *possibility* of the situation, which has been misunderstood as "contingent future" or "indefinite future", as in

(1) ਜੇ ਮੈਂ ਖ਼ਤ ਲਿਖਾਂ...
je mã^{i} xat lik^{h}ã...
Sbjct
'If I write a letter...'

Since this form denotes a situation which is not time-bound or definite, it is used for seeking permission as well.

(2) ਮੈਂ ਵਾਪਸ ਜਾਵਾਂ?
mã^{i} vāpas jāvã?
Sbjct
'Shall I go back?'

While it is true that this verb form is used most often for making suggestions, getting permission and making conditional statements which may be described as "contingent future" or "indefinite future", it can refer to past situations as well to give an impression of repetitions and timelessness, as in the following lines from the Panjabi poet Bawa Balwant (1915–1972).

(3) ਰੋਜ਼ ਉਸਦਾ ਹਾਰ ਟੁੱਟ ਜਾਇਆ ਕਰੇ
ਮੁਸਕ੍ਰਾਂਦੀ ਆ ਕੇ ਬਣਵਾਇਆ ਕਰੇ
ਮੇਰੇ ਪੁੱਛਣ ਤੇ ਕਿ ਟੁੱਟਾ ਕਿਸ ਤਰ੍ਹਾਂ
ਪਾ ਕੇ ਵਲ਼ ਗਰਦਨ ਨੂੰ ਸ਼ਰਮਾਇਆ ਕਰੇ
roz usdā hār ṭuṭṭ jāiā *kare*
muskrā̃dī ā ke baṇvāiā *kare*
mere pucc^{h}aṇ te ki ṭuṭṭā kis tarhā̃
pā ke vaḷ gardan nū̃ śarmāiā *kare*
'Daily her necklace would break,
(And she) would come smiling to get it mended;
On my asking how it broke,
(She) would twist her neck and blush.'

The situation being depicted is clearly located in the past, but the use of the **subjunctive** form ਕਰੇ **kare** gives the poem an air of romantic timelessness. (The combination exemplified by ਜਾਇਆ ਕਰੇ **jāiā kare** will be discussed in **11.5.5** below.) It is not surprising that this form is a special favourite of many other Panjabi poets as well. A famous poem of another Panjabi poet Mohan Singh (1905–78) describes an evening scene with young women coming to a well in his farm. The time of the recurring scenario includes the present time as well. The use of the **imperfect participle** form (see **11.4** below) would have conveyed the same *factual* information but ruined all poetry.

(4) ਉਹ ਪੈਲਾਂ ਪਾਉਂਦੀਆਂ ਆਵਣ
ਕਦੇ ਗੁਟ੍ਹਕਣ ਤੇ ਕਦੇ ਗਾਵਣ
ਪਏ ਨੱਕ ਵਿਚ ਲੌਂਗ ਸੁਹਾਵਣ
ਤੇ ਝਿਲਮਿਲ ਕਰਦੇ ਨਗ ਨੀ।
uh pa^{i}lā̃ pāũdīā̃ *āvaṇ*
kade *guṭhkaṇ* te kade *gāvaṇ*
pae nakk vic lā̃^{u}g *suhāvaṇ*
te j^{h}ilmil karde nag nī
'They *come* dancing like peacocks,
Sometimes *cooing* and sometimes *singing*,
The golden cloves on their noses *look beautiful*
And the jewels (therein) glitter.'

11.2.2 Addition of the post-verb -ਗਾ -gā to the subjunctive (unmarked) form

The modal post-verb affix -ਗਾ **-gā** is added to the **subjunctive** form to derive what nearly all the Panjabi and Hindi-Urdu grammarians in the past called the "future tense" form. But -ਗਾ **-gā** simply adds the meaning **+definite** to the main verb indicating a possibility. Mostly, future is simply a definite possibility, and hence the name "future tense". But this can be a definite possibility in the past as well as the present time. So the use of the term "future tense" is misleading.

The affix -ਗਾ **-gā** gets the **adjectival** endings mentioned in the Magic Square in Chapter 7, but are mentioned below as well because they are also added to other **adjectival** verb forms discussed later.

	Singular	Plural
Masculine	-ਆ **-ā**	-ਏ **-e**
Feminine	-ਈ **-ī**	-ਈਆਂ **-īā̃**

The so-called "future tense" form is thus inflected *twice* – once as the **subjunctive** form with **personal** endings and again with the **adjectival** endings of -ਗਾ **-gā**. The **subjunctive** first person singular form with the -ਊਂ **-ū̃** ending and the **third person singular** form with the -ਊ **-ū** ending can have -ਗਾ **-gā** as with other **personal** endings. But many speakers use them with **emphasis** and **falling intonation** and without -ਗਾ **-gā** to convey the sense of 'definitely will'. But this use is mostly limited to spoken language only. You come across constructions both with and without -ਗਾ **-gā** having the same meaning. (Also see Chapter 16.)

(5) ਮੈਂ ਉੱਥੇ ਜਾਊਂ(ਗਾ)
mãi utthe jaū̃(gā)
Sbjct+**gā**
'I will definitely go there'

(6) ਅੱਜ ਮੀਂਹ ਪਊ(ਗਾ)
ajj mī̃h paū(gā)
Sbjct+**gā**
'It will definitely rain today'

But since a definite possibility can be located in the past time as well (as shown by the perfect participle ਕੀਤੀ **kītī** in (7) below, the name "future tense" is inappropriate.

(7) ਉਹਨੇ ਕਾਲਿਜ ਦੀ ਪੜ੍ਹਾਈ ਕੀਤੀ ਹੋਏਗੀ
uhne kālij dī parhāī kītī hoegī
PerP Sbjct+**gā**
'He would have received a college education'

refers to a strong possibility in the past.

The negative particles ਨਾ **nā** and ਨਹੀਂ **nahī̃** cannot be used interchangeably. ਨਹੀਂ **nahī̃** (ਨਾ +ਹੀ **nā+ hī**) is an **emphatic** form of ਨਾ **nā.** We can say

(8a) ਮੈਂ ਵਾਪਸ ਨਾ ਜਾਵਾਂ?
mæ̃ vāpas nā jāvā̃?
Sbjct
'Shall I not go back?'

But (8b) will sound odd because seeking permission emphatically is something odd.

(8b) (?) ਮੈਂ ਵਾਪਸ ਨਹੀਂ ਜਾਵਾਂ?
(?) **mæ̃ vāpas nahī̃ jāvā̃?**

But since the addition of -ਗਾ **-gā** makes the situation definite, the **emphatic negative particle** ਨਹੀਂ **nahī̃** sounds fine in (9a) and ਨਾ **na** sounds odd in (9b).

(9a) ਮੈਂ ਵਾਪਸ ਨਹੀਂ ਜਾਵਾਂਗਾ
mæ̃ vāpas nahī̃ jāvā̃gā
Sbjct+**gā**
'I will not go back'

(9b) (?) ਮੈਂ ਵਾਪਸ ਨਾ ਜਾਵਾਂਗਾ
(?) **mæ̃ vāpas na jāvā̃gā**

In all the examples given above, -ਗਾ **-gā** is **agglutinated** (glued or firmly bonded) to the **subjuntive** verb forms. Nothing (a **negative** or **emphatic particle**, for example) can intervene between the two. For example, you cannot say *ਜਾਵਾਂ ਨਹੀਂ ਗਾ *jāvā̃ nahī̃ gā. But, as we saw in Chapter 11, -ਗਾ **-gā** is **agglutinated** in ਸੀਗਾ **sīgā**, but not in ਹੈਗਾ **hægā**. In Shahmukhi script (the name used for the Urdu script when used for writing Panjabi in Pakistan) -ਗਾ **-gā** is not joined to the verb and is written separately. The verb form often ends in a non-connector letter to which another letter cannot be joined and has to be written separately. (See Chapter 18.) So they have made it a rule to always write **-gā** separately. For example, they write ਜਾਵਾਂਗਾ **jāvā̃gā** as جاواں گا.

Agglutination and pronunciation tend to give the impression that **subjunctive+gā** is a single verb form which should have only one **TMA** (or *kāla*) **inflection** at the end. Throughout the history of North Indian languages, the **personal verb inflections** have been giving way to the **adjectival** (or **participial**) **inflections**. So the **personal inflection** in **subjuncitve+gā** is likely to disappear and signs of this have already started appearing. By adding the **singular masculine -gā** to the **first personal singular** ਕਰਾਂ **karā̃** we get ਕਰਾਂਗਾ **karā̃gā**. But by adding the **masculine plural -ge** to the first person plural ਕਰੀਏ **karīe**, we do not get *ਕਰੀਏਗੇ ***karīege**, but ਕਰਾਂਗੇ **karā̃ge**. The **subjunctive *plural* personal inflection** has given way to the ***singular***. This may be a sign of a change taking place. But such changes take centuries to show any visible and audible results. We can *speculate* that the **internal personal endings** in **subjunctive+gā** may disappear, and a Panjabi grammarian in 2200 AD may be dealing with *ਕਰਗਾ **kargā**, *ਕਰਗੇ **karge**, *ਕਰਗੀ **kargā** and *ਕਰਗੀਆਂ **kargīā̃**!

Some Western Panjabi dialects have retained the **future tense** form inherited from the Sanskrit **future tense**. Each inflected personal form has the sound ਸ **s** which comes from the Sanskrit **future tense** affix *-ṣ* or *-s*. In the Mirpuri dialect of Panjabi, we have

(10) ਮੈਂ ਜਾਸਾਂ **mā̃ⁱ jāsā̃**
'I will go'

ਅਸਾਂ ਜਾਸਾਂ **asā̃ jāsā̃**
'We will go'

ਤੁਸਾਂ ਜਾਸੋ **tusā̃ jāsõ**
'You will go'

ਉਹ ਜਾਸੀ **uh jāsī**
'He will go'

ਉਹ ਜਾਸਣ **uh jāsaṇ**
'They will go'

In some other Western dialects the endings are

	Singular	Plural
First person	-ਸਾਂ **-sā̃**	-ਸੂੰ **-sū̃**
Second person	-ਸੇਂ **-sẽ**	-ਸੋ **-so**
Third person	-ਸੀ **-sī**	-ਸਨ/ਸਣ **-san/saṇ**

11.2.3 The copula

The Panjabi **copula** is a verb with **personal** inflections shown in the following tables.

(1) **-remote**

	Singular	**Plural**
First person	ਹਾਂ **hā̃**	ਹਾਂ **hā̃**
Second person	ਹੈਂ **hæ̃**	ਹੋ **ho**
Third person	ਹੈ **hæ**	ਹਨ **han** / ਨੇ **ne**

(2) **+remote**

	Singular	**Plural**
First person	ਸਾਂ **sā̃**	ਸਾਂ **sā̃**
Second person	ਸੈਂ **sæ̃**	ਸੋ **so**
Third person	ਸੀ **sī**	ਸਨ **san**

These are the forms used in writing and in very formal spoken Panjabi. In the more colloquial style, the dialectal unstressed variants ਆਂ **ā̃**, ਆ **ā**, ਵਾਂ **vā̃**, ਜੇ **je** (for ਹੈ **hæ**) and ਸੀ **sī** are mostly used. Some speakers inflect ਸੀ **sī** for **number** and **gender** as they do with **participial** forms and use ਸੇ **se** and ਸੀਆਂ **sīā̃** as well.

Interestingly, while more conservative Panjabi has retained the older **personal +remote** forms (inflected for **person** and **number**) of the **copula** given above, Hindi-Urdu has evolved further and has adopted the **adjectival +remote** forms (inflected for **number** and **gender**) – था **tʰā** ('was' *Mas*), थे **tʰe** ('were' *Mas*), थी **tʰī** ('was' *Fem*) and थीं **tʰī̃** ('were' *Fem*).

The Panjabi **copula** is an idiosyncratic verb and has been so ever since the time of Sanskrit (or perhaps earlier). It is also the most misunderstood and misanalysed verb in Panjabi (and Hindi-Urdu as well). As also pointed out in Chapter 2, it comes from the Sanskrit root √*as*, which was conjugated in the 'general' (*sārvadhātuka*) tenses only. In the 'special' (*ārdhādhātuka*) tenses, √*bhū* was a substitute of √*as* (Pāṇini II.4.52). This continues to be the case in Panjabi. ਹੋ **ho**, which comes from √*bhū*, is a substitute of ਹੈ **hæ** where an **adjectival** (**participial**) form is needed. This has led some grammarians to confuse ਹੋ **ho** and ਹੈ **hæ** and assert that ਹੈ **hæ** (or ਹੋ **ho**) has "two additional forms". Interestingly, ਹੈ **hæ** is the only Panjabi verb inflected for **tense**, but has no **participial** forms.

But this ignorance about the *history* of the verb is not as serious as the misunderstanding about its *present* semantics.

Many past grammarians of Panjabi have regarded ਹੈ **ha^{i}** as the "present tense form", ਸੀ **sī** as the "past tense form" and ਗਾ **gā** as a "marker of the future tense". But (11) is a serious challenge to this misanalysis.

(11) ਉਹ ਘਰ ਹੈਗਾ ਸੀ
uh g^{h}ar ha^{i}gā sī
'He was definitely at home'

Surely (11) does not have three "tenses". Actually, the so-called "present tense" form ਹੈ **ha^{i}** is a **subjunctive** form with **-remote** as its *prototypical* meaning indicating simple existence without specifying its time. In the absence of any contextual and co-textual clues to the contrary, the *default* meaning of ਹੈ **ha^{i}** is "existence at the present moment". But in (11), the presence of ਸੀ **sī** indicates definite existence in the past time. Also, we can regard the meaning of ਸੀ **sī** as **+remote**, with "existence in the past time relative to the present moment" as its *default* meaning. But this form can place that existence prior to *any* point in time even in the past or the future.

(12) ਉਹਨੇ ਅਗਲੇ ਹਫ਼ਤੇ ਆਉਣਾ ਸੀ
uhne agle hafte āuṇā si
PotP
'He was to come next week'

Similarly the *default*, but not *the only*, meaning **subjunctive+ਗਾ gā** is "future".

Ever since the time of Sanskrit, √*bhū* (modern form ਹੋ **ho**) has been a substitute for √*as* (modern form ਹੈ **ha^{i}**) in many situations where √*as* lacked the inflected forms. This continues in Panjabi. ਹੋ **ho** and ਹੈ **ha^{i}** complement each other; each has the forms which the other lacks. Their meanings and pronunciation are so similar that many grammarians can be forgiven for getting confused.

(13a) ਉਹ ਘਰ ਹੈ
uh g^{h}ar ha^{i}
'He is at home'

indicates his presence at home at the *moment of speaking*. But to put the situation into the *future time*, we would have to bring in ਹੋ **ho**, as in

(13b) ਉਹ ਘਰ ਹੋਵੇਗਾ
uh g^{h}ar hovegā
Sbjct+gā
'He will be at home'

As will be shown later in (22b), ਹੋ **ho** and ਹੈ **ha^i** can also occur together in a **VP**.

11.2.3.1 Omission of ਹੈ ha^i in negative clauses

ਹੈ **ha^i** can be optionally omitted in negative clauses with the negative particle ਨਹੀਂ **nahī̃** even when -ਗਾ **-gā** could be added to ਹੈ **ha^i**. For example, (14a) and (14b) can be negated as (15a) and (15b) respectively

(14a) ਉਹ ਘਰ ਹੈ
uh g^{h}ar ha^i
'He is at home'

(14b) ਉਹ ਘਰ ਨਹੀਂ
uh g^{h}ar nahī̃
'He is not at home'

(15a) ਉਹ ਘਰ ਹੈਗਾ
uh g^{h}ar ha^{i}gā
'He is certainly at home'

(15b) ਉਹ ਘਰ ਨਹੀਂ ਗਾ
uh g^{h}ar nahī̃ gā
'He is certainly not at home'

But you cannot omit ਸੀ **sī** in a negative clause. The reason seems to be that ਹੈ **ha^i** indicates existence *unrelated to* time, its default interpretation is the *present* time. So the **emphatic negative particle** ਨਹੀਂ **nahī̃** should be enough. But ਸੀ **sī** conveys the idea of *remote* time as well, whose default interpretation is the past time. So it is not possible to omit ਸੀ **sī** in a negative clause.

11.3 The imperative

The **imperative** form is a **personal** form. But, for obvious reasons, it is inflected for **second person** (singular and plural) only. There are two types of imperative forms in Panjabi: **plain** and **suggestive**. The latter is regarded as more polite.

The imperative endings are

	Singular	Plural
Plain Imperative	Ø	-ਓ **-o** / -ਵੋ **-vo**
Suggestive Imperative	-ਈਂ **-ī̃** / -ਵੀਂ **-vī̃**	-ਈਓ **-īo**

As in English, the **plain singular** form has zero affix and it sounds and looks identical to the stem of the verb. But this was not always the case. In the 16th century Panjabi, the **plain imperative** ending was -ਹੁ **-hu** or -ਉ **-u**. This is discussed later in this chapter. With historical phonetic changes, these endings have disappeared. Some modern Panjabi examples of the plain imperative are

(16a) (ਤੂੰ) ਜਾ
(tū̃) jā
Imper(P)
'(You) go'

(16b) (ਤੁਸੀਂ) ਜਾਓ/ਜਾਵੋ
(tusī̃) jāo/jāvo
Imper(P)
'(You) go'

The **suggestive imperative** forms are used in

(17a) ਤੂੰ ਜਾਈਂ/ਜਾਵੀਂ
tū̃ jāī̃/jāvī̃
Imper(S)
'You please go'

(17b) ਤੁਸੀਂ ਜਾਈਓ
tusī̃ jāīo
Imper(S)
'You please go'

ਤੂੰ **tū̃** or ਤੁਸੀਂ **tusī̃** is less frequently omitted in such sentences with the suggestive imperative.

11.4 Imperfect participle form

11.4.1 Morphology of the imperfect participle form

The **imperfect participle** affix is -ਦ- **-d-**, which is followed by a **number-gender affix** given in section **11.2.2** above. If the stem ends in a consonant, just -ਦ- **-d-** and the number-gender affix are added. In some verb stems ending in a vowel, the vowel is nasalised before the addition of -ਦ- **-d-**. In some other stems ending in a vowel (and all the ones ending in -ਆ **-ā** or -ਵਾ **-vā**), the final vowel is not nasalised but -ਉਂ- **-ū̃-** is added. Following are the examples of the **masculine singular** forms of the **imperfect participle**.

ਬਣ **baṇ**	ਬਣਦਾ **baṇdā** 'becoming'
ਉੱਠ **uṭṭ^h**	ਉੱਠਦਾ **uṭṭ^{h}dā** 'rising'
ਚਲ **cal**	ਚਲਦਾ **caldā** 'moving'
ਪੜ੍ਹ **parh**	ਪੜ੍ਹਦਾ **paṛhdā** 'reading'
ਜਾ **jā**	ਜਾਂਦਾ **jā̃dā** 'going'
ਖਾ **k^{h}ā**	ਖਾਂਦਾ **k^{h}ā̃dā** 'eating'
ਪੀ **pī**	ਪੀਂਦਾ **pī̃dā** 'drinking'
ਲੈ **la^i**	ਲੈਂਦਾ **lã^{i}dā** 'taking'
ਜੀ **jī**	ਜੀਉਂਦਾ **jīū̃dā** 'living'
ਸੀ **sī**	ਸੀਉਂਦਾ **sīū̃dā** 'sewing'
ਆ **ā**	ਆਉਂਦਾ **āū̃dā** 'coming'
ਬਣਾ **baṇā**	ਬਣਾਉਂਦਾ **baṇāū̃dā** 'making'

Many speakers pronounce the vowel sequence **āū̃** as a single vowel **ã^u** (pure vowel or glide, depending upon the area). If **ū̃** is already there in the stem, only -ਦ- **-d-** is added.

ਭਿਉਂ b^hiũ **ਭਿਉਂਦਾ b^hiũdā** 'making wet'

A few more changes take place in some other stems.

ਦੇ de **ਦਿੰਦਾ dindā** 'giving'

ਹੋ ho **ਹੁੰਦਾ hundā** 'becoming'

11.4.2 Semantics of the imperfect participle form

The semantics of this verb form in Panjabi, like that of the other verb forms, was misunderstood by the European grammarians of Indian languages and by the Indian grammarians who uncritically followed them. By itself, it was called "conditional past tense" and various other types of "continuous" tenses in combination with **ਹੈ ha^i** and **ਹੋ ho**.

But if we keep in mind the *prototypical* meaning **-completed** of this form, we can explain all these "tense"-related meanings and many more. Basically, it denotes an **uncompleted** action or situation, which can be interpreted as "ongoing", "recurring", "habitual" and even "not started".

(18) ਤੁਸੀਂ ਕੀ ਕੰਮ ਕਰਦੇ ਹੋ?

tusī̃ kī kamm karde ho?

ImP Cop

'What work do you do?'

To emphasise that the work is ongoing at the moment, a construction with **ਰਹਿ rahi** can be used, as will be discussed in a later chapter. In (17), (18) and (19) below, this form is used in combination with **ਹੈ ha^i** and **ਸੀ sī**.

(19) ਮੈਂ ਸਵੇਰੇ ਪੰਜ ਵਜੇ ਉੱਠਦਾ ਹਾਂ

mã^i savere panj vaje uṭṭ^{h}dā hã̄

ImP Cop

'I get up at five in the morning'

(20) ਉਹ ਬਹੁਤ ਜ਼ਿਆਦਾ ਸ਼ਰਾਬ ਪੀਂਦਾ ਹੈ

uh bahut ziādā śarāb pī̃dā ha^i

ImP Cop

'He drinks too much alcohol'

(21) ਉਹ ਰੋਜ਼ ਮੰਦਰ ਜਾਂਦਾ ਸੀ
uh roz mandar jā̃dā sī
ImP Cop
'He used to go to the temple daily'

The form by itself has been described as "conditional past" as in

(22) ਜੇ ਉਹ ਸ਼ਹਿਰ ਜਾਂਦਾ . . .
je uh śahir jā̃dā...
ImP
'If he had gone to the city...'

But the "conditional past" meaning is imparted by the *context* and the **conjunction ਜੇ je** 'if'. The **main verb** itself (used without **ਸੀ sī** in (22)) denotes an uncompleted action which by implication can refer to an action that did not take place.

In the following brief passage, the writer describes his experience of his boyhood days in his native village. Once the context sets the whole story in the past time he does not have to mark every sentence for tense like a speaker of English. (This is not possible in Panjabi, anyway.) He gets *inside* the situation and views every happening in this way, expressing this by using the **imperfect participle** *without* **ਸੀ sī**. There is not even the slightest hint of any "conditional past". The relevant verb forms are printed in *italics* in Panjabi and in the (ungrammatical) English translation of (23) as well.

(23) ਸਾਡੇ ਪਿੰਡ ਹਰ ਸਾਲ ਛਿੰਝ *ਪੈਂਦੀ*। ਦੂਰੋਂ ਦੂਰੋਂ ਭਲਵਾਨ *ਆਉਂਦੇ*, ਇੱਕ ਦੋ ਪਾਕਿਸਤਾਨ ਤੋਂ ਵੀ *ਆਉਂਦੇ*। ਜ਼ੋਰਦਾਰ ਕੁਸ਼ਤੀਆਂ *ਹੁੰਦੀਆਂ*। ਜੇਤੂਆਂ ਨੂੰ ਇਨਾਮ *ਮਿਲ਼ਦੇ*। ਪਟਕੇ ਦੇ ਜੇਤੂ ਨੂੰ ਚੋਖੀ ਰਕਮ ਅਤੇ ਚਾਂਦੀ ਦਾ ਗੁਰਜ *ਮਿਲਦਾ*।
sāḍe pinḍ har sāl c^{h}inj^h *pā̃'dī*. dūrõ dūrõ b^{h}alvān *āū̃de*, ikk do pākistān tõ vī *āū̃de*. zordār kuśtīā̃ *hundīā̃*. jetūā̃ nū̃ inām *miḷde*. paṭke de jetū nū̃ cok^{h}ī rakam ate cā̃dī dā guraj *miḷdā*.
'A wrestling tournament *taking* place in our village every year. Wrestlers from far off places *coming*, one or two *coming* from Pakistan as well. Strong wrestling matches *taking* place. Winners *getting* prizes. The champion winner *getting* a huge amount of money and a silver club.'

The effect is somewhat similar to that of the "historic present" used in English. But this term will be as inappropriate in Panjabi grammar as the term "historic imperfective" will be in English grammar.

It is interesting to note that the Punjabi immigrants in the UK who had little education in India make an excessive use of the *-ing* forms in their English speech, even where the native speakers of English would use different forms. An examples is "I *coming* home very tired. My wife *telling* me you go do shopping. I *saying* no I *going* to bed."

The **imperfect participle** form of ਹੋ **ho** (like that of any other lexical verb) can be used with ਹੈ **ha^i**, as in (24b) below), proving that ਹੋ **ho** and ਹੈ **ha^i** are not the same verb as assumed by many grammarians. ਹੈ **ha^i** is *basically* a "state" verb and ਹੋ **ho** a "process" verb, though ਹੋ **ho** may act as a substitute for ਹੈ **ha^i** in some situations. The following sentences differ in meaning.

(24a) ਗੁੜ ਮਿੱਠਾ ਹੈ
guṛ miṭṭ^{h}ā ha^i
Cop
'The sugar is sweet'
i.e., 'This particular sample of sugar is sweet'

(24b) ਗੁੜ ਮਿੱਠਾ ਹੁੰਦਾ ਹੈ
guṛ miṭṭ^{h}ā hundā ha^i
ImP Cop
'Sugar is sweet'

(24b) means that 'It is the generic quality of sugar to be sweet'. Now it can be easily understood why (25a) makes perfect sense and (25b) is senseless.

(25a) ਈਸ਼ਵਰ ਅੰਤਰਯਾਮੀ ਹੈ
īśvar antaryāmī ha^i
Cop
'God is omniscient'

(25b) (?) ਈਸ਼ਵਰ ਅੰਤਰਯਾਮੀ ਹੁੰਦਾ ਹੈ
(?) īśvar antaryāmī hundā ha^i
ImP Cop

There are different samples of sugar which you may continually come across but there are no such samples of an omniscient God. Similarly you can say (26a) but not (26b).

(26a) ਮਹਾਤਮਾ ਗਾਂਧੀ ਦਾ ਨਾਂ ਅਮਰ ਹੈ
mahātmā gānd^hi dā nā̃ amar ha^i
Cop
'Mahatma Gandhi's name is immortal'

(26b) (?) ਮਹਾਤਮਾ ਗਾਂਧੀ ਦਾ ਨਾਂ ਅਮਰ ਹੁੰਦਾ ਹੈ
(?) mahātmā gānd^hi dā nā̃ amar hundā ha^i
ImP Cop

11.4.3 Imperfect participle and the subtractive verb phases of verb stems

A verb stem in the **subtractive phase** can have *only* the **imperfect participle** inflection. The agent of the verb in the subtractive stem is **eliminated** and idea conveyed is that of universal applicability or prohibition. If the SUBJECT is ਅਸੀਂ **asī̃** 'we', the boastful idea of doing something *repeatedly* is conveyed. So the imperfect participle is the ideal form here.

(27) ਗੁਰਦਵਾਰੇ ਵਿਚ ਸਿਰ *ਢਕੀਦਾ* ਹੈ
gurdvāre vich sir *ḍ^hakīdā* ha^i
SubPh ImP Cop
'Head should be covered in a Sikh temple'

(28) ਬੱਚਿਆਂ ਨੂੰ ਗੰਦੀ ਭਾਸ਼ਾ ਨਹੀਂ *ਸਿਖਾਈਦੀ*
bacciā̃ nū̃ gandī b^hāśā nahī̃ *sik^hāīdī*
SubPh ImP
'Foul language should not be taught to children'

(29) ਅਸੀਂ ਖ਼ੂਬ *ਨੱਚੀਦਾ* ਸੀ
asī̃ xūb *naccīdā* sī
SubPh ImP Cop
'We used to dance a lot'

11.4.4 Imperfect participle form as an adjective

Like the English *-ing* form, the **imperfect participle** form can be used as an **adjective** with the meaning 'engaged in this activity'.

(30) ਕੰਮ ਕਰਦੀਆਂ ਮਾਂਵਾਂ
kamm kardīā̃ mā̃vā̃
'working mothers'

(31) ਡੁੱਬਦਾ ਜਹਾਜ਼
ḍubbdā jahāz
'sinking ship'

11.5 Perfect participle form

Panjabi has three verb forms expressive of **perfective aspect** as Figure 11.2 shows.To repeat what was said in **11.1** above, **aspect** takes *situation-internal* perspective and marks the situation as completed, incomplete or ongoing, recurring etc. without relating it to any situation-external point in time. Perfective aspect views the situation as an undivided **complete** (or **completed**) whole. But such a situation can be viewed *from the end point* (**retrospective**) or *from the starting point* (**prospective**) or *as a whole* (**simulspective**). Panjabi has verb forms for all the three possibilities, as shown in Figure 11.2. In this section we consider the **perfect participle** form viewing the complete situation *retrospectively.*

11.5.1 Morphology of the perfect participle form

There are two types of **perfect participle** forms in Panjabi: the **regular** and the **irregular** ones. The number of the **irregular** forms is quite small and is falling. But they are *very* common, and this is probably the reason for their survival. While *all* the perfect participle forms have the **adjectival** or **participial endings** shown in the table of affixes given above, the **stems** of the irregular forms undergo some additional phonetic changes. One notable thing about the regular perfect participle forms is that the masculine singular affix used with them is **-iā**, and not **-ā**. The other three affixes shown in the table are used in their unchanged form. For example, the regular perfect participle forms of the stem ਪੜ੍ਹ **parh** 'read' are

ਪੜ੍ਹਿਆ **paṛhiā** (not *ਪੜ੍ਹਾ ***paṛhā**), ਪੜ੍ਹੇ **paṛhe**, ਪੜ੍ਹੀ **paṛhī** and ਪੜ੍ਹੀਆਂ **paṛhīā̃**. (But some younger speakers have started using ਪੜ੍ਹਾ **paṛhā**.)

The **masculine singular** forms of the most important **irregular** verbs are given below. The endings given in the table are applied to the changed stems.

ਸੌਂ **sã^{u}** 'sleep'	ਸੁੱਤਾ **suttā**	
ਕਰ **kar** 'do'	ਕੀਤਾ **kītā**	(regular ਕਰਿਆ **kariā** is also used)
ਕਹਿ **kahi** 'say'	ਕਿਹਾ **kihā**	
ਖਾ **k^{h}ā** 'eat'	ਖਾਧਾ **k^{h}ād^{h}ā**	(regular ਖਾਇਆ **k^{h}āiā** is also used)
ਜਾ **jā** 'go'	ਗਿਆ **giā**	
ਦੇ **de** 'give'	ਦਿੱਤਾ **dittā**	
ਧੋ **d^{h}o** 'wash'	ਧੋਤਾ **d^{h}otā**	(regular ਧੋਇਆ **d^{h}oiā** is also used)
ਪੀ **pī** 'drink'	ਪੀਤਾ **pītā**	
ਬਹਿ **bahi** 'sit'	ਬੈਠਾ **ba^{i}ṭ^{h}ā**	
ਰਿੰਨ੍ਹ **rinnh** 'cook'	ਰਿੱਧਾ **ridd^{h}ā**	(regular ਰਿੰਨ੍ਹਿਆ **rinnhiā** has almost completely replaced ਰਿੱਧਾ **ridd^{h}ā**)
ਲੈ **la^{i}** 'take'	ਲੀਤਾ **lītā**	(regular ਲਿਆ **liā** has almost completely replaced ਲੀਤਾ **lītā**)

11.5.2 Semantics of the perfect participle form

The prototypical meaning of this verb form is **+complete**, and the *default* interpretation, in the absence of any contextual and co-textual clues to the contrary, is "completed in the past". The interpretation of

(32) ਉਹ ਹੁਣੇ ਆਇਆ
uh huṇe āiā
PerP
'He came right now'

is that the action took place in the very recent past. But if you call a servant, and he replies

(33) ਹੁਣੇ ਆਇਆ, ਸਾਹਬ
huṇe āiā, sāhab
PerP
'I come right now, sir'

he intends to say, "Sir, kindly regard my action as if already completed." He has not even started yet. By using the verb **ਆਇਆ āiā** 'come', he has already imagined himself as having moved *spatially*. So regarding this form in the "past tense" does not make any sense.

But this mistake of regarding the Panjabi (and Hindi-Urdu) perfect participle form as the "past tense" form has been committed not only by ordinary grammarians but also by modern academic linguists. (34), (35) and (36) are even more interesting. The first clause is shared by (34) and (35), but the intonation makes a lot of difference.

(34) ਜੇ ਤੂੰ ਪਿੰਡ ਗਿਆ, ਤਾਂ ਪੁਲਿਸ ਤੈਨੂੰ ਫੜ ਲਏਗੀ
je tū̃ piṇḍ giā, tā̃ pulis ta'nū̃ pʰaṛ laegī
PerP Sbjct+gā
'If you go to the village, the police will arrest you'

Figure 11.4 Intonation of the "warning" adverb clause

(35) ਜੇ ਤੂੰ ਪਿੰਡ ਗਿਆ, ਤਾਂ ਉੱਥੇ ਰਿਹਾ ਕਿਉਂ ਨਹੀਂ?
je tū̃ piṇḍ giā, tā̃ uttʰe rihā kiũ nahī̃?
PerP PerP
'If you went to the village, why didn't you stay there?'
('I doubt whether you went there')

Figure 11.5 Intonation of the "taunting" adverb clause

The first clauses in both (34) and (35) are *phonematically* the same and differ in *prosody* only. The *context* and the *warning* intonation in (34) place the action in the future time. But the *context* and the *implicational* intonation in (35) places the action in the past time. (34) warns against the *completion* of the action and (35) doubts its *completion*. Both the situations are viewed *holistically* and *retrospectively*. The "past tense" interpretation of **ਗਿਆ giā** in (34) will be wrong. (36) is an extremely common expression in Panjabi.

(36) ਹੁਣ ਨਾ ਉਹ ਆਇਆ
huṇ nā uh āiā
PerP
'He is not going to come now'

His *not* coming is so certain that it is taken for granted. Enough about the "past tense" interpretation of this form.

11.5.3 Perfective participle form as an adjective

Like the **imperfect participle** form, the **perfect participle** form can be used as an **adjective** as in

(37) ਟੁੱਟਿਆ ਸ਼ੀਸ਼ਾ
ṭuṭṭiā śīśā
PerP
'broken glass'

(38) ਅੱਖੀਂ ਦੇਖਿਆ ਨਜ਼ਾਰਾ
akkʰī̃ dekʰiā nazārā
PerP
by eyes witnessed scene
'eye-witnessed scene'

11.5.4 Perfect participle form as a nominal

As we saw in Chapter 7, most **adjectives** in Panjabi can be used as **nouns** as well. This applied equally well to the **adjectival** perfect participle form. Guru Ram Das (16th century) wrote

(39) ਤੇਰਾ ਦਿਤਾ ਖਾਵਣਾ
PerP
terā ditā kʰāvṇā
your given to eat
'We will eat what is given by you'

As a **noun,** ਦਿਤਾ **ditā** (modern pronunciation and spelling ਦਿੱਤਾ **dittā**) is qualified by an **adjective** ਤੇਰਾ **terā** and is the OBJECT of the **potential participle** form ਖਾਵਣਾ **kʰāvṇā**. This form is discussed in section **11.7** below. There is a Panjabi proverb

(40) ਤੇਰਾ ਕੀਤਾ ਇਕ ਦਿਨ ਤੇਰੇ ਸਾਹਮਣੇ ਆਏਗਾ
terā kītā ik din tere sāhmaṇe āegā
PerP Sbjct+gā
'You will one day face the consequences of your deeds'
Lit. 'Your deed will one day come before you'

ਕੀਤਾ **kītā** 'done' qualified by the adjective ਤੇਰਾ **terā** 'your' acts as the SUBJECT of the verb ਆ **ā**.

The **nominal** use of the three verb forms expressive of **perfective aspect** is extremely important in Panjabi grammar and will be discussed in the next chapter. In fact, as we will see below, *all* the verb forms expressing **perfective aspect** can act as **nominals**, semantically as **initiators** and **patients** of an event or situation. Bhartṛhari said very clearly (*Vākyapadīya* III.7.3) that regarding a notion as a verb (*kriyā*) or a nominal accessory (*kāraka*) often depends upon the intention of the speaker. In English, for example, *singing* is a verb in *She is singing beautifully,* but a nominal accessory (SUBJECT of the clause) in *Her singing pleases me.* This happens in Panjabi as well.

11.5.5 The process of regularisation

There is a construction in Panjabi **perfect participle+ਕਰ kar** conveying the meaning of "performing some action as a matter of routine" in which *only the regular* or *regularised* forms of the **perfect participle** are used. Examples are

(41) ਮੈਂ ਉਹਨੂੰ ਪੈਸੇ *ਦਿਆ* ਕਰਦਾ ਸਾਂ
mã^{i} uhnū̃ pa^{i}se *diā* kardā sā̃
PerP ImP
'I used to give him money'

(42) ਨਾਨਕ ਸਿੰਘ ਗਰਮੀਆਂ ਵਿਚ ਡਲਹੌਜ਼ੀ *ਜਾਇਆ* *ਕਰਦਾ* ਸੀ
nanak sing^{h} garmīā̃ vic ḍalha^{u}zī *jāiā* *kardā* si
PerP ImP
'Nanak Singh routinely went to Dalhousie in summer'

It is notable that the *regularised* perfect participle forms of ਦੇ **de** and ਜਾ **jā** (ਦਿਆ **diā** and ਜਾਇਆ **jāiā** respectively) are used in (41) and (42) instead of the more common ਦਿੱਤਾ **dittā** and ਗਿਆ **giā** used outside this type of construction.

There is a comic Panjabi song

(43) ਮੱਖੀਆਂ ਤੋਂ ਡਰ ਲਗਦਾ
ਤੁਸੀਂ ਰੋਜ਼ ਨਹਾਇਆ ਕਰੋ
ਮੱਖੀਆਂ ਤੋਂ ਡਰ ਲਗਦਾ
ਗੁੜ ਥੋੜਾ ਖਾਇਆ ਕਰੋ
makkʰīā̃ tõ ḍar lagdā
tusī̃ roz *nahāiā karo*
makkʰīā̃ tõ ḍar lagdā
guṛ tʰoṛā *kʰāiā karo*
'(If) you are afraid of flies
You should bathe daily
(If) you are afraid of flies
Eat less sugar'

The irregular forms mentioned in **11.5.1** above are not used in these examples. ਲੀਤਾ ਕਰ **lītā kar** 'used to take' and ਕੀਤਾ ਕਰ **kītā kar** 'used to do' are found in the writings of some older Panjabi writers, but modern Punjabi usage is ਲਿਆ ਕਰ **liā kar** and ਕਰਿਆ ਕਰ **kariā kar**. This construction may be the source from which regularised forms are moving out into general usage. An interesting dialectal usage is exemplified in

(44)

ਤੇਰਾ	ਲਾੜੂਆ	ਸ਼ਰਾਬ	ਪੀਂਦਾ	ਕਰਿਆ	ਕਰਦਾ
terā	**lāṛūā**	**śarāb**	**pī̃dā**	***kariā***	***kardā***
			ImP	PerP	ImP
your	husband	liquor	drinking	done	doing

'Your husband has been drinking liquor regularly'

11.5.6 Question of the "certainty" modality and the Panjabi reporting verb ਕਹਿ kahi

Modality is not far away from any of the verb forms in Panjabi, even if we have classified them as non-modal to make our analysis manageable. The meaning of the **subjunctive** form, for example, is inherently indefinite, indicating some sort or possibility. The post-verb -ਗਾ **-gā** is added to the **subjunctive** form to make this meaning definite. -ਗਾ **-gā** comes from the Sanskrit perfect participle form *gataḥ* 'gone'. Both the lexical and the grammatical meaning of -ਗਾ **-gā** convey some idea of definiteness, which has misled some grammarians into regarding it as a marker of the "future tense" and **subjunctive+ga** as the "future tense" form. A completed action is more definite than an uncompleted one. The use of the Panjabi reporting verb **ਕਹਿ kahi** 'say' in narrative discourse makes this very clear. The English translations *said* and *saying* in the following example are literal.

(45) ਮੈਂ *ਕਿਹਾ*, "ਅੱਜ ਮੌਸਮ ਸੁਹਣਾ ਹੈ। ਕਿਤੇ ਬਾਹਰ ਚਲੀਏ।"
ਉਹ *ਕਹਿੰਦਾ*, "ਨਹੀਂ, ਮੈਨੂੰ ਘਰ ਕੰਮ ਹੈ।"
ਤੁਸੀਂ *ਕਿਹਾ*, "ਕੰਮ ਤੂੰ ਕੱਲ੍ਹ ਨੂੰ ਕਰ ਲਈਂ।"

mã^{i} *kihā*, "ajj ma^{u}sam suhṇā ha^{i}. kite bāhar calīe."
PerP
uh *kahindā*, "nahī̃, ma^{i}nū̃ g^{h}ar kamm ha^{i}."
ImP
tusī̃ *kihā*, "kamm tū̃ kallh nū̃ kar laī̃."
PerP

'I *said*, "The weather is fine today. Let us go out somewhere"'
'He *saying*, "No, I have work to do at home"'
'You *said*, "You should do the work tomorrow"'

The notable thing is that the perfect participle **ਕਿਹਾ kihā** 'said' is used to report the words of the speaker 'I' and the listener 'you', but the imperfect participle **ਕਹਿੰਦਾ kahindā** 'saying' is used to report the words of a third person. The two participle forms indicate the *degree of certainty*. The words spoken by the speaker and the listener are more certain and can be verified. But the words spoken by a third (and absent) person are not so certain. This is again an argument against regarding **ਕਿਹਾ kihā** and **ਕਹਿੰਦਾ kahindā** as "tense" forms because both refer to a *past* situation. **ਉਹਨੇ ਕਿਹਾ uhne kihā** could also be used in (45). But the more frequent use of **ਕਿਹਾ kihā** and **ਕਹਿੰਦਾ kahindā** in (45) is significant.

The **perfect participle** agreeing or in **number** and **gender** with the OBJECT of the clause or *not* agreeing with any **NP** and remaining in the **neuter** (homophonous to the **masculine singular**) form is discussed in detail in the next chapter.

11.6 Conjunctive participle form

This most frequently used verb form in Panjabi has been an uninflected one since the days of Sanskrit. Its Sanskrit ancestor has been called an infinitive or a gerund. But we group it with the **participles**. Each name has some justification. Its *prototypical* meaning is "an action completed before another action".

11.6.1 Conjunctive participle with an explicator auxiliary

Like the singular form of the **plain imperative**, the **conjuctive participle** sounds like a bare stem. This is the result of historical phonetic changes which have not (yet) changed its role in grammar. Until the beginning of the 18th century, this form ended in short **-ਿ -i**, which has since disappeared.

Guru Nanak Dev wrote in the first half of the 16th century

(46a) ਕਰਿ ਕਰਿ ਕਰਣਾ ਲਿਖਿ ਲੈ ਜਾਹੁ

kari kari karṇā lik^{h}i la^{i} jāhu

ConjP (repeated) ConjP ConjP Imper(P)

'Having done (your) deeds repeatedly, you (will) carry them written (on your soul)'

In the modern Panjabi version in the dialect used in this book would be

(46b) ਕਰ ਕਰ ਕਰਨੀ ਲਿਖ ਲੈ ਜਾ

kar kar karnī lik^{h} la^{i} jā

Several points are notable in Guru Nanak Dev's writing.

1. The **conjunctive participle ਲਿਖਿ lik^{h}i** has now become **ਲਿਖ lik^{h}** and the **imperative ਜਾਹੁ jāhu** has become **ਜਾ jā**, both sounding like a stem, which has misled some grammarians. But their old grammatical behaviour continues.

2. The **ਲੈ ਜਾ la^{i} jā** (literally 'take go') has acquired a compound meaning 'to take away'. In Chapter 13, we discuss the same fate of **ਲੈ ਆ la^{i} ā** (literally 'take come') meaning 'to bring'. The monosyllabic **ਲੈ la^{i}** in the compound had one gliding vowel, which later became a pure vowel and the word became [lɛ] in most modern dialects. As we will argue in Chapter 13, **ਲਿਖਿ ਲੈ ਜਾਹੁ lik^{h}i la^{i} jāhu** can be bracketed as ((ਲਿਖਿ) (ਲੈ ਜਾਹੁ)) **((lik^{h}i) (la^{i} jāhu))**, like its modern version ((ਲਿਖ) (ਲੈ ਜਾ)) **((lik^{h}) (la^{i} jā))**. **Serial verb constructions** of Panjabi have quite a long history!

3. Words are repeated to indicate a repeated activity. This topic is dealt with in **Appendix 2.**

The older ending of the **conjunctive participle** is preserved in the following Panjabi nursery rhyme which seems quite old.

(47) ਬਿੱਲੀ ਨੇ ਰਿੱਧਾ ਸਾਗ ਅੱਲਣ *ਪਾਇ* ਕੇ
ਚੂਹੇ ਆਏ ਖਾਣ ਧੋਤੀ *ਲਾਇ* ਕੇ
ਇੱਲ੍ਹ ਚੜ੍ਹੀ ਅਸਮਾਨ ਟੱਲ *ਵਜਾਇ* ਕੇ
billī ne ridd^{h}ā sāg allaṇ *pāi* ke
cūhe āe k^{h}āṇ d^{h}otī *lāi* ke
illh carhī asmān ṭall *vajāi* ke
'The cat cooked ਸਾਗ **sāg** after putting in corn flour
The rats came to eat (it) after wearing *dhotis*
The kite soared into the sky after ringing a huge bell'

ਸਾਗ **sāg** is a classic Indian vegetarian dish. The contents of its Panjabi version are spinach and mustard leaves cooked with corn flour and salt and then pureed. Instead of the verb forms used in this nursery rhyme, modern Panjabi uses ਪਾ **pā**, ਲਾ **lā** and ਵਜਾ **vajā**. Also, ਰਿੱਧਾ **ridd^{h}ā** has been almost completely replaced by ਰਿੰਨ੍ਹਿਆ **rinnhiā** in most dialects. It could be argued that the forms used in the nursery rhyme are there for metrical reasons. But only *grammatically permissible* forms are used in metrical poetry.

Within a **verb phrase** (in our sense of the term clarified in Chapter 5, the meaning of the combination of the **conjunctive participle** and the (**explicator**) **auxiliary** is "an action denoted by the main verb in the conjunctive participle form taking place under the conditions specified by the **auxiliary**". It is a "blending" of the two semantic spaces. (Fauconnier and Turner 2002.) This "blending" is harmonious in some cases but looks unlikely in some others. ਖਾ ਲੈ **k^{h}ā la^{i}** 'eat+take' makes sense, because the benefit of eating can be "taken", but *ਖਾ ਦੇ ***k^{h}ā de** 'eat+give' does not make any sense because the semantic spaces of ਖਾ **k^{h}ā** and ਦੇ **de** do not blend.

(48)

ਖ਼ਤ	ਪੜ੍ਹ	ਲੈ
xat	**paṛ^{h}**	**la^{i}**
	ConjP	
letter	read	'take'

means 'read the letter (silently) for your own information', but

(49) ਖ਼ਤ ਪੜ੍ਹ ਦੇ
xat paṛ^{h} de
ConjP
letter read 'give'

means 'read the letter aloud for someone else'. ਦੇਖ ਲੈ **dek^{h} la^{i}** 'see+take' means 'look or see for yourself' but ਦੇਖ ਦੇ **dek^{h} de** 'see+give' means, depending upon the context, 'have a look at, take care of, examine, supervise etc. for someone else'. The presence of ਰੱਖ **rakk^{h}** 'keep' or ਛੱਡ **c^{h}aḍḍ** 'leave' in ਕਰ ਰੱਖ **kar rakk^{h}** and ਕਰ ਛੱਡ **kar c^{h}aḍḍ** affects our perception of the meaning of the main verb ਕਰ **kar** 'do', carefully, or with concern and devotion, or carelessly or disinterestedly or with abandon.

Needless to say, the blending of the semantic spaces is thoroughly metaphorical. Each combination of a **main verb** and an **auxiliary** results in a unique blend. This subject of "blending" is also taken up in Chapter 13 on **serial verb constructions.**

11.6.2 Conjunctive participle with the post Verb ਕੇ ke

The most obvious use of the **conjunctive participle** is with the post verb ਕੇ **ke**. In this construction, the conjunctive participle form is followed by ਕੇ **ke**, which itself has historically developed from the conjunctive participle form of ਕਰ **kar** 'do'. The meaning of the construction is 'having done X' (as in (46a) and (46b) too). There is no limit on how many such constructions can be strung together to indicate actions done in a sequence. The only limit is that of the memory and the amount of air in the lungs! Only the last verb is marked for aspect and/or agrees with an **NP**.

(50) ਮੈਂ ਕਮਰੇ ਵਿਚ *ਜਾ ਕੇ*, ਕੁਰਸੀ 'ਤੇ *ਬਹਿ ਕੇ*, ਚਾਹ *ਪੀ ਕੇ*, ਸਾਰੇ ਖ਼ਤ ਟਾਈਪ *ਕਰ ਕੇ*, ਬਾਹਰ *ਜਾ ਕੇ*, ਡਾਕ ਵਿਚ ਪਾਏ

mã^{i} kamre vic *jā ke*, kursī te *bahi ke*, cāh *pī ke*, sāre xat *tāīp kar ke*, bāhar *jā ke*, ḍāk vic pāe

Lit. 'I *having gone* into the room, *having sat* on a chair, *having drunk* tea, *having typed* all the letters, *having gone* out, posted them.'

The **conjunctive participle+ਕੇ ke** sequence does not become a part of the **VP** in our sense. It is not possible to decide whether the conjunctive participle in this use acts as a **participle** or a (nominal) **gerund** or **infinitive**. But, as was said above, the name is less important than its grammatical function or role. We regard the construction with **conjunctive participle+ਕੇ ke** as a **non-finite adverbial clause**. (See Chapter 14.)

11.6.3 Conjunctive participle form as a nominal

Like other Panjabi verb forms depicting a completed action, the **conjunctive participle** also works clearly as a nominal, as the SUBJECT of a clause, mostly conveying "incapabilitative" meaning (inability to do something or inability to stop oneself from doing something) or to avoid the responsibility for some action, making the whole action itself the SUBJECT of the clause and the actual **agent** of the action the *mere* **source** from whom the action proceeds or does not proceed.

(51)	ਦੁਖਦੇ	ਹੱਥਾਂ	ਨਾਲ	ਮੈਥੋਂ	ਠੀਕ	*ਲਿਖ*	ਨਹੀਂ ਹੁੰਦਾ
	duk^{h}de	**hatt^{h}ā̃**	**nāḷ**	**ma^{i}t^{h}õ**	**ṭ^{h}īk**	***lik^{h}***	**nahī̃ hundā**
						ConjP	ImP
	aching	hands	with	me-from	correct	'writing'	not happening

'I cannot write correctly with aching hands'
Lit. 'With aching hands, correct writing does not happen from me'

'Writing' in the glosses of (51) is only a rough translation of **ਲਿਖ lik^{h}**, which is clearly the grammatical subject of (51). As a nominal it is qualified by the adjective **ਠੀਕ ṭ^{h}īk**. The verb in the **imperfect participle** form agrees in number and gender with this subject. As we see in the next chapter, a **participle** used as a nominal is a **masculine singular** noun.

(52)	ਮੈਥੋਂ	ਸੱਚ	*ਬੋਲ*	ਹੋ	ਗਿਆ
	ma^{i}t^{h}õ	**sacc**	***bol***	**ho**	**giā**
				ConjP	PerP
	me-from	truth	speaking	happening	gone

'I could not stop myself from speaking the truth'
Lit. 'Truth-speaking happened from me.'

There is a Panjabi song in which a young unmarried woman confesses to her older brother's wife.

(53) ਮੈਥੋਂ ਹਾਣ ਦੇ ਮੁੰਡੇ ਨਾ' *ਹੱਸ* ਹੋ ਗਿਆ,
ਨੀ ਭਾਬੀ ਕਿਤੇ ਗੱਲ ਨਾ ਕਰੀਂ
ma^{i}t^{h}õ hāṇ de muṇḍe nā' *hass* ho giā
nī b^{h}ābī kite gall nā karī̃
'I happened to smile to a youth of my age;
O sister-in-law, please don't tell anyone (about this)'

The literal translation of the first line of (53) would be, 'Smiling to a youth of my age happened from me'.

11.6.4 Special cases of ਕਰ ਕੇ kar ke and ਰੱਜ ਕੇ rajj ke

ਕਰ ਕੇ **kar ke** ('having done') and ਰੱਜ ਕੇ **rajj ke** ('having filled the belly'), because of their frequent use, have also developed special idiomatic meanings and grammatical behaviour. ਕਰ ਕੇ **kar ke** (now written as one word ਕਰਕੇ by many Panjabi writers) is also used as a **postposition** meaning 'because of', while ਰੱਜ ਕੇ **rajj ke** (generally written as two words) also functions as an adverb meaning 'to one's full satisfaction' or 'to one's heart's content'.

(54) ਮੀਂਹ *ਕਰਕੇ* ਮੈਚ ਨਾ ਹੋ ਸਕਿਆ
mī̃h *karke* ma^{i}c nā ho sakiā
'The match could not take place because of rain'

(55) ਅਸੀਂ *ਰੱਜ ਕੇ* ਨੱਚੇ
asī̃ *rajj ke* nacce
'We danced to our heart's content'

The original meanings are clearly metaphorically extended.

11.7 Potential participle form

The last form of the **perfective** family in our list is the **potential participle** form, whose semantics we describe as **prospective**. As the name indicates, it views the situation holistically and *prospectively* i.e., *potentially completed.*

11.7.1 Morphology of the potential participle form

The **potential participle** affix is -ਣ- **-ṇ-** or -ਨ- **-n-** which is followed by the usual **number-gender** affix from the table of adjectival endings given earlier. Sometimes -ਉ- **-u-** is added to the stem before -ਣ- **-ṇ-** or -ਨ- **-n-**. The rules for the addition of this -ਉ- **-u-** are the same as for the **imperfect participle**. (See section **11.4.1**). The choice between -ਣ- **-ṇ-** or -ਨ- **-n-** is quite simple. Normally, -ਣ- **-ṇ-** is used except after ਣ **ṇ**, ਰ **r**, ੜ **ṛ** and ਲ਼ **ḷ**. All these four consonant sounds involve a quick flapping of the tongue, and flapping the tongue quickly twice in order to add ਣ **ṇ** is difficult. (This is a tongue-twister – literally!). So ਨ **n** is added as the participial affix.

There is another form homophonous and homographic to the **potential participle**. It is the **gerund**. Though the potential participle and the gerund historically come from different sources, the consequences of their phonetic and semantic similarity are interesting. As we have seen above, the other two members of the **perfective** family are often used as nominals. This is the case with the **potential participle** as well, and the **gerund** comes in very handy for this purpose. In the citation form and in a Panjabi dictionary, a Panjabi verb is mentioned in the **masculine singular** form of the **gerund**. (See Appendix 1.) ਹੈ **ha^{i}** is the only Panjabi verb which has no **potential participle** or the **gerund** form. So it is is grouped with ਹੋ **ho** and is mentioned as ਹੋਣਾ **hoṇā**.

The *prototypical* meaning of the **potential participle** is unrelated to any time in relation to the present time or the time of the speech moment. It refers to a potential situation at *any* time, present, past or future.

(56) ਉਹਨੇ ਹੁਣੇ ਆਉਣਾ ਹੈ
uhne huṇe āuṇā ha^{i}
PotP Cop
'He is coming right now'

(57) ਉਹਨੇ ਕੱਲ੍ਹ ਆਉਣਾ ਸੀ
uhne kallh āuṇā sī
PotP Cop
'He was to come yesterday'

(58) ਉਹਨੇ ਅਗਲੇ ਮਹੀਨੇ ਆਉਣਾ ਹੈ
uhne agle mahīne āuṇā ha^{i}
PotP Cop
'He is coming next month'

It is the context or accompanying verb or the adverbial that indicates the time of the potential action.

11.7.2 The gerund

A **gerund** grammatically behaves like a **masculine singular noun**, but with one major difference. It ends in **-ā**, but this does not change to **-e** before a **postposition** as other masculine singular nouns ending in **-ā** do for their oblique form. (See Chapter 6.) Most speakers would say

(59a) ਪੜ੍ਹਨ ਦਾ ਕੰਮ
paṛhan dā kamm
Ger
reading of work
'the work of reading'

(60a) ਖਾਣ ਵਾਲ਼ਾ ਤੇਲ
k^hāṇ vāḷā tel
Ger
eating of oil
'edible oil'

But in some dialects (and sometimes in poetry for metrical reasons) the speakers have started inflecting the **gerund** in this position like a **masculine singular noun** ending in **-ā**. They pronounce and write these expressions as

(59b) ਪੜ੍ਹਨੇ ਦਾ ਕੰਮ
paṛhne dā kamm
Ger

(60b) ਖਾਣੇ ਵਾਲ਼ਾ ਤੇਲ
k^hāṇe vālā tel
Ger

This inflection of the gerund for the oblique form is standard in Hindi-Urdu, in which पढ़ने का काम **paṛhne kā kām** and खाने वाला तेल **k^hāne vālā tel** are used.

11.7.3 Semantics of the potential participle and the gerund

As a **verbal noun**, the **gerund** presents a situation as a whole; so does the **potential participle**. They are homophonous as well. So their semantic functions are morphing into each other's. Often, it is impossible to say which of the two is used when the verb does not agree with any **NP** and is in the **neuter** (homophonous to the **masculine singular**) form. **Case-marking** and **verb-agreement** are discussed in the next chapter.

As we saw in section **11.2.2** above, the combination **subjunctive+gā** refers to a more or less definite potential situation as in

(61) ਮੈਂ ਕੱਲ੍ਹ ਵਾਪਸ ਜਾਵਾਂਗਾ
mãi kallh vāpas jāvā̃gā
Subjct+gā
'I will go back tomorrow'

By contrast, the the use of the **potential participle** form indicates some sort of compulsion or inevitability.

(62) ਮੈਂ ਕੱਲ੍ਹ ਵਾਪਸ ਜਾਣਾ ਹੈ
mãi kallh vāpas jāṇā hai
PotP Cop
'I am going to go back tomorrow'

The **postposition** ਵਾਲ਼ਾ **vāḷā** means 'possessor' or 'in possession of' as in ਦਾਹੜੀ ਵਾਲ਼ਾ ਬੰਦਾ **dāhṛī vāḷā bandā** 'the bearded man' (*lit.* 'the man possessing a beard'). When ਵਾਲ਼ਾ **vāḷā** is added to a **gerund**, the meaning is "an imminent or inevitable action" as in

(63) ਗੱਡੀ ਚੱਲਣ ਵਾਲ਼ੀ ਹੈ
gaḍḍī callaṇ vāḷī hai
Ger
'The train is about to start'

That the meanings conveyed by the combination **subjunctive+gā** and the **potential participle** or the **gerund** are different is clear in the following examples.

(64) ਜੋ ਹੋਣਾ ਹੈ ਉਹ ਹੋਏਗਾ
jo hoṇā hai uh hoegā
PotP Subjct+gā
'What is certain to happen will happen'
'The inevitable will happen'

(65) ਜਾਣ ਵਾਲ਼ਾ ਜਾਏਗਾ, ਆਉਣ ਵਾਲ਼ਾ ਆਏਗਾ
jāṇ vāḷā jāegā; āuṇ vāḷā āegā
Ger Subjct+gā Ger Subjct+gā
'He who is to go will go; he who is to come will come'

There is a famous Hindi song आएगा आने वाला **āegā āne vālā** ('The man who is bound to come will come').

Two more examples of the frequently used constructions featuring the **gerund** are given below.

(66) ਮੈਨੂੰ ਹੁਣ ਜਾਣਾ ਪਏਗਾ
ma^{i}nū̃ huṇ jāṇā paegā
Ger Subjct+gā
me-to now going will fall
'I will have to go now'

(67) ਮੈਨੂੰ ਹੁਣ ਘਰ ਜਾਣ ਦਿਓ
ma^{i}nū̃ huṇ g^{h}ar jāṇ dio
Ger Imper(P)
me-to now home going please give
'Please allow me to go home now'

ਜਾਣਾ **jāṇā** is the SUBJECT of the clause in (66) and OBJECT in (67). So the accusative/oblique form ਜਾਣ **jāṇ** is used in (67). As mentioned above, the oblique form of the **gerund** in Panjabi is derived by removing the final **-ā**, and not by changing **-ā** into **-e**, as is done with other **masculine singular nouns**. But this has started happening in Panjabi and is already done in Hindi, in which (67) will be said as मुझे अब घर जाने दो **muj^{h}e ab g^{h}ar jāne do**. These, and most other, constructions involving **explicator auxiliaries** are unmistakably metaphorical.

Summing up and looking ahead

As pointed out several times earlier as well, our usage-based view regards Panjabi grammar as a dynamical and evolving complex system. This chapter presents simply a brief picture of Panjabi **verb phrase**, a subject which demands a thick book length study. There is a *dynamical* living semantic logic operating in this system which *simply seems* inconsistent at places. It has the living spirit of the logic of an evolving natural language, not the *rigor mortis* of a philosophical mathematical logic. We have not drawn attention to a fact which perceptive readers must have noted – that the verb in the clause sometimes agrees with the SUBJECT, sometimes agrees with the OBJECT and sometimes does not agree with any **NP** and remains in the **neuter** form, which is homophonous to the **masculine singular** form. In general and comparative linguistics, a language in which the verb consistently agrees with the grammatical SUBJECT or the semantic **agent** in a clause is called an **accusative** language, and a language in which the verb consistently agrees with the syntactic OBJECT or the semantic **patient** is called an **ergative** language. The Australian language Dyirbal is an example of such an ergative language. But Panjabi and other North Indian languages do not fit into this classification. Therefore, many theoretical linguists use all sorts of names (some of them sounding derogatory) for these language, such as "pseudo ergative", "superficially ergative", "just morphologically ergative but syntactically accusative" or having "split ergativity" etc. But the fault lies not in these languages but in the classification itself. This is like setting up two categories for cats – black and white – and then, unable to fit tabbies into either category, finding fault with God's creation. The following chapters deal with the *perfectly consistent* semantic logic behind the Panjabi way of case-marking and verb-agreement and show that there is nothing "pseudo" or "split" or "superficial" or "just morphological" in this part of Panjabi grammar.

For teachers and other more advanced learners

It will be interesting to have a look at the history of the Panjabi *lexical* **conjunctive participle** form ਕਰ **kar** 'having done' and the *grammaticalised* auxiliary particle ਕੇ **ke** 'having done', both coming from the Sanskrit gerund कृत्वा *kṛtvā* 'having done' through Prākrit and old Panjabi.

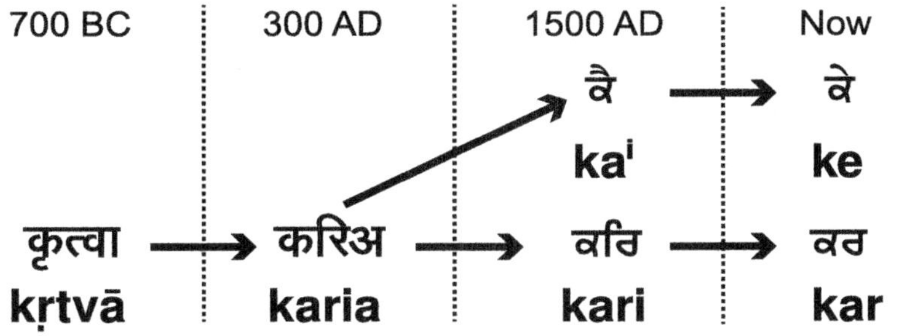

ਕਰ **kar** and ਕੇ **ke** can occur together in modern Panjabi as ਕਰ ਕੇ **kar ke**. In the 15th century, this combination was written as ਕਰਿ ਕੈ **kari ka^{i}** by Guru Nanak Dev.

> ਜਿਨਿ ਦਿਨੁ *ਕਰਿ ਕੈ* ਕੀਤੀ ਰਾਤਿ
>
> **jini din *kari ka^{i}* kītī rāti**
>
> 'He who, *having done* (created) the day, created the night'
>
> (*Srī Gurū Granth Sāhib* p. 349)

Sodhi Manohardas Meharban (d. 1640) wrote the earliest known hagiography of Guru Nanak Dev. An interesting passage from this book is

> ਬਾਬਾ ਨਾਨਕੁ ਜੀ ਪਗ *ਬਾਂਧਿ ਕਰਿ*, ਧੋਤੀ *ਕਰਿ ਕਰਿ*, ਚਾਦਰ *ਓਢਿ ਕਰਿ* , ਤਰਪਨ ਨੇਮ ਗਾਇਤ੍ਰੀ *ਪੜ੍ਹਿ ਕਰਿ*, ਸਿਮਰਨੁ ਧਿਆਨੁ ਪਰਮੇਸਰ ਕਾ *ਕਰਿ ਕਰਿ*, ਬਾਹਰਿ ਦਰੀਆਵ ਊਪਰਿ ਤੇ ਫੇਰਿ ਘਰਿ *ਆਇ ਕੈ* ਪਰਮੇਸਰ ਕਾ ਕੀਰਤਨੁ ਕਰਤਾ
>
> **bābā nānaku jī pag *bā̃di kari*, d^{h}otī *kari kari*, cādar *oḍ^{h}i kari*, rapan nem gāitrī *paṛ^{h}i kari*, simranu d^{h}iān parmesar kā *kari kari*, bāhrī darīāv ūpri te p^{h}iri g^{h}ari *āī ka^{i}* parmesar kā kīrtanu kartā**
>
> 'Baba Nanak Ji *having put on* a turban, *having worn* a shawl, *having recited* the ritual Gayatri prayer, *having meditated* on God, *having come* out of the river and then home, would sing praises God'
>
> (Kirpal Singh 1969, p. 84)

The writer uses both ਕਰਿ **kari** and ਕੈ **ka^{i}** in the positions where a modern writer would use only ਕੇ **ke**. In the whole passage there is only one finite verb (**imperfect participle**) ਕਰਤਾ **kartā** 'would do' at the end.

Such constructions started in Pali and classical Sanskrit (syntactically modelled on contemporary vernaculars) and are still used in all the modern Indic languages including Panjabi. See **14.2.6.**

Chapter 12

Case-marking and Verb-agreement

Preview of the chapter

This chapter deals with the fourth type of meaning conveyed by a sentence, called *dik* 'direction' by Bhartṛhari. It is significant, as far as Indian languages are concerned, that Bhartṛhari used the term *dik*, and not one of the numerous terms for 'space' (such as *ākāśa*) available in Sanskrit. We deal with the spatial symbolism (especially the metaphorical movement and location in space) in Panjabi case-marking and the agreement or lack of agreement of the verb with the SUBJECT or OBJECT **NP** in the clause, and with the so-called "split ergativity" and various "experiencer"-type constructions. An understanding of this spatial symbolism (especially the *Location Event Structure Metaphor* omnipresent in Panjabi grammar and discussed in the last section of this chapter) is extremely important for an understanding of the salient features of Panjabi grammar.

12.1 Agreement of the verb with an NP in the clause

Before we outline the rules for the **agreement** of the **verb** with an **NP**, making a crucial distinction between "no postposition" and "zero postposition" is necessary. The plural form of the English word "goat" is "goats" because we say "one goat" and "two goats". The form "goat" has no plural marker, and 'goats' has the plural marker -s. But we say "one sheep" and "two sheep". For historical reasons, the plural form "sheep" does not have the plural marker *-s*. But for grammatical consistency, we say that the plural "sheep" has the *zero* plural maker because most other nouns in the same position would have one. In grammar, we can describe the plural form "sheep" as "sheep+Ø"" Similarly, for historical reasons (which we are not going to discuss in detail in this book), the **first person pronouns** ਮੈਂ **mãi** and ਅਸੀਂ **asĩ** and the **second person pronouns** ਤੂੰ **tũ** and ਤੁਸੀਂ **tusĩ** do not get the postposition ਨੇ **ne** in the positions where **third person pronouns** and **nouns** have it. So these pronouns can occur *without* ਨੇ **ne** as well as with *zero* (Ø) postposition or *invisible/inaudible* ਨੇ **ne**. In the following rules, the invisible/inaudible **postposition** written as Ø is also regarded as a postposition. (See section **6.7**).

12.2 The meaning of an inflected verb form in Panjabi

Ancient Indian linguists had their views about the meaning of the agreement of the verb with the SUBJECT or the OBJECT of the clause. Their views are extremely useful for an analysis of the semantics of the **verb phrase** in Panjabi, especially the spatial symbolism and metaphors which characterise Panjabi grammar.

These linguists regarded a *verb root* as having two semantic components: *vyāpāra* (activity) and *phala* ('fruit' or result of the activity). The agreement of the inflected form with an **NP** indicates *vyāpārāśraya* (*vyāpāra+āśraya*) and *phalāśraya* (*phala+āśraya*) (Rao 1969). The Sanskrit word *āśraya* means 'something you lean upon', 'support', 'shelter' etc. We can translate *vyāpārāśraya* as **'substratum of activity'** and *phalāśraya* as **'substratum of result'**. In addition to these two concepts, we also make use of the concept of the **goal of the result**, for which there is no Sanskrit term presumably because the concept was not needed for Sanskrit grammar. There is no need to create a new Sanskrit term here (though there is a temptation to create *phalalakṣya*!). These concepts will make our analysis extremely easy. In our analysis, we are not going to use the Sanskrit terms but their English translations.

We have seen in earlier chapters that the activity or action denoted by a verb can be started by an **agent** or a **causing agent**. Also, an inanimate object or abstract idea or notion may start an activity or cause it to start. So we can use the term **initiator** (or **initiating agent**) of an activity for all these. The initiator may or may not be an **agent** as traditionally understood. The traditional term **patient** seems fine for the *affected* person or entity.

The **initiator** is *always* the **substratum of activity (SA)**. But if the action or the activity is viewed as *incomplete* or *uncompleted*, the **initiator** is the **substratum of result (SR)** as well. If the action or activity is viewed as *complete* or *completed*, there are three possibilities – (i) the **initiator** remains the **substratum of result**, in which case it is ***not*** marked by a **postposition**, (ii) the **patient** becomes the **substratum of result**, and is ***not*** marked by a **postposition**, or (iii) the **patient** is the **goal** towards which the result of the activity *viewed as an entity* is directed; it is not the **substratum** for the result to "lean upon" or "take shelter in". Such a **goal** is marked by the **postposition ਨੂੰ nū̃** 'to'.

When the **initiator** is *not* the **substratum of result (SR)**, it is marked by the postposition **ਨੇ ne** (or Ø). In this chapter we abbreviate the extremely important concept **substratum of result** as **SR.**

12.3 Agreement of the verb

The agreement of the verb with an **NP** (or lack of it) depends on (i) the form of the verb, (ii) whether the verb is **transitive** or **intransitive**, and (iii) whether or not the **patient** is marked with **ਨੂੰ nū̃**. When the **patient** is **definite** for any reason – contextual, or being unique or being a pronoun, or any other reason – it is regarded as a **goal** of the result of the activity and is marked with **ਨੂੰ nū̃** 'to'.

12.3.1 Agreement of subjunctive form and subjunctive+ਗਾ gā form

The action or activity denoted by this verb form is viewed as rather **potential** and **uncompleted.** So the **subjunctive** form agrees with the **initiator** in **person** *and* **number**. **-ਗਾ -gā**, which makes the activity **definite**, also agrees with the **initiator** in **number** *and* **gender**. Whether the verb is **transitive** or **intransitive** or the **patient** is definite or indefinite makes no difference. The **initiator** does *not* take **ਨੇ ne**.

(1)	ਕੁੜੀਆਂ	ਗੀਤ	ਗਾਉਣ. . . ਗੀਆਂ
	kuṛīā̃	**gīt**	**gāuṇ...gīā̃**
	3rd Per Fem Pl	3rd Per Sg	Fem Pl
	'The girls will sing a song'		

The **number** and **gender** of the OBJECT **ਗੀਤ gīt** (or even if it were followed by **ਨੂੰ nū̃**) make no difference.

(2)	ਅਸੀਂ	ਚਾਹ	ਪੀਆਂ.....ਗੇ
	asī̃	**cāh**	**pīā̃....ge**
	1st Per Mas Pl	3rd Per Sg	Mas Pl
	'We will drink tea'		

(3)	ਇਹ ਮੁੰਡੇ	ਹਾਕੀ	ਖੇਡਣ.....ਗੇ
	ih muṇḍe	**hākī**	**k^heḍaṇ...ge**
	3rd Per Mas Pl	3rd Per Fem Sg	Mas Pl
	'These boys will play hockey'		

12.3.2 Agreement of the imperfect participle form

The action or activity denoted by this form of the verb is viewed as uncompleted, ongoing, recurring, not started etc. The verb agrees with the **initiator** in **number** and **gender** irrespective of whether it is **intransitive** or **transitive**.

(4)	ਮੇਰੀ ਪਤਨੀ	ਰੋਜ਼	ਮੰਦਰ	ਜਾਂਦੀ	ਹੈ
	merī patnī	**roz**	**mandar**	**jā̃dī**	**ha^i**
	3rd Per Fem Sg			Fem Sg	3rd Per Sg
	'My wife goes to the temple every day'				

It is notable that while the main verb ਜਾ **jā** in the **imperfect participle** form agrees with the **initiator** SUBJECT in **number** and **gender,** ਹੈ **ha^i**, being a **subjunctive** form (see the last chapter), agrees with the **initiator** in **person** and **number**.

(5)	ਅਸੀਂ	ਸ਼ਤਰੰਜ	ਖੇਡਦੇ	ਹਾਂ
	asī̃	**śatranj**	**k^heḍde**	**hā̃**
	1st Per Mas Pl	Fem Sg	Mas Pl	1st Per Pl
	'We play chess'			

The agreement of the verb with the **initiator** of the activity is not a "superficial surface structure phenomenon", as some linguists would say. Rather, the **initiator**, being the **SR** of an uncompleted activity is viewed an **SR** *characterised* by the result of activity. The result of the activity "leans upon" this **NP**.

We pointed out in Chapter 5 that the SUBJECT of a clause in Panjabi is the **NP** which is *either* marked with the postposition ਨੇ **ne**, *or* if this is not the case, the verb agrees with this NP in **person** and **number** *or* **number** and **gender** *or* both. In all the example sentences given above, the **initiator** is the SUBJECT of the clause.

12.3.3 Agreement of the perfect participle form

Now we come to the verb-forms whose agreement with the **initiator** or the **patient** or with neither is a bit more complicated but perfectly logical by the standards of the internal logic of Panjabi grammar.

As we saw in the last chapter, the **perfect participle** views a situation as complete or completed *retrospectively* or from the end point. If the verb is **intransitive**, the **initiator** is the **SR**. But if the verb is **transitive**, it is mostly the **patient** that is the **SR**. But if the **patient** is **definite** for any reason, it is symbolically viewed as the **goal** towards which the result of the activity is *directed*. Then it is not simply an entity for the result of the activity to "lean upon". It is marked with ਨੂੰ **nū̃** 'to'. The activity viewed as completed and carrying the result (or "pregnant with the result" – to speak metaphorically) is a **nominal** in the **neuter** form with **zero agreement** with the verb. The **neuter** form in Panjabi is homophonous to the **masculine singular** form. In the last chapter, we saw that all the three Panjabi verb forms expressing the **perfective aspect** can act as nominals. The following examples illustrate this.

(6) ਮੇਰਾ ਛੋਟਾ ਪੁੱਤਰ ਕੱਲ੍ਹ ਘਰ ਆਇਆ
merā c^hoṭā puttar kallh g^har āiā
Mas Sg Mas Sg
'My younger son came home yesterday'

(7) ਘਰ ਆ ਕੇ ਉਹਨੇ ਦੋ ਕਵਿਤਾਵਾਂ ਲਿਖੀਆਂ
g^har ā ke uhne do kavitāvā̃ lik^hīā̃
Mas Sg Agt Fem Pl Fem Pl
'After coming home, he wrote two poems'

(8) ਮੈਂØ ਉਹਨਾਂ ਕਵਿਤਾਵਾਂ ਨੂੰ ਗਾਇਆ

mã^{i}Ø uhnā̃ kavitāvā̃ nū̃ gāiā

Fem Pl Def Neu

'I sang those poems'

The verb in (6) is **intransitive**. So the **initiator** is also the **SR** and the verb agrees in **number** and **gender** with this **SR**. The verb in (7) is **transitive**. The **initiator** is marked by the **agentive postposition ਨੇ ne**. The **patient** is the **SR** of an activity viewed as completed and is not marked by any postposition. The verb agrees in **number** and **gender** with the **SR**. The patient in (8) has become contextually **definite,** having been already mentioned. So it is regarded as the **goal** towards which the result is directed. So it is marked with the postposition **ਨੂੰ nū̃** 'to' and the verb does not agree with it and remains in the **neuter** form. The **first person** initiator **ਮੈਂ mã^{i}** 'I' does not get the agentive postposition **ਨੇ ne** for historical reasons. But it is regarded as having the zero postposition Ø. The verb does not agree with the **initiator** either. It is not possible to know whether the narrator ('I') in (8) is the father or the mother of the poet because the **gender** of the initiator is not indicated by the **pronoun** and is not marked on the **verb** either.

It needs pointing out here that in some Western dialects of Panjabi, the use of the postposition **ਨੇ ne** has been stopped. But the **oblique form** of the **nouns** shows that the **postposition** was once there.

(9) ਰਾਂਝੇ Ø ਵੰਝਲੀ ਵਜਾਈ

rā̃jʰe Ø vanjʰalī vajāī

Mas Sg Fem Sg Fem Sg

'Ranjha played the flute'

The verb agrees with the patient OBJECT. The **initiator** SUBJECT **ਰਾਂਝਾ rā̃jʰā** is a masculine noun ending in **-ā**. But in (9) it is in the **oblique form** as it should be if followed by a **postposition. ਨੇ ne** is also frequently omitted in poetry for metrical reasons.

(10) ਕੁੱਕੜ Ø ਖੇਹ ਉੜਾਈ, ਆਪਣੇ ਹੀ ਸਿਰ ਪਾਈ

kukkaṛ Ø kʰeh uṛāī, āpṇe hī sir pāī

Mas Sg Fem Sg Fem Sg Fem Sg

'The rooster raised the dust, and put it on its own head'
i.e., 'The trouble-maker ultimately disgraced himself as a result of his mischief'

Again ਨੇ **ne** is missing after the initiator SUBJECT ਕੁੱਕੜ **kukkaṛ** 'rooster' not ending in **-ā**. So its **oblique form** is not different from the **direct form**. Some other masculine nouns ending in **-ā** (ਕੁੱਤਾ **kuttā** 'dog', for example) would have got the **-e** ending in (10) and become ਕੁੱਤੇ **kutte**.

The omission of ਨੇ **ne** in some dialects could have happened on the analogy of the first and second person pronouns, which do not get this agentive postposition for historical reasons. Interestingly, Hindi-Urdu has started adding ਨੇ **ne** to the first and second person pronouns apparently on the analogy of nouns and third person pronouns.

12.3.4 Agreement of the potential participle form

The rules of the agreement of the **perfect participle** form are quite simple. The rules for the agreement of the **potential participle** form are similar but with some minor differences. To repeat what has already been said in the previous chapter, the **potential participle** views a situation as complete or completed *prospectively* or from the starting point.

(i) Intransitive verbs

The patient or the **SR** of a **transitive verb** in the **potential participle** form is marked in the same way as the patient or **SR** of a verb in the **perfect participle** form. But the marking of an **agentive initiator** of an **intransitive** verb is different from that of a **non-agentive initiator**. An **agentive initiator** is one that is viewed as capable of taking a decision to start the activity. A **non-agentive initiator**, such as a force or object of nature, does not start an activity in this way. Examples are

(11) ਕੱਲ੍ਹ ਸੂਰਜ ਸਵੇਰੇ ਪੰਜ ਵਜੇ ਚੜ੍ਹਨਾ ਹੈ
kallh sūraj savere panj vaje carḥnā ha^{i}
Mas Sg Mas Sg Cop Sg
'Tomorrow, the sun is going to rise at five in the morning'

(12) ਅੱਜ ਰਾਤੀਂ ਤੇਜ਼ ਹਵਾ ਚੱਲਣੀ ਹੈ
ajj rātī̃ tez havā callṇī ha^{i}
Fem Sg Fem Sg Cop Sg
'Strong wind is going to blow tonight'

If sentient beings capable of taking decisions are viewed as working according to a set programme, this pattern can be used.

(13) ਮੀਟਿੰਗ ਵਿਚ ਬਹੁਤ ਲੋਕ ਆਉਣੇ ਹਨ
mīting vich bahut lok āuṇe han
Mas Pl Mas Pl Cop PL
'Many people are coming in the meeting'

The verb agrees with the **initiator** in **number** and **gender**.

But if the **initiator** of an **intransitive** verb is **agentive**, it is marked with ਨੇ **ne** and the verb is in the **neuter form.**

(14) ਮੇਰੀ ਪਤਨੀ ਨੇ ਕਿਸੇ ਮੀਟਿੰਗ ਵਿਚ ਜਾਣਾ ਹੈ
meri patnī ne kise mīting vic jāṇā ha^{i}
Fem Sg Agt Neu Cop
'My wife is going to some meeting'

(15) ਅੱਜ ਮੈਂØ ਘਰ ਰਹਿਣਾ ਹੈ
ajj mã^{i}Ø g^{h}ar rahiṇā ha^{i}
Mas Sg Agt Neu Cop
'I am going to stay at home today'

The **verb** will be in this form whatever the **number** and **gender** of the initiator may be. ਹੈ **ha^{i}** is used in these sentences to indicate the point in time (the present moment) from where the situation is viewed.

(ii) Transitive verbs

The pattern is the same as for the transitive verbs in the **perfect participle** form. The verb agrees in **number** and **gender** with the **patient** or **SR.** But if the **patient** is **definite** it does not become the **SR**, is regarded as a **goal** of the result of the activity and is marked ਨੂੰ **nū̃**. The verb does not agree with any NP and remains in the **neuter** form.

(16) ਅੱਜ ਮੈਂØ ਬਹੁਤ ਸਾਰੇ ਖ਼ਤ ਲਿਖਣੇ ਹਨ
ajj mã^{i}Ø bahut sāre xat lik^{h}ṇe han
Mas Sg Agt Mas Pl Mas Pl Cop Pl
'I am going to write many letters today'

(17) ਉਹਨਾਂ ਖ਼ਤਾਂ ਨੂੰ ਮੇਰੇ ਕਲਰਕ ਨੇ ਟਾਈਪ ਕਰਨਾ ਹੈ
uhnā̃ xatā̃ nū̃ mere kalark ne ṭāīp karnā ha^{i}
Mas Pl Def Neu
'My clerk is going to type those letters'

The OBJECT or **patient NP** in (17) has become contextually definite, so it is the goal of the **result** of the activity and is marked with ਨੂੰ **nū̃**. According to the rules of Panjabi grammar, the **potential participle** form of the verb does not agree with this **patient** and remains in the **neuter form**.

As pointed out above, ਨੇ **ne** is not used in some Western dialects of Panjabi. But the NP with which ਨੇ **ne** was used in the past continues to be in the **oblique case form**.

12.3.5 The imperative use of the potential participle or gerund

These forms can be used as an **imperative**, mostly for giving advice about something to be completed in the *future* time.

(18) ਤੁਸੀਂ ਜ਼ਰੂਰ ਜਾਣਾ, ਪਰ ਚੁੱਪ ਰਹਿਣਾ, ਬੋਲਣਾ ਕੁਝ ਨਹੀਂ
tusī̃ zarūr jāṇā, par cupp rahiṇā, bolṇā kuj^h nahī̃
PotP PotP PotP
'You must go, but keep quiet, say nothing'

(19a) ਤੁਸੀਂ ਸਵੇਰੇ ਉੱਥੇ ਜਾਣਾ, ਤੇ ਕੰਮ ਕਰ ਕੇ ਮੁੜ ਆਉਣਾ
tusī̃ savere utt^{h}e jāṇā, te kamm kar ke muṛ āuṇā̃
PotP PotP
'You should go there in the morning, and come back after finishing the work'

Interestingly, if ਅਸੀਂ **asī̃** 'we' is used in place of ਤੁਸੀਂ **tusī̃** 'you' as in (19b), the sentence, quite obviously, will not have the meaning of a piece of advice but will refer to some activity regularly completed by 'us' in the *past*.

(19b) ਅਸੀਂ ਸਵੇਰੇ ਉੱਥੇ ਜਾਣਾ, ਤੇ ਕੰਮ ਕਰ ਕੇ ਮੁੜ ਆਉਣਾ
asī̃ savere utt^{h}e jāṇā, te kamm kar ke muṛ āuṇā
PotP PotP
'We used to go there in the morning, and come back after finishing the work'

Indicating or inferring the time of an event is not a straightforward matter in Panjabi. A lot depends upon the participants and the context of use (and very often intonation as well). So much for "tenses" in Panjabi!

12.4 Spatial symbolism and metaphors elsewhere in Panjabi sentence structure

Different languages are often said to symbolically and metaphorically present the same "extralinguistic" or "language independent reality". But many thinkers doubt the existence of any such well-defined and well-structured reality and believe that while the "real" world independently exists "out there", it *reveals itself* in different ways in different languages; so what *counts as* the reality is symbolised by each language and culture in its own way. In other words, the world "out there" is *experienced* in different ways by the speakers of different languages for the purpose of "thinking for speaking". This is not "subjectivism" or "relativism" but "experientialism" (Lakoff and Johnson 1980).

12.4.1 "Experiencer" constructions in Panjabi

In this section, we take up one of the most misunderstood, misanalysed and misrepresented constructions in Panjabi and other North Indian languages (by those who use English as a *filter* language, regarding the English translation of a construction as its "real underlying meaning" or "logical structure"). This construction is said to have a "dative subject". For example, while a speaker of English would say

(20) I became angry

A speaker of Panjabi would present the "same" (?) situation as

(21)			
	ਮੈਨੂੰ	ਗੁੱਸਾ	ਆਇਆ
	maˈnū̃	**gussā**	**āiā**
	Expcr	SUB	PRED
	me-to	anger	came

Lit. 'Anger came to me'

Another example of a "dative subject" can be found in (22).

(22)			
	ਮੈਨੂੰ	ਹਾਸਾ	ਆਇਆ
	maˈnū̃	**hāsā**	**āiā**
	Expcr	SUB	PRED
	me-to	laughter	came

'I felt like laughing'

Some other mental states can also be depicted using such a construction.

(23) ਮੈਨੂੰ ਯਕੀਨ ਹੈ ਕਿ...

ma^{i}nū̃ yakīn ha^{i} ki ...

Expcr	SUB	PRED	
me-to	belief	is	that ...

'I believe that ...'

(24) ਵਰਿੰਦਰ ਦੀ ਕਵਿਤਾ ਮੈਨੂੰ ਬਹੁਤ ਪਸੰਦ ਹੈ

varindar dī kavitā ma^{i}nū̃ bahut pasand ha^{i}

		SUB	Expcr			PRED
Varindar	of	poetry	me-to	very	likeable	is

'I like Varindar's poetry very much'

Many grammarians dealing with Indian languages who use English not only as a *meta*language (which we are also doing here) but also as a *filter* language, go to great lengths to argue with the help of numerous "tests", "deep structures", "logical representations", "transformations" etc. to argue that ਮੈਂ **mã^{i}** 'I' is the "subject" of (21)–(24), albeit a "subject" of a special type known as the "dative subject". Some of their arguments are so naive and shallow that they can be summarily dismissed – such as ਮੈਨੂੰ **ma^{i}nū̃** in (21) comes before ਗੁੱਸਾ **gussā**. Since, they argue, the the "normal" order of words in Panjabi is SOV (Subject Object Verb), ਮੈਂ **mã^{i}** is the SUBJECT of the clause in (21). Now, if we look at (24) above, the word order could be regarded as OSV because the the "OBJECT" comes before the "SUBJECT". As we will see in Chapter 16, word order in Panjabi is *very* (but not completely) flexible and depends on many factors. SOV is simply a *tendency*, and not a *rule*, in Panjabi grammar. This happens *as a rule*, which means that this is *not* a rule. One of the reasons why ਮੈਨੂੰ **mãnū̃** comes before ਗੁੱਸਾ **gussā** in (21) is that a human being is more significant than an abstract concept. For us, ਗੁੱਸਾ **gussā** is the semantic **initiator** (if not the **agent** in the traditional sense) of the activity or the situation and the grammatical SUBJECT by the rules of Panjabi grammar. The person feeling the anger is the symbolic or metaphorical goal of anger (indicated by the postposition ਨੂੰ **nū̃** 'to' of the movement indicated by the verb ਆ **ā**).

The experiences referred to in such a construction are mental as in (21)–(24) above. The crucial thing is that the experiencer has no control (at least no *conscious* control) over the experience. Feeling angry, sad, happy, or having certain beliefs, doubts, love, hatred, moods etc. are such experiences. The experiences may be physical too, such as having a cold or flu, feeling pain, an itch, hunger, thirst or some other type of bodily sensation. Such experiences may be viewed as states or events.

(25) ਮੈਨੂੰ ਸਿਰ ਪੀੜ ਹੈ
maⁱnũ sir pīṛ haⁱ
Expcr SUB PRED
me-to headache is
'I have a headache'

(26a) ਮੈਨੂੰ ਫ਼ਲੂ ਹੋਇਆ
maⁱnũ flū hoiā
Expcr SUB PRED
me-to flu happened
'I got flu'

The human being in (26a) is pragmatically more significant than the illness. So it is mentioned first. Its mention is obligatory for *pragmatic* reasons because the sentence is "about" her/him. This is not an argument for regarding ਮੈਂ **mãⁱ** as a SUBJECT of whatever variety. (26a) is an **intransitive** clause – an expanded version of the **canonical clause pattern 1** – with ਮੈਨੂੰ **maⁱnũ** as an ADJUCNT NP. It is possible to say

(26b) ਸਿਆਲ਼ ਵਿਚ ਫ਼ਲੂ ਬਹੁਤ ਹੁੰਦਾ ਹੈ
siāḷ vic flū bahut hundā haⁱ
ADJCT SUB PRED
'In winter, flu happens a lot'

No "dative" or "experiencer" SUBJECT is *syntactically* necessary in (26b).

There was a satirical Panjabi comedy film about an old man who behaved romantically like a young man.

(27) ਚੜ੍ਹੀ ਜਵਾਨੀ ਬੁੱਢੇ ਨੂੰ
caṛhī javānī buḍḍʰe nũ
PRED SUB Expcr
ascended youth old man to
'The old man became young'

(28)

ਮੁੰਡੇ	ਨੂੰ	ਭੁੱਖ	ਲੱਗੀ
munḍe	**nũ**	**b^{h}ukk^h**	**laggī**
Expcr		SUB	PRED
boy	to	hunger	struck

'The boy got hungry'

(29)

ਧੂਏਂ	ਵਿਚ	ਮੁੰਡੇ	ਨੂੰ	ਖੰਘ	ਆਈ
d^{h}ūẽ	**vic**	**munḍe**	**nũ**	**k^{h}ang^h**	**āī**
ADJCT		Expcr		SUB	PRED
smoke	in	boy	to	cough	came

'The boy coughed (involuntarily) in the smoke'

But if the boy coughed knowingly, his action can be described as

(30)

ਕੁੜੀ	ਨੂੰ	ਦੇਖ	ਕੇ	ਮੁੰਡਾ	ਖੰਘਿਆ
kuṛī	**nũ**	**dek^h**	**ke**	**munḍā**	**k^{h}ang^{h}iā**
				SUB	PRED

'After seeing the girl, the boy coughed (to attract her attention)'

ਖੰਘ **k^{h}ang^h** is used as a verb in (30).

(31)

ਮੈਥੋਂ	ਹੱਸ	ਹੋ	ਗਿਆ
ma^{i}t^{h}õ	**hass**	**ho**	**giā**
	CnjP		
	SUB		PRED
me-from	laughing	having happened	'gone'

'I laughed (involuntarily)'

The use of the combination **verb+auxiliary ਜਾ jā** is discussed in the next chapter. This **auxiliary** shows the completion of an activity. It does not always literally mean 'go', as we will see in the next chapter. But even after **ਜਾ jā** 'go' becomes metaphorical, some traces of its original meaning often linger on. In the glosses to the following examples, it is put within single quotes.

The symbolism and metaphors of location or movement in space are clearly and unmistakably present in all these constructions.

12.5 Other "experiencer"-like constructions

12.5.1 Physical and mental perception, acts of remembering and forgetting

Acts of physical and mental perception and acts of remembering and forgetting are also grammatically treated as experiences.

(32) ਮੈਨੂੰ ਤੇਰੀ ਬਹੁਤ ਯਾਦ ਆਉਂਦੀ ਹੈ
ma^{i}nū̃ terī bahut yād āū̃dī ha^{i}
Expcr SUB PRED
me-to your much memory coming
'I remember (miss) you a lot'

(33) ਮੈਨੂੰ ਉਹਦਾ ਨਾਂ ਭੁੱਲ ਗਿਆ
ma^{i}nū̃ uhdā nā̃ b^{h}ull giā
Expcr SUB PRED
me-to his name forgotten 'gone'
'I forgot his name'

(34) ਉਹਨੂੰ ਛੇਤੀ ਅਕਲ ਆ ਗਈ
uhnū̃ c^{h}etī akal ā gaī
Expcr SUB PRED
him-to soon wisdom having come 'gone'
'Wisdom soon dawned upon him'

(35) ਸਾਨੂੰ ਪਤਾ ਲੱਗਿਆ ਕਿ . . .
sānū̃ patā laggiā ki ...
Expcr SUB PRED
us-to information struck that ...'
'We came to know that...'

(36) and (37) may also be regarded as expressing slightly different types of experiences.

(36) ਮੈਨੂੰ ਜਾਣਾ ਪਿਆ
ma^{i}nū̃ jāṇā piā
Expcr Ger SUB PRED
me-to going 'fell'
'I had to go'

(37)	ਉਹਨੂੰ	ਮੁਸੀਬਤ	ਆ	ਪਈ
	uhnū̃	**musībat**	**ā**	**paī**
	Expcr	SUB	PRED	
	him-to	trouble	having come	'fell'
	'Trouble befell him'			

The experiencer of the verb ਦਿਸ **dis** 'be visible' and ਸੁਣ **suṇ** 'be audible' is also marked with ਨੂੰ **nū̃**.

(38a)	ਇੱਥੇ	ਸਾਨੂੰ	ਕੁਝ	ਨਹੀਂ	ਦਿਸਦਾ
	itt^{h}e	**sānū̃**	**kuj^h**	**nahī̃**	**disdā**
		Expcr	SUB		PRED
	here	us-to	anything	not	being visible
	'We cannot see anything here'				

(39a)	ਮੈਨੂੰ	ਕੁਝ	ਆਵਾਜ਼ਾਂ	ਸੁਣੀਆਂ
	ma^{i}nū̃	**kuj^h**	**āvāzā̃**	**suṇīā̃**
	Expcr		SUB	PRED
	me-to	some	voices	were audible
	'I heard some voices'			

(38a) and (39a) also have the following variants.

(38b)	ਇੱਥੇ	ਸਾਨੂੰ	ਕੁਝ	ਦਿਖਾਈ	ਨਹੀਂ	ਦਿੰਦਾ
	itt^{h}e	**sānū̃**	**kuj^h**	**dik^{h}āī**	**nahī̃**	**dindā**
		Expcr	SUB			PRED
	here	us-to	anything	(?) visibility	not	giving

(39b)	ਮੈਨੂੰ	ਕੁਝ	ਆਵਾਜ਼ਾਂ	ਸੁਣਾਈ	ਦਿੱਤੀਆਂ
	ma^{i}nū̃	**kuj^h**	**āvāzā̃**	**suṇāī**	**dittīā̃**
	Expcr		SUB		PRED
	me-to	some	voices	(?) audibility	given

It is impossible to find exact glosses of ਦਿਖਾਈ **dik^{h}āī** and ਸੁਣਾਈ **suṇāī** in English. The ones given above are approximate.

12.5.2 Skills

Some skills, once properly acquired, are believed to become unconscious and automatic. In Panjabi, they are said to 'come to' a fully skilled person.

(40a) ਮੈਨੂੰ ਹਿੰਦੀ ਆਉਂਦੀ ਹੈ
ma^{i}nū̃ hindī āū̃dī ha^{i}
Expcr SUB PRED
'I know Hindi'
Lit. 'Hindi comes to me'

(41a) ਤੁਹਾਨੂੰ ਤਰਨਾ ਆਉਂਦਾ ਹੈ?
tuhānū̃ tarnā āū̃dā ha^{i}?
Expcr Ger SUB PRED
'Do you know how to swim?'

(42a) ਉਹਨੂੰ ਪਿਆਨੋ ਵਜਾਉਣਾ ਆਉਂਦਾ ਹੈ
uhnū̃ piāno vajāuṇā āū̃dā ha^{i}
Expcr OBJ Ger SUB PRED
'He knows how to play a piano'

It is possible to use the verb ਜਾਣ **jāṇ** 'know' in order to emphasise the *knowledge* aspect or the person's skill.

(40b) ਮੈਂ ਹਿੰਦੀ ਜਾਣਦਾ ਹਾਂ
mā̃^{i} hindī jāṇdā hā̃
SUB OBJ PRED
'I know Hindi'

(41b) ਤੁਸੀਂ ਤਰਨਾ ਜਾਣਦੇ ਹੋ
tusī̃ tarnā jāṇde ho
SUB Ger OBJ PRED
'You know how to swim'

(42b) ਉਹ ਪਿਆਨੋ ਵਜਾਉਣਾ ਜਾਣਦਾ ਹੈ
uh piāno vajāuṇā jāṇdā ha^{i}
SUB Ger OBJ PRED
'He knows how to play a piano'

Since a piano (especially a small one) is also feminine in Panjabi, some speakers say (42a) as (42c).

(42c) ਉਹਨੂੰ ਪਿਆਨੋ ਵਜਾਉਣੀ ਆਉਂਦੀ ਹੈ
uhnū̃ piāno vajāuṇī āū̃dī ha^{i}
Expcr OBJ Ger SUB PRED

12.5.3 The verb ਚਾਹੀਦਾ cāhīdā

ਚਾਹੀਦਾ **cāhīdā** is the **subtractive phase** of ਚਾਹ **cāh** 'desire' dealt with in Chapter 12, where it was pointed out that a verb in this phase can have only the **imperfect participle** form and the **agent** is either **eliminated** (not mentioned at all) or the **agent** is ਅਸੀਂ **asī̃** 'we'. The **verb** agrees with the **patient**, which is the SUBJECT of the clause. But ਚਾਹੀਦਾ **cāhīdā** is an exception in some respects. The **agent** or 'desirer' can be other than ਅਸੀਂ **asī̃** as well. It is mentioned but is followed by the postposition ਨੂੰ **nū̃** and is in the **oblique form**. The following examples make this rather abstract description clear. (No "boastful" meaning is expressed here!)

(43) ਸਾਨੂੰ ਖਾਣਾ ਚਾਹੀਦਾ ਹੈ
sānū̃ k^{h}āṇā cāhīdā ha^i
Expcr Mas Sg Mas Sg Cop Sg
'We want food'
Lit. 'Food is desirable to us'

(44) ਮੈਨੂੰ ਹਰੀਆਂ ਮਿਰਚਾਂ ਚਾਹੀਦੀਆਂ ਹਨ
ma^{i}nū̃ harīā̃ mircā̃ cāhīdīā̃ han
Expcr Fem Pl Fem Pl Cop Pl
'I want green chillies'
Lit. 'Green chillies are desirable to me'

(45) ਹੁਣ ਤੁਹਾਨੂੰ ਜਾਣਾ ਚਾਹੀਦਾ ਹੈ
huṇ tuānū̃ jāṇā cahīdā ha^i
Expcr Mas Sg Mas Sg Cop Sg
'Now you should go'
Lit. 'Going is desirable to you now'

While

(46a) ਤੁਹਾਨੂੰ ਕੀ ਚਾਹੀਦਾ ਹੈ?
tuānū̃ kī cāhīdā ha^i?
Expcr OBJ PRED
'What is desired by you/is desirable to you?'

is the normal *polite* way of questioning someone in Panjabi, (46b) is as *impolite* (though fully grammatical) as its English translation.

(46b)	ਤੁਸੀਂ	ਕੀ	ਚਾਹੁੰਦੇ	ਹੋ?
	tusī̃	**kī**	**cāhũde**	**ho?**
	SUB	OBJ	PRED	

‘What do you want?’

12.5.4 Compulsion and obligation

Constructions expressing compulsion and obligation also make use of ਨੂੰ **nū̃** and **gerund**+ਪੈ **pa^{i}** ‘fall’ because compulsion and obligation metaphorically “fall” upon someone, especially when the performer of the action is not very happy with this.

(47)	ਹੁਣ	ਤੁਹਾਨੂੰ	ਇੱਥੋਂ	ਜਾਣਾ	ਪਏਗਾ
	huṇ	**tuānū̃**	**itt^{h}õ**	**jāṇā**	**paegā**
		Expcr		Ger OBJ	PRED
	now	you-to	here-from	going	‘will fall’

‘You will have to go from here now’

(48)	ਖਾਣਾ	ਅੱਜ	ਮੈਨੂੰ	ਪਕਾਉਣਾ	ਪੈਣਾ	ਹੈ
	k^{h}āṇā	**ajj**	**ma^{i}nū̃**	**pakāuṇā**	**pa^{i}ṇā**	**ha^{i}**
	OBJ		Expcr	Ger OBJ		PRED
	food	today	me-to	cooking	‘to fall’	is

‘I am going to have to cook the food today’

All the examples given above show that the unnecessary category of the “dative subject” or “experiencer subject” is best shaved off with Occam’s Razor.

12.6 Causative constructions

While the past Panjabi and Hindi grammarians dealt with the **semantic valency** of causative verbs in these languages in some detail, virtually nothing has been said about the **syntactic valency** of the constructions involving the causative phases of these verbs. A full-length study of this subject will need a lot more pages than are available to us. So we deal with it very briefly here. A knowledge of the morphology and semantics of these phases described in earlier chapters is assumed here.

The **semantic valency** of the phase of a verb is the set of the *kārakas* or participants involved in the activity denoted by the verb. Its **syntactic valency** is the set of the **NPs** (denoting those participants) which are *grammatically obligatory* (unless they are *contextually* omitted). (See Chapter 16.) Chapter 9 deals with the two types of Panjabi verbs and their phases. The information is not repeated here. But briefly,

1. The Panjabi verbs can be grouped into two categories, (i) **Class 1** (*parsmaipada*) verbs, e.g., **ਚੁੱਕ cukk** 'lift' the benefit of the activity of which can be "given" to others as well as "taken" by the performer, and (ii) **Class 2** verbs (*ātmanepada*), e.g **ਸਿੱਖ sikk^h** 'learn', the benefit of which can be "taken" by the performer only. But this is a *very rough* characterisation because the meaning of the verb is also important. The Sanskrit terms from the old Indian tradition are not used below.
2. Within each class, a verb is either *basically* **intransitive** or **transitive**.
3. The **Class 1** verbs can be put into subgroups on the basis of their morphological behaviour.
4. The **semantic valency** of a verb *increases* with an **additive phase** and *decreases* with a **subtractive phase** with the elimination of the **agent**. (For exceptions, see **12.5.3** above.)

12.6.1 Class 1 verbs

(a) Intransitive verbs

Let us take a verb **ਚਲ cal** 'move' from the lists in Chapter 9. In (49) below, it is an **intransitive** verb with only the **(immediate) agent**, the 'mover' in the **semantic valency** set. This agent is the initiator of the activity. In (50), its **additive Phase 1 ਚਲਾ calā** 'drive' has an **initiator (agent)** or **causer** of the activity as well. With the **additive phase 2** in (51), the older **causer** or **initiator (agent)** of **phase 1** becomes the **intermediate agent** and another **causer** (or **causing agent**) assumes the role of the **initiator (agent)**. The following examples will make this clear.

(49) ਗੱਡੀ ਤੇਜ਼ ਚਲਦੀ ਹੈ
gaḍḍī tez caldī ha^i
ImmAgt VP
SUB PRED
'The car moves fast'

(50)

ਮੈਂ	ਗੱਡੀ	ਤੇਜ਼	ਚਲਾਉਂਦਾ	ਹਾਂ
mã^{i}	**gaḍḍī**	**tez**	**calāũdā**	**hā̃**
IniAgt	Pat		Verb	
SUB	OBJ		PRED	

'I drive the car fast'
Lit. 'I make the car move fast'

(51)

ਮੇਰੀ	ਪਤਨੀ	(ਮੈਥੋਂ)	ਗੱਡੀ	ਤੇਜ਼	ਚਲਵਾਉਂਦੀ	ਹੈ
merī	**patnī**	**(ma^{i}t^{h}õ)**	**gaḍḍī**	**tez**	**calvāũdī**	**ha^{i}**
IniAgt		IntAgt	Pat		Verb	
SUB		ADJCT	OBJ		PRED	

'My wife makes me drive the car fast'
Lit. 'My wife causes me to cause car move fast'

The **causativisation** process is worth looking at again.

1. The **initiator** SUBJECT of (49) becomes the **patient** OBJECT in (50).
2. With the introduction of a new **initiator causing agent** SUBJECT in (51), the original **patient** OBJECT retains it role, but the *older* **initiator causing agent** of (50) gets **backgrounded**. It is there in the **semantic valency** set but is a *syntactically optional* ADJUNCT NP marked with the **postposition ਤੋਂ tõ** 'from', which is pronounced and written as **ਥੋਂ t^{h}õ** when used with some pronouns. This use of **ਤੋਂ tõ** or **ਥੋਂ t^{h}õ** indicating the **intermediate agent** ADJUNCT is significant.
3. (49) represents the **canonical clause pattern 1** mentioned in Chapter 4, and (50) and (51) both represent the **canonical clause pattern 3**.

(b) Transitive verbs

We take up the verb **ਚੁੱਕ cukk** 'lift' which has only two phases. (See Chapter 9.)

(52)

ਮਜ਼ਦੂਰਾਂ	ਨੇ	ਮਲ਼ਬਾ	ਚੁੱਕਿਆ
mazdūrā̃	**ne**	**maḷbā**	**cukkiā**
ImmAgt	Agt	Pnt Mas Sg	Verb Mas Sg
SUB		OBJ	PRED

'The labourers lifted the debris'

The **perfect participle** of the verb agrees with the **patient** OBJECT as per the rules of agreement discussed above.

(53)

ਠੇਕੇਦਾਰ	ਨੇ	(ਮਜ਼ਦੂਰਾਂ ਤੋਂ)	ਮਲ਼ਬਾ	ਚੁਕਵਾਇਆ
ṭ^{h}ekedār	**ne**	**(mazdūrā̃ tõ)**	**maḷbā**	**cukvāiā**
contractor		labourers from	debris	got lifted
IniAgt	Agt	ImmAgt	Pnt	Verb
SUB		ADJCT	OBJ	PRED

'The contractor made the labourers lift the debris'

The **immediate agent** (labourers) is a part of the **semantic valency** set of the verb here but not of **syntactic valency**. Semantically it is a **source** marked with ਤੋਂ **tõ**. It is a *syntactically optional* ADJUNCT **NP**. The **perfect participle** of the verb agrees with the **patient** OBJECT.

12.6.2 Class 2 verbs

Most verbs in this group are **transitive**. Two important **intransitive** verbs of this group, ਸੁਣ **suṇ** 'be audible' and ਦਿਸ **dis** 'be audible', have been discussed in **12.5.1** above. But ਸੁਣ **suṇ** 'hear', 'listen to' is **transitive** as well. Here we give examples of the use of the verb ਸਿੱਖ **sikk^h** 'learn'.

(54)

ਬੱਚੇ	ਸੰਗੀਤ	ਸਿੱਖਦੇ ਹਨ
bacce	**sangīt**	**sikk^{h}de han**
ImmAgt	Pnt Mas Sg	Verb Mas Sg
SUB	OBJ	PRED

'Children are learning music'

(55)

ਉਸਤਾਦ	(ਬੱਚਿਆਂ ਨੂੰ)	ਸੰਗੀਤ	ਸਿਖਾਉਂਦਾ ਹੈ
ustād	**(bacciā̃ nū̃)**	**sangīt**	**sik^{h}āũdā ha^i**
IniAgt	ImmAgt	Pnt	Verb
SUB	ADJCT	OBJ	PRED

'The teacher teaches music to the children'
Lit. 'The teacher causes the children to learn music'

(56)

ਨਜ਼ੀਰ	(ਉਸਤਾਦ ਤੋਂ)	(ਬੱਚਿਆਂ ਨੂੰ)	ਸੰਗੀਤ	ਸਿਖਵਾਉਂਦਾ ਹੈ
nazīr	**(ustād to)**	**(bacciā̃ nū̃)**	**sangīt**	**sik^{h}vāũdā ha^i**
IniAgt	IntAgt	ImmAgt	Pnt	Verb
SUB	ADJCT	ADJCT	OBJ	

'Nazir gets the teacher to teach music to the children'

'Nazir gets music taught to the children by the teacher'
Lit. 'Nazir causes the teacher to cause the children to learn music'

The immediately notable thing is that the **intermediate agent** is regarded as a **goal** (and not a **source**), as in (55) above and is marked with ਨੂੰ **nū̃** 'to'. Another notable thing is that both the **intermediate agent** regarded as a **source** and marked with ਤੋਂ **tõ** 'from' and the **immediate agent** regarded as a **goal** and marked ਨੂੰ **nū̃** 'to' are *syntactically optional* ADJUNCTS in (56). Without the mention of the **immediate agent** (children), (55) can be used to talk about the subject taught by the teacher. (56) makes perfect sense without the syntactically optional elements put within brackets if Nazir is the principal of a music school not doing any teaching himself.

The most important conclusion we derive from this discussion of causative clauses is that a **causative clause** always represents the **canonical clause pattern 3**. (See Chapter 5). The most natural English translation of (56) is in the **passive voice**. We do not set up a separate category called **passive voice** in this book. "Passive voice" is simply an amalgam of a few logically independent semantic and syntactic features which we will discuss in the next chapter.

Summing up and looking ahead

The following diagrams summarise our discussion of verb-agreement and case-marking in Panjabi.

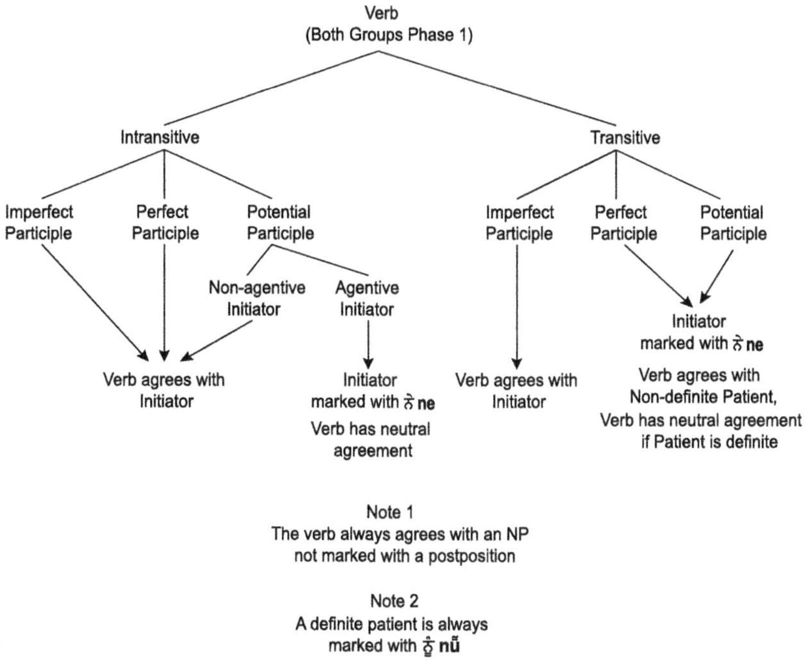

Figure 12.1 Verb-agreement and case-marking for the verbs in Phase 1

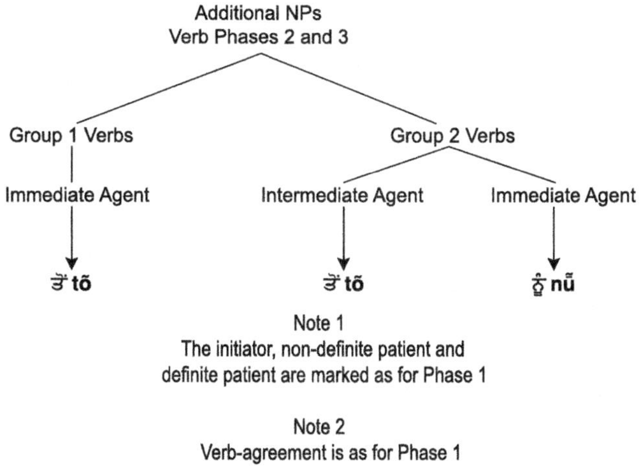

Figure 12.2 Case-marking for the additional NP in verb phases 2 and 3

We have shown that there is nothing "split" or "simply morphological" or "pseudo" about **verb-agreement** (or lack of it) in Panjabi. As we have shown above, this happens according to the internal semantic logic of Panjabi grammar. Moreover, the use of **verb-agreement** and **case-marking postpositions** in Panjabi show how Panjabi views **transitivity** (*the symbolical transfer* of the result of an activity indicated by the verb). The **experiencer NP** in a clause is not the SUBJECT of the clause according to our theoretical framework. The use of the postposition ਨੂੰ **nū̃** 'to' to mark an **experiencer** or the **recipient** of an experience is thoroughly metaphorical. If the equivalent of an **experiencer NP** is the SUBJECT of the clause in English translation, the grammarian should not become desperate to prove with the help of "tests", "transformations", "deep structure", "logical structure" and every other intellectual trick to prove that the "experiencer" is the "experiencing subject" or the "dative subject" of the clause. While it is fine to use English as a *meta*language to present our views, no serious grammarian should use English as a *filter* language. The "fully ergative" languages like Dyirbal must have their own and different internal semantic logic and ways of *metaphorising* transitivity, with which we are not concerned here.

For teachers and other more advanced users

12.7 The Location Event Structure Metaphor

We started a discussion of metaphor in Chapter 8. We continue and elaborate it below, repeating some of the things said earlier.

When European scholars (mostly Christian missionaries) came across ergative languages in the 18th and 19th centuries, they regarded these languages as evidence of the primitive mentality and twisted souls of their speakers. Strange though this may seem, it *is* true. The fact is documented by Seely (1977). It was regarded as an abomination that a verb should agree with the OBJECT in a sentence in the **active voice**. The motivation behind this thinking must have been political – that the speakers of the ergative languages should be brought under the European rules and into the fold of Christianity to make them civilised enough for this world and to save their souls from the eternal fire in the next! If these well-intentioned gentlemen were to rise from their graves today, they would borrow a term from psychiatry and characterise the speakers of North Indian languages as having "split personalities" because of "split ergativity" in their languages.

We introduced the subject of metaphor in Chapter 8. To recall briefly, a metaphor involves a mapping between two conceptual domains – the SOURCE DOMAIN and the TARGET DOMAIN. Lakoff and Johnson's basic formula (now conventionally written in SMALL CAPITALS) is TARGET DOMAIN IS THE SOURCE DOMAIN. When, for example, someone says

(57) ਅਸੀਂ ਇੱਕੀਵੀਂ ਸਦੀ ਵਿਚ ਦਾਖ਼ਿਲ ਹੋ ਗਏ ਹਾਂ
asī ikkīvī̃ sadī vic dāxil ho gae hā̃
'We have entered the 21st century'

she/he views time in terms of space; **space** being the SOURCE DOMAIN and **time** being the TARGET DOMAIN. So the metaphor is TIME IS SPACE.

The metaphor in

(58) ਉਹਨੇ ਆਪਣਾ ਸਾਰਾ ਸਮਾਂ ਬਰਬਾਦ ਕੀਤਾ
uhne āpṇā sārā samā̃ barbād kītā
'He wasted all his time'

is TIME IS MONEY.

Often two or more metaphors can be combined.

(59) ਸਾਡਾ ਕੰਮ ਹੁਣ ਇੱਥੇ ਹੀ ਅੜ ਗਿਆ ਹੈ, ਹੋਰ ਅਗਾਂਹ ਨਹੀਂ ਜਾ ਸਕਦਾ
sāḍā kamm huṇ itt^{h}e hī aṛ giā ha^{i}, hor agā̃h nahī̃ jā sakdā
'Our work is stuck right here now; (it) cannot go any further'

The metaphors involved in (59) are STATES ARE LOCATIONS, DIFFICULTIES ARE IMPEDIMENTS TO MOTION and PROGRESS IS FORWARD MOTION.

The group of metaphors used in Panjabi grammar dealt with in this chapter can collectively be called the Location Event Structure Metaphor, which involves "a mapping between States and Locations, and Change of Action and Motion" (Dancygier and Sweetser 2014: 45).

The Location Event Structure Metaphor in Panjabi grammar operates in the following manner.

1. **Transitivity** is the movement of the **result** of an activity from the **initiator** to or towards a **goal**.
2. The verb agreeing with an **NP** signifies that the **participant** denoted by that NP is in a **state** of being the **substratum** or **location** of the result of the activity, i.e, is characterised as being affected by the result, whether or not it is the originator or source of the activity or of its result. We have already pointed out in Chapter 8 that the **state** of transferable possession is metaphorised as a **location** in Panjabi, as TRANSFERRABLE POSSESSION IS CONTIGUITY IN SPACE.
3. The **NP** marked with ਨੇ **ne** or ਤੋਂ **tõ** 'from' is the **source** of the activity and its result but *not* its **substratum** or **goal**.
4. The **NP** marked with ਨੂੰ **nū̃** 'to' is the **goal** towards which the result is aimed or directed, but not its **substratum**.
5. The metaphorical movement of the result may be viewed as *horizontal* as in (32), (34) and (35) or *vertical* as in (36) or *both* as in (37).
6. The verb in the **nominal form** showing **neutral agreement** is syntactically a nominal and semantically a participating entity in the process.

It would be interesting to make an elaborate study of spatial metaphorisation in Panjabi grammar, using the Lakoff and Johnson notation. But we have no space for this. The examples given in this chapter should be enough to prove our point.

I must add here that the interpretation of Bhartṛhari's semantic-grammatical notion of *dik* 'direction', on which this chapter is based, is my own. It is clear from his writings that he recognised the role of spatial metaphor as a grammatical device. But many philosophers may not agree with me. Over centuries, Bhartṛhari has been over-discussed as a philosopher and underestimated and misunderstood as a linguist, though he himself said very clearly that he was not a philosopher but a grammarian firmly believing in studying language in *lokavyavahāra* (social behaviour of the people).

Chapter 13

Serial Verb Constructions

> It is not that the whole is more than the sum of its parts, but that the *parts* acquire new properties. But as the parts acquire new properties by being together, they impart to the whole new properties, which are reflected in the changes in the parts, and so on. Parts and wholes evolve in consequence of their relationship and the relationship itself evolves. These are properties of things that we call dialectical...
>
> Levins and Lewontin (1985: 3)

Preview of the chapter

This chapter is a climax or culmination of the story of the Panjabi verb and verb phrase we began in Chapter 9. As in all these previous chapters, we start with Bhartṛhari's views. No better description of the semantics of a **serial verb construction** (**SVC**) has ever been given.

> What is called an action is a collection of parts produced in a sequence and mentally conceived as one and identical with parts which are subordinate to it.
>
> (*Vākyapadīya* III.8.4)

As pointed out earlier, Bhartṛhari lived in 5th–6th century when the Indian concept of time (dividing time into a succession of moments, described in Chapter 2) was fully established in Indian culture and had started affecting Indian languages, and classical Sanskrit written at that time was modelled on contemporary vernaculars. The result was a long series of uninflected gerunds ending in *-tvā* in classical Sanskrit, each verb depicting a fragment of the activity. The trend continues even today in all the North Indian languages, with the difference that, in Panjabi, the direct descendants of the *-tvā* constructions are the constructions involving the **conjunctive participle** followed by the uninflected ਕੇ **ke**. The **conjunctive participle** form comes from the Sanskrit gerund form ending in *-tvā*. ਕੇ **ke**, too, comes from the Sanskrit gerund *kṛtvā* 'having done'. But our definition of a **serial verb construction** or **SVC** is "one in which two or more successive verbs (other than the **copula**) are joined together with no connecting conjunction or ਕੇ **ke**". Since ਕੇ **ke** acts simply as a connecting affix (or a sort of particle generally written separately), **conjunctive participle**+ਕੇ **ke** is not an **SVC** in our sense. This is explained below.

Levins and Lewontin's above-mentioned "dialectical" view related to biology can be applied to Panjabi **SVC**s as well if viewed holistically like a living organism.

13.1 What is *not* included in an SVC

The inner semantics and syntax of serial verb constructions are so complex that they require a book-length study. They can be dealt with only in an outline form in this chapter. Before we analyse the structure of the SVCs or **serial verb** groups or clusters or sequences, certain verbs or verb sequences have to be *excluded* from membership of the group. In Panjabi, these verbs or verb sequences are

1. ਹੈ **ha**^{i}, ਸੀ **sī** *appended* to a proper **SVC**, and ਹੋਵੇਗਾ **hovegā** when used in this position because ਹੈ **ha**^{i}and ਸੀ **sī** have no form that can be used there. (See Chapter 10.) For example, in

   (1) ਉਹ ਜਾਂਦਾ ਹੈ
   uh jā̃dā ha^{i}
   'He is going'

the sequence of these verbs (like their translation in English) is not regarded as a **serial verb (SV)**. Such a **tense-marked** verb is not obligatory in a Panjabi clause. Its integration with the main verb is not of an **SV** type as discussed below.

2. **Conjunctive participle+ਕੇ ke**. This sequence functions more as an **adverbial of time**. It is regarded as a **non-finite clause** (Chapter 14), which is not a part of the **core verb group** in a clause. This is made clear in

(2a) ਉਹ ਆ ਕੇ ਬੈਠਾ
uh ā ke ba^{i}ṭ^{h}ā
'He came and sat down'
Lit. 'Having come, he sat down'

ਆ ਕੇ **ā ke** is simply an **adverbial of time**. But the following sequence *without* ਕੇ **ke** is an **SV**.

(2b) ਉਹ ਆ ਬੈਠਾ
uh ā ba^{i}ṭ^{h}ā

The meaning is not simply a sum of ਆ **ā** 'come' and ਬੈਠ **ba^{i}ṭ^{h}** 'sit' but more than this. The sentence has slightly negative connotations such as 'He came and sat down. But he is not welcome, or his presence is undesirable.'

The following sections will make additionally clear why sequences like (2a) are excluded.

13.2 The inner dialectics of an SVC

We will start with two-member clusters involving the main verb in the **conjunctive participle** form and an (**explicator**) **auxiliary**. They were briefly discussed in Chapter 10 as well. This cluster can occur by itself or as the first (and less frequently the second) member of a longer **serial verb construction**. But the meaning of the pair is not always a sum of the meanings of the parts. There are many verbs and explicator auxiliaries and the combination of each pair of "parents" results in unique semantic features. Context and co-text also play their role. It will be useful to divide our topic into sub-topics

13.2.1 General semantics

To avoid starting the discussion with an abstract description, we start with some examples.

(3) ਮੈਂ ਕੁਝ ਬੋਲ ਪਿਆ
mã^{i} kuj^{h} bol piā
ConjP PerP
I something 'speak-fall'
'I impulsively spoke something'

(4) ਮੈਂ ਕੁਝ ਬੋਲ ਬੈਠਾ
mã^{i} kuj^{h} bol ba^{i}ṭ^{h}ā
ConjP PerP
I something 'speak-sit'
'I spoke something, which I now regret'

It is clear that while the SVC inherits a few rather abstract semantic features ("genes") of the components ("parents"), the resulting construction has a unique individual meaning. For example, ਬੋਲ ਬੈਠਾ **bol ba^{i}ṭ^{h}ā** does not mean "spoke and then sat". To convey that meaning, the speaker would say ਬੋਲ ਕੇ ਬੈਠਾ **bol ke ba^{i}ṭ^{h}ā**. We have already seen (in Chapter 10) that ਪੜ੍ਹ ਦੇ **paṛ^{h} de** 'read-give' means 'read aloud for someone else' and ਪੜ੍ਹ ਲੈ **paṛ^{h} la^{i}** 'read-take' means 'read (generally silently) for one's own information'.

Sentence (5) below may be said about the working of a washing machine.

(5) ਇਹ ਮਸ਼ੀਨ ਕਪੜੇ ਸਿਰਫ਼ ਧੋ ਹੀ ਨਹੀਂ ਦਿੰਦੀ,
ih maśīn kappṛe sirf d^{h}o hī nahī̃ dindī,
ConjP Par ImP
this machine clothes only wash not 'giving'

ਪਾੜ ਵੀ ਦਿੰਦੀ ਹੈ
pāṛ vī dindī ha^{i}
ConjP Par ImP
rip also 'giving' is
'This machine not only washes clothes (for you) but also rips them'

While the meaning conveyed by an SVC is a unity (for which also see (3) and (4) above), it is still possible for **particles** and **adverbials** to intervene between the two components ਧੋ **d^{h}o** and ਦਿੰਦੀ **dindī** and ਪਾੜ **pāṛ** and ਦਿੰਦੀ **dindī** in (5) above. In other words, the members in an SVC sequence have not **agglutinated** (yet).

The influence of the context and the intervention of particles and adverbs is illustrated in (6) and (7).

(6) ਦੁਰਘਟਨਾ ਮਗਰੋਂ ਉਹ ਉੱਠ ਕਦੇ ਵੀ ਨਹੀਂ ਸਕਿਆ;
durg^{h}aṭanā magrõ uh uṭṭ^{h} kade vī nahī̃ sakiā;
ConjP AdvP Aux PerP
accident after he get up never could

ਤੇ ਹਫ਼ਤੇ ਬਾਅਦ ਦੁਨੀਆ ਤੋਂ ਉੱਠ ਗਿਆ
te hafte bād duniā tõ uṭṭ^{h} giā
ConjP Aux PerP
and week after world from arose gone
'After the accident, he was never able to get up, and died after a week'

There is no contradiction between ਉੱਠ ਕਦੇ ਵੀ ਨਹੀਂ ਸਕਿਆ **uṭṭ^{h} kade vī nahī̃ sakiā** 'was never able to get up' and ਉੱਠ ਗਿਆ **uṭṭ^{h} giā** 'arose-gone' i.e., 'died' because the meaning of ਉੱਠ **uṭṭ^{h}** is different in the two sequences. The adverbial ਕਦੇ ਵੀ ਨਹੀਂ **kade vī nahī̃** 'never' intervenes between the **conjunctive participle** ਉੱਠ **uṭṭ^{h}** and the (**explicator**) **auxiliary** ਸਕ **sak** in the first clause.

The context makes the meaning different in (7).

(7) ਉਹ ਅੱਧਾ ਘੰਟਾ ਸੌਂ ਕੇ ਉੱਠ ਗਿਆ
uh add^{h}ā g^{h}anṭā sā̃^{u} ke uṭṭ^{h} giā
ConjP ConjP Aux PerP
'He got up after sleeping half an hour'

The original meaning of ਜਾ **jā** 'go' or 'movement away from the time of reference' is completely absent in (7), but some of its traces can be found in (6), if death is viewed as a movement away from this world to the next. It could be argued that ਉੱਠ ਜਾ **uṭṭ^{h} jā** in the sense of dying is an idiom. But idioms develop from common usage becoming metaphorical and then idiomatic. The non-literal meaning of ਜਾ **jā** is clear in (8).

(8) ਮੈਂ ਆ ਗਿਆ ਹਾਂ
mā̃^{i} ā giā hā̃
ConjP Aux PerP Cop
I 'come-gone' am
'I have come'

After coming, the speaker has not literally 'gone' anywhere. ਜਾ **jā** refers to the completion of the event, as it does in (6) as well but with a combination of the movement metaphor.

13.2.2 *Special semantics of ਰਹਿ rahi* and of ਪੈ *pa^{i}*

The "special semantics" of the explicator auxiliary ਰਹਿ **rahi** [rɛ́] is slightly confusing. The meaning of the **full verb** ਰਹਿ **rahi** is 'stay'. As an **auxiliary**, it denotes a continuing situation. But the problem is that its **perfect participle** form (which ordinarily should refer to a *completed* situation or a situation viewed as completed) refers only to the *completion of the beginning or commencement* of a situation, not to the completion of the situation itself. In other words, ਰਿਹਾ **rihā** refers to a *continuing* situation as in

(9) ਮੈਂ ਕਿਤਾਬ ਲਿਖ ਰਿਹਾ ਹਾਂ
mã^{i} kitāb lik^{h} rihā hã
ConjP Aux ImP Cop
'write-stayed'
'I am writing a book'

Metaphorically, it means 'I am in an already started and now continuing situation involving the writing of a book'.

The constructions with the a**uxiliary** verb ਰਹਿ **rahi** do not warrant the special title of a "continuous tense" awarded to it by many Indian grammarians who learnt English from J.C. Nesfield's English grammar first published in 1898.

The semantics of ਪੈ **pa^{i}** is interesting in a somewhat similar as well as different way.

(10) ਕਿਤਾਬ ਮੇਜ਼ 'ਤੇ ਪਈ ਹੈ
kitāb mez te paī ha^{i}
'fallen' is
PerP Cop
'The book is lying on the table'

The original meaning of the full verb ਪੈ **pa^{i}** 'fall' is not reflected at all in (10). The situation is viewed as something like 'The book has fallen or has been placed on the table and is now lying there'. The 'fallen' interpretation may not be true, but the book, being an inanimate object, has certainly been placed there by someone. The dimensions of space and time cannot always be separated in grammar. In the following examples, the imperfect participle form ਪੈਂਦੀ **pã^{i}dī** indicates a *continuing process*, and the perfect participle form ਪਈ **pa^{i}** indicates a *continuing state* (resulting from a previous process).

(11) ਅਲਾਸਕਾ ਵਿਚ ਸਾਰਾ ਸਾਲ ਬਰਫ਼ ਪੈਂਦੀ ਰਹਿੰਦੀ ਹੈ
alāskā vic sārā sāl barf pã^{i}dī rahindī ha^{i}
ImP ImP Cop
Alaska in whole year snow falling staying is
'In Alaska snow keeps falling the whole year'

The form ਰਹਿੰਦੀ **rahindī** (imperfect participle form of ਰਹਿ **rahi** 'stay') indicates the repeated *process*. But in 12 below, ਪਈ **pãī** 'fallen' combines with ਰਹਿੰਦੀ **rahindī** to indicate a *continuing and never-ending state*.

(12) ਅਲਾਸਕਾ ਵਿਚ ਸਾਰਾ ਸਾਲ ਬਰਫ਼ ਪਈ ਰਹਿੰਦੀ ਹੈ
alāskā vic sārā sāl barf paī rahindī ha^{i}
PerP ImP Cop
Alaska in whole year snow fallen staying is
'In Alaska snow stays the whole year'

(11) and (12) clearly show that when ਰਹਿ **rahi** and ਪੈ **pa^{i}** are used as auxiliaries (together in these examples), their semantics undergoes considerable change. This happens with *all* the explicator auxiliaries. Each combination of a main verb and an explicator auxiliary (we call it a **construction**) has its own unique nuances, being a synthesis of the semantic and grammatical potentials of all the members, whose number can go up to five, as we shall see later on in the chapter. It is worth recalling here that each full verb in Panjabi can have three or four additive and subtractive **phases** discussed earlier in Chapter 9. This is the most complex and most interesting part of the grammar of Panjabi (and its sister Indic languages). Grammarians have so far either conveniently ignored them or handled some of them badly as "tenses" or "passive voice" etc. Our approach below is that all these constructions are syntactically first and foremost **serial verb constructions**. Their semantic peculiarities come from the grammatical and semantic interaction of their constituent members. We have used the term **blending** for this.

13.2.3 Two conjunctive participles in a cluster

In Chapter 11, we dealt with sentences like

(13) ਮੈਥੋਂ ਹੱਸ ਹੋ ਗਿਆ
mat^{h}õ hass ho giā
ConjP ConjP Aux PerP
ADJCT SUB PRED
'I happened to laugh'

Some other examples are

(14) ਮੈਥੋਂ ਝੂਠ ਬੋਲ ਹੋ ਗਿਆ
mat^{h}õ j^{h}ūṭ^h bol ho giā
ConjP ConjP Aux PerP
ADJCT SUB PRED
'I happened to tell a lie'

(15) ਉਹਤੋਂ ਹਰ ਰੋਜ਼ ਕੋਈ ਗ਼ਲਤ ਕੰਮ ਕਰ ਹੋ ਜਾਂਦਾ ਹੈ
uhtõ har roz koī ɣalat kamm kar ho jā̃dā ha^i
ConjP ConjP Aux ImP
ADJCT SUB PRED
'He happens to do something wrong every day'
Lit. 'Doing of some wrong action happens to proceed from him every day'

In such clusters, a **conjunctive participle** form is followed by another **conjunctive participle** form ਹੋ **ho** and some form of ਜਾ **jā**. We argued in Chapter 11 that the first **conjunctive participle** is the nominal SUBJECT of the clause. The ADJUNCT **agent** of the action is marked by the postposition ਤੋਂ **tõ** 'from'. It is not omitted for pragmatic reasons in (13), (14) and (15) because the **agent** is *situationally* significant.

The general semantics of a cluster can be regarded as a "blend" of the semantic potential of the members. (Fauconnier and Turner 2002).

13.2.4 Semantic valency

The "blending" of the semantics of the members of the cluster is a lot clearer in the **semantic valency** of the cluster. As already explained in Chapter 12, the **semantic valency** set of a verb-form consists of the **accessories** (or *kārakas*) involved in the **action** (*kriyā*) denoted by the form of the **verb**. The number in the set can be from one (**intransitive** verb-form) to four (**Phase 3** of a verb in **Group 2**). For example, the **valency set** of the verb-form ਜਾ **jā** 'go' has one member, the **agent**. We can say that its **semantic valency** is *one*. ਕਰਵਾ **karvā** 'get something done' has the **semantic valency** *three* (the **initior agent** who gets the job done, the **immediate agent** who does the job, and the **patient** affected by the work that is done.) The **semantic valency** of ਸਿਖਵਾ **sik^{h}vā** 'get something taught' is *four* (the **initiator agent**, the **intermediate agent** or the teacher, the **immediate agent** or the learner, and the **patient** or the skill being taught/learnt). The number of the accessories in the **valency set** of a **verb-form** make up its **semantic weight.**

The rule of the **semantic weight** of a **serial verb** in Panjabi is:

> *The semantic weight of a member verb following another member in a **serial verb cluster** is either equal to or lighter than the semantic weight of the preceding member.*

In other words, the **semantic valency** of a member following another can *never* be more than that of the preceding member. But, in addition to **semantic valency**, the **syntactic** behaviour of an **SVC** also needs to be understood.

13.3 Syntactic behaviour of an SVC

The **syntactic behaviour** of a set of verb-forms consists of (i) assigning the status of ARGUMENTS or COMPLEMENTS which a verb PREDICATE must have in order to form a grammatical clause, (ii) the agreement of the verb with one of the COMPLEMENTS and (iii) the use of **case-marking postpositions** for the *obligatory* COMPLEMENTS and the *optional* ADJUNCTS (the remaining accessories). Chapter 12 deals with this in detail. Briefly, the factors influencing this behaviour are the **phase** of the verb (whether the verb is **intransitive**, **transitive** or **causative**) and the **form** of the verb indicating TMA categories.

13.3.1 The pivot of an SVC

We are going to introduce an important theortical concept, the **pivot**, in this chapter. This concept is not new in linguistics (Matthews 2007: 305). But we have *adapted* it to suit our purpose.

*A **pivot** is a nominal with which every capable verb form in an SVC agrees in number and person/gender irrespective of its normal agreement behaviour outside the SVC.*

A *capable* verb form is the one capable of this type of agreement. In other words, the **pivot** of an SVC **controls** verb agreement.

Examples are needed to illustrate the working of a **pivot** in an SVC.

(16a) ਨੌਕਰ ਨੇ ਆਲੂ ਉਬਾਲ਼ੇ
na^{u}kar ne ālū ubāḷe
Mas Pl Mas Pl
'The servant boiled the potatoes'

(16b) ਨੌਕਰ ਨੇ ਆਲੂ ਉਬਾਲ਼ ਦਿੱਤੇ
na^{u}kar ne ālū ubāḷ ditte
Mas Pl Mas Pl
'The servant boiled the potatoes (for others)'

(16c) ਆਲੂ ਉਬਾਲ਼ ਦਿੱਤੇ ਗਏ
ālū ubāḷ ditte gae
Mas Pl Mas Pl
'The potatoes were boiled'

In (16a), the **transitive perfect participle** form agrees with the patient OBJECT ਆਲੂ **ālū**, and the agent SUBJECT is marked with ਨੇ **ne**, *as usual*. (16b) introduced the ***transitive*** explicator auxiliary ਦੇ **de** in the **perfect participle** form, which now controls the syntactic behaviour of the cluster. The verb agrees with the patient OBJECT, and the agent SUBJECT is marked with ਨੇ **ne**, *as usual*. The main verb ਉਬਾਲ਼ **ubāḷ** is now in the conjunctive participle form and is not capable of agreement with any nominal. But (16c) introduces an *intransitive* **explicator auxiliary** ਜਾ **jā**. As a result, the whole construction has become **intransitive**. The SUBJECT ਨੌਕਰ **na^{u}kar** of (16b) has been **backgrounded** or pushed out of the ***syntactic*** **valency set**. But both the *capable* verb forms agree with the masculine plural nominal ਆਲੂ **ālū**. Put differently, this nominal **controls** verb agreement in all three clauses (16a), (16b) and (16c). Normally (outside an SVC), an intransitive verb does not agree with a patient OBJECT. But it does in (16c). The last member of the SVC partly contributes its syntactic behaviour to the construction in the form of its syntactic valency and partly takes up the syntactic behaviour of the preceding members in the form of agreement. This imparts unity to an SVC.

If the patient OBJECT of a **transitive** verb in the **perfect participle** form is **definite**, the verb does not agree with it and remains in the **neuter** (homophonous to the masculine singular) form.

(17a) ਨੌਕਰ ਨੇ ਆਲੂਆਂ ਨੂੰ ਉਬਾਲ਼ਿਆ

na^{u}kar ne ālūā̃ nū̃ ubāḷiā

Mac Pl Def Neu

'The servant boiled the potatoes'

(17b) ਨੌਕਰ ਨੇ ਆਲੂਆਂ ਨੂੰ ਉਬਾਲ਼ ਦਿੱਤਾ

na^{u}kar ne ālūā̃ nū̃ ubāḷ dittā

Mac Pl Def Neu

'The servant boiled the potatoes (for others)'

(17c) ਆਲੂਆਂ ਨੂੰ ਉਬਾਲ਼ ਦਿੱਤਾ ਗਿਆ

ālūā̃ nū̃ ubāḷ dittā giā

Mac Pl Def Neu Neu

'The potatoes were boiled'

For some reason, the patient OBJECT is definite in (17a). So the verb is in the neuter form. This neuter verb agreement continues in (17b) and (17c).

13.3.2 Blending of semantic and syntactic behaviour of the members of an SVC

Now let us take up the serial verb cluster ਲੈਆ **la^i ā** 'bring' ('take-come')

(18) ਕੁੜੀ ਦੁੱਧ ਲੈ ਆਈ

kuṛī dudd^h lai āī

ConjP Aux PerP

'The girl brought milk'

Lit. 'Having taken the milk, the girl came'

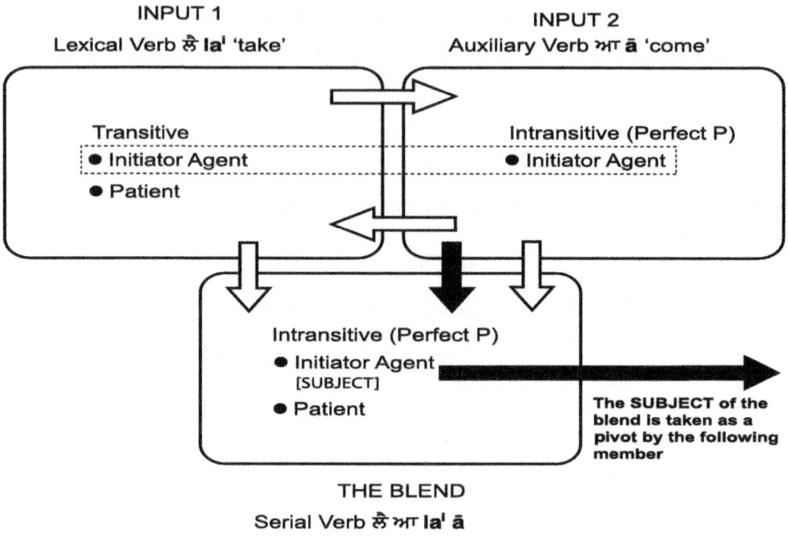

Figure 13.1 Blending in a main verb+auxiliary cluster 1

The upper two boxes show each member's **semantic valency**. The horizontal hollow arrows indicate that the members influence each other's general semantics. The lower box shows the *semantic* contribution (indicated by the downward vertical hollow arrows) of each member to the **blend**. The dotted rectangle shows the shared accessory or the accessories. The dark downward arrow shows that the **syntactic** behaviour of the second member is the syntactic behaviour of the **blend** as well. The **pivot** mentioned in Figure 13.1 has been discussed above and will be taken up again in **13.4.1** below.

ਲੈ la 'take' is **transitive** with the **initiator agent ਕੁੜੀ kuṛī** 'girl' and the **patient ਦੁੱਧ duddʰ** 'milk' in its **semantic valency** set. The second member **ਆ ā** 'come' is **intransitive** with only one accessory **ਕੁੜੀ kuṛī**, which it shares with the first member. Both the accessories are present in the **semantic valency set** of the **blend**. But *syntactically* the blend acts as an **intransitive** verb as far as the agreement of the verb is concerned because the second member contributing its **syntactic** behaviour to the **blend** is **intransitive**. A transitive verb expressing **perfective aspect** (such **ਲੈ la'**) *by itself* should agree with the **patient** OBJECT (see Chapter 12), but the **blend ਲੈ ਆ la' ā**, being an **intransitive verb**, does not.

Later on, we will see what has happened to the syntactic behaviour of **ਲੈ ਆ la' ā** regarded by the speakers of Panjabi as a *single semantic unit* because of its extremely frequent use.

(19) ਕੁੜੀ ਨੇ ਸੰਗੀਤ ਸਿੱਖ ਲਿਆ
kuṛī ne sangīt sikk^h liā
ConjP Aux PerP
'The girl learnt music'

This should be quite unproblematic. Both the members are **transitive** and have shared accessories.

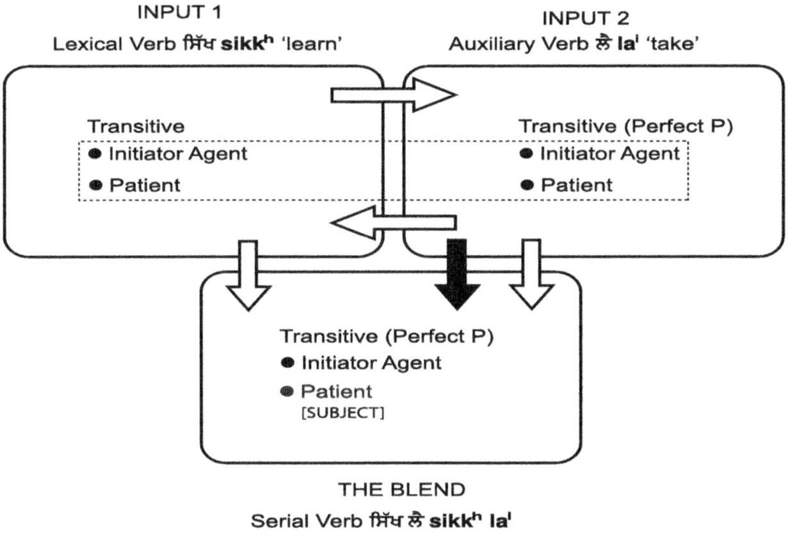

Figure 13.2 Blending in a main verb+auxiliary cluster 2

The blend is **transitive** because of the *second* member. The verb in the **perfect participle** form agrees with the **patient** OBJECT. The agent SUBJECT is marked with ਨੇ **ne**.

(20) ਕੁੜੀ ਨੇ (ਨੌਕਰ ਤੋਂ) ਕੰਮ ਕਰਵਾ ਲਿਆ
kuṛī ne (na^{u}kar tõ) kamm karvā liā
ConjP Aux PerP
'The girl got the work done (for her) (by the servant)'

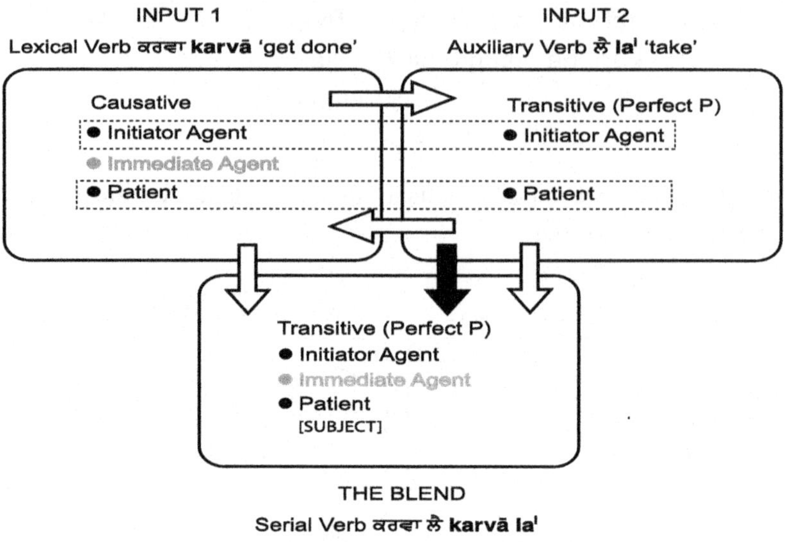

Figure 13.3 Blending in a main verb+auxiliary cluster 3

The first member is **causative** with three **semantic accessories** shown in the first box, two of which are shared by the second **transitive** member. It is notable that the **immediate agent** (ਨੌਕਰ **na^{u}kar** 'servant') is already **syntactically backgrounded** (an optional ADJUNCT "greyed out" in Figure 13.3 above) even with the **causative form** ਕਰਵਾ **karvā** 'get done' (see Chapter 9). The **blended** verb ਕਰਵਾ ਲੈ **karvā la^{i}** is **transitive** and in the **perfect participle** form. So the verb agrees with the patient OBJECT, but the agent SUBJECT is also a necessary COMPLEMENT of the verb PREDICATE. The agent SUBJECT is marked with ਨੇ **ne**.

But in (21) below, the **blended transitive** verb ਕਰਵਾ ਲੈ **karvā la^{i}** is in the **imperfect participle** form (because ਲੈ **la^{i}** in the right parent box is in this form). So the verb agrees with the agent SUBJECT.

(21) ਕੁੜੀ (ਨੌਕਰ ਤੋਂ) ਕੰਮ ਕਰਵਾ ਲੈਂਦੀ (ਹੈ)
kuṛī (na^{u}kar tõ) kamm karvā lã^{i}dī (ha^{i})
ConjP Aux ImP Cop
'The girl gets the work done (for her) (by the servant)

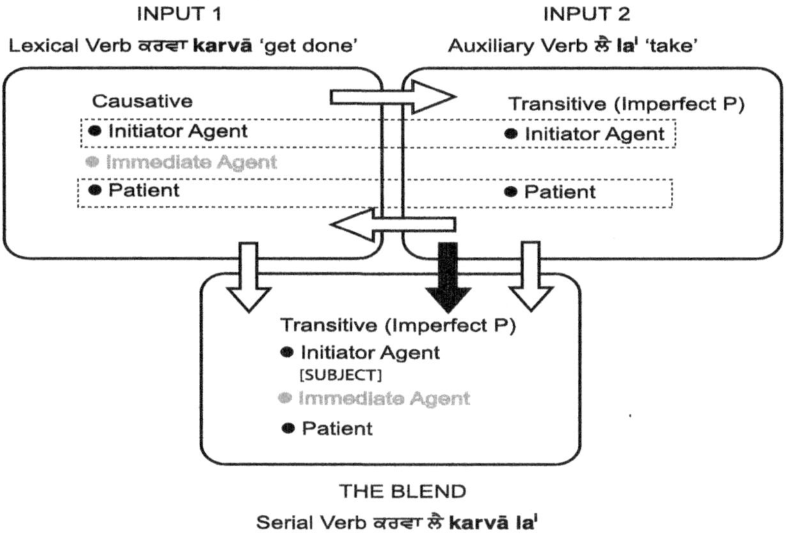

Figure 13.4 Blending in a main verb+auxiliary cluster 4

Now we deal below with the case when the verb in the second box has a **subtractive phase**. (See Chapter 9 for details.) To repeat briefly what we have already said, the **initiator agent** of the verb in this phase is *eliminated* (and not simply *backgrounded*), and is crossed out in the blend box in Figure 13.5 given below. To repeat what has been said several times before, a **backgrounded** agent is *syntactically optional* but an ***eliminated*** agent *must not* be mentioned (unless it is ਅਸੀਂ **asī̃** 'we' in a "boastful" sentence). The non-boastful sentence expresses an idea which is regarded as universally applicable and hence the elimination of the **initiating agent**. Another important thing about this phase is that a verb occurs only in the **imperfect participle** form.

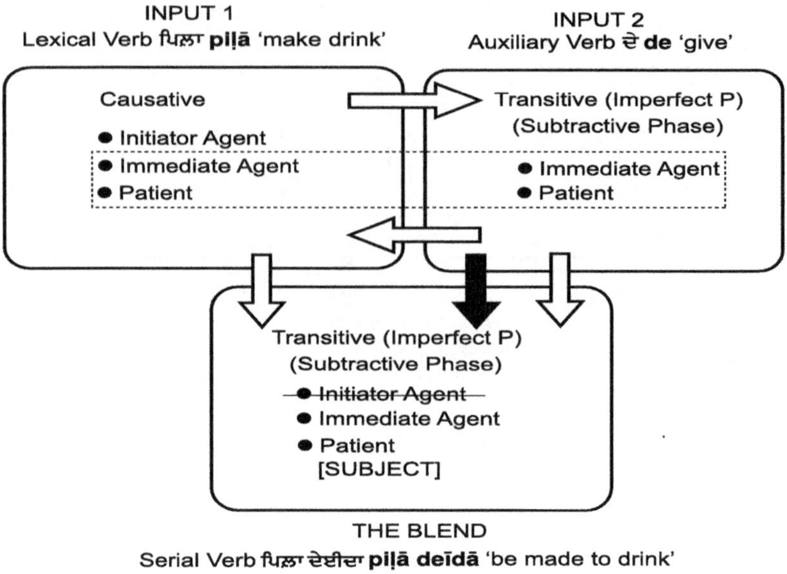

Figure 13.5 Blending in a main verb+auxiliary cluster 5

Two accessories are shared in the **semantic valencies** of the verbs contributing to the **blend**. But the blend inherits its *syntactic behaviour* from the **auxiliary** verb ਦੇ **de** in the second box, whose **subtractive phase** is ਦੇਈ **deī**.

Using the **transitive** form of the **normal phase** of the verb ਦੇ **de**, the speaker would say

(22) ਮੈਂ ਪਿਆਸੇ ਨੂੰ ਪਾਣੀ ਪਿਲ਼ਾ ਦਿੰਦਾ ਹਾਂ
mãˡ piāse nū̃ pāṇī piḷā dindā hā̃
ConjP Aux ImP Cop
'I offer water to a thirsty man to drink (for his benefit)'
Lit. 'I make a thirsty man drink water'

As per the rules, the **causative verb** in the **imperfect participle** form should agree with the **initiating agent**. But the use of the **subtractive phase** in (23) below forces the **initiating agent** out, and the verb agrees with the **patient**. A verb in the **imperfect participle** form agreeing with the **patient** appears to be slightly abnormal in Panjabi grammar, but such is the syntactic behaviour of a verb in the **subtractive phase**. The blend shown in Figure 13.5 above is exemplified in

(23) ਪਿਆਸੇ ਨੂੰ ਪਾਣੀ ਪਿਲ਼ਾ ਦੇਈਦਾ (ਹੈ)
piāse nū̃ pāṇī piḷā deīdā (ha^{i})
ConjP SubP ImP Cop
'A thirsty man should be offered water to drink
(for his benefit)'

13.3.3 The interesting history of ਲਿਆ liā

The interesting history of the verb **ਲਿਆ liā** is a clear proof that the blend of a **lexical verb** in the **conjunctive participle** form and an **explicator auxiliary** starts it journey towards becoming a single verb. Members in most such blends have not yet fused or **agglutinated** with each other, and particles can still intervene between the two, as in examples (5) and (6) above. But the great frequency of use of the **blend ਲੈ ਆ la^{i} ā** hastened this fusion or **agglutination**. This has happened in many other languages as well (Bybee 2010).

The **blend ਲੈ ਆ la^{i} ā** started, like all such blends discussed so far, as a construction involving **ਕੇ ke**, as **ਲੈ ਕੇ ਆ la^{i} ke ā** 'having taken, come', which is still used when the sequence and order of the two actions is highlighted. The primary stress is on **ਲੈ la^{i}**, the secondary stress is on **ਆ ā** and **ਕੇ ke** is unstressed. Only **ਆ ā** in the sequence is inflected; **ਲੈ la^{i}** and are **ਕੇ ke** are not.

(24a) ਕੁੜੀ ਮੇਰੇ ਲਈ ਦੁੱਧ ਲੈ ਕੇ ਆਈ
kuṛī mere laī dudd^{h} la^{i} ke āī
ConjP PerP
Fem Sg Fem Sg
'The girl got milk for me and (then) came'
'Having got the milk for me, the girl came'

The first step towards "mentally conceiving" the two actions as one (or as the two verbs having "one soul in two bodies", as a perfect marriage is described in Panjabi culture) was to eliminate **ਕੇ ke**. As already mentioned above, the sequence containing **ਕੇ ke** is not regarded as a serial verb construction in our system.

All the SVCs we have discussed so far are like

(24b) ਕੁੜੀ ਮੇਰੇ ਲਈ ਦੁੱਧ ਲੈ ਆਈ
kuṛī mere laī dudd^{h} la^{i} āī
ConjP PerP
Fem Sg Fem Sg

The **blend ਲੈ ਆਈ la^{i} āī** is an **intransitive verb** because the *second member* is **intransitive**. The stress is on **ਲੈ la^{i}** and **ਆ ā** is unstressed. But the great frequency of use led to the **phonetic agglutination** in **ਲਿਆ li'ā**, with stress shifted to the second syllable, as is the case with all the **Phase 2** Panjabi verbs ending in **-ਆ -ā**. Now no **particle** can be inserted inside this single word. But the **syntactic** behaviour continues to be that of an **intransitive** verb **ਲੈਆ la^{i} ā**, as in

(24c)	ਕੁੜੀ	ਮੇਰੇ	ਲਈ	ਦੁੱਧ	ਲਿਆਈ
	kuṛī	**mere**	**laī**	**dudd^{h}**	**liāī**
					PerP
	Fem Sg				Fem Sg

'The girl brought milk for me'

But this **syntactic** behaviour of the **perfect participle** form of a transitive-*looking* verb agreeing with agent SUBJECT seems rather anomalous and was bound to change. Quite justifiably, people started making **ਲਿਆ liā** behave like a *real* **transitive** verb. So

(24d)	ਕੁੜੀ	ਨੇ	ਮੇਰੇ	ਲਈ	ਦੁੱਧ	ਲਿਆਂਦਾ
	kuṛī	**ne**	**mere**	**laī**	**dudd^{h}**	**liā̃dā**
	Fem Sg	Agt				PerP
					Mas Sg	Mas Sg

'The girl brought milk for me'

is also used. As with any other **transitive** verb, the **perfect participle** form now agrees with the **patient** OBJECT and the **agent** SUBJECT is marked with the **agentive postposition ਨੇ ne**.

Since both (24c) and (24d) are in use, and can be regarded as referring to the "same" situation (or they are *truth conditionally* equivalent and express the same *proposition*, as a philosopher would say), it is interesting to ask whether the two differ in meaning. So they were presented to a number of native speakers of Panjabi, who were asked what difference in meaning, *if any*, they found between the two. While all these speakers agreed that the two referred to the same situation, interesting differences in meaning were also pointed out, such as "(24c) is about the girl and (24d) is about the milk"; "(24c) is more poetic and romantic than (24d)"; "their overhead meanings differ subtly, but it is difficult to say how".

The case of ਲਿਜਾ **lijā** (ਲੈ+ਜਾ **la^{i}+jā** 'take go') 'take away', with stress on the second syllable as in ਲਿਆ **liā**, is the same. We saw in Chapter 11 that Guru Nanak Dev used ਲੈ ਜਾਹੁ **la^{i} jāhu** in the 16th century. Later on it became ਲੈ ਜਾ **la^{i} jā** and finally ਲਿਜਾ **lijā**.

Leaving the "truth conditional" or "propositional" meaning for philosophers and the "overhead" or "poetic and romantic" meaning for literary critics, the grammarian should be concerned with the fact that the verb agrees with an accessory that is regarded as the **substratum of the result** of the activity denoted by the verb. The native speakers' intuition that (24c) is *about* the girl and (24d) is *about* the milk is extremely significant in Panjabi grammar, and is not simply a "superficial surface structure morphological phenomenon". It is this intuition that is responsible for the evolution of language. The next section is all about this "about" feeling.

13.3.4 Main features of the conjunctive participle+ (explicator) auxiliary cluster

Before we move further, let us review the main features of the cluster **conjunctive participle+(explicator) auxiliary** we have covered so far.

1. This cluster can be the only member in an **SVC**;
2. In a longer **SVC**, it is mostly the first member, and less frequently a second member;
3. It is very rare to find two such clusters in a longer **SVC**;
4. The first member inside this cluster may be **causative**, or **transitive** or **intransitive**, but the cluster as a whole can behave only as a **transitive** or **intransitive** verb.

13.4 Structure and features of a longer SVC

It will be useful to preview and summarise the features of an **SVC** consisting of three or more members.

1. In an **SVC** with more than two members, the maximum number of members is five (or four if a conjunctive participle+explicator auxiliary **blend** sequence is regarded as one member); there can be nesting within an SVC that can be represented by the use of different brackets used in algebra – ( ), [ ] and { }. However, this is

not possible if a word order other than the normal unmarked one is used because of contextual and rhetorical reasons.

2. Particles can intervene between the members of an **SVC**.
3. It is rare (but possible) for two **conjunctive participle+(explicator) auxiliary** clusters (or **blends**) to be present in an SVC. If they are present, they must be the first and/or the second members.
4. If ਹੈ **haⁱ**, or ਸੀ **sī** or a variant of ਹੋਵੇਗਾ **hovegā** follows an SVC, it is not a member of the construction.
5. In a longer SVC, the first member (or a blend) can be **causative**, or **transitive** or **intransitive**, but all other members are **intransitive**.
6. Since the last member of an SVC with more than one member (regarding a **blend** as one member) is always **intransitive,** and since the syntactic behaviour of an SVC is determined by the *last* member, such a longer SVC as a whole is always **intransitive**.
7. As regards the SUBJECT of the full SVC, we have to look at what the first member verb (or a **blend** as a whole) agrees with. This was discussed above and also in detail in Chapter 12. But it needs to be emphasised here that the verb in the **neuter form** carrying the result of the completed activity directed at the goal of the result (marked with ਨੂੰ **nū̃**) and not agreeing with any **NP** is regarded as a **nominal.**

13.4.1 The pivot in a longer SVC

As should be clear from the examples given above, the **substratum of result** (**SR**) of the activity indicated by the first single verb member or a blend with which the verb agrees is taken as *single* **syntactic** ARGUMENT by the following member, whatever **TMA** categories it may express. Consider these **single verb** clauses first.

(25a) ਧੋਬਣ ਕੱਪੜੇ ਧੋਂਦੀ ਹੈ

dʰobaṇ	**kappṛe**	**dʰõdī**	**haⁱ**
Fem Sg	Mas Pl	Fem Sg	

'The washerwoman washes the clothes'

(25b) ਧੋਬਣ ਨੇ ਕੱਪੜੇ ਧੋਤੇ ਹਨ
d^h^obaṇ ne kappṛe d^h^ote han
Fem Sg Agt Mas Pl Mas Pl
'The washerwoman has washed the clothes'

(25c) ਧੋਬਣ ਨੇ ਕੱਪੜਿਆਂ ਨੂੰ ਧੋਤਾ ਹੈ
d^h^obaṇ ne kappṛiā̃ nū̃ d^h^otā ha^i^
Fem Sg Agt Mas Pl (Def) Neu
'The washerwoman has washed the clothes (already mentioned)'

The main verb in all these clauses is a single verb, and not a blend. Now add the **intransitive auxiliary** ਜਾ **jā** in the **imperfect participle** form, emphasising the progress towards the completion of the activity.

(26a) ਧੋਬਣ ਕੱਪੜੇ ਧੋਂਦੀ ਜਾਂਦੀ ਹੈ
d^h^obaṇ kappṛe d^h^õdī jā̃dī ha^i^
Fem Sg Mas Pl Fem Sg Fem Sg
'The washerwoman has gone on washing the clothes'

(26b) ਕੱਪੜੇ ਧੋਤੇ ਜਾਂਦੇ ਹਨ
kappṛe d^h^ote jā̃de han
Mas Pl Mas Pl Mas Pl
'The clothes are washed'

(26c) ਕੱਪੜਿਆਂ ਨੂੰ ਧੋਤਾ ਜਾਂਦਾ ਹੈ
kappriā̃ nū̃ d^h^otā jā̃dā ha^i^
Mas Pl (Def) Neu Neu
'The clothes are washed'

The English translation does not fully capture the nuances of the Panjabi sentences. The verb ਹੈ **ha^i^** is not a part of the **SVC**, but it is added here to help us make a sensible English translation. The notable thing in (26a) and (26b) is that the **substratum of the result** of the activity of the first member verb becomes the **pivot** of the whole SVC. Since the SVC is regarded as mono-clausal which should have a single SUBJECT, the term **pivot** is used for discussing the syntactic behaviour of the individual constituent members of an SVC. There is no **substratum of the result** (**SR**) of the activity in (26c); the verb in the neuter form along with the goal of the result has been adopted as the **pivot**. The **agent** of the activity has been backgrounded in (26b) and (26c).

The same thing happens if we add the **intransitive (explicator) auxiliary** ਜਾ **jā** in the **perfect participle** form, emphasising the progress towards the completion of the activity. The verb form being the **perfect participle** makes no difference.

(27a) ਧੋਬਣ ਕੱਪੜੇ ਧੋਂਦੀ ਗਈ ਹੈ
d^{h}obaṇ kappṛe d^{h}õdī gaī ha^i
Fem Pl Mas Pl Fem Sg Fem Sg Cop
'The washerwoman has gone on washing the clothes'

(27b) ਕੱਪੜੇ ਧੋਤੇ ਗਏ ਹਨ
kappṛe d^{h}ote gae han
Mas Pl Mas Pl Mas Pl Cop
'The clothes have been washed'

(27c) ਕੱਪੜਿਆਂ ਨੂੰ ਧੋਤਾ ਗਿਆ ਹੈ
kappriā̃ nū̃ d^{h}otā giā ha^i
Mas Pl Neu Neu Cop
'The clothes have been washed'

The same rule (**the substratum of the result** or **SR** of the activity of the preceding verb being the *single* ARGUMENT of the following one) applied if the first member is a **blend**.

(28a) ਕੁੜੀ ਨੇ ਕੰਮ ਕਰਵਾ ਲਿਆ (ਹੈ)
kuṛī ne kamm karvā liā (ha^i)
Mas Sg ConP Mas Sg Cop
'The girl has got the the work done'

The **blend** is **transitive** because the auxiliary ਲੈ **la^i** is **transitive** in (28a), though the main verb is **causative**. If we add ਜਾ **jā**, whether in the **imperfect participle** or the **perfect participle** form, the **SR** of (28b) and (28c) will be the **pivot**, but the meaning will be different in the two cases.

(28b) ਕੰਮ ਕਰਵਾ ਲਿਆ ਜਾਂਦਾ (ਹੈ)
kamm karvā liā jā̃dā (ha^i)
Mas Sg ConjP Mas Sg Mas Sg Cop
'(It is often the case that) the work gets completed'

(28c) ਕੰਮ ਕਰਵਾ ਲਿਆ ਗਿਆ (ਹੈ)
kamm karvā liā giā (ha^{i})
Mas Sg ConjP Mas Sg Mas Sg Cop
'The work has been completed'

The **imperfect participle** form of ਜਾ **jā** in (28b) indicates the repeated nature of the activity. But the important point is that the **SR** of the activity of the **blend** is taken as the **pivot** of the longer **serial verb**. (28c) refers to an action done once, but the **pivot** is the same in both the cases.

Using the brackets used in algebra, we can represent the structure of the verb in (28c) as

[(karvā liā) (giā)] (ha^{i})

A **blend** can be a second member in an SVC.

(29) ਮਕਾਨ ਬਣਦਾ ਜਾ ਰਿਹਾ (ਹੈ)
makān baṇdā jā rihā (ha^{i})
Mas Sg ImP ConjP Aux PerP Cop
'The house is getting built'
Lit. 'The becoming of the house is continuing'

[(baṇdā) (jā rihā)] (ha^{i})

ਮਕਾਨ **makān**, the **SR** of the activity of the first verb in the **imperfect participle** form is the **pivot** of the **blend** ਜਾ ਰਿਹਾ **jā rihā**, whose verb in the **perfect participle** form indicates a continuing activity. Even in its rather metaphorical use, the **auxiliary** ਜਾ **jā** has not entirely lost its original meaning as 'movement away from the point of reference'.

The metaphorical movement *towards* the point of reference can be seen in

(30) ਇਹ ਝਗੜਾ ਕਈ ਸਾਲਾਂ ਤੋਂ ਚਲਿਆ ਆ ਰਿਹਾ (ਹੈ)
ih j^{h}agaṛā kaī sālā̃ tõ caliā ā rihā (ha^{i})
PerP ConjP PerP Cop
'come' 'stayed'
'This dispute has been continuing for many years'

[(caliā) (ā rihā)] (ha^{i})

The dispute is metaphorically viewed as ‘coming’ from the past to the present time.

There can be four or even five members in a **SVC**. They all contribute their semantic potential to the whole SVC. But each individual member takes its **syntactic behaviour** (including the **syntactic pivot**) from the preceding member. This pivot ultimately becomes the SUBJECT of the **SVC** *as a whole.*

(31)

ਕੱਪੜੇ	ਧੋ	ਦਿੱਤੇ	ਜਾ	ਰਹੇ	ਹੁੰਦੇ	(ਸਨ)
kappṛe	**{[(d^{h}o**	**ditte)**	**(jā**	**rahe)]**	**(hunde)}**	**(san)**
	ConjP	Aux PerP	ConjP	Aux	PerP ImP	Cop
Mas Pl		Mas Pl		Mas Pl	Mas Pl	Mas Pl

‘It used to be case that the action of washing of the clothes for someone else continued happening repeatedly’

Now let us make a rather cumbersome analysis this five-member **SVC**. All the verbs have the plural noun ਕੱਪੜੇ **kappṛe** ‘clothes’ as their **pivot**. The fact that clothes are washed by some agent is irrelevant. In other words, the agent is **backgrounded** and can be optionally mentioned by a **postpositional phrase**.

1. ਧੋ ਦਿੱਤੇ **d^{h}o ditte**. The washing of the clothes is for someone else. The auxiliary verb ਦਿੱਤੇ **ditte** in the **perfect participle** form agrees with the clothes, the **SR** of the activity.
2. ਜਾ ਰਹੇ **jā rahe**. The process, once started, is depicted as continuing to move forward in time.
3. ਹੁੰਦੇ **hunde**. The process is presented as being repeated again and again.
4. ਸਨ **san** ‘were’. We are talking about what used to happen in the past time. But ਸਨ **san** ‘were’ is not a part of the **SVC**. ਹਨ **han** ‘are’ and ਹੋਣਗੇ **hoṇge** ‘will be’ are also grammatically possible here.

In this **SVC** ਦਿੱਤੇ **ditte** and ਰਹੇ **rahe** are in the **perfect participle** form and ਹੁੰਦੇ **hunde** is in the **imperfect participle** form. The nominal entity ਕੱਪੜੇ **kappṛe** ‘clothes’ (the **SR** of ਦਿੱਤੇ **ditte**) is taken as a pivot by all the subsequent members, though some of them as **transitive** or **intransitive** verbs in **perfective participle** or **imperfective participle** forms could have different **SR**s or SUBJECTS if they were working alone. (See Chapter 12).

Semantically and syntactically the **SVC** presents a *single action* and (31) is a simple or **mono-clausal** sentence, a good example of what Bhartṛhari insightfully described as "a collection of parts produced in a sequence and mentally conceived as one and identical with parts which are subordinate to it". According to Bhartṛhari, the meaning of the whole is grasped as an undivided gestalt (*akhaṇḍa vākya sphoṭa*) by our intuition (*pratibhā*), and is not computed by adding the meanings of the individual components.

Advanced learners of Panjabi are advised to study the meaning potential of each component, whose number is quite small, and get used to their various combinations *by practice and experience*. Any language (and not just Panjabi) is learnt in this way.

13.5 Order of the members and the use of particles within an SVC

Consider the quite straightforward

(32a) ਤੇਰਾ ਕੰਮ ਕਰਵਾ ਦਿੱਤਾ ਜਾਣਾ (ਸੀ)
terā kamm [(karvā dittā) (jāṇā)] (sī)
ConjP Aux PerP PotP Cop
'Your work would have been got done'

But in actual speech situations and because of contextual and rhetorical reasons, it can be said as

(32b) ਕਰਵਾ ਤਾਂ ਕੰਮ ਤੇਰਾ ਦਿੱਤਾ ਹੀ ਜਾਣਾ (ਸੀ)
karvā tā̃ kamm terā dittā hī jāṇā (sī)
Part Part
'Of course, your work would have been got done'

The particle ਤਾਂ **tā̃** and the **pivot NP** (with the order of the noun and the adjective reversed) intervene between the members of the blend ਕਰਵਾ ਦਿੱਤਾ **karvā dittā**, and ਹੀ **hī** intervenes between the members of the **blend** and following verb ਜਾਣਾ **jāṇā**. Sentence stress and intonation accompany this process. It is impossible to use brackets in (32b) to mark the members of the SVC. Contextual and rhetorical factors are responsible for this word order. (See Chapter 16.)

The complicated subject of word order and the use of particles and intonation is *very briefly* touched on in Chapter 16. But the use of the word order and the particles in (32b) is notable. This shows that an SVC in Panjabi is not *yet* an **agglutinated** whole. What gives an SVC its unity is its semantics and **syntactic pivot** shared by all the members.

This ***pivot*** *ultimately becomes the* SUBJECT *of the whole SVC, whatever the* SUBJECT(s) *of the member verbs might have been if they had been used alone. This shows the semantic as well syntactic integration of the constituent members inside an SVC.*

How each verb member contributes to the overall semantics and syntactic behaviour of an SVC is a fascinating subject which has only been briefly sketched above.

13.5.1 How to go on doing something in Panjabi

The emphatic particle ਹੀ **hī** is added to the **conjunctive participle** form (which historically ended in short **-i**). In this combination, the ਹ **h** sound is lost and the combination ends in long **-ī**. For example, ਕਰਿ **kari** plus ਹੀ **hī** becomes ਕਰੀ **karī**. When the explicator auxiliary ਜਾ **jā** or some other auxiliary indicating actual or metaphorical movement follows this form, the sequence conveys the meaning of 'to go on doing something', as in the English translation as well.

(33)	ਤੁਸੀਂ ਆਪਣਾ ਕੰਮ	ਕਰੀ	ਜਾਓ
	tusī̃ āpṇā kamm	**karī**	**jāo**
		ConjP+Part	Aux Imper(P)

'You (should) go on doing your work'

Here, ਕਰ+ਈ **kar+ī** is followed by a plain imperative form ਜਾਓ **jāo**.

(34a)	ਬੱਚਾ	ਰੋਈ	ਜਾਂਦਾ	ਹੈ
	baccā	**roī**	**jā̃dā**	**ha^{i}**
		ConjP+Part	Aux ImP	Cop

'The child keeps crying'

ਰਿਹਾ **rihā** can be added to emphasise the prolonged nature of the activity.

(34b)	ਬੱਚਾ	ਰੋਈ	ਜਾ	ਰਿਹਾ	ਹੈ
	baccā	**roī**	**jā**	**rihā**	**ha^{i}**
		ConjP+Part	ConjP	Aux PerP	Cop

'The child goes on crying'

The **conjunctive participle+ī** followed by some form of **ਜਾ jā** is a **blend** of the type discussed above. There can be two conjunctive participle+ī in the blend.

(34c) **ਮੈਂ mā̃ⁱ** **ਕਈ kaī** **ਮੀਲ mīl** **ਬੱਚੇ bacce** **ਨੂੰ nū̃** **ਚੁੱਕੀ cukkī** (ConjP +Part) **ਲਈ laī** (ConjP +Part) **ਚਲਦਾ caldā** (ImpP) **ਗਿਆ giā** (PerP)

I several miles child-to lift+ī 'take'+ī walking gone
'For several miles, I kept walking with the child lifted by me'
'I kept carrying the child for several miles'

ਚੁੱਕ ਲੈ cukk laⁱ means 'lift for one's own sake'. **-ī** is added to each member of the blend to make it **ਚੁੱਕੀ ਲਈ cukkī laī**. This is followed by the imperfect participle form **ਚਲਦਾ caldā** 'moving' and the perfect participle form of **ਜਾ jā** 'gone'. Some of the sentences discussed in this section can be taken both literally and metaphorically. As has been pointed out earlier, it is often difficult to clearly differentiate the literal from the metaphorical in an **SVC**.

Here is a semi-idiomatic expression.

(34d) **ਖਾਈ kʰāī** (ConjP+Part) **ਜਾਓ, jāo** **ਹੱਗੀ haggī** (ConjP+Part) **ਜਾਓ jāo** (ConjP)

eat+ī go defecate+ī go
'Go on eating and defecating'
('Do nothing other than these two things')

13.6 "Passive voice" in Panjabi

Wielding the principle known as Occam's Razor (that we should have no more theoretical entities and categories than are strictly necessary) we have shaved off the separate grammatical category "passive voice" from our analysis of Panjabi grammar. Some ideas picked from what we have said about the Panjabi verb and verb phrase from Chapter 7 onwards should take care of the features associated with the general and "universal" (?) notion of **passive voice.**

Basically, and cross-linguistically, *three* features (using our terms) are associated with passive voice.

1. The **agent** SUBJECT is "demoted" to the role of an optional ADJUNCT NP.
2. The **patient** is the **substratum** or the **goal** of the result of the activity.
3. The **patient** OBJECT is "promoted" to the role of the SUBJECT.

As should be clear by now, *not all the three* may be present in particular cases in Panjabi. For example, in

(35)	ਮੁੰਡੇ	ਨੇ	ਕਿਤਾਬ	ਪੜ੍ਹੀ
	munḍe	**ne**	**kitāb**	**paṛhī**
	SUB		OBJ	PRED
	Mas Sg		Fem Sg	Fem Sg

'The boy read the book'

the patient OBJECT is the **substratum of the result (SR)** of the activity in the ergative constructions. But the agent SUBJECT is very much there and has not been "demoted" to vacate its seat for any "promoted" NP. In (36), the verb is in the **subtractive phase** (which can have only the **imperfect participle** form).

(36)	ਜ਼ਿਆਦਾ	ਸ਼ੱਕਰ	ਨਹੀਂ	ਖਾਈਦੀ
	ziādā	**śakkar**	**nahī̃**	**k^{h}aīdī**
	Fem Sg	SUB		PRED
				SubPh ImP Fem Sg

'Too much sugar should not be eaten'

The **patient** is indeed the SUBJECT of the clause. But it is difficult to find the original active sentence whose agent SUBJECT is "demoted". The **agent** (a sort of Everyman) is *eliminated*, and not "demoted". It *must not* be mentioned. Another version employing the **subtractive phase** of the verb is

(37)	ਅਸੀਂ	ਰੱਜ	ਕੇ	ਮਠਿਆਈ	ਖਾਈਦੀ	ਸੀ
	asī̃	**rajj**	**ke**	**$maṭ^{h}$iāī**	**k^{h}āīdī**	**sī**
				SUB	PRED	
				Fem Sg	SubPh ImP Fem Sg	

'We used to eat the sweet stuff to our heart's content'

This "boastful" sentence is somewhat like (36). The **patient** is the **SR** of the activity and the verb agrees with it. But the **obligatory agent** is present and cannot be backgrounded, as in other **passive constructions**. Now comes the most interesting case.

(38)	ਬਹੁਤਾ	ਹੱਸੀਦਾ	ਨਹੀਂ
	bahutā	**hassīdā**	**nahī̃**
		SUB/PRED	
	too much	laughing	not
	'One should not laugh too much'		

It is difficult to find a good English gloss for ਹੱਸੀਦਾ **hassīdā**. The agent SUBJECT of **Phase 1** of the **intransitive** verb ਹੱਸ **hass** is *eliminated* as per the rules. But there is no **patient** OBJECT to be "promoted" to the role of the SUBJECT of the clause. We have seen that the action viewed as completed and denoted by a verb expressing **perfective aspect** (**perfect participle**, **potential participle** and **conjunctive participle**) can act as a nominal accessory. (See Chapter 11.) But the verb in (38) is in the **imperfect participle** form expressing not a completed but a supposedly recurring action. And yet it acts (or appears to act) like a nominal accessory. If (38) appears to behave oddly, this should not be surprising. Languages did not develop to fit into any grammarian's framework. It should be the other way round. All grammars are said to "leak" because all natural languages have "rogue" constructions which do not obey the rules governing the majority. On page 93, we mentioned the English ***were*-subjunctive** and the **mandative subjunctive** to which the usual rules of the agreement of the verb with the subject of the clause do not apply.

The following **causative clause** (already discussed in detail in Chapter 12) is also worth considering.

(39)	ਠੇਕੇਦਾਰ	ਨੇ	(ਮਜ਼ਦੂਰਾਂ ਤੋਂ)	ਮਲ਼ਬਾ	ਚੁਕਵਾਇਆ
	ṭʰekedār	**ne**	**(mazdūrā̃ tõ)**	**maḷbā**	**cukvāiā**
	IntAgt	Agt	ImmAgt	Patient	Verb PerP
				Mas Sg	Mas Sg
	'The contractor made the labourers pick up the debris'				
	'The contractor got the debris picked up by the labourers'				

The **immediate agent** (enclosed within brackets) in (39) is **back-grounded** or is an optional ADJUNCT NP. The **transitive verb** in the

perfect participle form agrees with the **patient** OBJECT, which is the **substratum of the result** of the action. The **initiating agent** is the SUBJECT of this clearly **active** clause. But the second English translation given above *sounds more natural*. Some English students of Indian languages would feel that (39) is in **passive voice**. This is because it has two of the three features of **passive voice** mentioned above. What we conclude from this section is that it is not necessary to set up a separate category of passive voice in Panjabi grammar.

13.6.1 The Panjabi SVC with prototypical "passive" meaning

An **SVC** involving a full lexical verb in the **perfect participle** form with the **patient** as the **substratum** or the **goal** of the result of the activity, followed by an **intransitive auxiliary** (especially **ਜਾ jā**) satisfies *all* the three criteria of a **passive construction**. If a speaker of Panjabi who knows some English grammar (and is thus familiar with the concept of passive voice) is asked to convert (40a) into passive voice,

(40a) ਮੈਂ ਫਲ਼ ਕੱਟੇ
mã^{i} p^{h}aḷ kaṭṭe
SUB OBJ PRED
'I cut the fruits'

she/he is most likely to say

(40b) ਮੈਥੋਂ ਫਲ਼ ਕੱਟੇ ਗਏ
ma^{i}t^{h}õ p^{h}aḷ kaṭṭe gae
ADJCT SUB PRED
'The fruits were cut by me'

or even

(40c) ਫਲ਼ ਕੱਟੇ ਗਏ
p^{h}aḷ kaṭṭe gae
SUB PRED
'The fruits were/got cut'

In (40a) the **patient** OBJECT **ਫਲ਼ p^{h}aḷ** 'fruits' is the **substratum of the result (SR)** of the activity. The **transitive** verb in the **perfect participle** form agrees with the **patient** OBJECT. The **auxiliary ਜਾ jā** in (40b) takes it as a **pivot**, which becomes the SUBJECT of the **serial verb ਕੱਟੇ ਗਏ kaṭṭe gae**, which agrees with its own SUBJECT **ਫਲ਼ p^{h}aḷ**. The **agent** of (40a), which now appears as a **postpositional phrase** in (40b), is a syntactically **optional** ADJUNCT and can be omitted, as in (40c).

But the **patient** can be the (contextually definite) **goal** of the result of the activity. The verb does not agree with any **NP** and is in the neuter form.

(41a)	ਮੈਂ	ਫਲ਼ਾਂ	ਨੂੰ	ਕੱਟਿਆ
	mã^{i}	**p^{h}aḷã**	**nū̃**	**kaṭṭiā**
	ImmAgt	Pnt	(Def)	Verb

'I cut the fruits'

Its passive version is

(41b)	(ਮੈਥੋਂ)	ਫਲ਼ਾਂ	ਨੂੰ	ਕੱਟਿਆ	ਗਿਆ
	(ma^{i}t^{h}õ)	**p^{h}aḷã**	**nū̃**	**kaṭṭiā**	**giā**
	ADJCT	SUB		PRED	

'The fruits were cut by me'

The verb is in the **neuter form** in both (41a) and (41b).

But **ਜਾ jā** is not the only verb that does this "passivising" business. Some other frequently used **intransitive auxiliary** verbs in this business are **ਹੋ ho** 'happen' and **ਪੈ pa^{i}** 'lie', (for which also see **13.2.2** above). The meanings are different from those imparted by **ਜਾ jā**, but the resulting constructions are "passive" in equal measure.

(42a)	ਫਲ਼	ਕੱਟੇ	ਹੋਏ	ਹਨ
	p^{h}aḷ	**kaṭṭe**	**hoe**	**han**
		cut	happened	are

'The fruits have been cut'

(42b)	ਫਲ਼	ਕੱਟੇ	ਪਏ	ਹਨ
	p^{h}aḷ	**kaṭṭe**	**pae**	**han**
		cut	lying	are

'The fruits are lying cut'

It is also possible to use a longer **SVC** and say

(42c)	ਫਲ਼	ਕੱਟੇ	ਹੋਏ	ਪਏ	ਹਨ
	p^{h}aḷ	**kaṭṭe**	**hoe**	**pae**	**han**
		cut	happened	lying	are

'The fruits (already cut) are lying'

Another **serial verb** can also be used to convey the "passive" meaning.

(42d)	ਧੋਤੇ	ਗਏ	ਫਲ਼	ਮੇਜ਼	'ਤੇ	ਰੱਖੇ	ਹੋਏ	ਹਨ
	d^{h}ote	**gae**	**p^{h}aḷ**	**mez**	**te**	**rakk^{h}e**	**hoe**	**han**
	washed	'gone'				placed	happened	are

'The washed fruits are lying on the table'
Lit. 'The washed fruits have been placed on the table'

But, unlike its literal English translation, (42d) concentrates on the *state* resulting from the previous action. It is simply a Panjabi way of saying – "By the way, the present state is the result of a previous action".

The structure of the **SVC** in (42c) is **{[(kaṭṭe) (hoe)] (pae)} (han)**. The pivot of **kaṭṭe** is taken by ਹੋਏ **hoe** and the **pivot** of the combination ਕੱਟੇ ਹੋਏ **kaṭṭe hoe** is taken by ਪਏ **pae**. The common **pivot** of the members of the **SVC** becomes the SUBJECT of this prototypical passive clause. In (42d), the patient OBJECT of the **perfect participle** of the **transitive** ਰੱਖੇ **rakk^{h}e** is the **pivot** for the following **intransitive verb** ਹੋਏ **hoe**. So the **patient** OBJECT of ਰੱਖੇ **rakk^{h}e** becomes the SUBJECT of the **SV** ਰੱਖੇ ਹੋਏ **rakk^{h}e hoe**.

An analysis of **SVC** in Panjabi can cover all the three features of the prototypical "passive" meaning. So a separate grammatical category of "**passive voice**" is redundant.

(42d) is open to another (and perfectly valid) analysis. The **NP** ਧੋਤੇ ਗਏ ਫਲ਼ **d^{h}ote gae p^{h}aḷ** 'the washed fruits' could be regarded as a contraction of the finite clause ਫਲ਼ ਧੋਤੇ ਗਏ **p^{h}aḷ d^{h}ote gae** 'The fruits were washed'. So this NP could be regarded as a **non-finite clause** with the SUBJECT missing. If followed consistently, this analysis would regard *any* phrase containing *any* form of a **verb** (for example ਵਗਦਾ ਪਾਣੀ **vagdā pāṇī** 'flowing water' or ਟੁੱਟਿਆ ਹੋਇਆ ਪੱਖਾ **ṭuṭṭiā hoiā pakk^{h}ā** 'broken fan') as a non-finite clause, thus leading to an unmanageable crowd of non-finite clauses of various types. So, in the interests of simplicity and economy, we regard ਧੋਤੇ ਗਏ ਫਲ਼ **d^{h}ote gae p^{h}aḷ**, like its English translation 'washed fruits', as a sequence of a **participial adjective** and a **noun**. We reserve the term **non-finite clause** for a **conjunctive participle+ke** cluster and for an adverbial construction involving the verb forms we call **derived free forms**. The defining characteristic of a non-finite clause in our system is that the verb or the verb+ਕੇ **ke** in such a clause is invariable and does not inflect. (See Chapter 14.)

13.6.2 Remnants of the older passive voice in modern Panjabi

Sanskrit had a genuine **passive** verb form in which *-ya-* was inserted between the verb root and the the **conjugational suffix**. Modern Panjabi infix **-ਈ- -ī-** in the **subtractive phase** of a verb appears to have come from this *-ya-*, though historical records are incomplete. This vowel in the infix **-ਈ- -ī-** is *unstressed*. For example, it is the first syllable that is stressed in **ਕਰੀਦਾ karīdā**, and the pronunciation is **'ka.rī.dā**.

But **passive verb forms** with *stressed* **-ਈ- -ī-** also occur in some Western dialects, in which **-ਈ- -ī-** is either sometimes nasalised or becomes **-ਈਜ- -īj-** . An example is **ਕੁਟੀਂਦਾ kuṭī̃dā [ku.'ṭī̃.dā]** or **ਕੁਟੀਜਦਾ kuṭījdā [ku.'ṭīj.dā]** 'being beaten'. These are the dialectal variants of the adjectival **imperfect participle** form.

The older **passive** form also survives in the skeleton of a Panjabi folk song starting with **ਪਿੰਡਾਂ ਵਿਚੋਂ ਪਿੰਡ ਸੁਣੀਂਦਾ pinḍā̃ vicõ pinḍ suṇī̃dā**, in which a writer or a singer can fill any details. The skeleton, still productive, appears to have survived from the days when this passive verb form was used in the Eastern dialects as well. An example given below with details filled in the first two lines. In the italicised passive forms, the syllable with nasalised **-ਈਂ- -ī̃-** is stressed.

(43) ਪਿੰਡਾਂ ਵਿਚੋਂ ਪਿੰਡ *ਸੁਣੀਂਦਾ*, ਪਿੰਡ *ਸੁਣੀਂਦਾ* ਮਾਨਾ
ਉਥੋਂ ਦਾ ਇਕ ਸਾਧ *ਸੁਣੀਂਦਾ*, ਨਾਮ ਹੈ ਜਿਸਦਾ ਭਾਨਾ
....
pinḍā̃ vicõ pinḍ *suṇī̃dā*, pinḍ *suṇī̃dā* mānā;
uttʰõ dā ik sādʰ *suṇī̃dā*, nām haⁱ jīsdā bʰānā
....

'A village among villages *is heard of*; the village *heard of* is Mana;
A hermit from there *is heard of*, whose name is Bhana.'

This ਸੁਣੀਂਦਾ **suṇī̃dā [su. ˈṇī̃.dā]** 'is heard of' is not ਸੁਣੀਦਾ **suṇīdā [ˈsu.ṇī.dā]** 'should be heard', as is often mispronounced and misunderstood by speakers of Eastern Panjabi.

Summing up and looking ahead

The complexity outlined above in this chapter is *certainly and unmistakably* there in the grammatical structure of Panjabi and (in different forms) in the grammatical systems of Panjabi's sister Indic languages. The fact that many grammarians have conveniently chosen to ignore it in order to write "simple" and "user-friendly" grammars does not wish it away. But the bull must be taken by the horns one day. And this is what has been attempted in this chapter. It is not claimed here that the subject has been dealt with exhaustively here or that this is the only correct way of dealing with it. Other grammarians may handle the beast differently.

The story featuring the Panjabi verb started in Chapter 9 and concluded in this chapter (only *tentatively*, because a language goes on evolving and the work of scientific research should never stop) demonstrates the futility of setting up a small number of "tenses" in Panjabi. But we do not claim to have found the final answer to the problem.

We started with the form-meaning complexes *actually* found in the language, without recourse to any supposedly "universal" and "language-independent" Platonic categories. But there is no need to reject *all* the theoretical categories used by past linguists. Some of them (such as **aspect**, **copula** and **serial verb construction** and some others we made use of after careful testing) are indeed applicable to Panjabi. Others like **passive voice** are redundant as we argued above.

The story of the **serial verb constructions** began in the Prākrit and Apabhraṁśa Indic languages centuries ago. The insights of the linguists who were native speakers of these languages (though they wrote in Sanskrit syntactically modelled on the vernaculars they spoke) are valuable, and we have made use of these insights in our effort to understand the genesis or "coming into being" (*svarūpadhāraṇaṁ karoti*) of serial verb constructions in Panjabi. The complicated semantic and syntactic features of the Panjabi verb and the creativity inherent in a living language make literally *hundreds* of such constructions possible. The inner dialectics of the parts and the whole in each SVC can be as fascinating for linguists as its biological counterpart for a biologist. No grammarian can *list* all such actual and possible SVCs in Panjabi (let alone analyse them in detail). All that they can do is offer *generalisations*. And exactly this has been attempted in this chapter.

The structure of the Panjabi **VP** demanded our approach of dealing with form-meaning pairings (again inherited from Pāṇini) to be what it is. But our approach in the next chapter dealing with compound and complex sentences will look familiar to users.

For teachers and other more advanced users

Many linguists will be surprised to learn about **serial verb constructions** in Panjabi. They are found in all the major Indian languages. But the fact will come as a shock to those Indian linguists who have been blissfully unaware of the existence of **SVCs** in the languages they analysed, *or worse*, wilfully ignored them as an inconvenient nuisance.

This chapter should have amply demonstrated that an SVC should be taken *holistically* and not *compositionally*. At both the linguistic poles – phonetic and semantic – it is not simply a sum of its parts. While the parts make up the whole, it is the whole that controls the meaning and phonetic realisation of each part. A spectrogram of the spoken form of an SVC (not presented here) will show that the phonetic realisation of each word (and of a phoneme in each word) is determined by its place in the structure of the whole. Levins and Lewontins's dialectical view about biology quoted earlier is fully applicable to an SVC. A comparison with Indian classical music will not be out of place here. While the musical notes build a *rāga*, the precise acoustic realisation of each note is determined by the *rāga*. The same note will sound different in different *rāga*s. Flat E, for example, sounds very different in Raga Darbari and Raga Jaunpuri. In the ascending scale in Darbari, it sounds "flatter" than in the descending scale. This makes it impossible to play an Indian *rāga* accurately on a Western keyboard instument with *fixed* notes. The fault lies neither with the Western keyboard instruments nor with the Indian classical music. They were simply not "made for each other". Instruments of the violin family (whose proto-form is believed to have come from the East) without any fixed notes are fine for playing classical Indian music. Violin is widely used very successsfully in South India for this purpose. Coming to **serial verb constructions**, linguists should *seriously* re-examine their existing theoretical frameworks and approaches (the equivalents of the keyboard instuments) created for European languages, which are without SVCs.

The fairly recently published book *Serial Verb Constructions: A Cross-linguistic Typology* (Aikhenvald and Dixon 2006) analyses SVCs in more than two dozen languages from some different areas. This book was mentioned in Chapter 2 as well.

This book is extremely technical and is meant for professional theoretical linguists and very advanced students of linguistics. Interested readers are referred to this book. In the first chapter, Aikhenvald summarises the features found in these languages, though the structure of the SVCs found in each language is also different. The Panjabi SVCs do not have all these features, but the ones that they have firmly place them in this group. Some features that Panjabi has are not included in Aikhenvald's summary, which is not engraved on a stone tablet and can be modified and extended, as Aikhenvald and Dixon would be the first to admit.

One of the languages analysed in this book is Tariana. What in English could be expressed as one action (p.182)

(44a) I managed to return passing over and up away (from here), up until that place

using one finite and two non-finite verbs, is expressed in Tariana literally as something like

(44b) I return—I arrive—I pass—I go up—I go

using what clearly look like five finite verbs, all in the first person singular form. In terms of our system, they all share the same **pivot**.

What is more significant is that one of Aikhenvald's Tariana consultants told her, ***"It is not like Portuguese, we just cannot say it with one verb."***

This reminds me of what Daniel Everett (2013) reports about Pirahã. The Pirahã equivalent of the English 'That smells good' is

(45) It please me, the smoke, which hits my nose, as I pass by your fire (p.132).

Everett does not present a detailed grammatical analysis of this Pirahã utterance. So it is not possible to say whether it is a true **SVC** in our sense.

But the overall thrust of of Everett's book – regarding a language as a cultural tool – is unmistakably powerful.

(44b) and (45) are uncannily reminiscent of what Bhartṛhari (quoted at the beginning of this chapter) insightfully said.

It is possible that viewing an action as a series of parts produced in a sequence but mentally conceived as one and subordinate to the action may be the basis of the grammar of SVCs in ***all*** *the languages in which SVCs occur.*

This is simply a speculation, and is not put forth as a hypothesis. Aikhenvald's Tariana consultant's words mentioned above remind us of what Bhartṛhari said fifteen centuries earlier:

> There is no cognition in the world in which word does not figure. All knowledge, as it were, is intertwined with the word.
>
> *Vākyapadīya* (1.110)

> It is through the word that the object is established.
>
> *Vākyapadīya* (1.115)

Bhartṛhari's views were echoed in the much maligned "Sapir-Whorf hypothesis". Actually, Sapir and Whorf did not invent this "hypothesis" and did not hold it in the extreme form attributed to it by their critics. Whorf took the idea from his teacher Sapir, who learnt it from his teachers in Germany. But it is Bhartṛhari who is the first known proto-"Whorfian" linguist (unless he was following an earlier lingust, which is possible).

Aikhevald's Tariana consultant has no choice but to use five finite verbs to describe a situation which she could describe with one finite verb as a competent speaker of a European language as well. But does a situation remain the "same" when cognised and described in two very different languages such as Tariana and Portuguese?

Leaving this philosophical question aside and coming back to grammatical analysis, this chapter has amply demonstrated that the individuality of every language (as a cultural tool or social semiotic) must be respected and it must not be forced into any Euro-centred and supposedly "language-independent" Procrustean bed. One such fairly recent detailed and ambitious framework of "language-independent" temporal categories is Wolfgang Klein's *Time in Language* (1994). Try fitting the Panjabi **SVC**s into this or any other such framework and you will see how woefully inadequate it is. There may be in the world

1000 or more such languages each with its own special types of **SVC**s. "[L]anguages could differ from each other without limit and in unpredictable ways." (Joos 1957: 96). No armchair semantic and syntactic framework, however detailed and ambitious, can encompass the great diversity found in the languages of the world, as the latest cross-linguistic research is now making very clear.

The actual and possible number of **SVC**s in Panjabi is difficult to catalogue here. Beames (quoted earlier) was probably right that the number of such verb-combinations in North Indian languages, if regarded as "tenses", is infinite. Each dialect of Panjabi has a few special combinations. New combinations keep coming up in different dialects and in the speech of creative individuals, especially children. *But they are always easily comprehensible*, most probably because of their context of use and also because the number of the *forms* of the main verbs and the auxiliaries entering these clusters is quite small, and each member contributes its *meaning potential* to the whole, which is not just a sum of its parts and is perceived as gestalt. The inherent creativity of the living language manifests itself here. As we have seen, a great deal more than pure temporality is involved in these constructions. But there is no need to look for a single "language-independent" theory of **SVC**s lying *behind* them. A *critical* consideration of the work done by other grammarians on other languages sharing some features with our language should be enough to guide us in our analysis. But their work must not be taken as a well-defined "theory" in the sense of a Procrustean bed. Ultimately, each language is unique and carries its own theory *inside* it (as Goethe would have said).

Chapter 14

Expanding Basic Clauses or Simple Sentences

Preview of the chapter

In Chapter 5, we mentioned four basic **canonical clause patterns** in Panjabi with triangles diagrammatically showing that **NPs** and **VPs** in them can be expanded and elaborated. We did not give any examples because the words and phrases they can be expanded and elaborated with were to be dealt with in the subsequent chapters. Now that we have done this, we can take up the subject here.

14.1 Expanding a canonical clause pattern

It should first be mentioned that this section deals with the expansion of a **single finite clause** or a **simple sentence**. We will use these terms interchangeably. A **finite clause** in our system of Panjabi grammar, already defined in Chapter 5, is the one which has a SUBJECT, which is either (i) marked with the **postposition ਨੇ ne**, or (ii) *if this is not the case*, controls **verb-agreement**. It is *not* necessary for a **finite** clause in Panjabi to have a **verb** marked for **tense**, as it is in English. A multi-member **serial verb** is regarded as *single* **finite verb** of a mono-clausal or simple sentence. If **ਹੈ ha^{i}** or **ਸੀ sī** or **ਹੋਵੇਗਾ hovegā** follows it, it is *not* regarded as a part of a **serial verb**, and it does not affect the status of the clause as a simple sentence. It works more like an **adverb** of time than a **verb**.

14.1.1 Expanding and elaborating an NP in a simple sentence

It should first be mentioned that

1. **Nouns** in the **NPs** are qualified with **adjectives** and **postpositional phrases (PPs)** working like **adjectives;**
2. **Adjectives** are qualified with **adverbs** and **PPs** working like **adverbs;**
3. **Adverbs** are qualified with other **adverbs** and **PPs** working like **adverbs;**
4. **VPs** are qualified with **adverbs** and **PPs** working like **adverbs.**
5. **Finite clauses** can be compressed into **adjectival** and **adverbial phrases** and **non-finite clauses** and then inserted into finite clauses, which still remain simple sentences.

A **PP** contains a **noun** or **nouns** which can be further qualified like other **nouns**, by ... and so on.

Examples are needed to illustrate the process. Let us start with a **canonical clause pattern (pattern 2).**

(a) PPs working as adjectives

(1a) ਬੰਦਾ ਵਿਦਵਾਨ ਹੈ
bandā vidvān ha^{i}
'The man is a scholar'

Now let us expand it with the elements mentioned above

(1b) (ਲੰਮੀ ਚਿੱਟੀ ਦਾਹੜੀ ਵਾਲਾ) ਇਹ ਬਜ਼ੁਰਗ ਬੰਦਾ
(lammī ciṭṭī dāhṛī vāḷā) ih bazurg bandā
(..................PP...................)
(...................................... NP......................................)
(having a long white beard) this elderly man

ਕਈ ਭਾਸ਼ਾਵਾਂ ਦਾ ਬਹੁਤ ਵੱਡਾ ਵਿਦਵਾਨ ਹੈ
(kaī b^{h}āśāvā̃ dā) bahut vaḍḍā vidvān hai
(............PP...........)
(................................ NP................................)
(of several languages) very great scholar is

'This elderly man with a long white beard is a very great scholar of several languages'

An example of the use of **adverbials** expanding a **VP** can be constructed by combining several clauses into a single one (from a **canonical pattern**).

(b) Imperfect participles working as adjectives

Consider the following

(2a) ਚਾਹ ਉਬਲ਼ਦੀ ਹੈ
cāh ubaḷdī ha^{i}
'Tea is boiling'

(2b) ਇਸ ਵਿਚ ਖੰਡ ਪਾਓ
is vich k^{h}anḍ pāo
'Put sugar into it'

The **imperfect participle** (2a) can be turned into a **participial adjective** and inserted into (2b) to create

(2c) ਉਬਲ਼ਦੀ ਚਾਹ ਵਿਚ ਖੰਡ ਪਾਓ
***ubaḷdī* cāh vich k^{h}anḍ pāo**
'Put sugar into the *boiling* tea'

More than one clause can be involved in the process.

(3a) ਲੋਕ ਆਉਂਦੇ ਹਨ
lok āũde han
'People come'

(3b) ਲੋਕ ਜਾਂਦੇ ਹਨ
lok jā̃de han
'People go'

(3c) ਆਉਂਦੇ ਜਾਂਦੇ ਲੋਕਾਂ ਵਲ ਧਿਆਨ ਦਿਓ
***āũde jā̃de* lokā̃ val d^{h}iān dio**
'Pay attention to the "*coming* and *going*" people'

(c) Perfect participles working as adjectives

A clause with the **perfect participle** can also be turned into a **participial adjective** or adjectival phrase to play this role.

(4a) ਇਹ ਬੱਚਾ ਸੁੱਤਾ ਪਿਆ ਹੈ
ih baccā suttā piā hai
'This child has fallen asleep'

(4b) ਇਹਨੂੰ ਨਾ ਜਗਾਓ
ihnū̃ nā jagāo
'Don't wake him up'

(4c) ਇਸ *ਸੁੱਤੇ ਪਏ* ਬੱਚੇ ਨੂੰ ਨਾ ਜਗਾਓ
is *sutte pae* bacce nū̃ nā jagāo
'Don't wake up this sleeping child'

There can be longer chains involving both these participles working as adjectives.

(5a) ਉਹ ਬੰਦਾ ਮਰ ਗਿਆ ਹੈ
uh bandā mar giā ha^{i}
'That man has died'

(5b) ਉਸ *ਮਰ ਗਏ* ਬੰਦੇ ਦਾ ਭੂਤ ਇਸ ਘਰ ਵਿਚ ਰਹਿੰਦਾ ਹੈ
us *mar gae* bande dā b^{h}ūt is g^{h}ar vich rahindā ha^{i}
'That *dead* man's ghost lives in this house'

(5c) ਇਸ ਘਰ ਵਿਚ *ਰਹਿੰਦਾ* ਉਹਦਾ ਭੂਤ ਲੋਕਾਂ ਨੂੰ ਡਰਾਉਂਦਾ ਹੈ
is g^{h}ar vich *rahindā* uhdā b^{h}ūt lokā̃ nū̃ ḍarāū̃dā ha^{i}
'His ghost *living* in this house frightens the people'

(5d) *ਡਰੇ ਹੋਏ* ਲੋਕ ਕਿਸੇ ਤਾਂਤ੍ਰਿਕ ਕੋਲ਼ ਜਾਂਦੇ ਹਨ
***ḍare hoe* lok kise tā̃trik koḷ jā̃de han**
'The *frightened* people go to some exorcist'

The results of this embedding of words and phrases within a clause or simple sentences can be quite complicated.

(6a) ਤਾਨਸੈਨ ਨੇ ਰਾਗ ਦਰਬਾਰੀ ਸਿਰਜਿਆ
tānsa^{i}n ne rāg darbārā sirjiā
N Agt N N Vtr
'Tansen composed Raga Darbari'

Let us first expand it with two **postpositional phrases** acting as **adverbials** of **time** and **purpose**.

(6b) ਤਾਨਸੈਨ ਨੇ ਸੋਲ੍ਹਵੀਂ ਸਦੀ ਵਿਚ ਅਕਬਰ ਦੇ ਦਰਬਾਰ ਲਈ
tānsa^{i}n ne solhvī̃ sadī vich ((akbar de darbār) laī))
N Agt Adj N P N P N P
(.......... PP.........) (..........PP................)
(..................PP................)
'Tansen Agt (in the 16th century) ((Akbar's court) for))

ਬਹੁਤ ਗੰਭੀਰ ਰਾਗ ਦਰਬਾਰੀ ਸਿਰਜਿਆ
bahut gamb^{h}īr rāg darbāri sirjiā
Adv Adj N N Verb
very serious Raga Darbari composed
'Tansen composed a very serious Raga Darbari in the 16th century for Akbar's court'

Now a separate clause about Raga Darbari

(6c) ਦਰਬਾਰੀ ਨੀਵੀਆਂ ਸੁਰਾਂ ਅਤੇ ਵਿਲੰਬਿਤ ਲੈਅ ਵਿਚ ਗਾਇਆ ਜਾਂਦਾ ਹੈ
darbāri nīvīā̃ surā̃ ate vilambit la^{i}y vic gāiā jā̃dā ha^{i}
N Adj N Co-or Adj N P SVC
(..........................PP........................)
Darbari low notes and slow tempo in is sung
'Darbari is sung in low notes and slow tempo'

ਗਾਇਆ ਜਾਂਦਾ gāiā jā̃dā is a **serial verb**. The substratum of the activity of the verb **ਗਾ gā** 'sing' is taken as the **pivot** by the **intransitive auxiliary ਜਾ jā** 'go'. This **pivot** becomes the SUBJECT of the clause with a "passive" meaning. But the fact remains that Darbari is viewed as a **noun** qualified by the result of the activity (which itself is qualified by the **adverbial** in the form of a **postpositional phrase** with two **nouns** qualified by **adjectives**). It sounds like 'Darbari is X'.

Now let us combine (6a), (6b) and (6c) into (6d).

(6d) ਨੀਵੀਆਂ ਸੁਰਾਂ ਅਤੇ ਵਿਲੰਬਿਤ ਲੈਯ ਵਿਚ ਗਾਇਆ ਜਾਂਦਾ
nīvīā̃ surā̃ ate vilambit la^{i}y vic gāiā jā̃dā
Adj N Co-or Adj N P SV
(............................PP..........................)
low notes and slow tempo in being sung

ਬਹੁਤ ਗੰਭੀਰ ਰਾਗ ਦਰਬਾਰੀ
bahut gamb^{h}īr rāg darbāri
Adv Adj N N
(..................NP OBJ..............)
very serious Raga Darbari

ਤਾਨਸੈਨ ਨੇ ਸੋਲ੍ਹਵੀਂ ਸਦੀ ਵਿਚ
tānsa^{i}n ne solhvī̃ sadī vich
N Agt Adj N P
(................PP............)
Tansen Agt 16th century in

ਅਕਬਰ ਦੇ ਦਰਬਾਰ ਲਈ ਸਿਰਜਿਆ
akbar de darbār laī sirjiā
N P N P Vern
(............PP............)
(.............PP.................)
Akabr of court for composed

'The very serious Raga Darbari, sung in lower notes and slow tempo, was composed by Tansen in the 16th century for Akbar's court'

Since the OBJECT Raga Darbari is the main topic under discussion, the Panjabi word order allows it to be placed before the SUBJECT in (6d).

It must be made very clear here that (6a), (6b) and (6c) are not here regarded as lying in the "Deep Structure" of (6d). Each of the first three can stand as an independent sentence by itself, and they can also be combined into (6d) by making certain grammatical and prosodical changes in each.

14.1.2 Gerund used in place of a noun

The situation presented in

(7a) ਉਹ ਕਾਹਲ਼ੀ ਕਾਹਲ਼ੀ ਵਾਪਸ ਚਲੀ ਗਈ
uh kāhḷī kāhḷī vāpas calī gaī
AdvP SVC
'She went back in a great hurry'

ਚਲੀ ਗਈ **calī gaī** 'started gone' is a **serial verb (SV)**. The repetition of the adverb ਕਾਹਲ਼ੀ **kāhḷī** 'in a hurry' is done to intensify its meaning as 'in a great hurry'. The whole action can be regarded as a complete action (grammatically turned into a **gerund**) to be used as the SUBJECT **NP** in

(7b) ਉਹਦਾ ਕਾਹਲ਼ੀ ਕਾਹਲ਼ੀ ਵਾਪਸ ਚਲੀ ਜਾਣਾ ਠੀਕ ਨਹੀਂ ਸੀ
uhdā kāhḷī kāhḷī vāpas calī jāṇā ṭ^{h}īk nahī̃ sī
Adj AdvP ConjP Ger Adj Cop
(..........................NP SUB........................)
'Her going back hurriedly was not right'

This is **clause pattern 2**. Only the second member of the **SV** is turned into the **gerund** ਜਾਣਾ **jāṇā** 'going' (in the **neuter form**, which is homophonous to the **masculine singular**). The **gerund**, a **verb** turned **noun**, enjoys the best of both worlds. It can still be qualified by adverbs and also have a **demonstrative adjective**.

We can also say

(7c) ਉਹਦੇ ਕਾਹਲ਼ੀ ਕਾਹਲ਼ੀ ਵਾਪਸ ਚਲੀ ਜਾਣ ਨੇ ਮੈਨੂੰ ਦੁਖੀ ਕੀਤਾ
uhde kāhḷī kāhḷī vāpas calī jāṇ ne ma^{i}nū̃ duk^{h}ī kītā
Adj AdvP ConjP Ger Agt Pnt Adj Verb
(.............................SUB.............................) OBJ COMP (O)
PRED
'Her going back hurriedly made me upset'

This is **clause pattern 4**. If the **gerund** ending in **-ā** is followed by a **postposition**, this **-ā** is dropped; it does not turn into **-e** (see Chapter 11) as is the case with a masculine singular noun. So ਜਾਣਾ **jāṇā** in the SUBJECT position followed by ਨੇ **ne** becomes ਜਾਣ **jāṇ**. But the **demonstrative adjective** ਉਹਦਾ **uhdā** becomes **uhde** ਉਹਦੇ. The more notable thing is that the **adverbs** ਕਾਹਲ਼ੀ ਕਾਹਲ਼ੀ **kāhḷī kāhḷī** and ਵਾਪਸ **vāpas** 'back' qualifying the action are still there.

14.2 Qualifying a VP in a clause or simple sentence

The broad definition of an **adverb** or **adverbial** is "a word or phrase or clause whose most characteristic role is traditionally that of modifying a verb or verb phrase". In this section, we will deal with the role of the **adverbs** like the ones presented in Chapter 7. There are single-word adverbs like ਪਹਿਲਾਂ **pahilā̃** 'before' or multi-word adverbs like ਤਾਂ ਜੋ **tā̃ jo** 'so that' (written as ਤਾਂਜੁ by some writers). As already indicated previously, an **adverb** can be modified by another **adverb**, as in ਬਹੁਤ ਪਹਿਲਾਂ **bahut**

pahilā̃ 'long before' or ਕੁਝ ਕੁ ਪਹਿਲਾਂ **kuj^h ku pahilā̃** 'a little before'. We use the term **adverbial phrase** for this type of construction. To avoid any confusion, we repeat here what was pointed out earlier. Our concept of a **verb phrase** or a **VP** is different from that found in Transformational Generative Grammar in which what is left after taking out the SUBJECT **NP** from the clause is the **VP**, which includes the OBJECT and other COMPLEMENTS. Our VP is a single verb or an **SV** acting like a single finite verb, which can be modified by adverbs or adverbials. Full finite clauses can act as adverbials or adverbial clauses. They are dealt with later in Chapter 15. But Panjabi also has **non-finite adverbial clauses** which we take up below (in **14.2.3**). A **postpositional phrase** (**PP**) can also do the job of an adverb or adverbial. A **PP** contains a noun, and this noun can be qualified by an adjective etc..., or by another **PP** etc..., as we have seen above.

14.2.1 Qualifying a VP with an adverb in a clause or simple sentence

(8) ਉਹ ਬਹੁਤ ਛੇਤੀ ਕਾਹਲ਼ੀ ਕਾਹਲ਼ੀ ਵਾਪਸ ਚਲਾ ਗਿਆ
uh bahut c^{h}etī kāhḷī kāhḷī vāpas calā giā
Adv Adv Adv Adv Adv SV
(..........................AdvP.........................)
he very soon hurriedly hurriedly back gone away
'Very soon, he went back in a great hurry'

The **SV** ਚਲਾ ਗਿਆ **calā giā** is qualified by a series of adverbs qualified by other adverbs.

A **gerund** acting as an NP can be qualified by adverbs, as in (7c) above.

14.2.2 Postpositional phrase in an adverbial role

This is something fairly straightforward.

(9) ਮੈਂ ਨੌਂ ਵਜੇ ਤੋਂ ਪੰਜ ਵਜੇ ਤਕ ਕੰਮ ਕਰਦਾ ਹਾਂ
mã^i nã^u vaje tõ panj vaje tak kamm kardā hā̃
(................PP as an AdvP.............)
I nine o'clock from five o'clock till work doing am
'I work from nine o'clock till five o'clock'

(10) ਅਸੀਂ ਸੜਦੀ ਧੁੱਪ ਵਿਚ ਬੈਠਦੇ ਹਾਂ
asī̃ saṛdī dʰupp vic baiṭʰde hā̃
(...PP as an AdvP.....)
we scorching sunshine in sitting are
'We sit in the scorching sunshine'

14.2.3 Non-finite clauses

A **non-finite clause** has one of the three verb forms discussed below and is parasitic upon the main clause or the context for the choice of its SUBJECT which is either not explicitly expressed or is expressed in a way different from that of a **finite clause**. The first two discussed below are derived from participles. Duni Chandra (1964) calls them ਸੁਤੰਤਰ ਰਚਨਾਵਾਂ **sutantar rachnāvā̃**, which we translate as "derived free forms". We adopt this term and call them **derived free form 1 (Deff1)** and **derived free form 2 (Deff2)**. These clauses are **adverbials of time**.

The verb forms used in a **non-finite clause** are

1. **Imperfect participle** plus -ਆਂ **-ā̃**
   ਰੋਂਦਿਆਂ **rõdiā̃** (ਰੋਂਦਾ+ਆਂ **rõdā+ā̃**) 'by weeping'
   ਹੁੰਦਿਆਂ **hundiā̃** (ਹੁੰਦਾ+ਆਂ **hundā+ā̃**) 'by being'
   ਜਾਂਦਿਆਂ **jā̃diā̃** (ਜਾਂਦਾ+ਆਂ **jā̃dā+ā̃**) 'by going'

2. **Perfect participle** plus -ਆਂ **-ā̃**
   ਰੋਇਆਂ **roiā̃** (ਰੋਇਆ+ਆਂ **roiā+ā̃**) 'by having wept'
   ਹੋਇਆਂ **hoiā̃** (ਹੋਇਆ+ਆਂ **hoiā+ā̃**) 'by having been'
   ਗਿਆਂ **giā̃** (ਗਿਆ+ਆਂ **gi+ā̃**) 'by having gone'

The English glosses are very rough and approximate. The use of these forms is best understood in examples.

3. **Conjunctive participle** plus ਕੇ **ke**
   ਰੋ ਕੇ **ro ke** 'having wept'
   ਹੋ ਕੇ **ho ke** 'having been'
   ਜਾ ਕੇ **jā ke** 'having gone'

The feature shared by all three types of non-finite clauses is that the main verb forms featuring in these clauses (the two **derived free forms** and the

conjunctive participle+ਕੇ **ke**) are *invariable*. They are not inflected for **person** or **number** or **gender**. Other forms used in finite clauses, even when they do not agree with any NP, are *capable of being inflected* to do so. As we saw in earlier chapters, the **perfect participle** and the **potential participle** forms not agreeing with any NP are in the **neuter** form (homophonous to the **masculine singular** form). So they are inflected forms. Even in their adjectival role, they are inflected for number and gender as we have seen above.

14.2.4 Imperfect participle plus -ਆਂ -ā̃

Examples of the **non-finite** use of this **verb** form are

(11)   ਉਹਦੀ ਸਾਰੀ ਉਮਰ   ਰੋਂਦਿਆਂ   ਗੁਜ਼ਰੀ
(............NP..........)   Deff 1   Verb
uhdī sārī umar rõdiā̃ guzrī
                              weeping
'All his life passed while weeping'

The context makes it very clear who was weeping.

(12)   ਮੇਰੇ   ਹੁੰਦਿਆਂ ਤੈਨੂੰ ਕੋਈ ਨਹੀਂ ਛੇੜ ਸਕਦਾ
mere   hundiā̃ ta'nū̃ koī nahī̃ cʰeṛ sakdā
            Deff 1
my   being
'Nobody can touch you while I exist'

(13)   ਕਮਰੇ ਵਿਚ   ਵੜਦਿਆਂ   ਸਾਰ ਹੀ   ਮੈਨੂੰ   ਬਦਬੂ   ਆਈ
kamre vich vaṛdiā̃   sār hi ma'nū̃ badbū   āī
                        Deff 1
room   in   entering   at once   me-to foul smell came
'I felt the foul smell the moment I entered the room'

This **verb** form followed by ਸਾਰ ਹੀ **sār hi** 'the very moment' is a semi-idiomatic construction. Some speakers use the ending -ਏ **-e** instead of -ਇਆਂ **-iā̃** with this form and would use ਵੜਦੇ **vaṛde** in (13). But the meaning is the same.

14.2.5 Perfect participle plus -ਆਂ **-ā̃**

(14) ਰੋਇਆਂ ਕੁਝ ਨਹੀਂ ਬਣਨਾ
roiā̃ kuj^{h} nahī̃ baṇnā
Deff 2
having wept anything not going to become
'The act of weeping will not achieve anything'

The context makes it very clear whose weeping is being talked about. It is being emphasised that the act of weeping, viewed as a completed action, will be ineffectual.

(15) ਇਹ ਸੁਹਣੀ ਕੁੜੀ ਹੱਥ ਲਾਇਆਂ ਮੈਲ਼ੀ ਹੁੰਦੀ ਹੈ
ih suhṇī kuṛī hatt^{h} lāiā̃ ma^{i}ḷī hundī ha^{i}
Deff 2
(by) hand having been touched
Lit. 'This beautiful girl starts looking dirty even if touched by hand'

This is a semi-idiomatic expression meaning 'She is extremely beautiful'. ਹੱਥ ਲਾ **hatt^{h} lā** means 'to touch by hand'. The result of the completed action of touching by hand is mentioned. It is not necessary to mention the SUBJECT, which is clearly understood as 'any one'.

(16) ਇਹ ਕੰਮ ਕੀਤਿਆਂ ਹੀ ਹੋਣਾ ਹੈ
ih kamm kītiā̃ hī hoṇā ha^{i}
Deff 2
'This task will be accomplished only if it is done'

The clauses containing these verb forms are not **finite** clauses. The SUBJECT of such a **non-finite clause** is either marked differently or is implicit within the context.

There is a famous line from a Pakistani Punjabi song which has attained the status of a proverb.

(17) ਦੁਸ਼ਮਣ ਮੋਇਆਂ ਖ਼ੁਸ਼ੀ ਨਾ ਕਰੀਏ; ਸੱਜਣਾਂ ਵੀ ਮਰ ਜਾਣਾ
duśmaṇ moiā̃ xuśī nā karīe; sajjṇā̃ vā mar jāṇā
Deff 2
'Do not celebrate when an enemy has died; dear ones are also going to die.'

It is possible for such non-finite clause to have a **serial verb** with two members, one member being in the first **derived free form** and the second member in the other.

(18a) ਬਾਹਰ ਜਾਂਦਿਆਂ ਹੋਇਆਂ ਮੇਰੀ ਜੇਬ 'ਚ ਮੋਬਾਈਲ ਫ਼ੋਨ ਹੁੰਦਾ ਹੈ
bahar jā̃diā̃ hoiā̃ merī jeb c mobāīl fon hundā ha^{i}
Deff 1 Deff 2
'While going out, I keep a mobile phone in my pocket'

Since the natural English translation grossly misrepresents the grammatical structure (though not the meaning) of the Panjabi sentence, let us look at the possible component clauses.

(18b) ਮੈਂ ਬਾਹਰ ਜਾਂਦਾ ਹੁੰਦਾ ਹਾਂ
mā̃^{i} bāhar jā̃dā hundā hā̃
Mas Sg Mas Sg
'I (habitually) go out'

or

(18c) ਮੈਂ ਬਾਹਰ ਜਾਂਦੀ ਹੁੰਦੀ ਹਾਂ
mā̃^{i} bāhar jā̃dī hundī hā̃
Feb Sg Fem Sg
'I (habitually) go out'

(18d) ਮੇਰੀ ਜੇਬ 'ਚ ਮੋਬਾਈਲ ਫ਼ੋਨ ਹੁੰਦਾ ਹੈ
merī jeb c mobāīl fon hundā ha^{i}
Mas Sg Mas Sg
'There is (habitually) a mobile phone in my pocket (at that time)'

The context makes it clear that the agent SUBJECT of the first non-finite clause in (18a) is **ਮੈਂ mā̃^{i}** 'I', i.e., who habitually goes out and keeps a mobile phone in her/his pocket at that time. Gender cannot be marked in the **non-finite clause** in (18a), though it has to be marked in the **finite clauses** in (18b) or (18c).

It is important to remember that the **derived free forms** in such non-finite clauses are *incapable* of being inflected and are in the **neuter** form. The ones that inflect for number and gender, are **participial adjectives** characterising a nominal. (19a), (19b), (19c) and (19d) below should be compared carefully.

(19a) ਮੁੰਡਾ ਜਾਂਦਾ ਹੋਇਆ ਕੁਝ ਕਹਿ ਗਿਆ
munḍā jā̃dā hoiā kujʰ kahi giā
Mas Sg Mas Sg Mas Sg Mas Sg
'The "going out" boy said something before going'

(19b) ਕੁੜੀ ਜਾਂਦੀ ਹੋਈ ਕੁਝ ਕਹਿ ਗਈ
kuṛī jā̃dī hoī kujʰ kahi gaī
Fem Sg Fem Sg Fem Sg FemSg
'The "going out" girl said something before going'

(19c) ਮੁੰਡਾ ਜਾਂਦਿਆਂ ਹੋਇਆਂ ਕੁਝ ਕਹਿ ਗਿਆ
munḍā jā̃diā̃ hoiā̃ kujʰ kahi giā
Mas Sg Neu Neu Mas Sg
'While going out, the boy said something'

(19d) ਕੁੜੀ ਜਾਂਦਿਆਂ ਹੋਇਆਂ ਕੁਝ ਕਹਿ ਗਈ
kuṛī jā̃diā̃ hoiā̃ kujʰ kahi gaī
Fem Sg Neu Neu Fem Sg
'While going out, the girl said something'

The **participial adjecvtives** in (19a) and (19b) agree with the nominal SUBJECT in number and gender. But the **derived free forms** in in (19c) and (19d) are invariable (or in the **neuter** form). The derived free forms and the participial adjectives may mean 'more or less the same' in these examples, but their grammatical functions are different.

14.2.6 Conjunctive participle plus ਕੇ ke

These constructions are one of the distinguishing marks of India as a linguistic area (Masica 1976) and are found in all the languages of all the families spoken in India. There is no grammatical limit on the number of these **non-finite clauses** that can be strung together. They all *mostly* (but not invariably) share their SUBJECT with the **finite verb** at the end. They are also arranged *mostly* according to the principle of iconicity or the natural temporal order.

(20) ਆਲੂ ਧੋ ਕੇ, ਉਬਾਲ਼ ਕੇ, ਛਿੱਲ ਕੇ, ਕੱਟ ਕੇ, ਲੂਣ ਮਿਰਚ ਲਾ ਕੇ ਖਾ ਲਓ
ālū d^{h}o ke, ubāḷ ke, c^{h}ill ke, kaṭṭ ke, lūṇ mirc lā ke, k^{h}ā lao
'Having washed, boiled, peeled and cut the potatoes, and having added salt and pepper, eat them'

The **adverbial** status of the non-finite ਕੇ **ke**-clause is clear in (21).

(21) ਖਾਣੇ ਤੋਂ ਪਹਿਲਾਂ ਕੁਝ ਪੀ ਲਓ, ਫ੍ਰਿਜ ’ਚੋਂ ਕੱਢ ਕੇ
k^{h}āne tõ pahilā̃ kuj^h pī lao, frij cõ kaḍḍ^h ke
meal before something drink fridge from having taken out
'Before the meal, drink something, after taking it out of the fridge'

The actual order of the events (eating the meal and drinking something before it) is reversed. The main event is mentioned first and the less significant event is represented by an **adverbial** of time. But the grammatical marking and intonation ensure that there is no confusion regarding their temporal order.

The SUBJECT is generally shared by the ਕੇ **ke-clause(s)** and the main **finite verb.** But this is not strictly necessary.

(22a) ਮਲੇਰੀਆ ਬੁਖ਼ਾਰ ਕਾਂਬਾ ਲਗ ਕੇ ਚੜ੍ਹਦਾ ਹੈ
maleriā buxār kā̃bā lag ke caṛhdā ha^i
malaria fever shivering having happened attacks
'Shivering happens before the attack of the malaria fever'

The natural order of the events is

(22b) (ਪਹਿਲਾਂ) ਕਾਂਬਾ ਲਗਦਾ ਹੈ
(pahilā̃) kā̃bā lagdā ha^i
'(At first) shivering happens'

(22c) (ਫਿਰ) ਮਲੇਰੀਆ ਬੁਖ਼ਾਰ ਚੜ੍ਹਦਾ ਹੈ
(phir) maleriā buxār caṛhdā ha^i
'(Then) the malaria fever attacks'

The SUBJECT is different in each clause. The **non-finite** ਕੇ **ke clause** acting as an **adverbial** is embedded within the main clause, as is often the case in Panjabi. Here, too, there is no confusion regarding the temporal order.

The use of these three types of non-finite clauses is extremely widespread (and has been so for centuries) in Panjabi. An example of the use of the **derived free form 1** from 16th century Panjabi poetry is

(23) ਹਸੰਦਿਆ ਖੇਲੰਦਿਆ ਪੈਨੰਦਿਆ ਖਾਵੰਦਿਆ ਵਿਚੇ ਹੋਵੈ ਮੁਕਤਿ
hasandiā k^helandiā pa^{i}nandiā k^hāvandiā vice hova^i mukti
'While laughing, playing, wearing (clothes), eating, one attains liberation'
(*Sri Guru Granth Sahib,* p 522)

This verse was written by Guru Arjan Dev (1563–1606) to argue against those who believed that asceticism was necessary in order to attain liberation. In the typical centuries-old Indian fashion, the author chains together four uninflecting verbs. The Panjabi prose literature (without any metrical constraints) is full of even longer and more complicated examples of all types of non-finite clauses, especially of **conjunctive participle+ਕਰਿ/ਕੈ** (now pronounced and written as **ਕੇ ke**) in which only the *last* verb is inflected for tense/aspect. The trend exemplified in (20) and (23) above continues in Panjabi and other North Indian languages. John Beames observed the use of the **conjunctive participle** in all the major North Indian languages:

> It implies "having done," and the sense of the clause in which it is used remains incomplete until another clause containing a finite verb is added; thus, instead of saying, "Next morning he woke and arose, bathed, ate, dressed, collected his goods, loaded them on his camel, bade farewell to his friend, and started on his journey," the Indian languages would say, "Having woken, having risen, having bathed, having eaten, having dressed, having collected his goods, having loaded them on his camel, having bidden farewell to his friend, having started on his journey, he went."
>
> (Beames 1879: 229)

As a magistrate in Calcutta, he found in the police reports written in Bengali:

> All the verbs throughout the report are in the conjunctive participle "having done," and at the end of perhaps the fouth page one comes at last to the only finite verb in the whole, "I have reported it"!
>
> (Beames 1875: 249)

Similar examples can be found in prose writings in classical Sanskrit, Pali and later Prakrit and Apabhraṁśa languages. The Indian view of time, outlined in Chapter 2, has strongly influened the grammatical structure of *all* the Indian languages, including the Dravidian languages of South India.

14.2.7 ਕਰਕੇ *karke* as postposition

Having been used extremely frequently, the phrase **ਕਰ ਕੇ kar ke** 'having done' has also become a postposition (with the related meaning 'because of') written as one word **ਕਰਕੇ karke** by many writers. But both are pronounced as one word with no phonetic "juncture". In spoken form, there is rarely any confusion regarding which of the two is used. But an ambiguity *can* sometimes happen as in

(24) ਉਹ ਕੰਮ ਕਰਕੇ ਨਾ ਆ ਸਕਿਆ
uh kamm *karke* na ā sakiā

which can mean either (i) 'He could not come *after doing* the work' or (ii) 'He could not come *because of* the work'.

Summing up and looking ahead

This chapter described how the constituents of a **mono-clausal** or **simple** sentence are expanded so that the sentence as a whole remains mono-clausal. The verb-forms used in this process of expansion are **non-finite** and so that the clause has a single **finite verb** (even if it is a **serial verb**). The rules of grammar set no limit on how many phrases (and phrases within phrases) or non-finite clauses (and non-finite clauses withn non-finite clauses) can be adjusted into a simple sentence in this way – this process is known as **recursion** – or how many phrases and non-finite clauses can be chained together within a simple sentence. The only limit is that of human memory. These processes can result in extremely *complicated* structures, which remain grammatically *simple* sentences. (What a joke!)

But **finite clauses** can also be **embedded** within a clause. These embedded clauses are known as **subordinate clauses** of different types. The result is known a **complex sentence**. Two or more finite clauses of equal rank known as **co-ordinate clauses** can also be **joined** together to form a **compound sentence**. These **subordination** and **co-ordination** processes are the subject of the next chapter.

Chapter 15

Compound and Complex Sentences

Preview of the chapter

Chapter 14 dealt with how a basic clause pattern can be expanded with words, phrases and non-finite clauses, so that the clause remains a *single* **finite clause** or a **simple sentence**. But a simple sentence can be expanded with a **finite clause** as well in two ways – (1) another finite clause (already expanded or otherwise) can be added to it, or (2) another finite clause can be **embedded** into it. In the first case, the result is a **compound** sentence and the attached clause is called a **co-ordinate** clause. More than one co-ordinate clause can be added in this way. If a finite clause is embedded within a finite clause, this **embedded** clause is called a **subordinate** clause and the result is a **complex** sentence. The host clause in a complex sentence is called the **main clause** or the **matrix clause**. More than one clause can be embedded in this way. The sentence resulting from both these processes is called a **compound complex** or **mixed** sentence.

Since the resulting sentence is a *single* sentence, the process of adding a co-ordinate clause or embedding a subordinate clause is also accompanied by some other processes or changes dealt with in this chapter. But since the adding of a co-ordinate clause is a slightly simpler process, we take it up first.

15.1 Compound sentences

As mentioned above, a **compound** sentence is formed by linking two or more **co-ordinate** clauses with the help of conjunctions known as **co-ordinating conjunctions** or **co-ordinators.**

15.1.1 Co-ordination and co-ordinators

A **co-ordinator** or **co-ordinating conjunction** is a word or group of words or phrases (not always a single unbroken one). These co-ordinators can be divided into three groups.

(a) **Additive**, with the subgroup **cumulative**;

(b) **Contrastive**, with the subgroup **alternative**;

(c) **Consequential**

Since the result of **co-ordination** of clauses is a single sentence, there is internal **cohesion** within it, a sense of its being one unit. Cohesion is achieved in several ways, such as

1. **Semantics**. The clauses are meaningfully related;
2. **Intonation**. The first clause usually ends with a 'non-final' intonation contour. (See Chapter 4);
3. **Discontinuous co-ordinator phrases**, similar to the English *not only ... but also* or *either ... or* with one part in the first clause and the other part in the second;
4. Panjabi **particles ਹੀ hī, ਵੀ vī** and **ਤਾਂ tā̃**;
5. **Emphatic** words like **ਕਾਹਦਾ kāhdā** and **ਥੋੜ੍ਹੇ t^hoṛhe**;
6. **Co-referential omission** from one clause of the elements present in the other.

This omission is mostly **anaphoric** or **backward-looking.** The omitted elements are **recovered** from the *preceding* clause. But it can be **cataphoric** or **forward-looking** as well if the omitted elements are given in the *following* clause.

15.1.2 Additive and cumulative co-ordinators

(a1) The additive co-ordinator

The most common **additive co-ordinator** is ਅਤੇ **ate** 'and', which is often pronounced ਤੇ **te** in the unstressed form, or Ø when ਅਤੇ **ate** is omitted. In the following examples, the word or phrase usually omitted is put in brackets. The arrow ❮ or ❯ indicates which way a pro-form (pronoun or an expression whose referent lies elsewhere) "looks" to recover the meaning of the omitted part.

Examples are

(1) ਉਹ ਰੋਜ਼ ਸਵੇਰੇ ਮੰਦਰ ਜਾਂਦਾ ਹੈ
uh roz savere mandar jā̃dā ha^{i}
ਅਤੇ ❮ (ਉਹ) ਪੂਜਾ ਕਰਦਾ ਹੈ
***ate* ❮(uh) pūjā kardā ha^{i}**
'He goes to the temple every morning and worships'

Since the two clauses share the subject ਉਹ **uh** 'he', it is **co-referentially omitted** in the second. The symbol ❮ indicates that it is recovered by looking back (or **anaphorically**).

The **co-ordiantor** ਅਤੇ **ate** is often omitted. The non-final intonation contour and a slight pause does the job of the co-ordinator.

(2) ਉਹ ਗਾਉਂਦਾ ਰਿਹਾ, Ø ਮੈਂ ਤਬਲਾ ਵਜਾਉਂਦਾ ਰਿਹਾ
uh gāũdā riha, Ø mā^{i} tablā vajāũda rihā
'He went on singing; I went on playing the drums'

Many Panjabi proverbs have this form, such as

(3) ਦਾਤਾ ਦਾਨ ਕਰੇ, Ø ਭੰਡਾਰੀ ਕਿਉਂ ਸੜੇ?
dātā dān kare, Ø b^{h}aṇḍārī kiũ saṛe?
'The charitable man gives the charity; why should (his) store manager burn (with envy?)

Many lines from the poetry of Guru Nanak Dev (1469–1539) have become proverbs. One of them is

(4) ਕੂੜ ਨਿਖੁਟੇ ਨਾਨਕਾ, Ø ਓੜਕਿ ਸਚਿ ਰਹੀ
kūṛ nik^{h}uṭe nānakā, Ø oṛaki saci rahī
'O Nanak, falsehood ends; truth ultimately stays'

There is a Panjabi folk song

(5) ਲੋਕਾਂ ਦੀਆਂ ਰੋਣ ਅੱਖੀਆਂ, Ø ਸਾਡਾ ਰੋਂਦਾ ਈ ਦਿਲ ਮਾਹੀਆ
lokā̃ dīā̃ roṇ akkʰīā̃, Ø **sāḍā rõdā ī dil māhīā**
people -of weep eyes, our weeping is heart O sweetheart
'O sweetheart, people weep with their eyes, (but) I weep with my heart'

(a2) The cumulative co-ordinators (discontinuous)

The most common **cumulative co-ordinators** are

ਉੱਤੋਂ **uttõ** 'moreover', 'additionally'

ਨਾ ਸਿਰਫ਼ ... ਸਗੋਂ **na sirf ... sagõ** 'not only ... but also'

ਸਿਰਫ਼ X ਹੀ ਨਹੀਂ, ਸਗੋਂ Y ਵੀ **sirf X hī nahī̃, sagõ Y vī** 'not only X, but also Y'

X ਹੀ ਨਹੀਂ, Y ਵੀ, **X hī nahī̃, Y vī** 'not only X, but also Y'

ਨਿਰਾ X (ਹੀ) ਨਹੀਂ, (ਸਗੋਂ) Y ਵੀ **nirā X (hī) nahī̃, (sagõ) Y vī** 'not only X, but also Y'

ਨਾਲ਼ੇ X ਨਾਲ਼ੇ Y **nāḷe X nāḷe Y** 'X as well as Y'

ਸਿਰਫ਼ **sirf** and ਨਿਰਾ **nirā** mean 'only' and ਸਗੋਂ **sagõ** means 'but additionally'. ਹੀ **hī** is the 'exclusive' or 'emphatic' particle and ਵੀ **vī** is the 'inclusive' particle. ਤਾਂ **tā̃** roughly means 'as far as X is concerned'.

(4) ਮੈਂ ਵਾਇਲਿਨ ਹੀ ਨਹੀਂ (ਵਜਾਉਂਦਾ ਹਾਂ)➤,
mãⁱ vāilin hī nahī̃ (vajāūdā hā̃)➤
◄(ਮੈਂ) ਚੈਲੋ ਵੀ ਵਜਾਉਂਦਾ ਹਾਂ
◄(mãⁱ) caⁱlo vī vajāūdā hā̃
'I play not only the violin, I play the cello as well'

The verb is **co-referentially** (**cataphorically**) omitted in the first clause and the subject is **anaphorically** omitted in the second. Any of the four discontinuous pairs given above could be used in (4).

(5) ਇਹ ਬੰਦਾ ਨਿਰਾ ਸ਼ਰੀਫ਼ ਹੀ ਨਹੀਂ, ◄(ਇਹ ਬੰਦਾ) ਸਿਆਣਾ ਵੀ ਬਹੁਤ ਹੈ
ih bandā nirā śarīf hī nahī̃, ◄(ih bandā) siāṇā vī bahut haⁱ
'This man is not only gentle, but very wise as well'

ਉੱਤੋਂ uttõ (literally 'from above') is also used as a **co-ordinating conjunction** or **co-ordinator** (meaning 'moreover' or 'additionally') to connect a clause referring to something unpleasant or undesirable, something 'from above'.

(6) ਮੈਂ ਪਹਿਲਾਂ ਹੀ ਬੀਮਾਰ ਸਾਂ; ਉੱਤੋਂ ਮੇਰੇ ਸੱਟ ਲਗ ਗਈ
mã^{i} pahilā̃ hī bīmār sā̃; *uttõ* mere saṭṭ lag gaī
'I was already ill; additionally, I got injured'

15.1.3 Contrastive and alternative co-ordinators

(b1) The contrastive co-ordinator

The most common **contrastive co-ordinators** are **ਪਰ par** 'but' and **ਸਗੋਂ sagõ** 'but in addition to that'.

(7) ਮੈਂ ਪਾਰਟੀ ਵਿਚ ਗਿਆ ਜ਼ਰੂਰ, ਪਰ ◄(ਮੈਂ) ਉੱਥੇ ਖਾਧਾ ਕੁਝ ਨਹੀਂ
mã^{i} partī vich gia zarūr, par ◄(mã^{i}) utt^{h}e k^{h}ād^{h}ā kuj^{h} nahī̃
'I did go to the party, but I did not eat anything there'

(8) ਮੇਰਾ ਮੁਵੱਕਿਲ ਚੋਰ ਹੋ ਸਕਦਾ ਹੈ, Ø ਕਾਤਿਲ ਨਹੀਂ (ਹੋ ਸਕਦਾ)
merā muvakkil cor ho sakdā ha^{i}, Ø kātil nahī̃ (ho sakdā)
'My client may be a thief, (but) not a murderer'

(9) ਹਾਈ ਕੋਰਟ ਵਿਚ ਉਹਦੀ ਸਜ਼ਾ ਘਟੀ ਨਹੀਂ, *ਸਗੋਂ* ◄(ਉਹਦੀ ਸਜ਼ਾ) ਵਧ ਗਈ
hāī korṭ vic uhdī sazā g^{h}aṭī nahī̃, *sagõ* ◄(uhdī sazā) vad^{h} gaī̃
'In the high court, his punishment did not become less; it increased rather'

(b2) The alternative co-ordinator

The most commonly used pairs of alternative co-ordinators are

ਜਾਂ ... ਜਾਂ jā̃ ... jā̃ 'either ... or'
ਚਾਹੇ ... ਚਾਹੇ cāhe ... cāhe 'either ... or'
ਜਾਂ ਤਾਂ ... ਜਾਂ ਫਿਰ jā̃ tā̃ ... jā̃ p^{h}ir 'either ... or'
ਨਾ (ਤਾਂ) ... ਨਾ (ਹੀ) nā (tā̃) ... nā (hī) 'neither ... nor'

(10) ਜਾਂ ਉਹ ਸਚਮੁੱਚ ਬੀਮਾਰ ਹੈ, *ਜਾਂ* ◄(ਉਹ) ਬਹਾਨਾ ਬਣਾ ਰਿਹਾ ਹੈ
_jā̃_ uh sacmuc bīmār ha^{i}, _jā̃_ ◄(uh) bahānā baṇā rihā ha^{i}
'*Either* he is really ill, *or* is making an excuse'

(11) ਨਾ ਉਧਾਰ ਅਸੀਂ ਲੈਂਦੇ ਹਾਂ, ਨਾ ◄(ਉਧਾਰ ਅਸੀਂ) ਦਿੰਦੇ ਹਾਂ
_na_ ud^{h}ār asī̃ lā̃^{i}de hā̃, _na_ ◄(ud^{h}ār asī̃) dinde hā̃
'We neither borrow nor lend'

15.1.4 Consequential co-ordinators

(c) The **consequential co-ordinators** do not occur in pairs. The most commonly used ones are

ਸੋ **so** 'so'
ਇਸ ਕਰਕੇ **is karke** 'therefore'
ਇਸ ਵਾਸਤੇ **is vāste** 'because of this'
ਤਾਹੀਂਓਂ **tāhīõ** 'this is why'

(12) ਉਹ ਗੰਜਾ ਹੈ, *ਤਾਹੀਂਓਂ* ◄(ਉਹ) ਸਿਰ ਤੇ ਸਦਾ ਟੋਪੀ ਰੱਖਦਾ ਹੈ
uh ganjā ha^{i}, _tāhī̃õ_ ◄(uh) sir te sadā ṭopī rakk^{h}dā ha^{i}
'He is bald, *this is why* he always keeps a hat on his head'

(13) ਸਾਡੇ ਕਰਨ ਲਈ ਉੱਥੇ ਕੋਈ ਕੰਮ ਨਹੀਂ ਸੀ, *ਇਸ ਕਰਕੇ* ਅਸੀਂ ਚਲੇ ਗਏ
sāḍe karan laī utt^{h}e koī kamm nahī̃ sī, _is karke_ asī̃ cale gae
'We had no work to do there; *therefore* we went away'

15.1.5 Restrictions on co-referential omission

It has been pointed out several times in the past chapters that the SUBJECT of a clause in Panjabi is marked in two ways: either by adding the postposition ਨੇ **ne**, or *if this is not the case*, by making the verb agree with it. Examples are

(14) ਉਹਨੇ ਚੋਰੀ ਕੀਤੀ
uhne corī kītī
'He committed a theft'

(15) ਉਹਨੇ ਆਪਣੇ ਜੁਰਮ ਦੀ ਸਜ਼ਾ ਭੁਗਤੀ
uhne āpṇe juram dī sazā b^{h}ugtī
'He suffered the punishment of his crime'

(16) ਉਹ ਜੇਲ ਗਿਆ
uh jel giā
'He went to prison'

(14) and (15) can be combined with ਅਤੇ **ate** 'and' and ਉਹਨੇ **uhne** can be **co-referentially omitted**. (14) can precede either (15) or (16) by being joined with ਅਤੇ **ate**, again without any problem and ਉਹ **uh** can be omitted. But if we co-referentially omit ਉਹਨੇ **uhne** in the second clause in (17a) and say

(17a) (?) ਉਹ ਜੇਲ ਗਿਆ ਅਤੇ ਆਪਣੇ ਜੁਰਮ ਦੀ ਸਜ਼ਾ ਭੁਗਤੀ
(?) uh jel giā ate āpṇe juram dī sazā b^{h}ugtī
'He went to prison and he suffered the punishment of his crime'

a native speaker of Panjabi may not reject (17a) as ungrammatical but may feel "uneasy" about it, or say that (17a) somehow "feels odd". It appears that the form and meaning of ਉਹ **uh** are contained in ਉਹਨੇ **uhne**, *but not vice versa.* So omitting ਉਹ **uh** after ਉਹਨੇ **uhne** is fine, *but not vice versa.* So it has to be

(17b) ਉਹ ਜੇਲ ਗਿਆ ਅਤੇ ਉਹਨੇ ਆਪਣੇ ਜੁਰਮ ਦੀ ਸਜ਼ਾ ਭੁਗਤੀ
uh jel giā ate uhne āpṇe juram dī sazā b^{h}ugtī
'He went to prison and he suffered the punishment of his crime'

Another similar-looking example can also be given. A non-definite OBJECT in a clause is not marked with any **postposition**. But if it becomes definite for any reason, it is marked with ਨੂੰ **nū̃**. Now imagine a situation. A marriage bureau arranged a meeting between a young man and a young woman previously unknown to each other. This happened there:

(18) ਮੁੰਡੇ ਨੇ ਕੁੜੀ ਪਸੰਦ ਕੀਤੀ,
muṇḍe ne kuṛī pasand kītī,
Fem Sg Fem Sg
ਤੇ ਉਹਨੂੰ ਖਾਣੇ ਤੇ ਬੁਲਾਇਆ
te uhnū̃ kʰāṇe te bulāiā
Def Neu
'The boy liked the girl and invited her to dinner'

The OBJECT ਕੁੜੀ **kuṛī** in the first clause is not a previously known definite girl. The verb in the **perfect participle** form agrees with the **indefinite** OBJECT, which is *not* marked with ਨੂੰ **nū̃**. She could be referred to with the pronoun ਉਹ **uh**. But by the time she is invited to dinner, she has become **definite** and is referred to as ਉਹਨੂੰ **uhnū̃**, which cannot be **co-referentially omitted** in the second clause. As is the case with ਉਹਨੇ **uhne** mentioned above, ਉਹ **uh** is contained in ਉਹਨੂੰ **uhnū̃** *but not vice versa*. It is, however, difficult to imagine a situation where an OBJECT is definite in the first clause and indefinite in the second.

15.1.6 Emphatic words ਕਾਹਦਾ kāhdā and ਥੋੜ੍ਹੇ tʰoṛhe

These emphatic words are mostly used for contrasting two **co-ordinate clauses**. The second clause may not be explicitly stated but simply implied.

(19) ਉਹ ਬੰਦਾ *ਕਾਹਦਾ* (ਸੀ), ◄(ਉਹ) ਦੈਂਤ ਸੀ
uh bandā *kāhdā* (si), ◄(uh) dãᶦt si
'He was not a man but a giant'
Lit. 'What sort of man (was) he, (but he) was a giant'

(20) ਇਹ ਬੰਦਾ ਪੁਲ਼ਸੀਆ *ਕਾਹਦਾ*, ◄(ਇਹ ਤਾਂ) ਕਸਾਈ ਹੈ
ih bandā puḷsīā *kāhdā*, ◄(ih tā̃) kasāī haᶦ
'This man is not a police officer, but a butcher'

ਕਾਹਦਾ is a **black adjective** and agrees with the following **noun** in **number** and **gender**.

ਥੋੜ੍ਹੇ **tʰoṛe** acts like a negator. The second clause in the brackets in the following examples may not be explicitly said. But it is always implied.

(21) ਇਹ ਕੰਮ ਮੈਂ ਥੋੜ੍ਹੇ ਕੀਤਾ ਹੈ? (ਕਿਸੇ ਹੋਰ ਨੇ ਕੀਤਾ ਹੈ)
ih kamm mãⁱ t^h*oṛhe* kītā haⁱ? (kise hor ne kītā haⁱ)
'This work has not been done by me, (but by someone else)'

(22) ਮੈਂ ਜੇਲ੍ਹ 'ਚ ਮੁਜਰਿਮ ਬਣ ਕੇ ਥੋੜ੍ਹੇ ਗਿਆ ਸਾਂ?
mãⁱ jelh c mujrim baṇ ke t^h*oṛhe* giā sã̄?
'I did not go to the jail as a criminal, (but in some other capacity)'

ਥੋੜ੍ਹਾ **t^hoṛhā** and ਥੋੜ੍ਹੀ **t^hoṛhī** are other dialectal variations of ਥੋੜ੍ਹੇ **t^hoṛhe**.

15.2 Complex sentences

A **complex sentence** is formed by **embedding** one or more **finite subordinate clauses** (also known as **embedded clauses**) within a **main clause** (also known as the **matrix clause**). The **conjunctions** aiding this process are known as **subordinating conjunctions** or **subordinators**. Since the result is a *single* sentence (though multi-clausal), devices for achieving internal **cohesion** are also used. These devices, though performing the same cohesive function as in compound sentences (discussed above), work in considerably different ways here. The basic or default word order in Panjabi is said to be SOV (Subject Object Verb). Though this word order is considerably flexible in actual practice, as we have already seen at numerous places in the previous chapters and are going to discuss in some detail in the next chapter as well, this basic word order makes itself felt as a *constraining* factor in the organisational structure of a complex sentence in Panjabi.

In Chapter 5, we mentioned four types of **canonical finite clause patterns** found in Panjabi. Here we take up the first of these patterns involving SUBJECT **NP** and PREDICATOR **VP** and see how subordinate clauses can be embedded in it. This pattern consists of two constituents.

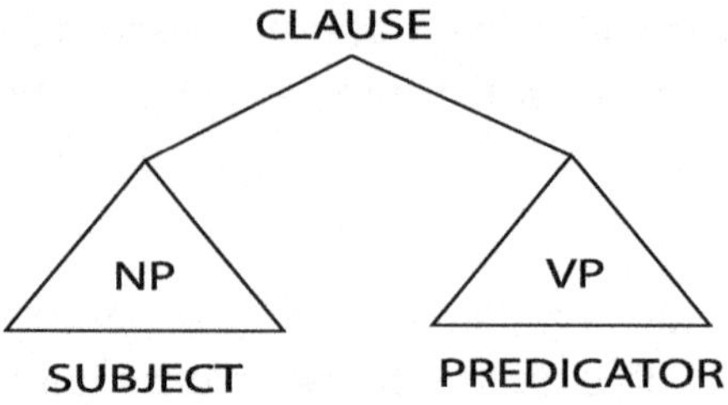

Figure 15.1 Canonical finite clause pattern 1

The SUBJECT **noun phrase** in this pattern can be expanded with a **finite subordinate clause** in two ways.

1. A full **finite clause** (known as a **nominal clause**) can work as an **NP**.
2. The **noun(s)** within the NP can be restricted (made more specific) in their reference, or their meaning can be expanded, by finite clauses acting like **adjectives**. Such clauses are known as **adjectival** or **relative** clauses.

15.2.1 Subordinate nominal clause as the SUBJECT

Let us start with a canonical clause.

(23a) ਕੁਝ ਹੋਇਆ
kuj^{h} hoiā
'Something happened'

One the ways of expanding the **VP** is using a serial verb followed by a form of the **copula** to relate it to the present or the past time.

(23b) ਕੁਝ ਹੋ ਗਿਆ ਹੈ
kuj^{h} ho giā ha^{i}
'Something has happened'

We can use a **finite clause** in the position of the SUBJECT (with its own SUBJECT and PREDICATOR).

(23c) ਜੋ ਹੋਣਾ ਸੀ, ◀(ਉਹ) ਹੋ ਗਿਆ ਹੈ
jo hoṇā si ◀(uh) ho giā ha^{i}
SUB PRED
'What was going to happen has happened'

There is a *strong tendency* (but not a strict rule) in Panjabi to *avoid* embedding a **subordinate clause** (especially a longish one) *within* the main clause. A **dummy** is placed to mark the spot where the **subordinate clause** should have been embedded. This dummy indicates **anaphorically** (looking backward) or **cataphorically** (looking forward) what is supposed to be at the position of the embedded clause. The reason for this seems to be the basic **SOV** word order of a Panjabi clause. The final verb of the embedded clause coming adjacent to the final verb of the main clause has to be avoided to avert confusion. The dummy <(ਉਹ) **<(uh)** is not necessary in (23c). It is optional, but we are going to see cases where it becomes absolutely necessary in the interests of good communication. The **subordinate clause** mostly starts with a **J-word** in such cases. This J-word indicates the omitted or present (as a dummy) SUBJECT of the **main clause**.

(24) ਜੋ ਇਸ ਦੁਨੀਆ ਨੂੰ ਹਮੇਸ਼ਾ ਲਈ ਛੱਡ ਗਿਆ ਹੈ,
jo is duniā nū̃ hameśā laī c^{h}aḍḍ giā ha^i,
(..................................SUB................................)

<ਉਹ ਹੁਣ ਵਾਪਸ ਨਹੀਂ ਆਏਗਾ
<uh huṇ vāpas nahī̃ āegā
(dummy) PRED
'He who has left this world for ever will not come back now'

The dummy SUBJECT <ਉਹ **<uh** in such a sentence is not grammatically obligatory but is communicatively very effective. Most Indian speakers and writers of English would start the main clause with 'he' in the SUBJECT position because of the influence of their first language (e.g., **The person who is dead he will not come back*).

Now let us see what happens when the **verb** in the **main clause** is a **serial verb** (with a typically 'passive' meaning)

(25a) ਚੋਰ ਫੜਿਆ ਗਿਆ ਹੈ
cor p^{h}aṛiā giā ha^i
SUB PRED
'The thief has been caught'

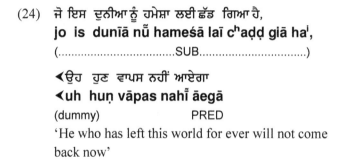

(25b) ਜਿਹਨੇ ਚੋਰੀ ਕੀਤੀ ਸੀ <ਉਹ ਫੜਿਆ ਗਿਆ ਹੈ
jihne corī kītī sī <uh p^{h}aṛiā giā ha^{i}
(...........SUB..........) (dummy) PRED
'The doer of the theft has been caught'

There is a famous Panjabi song (probably centuries old).

(26a) ਮਰਨੋਂ ਨਾ ਡਰਦੇ ਜਿਹੜੇ ਪ੍ਰੇਮ ਦੀ ਨਦੀ ਦੇ ਵਿਚ ਤਰਦੇ
marnõ na ḍarde jihṛe prem dī nadī de vic tarde
'Those who swim in the river of love are not afraid of dying'

The word order manipulated for metrical purposes makes the dummy SUBJECT unnecessary. But it would be communicatively necessary in the ordinary prose version (26b).

(26b) ਜਿਹੜੇ ਪ੍ਰੇਮ ਦੀ ਨਦੀ ਦੇ ਵਿਚ ਤਰਦੇ (ਹਨ),
jihṛe prem dī nadī de vic tarde (han)
(............................SUB................................)
<(ਉਹ) ਮਰਨੋਂ ਨਹੀਂ ਡਰਦੇ
<(uh) marnõ nahĩ ḍarde
(dummy) PRED

Here is a line from the Panjabi poet Mohan Singh.

(27a) ਕਦੇ ਨਾ ਕੰਢੀਂ ਉਹ ਲਗ ਸੱਕਣ ਜਿਹੜੇ ਆਸ ਬਿਗਾਨੀ ਧਰਦੇ
kade na kaṇḍ^{h}ĩ uh lag sakkaṇ jihṛe ās bigānī d^{h}arde
'Those who pin their hopes upon others can never reach the shores'

Its prose version is

(27b) ਜਿਹੜੇ ਬਿਗਾਨੀ ਆਸ ਧਰਦੇ ਹਨ
jihṛe bigānī ās d^{h}arde han
(....................SUB......................)
<ਉਹ ਕਦੇ ਕੰਢੀਂ ਨਹੀਂ ਲਗ ਸਕਦੇ
<uh kade kaṇḍ^{h}ĩ nahĩ lag sakde
(dummy) PRED
'Those who pin their hopes upon others can never reach the shores'

Canonical finite clause pattern 2 can also be expanded.

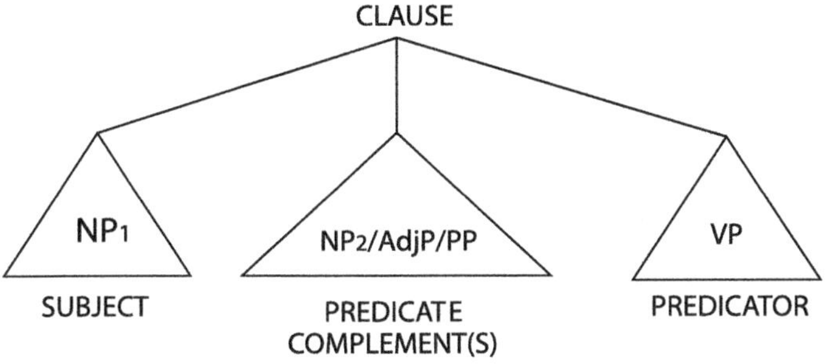

Figure 15.2 Canonical finite clause pattern 2

(28a) ਤੂੰ ਰੋਜ਼ ਦੇਰ ਨਾਲ਼ ਆਉਂਦਾ ਏਂ। ਇਹ ਬੁਰੀ ਗੱਲ ਹੈ
tū̃ roz der nāḷ āū̃dā ẽ. ih burī gall ha^i
'You come late every day. This is bad.'

(28b) ਇਹ➤ ਬੁਰੀ ਗੱਲ ਹੈ ਕਿ ਤੂੰ ਰੋਜ਼ ਦੇਰ ਨਾਲ਼ ਆਉਂਦਾ ਏਂ
ih➤ burī gall ha^i ki tū̃ roz der nāḷ āū̃dā ẽ
(.................SUB.................)
'It is bad that you come late every day.'

(28b) starts with the forward-looking dummy SUBJECT ਇਹ➤ **ih➤** and the real SUBJECT clause is put at the end with the help of the **subordinator** ਕਿ **ki** 'that'. In more colloquial speech the **subordinator** ਪਈ **paī** may be used in this position.

15.2.2 Subordinate nominal clause as the OBJECT

The **subordinate clause** working as the OBJECT is mostly (but not invariably) connected with the subordinator ਕਿ **ki** 'that'. A **K-word** acting as a **pronoun** or **adjective** or **adverb** *minus* its interrogative function can be used in the **subordinate clause** introduced with ਕਿ **ki**. But it cannot by itself act as a **subordinator** like an English **Wh-word**. Panjabi **J-words**, on the other hand, can act as **subordinators** and do not occur in the **subordinate clauses** starting with ਕਿ **ki**.

(29) ਮੈਂ ਜਾਣਦਾ ਹਾਂ ਕਿ ਇਹ ਖ਼ਤ ਕਿਹਨੇ ਲਿਖਿਆ ਹੈ
mã^i jāṇdā hā̃ ki ih xat kihne lik^{h}iā ha^i
'I know who has written this letter'
Lit. 'I know that who has written this letter'

Many Indian speakers and writers of English use both 'that' and a Wh-word in such cases because of the influence of the mother tongue. (e.g., **I know that who has written this letter*).

A **J-word** is often used, and a **dummy** OBJECT can be used for greater clarity.

(30a) ਤੁਸੀਂ ਜੋ ਕਿਹਾ ਸੀ, ◄(ਉਹ) ਮੈਂ ਸੁਣ ਲਿਆ ਹੈ
tusī̃ jo kihā sī, ◄(uh) mã^{i} suṇ liā ha^{i}
(........OBJ........) (dummy)
'I have heard what you said'
Lit. 'What you said (that) I have heard'

Another way of saying this is

(30b) ਮੈਂ (ਉਹ)► ਸੁਣ ਲਿਆ ਹੈ ਜੋ ਤੁਸੀਂ ਕਿਹਾ ਸੀ
mã^{i} (uh)► suṇ liā ha^{i} jo tusī̃ kihā sī
(dummy) (............OBJ...........)
'I have heard what you said'
Lit. 'What you said (that) I have heard'

Co-referential omission is often possible, as in a **compound sentence**.

(31a) ਤੁਸੀਂ ਕੁਝ ਕਹਿਣਾ ਚਾਹੁੰਦੇ ਹੋ। ਉਹ ਤੁਸੀਂ ਬੇਖ਼ੌਫ਼ ਕਹੋ।
tusī̃ kuj^{h} kahinā cāhunde ho. uh tusī̃ bexa^{u}f kaho
'You wish to say something. You should say that fearlessly'

(31b) ਤੁਸੀਂ ਜੋ ਕਹਿਣਾ ਚਾਹੁੰਦੇ ਹੋ, ◄(ਉਹ ਤੁਸੀਂ) ਬੇਖ਼ੌਫ਼ ਕਹੋ।
tusī̃ jo kahinā cāhunde ho, ◄(uh tusī̃) bexa^{u}f kaho
(....................OBJ....................)
'You should say fearlessly what you wish to say'

Indirect speech, now often used by educated Panjabi writers in their writings (and much less frequently in their informal speech), was not traditionally there in Panjabi. Quoted direct speech is a **subordinate object clause**. (25a) is common in writing

(32) ਮੁੰਡੇ ਨੇ ਕਿਹਾ, "ਮੈਂ ਕੱਲ੍ਹ ਸਵੇਰੇ ਆਵਾਂਗਾ"
muṇḍe ne kihā, "mã^{i} kallh savere āvā̃gā"
'The boy said, "I will come tomorrow"'

In ordinary informal conversation, a typical Panjabi *situation-internal perspective* is adopted. Only the subordinator **ਕਿ ki** 'that' is added and nothing else is changed. (Often the quoted speaker's intonation and "style" is also imitated.)

15.2.3 Relative (or adjectival) clauses

A **relative clause** either gives *additional* information (**non-defining** relative clause) or *restricts* the reference of a noun (**defining** relative clause).

(a) Non-defining relative clause

(33) ਮੇਰੇ ਚਾਚਾ ਜੀ, ਜੋ ਮਸ਼ਹੂਰ ਵਕੀਲ ਸਨ,
mere cācā jī, jo maśhūr vakīl san,

ਬਾਦ ਵਿਚ ਹਾਈ ਕੋਰਟ ਦੇ ਜੱਜ ਬਣੇ
bād vic hāī korṭ de jajj baṇe
'My uncle, who was a famous lawyer, became a high court judge later'

In speech, short pause or pauses separate the **non-defining relative clause** from the main clause. In writing commas are used for this purpose. It is rare to use a dummy (but it is not prohibited) in such a complex sentence.

(b) Defining relative clause

(34a) ਉਹ➤ ਬੱਚੇ ਅਗਲੀ ਕਲਾਸ ਵਿਚ ਜਾਣਗੇ
uh➤ bacce aglī kalās vich jāṇge

ਜੋ ਚੰਗੇ ਨੰਬਰ ਲੈਣਗੇ
jo cange nambar la^{i}ṇge
'Those children will go to the next class who get good marks'

It could also be rephrased as

(34b) ਜੋ ਬੱਚੇ ਚੰਗੇ ਨੰਬਰ ਲੈਣਗੇ
jo bacce cange nambar la^{i}ṇge

◀ਉਹ ਅਗਲੀ ਕਲਾਸ ਵਿਚ ਜਾਣਗੇ
◀uh aglī kalās vich jāṇge

The forward-looking or backward-looking **dummy** is necessary in both (34a) and (34b).

This the first line of a well-known poem from the modern Panjabi poet Shiv Kumar (1936–1973)

(35a) ਇਕ ਕੁੜੀ ਜਿਹਦਾ ਨਾਂ ਸੀ ਮੁਹੱਬਤ
ik kuṛī jihdā nā̃ sī muhabbat

ਗੁੰਮ ਹੈ, ਗੁੰਮ ਹੈ, ਗੁੰਮ ਹੈ
gumm ha^{i}, gumm ha^{i}, gumm ha^{i}
'A girl whose name was love is missing, missing, missing'

The inserted relative clause is short and is kept away from the verb of the main clause by the intervening word ਮੁਹੱਬਤ **muhabbat**. So a **dummy** is not needed. But a **dummy** would become necessary if the line (disregarding the poetic rhythm) were

(35b) ਇਕ ਕੁੜੀ ਜਿਹਦਾ ਨਾਂ ਜਨਮਾਂ ਜਨਮਾਂ ਦੀ ਅਮਰ ਪਾਕ ਮੁਹੱਬਤ ਸੀ
ik kuṛī jihdā nā̃ janmā̃ janmā̃ dī amar pāk muhabbat sī

◀ਉਹ ਗੁੰਮ ਹੈ
◀uh gumm ha^{i}
'A girl whose name was many lives old immortal sacred love is missing'

Now this couplet from a poem by the modern Panjabi poet Rajinderjeet (1972–) should be easily comprehensible.

(36) ਜੀਹਨੇ ਮੈਨੂੰ ਮਾਰਿਆ ਤਲਵਾਰ ਉਹ ਤੇਰੀ ਹੀ ਸੀ, ਪਰ
ਜੀਹਨੇ ਤੈਨੂੰ ਮਾਰਿਆ ਉਹ ਬਦ-ਦੁਆ ਮੇਰੀ ਨਹੀਂ ਸੀ
jīhne ma^{i}nū̃ māriā talvār uh terī hī si, par
jīhne ta^{i}nū̃ māriā uh bad-duā merī nahī̃ sī

'The sword that killed me was certainly yours, but the curse that killed you was not mine'

ਜੀਹਨੇ **jīhne = ਜਿਸ ਨੇ jīs ne**
ਤਲਵਾਰ **talvār** = sword
ਬਦ-ਦੁਆ **bad-duā** = curse

The reason for a typical error made by many Indian speakers of English

**The man who stole your money he has been caught by the police*

can now be understood.

15.2.4 Adverbial clauses

Like an **adverb** or **adverbial phrase**, an **adverbial clause** introduced by an appropriate **subordinator** can modify the meaning of the **VP** in various ways.

(a) Cause

(37) ਮੈਂ ਅੱਜ ਕੰਮ 'ਤੇ ਨਹੀਂ ਜਾ ਸਕਦਾ *ਕਿਉਂਕਿ* ਮੈਂ ਬੀਮਾਰ ਹਾਂ
mã^{i} ajj kamm te nahī̃ jā sakdā *kiū̃ki* mã^{i} bīmār hā̃
'I cannot go to work today *because* I am unwell'

(b) Effect

(38) ਉਹਨੇ *ਇੰਨੀ* ਮਿਹਨਤ ਕੀਤੀ *ਕਿ* ਚੰਗੇ ਨੰਬਰ ਲੈ ਗਿਆ
uhne *innī* mihnat kītī *ki* cange nambar la^{i} giā
'He worked *so* hard *that* he got good marks'

(c) Purpose

(39) ਉਹਨੇ ਬਹੁਤ ਮਿਹਨਤ ਕੀਤੀ *ਤਾਂਕਿ* ਚੰਗੇ ਨੰਬਰ ਲੈ ਸਕੇ
uhne bahut mihnat kītī *tā̃ki* cange nambar la^{i} sake
'He worked very hard *so that* he could get good marks'

ਤਾਂ ਜੁ **tā̃ ju** can also be used here. Even without the use of a **subordinator** the context can make the meaning clear, as in the female Panjabi song

(40) ਬੱਤੀ ਬਾਲ਼ ਕੇ ਬਨੇਰੇ ਉੱਤੇ ਰੱਖਨੀ ਆਂ
ਗਲ਼ੀ ਭੁੱਲ ਨਾ ਜਾਵੇ ਚੰਨ ਮੇਰਾ
battī bāḷ ke banere utte rakk^{h}nī ā̃
gaḷhī b^{h}ull nā jāve cann merā
'I put a lighted lamp on the edge of my roof
lest my sweetheart misses my street'

ਰੱਖਨੀਆਂ **rakk^{h}nī ā̃** is a colloquial version of ਰੱਖਦੀ ਹਾਂ **rakk^{h}dī hā̃** 'I place'.

(d) Condition

(41) ਮੈਂ ਕੰਮ ਕਰਾਂਗਾ *ਜੇ* ਤੁਸੀਂ ਮੈਨੂੰ ਪੰਜ ਸੌ ਰੁਪਏ ਫ਼ੀ ਘੰਟਾ ਦਿਓ
mã^{i} kamm karā̃gā *je* tusī̃ ma^{i}nū̃ panj sa^{u} rupae fī g^{h}aṇṭā dio
'I will do the job *if* you pay me five hundred rupees per hour'

ਜੇਕਰ **jekar** and ਬਸ਼ਰਤਿ **baśarti** can also be used.

(e) Concession

(42) ਅਸੀਂ ਸਮੇਂ 'ਤੇ ਪਹੁੰਚ ਨਾ ਸਕੇ, *ਹਾਲਾਂਕਿ* ਮੈਂ ਗੱਡੀ ਬਹੁਤ ਤੇਜ਼ ਚਲਾਈ
asī̃ samẽ te pahũc na sake, *hālā̃ki* mã^{i} gaḍḍī bahut tez calāī
'We could not reach on time, *although* I drove the car very fast'

(f) Manner

(43) ਉਹ ਉੱਚੀ ਉੱਚੀ ਹੂੰਘ ਰਿਹਾ ਸੀ, *ਜਿਵੇਂ ਕਿ* ਉਹਨੂੰ ਸੱਚਮੁਚ ਦਾ ਦਰਦ ਹੋਵੇ
uh uccī uccī hũg^{h} rihā sī, *jivẽ ki* uhnū̃ saccmuch dā dard hove
'He was groaning loudly *as if* he had a real pain'

(g) Time

(44) *ਜਦ* ਦੁਰਘਟਨਾ ਹੋਈ, ◄*ਉਸ ਵੇਲੇ* ਗੱਡੀ ਉਹਦੀ ਪਤਨੀ ਚਲਾ ਰਹੀ ਸੀ
***jad* durg^{h}aṭanā hoī ◄*us vele* uhdī patnī gaḍḍī calā rahī si**
'*When* the accident happened, *at that time* his wife was driving the car'

(h) Place

(45a) *ਜਿੱਥੇ* ਦੁਰਘਟਨਾ ਹੋਈ ਸੀ, ◄*ਉੱਥੇ* ਪੁਲਿਸ ਗਈ
***jitt^{h}e* durg^{h}aṭanā hoī sī ◄*utt^{h}e* pulis gaī**
'The police went to the place *where* the accident had happened'
Lit. '*Where* the accident had happened, the police went *there*'

(45a) can also be rephrased as

(45b) ਪੁਲਿਸ *ਉੱਥੇ➤* ਗਈ *ਜਿੱਥੇ* ਦੁਰਘਟਨਾ ਹੋਈ ਸੀ,
pulis *uttʰe➤* gaī *jittʰe* durgʰaṭanā hoī sī

15.3 Mixed sentences

Very often you can come across mixed sentences of the following types.

15.3.1 Compound-complex sentences

A **subordinate clause** or **sentence** can be attached to a **compound sentence.**

(46) (ਉਹ ਆਇਆ, ਪਰ ਛੇਤੀ ਮੁੜ ਗਿਆ) (ਕਿਉਂਕਿ ਉਹਨੇ ਕਿਸੇ ਹੋਰ ਥਾਂ ਵੀ ਜਾਣਾ ਸੀ)
(uh āīā, par cʰetī muṛ giā) (kiũki uhne kise hor tʰā̃ vī jāṇā sī)
Compound Sentence (Subo) Complex Sentence
'(He came, but went back soon) (because he had to go somewhere else as well)'

15.3.2 Complex-compound sentences

A **compound sentence** can be embedded in clauses, resulting in **complex-compound** sentences as in this sweetly romantic female Panjabi folk song.

(47) ਸੂਹੇ ਵੇ ਚੀਰੇ ਵਾਲ਼ਿਆ, ਮੈਂ ਕਹਿੰਨੀ ਆਂ
ਕਰ ਛਤਰੀ ਦੀ ਛਾਂ, ਮੈਂ ਛਾਂਵੇਂ ਬਹਿੰਨੀ ਆਂ
sūhe ve cīre vāḷiā, mãi kahinī ā̃
kar cʰatrī dī cʰā̃, mãi cʰā̃vẽ bahinī ā̃
'O wearer of red turban, I say (to you) –
Make a shade with an umbrella, (and) I will sit in the shade'

Colloquial versions are used in the song.

ਕਹਿੰਨੀ ਆਂ **kahinī ā̃** 'am saying' is a colloquial version of ਕਹਿੰਦੀ ਹਾਂ **kahindī hā̃**
ਬਹਿੰਨੀ ਆਂ **bahinī ā̃** 'am or will be sitting' is a colloquial version of ਬਹਿੰਦੀ ਹਾਂ **bahindī hā̃**

But nothing more anti-romantic can be imagined than the Panjabi version of the oath taken by a witness in a court of law. In this mixed sentence, (ਮੈਂ) **(mã^{i})** in the brackets is co-referentially omitted in the embedded compound sentence.

(48) ਮੈਂ ਕਸਮ ਖਾਂਦਾ ਹਾਂ ਕਿ ਮੈਂ ਸੱਚ ਕਹਾਂਗਾ, (ਮੈਂ) ਪੂਰਾ ਸੱਚ ਕਹਾਂਗਾ, ਅਤੇ (ਮੈਂ) ਸੱਚ ਤੋਂ ਬਿਨਾਂ ਹੋਰ ਕੁਝ ਨਹੀਂ ਕਹਾਂਗਾ
mã^{i} kasam k^{h}ā̃dā hā̃ ki mã^{i} sacc kahā̃gā, (mã^{i}) pūrā sacc kahā̃gā, ate (mã^{i}) sacc tõ binā̃ hor kuj^{h} nahī̃ kahā̃gā
'I take an oath that I will speak the truth, (I will) speak the whole truth, and (I will) speak nothing except the truth'

Summing up and looking ahead

A sentence has traditionally been (implicitly or explicitly) regarded as the upper limit of grammatical analysis. A grammarian's dilemma about the sentence is like St Augustine's about time – they know what a sentence is so long as you do not ask them to define it! Accordingly, no definition of the sentence is attempted in this book. But it is hoped that users will have formed a fairly good idea about what a simple, compound and complex sentence in Panjabi is.

We have seen how **mono-clausal simple sentences** are expanded into **multi-clausal compound** and **complex sentences**. But, *as far as possible*, we have tried to follow the tradition of regarding the sentence as the upper limit of grammatical analysis and kept the textual and discoursal determinants of the structure of the sentence out of our analysis. But *keeping them out* is different from *denying their existence or importance.* We have seen how **cohesive devices** such as **pronouns**, and **dummies** and **particles** are used. The different marking of a **definite object** is also a **discoursal** feature. In the next chapter, we will look *very briefly* at how the **particles** in combination with **intonation** and other **prosodic features** are used to organise discourse and give it particular nuances.

Chapter 16

Above and Beyond the Sentence: Discourse, Text and Cohesion

Preview of the chapter

As pointed out at the end of the last chapter, the sentence has traditionally been (implicitly or explicitly) regarded as the upper limit of grammatical analysis. But human languages developed to satisfy socio-cultural (and hence communicative) human needs, not to fit into grammarians' frameworks. In real life, nobody utters isolated and unrelated sentences. Typically, sentences are a part of **discourse** and **text**. The terms "discourse" and "text" used here are for a *linguistic* or *grammatical* analysis, and not a *philosophical* analysis (especially of the type practised by some modern "Continental" philosophers).

16.1 "Above" and "beyond" the sentence

What lies "above" or "beyond" the sentence in discourse or text greatly influences the structure of the sentence in Panjabi (and probably in all languages). For our purpose, **discourse** means any coherent spoken or written succession of sentences. The term **text** is commonly used for a written text, but we extend it here to "cover a coherent stretch of speech, including a conversation or other interchange involving two or more participants, as well as stretches of writing" (Matthews 2007: 405–6). **Cohesion** is the connection between successive sentences in a text *achieved with linguistic devices*. Cohesion is different from **coherence**, which is "the way in which the content of connected speech or text hangs together, or is interpreted as hanging together, as distinct from that of random assemblage of sentences" (*ibid.* 62). **Coherence** in text is not our business here, but **cohesion** is, insofar as it affects the structure of individual sentences connected in text or discourse.

Before we move any further, it must be mentioned that this area is a vast minefield where most linguist angels fear to tread. So we do not wish to rush in there. Only *a few* points relevant to Panjabi grammar will be dealt with *very briefly* in this chapter.

16.2 Definite patient OBJECT

An entity's being **definite** is partly a discoursal phenomenon. Once it is mentioned in the discourse, it becomes definite. We have already seen in Chapter 12 that a definite OBJECT is marked with ਨੂੰ **nū̃** 'to' and the verb in the **perfect participle** or the **potential participle** form does not agree with such an NP and is in the **neuter** number-gender form, which is homophonous to the **masculine singular** form. It agrees only with a non-definite OBJECT. **Pronouns** in the OBJECT position are always definite for discoursal reasons. Since this topic has already been dealt with in detail, we do not wish to repeat it here.

16.3 Tinkering with the SOV word order

The basic word order in Panjabi is classified as **SOV** (Subject Object Verb) in modern linguistics literature. Panjabi also has some other features associated with this word order – such as the language having **postpositions** and not **prepositions**, **adjectives** preceding the **nouns** in **adjective phrases**, **auxiliaries** following the **main verb** etc.) We have also seen that this word order *seems to* have its influence in the construction of complex sentences in Panjabi. (See Chapter 15.)

But in actual practice, a speaker or writer of Panjabi enjoys considerable freedom to tinker with this basic word order for various pragmatic, discoursal and textual reasons. In this section, we briefly mention a topic already dealt with in detail.

16.3.1 The "dative subject" or "experiencer subject"

This topic has already been dealt with in great detail in Chapter 12. Since human beings are *pragmatically* more significant than their mental attitude or physical condition or ailments, they are mentioned first. It is wrong to invoke the **SOV** word order to regard an **NP** denoting the human being(s) as the SUBJECT (of whatever variety) of the clause.

16.4 Cohesion in text and discourse

Two sentences A and B in a text or discourse have **cohesion** if, in order to understand the meaning of one of them, you have to refer to the other. Two main devices are used for creating this type of cohesion.

16.4.1 Co-referential omission

We have already come across (in Chapter 15) **co-referential omission** used for creating **cohesion** between two **co-ordinate clauses** or intra-sentential cohesion. The same method can be used to create inter-sentential cohesion between two sentences in a text or discourse.

(1a) A: ਤੁਸੀਂ ਮੇਰਾ ਨਵਾਂ ਨਾਵਲ ਪੜ੍ਹਿਆ ਹੈ?
tusī̃ merā navā̃ nāval paṛhiā ha^{i}?
'Have you read my new novel?'

B: ਹਾਂ, ਦੋ ਵਾਰ
hā̃, do vār
'Yes, twice'

Without omission, B's response in (1a) would be

(1b) ਹਾਂ, (ਮੈਂ ਤੁਹਾਡਾ ਨਵਾਂ ਨਾਵਲ) ਦੋ ਵਾਰ (ਪੜ੍ਹਿਆ ਹੈ)
hā̃, (mã^{i} tuhāḍā navā̃ nāval) do vār (paṛhiā ha^{i})
'Yes (I have read your new novel) twice.'

(2) A: ਤੁਸੀਂ ਬਲਦੇਵ ਨੂੰ ਜਾਣਦੇ ਹੋ?
tusī̃ baldev nū̃ jāṇde ho?
'Do you know Baldev?'

B: (ਮੈਂ ਬਲਦੇਵ ਨੂੰ) ਬਹੁਤ ਚੰਗੀ ਤਰ੍ਹਾਂ (ਜਾਣਦਾ ਹਾਂ), ਤੇ (ਮੈਂ ਬਲਦੇਵ ਨੂੰ) ਸਮਝਦਾ ਵੀ ਹਾਂ
(mã^{i} baldev nū̃) bahut cangī tarhā̃ (jāṇdā hā̃) te (mã^{i} baldev nū̃) samj^{h}dā vī hā̃
'(I know Baldev) very well, and (I) also understand (Baldev)'

The words enclosed within brackets in the examples given above are not repeated by the speakers. The *old* information that needs to be repeated in the response is omitted. Only the *new* information is given. **Cohesion** is established by the fact that the information missing in the later sentence has to be recovered from the earlier sentence.

16.4.2 Pro-forms

Pro-forms are words or phrases whose referents (or antecedents) are located outside the sentence. Pronouns belong to this group. These pro-forms are italicised in the following examples.

(3) ਗੱਡੀ ਸਵੇਰੇ ਦਸ ਵਜੇ ਸਟੇਸ਼ਨ 'ਤੇ ਪੁੱਜੀ। <*ਤਦ ਤਕ* <*ਉੱਥੇ* ਕਾਫ਼ੀ ਭੀੜ ਜਮ੍ਹਾ ਹੋ ਗਈ ਸੀ।
gaḍḍī savere das vaje sateśan te pujjī. <*tad* tak <*utt^{h}e* kāfī b^{h}īṛ jamhā ho gaī si
'The train arrived at the station at 10 am. By *then* a large crowd had gathered *there*'

In the second sentence in (3) you need to refer to the first in order to know that ਤਦ **tad** 'then' has been used for ਸਵੇਰੇ ਦਸ ਵਜੇ **savere das vaje** 'at ten am' and ਉੱਥੇ **utt^{h}e** 'there' has been used for ਸਟੇਸ਼ਨ 'ਤੇ **sateśan te** 'at the station'.

(4) A: ਬਲਦੇਵ ਨੇ ਤੁਹਾਡਾ ਬਹੁਤ ਅਪਮਾਨ ਕੀਤਾ ਹੈ
baldev ne tuhāḍā bahut apmān kītā ha^{i}
'Baldev has insulted you a lot'

B: <*ਉਹਨੇ* <*ਇਹ* ਪਹਿਲੀ ਵਾਰ ਨਹੀਂ ਕੀਤਾ
<*uhne* <*ih* pahilī vār nahī̃ kītā
'*He* has not done *this* for the first time'

In B's response, the pronoun ਉਹ **uh** stands for Baldev mentioned in A's statement. The pro-form ਇਹ **ih** 'this' stands for the action of insulting mentioned earlier.

Pro-forms are mostly backward-looking (or **anaphoric**) and they are said to have **antecedents**. But it is possible (though less common) to use forward-looking (or **cataphoric**) pro-forms.

(5) ਅਸੀਂ *ਇਹ*➤ ਕਰਾਂਗੇ – ਮੈਂ ਪਹਿਲਾਂ ਜਾ ਕੇ ਟਿਕਟਾਂ ਖ਼ਰੀਦਾਂਗਾ, ਤੇ ਤੁਸੀਂ ਸਾਰੇ ਮਗਰੋਂ ਆਓਗੇ
asī̃ *ih*➤ karā̃ge – mã^{i} pahilā̃ jā ke ṭikṭā̃ xarīdā̃gā, te tusī̃ sāre magrõ āoge
'We will do *this* – I will go first and buy the tickets, and you all will come later'

16.4.3 Particles and echoing of old information

The Panjabi particles ਵੀ **vī**, ਹੀ **hī** and ਤਾਂ **tā̃** can be used to echo old information or a part of it in the new sentence and thus help in creating cohesion. This is the opposite of co-referential omission. ਵੀ **vī** is called the **inclusive particle** and roughly means 'also'. ਹੀ **hī** is called the **exclusive particle** and roughly means 'only'. It is also used for laying emphasis. ਤਾਂ **tā̃** is used to mark the information in the sense of 'as far as X is concerned...'.

(6) A: ਕੀ ਤੁਸੀਂ ਜਗਮੋਹਨ ਨੂੰ ਮਿਲ਼ੇ ਸੀ?
kī tusī̃ jagmohan nū̃ miḷe sī?
'Did you meet Jagmohan?'

B: ਹਾਂ, ਮਿਲ਼ਿਆ ਹੀ ਨਹੀਂ, ਸਗੋਂ ਉਹਦੇ ਕੋਲ਼ ਠਹਿਰਿਆ ਵੀ ਸਾਂ
hā̃, miḷinā hī nahī̃, sagõ uhde koḷ ṭ^{h}ahiriā vī sā̃
'Yes. I not only met him, but also stayed with him'

B's answer first partly echoes what A says and then adds to it.

ਤਾਂ **tā̃** can be used to pick out any relevant part of the older information for echoing it.

(7) A: ਮੈਂ ਕਿਤਾਬ ਲਿਖ ਲਈ ਹੈ
mã^{i} kitāb lik^{h} laī ha^{i}
'I have written the book'

B: ਲਿਖ ਤਾਂ ਲਈ ਹੈ, ਹੁਣ ਛਪਵਾਓਗੇ ਕਦ?
lik^{h} tā̃ laī ha^{i}, huṇ c^{h}apvāoge kad?
'You have written it, but when will you get it printed?'

A: ਛਪਵਾਉਣਾ ਤਾਂ ਕੋਈ ਮਸਲਾ ਹੀ ਨਹੀਂ
cʰapvāuṇā tā̃ koī maslā hī nahī̃
'Getting it printed is not a problem'
Lit. 'As for getting it printed, it is not a problem'

B: ਤਾਂ ਫਿਰ ਦੇਰ ਕਿਉਂ?
tā̃ phir der kiũ?
'Why is the delay then?'

B first repeats ਲਿਖ ਲਈ ਹੈ **likʰ laī haⁱ** with the help of ਤਾਂ **tā̃** to say "Well, as far as writing is concerned, you have done it". Then he builds upon this information to ask the question "When will you get it printed?". Each speaker, in turn, echoes a part of the previous utterance before building upon it. Very often, ਤਾਂ **tā̃** is not used; only some part of the earlier information is repeated for the purpose of linkage.

16.5 Word order again: the "given" and the "new" information

So far, we have come across two *tendencies* (not rules) used for tinkering with the basic **SOV** word order and building up cohesive text or discourse in Panjabi.

1. Pragmatically more salient information tends to precede the less salient information, and
2. Contextually given information is either omitted (and sometimes its omission is indicated by using pro-forms) or echoed and built upon.

Now let us consider this dialogue.

(8) Mr B: ਮੈਨੂੰ ਸਿਰ ਦਰਦ ਹੈ
maⁱnū̃ sir dard aⁱ
'I have a headache'

Mrs B: ਔਹ ਗੋਲ਼ੀਆਂ ਲੈ ਲਓ, ਪਾਣੀ ਨਾਲ਼
aⁱh goḷiā̃ laⁱ lao, pāṇī nāḷ
these tablets take water with
'Have these tablets, with water'

Mr B:	ਗੋਲ਼ੀਆਂ	ਲਊਂ	ਮੈਂ	ਘਰ	ਜਾ ਕੇ,
	goḷīā̃	**laū̃**	**mā̃ⁱ**	**gʰar**	**jā ke,**
	tablets	will take	I	home	having gone
	ਚਾਹ ਦੇ ਨਾਲ਼				
	cāh de nāḷ				
	tea with				

'I will take the tablets after going home; with tea'
Lit. 'As for the tablets, I will take them after going home, (and) with tea'

Mr B mentions the taking of the tablets, the information "given" in the context, and then adds the more significant part of "new" information, i.e., after going home. The less significant part of the "new" information is taking the tablets with tea instead of water. ਚਾਹ ਦੇ ਨਾਲ਼ **cāh de nāḷ** 'with tea' seems to be added as an afterthought and it has a separate intonation contour starting after a very short pause. Mrs B, too, puts ਪਾਣੀ ਨਾਲ਼ **pāṇī nāḷ** 'with water' in a separate intonation unit. Mr B does the same for its equivalent ਚਾਹ ਦੇ ਨਾਲ਼ **cāh de nāḷ** 'with tea'. Echoing the *style* is also a **cohesive** device. The **nuclear sentence stress** in the first intonation contour occurs on ਘਰ **gʰar** 'home', where the contour changes direction.

This is a *simplified* picture of the intonation contours. The **tonal** pitch contours of ਘਰ **gʰar** [kὲr] and ਚਾਹ **cāh** [ʧá] are ignored here.

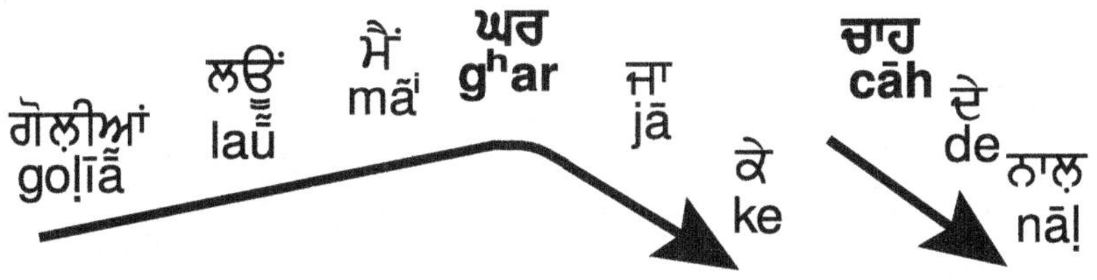

Figure 16.1 Intonation of (8)

The two tendencies are in co-operation here. If they are in opposition, the word order and the use of the particle (if any) depends on the situational context. There are no hard and fast rules. Whether or not this happens in any other language is worth investigating. This is certainly not a "language universal", but it does not become theoretically any less interesting simply because it is not a "universal".

As for the other factors "above and beyond" the sentence affecting the structure of the sentence in Panjabi, an honest grammarian can be sure of only one thing: that she/he can never be absolutely sure!

The situation described in (8) above actually happened two days before I started typing this chapter. I (Mr B) was going back home with my wife on a local bus, and the exchange took place on the bus. On learning about my headache, Mrs B took out two paracetamol tablets and a small bottle of water from her bag and asked me to take the tablets with water. I said that I would take them a few minutes later at home, and with tea. After saying this, I started introspecting why I used this expression, and not any other grammatically possible one. I could have expressed the same idea by arranging my words differently. For example, I prefer to use the **subjunctive** form with **ਗਾ gā** (**ਲਵਾਂਗਾ lavā̃gā** or **ਲਊਂਗਾ laū̃gā**). Putting the SUBJECT after the verb is fine in Panjabi, and **ਲਊਂ ਮੈਂ laū̃ mā̃ˡ** is as grammatical as the more normal **ਮੈਂ ਲਊਂ mā̃ˡ laū̃**. There must be reason for this "marked" word order. It is worth investigating whether this is related to the natural rhythm of the language.

To whom it may concern

It is logically impossible to refine and regularise a non-existing entity. The rhythm of Panjabi poetry is a regularised and refined form of what *already* exists in the language. The Panjabi-speaking linguist Banarsi Das Jain, the first native speaker of Panjabi to receive a doctorate in a linguistic science in 1926 from the University of London, presented his views on the subject nearly a century ago in his Ph.D. thesis *Phonology of Panjabi as Spoken about Ludhiana*. He wrote that in a Panjabi utterance, stressed syllables tend to occur at approximately equal intervals and *this may be effected by changing the order of words if it is permissible by grammar*. Jain must have used his ear to arrive at this hypothesis. Though he does mention the instrumental analysis he made, this type of analysis in his days was relatively primitive as compared with what we can do now with today's electronic devices. I actually did analyse this sentence recorded in my voice with PRAAT, a program for phonetic analysis developed by the University of Amsterdam and downloadable free from the Internet, and the results support Jain's thesis that in spoken Panjabi, the stressed syllables *tend to* occur at *approximately* equal intervals. (Jain himself used the words "tend to" and "approximately".) A discussion of the technicalities of this acoustic analysis will be beyond the scope of this book. But one point needs a mention here – that the Panjabi vowels normally classified as "long" and "tense" (Chapter 2) become considerably weakened and shortened in the words and syllables unstressed in the sentence.

In ਗੋਲ਼ੀਆਂ ਲਊਂ ਮੈਂ ਘਰ ਜਾ ਕੇ, ਚਾਹ ਦੇ ਨਾਲ਼ **goḷīā̃ laū̃ mã^{i} g^{h}ar jā ke, cāh de nāḷ** the first intonation unit has three rhythmic feet of three syllables each, a stressed syllable followed by two unstressed ones. Pronouns, auxiliaries and postpositions are normally unstressed in speech and nouns and main verbs are stressed. So the more "normal" word order of SUBJECT preceding the verb in ਮੈਂ ਲਊਂ **mã^{i} laū̃** would have disturbed the natural rhythm analysed below. ਲਊਂਗਾ **laū̃gā** or ਲਵਾਂਗਾ **lavā̃gā** would have added an extra syllable, again with the same result. The nuclear stress in the first intonation contour is on "ਘਰ **"g^{h}ar** as shown in Figure 16.1 on p.335.

'ਗੋ ਲ਼ੀ ਆਂ 'ਲ ਊਂ ਮੈਂ "ਘਰ ਜਾ ਕੇ, | 'ਚਾਹ ਦੇ ਨਾਲ਼
'go ḷī ā̃ 'la ū̃ mã^{i} "g^{h}ar jā ke, | 'cāh de nāḷ

Out of the many possible (and grammatically equally permissible) word orders, I *instinctively* chose this one. I had read Jain's observation about twenty years earlier. But I obviously did not speak according to his prescription!

Critically examining past scholars' ideas is the best tribute that can be paid to them. So there can be no better way of ending this last chapter on Panjabi syntax than paying this ultimate tribute to Banarsi Das Jain, the most dedicated and perceptive, and now nearly forgotten, first modern native Panjabi linguist, sixty years after his death.

But what Jain observed may simply be a proverbial tip of the iceberg. More may be hidden than meets the eye (or the ear in this case). Panjabi appears to be moving towards an English-like "stress-timed rhythm". Any careful observer of Panjabi and Hindi-Urdu speech can hear that stressed syllables as compared to the unstressed ones in Panjabi are a lot stronger than in Hindi-Urdu. This is accompanied by Panjabi's preference for closed syllables even in words having long and tense vowels (Chapter 4). Word stress was less prominent in Panjabi four of five hundred years ago (Harkirat Singh 2011). Tones became prominent in Panjabi over the period in which strong stress (along with the related phenomena like preference for closed syllables) was also becoming prominent. The Panjabi tones developed in the words with breathy voiced (or voiced aspirated) consonants. So it is possible that breathy voice become incompatible with strong stress, and tones were the outcome of this. These may not be just isolated facts, and they may actually be intimately connected. But a lot of research is needed to establish this. It appears that there lies a great deal in the "beyond" than has been sketchily presented in this chapter.

Chapter 17

A Little Bit of Derivational Morphology

Preview of the chapter

This chapter describes some of the **semi-productive** *derivational* morphological processes and the formation of some phrases doing the work of single lexical items in Panjabi.

17.1 Some productive tendencies in Panjabi derivational morphology

Chapter 4 mentions two types of morphological processes – the **inflectional** and the **derivational**. When a lexeme (or dictionary word) is **inflected**, the result is a *different grammatical form* of the *same* lexeme. But the process of **derivation** creates a *different lexeme*. For example, we can **inflect** the verb *create* to derive its **past tense** form *created* and the **present participle** form *creating*. But we can also **derive** the adjective *creative* from the verb *create*. From the adjective *creative*, we can derive the abstract noun *creativity*. *Creative* and *creativity* are different lexemes ultimately derived from *create*. Every English grammarian would agree that *created* is simply a past tense form of the lexeme *create*, and not a different lexeme. But what about the cases involving **suppletion**, like *went* being the past tense form of *go*? A surviving form of an extinct lexeme has become the past tense form of *go*. A morphological process changes the *form* of a lexeme. But, strictly speaking, suppletion is not a morphological process.

There are no absolute *rules* of **inflection** just some *strong tendencies* creating *regularities* in English and Panjabi. The **gerund** form of the Panjabi verb ਜਾ **jā** is ਜਾਣਾ **jāṇā**, but the **perfect participle** form is ਗਿਆ **giā**, which comes from a different root. This, too, is a case of suppletion, like *went* being the past tense form of *go*. Some Western Panjabi dialects have ਵੰਞਸਾਂ **vaññsā̃** 'I will go' and its variants for person and number.

As far as the processes of **derivation** are concerned, there are not even strong tendencies. The abstract noun related to the adjective *good* is *goodness*. But the one related to *difficult* is *difficulty*, and not **difficultness*. The same applies to Panjabi. The **adjective** related to the noun ਗੰਦ **gand** 'dirt' is ਗੰਦਾ **gandā** 'dirty' and the adjective related to ਗੰਢ **gaṇḍ^h** 'knot' is ਗੰਢਲ਼ **gaṇḍ^{h}aḷ** 'knotty', and not ਗੰਢਾ **gaṇḍ^{h}ā**, which is an altogether different lexeme meaning 'onion'. ਗੰਦਲ਼ **gandaḷ** 'tender stem of a plant' is also a different and unrelated lexeme. The period of childhood is ਬਚਪਨ **bacpan** related to the lexeme ਬੱਚਾ **baccā**. But the word for old age in Panjabi is ਬੁਢਾਪਾ **buḍ^{h}āpā** or ਬੁਢੇਪਾ **buḍ^{h}epā**, related to ਬੁੱਢਾ **buḍḍ^{h}ā** 'old man'. There are no Panjabi words *ਬਚੇਪਾ ***bacepā** and *ਬੁੱਢਪਨ ***buḍḍ^{h}pan**. In derivational processes, we can find some **prefixes** and **suffixes**, each used with a few words. We can take note of some of them here.

17.2 Some commonly used prefixes and suffixes

17.2.1 Commonly used prefixes

ਉਪ- **up-** ('smaller', 'sub-')

ਉਪ-ਮੰਤਰੀ **up-mantarī** 'junior minister'
ਉਪ-ਪ੍ਰਧਾਨ **up-prad^{h}ān** 'vice president'
ਉਪ-ਮੰਡਲ **upmanḍal** 'subdivision'

ਅ- **a-** ('not')

ਅਪਮਾਨ **apmān** 'disrespect'
ਅਸਹਿ **asahi** 'unbearable'
ਅਨਾਥ **anāt^h** 'orphan', 'without any guardian'

ਅਣ- **aṇ-** ('not')

ਅਣਹੋਂਦ **aṇhõd** 'non-existence'
ਅਣਗਿਣਤ **aṇgiṇat** 'uncountable', 'innumerable'
ਅਣਜਾਣ **aṇjāṇ** 'ignorant', 'without knowledge'

ਅਪ- **ap-** ('bad')

ਅਪਮਾਨ **apmān** 'disrespect', 'insult'
ਅਪਸ਼ਬਦ **apśabad** 'bad words'
ਅਪਸ਼ਗਨ **apśagan** 'bad omen'

ਅੱਧ- **add^h-** ('half')

ਅੱਧਵਾਟੇ **add^{h}vāṭe** 'half way through'
ਅੱਧਮੋਇਆ **add^{h}moiā** 'half dead'
ਅੱਧਖੜ **add^{h}k^{h}aṛ** 'middle aged'

ਅਵ- **av-** ('bad')

ਅਵਗਤ **avgat** 'bad treatment'
ਅਵਗੁਣ **avguṇ** 'bad trait'
ਅਵਸਾਦ **avsād** 'listlessness'

ਸੁ- **su-** ('good')

ਸੁਆਗਤ **suāgat** 'welcome'
ਸੁਲੱਖਣੀ **sulakk^{h}aṇī** '(woman) with good qualities'
ਸੁਭਾਗ **sub^{h}āg** 'good fortune'

ਸਵੈ- **sva^i-** ('own')

ਸਵੈ-ਜੀਵਨੀ **sva^i-jīvanī** 'autobiography'
ਸਵੈ-ਸ਼ਾਸਨ **sva^i-śāsan** 'home rule'
ਸਵੈ-ਮਾਣ **sva^i-māṇ** 'self-respect'

ਕੁ- **ku-** ('bad')

ਕੁਕਰਮ **kukaram** 'bad deed'
ਕੁਰੂਪ **kurūp** 'bad looking'
ਕੁਬੋਲ **kubol** 'bad words'

ਦੁਰ- **dur-** ('bad')

ਦੁਰਦਸ਼ਾ **durdaśā** 'bad condition'
ਦੁਰਜਨ **durjan** 'bad man'
ਦੁਰਗੰਧ **durgand^h** 'bad smell'

ਨਿਸ਼- **niś-** ('without')

ਨਿਸ਼ਚਿੰਤ **niścint** 'without worry'
ਨਿਸ਼ਕਾਮ **niśkām** 'selfless'
ਨਿਸ਼ਕਪਟ **niśkapaṭ** 'without deception'

ਨਿਰ- **nir-** ('without')

ਨਿਰਦਈ **nirdaī** 'merciless'
ਨਿਰਧਨ **nird^{h}an** 'penniless'
ਨਿਰਭੈ **nirb^{h}a^i** 'fearless'

ਪੜ- **paṛ-** ('one place behind')

ਪੜਦਾਦਾ **paṛdādā** 'great grandfather'
ਪੜਨਾਂਵ **paṛnā̃v** 'pronoun'
ਪੜਵਾਲ਼ **paṛvāḷ** 'hair growing behind eyelashes'

ਮਹਾ- **mahā-** ('great')

ਮਹਾਤਮਾ **mahātmā** 'great soul'
ਮਹਾਰਾਜਾ **mahārājā** 'great king'
ਮਹਾਜਨ **mahājan** 'eminent person'

ਮਹਾਂ- **mahā̃-** ('great')

ਮਹਾਂਪਾਪ **mahā̃pāp** 'great sin'
ਮਹਾਂਯੁੱਧ **mahā̃yudd^h** 'great war'
ਮਹਾਂਸਾਗਰ **mahā̃sāgar** 'great ocean'

ਵਿ- **vi-** ('without')

ਵਿਅਰਥ **viart^h** 'to no avail'
ਵਿਯੋਗ **viyog** 'non-union, separation'
ਵਿਕਾਰ **vikār** 'bad symptom'

17.2.1.1 Prefixes borrowed from or via Persian

Languages borrow words from other languages. But the borrowing of grammar (in the form of *productive* sentence patterns, grammatico-semantic features of grammatical words, case-endings and tense and aspect markers) is quite rare, though not unknown. Below we give some prefixes borrowed from and/or via Persian. The Panjabi-speaking population has been learning Persian and Arabic for centuries. Persian was the language of administration for more than eight centuries in North India. So Panjabi has been borrowing Persian words (and Arabic words mostly via Persian) for centuries. Some of them have become extremely common (and Panjabi-ised) in the speech of the common people. When this happens, the prefix or the suffix in the word tends to become productive and used with the native non-Persian words as well.

ਹਮ- **ham-** ('equal')

ਹਮਸ਼ਕਲ **hamśakal** 'resembling'
ਹਮਨਾਮ **hamnām** 'namesake'
ਹਮਦਰਦ **hamdard** 'sympathiser'

ਕਮ- **kam-** ('less')

ਕਮਜ਼ੋਰ **kamzor** 'weak'
ਕਮਅਕਲ **kamakal** 'less intelligent'
ਕਮਖ਼ਰਚ **kamxarc** 'economical'

ਖ਼ੁਸ਼- **xuś-** ('good')

ਖ਼ੁਸ਼ਕਿਸਮਤ **xuśkismat** 'fortunate'
ਖ਼ੁਸ਼ਬੂ **xuśbū** 'fragrance'
ਖ਼ੁਸ਼ਖ਼ਤ **xuśxat** 'good handwriting'

ਬਦ- **bad-** ('bad')

ਬਦਨਾਮ **badnām** 'with bad reputation'
ਬਦਬੂ **badbū** 'bad smell'
ਬਦਚਲਨ **badcalan** 'with bad character'

ਬਾ- **bā-** ('with')

ਬਾਕਾਇਦਾ **bākāidā** 'regularly'
ਬਾਇੱਜ਼ਤ **bāizzat** 'honourably'
ਬਾਅਸਰ **bāasar** 'effective'

ਬੇ- **be-** ('without')

ਬੇਕਾਰ **bekār** 'useless'
ਬੇਸ਼ਰਮ **beśaram** 'shameless'
ਬੇਗੁਨਾਹ **begunāh** 'guiltless'

17.2.2 Commonly used suffixes

Commonly used suffixes in Panjabi are more numerous and less regular or productive. We list some of them below.

This list of Panjabi prefixes and suffixes is not exhaustive. A good grammar book for college students (such as Duggal 2011) can provide a more comprehensive list.

-ਊ -ū ('doer', 'for')
ਕਮਾਊ **kamāū** 'earner'
ਗੁਆਊ **guāū** 'waster'
ਵਿਕਾਊ **vikāū** 'for sale'

-ਆਈ -āī ('action/quality of')
ਸਚਾਈ **sacāī** 'truth'
ਧੁਆਈ **d^huāī** 'action of washing'
ਵਡਿਆਈ **vadiāī** 'action of praising'

-ਆਰ -ār ('doer of')
ਸੁਨਿਆਰ **sūniār** 'goldsmith'
ਲੁਹਾਰ **luhār** 'blacksmith'
ਚਮਾਰ **camār** 'leather worker'

-ਆਲੂ -ālū ('full of')
ਸ਼ਰਧਾਲੂ **śard^hālū** 'full of devotion'
ਝਗੜਾਲੂ **j^hagṛālū** 'quarrelsome'
ਕਿਰਪਾਲੂ **kirpālū** 'full of mercy'

-ਆਵਲੀ -āvalī ('row/collection of')
ਸ਼ਬਦਾਵਲੀ **śabdāvalī** 'glossary'
ਬੰਸਾਵਲੀ **bansāvalī** 'family tree'
ਦੀਪਾਵਲੀ **dīpāvalī** 'row of lamps'

-ਈਅਲ -īal ('habituated')
ਅੜੀਅਲ **aṛīal** 'unbending'
ਸੜੀਅਲ **saṛīal** 'irritable'
ਮਰੀਅਲ **marīal** 'extremely weak'

-ਈਲਾ -īlā ('full of')
ਜੋਸ਼ੀਲਾ **jośīlā** 'full of vigour'
ਸ਼ਰਮੀਲਾ **śarmīlā** 'shy'
ਅਣਖੀਲਾ **aṇk^hīlā** 'full of sense of honour'

-ਹਾਰ -hār ('doing')
ਸਿਰਜਨਹਾਰ **sirjanhār** 'creator'
ਹੋਣਹਾਰ **hoṇhār** 'promising'
ਰੱਖਣਹਾਰ **rakk^hṇhār** 'saviour'

-ਹੀਣ **-hīṇ** ('without')

ਧਨਹੀਣ **d^{h}anhīṇ** 'poor'
ਬਲਹੀਣ **balhīṇ** 'weak'
ਮੱਤਹੀਣ **matthīṇ** 'unwise'

-ਕਾਰ **-kār** ('doer')

ਕਲਾਕਾਰ **kalākār** 'artist'
ਆਗਿਆਕਾਰ **āgiākār** 'obedient'
ਕਹਾਣੀਕਾਰ **kahāṇikār** 'story writer'

-ਕਾਰੀ **-kārī** ('act of')

ਨਿਰਤਕਾਰੀ **niratkārī** 'dancing'
ਚਿਤ੍ਰਕਾਰੀ **citrakārī** 'painting'
ਗੁਣਕਾਰੀ **guṇkārī** 'beneficial'

-ਚੀ **-cī** ('operator')

ਖ਼ਜ਼ਾਨਚੀ **xazāncī** 'treasurer'
ਤੋਪਚੀ **topcī** 'cannon operator'
ਨਿਸ਼ਾਨਚੀ **niśancī** 'marksman'
ਖ਼ਬਰਚੀ **xabarcī** 'news correspondent'

-ਤਾਈ **-tāī** ('quality of')

ਸੂਰਮਤਾਈ **sūramtāī** 'bravery'
ਮੂਰਖਤਾਈ **mūrak^{h}tāī** 'stupidity'
ਮਿੱਤਰਤਾਈ **mittartāī** 'friendship'

-ਦਾਨ **-dān** ('container')

ਕਦਰਦਾਨ **kadardān** 'appreciator'
ਪਾਨਦਾਨ **pāndān** 'container for paans'
ਫੂਲਦਾਨ **p^{h}ūldān** 'vase for flowers'

-ਦਾਇਕ **-dāik** ('giver')

ਅਸਰਦਾਇਕ **asardāik** 'effective'
ਸਿੱਖਿਆਦਾਇਕ **sikk^{h}iādaik** 'didactic'
ਲਾਭਦਾਇਕ **lāb^{h}daik** 'beneficial'

-ਪਨ **-pan** ('quality of')

ਸਾਦਾਪਨ **sādāpan** 'simplicity'
ਕਚੇਰਾਪਨ **kacerāpan** 'immaturity'
ਬਚਪਨ **bacpan** 'childhood'

-ਪੁਣਾ **-puṇā** ('bad trait of')

ਗੁੰਡਪੁਣਾ **gunḍpuṇā** 'bullying behaviour'
ਢੀਠਪੁਣਾ **ḍ^{h}īṭ^{h}puṇā** 'being shameless'
ਮੁੰਡਪੁਣਾ **munḍpuṇā** 'bad boyish behaviour'

-ਮਾਨ **-mān** ('full of')

ਸ਼ਕਤੀਮਾਨ **śaktimān** 'powerful'
ਬੁੱਧੀਮਾਨ **budd^{h}īmān** 'wise'

-ਮਾਰ **-mār** ('killer')

ਚੂਹੇਮਾਰ **cuhemār** 'rat killer'
ਮੱਖੀਮਾਰ **makk^{h}āmār** 'fly killer'
ਮੱਛਰਮਾਰ **mcc^{h}armār** 'mosquito killer'

-ਵਰ **-var** ('possessor')

ਜ਼ੋਰਾਵਰ **zorāvar** 'powerful'
ਤਾਕਤਵਰ **takatvar** 'powerful'
ਨਾਮਵਰ **nāmvar** 'famous'

-ੜਾ **-ṛā** ('diminutive/darling)

ਬੱਚੜਾ **baccṛā** 'little child'
ਬਾਲੜੀ **bālṛī** 'lovely little girl'
ਬੁੱਢੜਾ **buḍḍṛā** 'weak old man'
ਯਾਰੜਾ **yārṛā** 'dear friend'

17.2.2.2 Suffixes borrowed from or via Persian

-ਆਨਾ **-ānā** ('related to')

ਸੂਫ਼ੀਆਨਾ **sūfīānā** 'related to Sufi way of thinking
ਸ਼ਾਇਰਾਨਾ **śāirānā** 'poetic'
ਆਸ਼ਿਕਾਨਾ **āśikānā** 'romantic'

-ਆਨੀ **-ānī** ('related to')

ਰੂਹਾਨੀ **rūhānī** 'spiritual'
ਨੂਰਾਨੀ **nūrānī** 'resplendent'
ਜਿਸਮਾਨੀ **jismānī** 'bodily, physical'

-ਖ਼ਾਨਾ **-xānā** ('house of')

ਡਾਕਖ਼ਾਨਾ **dākxānā** 'post office'
ਦਵਾਖ਼ਾਨਾ **davāxānā** 'hospital, dispensary'
ਬੁੱਚੜਖ਼ਾਨਾ **buccaṛxānā** 'slaughter house'

-ਖ਼ੋਰ **-xor** ('eater')

ਆਦਮਖ਼ੋਰ **ādamxor** 'man eater'
ਹਰਾਮਖ਼ੋਰ **harāmxor** 'living on illegal income'
ਰਿਸ਼ਵਤਖ਼ੋਰ **riśvatxor** 'bribe taker'

-ਗਰ **-gar** ('practitioner')

ਜਾਦੂਗਰ **jādūgar** 'magician'
ਕਾਰੀਗਰ **kārīgar** 'expert'
ਸਿਤਮਗਰ **sitamgar** 'tormenter'

-ਦਾਰ **-dār** ('owner')

ਦੁਕਾਨਦਾਰ **dukāndār** 'shopkeeper'
ਜ਼ਿਮੀਂਦਾਰ **zimīdār** 'land owner'
ਸਰਮਾਏਦਾਰ **sarmāedār** 'capitalist'

-ਬਾਜ਼ **-bāz** ('practitioner')

ਚਾਲਬਾਜ਼ **calbāz** 'trickster'
ਜੰਗਬਾਜ਼ **jangbāz** 'warmonger'
ਪੱਤੇਬਾਜ਼ **pattebāz** 'deceiver in card games'

-ਬਾਨ **-bān** ('carer')

ਬਾਗ਼ਬਾਨ **baɣbān** 'gardener'
ਮੇਹਰਬਾਨ **meharbān** 'merciful'

-ਮੰਦ **-mand** ('full of')

ਅਕਲਮੰਦ **akalmand** 'intelligent'
ਸਿਹਤਮੰਦ **sihatmand** 'healthy'
ਦੌਲਤਮੰਦ **daulatmand** 'wealthy'

17.2.3 Arabic and Persian suffixes used by speakers of Panjabi

Many speakers of Panjabi who also speak Urdu use Arabic and Persian grammatical endings (especially plural endings) in the words borrowed from Arabic and Persian in their Panjabi speech as well. The most commonly used words with the Arabic and Persian grammatical endings are given below.

ਅਖ਼ਬਾਰ **axbār** 'newspaper'	ਅਖ਼ਬਾਰਾਤ **axbārāt** 'newspapers'
ਆਲਿਮ **ālim** 'scholar'	ਉਲਮਾ **ulmā** 'scholars'

ਇੰਤਜ਼ਾਮ **intzām** 'arrangement'	ਇੰਤਜ਼ਾਮਾਤ **intzāmāt** 'arrangements'
ਸਵਾਲ **savāl** 'question'	ਸਵਾਲਾਤ **savālāt** 'questions'
ਸ਼ਖ਼ਸ **śaxs** 'person'	ਸ਼ਖ਼ਸਾਤ **śaxāt** 'persons'
ਕ਼ਾਇਦਾ **qāidā** 'rule'	ਕ਼ਵਾਇਦ **qavāid** 'rules'
ਖ਼ਰਚ **xarc** 'expense'	ਅਖ਼ਰਾਜਾਤ **axrājāt** 'expenses'
ਖ਼ਾਤੂਨ **xātūn** 'woman'	ਖ਼ਵਾਤੀਨ **xavātīn** 'women'
ਮੁਲਕ **mulk** 'country'	ਮੁਮਾਲਿਕ **mumālik** 'countries'
ਮੋਮਿਨ **momin** 'believer'	ਮੋਮਿਨੀਨ **mominīn** 'believers'
ਵਕੀਲ **vakīl** 'lawyer'	ਵੁਕਲਾ **vuklā** 'lawyers'
ਵਜ਼ੀਰ **vazīr** 'minister'	ਵੁਜ਼ਰਾ **vuzrā** 'ministers'

17.2.4 Summing up the Arabic and Persian "influence" on Panjabi grammar

There is a lot of misunderstanding about the "influence" of Persian and Arabic on Panjabi, even among some educated speakers of the language. So this alleged "influence" needs to be carefully examined.

1. Arabic and Persian contributed the Perso-Arabic script (mostly in the Persian or Nastaliq style) to Indian languages including Panjabi. For centuries, nearly all the Muslim writers and many Sikh and Hindu writers have been using this script for writing Panjabi. But this script (now known as Shahmukhi when used for writing Panjabi in Pakistan) has been unable to replace the native Gurmukhi script, which is now used a lot more than Shahmukhi for writing Panjabi.

2. Arabic and Persian contributed hundreds of words to the Panjabi word stock. Many of these words have become so common in everyday speech that they are not felt to be of foreign origin. But other languages like Turkish, Portuguese and, more recently English, also contributed words to Panjabi. Many Panjabi words come from the Indian languages of the Dravidian and Munda families as well.

3. But the "influence" of Arabic and Persian on Panjabi *grammar* is extremely limited and almost negligible. The borrowed prefixes and suffixes mentioned above are used almost exclusively in the

borrowed words. Only a few like ਬੇ- **-be** 'without', -ਖ਼ਾਨਾ **-xānā** and -ਖ਼ੋਰ **-xor** (mostly pronounced as -ਖਾਨਾ **-k^{h}ānā** and -ਖੋਰ **-k^{h}or** respectively) have become productive and are used with the native Panjabi words as in ਬੇਘਰ **beg^{h}ar** 'homeless', ਕੰਜਰਖਾਨਾ **kanjark^{h}ānā** 'brothel' and ਵੱਢੀਖੋਰ **vaḍḍ^{h}ik^{h}or** 'bribe taker'.

4. An example of a serious and deep influence of one language or a group of languages on the *grammar* of another language or group of language is the **serial verb constructions** in the Indian languages of all the families. As we saw in Chapter 13, serial verbs are the hub of a clause-level construction in Panjabi. This is the case with all the languages spoken in the Indian sub-continent. Most serial verb constructions in the South Indian Dravidian languages are at a more advanced agglutinative stage. So it is possibe that the North Indian Indo-European languages borrowed this grammatical feature from their Dravidian neighbours through millennia of extremely close *geographical* and *cultural* contact. But more research and analysis is needed to establish this influence. Masica (1976) made a detailed study of the grammatical features shared by all the major (and possibly all) Indian languages. Some of these features may be related to the influence of the common and shared culture. The grammar of a language enshrines a culture's way of conceptualising and symbolising reality. The "influence" of Arabic and Persian on Panjabi *grammar* (the subject of this book) in this sense is non-existent (and would have been historically impossible anyway). It is limited to a few *deliberately* used morphological endings in some borrowed words in the speech of some educated people. But common people use the Panjabi endings with these words. If an educated Panjabi speaker says *buses*, *trains*, *schools*, *colleges*, *copies*, *telephones* etc. instead of the Panjabi-ised versions **basā̃**, **ṭrenā̃**, **sakūlā̃**, **kālijā̃**, **kāpīā̃**, **ṭa^{l}līfonā̃**, this does not constitute the "influence" of English on Panjabi grammar.

Grammatically, Panjabi is an Indic language descended from Vedic. The work of the great Sanskrit linguists can help us understand the grammatical structure of Panjabi. The great and insightful work of the Arab and Persian linguists over the past centuries is useful for understanding *their* languages, but is irrelevant in a study of the grammar of modern Indic languages including Panjabi.

17.3 A semi-productive way of deriving verbs in Panjabi

In Panjabi, you can add the **verb** ਹੋ **ho** 'become' or ਕਰ **kar** 'do' to many **nouns** or **adjectives** to derive **intransitive** and **transitive verbs** respectively. For example, you can add ਹੋ **ho** or ਕਰ **kar** to the **adjective** ਬੀਮਾਰ **bīmār** 'ill' to derive the verbs ਬੀਮਾਰ ਹੋ **bīmār ho** 'become ill' and ਬੀਮਾਰ ਕਰ **bīmār kar** 'make ill'.

Since verbs are listed in the gerund form in a Panjabi dictionary (and are also cited in this form by speakers of Panjabi), we will refer these verbs as ਬੀਮਾਰ ਹੋਣਾ **bīmār hoṇā** and ਬੀਮਾਰ ਕਰਨਾ **bīmār karnā** respectively in this order (see Appendix 1). Other examples are ਪੈਦਾ ਹੋਣਾ **pa^{i}dā hoṇā** 'being born' and ਪੈਦਾ ਕਰਨਾ **pa^{i}dā karnā** 'give birth to'. ਹੋਣਾ **hoṇā** and ਕਰਨਾ **karnā** are both used with **adjectives**, but ਕਰਨਾ **karnā** is also, and more often, used with **nouns** to derive **transitive verbs** such as ਮਦਦ ਕਰਨਾ **madad karnā** 'doing help' or 'helping' and ਰੰਗ ਕਰਨਾ **rang karnā** 'doing colour' or 'painting' and ਵਿਆਹ ਕਰਨਾ **viāh karnā** 'doing marriage' or 'marrying'. An example will make this grammatical process clear.

> ਪਹਿਲਾਂ ਅਸੀਂ *ਵਿਆਹ ਕੀਤਾ*, ਤੇ ਫਿਰ ਦੋ ਬੱਚੇ *ਪੈਦਾ ਕੀਤੇ*, ਜਿਹਨਾਂ ਨੇ ਵੱਡੇ ਹੋ ਕੇ ਸਾਡੀ ਜ਼ਿੰਦਗੀ ਨੂੰ ਬਹੁਤ *ਸੁਖੀ ਕੀਤਾ*।
> **pahilā̃ asī̃ *viāh kītā*, te p^{h}ir do bacce *pa^{i}dā kīte*, jihnā̃ ne *vaḍḍe ho* ke sāḍī zindagī nū̃ bahut *suk^{h}ī kītā***
> 'At first we married, and then gave birth to two children, who, after growing up, made our life very happy'

In this sentence the speaker uses

> ਵਿਆਹ ਕੀਤਾ **viāh kītā** 'marriage did'
> ਪੈਦਾ ਕੀਤੇ **pa^{i}dā kīte** 'born did'
> ਵੱਡੇ ਹੋ ਕੇ **vaḍḍe ho ke** 'after becoming grown up'
> ਸੁਖੀ ਕੀਤਾ **suk^{h}ī kītā** 'happy did'

This process, is only *semi-productive*. It cannot be used with all adjectives and nouns.

It is worth mentioning that ਕਰਨਾ **karnā** 'doing', 'making' is a suppletive causative form of ਹੋਣਾ **hoṇā** 'becoming' as shown in the tables in the next section.

17.4 Other frequently used combinations and "ingestive" verbs

Some other frequently used **noun+verb** or **adjective+verb** or **adverb+verb** combinations are attaining or have attained the status of verbs. Examples are

ਅਗਾਂਹ ਵਧਣਾ **agā̃h vad^{h}ṇā** 'moving forward'
ਪਿਛਾਂਹ ਪਰਤਣਾ **pic^{h}ā̃h partṇā** 'coming back'
ਠੋਕਵਾਂ ਜਵਾਬ ਦੇਣਾ **ṭ^{h}okvā̃ javāb deṇā** 'giving a befitting answer'
ਧੋਖਾ ਦੇਣਾ **d^{h}ok^{h}ā deṇā** 'giving deception'
ਬਦਲਾ ਲੈਣਾ **badlā la^{i}ṇā** 'taking revenge'

"Ingestive" verbs

Many idiomatic expressions in Panjabi, Hindi-Urdu and other Indian languages involve the use of the verbs ਖਾਣਾ 'to eat' and ਪੀਣਾ 'to drink'. But the actions denoted by such idioms do not literally involve eating and drinking, just as the English idiom *kick the bucket* does not involve the actual kicking of a physical bucket! Some examples of "ingestive" idioms in Panjabi are:

ਸਿਗਰਟ ਪੀਣਾ **sigraṭ pīṇā**	'to smoke a cigarette' (*Lit.* 'drinking a cigarette')
ਸਿਰ ਖਾਣਾ **sir k^{h}āṇā**	'to bore with non-stop talking' (*Lit.* 'eating the head')
ਹੁੱਕਾ ਪੀਣਾ **hukkā pīṇā**	'to smoke a hookah' (*Lit.* 'drinking a hookah')
ਕੰਨ ਖਾਣਾ **kann k^{h}āṇā**	'to talk noisily, to make a noise' (*Lit.* 'eating ears')
ਕੁੱਟ ਖਾਣਾ **kuṭṭ k^{h}āṇā**	'to receive a beating' (*Lit.* 'eating a beating')
ਖੇਹ ਖਾਣਾ **k^{h}eh k^{h}āṇā**	'to indulge in useless activities' (*Lit.* 'eating dust')
ਗਰਮੀ ਖਾਣਾ **garmī k^{h}āṇā**	'to lose one's cool' (*Lit.* 'eating heat')
ਗਾਹਲ਼ਾਂ ਖਾਣਾ **gāhḷā̃ k^{h}āṇā**	'to receive verbal abuse' (*Lit.* 'eating abuses')
ਗਾਂਜਾ ਪੀਣਾ **gā̃jā pīṇā**	'to smoke cannabis' (*Lit.* 'drinking cannabis')

ਛਿੱਤਰ ਖਾਣਾ **c^{h}ittar k^{h}āṇā**	'to be beaten' (*Lit.* 'eating broken shoes')

(ਲਿੱਤਰ ਖਾਣਾ **littar k^{h}āṇā** is also used in some areas)

ਜੁੱਤੀਆਂ ਖਾਣਾ **juttīā̃ k^{h}āṇā**	'to be beaten' (*Lit.* 'eating shoes')
ਝਿੜਕਾਂ ਖਾਣਾ **j^{h}iṛkā̃ k^{h}āṇā**	'to receive rebukes' (*Lit.* 'eating rebukes')
ਠੋਕਰ ਖਾਣਾ **ṭ^{h}okar k^{h}āṇā**	'to stumble' (*Lit.* 'eating a knock')
ਡੰਡੇ ਖਾਣਾ **ḍaṇḍe k^{h}āṇā**	'to be beaten' (*Lit.* 'eating rods')

(Real shoes or rods may or may not be used in the act)

ਧੋਖਾ ਖਾਣਾ **d^{h}ok^{h}ā k^{h}āṇā**	'to be deceived' (*Lit.* 'eating deception')
ਭੁਲੇਖਾ ਖਾਣਾ **b^{h}ulek^{h}ā k^{h}āṇā**	'to misunderstand' (*Lit.* 'eating misunderstanding')
ਰਿਸ਼ਵਤ ਖਾਣਾ **riśvat k^{h}āṇā**	'to receive a bribe' (*Lit.* 'eating bribe')
ਵੱਢੀ ਖਾਣਾ **vaḍḍ^{h}ī k^{h}āṇā**	as above
ਲਹੂ ਪੀਣਾ **lahū pīṇā**	'to torment someone' 'to exploit someone financially' (*Lit.* 'drinking blood')

These actions are frequently cited this way. But, syntactically, they are used as **transitive verb**+OBJECT as in

ਅੱਜ ਉਹਨੇ ਚੰਗੀ ਕੁੱਟ ਖਾਧੀ
ajj uhne cangī kuṭṭ k^{h}ād^{h}ī
'He received a sound beating today'
Lit. 'He ate a good beating today'

ਤੁਸੀਂ ਸਿਗਰਟ ਬਹੁਤ ਪੀਂਦੇ ਹੋ
tusī̃ sigraṭ bahut pī̃de ho
'You smoke too much'
Lit. 'You drink cigarette too much'

17.5 Phases of Panjabi verbs

Additive and **subtractive phases** of some Panjabi verbs were discussed in Chapter 9, where the additive phases of some important verbs were given and it was mentioned that every additive phase has a corresponding subtractive phase derived by adding the infix -ਈ- **-ī-** to the stem before the inflectional ending.

But the nice picture of some verbs having regular phases given in that chapter is far from the real situation. There is considerable irregularity in the application of the productive rule. In reality, some verbs do not have one or two phases, and some *possible* phases of some verbs are not *actually* used at all. The following tables show this. The addition of the productive endings -ਆ **-ā** and -ਵਾ **-vā** to some verbs would produce unpronounceable results. ਆ **ā** 'come', ਜਾ **jā** 'go' and ਲੈ **la[i]** 'take' are such verbs. So suppletion has to be resorted to, as the tables show. For example, the causative form of ਲੈ **la[i]** 'take' is ਦੇ **de** 'give'. 'Giving' something to someone is the same thing as making them 'take' it. Perfectly logical!

The exact nature of the process of the creation of the different **phases** of a Panjabi verb can be a debatable issue – whether it is **inflection** or **derivation**. Arguments can be given in favour of both the processes. It would be like debating whether the tomato is a fruit or a vegetable. Sensible people *use* the tomato without asking this question. Similarly, as sensible learners you should *use* these phases correctly without wasting your time in asking whether the process of deriving these phases is inflection or derivation.

The following tables give the **basic** and **additive phases** of Panjabi verbs classified as **intransitive** (*vi*) or **transitive** (*vt*). The tables are arranged in the order followed by the modern Panjabi dictionaries. (See Appendix 1). The words put in the brackets in these tables are **suppletives**.

ੳ				
ਉੱਠਣਾ **uṭṭʰṇā**	*vi*	rise	ਉਠਾਉਣਾ **uṭʰāuṇā**	ਉਠਵਾਉਣਾ **uṭʰvāuṇā**
ਉਡੀਕਣਾ **uḍīkṇā**	*vi*	to wait		
ਉਤਰਨਾ **utarnā**	*vi*	come down	ਉਤਾਰਨਾ **utārnā**	ਉਤਰਵਾਉਣਾ **utarvāuṇā**

ਉਬਲਣਾ **ubalṇā**	*vi*	boil	ਉਬਾਲਣਾ **ubālṇā**	
ਉਲਟਣਾ **ulṭṇā**	*vi/vt*	reverse	ਉਲਟਾਉਣਾ **ulṭāuṇā**	ਉਲਟਵਾਉਣਾ **ulṭvāuṇā**
ਉੜਨਾ **uṛṇā**	*vi*	fly	ਉੜਾਉਣਾ **uṛāuṇā**	ਉੜਵਾਉਣਾ **uṛvāuṇā**

ਅ				
ਅਟਕਣਾ **aṭkṇā**	*vi*	stop	ਅਟਕਾਉਣਾ **aṭkāuṇā**	
ਆਉਣਾ **āuṇā**	*vi*	come		(ਮੰਗਵਾਉਣਾ) **(mãgvāuṇā)**
ਆਖਣਾ **āk^{h}ṇā**	*vt*	say		ਅਖਵਾਉਣਾ **ak^{h}vāuṇā**

ਸ				
ਸਕਣਾ **sakṇā**	*vi*	be able to		
ਸੱਦਣਾ **saddṇā**	*vt*	invite	ਸਦਾਉਣਾ **sadāuṇā**	ਸਦਵਾਉਣਾ **sadvāuṇā**
ਸੰਭਾਲਣਾ **sam-** **b^{h}ālṇā**	*vt*	take care of		
ਸਮਝਣਾ **samj^{h}ṇā**	*vi*	understand	ਸਮਝਾਉਣਾ **samj^{h}āuṇā**	
ਸਾਂਭਣਾ **sā̃b^{h}ṇā**	*vt*	take care of		
ਸਿਕਣਾ **sikṇā**	*vi*	get warmed/ heated	ਸੇਕਣਾ **sekṇā**	ਸਿਕਾਉਣਾ **sikāuṇā** ਸਿਕਵਾਉਣਾ **sikvāuṇā**
ਸਿੱਖਣਾ **sikk^{h}ṇā**	*vt*	learn	ਸਿਖਾਉਣਾ **sik^{h}āuṇā**	ਸਿਖਵਾਉਣਾ **sik^{h}vāuṇā**
ਸਿਮਰਨਾ **simarnā**	*vt*	mutter		

ਸੁਆਰਨਾ **suārnā**	*vt*	brush up		
ਸੁੱਟਣਾ **suṭṭṇā**	*vt*	throw	ਸੁਟਾਉਣਾ **suṭāuṇā**	ਸੁਟਵਾਉਣਾ **suṭvāuṇā**
ਸੁਣਨਾ **suṇnā**	*vi/vt*	hear	ਸੁਣਾਉਣਾ **suṇāuṇā**	ਸੁਣਵਾਉਣਾ **suṇvāuṇā**
ਸੌਣਾ **saᵘṇā**	*vi*	sleep	ਸੁਲ਼ਾਉਣਾ **suḷāuṇā**	ਸੁਲ਼ਵਾਉਣਾ **suḷvāuṇā**
ਹ				
ਹੱਸਣਾ **hassṇā**	*vi*	laugh	ਹਸਾਉਣਾ **hasāuṇā**	
ਹਟਣਾ **haṭṇā**	*vi*	move away	ਹਟਾਉਣਾ **haṭāuṇā**	ਹਟਵਾਉਣਾ **haṭvāuṇā**
ਹਾਰਨਾ **hārnā**	*vi*	lose	ਹਰਾਉਣਾ **harāuṇā**	ਹਰਵਾਉਣਾ **harvāuṇā**
ਹਿੱਲਣਾ **hillṇā**	*vi*	move	ਹਿਲਾਉਣਾ **hilāuṇā**	ਹਿਲਵਾਉਣਾ **hilvāuṇā**
ਹੋਣਾ **hoṇā**	*vi*	be, happen	(ਕਰਨਾ) **karnā**	(ਕਰਵਾਉਣਾ) **karvāuṇā**
ਕ				
ਕਹਿਣਾ **kahiṇā**	*vt*	say	ਕਹਾਉਣਾ **kahāuṇā**	
ਕੱਜਣਾ **kajjṇā**	*vt*	cover		
ਕੱਟਣਾ **kaṭṭṇā**	*vt*	cut	ਕਟਾਉਣਾ **kaṭāuṇā**	ਕਟਵਾਉਣਾ **kaṭvāuṇā**
ਕੱਢਣਾ **kaḍḍʰṇā**	*vt*	take out	ਕਢਾਉਣਾ **kaḍʰāuṇā**	ਕਢਵਾਉਣਾ **kaḍʰvāuṇā**
ਕੱਤਣਾ **kattṇā**	*vt*	spin	ਕਤਾਉਣਾ **katāuṇā**	ਕਤਵਾਉਣਾ **katvāuṇā**
ਕੁਤਰਨਾ **kutarnā**	*vt*	cut into small pieces		ਕੁਤਰਵਾਉਣਾ **kutarvāuṇā**

ਕੰਬਣਾ **kambaṇā**	*vi*	tremble		
ਕਰਨਾ **karnā**	*vt*	do	ਕਰਾਉਣਾ **karāuṇā**	ਕਰਵਾਉਣਾ **karvāuṇā**
ਕੁੱਦਣਾ **kuddṇā**	*vi*	jump	ਕੁਦਾਉਣਾ **kudāuṇā**	ਕੁਦਵਾਉਣਾ **kudvāuṇā**
ਖ				
ਖੱਟਣਾ **k^{h}aṭṭṇā**	*vt*	earn		
ਖ਼ਰਚਣਾ **xarcṇā**	*vt*	spend	ਖ਼ਰਚਾਉਣਾ **xarcāuṇā**	ਖ਼ਰਚਵਾਉਣਾ **xarcvāuṇā**
ਖੜ੍ਹਨਾ **k^{h}aṛhnā**	*vi*	to stand		
ਖੜਕਾਉਣਾ **kaṛkā-** **uṇā**	*vi*	to knock at		ਖੜਕਵਾਉਣਾ **k^{h}aṛkvāuṇā**
ਖਾਣਾ **k^{h}āṇā**	*vt*	eat	ਖਿਲ਼ਾਉਣਾ **k^{h}iḷāuṇā** ਖੁਆਉਣਾ **k^{h}uāuṇā**	ਖਿਲ਼ਵਾਉਣਾ **k^{h}iḷvāuṇā**
ਖਿੱਚਣਾ **k^{h}iccṇā**	*vt*	pull	ਖਿਚਾਉਣਾ **k^{h}icāuṇā**	ਖਿਚਵਾਉਣਾ **k^{h}icvāuṇā**
ਖੇਡਣਾ **k^{h}eḍṇā**	*vi/vt*	play	ਖਿਡਾਉਣਾ **k^{h}iḍāuṇā**	ਖਿਡਵਾਉਣਾ **k^{h}iḍvāuṇā**
ਖੇਲ੍ਹਣਾ **k^{h}elhṇā**	*vi/vt*	play	ਖਿਲਾਉਣਾ **k^{h}ilhāuṇā**	ਖਿਲਵਾਉਣਾ **k^{h}ilhvāuṇā**
ਖੁੱਭਣਾ **k^{h}ubb^{h}ṇā**	*vi*	get pushed in	ਖੋਭਣਾ **k^{h}ob^{h}ṇā** ਖੁਭੋਣਾ **k^{h}ub^{h}oṇā**	ਖੁਭਵਾਉਣਾ **k^{h}ub^{h}vāuṇā**
ਖੁੱਲ੍ਹਣਾ **k^{h}ullhṇā**	*vi*	open	ਖੋਲ੍ਹਣਾ **k^{h}olhṇā**	ਖੁਲ੍ਹਾਉਣਾ **k^{h}ulhāuṇā** ਖੁਲ੍ਹਵਾਉਣਾ **k^{h}ulhvāuṇā**

ਗ				
ਗਾਉਣਾ **gāuṇā**	*vt*	sing	ਗਵਾਉਣਾ **gavāuṇā**	
ਗਿਣਨਾ **giṇnā**	*vt*	count	ਗਿਣਾਉਣਾ **giṇāuṇā**	ਗਿਣਵਾਉਣਾ **giṇvāuṇā**
ਗਿਰਨਾ **girnā**	*vi*	fall	ਗਿਰਾਉਣਾ **girāuṇā**	ਗਿਰਵਾਉਣਾ **girvāuṇā**
ਗੁਆਚਣਾ **guācṇā**	*vi*	become lost	ਗੁਆਉਣਾ **guāuṇā**	
ਗੁੰਨ੍ਹਣਾ **gunnhṇā**	*vt*	knead	ਗੁੰਨ੍ਹਾਉਣਾ **gunhāuṇā**	ਗੁੰਨ੍ਹਵਾਉਣਾ **gunhvāuṇā**

ਘ				
ਘੱਲਣਾ **g^{h}allṇā**	*vt*	send		
ਘੁੱਟਣਾ **g^{h}uṭṭṇā**	*vt*	hold tightly	ਘੁਟਾਉਣਾ **g^{h}uṭāuṇā**	ਘੁਟਵਾਉਣਾ **g^{h}uṭvāuṇā**
ਘੁੰਮਣਾ **g^{h}ummṇā**	*vi*	rotate	ਘੁਮਾਉਣਾ **g^{h}umāuṇā**	
ਘੁਲਣਾ **g^{h}ulṇā**	*vt*	dissolve	ਘੋਲਣਾ **g^{h}olṇā**	ਘੁਲ਼ਵਾਉਣਾ **g^{h}uḷvāuṇā**
ਘੇਰਨਾ **g^{h}ernā**	*vt*	surround		

ਚ				
ਚਖਣਾ **cak^{h}ṇā**	*vt*	taste	ਚਖਾਉਣਾ **cak^{h}āuṇā**	ਚਖਵਾਉਣਾ **cak^{h}vāuṇā**
ਚੱਟਣਾ **caṭṭṇā**	*vt*	lick	ਚਟਾਉਣਾ **caṭāuṇā**	ਚਟਵਾਉਣਾ **caṭvāuṇā**
ਚੱਬਣਾ **cabbṇā**	*vt*	chew	ਚਬਾਉਣਾ **cabāuṇā**	ਚਬਵਾਉਣਾ **cabvāuṇā**
ਚਲਣਾ **calṇā**	*vi*	move	ਚਲਾਉਣਾ **calāuṇā**	ਚਲਵਾਉਣਾ **calvāuṇā**

ਚੜ੍ਹਨਾ **caṛhṇā**	*vi*	climb, rise	ਚਾੜ੍ਹਨਾ **cāṛhṇā** ਚੜ੍ਹਾਉਣਾ **caṛhāuṇā**	ਚੜ੍ਹਵਾਉਣਾ **caṛhvāuṇā**
ਚਾਹੁਣਾ **cahuṇā**	*vt*	desire		
ਚੀਰਨਾ **cirṇā**	*vt*	saw		ਚਿਰਾਉਣਾ **cirāuṇā** ਚਿਰਵਾਉਣਾ **cirvāuṇā**
ਚੁੱਕਣਾ **cukkṇā**	*vt*	lift, pick up	ਚੁਕਾਉਣਾ **cukāuṇā**	ਚੁਕਵਾਉਣਾ **cukvāuṇā**
ਚੁਣਨਾ **cuṇnā**	*vt*	choose		ਚੁਣਵਾਉਣਾ **cuṇvāuṇā**
ਚੁਰਾਉਣਾ **curāuṇā**	*vt*	steal		

ਛ				
ਛਕਣਾ **c^hakṇā**	*vt*	relish	ਛਕਾਉਣਾ **c^hakāuṇā**	ਛਕਵਾਉਣਾ **c^hakvāuṇā**
ਛੱਡਣਾ **c^haḍḍṇā**	*vt*	give up	ਛੁਡਾਉਣਾ **c^huḍāuṇā** ਛੁੜਾਉਣਾ **c^huṛāuṇā**	ਛੁਡਵਾਉਣਾ **c^huḍvāuṇā** ਛੁੜਵਾਉਣਾ **c^huṛvāuṇā**
ਛਾਣਨਾ **c^hāṇnā**	*vt*	sieve		ਛਣਵਾਉਣਾ **c^hāṇvāuṇā**
ਛਾਪਣਾ **c^hāpṇā**	*vt*	print	ਛਪਾਉਣਾ **c^hapāuṇā**	ਛਪਵਾਉਣਾ **c^hapvāuṇā**
ਛਿੱਕਣਾ **c^hikkṇā**	*vi*	sneeze		
ਛਿੱਲਣਾ **c^hillṇā**	*vt*	peel		ਛਿਲਾਉਣਾ **c^hilāuṇā** ਛਿਲਵਾਉਣਾ **c^hilvāuṇā**

ਛੂਹਣਾ **c^{h}ūhṇā**	*vt*	touch	ਛੁਹਾਉਣਾ **c^{h}uhāuṇā**	
ਜ				
ਜਗਣਾ **jagṇā**	*vi*	light	ਜਗਾਉਣਾ **jagāuṇā**	ਜਗਵਾਉਣਾ **jagvāuṇā**
ਜਪਣਾ **japṇā**	*vt*	mutter	ਜਪਾਉਣਾ **japāuṇā**	ਜਪਵਾਉਣਾ **japvāuṇā**
ਜੰਮਣਾ **jammṇā**	*vi*	be born	ਜਮਾਉਣਾ **jamāuṇā**	ਜਮਵਾਉਣਾ **jamvāuṇā**
ਜਲਣਾ **jalṇā**	*vi*	burn	ਜਲ਼ਾਉਣਾ **jaḷauṇā**	ਜਲ਼ਵਾਉਣਾ **jaḷvāuṇā**
ਜਾਗਣਾ **jāgṇā**	*vi*	wake up	ਜਗਾਉਣਾ **jagāuṇā**	ਜਗਵਾਉਣਾ **jagvāuṇā**
ਜਾਣਾ **jāṇā**	*vi*	go	(ਭੇਜਣਾ) **(b^{h}ejṇā)**	(ਭਿਜਵਾਉਣਾ) **(b^{h}ijvāuṇā)**
ਜਾਣਨਾ **jāṇnā**	*vt*	know		
ਜਾਪਣਾ **jāpṇā**	*vt*	seem		
ਜਿੱਤਣਾ **jittṇā**	*vi/vt*	win, conquer	ਜਿਤਾਉਣਾ **jitāuṇā**	ਜਿਤਵਾਉਣਾ **jitvāuṇā**
ਜੀਉਣਾ **jīuṇā**	*vi*	live		
ਜੁੜਨਾ **juṛṇā**	*vi*	be joined	ਜੋੜਨਾ **joṛṇā**	ਜੁੜਾਉਣਾ **juṛāuṇā** ਜੁੜਵਾਉਣਾ **juṛvāuṇā**
ਝ				
ਝਗੜਨਾ **j^{h}agaṛṇā**	*vi*	quarrel		

ਝੜਨਾ **j^{h}aṛṇā**	*vi*	fall off	ਝਾੜਨਾ **j^{h}āṛṇā**	ਝੜਾਉਣਾ **j^{h}aṛāuṇā** ਝੜਵਾਉਣਾ **j^{h}aṛvāuṇā**
ਝਿੜਕਣਾ **j^{h}iṛkṇā**	*vt*	rebuke		
ਝੁਕਣਾ **j^{h}ukṇā**	*vi*	bow, bend	ਝੁਕਾਉਣਾ **j^{h}ukāuṇā**	ਝੁਕਵਾਉਣਾ **j^{h}ukvāuṇā**
ਝੱਲਣਾ **j^{h}allṇā**	*vi*	tolerate		
ਝੁੱਲਣਾ **j^{h}ullṇā**	*vi*	blow/wave	ਝੁਲਾਉਣਾ **j^{h}ulāuṇā**	ਝੁਲਵਾਉਣਾ **j^{h}ulvāuṇā**
ਟ				
ਟਕਰਾਉਣਾ **ṭakrāuṇā**	*vi*	collide		
ਟੰਗਣਾ **ṭangṇā**	*vt*	hang		ਟੰਗਾਉਣਾ **ṭãgāuṇā** ਟੰਗਵਾਉਣਾ **ṭãgvāuṇā**
ਟੱਪਣਾ **ṭappṇā**	*vi*	jump	ਟਪਾਉਣਾ **ṭapāuṇā**	ਟਪਵਾਉਣਾ **ṭapvāuṇā**
ਟਾਲਣਾ **ṭālṇā**	*vt*	put off		ਟਲ਼ਵਾਉਣਾ **ṭalvāuṇā**
ਟਿਕਣਾ **ṭikṇā**	*vi*	stay	ਟਿਕਾਉਣਾ **ṭikāuṇā**	ਟਿਕਵਾਉਣਾ **ṭikvāuṇā**
ਟੁੱਟਣਾ **ṭuṭṭṇā**	*vi*	break	(ਤੋੜਨਾ) **(toṛnā)**	(ਤੁੜਾਉਣਾ) **(tuṛāuṇā)** (ਤੁੜਵਾਉਣਾ) **(tuṛvāuṇā)**
ਠ				
ਠਹਿਰਨਾ **ṭ^{h}ahirnā**	*vi*	stay	ਠਹਿਰਾਉਣਾ **ṭ^{h}ahirāuṇā**	ਠਹਿਰਵਾਉਣਾ **ṭ^{h}ahirvāuṇā**

ਠਾਰਨਾ **ṭʰārnā**	*vt*	make cool		ਠਰਵਾਉਣਾ **ṭʰavāurṇā**
ਠੁਕਣਾ **ṭʰukṇā**	*vi*	to get beaten	ਠੋਕਣਾ **ṭʰokṇā**	ਠੁਕਾਉਣਾ **ṭʰukāuṇā** ਠੁਕਵਾਉਣਾ **ṭʰukvāuṇā**
ਡ				
ਡੱਸਣਾ **ḍassṇā**	*vt*	sting, bite		ਡਸਵਾਉਣਾ **ḍasvāuṇā**
ਡੱਕਣਾ **ḍakkṇā**	*vt*	stop		ਡਕਵਾਉਣਾ **ḍakvāuṇā**
ਡੰਗਣਾ **ḍangṇā**	*vt*	sting, bite		ਡੰਗਵਾਉਣਾ **ḍangvāuṇā**
ਡਟਣਾ **ḍaṭṇā**	*vi*	stand firm		
ਡਰਨਾ **ḍarṇā**	*vi*	be afraid	ਡਰਾਉਣਾ **ḍarāuṇā**	
ਡਾਂਟਣਾ **ḍā̃ṭṇā**	*vt*	rebuke		
ਡਿਗਣਾ **ḍigṇā**	*vi*	fall	ਡੇਗਣਾ **ḍegṇā**	ਡਿਗਾਉਣਾ **ḍigāuṇā** ਡਿਗਵਾਉਣਾ **ḍigvāuṇā**
ਡੁੱਬਣਾ **ḍubbṇā**	*vi*	sink	ਡੁਬੋਣਾ **ḍuboṇā**	
ਡੁੱਲ੍ਹਣਾ **ḍullhṇā**	*vi*	spill	ਡੋਲ੍ਹਣਾ **ḍolhṇā**	ਡੁਲ੍ਹਵਾਉਣਾ **ḍulhvāuṇā**
ਢ				
ਢਹਿਣਾ **ḍʰahiṇā**	*vi*	fall down	ਢਾਹੁਣਾ **ḍʰāhuṇā**	ਢਹਾਉਣਾ **ḍʰahāuṇā**
ਢਕਣਾ **ḍʰakṇā**	*vt*	to cover		

ਢਲਣਾ **ḍ^{h}alṇā**	*vi*	melt	ਢਾਲਣਾ **ḍ^{h}ālṇā**	ਢਲ਼ਾਉਣਾ **ḍ^{h}aḷāuṇā** ਢਲ਼ਵਾਉਣਾ **ḍ^{h}aḷvāuṇā**
ਤ				
ਤੱਕਣਾ **takkṇā**	*vt*	look		
ਤਰਨਾ **tarnā**	*vi*	swim, float	ਤਾਰਨਾ **tārnā** ਤਰਾਉਣਾ **tarāuṇā**	ਤਰਵਾਉਣਾ **tarvāuṇā**
ਤਲਣਾ **talṇā** ਤਲ਼ਨਾ **taḷṇā**	*vt*	deep fry	ਤਲ਼ਾਉਣਾ **taḷāuṇā**	ਤਲ਼ਵਾਉਣਾ **taḷvāuṇā**
ਤੜਫਣਾ **taṛp^{h}aṇā**	*vi*	writhe in pain	ਤੜਫਾਉਣਾ **taṛp^{h}auṇā**	
ਤੁੜਕਣਾ **tuṛakṇā**	*vt*	fry		
ਤਾੜਨਾ **tāṛnā**	*vt*	rebuke		
ਤਿਆਗਣਾ **tiāgṇā**	*vt*	abandon		
ਤਿਲ੍ਹਕਣਾ **tilhkṇā**	*vi*	slip		
ਤੁਰਨਾ **turnā**	*vi*	walk, move	ਤੋਰਨਾ **tornā** ਤੁਰਾਉਣਾ **turāuṇā**	ਤੁਰਵਾਉਣਾ **turvāuṇā**
ਤੋੜਨਾ **toṛṇā**	*vt*	break	ਤੁੜਾਉਣਾ **tuṛāuṇā**	ਤੁੜਵਾਉਣਾ **tuṛvāuṇā**

ਥ				
ਥੱਕਣਾ **t^{h}akkṇā**	*vi*	become tired	ਥਕਾਉਣਾ **t^{h}akāuṇā**	
ਥਾਪੜਨਾ **t^{h}āpaṛnā**	*vt*	tap, pat		
ਥਾਪੜਨਾ **t^{h}āpaṛnā**	*vt*	beat	ਥਪੜਾਉਣਾ **t^{h}āpṛāuṇā**	
ਥੁੱਕਣਾ **t^{h}ukkṇā**	*vi*	spit		

ਦ				
ਦੱਸਣਾ **dassṇā**	*vt*	tell		
ਦਫ਼ਨਾਉਣਾ **dafnāuṇā**	*vt*	bury (a dead body)		
ਦੱਬਣਾ **dabbṇā**	*vt*	bury, press down	ਦਬਾਉਣਾ **dabāuṇā**	
ਦਿਸਣਾ **disṇā**	*vi*	be visible		
ਦੁਹਰਾਉਣਾ **duhrāuṇā**	*vt*	revise, repeat		
ਦੁਖਣਾ **duk^{h}ṇā**	*vi*	ache	ਦੁਖਾਉਣਾ **duk^{h}āuṇā**	ਦੁਖਵਾਉਣਾ **duk^{h}vāuṇā**
ਦੇਖਣਾ **dek^{h}ṇā**	*vt*	see	ਦਿਖਾਉਣਾ **dik^{h}āuṇā**	ਦਿਖਵਾਉਣਾ **dik^{h}vāuṇā**
ਦੇਣਾ **deṇā**	*vt*	give	ਦੁਆਉਣਾ **duāuṇā**	
ਦੌੜਨਾ **dauṛnā**	*vi*	run	ਦੁੜਾਉਣਾ **duṛāuṇā**	ਦੁੜਵਾਉਣਾ **duṛvāuṇā**

ਧ				
ਧੱਕਣਾ **d^{h}akkṇā**	*vt*	push		

ਧੜਕਣਾ **d^haṛkṇā**	*vi*	palpitate		
ਧਾਰਨਾ **d^hārnā**	*vt*	resolve		
ਧੋਣਾ **d^hoṇā**	*vt*	wash	ਧੁਆਉਣਾ **d^huāuṇā**	

ਨ				
ਨੱਸਣਾ **nassṇā**	*vi*	run	ਨਸਾਉਣਾ **nasāuṇā**	
ਨਹਾਉਣਾ **nahāuṇā**	*vi*	have a bath		
ਨੱਚਣਾ **naccṇā**	*vi*	dance	ਨਚਾਉਣਾ **nacāuṇā**	ਨਚਵਾਉਣਾ **nacvāuṇā**
ਨਚੋੜਨਾ **nacoṛnā**	*vt*	squeeze		
ਨੱਠਣਾ **naṭṭ^{h}ṇā**	*vi*	run	ਨਠਾਉਣਾ **naṭ^{h}āuṇā**	ਨਠਵਾਉਣਾ **naṭ^{h}vāuṇā**
ਨ੍ਹਾਉਣਾ **nhāuṇā**	*vi*	have a bath	ਨਲ੍ਹਾਉਣਾ **naḷhāuṇā**	
ਨਾਪਣਾ **nāpṇā**	*vt*	measure		
ਨਬੇੜਨਾ **nabeṛṇā**	*vt*	finish		
ਨਿਗਲਣਾ **nigalṇā**	*vt*	to swallow		
ਨਿਚੋੜਨਾ **nicoṛnā**	*vt*	squeeze		
ਨਿਭਾਉਣਾ **nib^{h}āuṇā**	*vt*	fulfil		

ਪ				
ਪਹੁੰਚਣਾ **pahũcṇā**	*vi*	reach	ਪਹੁੰਚਾਉਣਾ **pahũcāuṇā**	
ਪਹਿਨਣਾ **pahinṇā**	*vt*	wear	ਪਹਿਨਾਉਣਾ **pahināuṇā**	
ਪੱਕਣਾ **pakkṇā**	*vi*	ripen	ਪਕਾਉਣਾ **pakāuṇā**	
ਪਕੜਨਾ **pakaṛnā**	*vt*	catch, hold	ਪਕੜਾਉਣਾ **pakaṛāuṇā**	ਪਕੜਵਾਉਣਾ **pakaṛvāuṇā**
ਪਚਣਾ **pacṇā**	*vi*	be digested	ਪਚਾਉਣਾ **pacāuṇā**	
ਪਛਤਾਉਣਾ **pac^htā-uṇā**	*vi*	repent		
ਪਰਖਣਾ **park^hṇā**	*vt*	judge		
ਪਰਤਣਾ **partṇā**	*vt*	turn over/ return	ਪਰਤਾਉਣਾ **partāuṇā**	
ਪੜ੍ਹਨਾ **parhṇā**	*vt*	read	ਪੜ੍ਹਾਉਣਾ **parhāuṇā**	ਪੜ੍ਹਵਾਉਣਾ **parhvāuṇā**
ਪਾਉਣਾ **pāuṇā**	*vt*	put in	ਪੁਆਉਣਾ **puāuṇā**	
ਪੀਣਾ **pīṇā**	*vt*	drink	ਪਿਆਉਣਾ **piāuṇā** ਪਿਲ਼ਾਉਣਾ **piḷāuṇā**	ਪਿਲ਼ਵਾਉਣਾ **piḷvāuṇā**
ਪੀਸਣਾ **pīsṇā**	*vt*	grind	ਪਿਸਾਉਣਾ **pisāuṇā**	ਪਿਸਵਾਉਣਾ **pisvāuṇā**
ਪੀਹਣਾ **pīhṇā**	*vt*	grind	ਪਿਹਾਉਣਾ **pihāuṇā**	ਪਿਸਵਾਉਣਾ **pisvāuṇā**
ਪੁੱਜਣਾ **pujjṇā**	*vi*	reach	ਪੁਚਾਉਣਾ **pucāuṇā**	ਪੁਚਵਾਉਣਾ **pucvāuṇā**
ਪੁੱਟਣਾ **puṭṭṇā**	*vt*	uproot	ਪੁਟਾਉਣਾ **puṭāuṇā**	ਪੁਟਵਾਉਣਾ **puṭvāuṇā**

ਪੂਜਣਾ **pūjṇā**	*vt*	worship		ਪੁਜਵਾਉਣਾ **pujvāṇā**
ਫ				
ਫਸਣਾ **p^hasṇā**	*vi*	be caught	ਫਸਾਉਣਾ **p^hasāuṇā**	ਫਸਵਾਉਣਾ **p^hasvāuṇā**
ਫਟਣਾ **p^haṭṇā**	*vi*	burst, get torn	ਫਾੜਨਾ **p^hāṛnā** ਫਟਾਉਣਾ **p^haṭāuṇā**	ਫੜਵਾਉਣਾ **p^haṛvāuṇā** ਫਟਵਾਉਣਾ **p^haṭvāuṇā**
ਫ਼ਰਮਾਉਣਾ **farmāuṇā**	*vt*	order		
ਫੜਨਾ **p^haṛnā**	*vt*	catch, hold	ਫੜਾਉਣਾ **p^haṛāuṇā**	ਫੜਵਾਉਣਾ **p^haṛvāuṇā**
ਫਿਰਨਾ **p^hirnā**	*vi*	turn	ਫੇਰਨਾ **p^hernā** ਫਿਰਾਉਣਾ **p^hirāuṇā**	ਫਿਰਵਾਉਣਾ **p^hirvāuṇā**
ਫੈਲਣਾ **p^haⁱlṇā**	*vi*	spread	ਫੈਲਾਉਣਾ **p^haⁱlāuṇā**	
ਫੁੱਲਣਾ **p^hullṇā**	*vi*	swell	ਫੁਲਾਉਣਾ **p^hulāuṇā**	ਫੁਲਵਾਉਣਾ **p^hulvāuṇā**
ਬ				
ਬਹਿਣਾ **bahiṇā**	*vi*	sit	ਬਿਠਾਉਣਾ **biṭ^hāuṇā**	ਬਿਠਵਾਉਣਾ **biṭ^hvāuṇā**
ਬਕਣਾ **bakṇā**	*vt*	talk incoherently, talk nonsense	ਬਕਾਉਣਾ **bakāuṇā**	ਬਕਵਾਉਣਾ **bakvāuṇā**
ਬਚਣਾ **bacṇā**	*vi*	avoid, be safe	ਬਚਾਉਣਾ **bacāuṇā**	
ਬੱਝਣਾ **bajj^hṇā**	*vi*	become bound	ਬੰਨ੍ਹਣਾ **bannhṇā**	ਬੰਨ੍ਹਵਾਉਣਾ **bannhvāuṇā**

ਬਣਨਾ **baṇnā**	*vi*	become	ਬਣਾਉਣਾ **baṇāuṇā**	ਬਣਵਾਉਣਾ **baṇvāuṇā**
ਬਦਲਣਾ **badalṇā**	*vi/vt*	change	ਬਦਲਾਉਣਾ **badalāuṇā**	ਬਦਲਵਾਉਣਾ **badalvāuṇā**
ਬਲਣਾ **balṇā**	*vi*	burn	ਬਾਲਣਾ **bālṇā**	
ਬਿਗੜਨਾ **bigaṛnā**	*vi*	be spoiled	ਬਿਗਾੜਨਾ **bigāṛnā**	
ਬੁਝਣਾ **buj^{h}ṇā**	*vt*	be extin-guished	ਬੁਝਾਉਣਾ **buj^{h}āuṇā**	ਬੁਝਵਾਉਣਾ **buj^{h}vāuṇā**
ਬੁੱਝਣਾ **bujj^{h}ṇā**	*vt*	guess	ਬੁਝਾਉਣਾ **buj^{h}āuṇā**	
ਬੁਣਨਾ **buṇnā**	*vt*	knit	ਬੁਣਾਉਣਾ **buṇāuṇā**	ਬੁਣਵਾਉਣਾ **buṇvāuṇā**
ਬੁਲਾਉਣਾ **bulāuṇā**	*vt*	call		ਬੁਲਵਾਉਣਾ **bulvāuṇā**
ਬੈਠਣਾ **ba^{i}ṭ^{h}ṇā**	*vi*	sit	ਬਿਠਾਉਣਾ **biṭ^{h}āuṇā**	ਬਿਠਵਾਉਣਾ **biṭ^{h}vāuṇā**
ਬੋਲਣਾ **bolṇā**	*vi*	speak	ਬੁਲਾਉਣਾ **bulāuṇā**	ਬੁਲਵਾਉਣਾ **bulvāuṇā**

ਭ				
ਭੱਜਣਾ **b^{h}ajjṇā**	*vi*	become broken	ਭੰਨਣਾ **b^{h}annṇā**	ਭੰਨਾਉਣਾ **b^{h}anāuṇā** ਭੰਨਵਾਉਣਾ **b^{h}anvāuṇā**
ਭੱਜਣਾ **b^{h}ajjṇā**	*vi*	run	ਭਜਾਉਣਾ **b^{h}ajāuṇā**	
ਭਰਨਾ **b^{h}arnā**	*vt*	fill	ਭਰਾਉਣਾ **b^{h}arāuṇā**	ਭਰਵਾਉਣਾ **b^{h}arvāuṇā**
ਭੁੰਨਣਾ **b^{h}unnṇā**	*vt*	roast	ਭੁੰਨਾਉਣਾ **b^{h}unāuṇā**	ਭੁੰਨਵਾਉਣਾ **b^{h}unvāuṇā**
ਭੇਜਣਾ **b^{h}ejṇā**	*vt*	send	ਭਿਜਾਉਣਾ **b^{h}ijāuṇā**	ਭਿਜਵਾਉਣਾ **b^{h}ijvāuṇā**

ਭੋਗਣਾ **b^{h}ogṇā**	*vt*	undergo, experience		
ਮ				
ਮੰਨਣਾ **mannṇā**	*vi*	agree	ਮਨਾਉਣਾ **manāuṇā**	ਮਨਵਾਉਣਾ **manvāuṇā**
ਮਰਨਾ **marnā**	*vi*	die	ਮਾਰਨਾ **mārnā**	ਮਰਾਉਣਾ **marāuṇā** ਮਰਵਾਉਣਾ **marvāuṇā**
ਮਾਪਣਾ **māpṇā**	*vt*	measure		
ਮਿਣਨਾ **miṇnā**	*vt*	measure		ਮਿਣਵਾਉਣਾ **miṇvāunā**
ਮਿਲਣਾ **milṇā**	*vi*	meet	ਮਿਲ਼ਾਉਣਾ **miḷāuṇā**	ਮਿਲ਼ਵਾਉਣਾ **miḷvāuṇā**
ਮੁੱਕਣਾ **mukkṇā**	*vi*	come to an end	ਮੁਕਾਉਣਾ **mukāuṇā**	
ਮੁੜਨਾ **muṛnā**	*vi*	turn	ਮੋੜਨਾ **moṛnā** ਮੁੜਾਉਣਾ **muṛāuṇā**	ਮੁੜਵਾਉਣਾ **muṛvāuṇā**
ਯ				
ਯਰਕਣਾ **yarkṇā**	*vi*	get frighten-ed	ਯਰਕਾਉਣਾ **yarkāuṇā**	
ਰ				
ਰਹਿਣਾ **rahiṇā**	*vi*	stay, live	ਰੱਖਣਾ **rakk^{h}ṇā**	ਰਖਵਾਉਣਾ **rak^{h}vāuṇā**
ਰੰਗਣਾ **rangṇā**	*vt*	dye	ਰੰਗਾਉਣਾ **rangāuṇā**	ਰੰਗਵਾਉਣਾ **rangvāuṇā**
ਰਗੜਨਾ **ragaṛnā**	*vt*	rub		ਰਗੜਵਾਉਣਾ **ragaṛvāuṇā**

ਰਟਣਾ **raṭṇā**	*vt*	learn by rote	ਰਟਾਉਣਾ **raṭāuṇā**	ਰਟਵਾਉਣਾ **raṭvāuṇā**
ਰਲਣਾ **ralṇā**	*vi*	mix	ਰਲ਼ਾਉਣਾ **raḷāuṇā**	ਰਲ਼ਵਾਉਣਾ **raḷvāuṇā**
ਰਿੱਝਣਾ **rijj^{h}ṇā**	*vi*	get cooked	ਰਿੰਨ੍ਹਣਾ **rinnhṇā**	ਰਿੰਨ੍ਹਵਾਉਣਾ **rinnhvāuṇā**
ਰੋਣਾ **roṇā**	*vi*	weep	ਰੁਆਉਣਾ **ruāuṇā**	

ਲ				
ਲੱਗਣਾ **laggṇā**	*vi*	attach	ਲਾਉਣਾ **lāuṇā** ਲਗਾਉਣਾ **lagāuṇā**	ਲਗਵਾਉਣਾ **lagvāuṇā**
ਲੰਗੜਾਉਣਾ **lãgṛāuṇā**	*vi*	limp		
ਲੰਘਣਾ **lang^{h}ṇā**	*vi*	pass through	ਲੰਘਾਉਣਾ **lang^{h}āuṇā**	ਲੰਘਵਾਉਣਾ **lang^{h}vāuṇā**
ਲੱਭਣਾ **labb^{h}ṇā**	*vt*	search, find	ਲਭਾਉਣਾ **lab^{h}āuṇā**	ਲਭਵਾਉਣਾ **lab^{h}vāuṇā**
ਲਮਕਣਾ **lamakṇā**	*vi*	be suspend-ed	ਲਮਕਾਉਣਾ **lamkāuṇā**	ਲਮਕਵਾਉਣਾ **lamkvāuṇā**
ਲੜਨਾ **laṛnā**	*vi*	fight	ਲੜਾਉਣਾ **laṛāuṇā**	ਲੜਵਾਉਣਾ **laṛvāuṇā**
ਲਾਉਣਾ **lāuṇā**	*vt*	fix	ਲੁਆਉਣਾ **luāuṇā**	ਲਗਵਾਉਣਾ **lagvāuṇā**
ਲਾਹੁਣਾ **lāhuṇā**	*vt*	bring down	ਲੁਹਾਉਣਾ **luhāuṇā**	
ਲਿਆਉਣਾ **liāuṇā**	*vt*	bring		
ਲਿਖਣਾ **lik^{h}ṇā**	*vt*	write	ਲਿਖਾਉਣਾ **lik^{h}āuṇā**	ਲਿਖਵਾਉਣਾ **lik^{h}vāuṇā**

ਲੁਕਣਾ **lukṇā**	*vi*	be hidden	ਲੁਕੋਣਾ **lukoṇā** ਲੁਕਾਉਣਾ **lukāuṇā**	ਲੁਕਵਾਉਣਾ **lukvāuṇā**
ਲੁੱਟਣਾ **luṭṭṇā**	*vt*	rob	ਲੁਟਾਉਣਾ **luṭāuṇā**	ਲੁਟਵਾਉਣਾ **luṭvāuṇā**
ਲੂਹਣਾ **lūhṇā**	*vt*	scorch		
ਲੈਣਾ **la^{i}ṇā**	*vt*	take	(ਦੇਣਾ) **(deṇā)**	(ਦੁਆਉਣਾ) **(duāuṇā)**
ਵ				
ਵਸਣਾ **vasṇā**	*vi*	live (dwell)	ਵਸਾਉਣਾ **vasāuṇā**	
ਵੱਜਣਾ **vajjṇā**	*vi*	to sound		
ਵਜਾਉਣਾ **vajāuṇā**	*vt*	play (musical instrument)		ਵਜਵਾਉਣਾ **vajvāuṇā**
ਵਟਾਉਣਾ **vaṭāuṇā**	*vt*	exchange		
ਵੰਡਣਾ **vanḍṇā**	*vt*	divide	ਵੰਡਾਉਣਾ **vanḍāuṇā**	
ਵੱਢਣਾ **vaḍḍ^{h}ṇā**	*vt*	cut	ਵਢਾਉਣਾ **vaḍ^{h}āuṇā**	ਵਢਵਾਉਣਾ **vaḍ^{h}vāuṇā**
ਵਧਣਾ **vad^{h}ṇā**	*vi*	increase	ਵਧਾਉਣਾ **vad^{h}āuṇā**	ਵਧਵਾਉਣਾ **vad^{h}vāuṇā**
ਵਰਤਣਾ **vartṇā**	*vt*	use		
ਵੜਨਾ **vaṛnā**	*vi*	enter	ਵਾੜਨਾ **vāṛnā**	ਵੜਾਉਣਾ **vaṛāuṇā** ਵੜਵਾਉਣਾ **vaṛvāuṇā**
ਵਿਸਰਨਾ **visarnā**	*vi*	be forgotten	ਵਿਸਾਰਨਾ **visārnā**	

ਵਿਚਾਰਨਾ **vicarnā**	*vt*	think		
ਵੇਖਣਾ **vek^{h}ṇā**	*vt*	see	ਵਿਖਾਉਣਾ **vik^{h}āuṇā**	ਵਿਖਵਾਉਣਾ **vik^{h}vāuṇā**

Summing up

Grammar deals with *productive* rules. But there are very few exceptionless rules in a living language, especially those governing the processes of derivational morphology. We can say that grammar deals with *strong productive tendencies*. This chapter describes some of such tendencies in some detail.

Chapter 18

On Shahmukhi

Preview of the chapter

The purpose of this chapter is not to give a detailed description of Shahmukhi script comparable to what has been said about Gurmukhi in Chapter 3. Since a great deal has been written by various writers about the past incarnations of Shahmukhi, only some important facts about Shahmukhi are given below.

18.1 A brief history of Shahmukhi

1. The name Shahmukhi (coined recently on the analogy of Gurmukhi) is given to the Urdu script when used for writing Panjabi in Pakistan. It is 100% Urdu script with no Panjabi-specific changes made to the script.
2. The Urdu script is the Indian variety of the Perso-Arabic (Nastaleeq) script with a few symbols for Indian consonants added. The original Arabic script is called Naskh.
3. The Persian (Nastaleeq) script itself was created by adding four letters for the Persian consonants not found in Arabic and by changing the style of writing. It is sometimes called Arabic+4 script.
4. Speakers of Persian could not pronounce some Arabic sounds in the words borrowed from Arabic. So they changed their pronunciation but retained the Arabic spelling.

5. The early Muslim rulers of India used the Persian script for writing the language spoken in and around Delhi, which they called Hindvi and **kʰaṛī bolī**. (The name Urdu came into use much later.) The designers of this script added three letters for the Urdu retroflex consonants. So the Urdu script can be described as Arabic+4+3 script. The aspirated consonants are written by combining the "Do Chashmi ('two-eyed') He" letter ھ with a consonant symbol. But the Arabic and Persian spellings were retained in the borrowed words. The Arabic words were borrowed in their Persianised versions. The result is that the Urdu script has four letters for [z], three letters for [s], two letters for [t] and two letters for [h].
6. Shahmukhi is 100% Urdu script with the Urdu writing conventions carried on *in toto* into the writing of Panjabi, even where the pronunciation of the words shared by the two languages is different in Panjabi. The Urdu script has no letter for the extremely important retroflex nasal sound **ṇ** [ɳ] (the equivalent of the Gurmukhi letter ਣ and the Devanagari letter ण). Some writers use the Unicode symbol 0768 ݨ for **ṇ** [ɳ] in Shahmukhi, but this is not a standard practice. A new Nastaleeq symbol shown in Figure 18.1 below has also been created, but has not been accepted by all Shahmukhi writers, who are quite happy managing without any symbol for [ɳ]. No attempt has been made to standardise the spellings of Panjabi words in Shahmukhi.

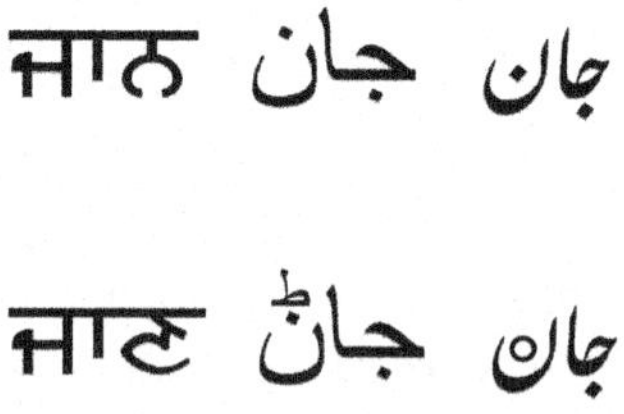

Figure 18.1 Two symbols for the Panjabi retroflex nasal

The first word is **jān** 'life' and the second word is **jāṇ** 'to know', written differently in Gurmukhi. But most writers go on writing both as جان, relying upon the context to indicate which word is written.

7. Arabic language has three long vowels [a:], [i:] and [u:], and three corresponding short vowels [a], [i] and [u]. It also has two

diphthongs [ai] and [au]. It has three letters ی , ا and و for these long vowels and uses the diacritics described below for writing short vowels. The letters for two high vowels [iː] ی and [uː] و are also used for the corresponding semi-vowels [j] and [w] respectively.

8. Panjabi (like Urdu) has ten vowels. The problem of writing these ten vowels has been solved by combining diacritical marks with the symbols for the long vowels. But the trouble is that in actual practice diacritical marks are generally omitted in writing and the reader has to depend upon the context to make sense of the text.

18.2 The Naskh and Nastaleeq styles

The Naskh (original Arabic) and the Nastaleeq (Persian) scripts are simply two different *styles* of writing. If you can read Naskh, you can also read Nastaleeq and *vice versa*. The latter style is also described as the "cascading" style of writing. The following diagram shows the word 'Pakistan' typed in the two styles. The diagram also shows the "cascading" nature of the Nastaleeq style.

Figure 18.2 Different looks of the Naskh and the ("cascading") Nastaleeq script

The following diagram gives a two-line Panjabi folk song **terii sajjari paˡṛ dā retā/cuk cuk lāvā̃ hikk nū̃** ('I pick up the sand from your fresh footprint and hold it to my heart'). A very careful comparison of the shapes of the letters in these two styles will show that they are simply two stylistic versions of the same system of writing.

تیری سَجری پیڑ دا ریتا
چُک چُک لاواں ہِک نوں

تیری سَجری پیڑ دا ریتا
چُک چُک لاواں ہِک نوں

Figure 18.3 Same text in the Naskh and the Nastaleeq scripts

In the rest of this chapter, as elewhwhere, we use the Naskh (Arabic) version. With the coming of the Internet and online dictionaries, the Naskh style has been gaining popularity at the cost of Nastaleeq over the past decade. In Iran itself (the birth place of Nastaleeq) people are switching to Naskh for printing popular books and newspapers. More Naskh fonts than the Nastaleeq ones are available these days for printing newspapers and books.

18.3 The Shahmukhi alphabet

As stated above, Shahmukhi is 100% Urdu script. Since excellent book-length descriptions of the Urdu script exist, the following information about Shahmukhi is quite brief and Panjabi-specific.

ح he (baṛī)	چ ce	ج jīm	ث se	ٹ ṭe	ت te	پ pe	ب be	ا alif
س sīn	ژ źe	ز ze	ڑ ṛe	ر re	ذ zāl	ڈ ḍāl	د dāl	خ xe
ق qāf	ف fe	غ ɣa'n	ع a'n	ظ zoe	ط toe	ض zvād	ص svād	ش śīn
	ہ he (cʰoṭī)	و vāo	ن nūn	م mīm	ل lām	گ gāf	ک kāf	
			ے ye (baṛī)	ی ye (cʰoṭī)	ھ he (do caśmī)			

Figure 18.4 The Shahmukhi alphabet

Readers can learn a great deal about Urdu from Bhatia and Koul (2013), Delacy (2001) and Matthews and Dalvi (2014).

The letters of the alphabet are supplemented by some diacritical marks. The most commonly used ones in Shahmukhi are shown below.

zabar	zer	peś	śadd	hamzā
َ	ِ	ُ	ّ	ء

Figure 18.5 Diacritical marks used in Shahmukhi

The Shadd or Tashdeed ّ is the Shahmukhi equivalent of the Gurmukhi Addhak ੱ. It marks a consonant as long or "double", as in سَتّ **[satt]** ਸੱਤ 'seven' contrasted with ست **[sat]** ਸਤ 'essence' and جَتّ **[jatt]** 'thick fur' contrasted with جت ਜਤ **[jat]** 'celibacy'. The diacritic ٔ (called Hamza) is used when one syllable in a word ends with a vowel sound and the following syllable starts with a vowel sound as in نائی **[nāī]** 'barber', and جاؤگے **[jāoge]** '(you) will go'.

The other diacritics related to vowels either mark short vowels or are added to the letters for the long vowels, as shown in Figure 18.6 below.

Shahmukhi Vowel Symbols

Vowel	Initial	Medial	Final
a ਅ	اَ	َ	
ā ਆ	آ	ا	ا
i ਇ	اِ	ِ	
ī ਈ	اِیـ	ِیـ	ی
u ਉ	اُ	ُ	
ū ਊ	اُو	ُو	ُو
e ਏ	ایـ	یـ	ے
a^i ਐ	اَیـ	َیـ	َے
o ਓ	او	و	و
a^u ਔ	اَو	َو	َو

Figure 18.6 Vowel symbols in Shahmukhi

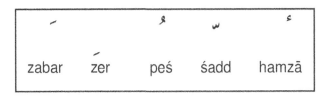

It is an ancient Arabic writing tradition (carried on in Persian, Urdu and Shahmukhi) to omit the diacritics (exept the Hamza) in ordinary writing and to depend on the context to interpret a word. For example, the word written as سر may be read as سر **[sar]** 'pool, lake' or سِر **[sir]** 'head' or سُر **[sur]** 'musical note'. The word written as پیڑ may be پیڑ **[peṛ]** 'tree' or پِیڑ, **[pīṛ]** 'pain' or پیَڑ **[pa^{i}ṛ]** 'footprint'. Similarly, موَت **[ma^{u}t]** 'death' and مُوت **[mūt]** 'urine' written without the diacrtical marks would look identical. Most writers are careful and they do use the appropriate diacritical marks when they foresee a possibility of ambiguity. But this is not always done.

18.4 Positional variants of the Shahmukhi letters

While the Gurmukhi letters are grouped *phonetically*, the Arabic (and hence the Persian, Urdu and Shahmukhi) letters are grouped *visually*.

We saw in Chapter 3 that only three letters of modern Gurmukhi (ਹ, ਰ and ਵ have positional variants ੍ਹ, ੍ਰ and ੍ਵ respectively) depending upon the syllabic structure of the word. But in Shahmukhi, *most* letters have positional variants, depending upon the position of the letter in the word. This positional *mutation* of letters is also very common in Gurmukhi's sister scripts like Devanagari (used for writing Hindi, Marathi, Nepali and Sanskrit), Bengali and Gujarati.

As far as positional mutation is concerned, the Shahmukhi letters are divided into the *connector* and the *non-connector* ones. A connector letter can join both the preceding and the following connector letter. But a *non-connector* letter can join only the preceding *connector* letter. In the Naskh script used in this chapter, each connector letter has an *intial* and *final* form. The medial form (except in the case of ع , غ and ھ) is the same as the initial form. The form of a non-connector letter does not change. Though ط and ظ are connector letters, their form remains invariant.

18.4.1 Positional variants of the connector letters

Arabic (and Shahmukhi) letters can be divided into groups or families, with members within the group looking very similar in shape. The families are shown in the boxes given below. The first group can be called the "Be Group" after its first member. Each group can be named in the same manner. The pronunciation of each letter appears with it. The presence of the star (*) is an indication that there is more to the pronunciation of the letter, which is discussed later.

ب	ﺑ	b
پ	ﭘ	p
ت	ﺗ	t
ٹ	ﭨ	ṭ
ث	ﺛ	s

ج	ﺟ	j
چ	ﭼ	c
ح	ﺣ	h
خ	ﺧ	x

س	ﺳ	s
ش	ﺷ	ś
ص	ﺻ	s
ض	ﺿ	z

ط	t
ظ	z

ع	ﻊ	ﻌ	ﻋ	*
غ	ﻎ	ﻐ	ﻏ	ɣ

ف	ﻓ	f
ق	ﻗ	q

ﻻ = ا + ل
←

ک	ﮐ	k
گ	ﮔ	g

ہ	ھ	ﮭ	ﮩ	ﮨ	h

ی	ے	ﯾ	y/i*

18.4.2 Non-connector letters

These letters have invariant shapes in the Naskh script, as shown in the following boxes. But the shape of ا does change when it is added to ل as is shown above.

ا	آ	a/ā*

د	d
ڈ	ḍ
ذ	z

ر	r
ڑ	ṛ
ز	z
ژ	ź

و	w/o*

The situation in the Nastaleeq script is a bit more complicated in the sense that some more letters have medial shapes as well. These complications are best learnt from a specialist book such as Delacy

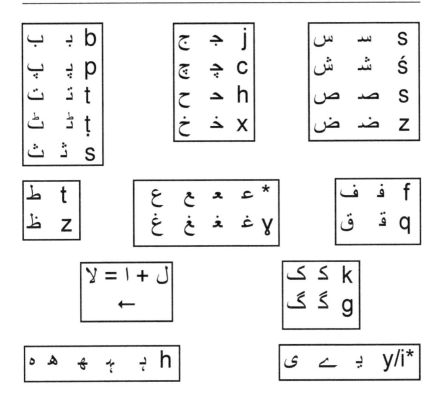

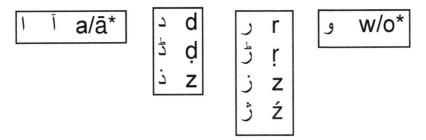

(2001). This subject is related to the structure of a borrowed script, and not to the phonological structure of the language as is the case with the Gurmukhi script.

18.5 The Gurmukhi and the Shahmukhi systems compared

It was pointed out earlier that people have strong religious feelings associated with the scripts used for writing Panjabi. Since Shahmukhi, whose use for writing Panjabi is older than Gurmukhi's, is a variant of the Arabic script used for writing the Holy Quran, the association of Muslim sentiments with this script is understandable. Similary, Gurmukhi is used for writing the Sikh holy book *Srī Gurū Granth Sāhib* and Sikhs have the same reverence for this script. Additionally, many Sikhs (including some well-known scholars) believe Guru Angad Dev, the second Guru of the Sikh faith, "invented the Gurmukhi letters". But this view is rejected by many Sikh scholars themselves (Nabha 1930, G.B. Singh 1950, Padam 1954, Sidhu 2004). Historical research shows that all the letters and symbols of this script existed centuries before Sikhism. Most probably, what Guru Angad Dev did was *assemble* the modern Gurmukhi writing *system* around 1530–35 (from the already existing scripts) under the guidance of his mentor and predecesor Guru Nanak Dev. Even this is a great linguistic achievement: Gurmukhi is an extremely simple and logical system ideally suited to Panjabi as it was spoken at that time. We can say that Gurmukhi was *tailor-made* for Panjabi.

Similarly, the original Arabic script must have been ideally suited to writing Arabic language. All the symbols of the alphabet and the diacritical marks were needed for writing the language. The morpho-phonological structure of the Arabic words (most of them derived from tri-consonantal roots) justified the three letters for the long vowels and diacritical marks for the corresponding short ones. The common practice of omitting the diacritics in writing (except when writing the verses from the Holy Quran and the Hadith books) was justified more in Arabic than in the languages which later borrowed the script. Taking into account the phonetic and morpho-phonological structure of Arabic, the original Arabic script is probably the best possible system designed for the language.

Now, while Gurmukhi (tailor-made for Panjabi) is used for writing only this language, the imported Arabic script, tailor-made for Arabic, was first altered for Persian and then the Persian variety was altered for

Urdu. The Urdu variety has been renamed as Shahmukhi for use in writing Panjabi in Pakistan. So Shahmukhi is *fourth-hand* Arabic script. As was inevitable, the alterations show up all over Shahmukhi, as was pointed out in Chapter 1, and they will be discussed in some detail below.

18.5.1 For an ordinary day-to-day use, no script is "better" than the other

Before attempting a comparative analysis of the two scripts, we wish to make it clear that for a *normal day-to-day use*, no script is "better" than the other. Both have been in use for centuries and have been serving the needs of their users well. It makes perfect sense to have only one script for all the languages spoken in Pakistan (but the Sindhi script, though based on the Arabic script, is different from the Urdu (Shahmukhi) script in some important respects). We read by scanning full words within the linguistic and the non-linguistic contexts, and not by adding up the letters in the spellings. So there need not be one-to-one correspondence between the letters of the alphabet used and their pronunciation. The context makes it clear whether the word spelt in English as *row* is used in the sense of 'line' [rəʊ] or 'fierce and noisy quarrel' [raʊ]. Similarly, a reader of English knows that *week* and *weak* have the same pronunciation. Retaining older spellings in the words borrowed from other languages, as in *psychology* and *pneumonia* is quite common in many languages. So if the diacritics for short vowels are usually omitted in Shahmukhi writing without creating any ambiguity or loss of proper communication, it is not a very serious matter for an *ordinary day-to-day use of the script.* Retaining the original spellings of the words borrowed from Arabic and Persian (with changed pronunciation in Panjabi) may sometimes serve a useful purpose. On the other hand, the claim made by the devotees of Gurmukhi, that in this script "you speak exactly as you write and write exactly as you speak" is no longer valid after the development of tones in Panjabi, as has been discussed in detail in Chapter 4.

18.6 Gurmukhi and Shahmukhi: structural comparison

The following chart compares the Gurmukhi and Shahamukhi systems. Reference should be made to this chart for the observations made in the following sub-sections. The letters shaded and marked with * are discussed below.

GURMUKHI AND SHAHMUKHI EQUIVALENTS

ੳ	ਅ	ੲ

Older Fricatives

*ਸ س	*ਹ ہ

CONSONANT SQUARE

	Voiceless Unaspirate	Voiceless Aspirate	Voiced Unaspirate	Voiced Aspirate	Nasal
Velar	ਕ ک	ਖ کھ	ਗ گ	ਘ گھ	ਙ None
Palatal	ਚ چ	ਛ چھ	ਜ ج	ਝ جھ	ਞ None
Retroflex	ਟ ٹ	ਠ ٹھ	ਡ ڈ	ਢ ڈھ	*ਣ ݨ
Dental	*ਤ ت	ਥ تھ	ਦ د	ਧ دھ	ਨ ن
Bilabial	ਪ پ	ਫ پھ	ਬ ب	ਭ بھ	ਮ م

Frictionless Continuants

*ਯ ے ی	ਰ ر	ਲ ل	ਵ و	ੜ ڑ

New Fricatives

ਸ਼ ش	ਖ਼ خ	ਗ਼ غ	*ਜ਼ ز	ਫ਼ ف

More recent additions

ਲ਼ None	ਕ਼ ق

Figure 18.7 Gurmukhi and Shahmukhi equivalents

18.6.1 Gurmukhi and Shahmukhi vowel systems

The system of writing the vowels sounds in Gurmukhi was discussed in detail in Chapter 3. The Shahmukhi system for writing the vowel sounds of Panjabi is mentioned briefly above. (See Figure 18.6.)

18.6.2 Absence of letters for some Panjabi consonants in Shahmukhi

Writing systems are created not simply for *ordinary day-to-day use in the present time*, but also for recording a language unambiguously for use out of the familiar present day context (e.g., for future generations) and for linguistic analysis. So, ideally, a writing system should mirror the phonetic and phonological structure of a language and help us understand the morpho-phonological processes operating in the language. When there are two competing writing systems for the same language, this consideration becomes all the more necessary for evaluating them.

A good writing system should mirror the phonetic and phonological system of a language (unless the writing system is ideographic like the Chinese system) as far as possible. Every writing system is used in a context, but the system in which appeal is made too often to the context as an escape route to hide the system's own inherent weaknesses is a badly designed system.

As we have already observed, Gurmukhi was based on a sound phonetic and phonological analysis of Panjabi as it was spoken in the 15th century. That changes occurred in the pronunciation of the language later on and there developed a slight (and still rule-governed) discrepancy between spelling and pronunciation is not the fault of the designers (Guru Nanak Dev and Guru Angad Dev, according to the tradition). As we mentioned in Chapter 1, Guru Nanak Dev knew the Perso-Arabic script well, which was fashionable at that time even among the non-Muslims. He may have rejected this script for two *linguistic* reasons. It did not have letters for the three very important Panjabi consonants ਙ **[ṅ]** [ŋ] , ਞ **[ñ]** [ɲ] and ਣ **[ṇ]** [ɳ] and it permitted the omission of short vowels, which are critically important for a correct understanding of the meaning of his poetry. Guru Nanak Dev probably feared that if he used the Perso-Arabic script, future generations might omit short vowel marks in his writings. As we saw in Chapter 1, ਙ **[ṅ]** and ਞ **[ñ]** were used as *independent* sounds in Guru Nanak Dev's writings. Now they have mostly been marginalised as independent sounds and occur mostly as homorganic nasals. (See Chapter 3.) However, they have survived in some words. Ironically, more words with these independent sounds occur in the Western dialects written in Shahmukhi, which lacks symbols for these sounds. But the absence of the symbol for the retroflex nasal **ṇ** [ɳ], for which Gurmukhi has ਣ, is a considerably more serious flaw in the Urdu (and Shahmukhi) script.

The writing systems of the Brahmi family to which Gurmukhi belongs were the result of millennia of the study of the science of phonetics in India (as documented by Varma (1961(1929)). The designers of the Urdu script were probably not familiar with this tradition. They may have been familiar with the Arabic tradition of linguistics, but that was not very helpful in designing a script for an Indic language. The Indian language spoken in and around Delhi which became the basis for the hodgepodge later called Urdu was an Indic language. (The word Urdu means an 'army camp' – an apt metaphorical name for the language.) A language does not change its family and basic phonological and grammatical ﬆructure by borrowing words from another language.

The designers of the Urdu script were irresponsible linguiﬆs and careless planners. They decided to use the diacrtic ؕ to mark the retroflex consonants of Hindvi (which became better known as Urdu later) – ٹ ڈ and ڑ. Thus they blocked their way for creating a letter for the retroflex nasal **ṇ**. The resulting symbol ݨ would have been troublesome because in the initial and the medial positions it would have appeared as ٹـ, which is also the shape of ٹ in these positions. So the Urdu script has no symbol for **ṇ**, not because the Urdu language (or Hindvi, as it was originally called) did not have this sound but because its script was planned badly. It is difficult to know what exactly the language of the people of Delhi was like at that time. But the sound **ṇ** is even now a prominent sound of the languages of the common rural people, now spoken in the areas around Delhi. So it is inconceivable that this sound did not occur in Hindvi. The Devanagari script (used for writing Hindi) has the letter ण for this sound and Gurmukhi has ਣ for it. The argument that the Urdu script has no letter for **ṇ** because the language has no sound **ṇ** is invalid. The Modern "high" variety of Urdu (especially as spoken in Pakiﬆan) is a highly artificial, pompous and ﬆilted language (loaded with Persian and Arabic words *with the original grammatical ending*s) and the speakers of this variety of Urdu try to follow the written texts in their speech. So it has no **ṇ** [ɳ] sound because the speakers carefully omit it. Leaving aside Urdu, this sound is extremely important in Panjabi. The escape route of "let the context help" does not always help a grammarian. There is a rule in Chapter 11 (page 223) which explains the choice between -ਨ- **-n-** [n] and -ਣ- **-ṇ-** [ɳ]. Including Shahmukhi without any letter for **-ṇ-** in the main body of the book would have made the writing of the following important morpho-phonological rule impossible.

> The potential participle affix is -ਣ- **-ṇ-** or -ਨ- **-n-** which is followed by the usual number-gender affix from the table of adjectival endings given earlier. Sometimes -ਉ- **-u-** is added to the ﬆem before -ਣ- **-ṇ-** or -ਨ- **-n-**. The rules for the addition of this -ਉ- **-u-** are the same as for the imperfect participle. (See section **11.4.1**.) The choice between -ਣ- **-ṇ-** or -ਨ- **-n-** is quite simple.

Normally, -ਣ- **-ṇ-** is used except after ਣ **ṇ**, ਰ **r**, ੜ **ṛ** and ਲ਼ **ḷ**. All these sounds involve a quick flapping of the tongue, and flapping the tongue quickly twice in order to add ਣ **ṇ** is difficult. So ਨ **n** is added as the participial affix.

When the script for Sindhi was designed by the famous orientalist Sir Richard Francis Burton with the help of Hindu and Muslim Sindhi scholars in the 19th century, the designers paid close attention to the fact that Sindhi was an Indic language. But, taking into account the fact that the majority of its users would be Muslims, they based the script on the Arabic script. They retained the letters for the Arabic sounds to write Muslim names and borrowed words, but they provided letters for *all* the special Sindhi sounds as well (including the implosive consonants for which breath is supposed to be drawn inwards). These consonant letters are [ɓ] ٻ , [ʄ] ڄ, [ɗ] ڏ and [ɠ] ڳ . They provided letters for the nasal sounds [ṅ] [ŋ] ڱ , [ñ] [ɲ] ڃ and [ṇ] [ɳ] ڻ as well, which were ignored by the designers of the Urdu script. They were careful not to use the diacritic ط to mark the symbol for ṭ [ʈ] and created the letter ٽ for this sound. So they were able to create the letter ڻ for **ṇ** [ɳ] without running into any difficulty. The result is an excellent writing system. A good writing system based on the Arabic script for an Indic language Sindhi and writing systems of the Brahmi family *can* be created for other Indic languages. But you need a good knowledge of the phonetic and phonological structure of the language *plus* good planning and foresight, which the 13th century designers of the Urdu script did not possess. Now the Urdu script with all the original flaws has been rechristened as Shahmukhi. The attempts of some writers to introduce a new symbol for **ṇ** (mentioned earlier in Chapter 1) or to use the Unicode symbol 0768 ڻ for this sound have not been accepted by those who would "let the context help". It is now too late to design a sensible Sindhi-like writing system for writing Urdu (and Panjabi in Pakistan), but adding some additional letters should not be a problem. But the attempt is likely to face considerable opposition.

It is interesting to note that short vowels are not omitted in the Holy Quran and the Hadith books. They contain serious writing meant for all time (in which context may change), not just for the present time, as children's books, newspaper articles and "light" literature are. Similary Guru Nanak Dev was writing for all time and he needed a system of writing which *must* express all the phonetic features of the language and should not rely upon the context for interpretation. Word-final short vowels (not found in Arabic) are extremely important in the grammar of his language. For example ਦੇਹਿ **dehi** means 'has given' and ਦੇਹੁ **dehu** means 'please give'. ਇਕੁ **iku** is a proper noun meaning 'One (God)', ਇਕ **ik** is an ordinary number meaning 'one', ਇਕਿ **iki** is the collective (plural) form meaning something like 'members of one particular group'. He chose a system which made it *impossible* to omit any vowel symbol, short or long. Instead of writing دیہ or اک in the Perso-Arabic script and then "letting the context decide" what he actually meant, he used a system of writing which allowed no omission of any vowel symbol and thus eliminated too much reliance on the context. As was mentioned in Chapter 1, he did not like those Hindus who blindly copied the dress, speech and mannerisms of the foreign rulers. Choosing an Indian script may be a part of his nationalism. Because of linguistic changes in Panjabi (mostly related to the stressing of the syllables) the word-final short vowels have now disappeared. But we still need to consider them while interpreting his writings and for analysing the syntactic behaviour of some modern Panjabi verb forms.

By choosing for his Indic language a Brahmi-based writing system based on the tradition of thousands of years of phonetic analysis, Guru Nanak Dev connected his writings to the great Indian tradition of inspired philosophical poetry. Moreover, the script he used in his writings connects us with the past stages of Panjabi. This is extremely important for any modern Panjabi grammarian. No serious linguist studying Panjabi can afford to ignore Guru Nanak Dev's writings and later Sikh literature *in Gurmukhi.* For example, the form ਕਰਿ **kari** 'having done' is written and pronounced as ਕਰ **kar** now and has become homophonous to the verb stem. But it continues to behave as a **conjunctive participle**. The whole Chapter 13 is based on regarding this stem-like form as a conjunctive participle. Not paying attention to the past of this form leads Puar (1990) to regard this form as a "root" form and produce misleading analysis. While every serious Panjabi grammarian should learn Shahmukhi (and as many other scripts as possible), they cannot do any serious work on Panjabi grammar without studying the writings of Guru Nanak Dev and other Gurus of the Sikh faith *in Gurmukhi*. The language of the prose biographies of Guru Nanak Dev, known as *Janamsākhīs*, is also extremely significant for a Panjabi grammarian. It is only through these writings that the roots of some significant features of modern Panjabi grammar can be discovered. This has been demonstrated repeatedly in this book (especially in Chapters 11 and 13). A knowledge of Shahmukhi is *useful* for reading the Panjabi literature written in this script and for studying the words borrowed from Arabic and Persian, but a knowledge of Gurmukhi and Devanagari (in which Vedic, Sanskrit, Prakrit and Apabhraṃsa literature is now available) is a *must* for connecting modern Panjabi to its roots in the past and for making use of the great deal of work on Panjabi done in the Indian Punjab. A linguist studying an Indic language in depth should look back to the *native Indian tradition* of linguistic analysis, and not to the Arab and Persian traditions, for guidance.

The Arabic script has serious flaws when it comes to writing other languages. Linguists who have studied the phonology of Turkish agree that the vowel signs of the Arabic alphabet are inadequate for representing the Turkish vowel sounds. In 1928, Kemal Atatürk replaced the Arabic script with the Latin script (with the addition of a few letters) for writing Turkish.

18.6.3 No "symbol for symbol" correspondence between the two systems

Iqbal Mahal published his Panjabi book ਸੁਰਾਂ ਦੇ ਸੁਦਾਗਰ ('Merchants of Musical Notes') in Gurmukhi in 1998 and as سُراں دے سوداگر in Shahmukhi in 2000. The "same" paragraph from the two editions is given below, with comments on how the two systems present the same information in the same language. The paragraph is on page 123 of the Gurmukhi edition and page 140 of the Shahmukhi edition. These paragraphs bring out the differences between how the two systems handle the language.

اسّی سالا گبھرو

ایہ گل 1991 دی ہے، جگت سنگھ ''جگا'' نال ٹی وی اُتے گل بات کردیاں میں اوس دی عمر پچھی ۔ اوہ بولیا ''جدوں اسیں جمیں ساں ، اوہنیں دنیں جنم تریکاں دا حساب کون رکھدا سی؟ ساڈی ماں نے واقیات دے ایڑ گیڑ نال جو کجھ دسیا، اوس توں لگدا اے کہ میرا جنم 1910-11 دے نیڑے تیڑے ہویا سی''۔

میں حیران ہو کے کہیا ''اسی سال! جگا جی، تسیں تاں ایس توں ادھی عمر دے وی نہیں لگدے''۔

ਅੱਸੀ ਸਾਲਾ ਗੱਭਰੂ

ਇਹ ਗੱਲ 1991 ਦੀ ਹੈ, ਜਗਤ ਸਿੰਘ "ਜੱਗਾ" ਨਾਲ ਟੀ. ਵੀ. ਉੱਤੇ ਗੱਲ ਬਾਤ ਕਰਦਿਆਂ ਮੈਂ ਉਹਦੀ ਉਮਰ ਪੁੱਛੀ। ਉਹ ਬੋਲਿਆ, "ਜਦੋਂ ਅਸੀਂ ਜੰਮੇ ਸਾਂ, ਉਹਨੀਂ ਦਿਨੀਂ ਜਨਮ ਤਰੀਕਾਂ ਦਾ ਹਿਸਾਬ ਕੌਣ ਰੱਖਦਾ ਸੀ? ਸਾਡੀ ਮਾਂ ਨੇ ਘਟਨਾਵਾਂ ਦੇ ਏੜ ਗੇੜ ਨਾਲ ਜੋ ਕੁਝ ਦੱਸਿਆ, ਉਸ ਤੋਂ ਲਗਦੈ ਕਿ ਮੇਰਾ ਜਨਮ 1901-11 ਦੇ ਨੇੜੇ ਤੇੜੇ ਹੋਇਆ ਸੀ।"

ਮੈਂ ਹੈਰਾਨ ਹੋ ਕੇ ਕਿਹਾ, "ਅੱਸੀ ਸਾਲ! ਜੱਗਾ ਜੀ, ਤੁਸੀਂ ਤਾਂ ਇਸ ਤੋਂ ਅੱਧੀ ਉਮਰ ਦੇ ਵੀ ਨਹੀਂ ਲਗਦੇ।"

Figure 18.8 "Same" text in Gurmukhi and Shahmukhi

<table>
<tr><td colspan="3">Each writing system has its own conventions, and there is no “symbol for symbol” correspondence between the two systems, as the first eight words in the table show. The differences become all the greater when the original Arabic spellings are used in the borrowed words in Shahmukhi. Keeping in view the target audience, a Hindi word likely to be unfamiliar to the readers is replaced by an Arabic word.</td></tr>
<tr><td></td><td>ਇਹ</td><td>ایہ</td></tr>
<tr><td></td><td>ਉਹ</td><td>اوہ</td></tr>
<tr><td></td><td>ਇਸ</td><td>ایس</td></tr>
<tr><td></td><td>ਉਸ</td><td>اوس</td></tr>
<tr><td></td><td>ਬੋਲਿਆ</td><td>بولیا</td></tr>
<tr><td></td><td>ਕਿਹਾ</td><td>کہیا</td></tr>
<tr><td></td><td>ਕਿ</td><td>کہ</td></tr>
<tr><td></td><td>ਲਗਦੈ</td><td>لگدا اے</td></tr>
<tr><td>Original Arabic spelling in Shahmukhi</td><td>ਉਮਰ</td><td>عُمر</td></tr>
<tr><td>Original Arabic spelling in Shahmukhi</td><td>ਹੈਰਾਨ</td><td>حیران</td></tr>
<tr><td>Original Arabic spelling in Shahmukhi</td><td>ਹਿਸਾਬ</td><td>حساب</td></tr>
<tr><td>An Arabic word is used in Shahmukhi in place of a Hindi word in Gurmukhi</td><td>ਘਟਨਾਵਾਂ</td><td>واقیات</td></tr>
</table>

Figure 18.9 Comments on the “same” text in Gurmukhi and Shahmukhi

The modern Panjabi pronunciation of the conjunction written as ਕਿ 'that' in Gurmukhi is **[ki]** [kɪ], and not **[kah]** [kəh], as indicated by the Shahmukhi spelling کہ. A truer representation of the pronunciation of this word as کِ would look extremely odd and inappropriate in the Urdu script because it would go against the norms of the Arabic wrtiting system. The Punjabi word **giā** written as ਗਿਆ in Gurmukhi is written with Urdu spelling as گیا in Shahmukhi. The written form گیا represents the Urdu pronunciation **gayā**, and not the Panjabi pronunciation **giā**, though the meaning of the word is the same in both the languages. Many examples of the misrepresenation of the Panjabi pronunciation in Shahmukhi can be given. This may not matter in actual day-to-day use of the script, but the Urdu spelling conventions transferred to Shahmukhi can seriously mislead a linguist basing their analysis on Shahmukhi written records.

An extreme case of a lack of correspondence between pronunciation and spelling in Shahmukhi (not exemplified in the paragraph from Mahal analysed above) is how some Arabic adverbs ending **[-an]** are spelt with اً at the end.

تقریباً **[taqrīban]** 'approximately'
حقیقتاً **[haqīqtan]** 'in reality'
مسلاً **[maslan]** 'for example'
عمؤماً **[amūman]** 'usually'

Almost all Panjabi speakers (and many Urdu speakers as well) pronounce the first two of these words with **[k]** instead of **[q]**.

18.6.4 Tonal pronuciation

Chapter 4 deals with the Panjabi tonal phenomena. Tones first developed in the words containing the consonants **h**, **g**^{h}, **j**^{h}, **ḍ**^{h}, **d**^{h} and **b**^{h}. The Gurmukhi and the Shahmukhi letters (or letter combinations) for these sounds are given in shaded boxes in Figure 18.7 on p.382. Since the tones are related to sounds, and not to the script, the information given in Chapter 4 cannot be repeated here. Some of the examples using words in Gurmukhi are given below with the relevant words in Shahmukhi.

گھوڑا **'g^{h}oṛā** → **[kòṛā]** 'horse'
گھٹا **'g^{h}aṭā** → **[kàṭā]** 'dark clouds'
گھٹا **g^{h}a'ṭā** → **[kaṭà]** 'to make less'

بھگوان **bʰag'vān** → **[pagvȁn]** 'God'

سنگھ **sangʰ** → **[sáng]** 'throat'

مجّھ **majjʰ** → **[májj]** 'buffalo'

جیبھ **jībʰ** → **[jī́b]** 'tongue'

ساہ **'sāh** **[sā́]** 'breath'

ویہ **'vīh** **[vī́h]** 'twenty'

لوہ **'lūh** **[lū́h]** 'to scorch'

18.6.5 More than one letter for a single sound

Some consonant letters in Figure 18.7 are marked with a *.

1. ے ی ਯ and و ਵ can represent either vowel sounds or semi-vowel consonants.
2. ݨ ਣ is used by some Shahmukhi writers for the retroflex nasal **ṇ** [ɳ], but it is rejected by most writers writing Panjabi in Shahmukhi who would "let the context help".
3. For the sounds represented by س ਸ, ہ ਹ, ت ਤ and ز ਜ਼, two or more letters are used, depending upon the spelling of the word in the language it is borrowed from. They are mostly Arabic words borrowed in the *Persianised phonetic form*. Some of such words are discussed below.

Summing up

This chapter has argued that

1. Both Shahmukhi and Gurmukhi are fine for *normal day-to-day use*; no system is "better" than the other in this respect, and a serious student of Panjabi should learn *both* the scripts;
2. Each system has its own conventions, and there is no exact "symbol for symbol" correspondence between the two systems;
3. But the native Gurmukhi system presents a better picture of the phonetic and phonological system of Panjabi than the imported and then badly adapted Shahmukhi system;
4. A good knowledge of Gurmukhi and the phonetic analyses of Indic languages underlying Gurmukhi and other Brahmi-based writing systems is a must for any serious scholar studying Panjabi and other Indian languages.

For teachers and other more advanced users

18.7 Spellings of the Arabic words in Shahmukhi

When Iranians borrowed Arabic words, they could not pronounce many of them in the original Arabic phonetic form. So they changed their pronunciation but retained their spelling.

1. One of these sounds is the interdental fricative [θ], which sounds like the first sound in the English word *think*. The Arabic letter for this sound is ث. The Iranians pronounced it as [s]. So they pronounce the Arabic word وارث (with final [θ]) with a final [s], as **[wāris]** 'inheritor'. The other troublesome interdental Arabic consonant [ð] is represented is by the letter ذ. This sound occurs at the beginning of the English word *this*. The Iranians ponounced it as [z], as in their pronunciation of ذلیل **[zalīl]** 'dishonourable', 'mean', 'accursed'. This pronunciation came to Urdu and Panjabi.
2. All other Arabic sounds which the Iranians could not pronounce are the *pharyngeal* or *pharyngealised* sounds. We need not go into the phonetic details here. Interested readers are referred to Ladefoged and Maddieson (1996). Briefly, the *pharyngeal* sounds are pronounced in the pharynx, the part of the throat above the epiglottis. The *pharyngealised* (or '*emphatic*') sounds are pronounced by retracting the tongue root. They are marked with the superscript IPA symbol ˁ, as in **[sˁ]** (*emphatic* or *pharyngealised* **[s]**).

   The Arabic *pharyngealised* (or *emphatic*) sounds changed their pronunciation in Persian and the Persian pronunciation was adopted in Urdu. This is why Urdu and Shahmukhi have two or more letters for some consonant sounds.

   ظ ðˁ → [z], as in ظاہر **[zāhir]** 'apparent'

   ط tˁ → [t], as in طوطا **[totā]** 'parrot'

   ض dˁ → [z] as in ضمیر **[zamīr]** 'conscience'

   ص sˁ → [s] as in صابن **[sābun]** 'soap'

3. Some proper pharyngeal sounds of Arabic changed their pronunciation in Persian.

ح ħ → [h] حرام **[harām]** 'forbidden'

The case of ع is more interesting. Generally, the Persian pronunciation is the glottal stop [ʔ].

ع ʕ → ʔ in Persian. ع has no particular sound in Urdu. The sound of the neighbouring vowel or consonant sound is used.

The Arabic word عام 'common' and the Indian word آم 'mango' are both pronounced as **[ām]** in Urdu.

More details can be found in the books designed for teaching Urdu, such as Bhatia and Koul (2013) and Delacy (2001).

Part IV

Appendices, Glossary and Indexes

Appendix 1

Using a Panjabi (Gurmukhi) Dictionary

Every advanced non-native learner of Panjabi who uses this grammar must also keep at least two bilingual dictionaries (Panjabi-English and English-Panjabi) on their desk or bookshelf *and frequently use them as well.* A few such dictionaries have been published since the middle of the 19th century, and some of them have been reprinted. They all use either Gurmukhi or some sort of phonetic transcription to write Panjabi. No bilingual dictionary using Shahmukhi (or what was previously known as the "Persian Script") has come to my attention.

The best bilingual dictionaries currently in use are

Punjabi-English Dictionary

English-Punjabi Dictionary

both prepared by reputed linguists and lexicographers working at Punjabi University, Patiala, India.

A dictionary follows the arrangement of the letters of the alphabet of the language. In the case of Gurmukhi, the problem is more complex than in English. Learners are advised to study Chapter 3 very carefully before going any further (and then go on looking at the relevant pages). The Gurmukhi "alphabet" has some special features. Actually, the name "alphabet" is not entirely appropriate for Gurmukhi because this script (like all its sister scripts of Indian origin) is neither alphabetic nor syllabic but a hybrid which can be described as alpha-syllabic.

1. Traditionally, the last letter of the alphabet was ੜ. The remaining letters following ੜ were added later to write the words borrowed from other languages.
2. Of these letters the sound represented by ਸ਼ was traditionally there in Sanskrit. (Actually, Sanskrit had two such sounds.) It went dormant for a few centuries but was probably always used by the Punjabis who knew Sanskrit.
3. The letters ਸ਼, ਖ਼, ਗ਼, ਜ਼ and ਫ਼ were added towards the close of the 19th century but were accepted by all Panjabi writers three decades later.
4. Not all the speakers of Panjabi use the retroflex lateral sound **ḷ** [ɭ] represented by ਲ਼, and many who do use it are not in favour of having a separate letter for this sound and use ਲ for both **l** [l] and **ḷ** [ɭ].
5. ਕ਼ representing the Arabic-Persian sound **q** [q] is used only by those writers in borrowed words who wish to "show off" their learning of Arabic and Persian in their writing (nearly all of them actually pronounce it as **k** [k]!). Those who use Shahmukhi to write Panjabi have to use the Arabic letter ق for **q** [q] in such borrowed words, though nearly all of them, too, pronounce it as **k** [k]. (It is said that the great modern Urdu poet Mohammad Iqbal (1877–1938), who was a fine scholar of Persian and Arabic as well, but whose mother tongue was Panjabi, pronounced his name effortlessly and unpretentiously as **ikbāl** [ɪkbɑl], with **k** [k] and not as **iqbāl** [ɪqbɑl] with **q** [q], as he should have "correctly" pronounced this Arabic word.)
6. There are ten vowel *symbols* (including an *invisible* one) added to the letters of the alphabet.
7. There are two subscript letters or "letters in the foot" ੍ਰ and ੍ਵ, which are now going out of fashion. Another subscript letter ੍ਹ is very much in use but is not pronounced. It adds a tone to the word. (See Chapter 4.)
8. There is a symbol known as Addhak (ੱ), used for representing a "double" or long consonant. There are also two symbols known as Tippi (ੰ) and Bindi (ਂ) to mark the nasalisation of a vowel.

The information about Gurmukhi given above may sound complicated, but the editors of the Panjabi-English dictionary mentioned above had no problem. They have followed these rules:

1. *Mostly*, they have followed the arrangement of the letters given in Chapter 3.
2. *But*, among the new letters, they regard only ਸ਼ as a *separate* letter and put it after ਸ, and not after ੜ as shown in the chart in Chapter 3. So, for example, the word ਸ਼ਰਮ is listed among the words which come under ਸ, but it comes after the words beginning with ਸ, such as ਸੈ.
3. In *most* cases, they use the letters with the dot, ਖ਼, ਗ਼, ਜ਼, ਫ਼ and ਲ਼ but treat them like ਖ, ਗ, ਜ, ਫ and ਲ respectively, as if the dot did not exist. (There is no Panjabi word beginning with ਲ਼.) There is an entry ਜਖਮ, following the usual arrangement of the Gurmukhi letters. But most educated speakers pronounce and write the word as ਜ਼ਖ਼ਮ. So the dictionary adds "also ਜ਼ਖ਼ਮ". The editors realise that their job is *descriptive*, and not *prescriptive*. They *describe* what most speakers and writers *actually do*, not *prescribe* what they *should do*. ਕ਼ does not appear anywhere in the dictionary.
4. The arrangement of the vowel symbols (including the invisible one) is followed. For example, ਘਟ comes before ਘਾਟ, which in turn comes before ਘੋਟ. ਬਾਵਾ comes before ਬਾਵੀ, which comes before ਬਾੜੂ.
5. The absence of Addhak, Tippi and Bindi and their presence are all used in this order – ਵਗ, ਵੱਗ and ਵੰਗ follow this order. ਘਟਾ comes before ਘੱਟਾ, which comes before ਘੰਟਾ. The Tippi and the Bindi are in complementary distribution because either the one or the other is used in one position. (See Chapter 3.) In the dictionary, ਬਾਗ comes before ਬਾਂਗ.
6. Entries of the words having the subscript letters ੍ਰ and ੍ਵ (in this order) come after the entries with the "full letters". For example, ਸ਼੍ਰਮ comes after ਸ਼ਲਾਘਾ (though the "full" ਰ comes before ਲ). The dictionary also gives the alternative spelling ਸ਼ਰਮ. ਸ੍ਰੀ comes after ਸੜੀਅਲ and ਸ੍ਵਰਗ comes after ਸ੍ਰੀ. The alternative spellings ਸਵਰਗ and ਸਿਰੀ are also given.
7. Words having the subscript ੍ਹ come after those without it. ਚੜ੍ਹ comes after ਚੜ.

The verb forms listed in Chapter 17 follow this dictionary order.

Appendix 2

Repetition of Words, Echo Words etc.

Repetition of words, the use of "echo words" and related phenomena for various semantic and stylistic effects is a characteristic feature of all the North Indian languages, though each language (or its dialects) uses them differently.

1. Repetition of words

(i) Repetition to express the idea of a prolonged state or activity

ਮੈਂ ਬੀਮਾਰ ਬੀਮਾਰ ਵੀ ਕੰਮ ਕਰੀ ਗਿਆ
mã^{i} *bīmār bīmār* vī kamm karī giā
I ill ill work went on doing
'I kept working even while I remained ill'

ਬੱਚਾ ਰੋਂਦਾ ਰੋਂਦਾ ਘਰ ਆਇਆ
baccā *rõdā rõdā* g^{h}ar āiā
child crying crying home came
'The child came home crying'

ਅਸੀਂ ਚਲਦੇ ਚਲਦੇ ਉੱਥੇ ਪਹੁੰਚ ਗਏ
asī̃ *calde calde* utt^{h}e pahũc gae
we walking walking there reached
'Walking continuously, we reached there'

The following two examples are from Pakistani Panjabi songs. The repeated verb ਤੱਕ **takk** is in the **conjunctive participle** form meaning 'having looked' or 'having watched'.

ਤੱਕ ਤੱਕ ਤੈਨੂੰ ਮੇਰੇ ਨੈਨ ਨਹੀਂਉਂ ਰੱਜਦੇ
takk takk **ta[i]nū̃ mere na[i]n nahiū̃ rajjde**
'(Even) after looking at you continuously, my eyes do not get satisfied'

ਅੱਖਾਂ ਥੱਕ ਗਈਆਂ ਤੱਕ ਤੱਕ ਰਾਹ ਸੱਜਣਾ
akkʰã tʰkk gaīã ***takk takk*** **rāh sajjṇā**
'O loved one, (my) eyes have got tired after continuously watching the path (of your expected arriving)

(ii) Repetition to convey the idea of intensity

ਲਾਲ ਲਾਲ ਟਮਾਟਰ
lāl lāl **ṭamāṭar**
red red tomatoes
'very red tomatoes'

ਡਰੇ ਡਰੇ ਲੋਕ
ḍare ḍare **lok**
frightened frightened people
'very frightened people'

ਤਾਜ਼ੇ ਤਾਜ਼ੇ ਗਰਮਾ ਗਰਮ ਪਕੌੜੇ
tāze tāze garmā garam **paka[u]ṛe**
fresh fresh hot hot fritters
'very fresh and very hot fritters'

(iii) Combining a Panjabi and a Persian word

Some Persian words are commonly used in Panjabi, which has its own synonymous words as well. Often a native Panjabi adjective is combined with a Persian one with the same meaning to convey the meaning of intensity.

ਲਾਲ ਸੁਰਖ਼
lāl surx
'deep red'

ਪੀਲ਼ਾ ਜ਼ਰਦ
pīḷā zard
'deep yellow'

ਕਾਲ਼ਾ ਸਿਆਹ
kāḷā siāh
'very dark black'

(iv) Repetition to express the idea of "all of them"

ਇਸ ਟੋਕਰੀ 'ਚੋਂ ਪੱਕੇ ਪੱਕੇ ਅੰਬ ਕੱਢ ਲਓ
is ṭokrī cõ *pakke pakke* amb kaḍḍ^{h} lao
this basket from ripe ripe mangoes take out
'Take out all the ripe mangoes from this basket'

There is a Panjabi proverb

ਮਿੱਠੀ ਮਿੱਠੀ ਹੜੱਪ, *ਕੌੜੀ ਕੌੜੀ* ਥੂਹ
***miṭṭ^{h}ī miṭṭ^{h}ī* haṛapp, *ka^{u}ṛī ka^{u}ṛī* t^{h}ūh**
sweet sweet swallow greedily, bitter bitter spit out
'Accept everything pleasant; reject everything unpleasant'

When some children get something to eat and others do not, the fortunate ones tease the others by saying

ਰਾਜੇ ਰਾਜੇ ਖਾਂਦੇ, *ਬਿੱਲੀਆਂ ਬਿੱਲੀਆਂ* ਝਾਕਦੀਆਂ
***rāje rāje* k^{h}ā̃de, *billīā̃ billīā̃* j^{h}ākdīā̃**
kings kings eat cats cats stare

2. Using synonymous or semantically related words

The meaning of the combination is deliberately vague

ਚਾਹ ਪਾਣੀ
cāh pāṇī
tea water
'light refreshment with a drink (not necessarily tea)'

ਮੱਖੀ ਮੱਛਰ
makk^{h}ī macc^{h}ar
fly mosquito
'winged insects (both or either of them)'

ਕੁੱਤਾ ਬਿੱਲਾ
kuttā billā
dog cat
'stray animal (either one or both or it could even be a fox)'

ਖਿੱਚ ਧੂਹ ਕਰਨਾ
k^{h}icc d^{h}uh karnā
pulling pulling doing
'manhandling someone (which may involve more than pulling)'

ਘਸੁੰਨ ਮੁੱਕੀ ਹੋਣਾ
g^{h}asunn mukkī hoṇā
fist blows fist blows happening
'coming to blows (possibly involving more than fists)'

ਨਿੱਕਾ ਮੋਟਾ ਕੰਮ
nikkā moṭā kamm
small fat work
'any type of work'

ਦਾਣਾ ਪਾਣੀ
grain water
'food allotted by fate'

ਤਨ ਮਨ ਧਨ ਵਾਰਨਾ
tan man d^{h}an vārnā
body mind wealth sacrificing
'sacrificing everything'

3. Echo words

In this pair, the second member sounds like the first but has no lexical meaning. The meaning of the pair is more vague – 'and all that'.

ਪਾਣੀ ਧਾਣੀ
pāṇī d^{h}āṇī
water (echo)
'drink etc.'

ਸਿਆਣਾ ਬਿਆਣਾ
siāṇā biāṇā
sensible (echo)
'having all the qualities of a sensible person'

ਮੁੰਡੇ ਖੁੰਡੇ
muṇḍe k^huṇḍe
boys (echo)
'typical boys'

4. Dismissive words

In a meaningless dismissive word, the stressed vowel (except **[u]** and **[ū]**) of the first word is replaced by the short **[u]** and long **[ū]** respectively, and **[u]** and **[ū]** are replaced by **[a]** and **[ā]** respectively. Some speakers replace **[o]** and **[a^u]** by **[ā]**. The meaning of the dismissive word is 'or something/anything like...' as in

ਮੈਂ ਕਿਸੇ ਭੂਤ ਭਾਤ ਤੋਂ ਨਹੀਂ ਡਰਦਾ
mã^i kise b^hūt *b^hāt* tõ nahī̃ ḍardā
ghost dismissive word
'I am not afraid of a ghost or anything like that'

Other examples are

ਡਰ ਡੁਰ
ḍar *ḍur*
'fear or any such feeling'

ਕੜਾਹ ਕੜੂਹ
ka'ṛāh *ka'ṛūh*
'pudding or anything like that'

ਜੇਬ ਜੂਬ
jeb *jūb*
'pocket or anything like'

ਚੁੱਕਣਾ ਚੱਕਣਾ
cukkṇā *cakkṇā*
'lifting or any such action'

ਮੋਹ ਮੂਹ *(ਮਾਹ)*
moh ***mūh*** ***(māh)***
'attachment or any such feeling'

ਪਕੌੜੇ ਪਕੂੜੇ *(ਪਕਾੜੇ)*
pa'kaᵘṛe ***pa'kūṛe*** ***(pa'kāṛe)***
'fritters and such things'

5. Insult words

The insult word precedes the main word. In an insult word, ੜਾ/ੜੇ/ੜੀ/ੜੀਆਂ **ṛā/ṛe/ṛī/ṛiā̃** (according to number and gender) is added to the first sound of the main word.

ਬੰਦ ਕਰੋ ਇਹ *ਸੜਾ* ਸੰਗੀਤ
band karo ih ***saṛā*** **sangīt**
'Stop this stupid music'

ਮੈਂ ਨਹੀਂ ਖਾਣੇ ਕੋਈ *ਅੜੇ* ਅੰਗੂਰ
mãⁱ nahī̃ kʰāṇe koī ***aṛe*** **angūr**
'I am not going to eat any damned grapes'

The information provided above is not exhaustive. Only some major processes are mentioned. Whether this information should be a part of grammar or lexicon is not the point in this and the next appendix. It is proper to include it in a grammar book meant for *reference*.

Appendix 3

Panjabi Numbers and Expressions of Time

Since the decimal number system originated in North India, you can expect the names for the Panjabi numbers to be in the form of 'multiple of ten plus a number smaller than ten' as you have in English after 20. Before 20 it is the opposite in English. You have 'twenty-four' (20+4) but 'eighteen', which may have originated as 'eight plus ten' (8+10). The names for the numbers in Panjabi seem to have originated in the same way, but with some differences. They are all in the pattern of 'eight plus ten' except those ending with 9. For example, 24 is literally 'four plus twenty', but 29 literally means 'below 30' or 'rising on to 30'. Since these names originated many centuries ago, phonetic changes have invariably changed their pronunciation, but have not entirely obscured their origin. ਚੌਵੀ **ca^{u}vī** still sounds somewhat like ਚਾਰ-ਵੀਹ **cār-vīh** 'four-twenty'.

1. Numbers

(i) Cardinal numbers

1	ਇੱਕ	**ikk**	6	ਛੇ	**c^{h}e**
2	ਦੋ	**do**	7	ਸੱਤ	**satt**
3	ਤਿੰਨ	**tinn**	8	ਅੱਠ	**aṭṭ^{h}**
4	ਚਾਰ	**cār**	9	ਨੌਂ	**nā̃^{u}**
5	ਪੰਜ	**panj**	10	ਦਸ	**das**

11	ਗਿਆਰਾਂ	**giārā̃**
12	ਬਾਰਾਂ	**bārā̃**
13	ਤੇਰਾਂ	**terā̃**
14	ਚੌਦਾਂ	**ca^{u}dā̃**
15	ਪੰਦਰਾਂ	**pandrā̃**
16	ਸੋਲ਼ਾਂ	**soḷā̃**
17	ਸਤਾਰਾਂ	**satārā̃**
18	ਅਠਾਰਾਂ	**aṭ^{h}ārā̃**
19	ਉੱਨੀ	**unnī**
20	ਵੀਹ	**vīh**
21	ਇੱਕੀ	**ikkī**
22	ਬਾਈ	**bāī**
23	ਤੇਈ	**teī**
24	ਚੌਵੀ	**ca^{u}vī**
	ਚਵ੍ਹੀ	**cavhī**
25	ਪੰਝੀ	**panj^{h}ī**
	ਪੱਚੀ	**paccī**
26	ਛੱਬੀ	**c^{h}abbī**
27	ਸਤਾਈ	**satāī**
28	ਅਠਾਈ	**aṭ^{h}āī**
29	ਉਣੱਤੀ	**uṇattī**
30	ਤੀਹ	**tīh**
31	ਇਕੱਤੀ	**ikattī**
32	ਬੱਤੀ	**battī**
33	ਤੇਤੀ	**tetī**
	ਤੇਂਤੀ	**tẽtī**
34	ਚੌਤੀ	**ca^{u}tī**
	ਚੌਂਤੀ	**cā̃^{u}tī**
35	ਪੈਂਤੀ	**pā̃^{i}tī**
36	ਛੱਤੀ	**c^{h}attī**
37	ਸੈਂਤੀ	**sā̃^{i}ntī**
38	ਅਠੱਤੀ	**aṭ^{h}attī**
39	ਉਂਤਾਲ਼ੀ	**untāḷī**
40	ਚਾਲ਼ੀ	**cāḷī**
41	ਇਕਤਾਲ਼ੀ	**iktāḷī**
42	ਬਤਾਲ਼ੀ	**batāḷī**
	ਬਿਆਲ਼ੀ	**biāḷī**
43	ਤਰਤਾਲ਼ੀ	**tartāḷī**
44	ਚੁਤਾਲ਼ੀ	**cutāḷī**
45	ਪੰਤਾਲ਼ੀ	**pantāḷī**
46	ਛਿਆਲ਼ੀ	**c^{h}iāḷī**
	ਛਤਾਲ਼ੀ	**c^{h}atāḷī**
47	ਸੰਤਾਲ਼ੀ	**santāḷī**
48	ਅਠਤਾਲ਼ੀ	**aṭ^{h}tāḷī**
49	ਉਣੰਜਾ	**uṇānjā**
50	ਪੰਜਾਹ	**panjāh,**
	ਪਜਾਹ	**ˈpajāh**
51	ਇਕਵੰਜਾ	**ikvanjā**
52	ਬਵੰਜਾ	**bavanjā**
53	ਤਰਵੰਜਾ	**tarvanjā**
54	ਚੁਰੰਜਾ	**curanjā**
55	ਪਚਵੰਜਾ	**pacvanjā**
56	ਛਪੰਜਾ	**c^{h}apanjā**
57	ਸਤਵੰਜਾ	**satvanjā**
58	ਅਠਵੰਜਾ	**aṭ^{h}vanjā**
59	ਉਣਾਹਟ	**uṇāhaṭ**
60	ਸੱਠ	**saṭṭ^{h}**
61	ਇਕਾਹਟ	**ikāhaṭ**
62	ਬਾਹਟ	**bāhaṭ**
63	ਤ੍ਰੇਹਟ	**trehaṭ**
64	ਚੌਹਟ	**ca^{u}haṭ**
	ਚੌਂਹਟ	**cā̃^{u}haṭ**
65	ਪੈਂਹਟ	**pā̃^{i}haṭ**
66	ਛਿਆਹਟ	**c^{h}iāhaṭ**
67	ਸਤਾਹਟ	**satāhaṭ**
68	ਅਠਾਹਟ	**aṭ^{h}āhaṭ**
69	ਉਣਹੱਤਰ	**uṇhattar**
70	ਸੱਤਰ	**sattar**

71	ਇਕਹੱਤਰ	**ikhattar**	86	ਛਿਆਸੀ	**c^{h}iāsī**
72	ਬਹੱਤਰ	**bahattar**	87	ਸਤਾਸੀ	**satāsī**
73	ਤਿਹੱਤਰ	**tihattar**	88	ਅਠਾਸੀ	**aṭ^{h}āsī**
74	ਚੁਹੱਤਰ	**cuhattar**	89	ਉਣੰਨਵੇਂ	**uṇanavẽ**
75	ਪੰਜਹੱਤਰ	**panjhattar**	90	ਨੱਬੇ	**nabbe**
76	ਛਿਹੱਤਰ	**c^{h}ihattar**		ਨੱਵੇ	**navve**
77	ਸਤੱਤਰ	**satattar**	91	ਇਕੰਨਵੇਂ	**ikannavẽ**
78	ਅਠੱਤਰ	**aṭ^{h}attar**		ਇਕਿਅੰਨਵੇ	**ikiannavẽ**
79	ਉਣਾਸੀ	**uṇāsī**	92	ਬੰਨਵੇਂ	**bannavẽ**
80	ਅੱਸੀ	**assī**	93	ਤਰੰਨਵੇਂ	**tarannavẽ**
81	ਇਕਿਆਸੀ	**ikiāsī**		ਤਿਰਿਅੰਨਵੇਂ	**tiriannavẽ**
	ਇਕਾਸੀ	**ikāsī**	94	ਚੁਰੰਨਵੇਂ	**curannavẽ**
82	ਬਿਆਸੀ	**biāsī**	95	ਪਚੰਨਵੇਂ	**pacannavẽ**
83	ਤਰਿਆਸੀ	**tariāsī**	96	ਛਿਅੰਨਵੇਂ	**c^{h}iannavẽ**
84	ਚੁਰਾਸੀ	**curāsī**	97	ਸਤੰਨਵੇਂ	**satannavẽ**
85	ਪਚਾਸੀ	**pacāsī**	98	ਅਠੰਨਵੇਂ	**aṭ^{h}annavẽ**
	ਪੰਜਾਸੀ	**panjāsī**	99	ਨੜ੍ਹਿੰਨਵੇਂ	**naṛhinnavẽ**
			100	ਸੌ	**sa^{u}**

0	ਸਿਫ਼ਰ	**sifar**
157	ਇਕ ਸੌ ਸਤਵੰਜਾ	**ikk sa^{u} satvanjā**
670	ਛੇ ਸੌ ਸੱਤਰ	**c^{h}e sa^{u} sattar**
837	ਅੱਠ ਸੌ ਸੈਂਤੀ	**aṭṭ^{h} sa^{u} sã^{i}tī**
1,000	(ਇੱਕ) ਹਜ਼ਾਰ	**(ikk) hazār**
1,213	ਇੱਕ ਹਜ਼ਾਰ ਦੋ ਸੌ ਤੇਰਾਂ	**ikk hazār do sa^{u} terā̃**
10,000	ਦਸ ਹਜ਼ਾਰ	**das hazār**
100,000 (a hundred thousand)	(ਇਕ) ਲੱਖ	**(ikk) lakk^{h}**
1,000,000 (a million)	ਦਸ ਲੱਖ	**das lakk^{h}**
10,000,000 (ten million)	(ਇਕ) ਕਰੋੜ	**(ikk) karoṛ**

100,000,000 (a billion)	ਦਸ ਕਰੋੜ	**das karoṛ**
1000,000,000 (ten billion)	(ਇਕ) ਅਰਬ	**(ikk) arab**

(ii) Ordinal numbers

(Masculine singular forms are given below)

first	ਪਹਿਲਾ	**pahilā**
second	ਦੂਸਰਾ, ਦੂਜਾ	**dūsarā, dūjā**
third	ਤੀਸਰਾ, ਤੀਜਾ	**tīsarā, tījā**
fourth	ਚੌਥਾ	**caᵘtʰā**
fifth	ਪੰਜਵਾਂ	**panjvā̃**
sixth	ਛੇਵਾਂ	**cʰevā̃**
		(Then go on adding -ਵਾਂ **-vā̃** up to ten. Beyond that, you omit the final -ਆਂ **-ā̃** before adding ਵਾਂ **-vā̃**. Some speakers also add the high tone, especially up to 19).
eleventh	ਗਿਆਰ੍ਹਵਾਂ	**giārhvā̃**
twelfth	ਬਾਰ੍ਹਵਾਂ	**bārhvā̃**
thirty-second	ਬੱਤੀਵਾਂ	**battīvā̃**
seventy-sixth	ਛਿਹੱਤਰਵਾਂ	**cʰihattarvā̃**
one hundred and tenth	ਇੱਕ ਸੌ ਦਸਵਾਂ	**ikk saᵘ dasvā̃**
thousandth	ਹਜ਼ਾਰਵਾਂ	**hazārvā̃**
one hundred and first	ਇੱਕ ਸੌ ਇੱਕਵਾਂ	But be careful with **ikk saᵘ ikkvā̃** (not ***ikk saᵘ pahilā)**

(iii) Fractions

¼ (a quarter)	ਇੱਕ ਚੌਥਾਈ	**ikk ca^{u}t^{h}āī**
½ (half)	ਅੱਧਾ	**add^{h}ā**
¾ (three quarters)	ਪੌਣਾ	**pa^{u}ṇā**
1¼	ਸਵਾ (ਇੱਕ)	**savā (ikk)**
1½	ਡੇੜ੍ਹ	**ḍeṛh**
1¾	ਪੌਣੇ ਦੋ	**pa^{u}ṇe do** (be careful, not ***pa^{u}ṇe ikk**)
2¼	ਸਵਾ ਦੋ	**savā do**
2½	ਢਾਈ	**ḍ^{h}āī**
2¾	ਪੌਣੇ ਤਿੰਨ	**pa^{u}ṇe tinn**
3¼	ਸਵਾ ਤਿੰਨ	**savā tinn**
3½	ਸਾਢੇ ਤਿੰਨ	**sāḍ^{h}e tinn**
3¾	ਪੌਣੇ ਚਾਰ	**pa^{u}ṇe cār** (not ***pa^{u}ṇe tinn**) Then follow the general pattern
number+¼	ਸਵਾ+number	**savā**+number
number+½	ਸਾਢੇ+number	**sāḍ^{h}e**+number
number+¾	ਪੌਣੇ+*next* number	**pa^{u}ṇe**+*next* number

(iv) Panjabi numerals

Panjabi has its own set of numerals. But they are rarely used these days except in some books on Sikh religion. These numerals are

੧	੨	੩	੪	੫	੬	੭	੮	੯	੦
1	2	3	4	5	6	7	8	9	0

The fundamental principle of the Sikh religion is written as ੴ which is pronounced as ਇੱਕ ਓਂਕਾਰ **ikk onkār** or ਇੱਕ ਓਅੰਕਾਰ **ikk oankār**. It means 'There is one God'. Since these numerals have been used in the Sikh holy book, they have religious significance for the Sikhs.

G.B. Singh (1950), who spent all his life researching the origin of Gurmukhi script, found something interesting that suggests that the numbers originated in the same area where Gurmukhi did.

The Panjabi word for 'two' is written as ਦੋ in Gurmukhi. The shape of the first letter ਦ of this word has some resemblance to the numeral in Panjabi and the so-called Arabic numeral 2. Its shape should be compared to the *actual* Arabic numeral ٢ as well. Turn the Arabic numeral 90 degrees anti-clockwise and the result will be interesting.

ਦ ੨ 2 ٢

Arabs learnt these numerals from India and still very honestly call them Hindsa or "Indian Art" and write their numbers left to right, as Indians do, and not right to left as their script is written.

Similarly the Panjabi word for 'three' is written in Gurmukhi as ਤਿੰਨ, starting with the letter ਤ. Let us compare the shapes again (after turning the *actual* Arabic numeral 90 degrees anti-clockwise).

ਤ ੩ 3 ٣

Interesting stuff. Time obscures origins, but not entirely!

2. Expressions of time

(i) Hours

o' clock	ਵਜੇ	**vaje** (which you add to the following)
1-15	ਸਵਾ	**savā (ikk)**
1-30	ਡੇੜ੍ਹ	**ḍeṛh**
1-45	ਪੌਣੇ ਦੋ	**pa^{u}ṇe do**
2-00	ਦੋ	**do**
2-15	ਸਵਾ ਦੋ	**savā do**
2-30	ਢਾਈ	**ḍ^{h}āī**
3-15	ਸਵਾ ਤਿੰਨ	**savā tinn**

3-30	ਸਾਢੇ ਤਿੰਨ	**sāḍ^{h}e tinn**
3-45	ਪੌਣੇ ਚਾਰ	**pa^{u}ṇe cār**
6-00 am	ਸਵੇਰ ਦੇ ਛੇ ਵਜੇ	**saver de c^{h}e vaje**
6-00 pm	ਸ਼ਾਮ ਦੇ ਛੇ ਵਜੇ	**śām de c^{h}e vaje**
at 6-00 pm	ਸ਼ਾਮ ਦੇ ਛੇ ਵਜੇ	**śām de c^{h}e vaje**
35 minutes *past* 5-00	ਪੰਜ ਵਜ ਕੇ ਪੈਂਤੀ ਮਿੰਟ	**panj vaj ke pā̃^{i}tī minṭ**
at 5-35	ਪੰਜ ਵਜ ਕੇ ਪੈਂਤੀ ਮਿੰਟ 'ਤੇ	**panj vaj ke pā̃^{i}tī minṭ te**
10 minutes *to* 7-00 (i.e., 6-50)	ਸੱਤ ਵਜਣ ਨੂੰ ਦਸ ਮਿੰਟ	**satt vajaṇ nū̃ das minṭ**
year	ਸਾਲ	**sāl** (*m*)
month	ਮਹੀਨਾ	**mahīnā** (*m*)
week	ਹਫ਼ਤਾ	**haftā** (*m*)
day	ਦਿਨ	**din** (*m*)
hour	ਘੰਟਾ	**g^{h}anṭā** (*m*)
minute	ਮਿੰਟ	**minṭ** (*m*)
second	ਸਕਿੰਟ	**sakinṭ** (*m*)
last week	ਪਿਛਲੇ ਹਫ਼ਤੇ	**pic^{h}ale hafte**
next week	ਅਗਲੇ ਹਫ਼ਤੇ	**agle hafte**
last month	ਪਿਛਲੇ ਮਹੀਨੇ	**pic^{h}ale mahīne**
next year	ਅਗਲੇ ਸਾਲ	**agle sāl**

(ii) Times of the day

morning	ਸਵੇਰ	**saver** (*f*)
	ਸਵੇਰਾ	**saverā** (*m*)
in the morning	ਸਵੇਰੇ	**severe**
	ਸਵੇਰ ਨੂੰ	**saver nū̃**
mid-day	ਦੁਪਹਿਰ	**dupahir** (*f*)
	ਦੁਪਹਿਰਾ	**dupahirā** (*m*)

at mid-day	ਦੁਪਹਿਰੇ	**dupahire**
	ਦੁਪਹਿਰ ਨੂੰ	**dupahir nū̃**
afternoon	ਲੌਢਾ ਵੇਲਾ	**la^{u}ḍ^{h}ā velā** (*m*)
in the afternoon	ਲੌਢੇ ਵੇਲੇ	**la^{u}ḍ^{h}e vele**
time of the	ਤਿਰਕਾਲ਼ਾਂ	**tirkāḷā̃** (*f/pl*)
sunset	ਤਕਾਲ਼ਾਂ	**takāḷā̃** (*f/pl*)
evening	ਸ਼ਾਮ	**śām** (*f*)
	ਸੰਝ	**sanj^h** (*f*)
in the evening	ਸ਼ਾਮੀਂ	**śāmī̃**
	ਸ਼ਾਮ ਨੂੰ	**śām nū̃**
	ਸੰਝ ਵੇਲੇ	**sanj^h vele**
night	ਰਾਤ	**rāt** (*f*)
at night	ਰਾਤ ਨੂੰ	**rāt nū̃**
	ਰਾਤੀਂ	**rātī̃**

(iii) Days of the week

Names of days marked as "Muslim" are used exclusively by Muslim speakers and by non-Muslim Panjabi speakers in Pakistan. The names of the days are masculine nouns.

Sunday	ਐਤਵਾਰ	**a^{i}tvār**
Monday	ਸੋਮਵਾਰ	**somvār**
	ਪੀਰ	**pīr** (Muslim)
Tuesday	ਮੰਗਲ਼ਵਾਰ	**mangaḷvār**
Wednesday	ਬੁਧਵਾਰ	**bud^{h}vār**
Thursday	ਵੀਰਵਾਰ	**vīrvār**
	ਜੁਮੇਰਾਤ	**jumerāt** (Muslim)
Friday	ਸ਼ੁੱਕਰਵਾਰ	**śukkarvār**
	ਜੁਮਾ	**jumā** (Muslim)
Saturday	ਛਨਿੱਛਰਵਾਰ	**c^{h}anicc^{h}arvār**
	ਸਨਿੱਚਰਵਾਰ	**saniccarvār**
	ਹਫ਼ਤਾ	**haftā** (Muslim)

(iv) Months

Names of the months of the Western calendar are pronounced slightly differently in Panjabi. But you can use the English pronunciation. These names of the months are **masculine nouns**.

Glossary

Explanation of Technical Terms and Abbreviations

The technical terms of phonetics, phonology, grammar and semantics used in book are described briefly in the following tables. These tables are for *quick reference only*. Each term is defined and explained with examples in the relevant chapters. The general Subject Index gives the page numbers where you can find such explanations. Only the chapters where the term is fully explained with examples are mentioned in these tables.

These definitions and explanations are Panjabi-specific and may not apply to other languages. For explanations of these terms applicable to a wider variety of languages, users/readers are advised to consult Matthews (2007).

1. Phonetics and phonology

Entries in the first table are not in the alphabetical order because you need to refer to the earlier ones before going to the later ones. But there are very few entries in this table. Technical terms explained elsewhere in these tables and the book are printed in **bold letters**.

Vowel (V)	A vowel is a linguistic sound articulated with the outgoing **voiced** airstream and without any obstruction in the throat or the mouth. CHAPTER 3.
Classification of Vowels	The acoustic quality of vowel sounds can be varied by (i) raising different parts of the tongue to different heights, (ii) by rounding or not rounding the lips, and (iii) by keeping the nasal passage closed or open. Thus you can have **high, mid, low, front** and **back** vowels, and **rounded** and **unrounded** vowels, all of which may be either **oral** or **nasalised**. The vowels articulated in the inner part of the vowel space are known as **centralised** vowels and the other vowels are contrastively known as **peripheral** vowels. CHAPTER 3.
Consonant (C)	For the articulation of the consonant sounds, the airstream is obstructed or stopped either in the throat or in the mouth. The nasal passage may be either open or closed. The open nasal passage results in **nasal consonants**. CHAPTER 3.
Place of Articulation of Consonants, Homorganic Consonants	The places where the airstream for the production of a consonant sound can be obstructed are (i) glottis or the space between the vocal cords (for glottal **h**) (ii) soft palate (**velar** consonants), (iii) hard palate (**palatal** consonants), (iv) with the underside of the curled back tongue touching the part of the palate above and behind the gum ridge (**retroflex** consonants), (v) upper and lower lips (**labial** consonants). Consonants having the same **place** of articulation are known as **homorganic** consonants. CHAPTER 3.

Manner of Articulation of Consonants	If the airstream is completley stopped, the resulting consonants are known as **stop** consonants. If the airstream is simply obstructed but goes out with an audible friction, the consonants are known as **fricatives**. But if there is no friction, the consonants are **frictionless continuants**. A stop consonant released with friction is known as an **affricate**. CHAPTER 3.
Voiced and Voiceless	For the production of **voiced** sounds, the vocal cords vibrate, but they do not vibrate for the production of **voiceless** consonants. All the **vowels**, **nasal** consonants and **frictionless** continuant consonants in Panjabi are **voiced**. The Panjabi **h** [ɦ] sound, unlike the English [h] sound, is **voiced.** CHAPTER 3.
Aspirated and Unaspirated	**Aspirated** consonants are produced with a *strong* puff of air. The outgoing airstream is controlled for the production of **unaspirated** consonants. CHAPTER 3.
Breathy Voiced	The Panjabi consonants which are both **voiced** and **aspirated** are also called **breathy voiced** consonants. CHAPTER 3.
Tense and Lax Vowels and Consonants	**Tense vowels** and **consonants** are pronounced with tense tongue muscles and the **lax vowels** and consonants are produced with lax tongue muscles. In Panjabi, only the tense vowels and consonants can be **geminated**. CHAPTERS 3, 4.
Syllable	A **syllable** in Panjabi is a phonological unit consisting of a **vowel** which may be accompanied by one or more **consonants** and is capable of being uttered alone. CHAPTER 3.
Stress (or Accent)	A **syllable** with **stress** or **accent** in Panjabi is uttered with more forceful articulatory effort than for an **unstressed** or **unaccented syllable**. It also generally sounds louder. CHAPTER 4.

Closed and Open Syllable	An **open syllable** ends with a **vowel** and a closed syllable ends with a **consonant**. CHAPTER 4.
Gemination	If a single **consonant** or vowel **sound** is stretched in speech in such a way that a **syllable** boundary lies in the middle of the sound, the process is known as gemination. A geminated consonant is also known as a **long consonant**. **Tense vowels** can also be geminated in Panjabi. CHAPTER 3.
Tone	If variation of the **pitch of voice** is involved in the stressing (or accenting) of the **vowel** of a **syllable**, the syllable is said to receive a **lexical pitch accent** if its presence makes a difference to the meaning of the word. Panjabi is not really a **tone language** in the sense Chinese is. But the term **"tone"** for a **pitch accent** is now an established term and is used in this book. Panjabi has two such tones, the **low tone** and the **high tone**. CHAPTER 4.
Intonation	The variation of pitch of voice generally over a **clause** or **sentence** (but sometimes over a smaller construction as well). CHAPTER 4.
Intonation Contour	The direction of **intonational pitch** movement (to express assertion, question, surprise, irony and many other attitudes and modalities) is known as **intonation contour**. The pitch contour generally changes direction at the **accented syllable** of the communicatively most sigificant word in the clause or sentence. This syllable is called the **nuclear** syllable of the contour. CHAPTER 4.
Nuclear Syllable	See '**intonation contour**'.

2. Grammar and semantics

The following table lists the technical terms in alphabetical order. The first column gives a brief explanation of the term and also mentions the chapter where a full explanation with examples can be found. The second column gives the abbreviations used in this book.

Ablative (Case Form) The notion of "movement away from a location" expressed either by the **synthetic** case form derived by adding -ਓਂ **-õ** to the **NP** *or* by the **analytic case form** by adding the **postposition** ਤੋਂ **tõ** 'from'. CHAPTER 6.	
Additive Phase (of a Verb) A **verb** phase derived from the basic **intransitive** or **transitive** phase by some morphological process and turning the basic phase into a **transitive** or **causative** phase. Also see **subtractive phase.** CHAPTER 9.	AdPh
Adjective A word class whose main role is to modify a noun. An adjective works as the HEAD of an **adjective phrase**. **Adjectives** which change their form are known as **black adjectives** and the ones which remain invariable are known as **red adjectives**. CHAPTER 7.	Adj
Adjective Phrase A phrase whose HEAD is an **adjective**. CHAPTER 7.	AdjP
Adjunct A modifier not strictly needed by the *structure* of a clause but giving additional information. CHAPTER 5.	ADJCT

Adverb A word or group of words modifying a **verb, verb phrase** or **adjective**. CHAPTER 7.	Adv
Adverb Phrase A **phrase** playing the role of an **adverb**. CHAPTER 7.	AdvP
Agentive Postposition ਨੇ ne The **postposition** marking the SUBJECT of an **ergative** clause. CHAPTER 12.	Agt
Agglutination Joining of segments with different grammatical functions in such a way that they are easily identifiable but no other elements can intervene between them. CHAPTERS 9, 10, 11.	
Agreement A **verb** or **adjective** having the same **number** and **gender** *or* **number** and **person** form as a **noun** or **pronoun**. CHAPTERS 11, 12.	
Analytic Case Form A case form derived by adding a **postposition** to an **NP**. Also see **synthetic case form**. CHAPTER 6.	
Anaphoric Reference Looking *backward* in order to know the meaning of a word or **phrase**. CHAPTERS 15,16.	
Aspect A grammatical category indicating the event as completed, or incomplete or recurring etc., contrasted with **tense**. It does *not* relate an event to an external point in time as **tense** does. CHAPTER 11.	
Auxiliary Verb A **verb** belonging to a small class which accompanies another verb and modifies its meaning. Also known as **explicator auxiliary.** CHAPTERS 9, 10.	Aux

Backgrounding
A case role expressible by an *optional* ADJUNCT. CHAPTER 11. Also see **elimination.**

Black Adjective
See **adjective**. CHAPTER 7.

Canonical Finite Clause
A **clause** is a syntactic unit whose structure is, or is regarded as, a reduced form of a sentence. A **canonical finite clause** in Panjabi is syntactically the most basic one and is a **declarative, positive,** non-**co-ordinate, main clause** whose **VP (verb phrase**) is not a **serial verb** or a verb in the **subtractive phase** and which has not undergone any of the **discourse-related** processes. CHAPTER 5.

Case Role (Semantic)
The entities denoted by **nouns** and **pronouns** involved in the event or situation denoted by the **verb**; not all of which may be required by the *structure* of the **clause**. CHAPTERS 5, 11, 12.

Cataphoric Reference
Looking *forward* in order to know the meaning of a word or phrase. CHAPTERS 15, 16.

Causative Verb V-cau
A verb form denoting an action in which the **causing agent** gets something done by the **immediate agent** or an **intermediate agent**. CHAPTERS 9, 12.

Complement

A linguistic element required by the *structure* of the clause unless it is left out for contextual reasons (and is thus "contextually recoverable"). COMPLEMENTS are said to be *licensed* by the verb PREDICATOR. COMPLEMENTS are opposed to syntactically *optional* ADJUNCTS. CHAPTER 5.

Complement (OBJECT) — COMP(O)

An **NP** or **AdjP** which is a *compulsory* COMPLEMENT in a clause and says something about the OBJECT of the **clause**. CHAPTER 5.

Complement (SUBJECT) — COMP(S)

An **NP** or **AdjP** which is a *compulsory* COMPLEMENT in a clause and says something about the SUBJECT of the clause. CHAPTER 5.

Conjunctive Participle — ConjP

A **verb** form which is now pronounced and written like a bare **stem** of the verb and is accompanied by an **explicator auxiliary** in a **serial verb construction** (**SVC**), or by ਕੇ **ke** in a **non-finite clause**. CHAPTERS 10, 11.

Co-ordinate Clause

A **clause** joined with another clause as its equal partner in a larger senetence. Also see **subordinate clause**. CHAPTER 15.

Co-ordinator — Co-or

A word or group of words which links syntactic units of equal standing (words, phrases or clauses) within a construction. CHAPTER 15.

Copula or **Copular-existential Verb** — Cop

The Panjabi **personal** verb ਹੈ **ha'** and its forms. This is the only verb form in Panjabi marked for **tense.** CHAPTERS 10, 11.

Definite Def

An **NP** whose referent has been contextually mentioned before or is unique. CHAPTER 12.

Demonstrative (Pronoun) Dem

A **pronoun** whose basic role is to locate a referent in relation to the speaker or the addressee. The so-called "third person pronouns" of Panjabi are actually **demonstratives** marked for *distance* and not person. CHAPTER 6.

Derived Free Form 1 Deff1

An uninflecting form of the verb derived by adding -ਦਿਆਂ **-diā̃** to the verb stem. It acts as the main verb in an **adverbial non-finite clause**. CHAPTER 14.

Derived Free Form 2 Deff2

An uninflecting form of the verb derived by adding -ਇਆਂ **-iā̃** to the verb stem. It acts as the main verb in an **adverbial non-finite clause**. CHAPTER 14.

Determiner Det

A **determiner** limits the potential referent of a **noun phrase**. CHAPTER 6.

Direct Form Dir

The form of a **noun, pronoun** or **adjective** which is *not* in the **oblique form**. CHAPTER 5.

Dual Case Form Dl

A case form which marks *two* individuals, i.e., more than one and fewer than three. CHAPTER 6.

Elimination

When the agent of the action denoted by the **verb** *must not* be mentioned, as opposed to **backgrounding**. CHAPTER 11.

Ergative Construction

A **clause** in which the **verb** does not agree with the **subject** in number and gender and either agrees with the **object** or is in the **neuter** form (homophonous to the masculine singular). CHAPTERS 11, 12.

Experiencer Expcr

A semantic case role of (generally) an animate being experiencing the effect of the action denoted by the verb. In Panjabi, it is mostly marked by the **postposition ਨੂੰ nū̃** 'to'. CHAPTER 12.

Explicator Auxiliary Verb

See **auxiliary verb**. CHAPTER 10.

Feminine (gender) Fem

Finite Clause

A **clause** in which *either* (i) the **subject** is marked with the postposition **ਨੇ ne** *or if this is not the case,* then (ii) the verb agrees with the **agent** SUBJECT. CHAPTER 5.

Gerund Ger

The **nominal** (functioning like a **noun** or **NP**) form of the **verb**. The **gerund** in Panjabi is homophonous to the **potential participle**. CHAPTER 11.

Goal of Result GR

The **semantic case role** towards which the result of the activity of a **verb** expressing the **perfective aspect** is regarded as aimed at or moving. In Panjabi it is also known as **definite object** and is marked by the **postposition ਨੂੰ nū̃** 'to'. CHAPTER 9, 11.

Immediate Agent ImmAgt

A case role marking a person or entity directly and immediately involved in carrying out an acvitity or event. CHAPTER 12.

Imperative (Plain) Imper(P)
A form of the verb used for giving orders or advice. The singular form of this type of imperative is homophonous to the **stem** form of the verb. CHAPTER 11.

Imperative (Suggestive) Imper(S)
An **imperative** in the form of a suggestion (regarded as more polite in Panjabi). CHAPTER 11.

Imperfect Participle ImP
An **adjectival** form of the verb denoting an activity regarded as incomplete or recurring (and sometimes as not even started). CHAPTERS 9, 11.

Initiator (Agent) IniAgt
A semantic case role marking a person or entity causing or intiating an activity or event carried out by the **immediate agent**. CHAPTER 12.

Instrumental (Case Form) Inst
A semantic case role marking an entity seen as being used as an instrument in an action or event. CHAPTER 6.

Intermediate Agent IntAgt
A semantic case role marking a person or entity acting as an intermediary between the **initiator agent** and the **immediate agent**. CHAPTER 12.

Intransitive Verb V-intr
A verb denoting an activity whose result stays with the **agent** SUBJECT and is neither aimed at nor passes on to a **patient** OBJECT. CHAPTER 9.

Locative (Case Form) Loc
A semantic case role locating the position of some entity in space. CHAPTER 6.

Masculine (Gender) Mas

Modality (Mood)
A grammatical category marking some action or event as definite, indefinite, possible, desirable, doubtful etc. It is a member of the trinity **TMA (Tense Mood Aspect)**.CHAPTER 11.

Neuter (agreement) — Neu
A verb in the **finite** form not agreeing with any **NP**. In Panjabi, such a verb is homophonous to the **masculine singular** form. CHAPTER 12.

Nominal (Subordinate) Clause — NomC
A **finite clause** playing the role of a **nominal** (SUBJECT, OBJECT or COMPLEMENT) in the main cluase. CHAPTER 14.

Non-finite Clause — NFC
An **adverbial clause** containing a verb in the uninflectable form and the SUBJECT either not mentioned or not marked as in a **finite clause**. CHAPTER 14.

Noun Phrase — NP
A **phrase** headed by a **noun** playing the role of a **nominal** in a **clause**. CHAPTER 6.

Object — OBJ
A **clause complement**, other than the SUBJECT which is involved in an action or event denoted by the **verb** and represents the semantic **patient**. CHAPTER 5.

Oblique Form — Obl
The form assumed by a **noun, pronoun** or **adjective** when it is followed by a **postposition**. Very often this form is homophonous to the **direct form**. CHAPTERS 6, 7, 8.

Particle — Part
Three members ਹੀ **hī**, ਵੀ **hī** and ਤਾਂ **tā̃** of the **adverb** class which organise the text and give it particular nuances. CHAPTERS 5, 16.

Passive Voice

Prototypically, in a **passive** clause (i) the semantic **patient** is the syntactic SUBJECT, (ii) the semantic **agent** is a **backgrounded** ADJUNCT and (iii) the patient is the **substratum** or the **goal** of the action/activity denoted by the **verb**. Not all the three features may be present in some clauses in Panjabi. CHAPTER 13.

Patient — Pnt

A semantic role of an NP seen as undergoing some process or action or the target of a process or action. CHAPTER 11.

Perfect Participle — PerP

A form of a verb stem indicating an action/event as a complete/completed whole and viewed from its *end point*. CHAPTER 11.

Person — Per

A grammatical system classifying a subset of pronouns in terms of the role of the speaker (**first person**), the addressee (**second person**) and the **third person** (with no reference to either). Panjabi "third person pronouns" are actually **demonstratives.** CHAPTER 6.

Phrase

A syntactic unit which is not a **clause** but functions as a whole within a larger construction.

Pivot

An **NP** with which all the inflecting **verb** members of an **SVC** agree in number and person/gender. A pivot is said to **control** verb-agreement in an **SVC**. CHAPTER 13.

Plural (Number) — Pl

Postposition P

A word or a group of words coming *after* an **NP** and basically indicating a spatial relation or (in the case of ਨੇ **ne**) marking the **agent** SUBJECT of an **ergative clause**. CHAPTER 8.

Postpositional Phrase PP

A **phrase** consisting of an **NP** followed by a **postposition** which acts as the HEAD of the phrase. CHAPTER 8.

Potential Participle PotP

A form of a verb stem indicating an action/event as a complete/completed whole and viewed from its *starting point*, or viewed as potentially complete/completed. CHAPTER 11

Predicator PRED

The **verb phrase (VP)** part of a **clause** viewed syntactically as requiring (or **licensing**) the **clause complements**. CHAPTER 5

Pronoun Pron

A member of a closed class of words whose members "stand for" or refer to **NPs** mostly **anaphorically** (by looking *backwards*) and sometimes **cataphorically** (by looking *forward*). CHAPTER 6.

Recipient Recipient

Semantic role of an **NP** which identifies an individual or individuals as receiving something. CHAPTER 12.

Red Adjective

See **adjective**. CHAPTER 7.

Relative Clause RelC

A clause that modifies an **NP** either by giving some extra information about it (**non-defining relative clause**) or by restricting its reference (**defining relative clause**). CHAPTER 15.

Relative Pronoun

A **pronoun** that introduces a **relative clause**. CHAPTER 15.

Serial Verb — SV

A construction in which two or more successive forms of verbs are joined together with no connecting ਕੇ **ke**. CHAPTER 13

Serial Verb Construction — SVC

A **clause** in which the main verb is **serial verb**. CHAPTER 13.

Singular (number) — Sg

Subject — SUB

In a Panjabi clause, the SUBJECT **NP** is *either* (i) marked with the postposition ਨੇ **ne**, *or if this is not the case*, then (ii) it is the **NP** the verb agrees with in number and person/or gender. CHAPTER 5.

Subjunctive Form — Sbjct

The form of the stem of a verb which does not express any **tense** or **aspect**. It is a **personal** form that agrees with the SUBJECT in person and number. CHAPTER 11.

Subordinate Clause

A **clause** which is a syntactic element within a larger clause (the **main clause** or the **matrix clause**). CHAPTER 15.

Subordinator — Subo

A word or group of words which introduces a **subordinate clause**. CHAPTER 15.

Substratum of the Activity (*vyāpārāśraya*) — SA

The **NP** referring to an entity that starts an event or activity. CHAPTER 12.

Substratum of the Result (*phalāśraya*) SR

The **NP** referring to an entity that is viewed as **affected** by an event or activity. CHAPTER 12.

Subtractive Phase of the Verb SubPh

A form of the stem derived by adding the infix **-ई- -i-** to the corresponding basic or **additive phase.** CHAPTER 11.

Synthetic Case Form

A case form derived by changing the form of the noun or pronoun instead of adding a **postposition.** Also see **analytic case form**. Examples are **synthetic** form ਘਰੋਂ (ਘਰ+ਓਂ) **gʰarõ (gʰar+õ)** and **analytic** form ਘਰ ਤੋਂ **gʰar tõ**. CHAPTER 6.

Tense

Inflectional category whose basic role is to locate a situation in time in relation to the *situation-external* moment of speech (and sometimes to another moment in time). In Panjabi, only the **copula** appears to be maked for **tense**. CHAPTER 11. Also see **aspect**.

Transitive Verb V-tr

A verb denoting an activity whose result passes on to, or is aimed at, a **patient** OBJECT. CHAPTER 9.

Verb V

One of the class of lexical units denoting actions and processes. In a Panjabi clause, the verb characteristically plays the role of the PREDICATOR. CHAPTER 9.

Verb Phrase VP

A **phrase** consisting of one or more **verbs** denoting a *single* action of event. CHAPTER 9.

Word Order

The order of syntactic elements in a **clause** or sentence. In Panjabi, it is a lot more flexible than in English, but it is not completely free and is determined by the context, discourse and rhetorical factors, often accompanied by the use of **particles** and **intonation**. Linguists generally regard Panjabi as having **SOV** (**Subject Object Verb**) word order. But this is simply a *tendency* which often makes itself felt in actual speech and writing. CHAPTER 16.

References

Agnihotri, R.K. (2007). *Hindi: An Essential Grammar.* London and New York: Routledge.

Aikhenvald, A.Y. and Dixon, R.M.W. (eds). (2006). *Serial Verb Constructions: A Cross-linguistic Typology*. Oxford: Oxford University Press.

Alhawary, M.T. (2011). *Modern Standard Arabic Grammar: A Learner's Guide.* Chichester: Wiley-Blackwell.

Allen, W.S. (1964). 'Tansitivity and Possession'. *Language 40*: 337-43.

Bahl, K.C. (1964). *A Grammatical Sketch of Punjabi.* Chicago: South Asia Centre, University of Chicago.

___ (1967). *A Reference Grammar of Hindi.* Chicago: South Asia Centre, University of Chicago.

___ (1969). 'Punjabi' in Sebeok, T.A. (ed.) *Current Trends in Linguistics 5*. The Hague: Mouton.

Bailey, T.G. (1904). *Panjabi Grammar: A Brief Grammar of Panjabi as Spoken in the Wazirabad District.* Lahore.

___ (1914). *A Panjabi Phonetic Reader.* London: Trübner.

___ and Cummings,T. (1912). *Panjabi Manual and Grammar: A Guide to the Colloquial Panjabi.* Calcutta: Baptist Mission Press.

Beames, John (1872–79). *A Comparative Grammar of the Modern Aryan Languages of India* (in 3 volumes). London: Trübner. Single volume Indian edition published in 1970 by Munshiram Manoharlal, New Delhi.

Bhardwaj, M.R. (1995). *Colloquial Panjabi*. London and New York: Routledge.

___ (2013). *Colloquial Panjabi 2*. London and New York: Routledge.

Bhartṛhari. See Iyer.

Bhatia, T.K. (1993). *Punjabi: A Cognitive-descriptive Grammar*. London and New York: Routledge.

___ and Koul, A. (2013). *Colloquial Urdu* (2nd edition). London and New York: Routledge.

Bloomfield, L. (1933). *Language*. New York: Holt, Rinehart and Winston.

Bortoft , H. (2012). *Taking Appearance Seriously: The Dynamic Way of Seeing in Goethe and European Thought*. London: Floris Books.

Brar, B.S. (2008). **ਪੰਜਾਬੀ ਵਿਆਕਰਨ: ਸਿਧਾਂਤ ਅਤੇ ਵਿਹਾਰ panjabi viakaran: sid^{h}ā̃t ate vihār.** Ludhiana: Chetna Prakashan.

Bybee, J.L. (1985). *Morphology: A Study of the Relation Between Meaning and Form*. Amsterdam: John Benjamin.

___ (2010). *Language, Usage and Cognition*. Cambridge: Cambridge University Press.

___ (2015). *Language Change*. Cambridge: Cambridge University Press.

Bybee, J.L., Perkins, R., and Paglicua, W. (1994). *The Evolution of Grammar: Tense, Aspect, and Modality in the Languages of the World*. Chicago: University of Chicago Press.

Carey, William (1812). *A Grammar of the Punjabee Language*. Serampore.

Cassirer, E. (1955). *The Philosophy of Symbolic Forms*. Vol 1. New Haven: University of Yale Press.

Chandra, Duni (1959). **ਪੰਜਾਬੀ ਭਾਸ਼ਾ ਦਾ ਵਿਕਾਸ panjabi b^{h}āśā dā vikās**. Chandigarh: Panjab University Publication Bureau.

___ (1964). **ਪੰਜਾਬੀ ਭਾਸ਼ਾ ਦਾ ਵਿਆਕਰਣ panjabi b^{h}āśā dā viākaraṇ**. Chandigarh: Panjab University Publication Bureau.

Chattopadhyaya, D.P., Embree, L., and Mohanty, J. (eds) (1992). *Phenomenology and Indian Philosophy.* Albany: State University of New York Press.

Court, Henry (1888). *History of the Sikhs or Translation of Sikkhan de Raj di Vikhia together with a Short Gurmukhi Grammar.* Lahore: Civil and Military Gazette Press.

Croft, W. (2001). *Radical Construction Grammar: Syntactic Theory in Typological Perspective.* Oxford: Oxford University Press.

___ and Cruse, D.A. (2004). *Cognitive Linguistics.* Cambridge: Cambridge University Press.

Dancygier, B., and Sweetser, E. (2014). *Figurative Language.* Cambridge: Cambridge University Press.

Dasgupta, S.N. (1922-1955). *A History of Indian Philosophy.* (Vol 1, 1922). London: Cambridge University Press.

Davison, A. (1981). 'Peculiar Passives'. *Language 56.* 42-66.

Delacy, R. (2001). *Read and Write Urdu Script.* London: Hodder Education.

Duggal, N.S. (2011). **ਪੰਜਾਬੀ ਵਿਆਕਰਨ ਤੇ ਰਚਨਾਵਲੀ panjābi viākaran te rachnāvalī**. Jalandhar: New Book Company.

Eliade, M. (1958). 'Time and Eternity in Indian Thought' in Campbell, J. (ed.) *Man and Time: Papers from the Eranos Yearbook.* London: Routledge & Kegan Paul.

Evans, V. (2014). *The Languge Myth: Why Language is Not an Instinct.* Cambridge: Cambridge University Press.

Evans, N. and Levinson, S.C. (2009). 'The Myth of Language Universals: Language Diversity and its Importance for Cognitive Science.' *Behavioural and Brain Sciences 32*: 429-92.

Everett, D. (2013). *Language The Cultural Tool.* London: Profile Books.

Fauconnier, G., and Turner, M. (2002). *The Way We think: Conceptual Blending and the Mind's Hidden Complexities.* New York: basic Books.

Feuerstein, G., Kak, S. and Frawley. D. (2005). *In Search of the Cradle of Civilisation: New Light on Ancient India.* New Delhi: Motilal Banarsidas.

Firth, J.R. (1957). *Papers in Linguistics 1934-1951.* London: Oxford University Press.

Gill, H.S. and Gleason, H.A. (1969). *A Reference Grammar of Punjabi.* Patiala: Punjabi University. (First published in Hartford in 1961.)

Goldberg, A.E. (1995). *Constructions: A Construction Grammar Approach to Argument Structure*. Chicago: University of Chicago Press.

Grierson, G. (1894–1927). *The Linguistic Survey of India.* Calcutta: Government of India Central Publication Branch.

Haas, W. (1957). 'Of Living Things'. *German Life and Letters 10* (89-96, 251–257).

Halliday, M.A.K. (1978). *Language as a Social Semiotic: The Social Interpretation of Language and Meaning.* London: Edward Arnold.

Huddleston, R. and Pullum, G.K. (2002). *The Cambridge Grammar of the English Language.* Cambridge: Cambridge University Press.

___ (2005). *A Student's Introduction to English Grammar.* Cambridge: Cambridge University Press.

Iyer, K.A.S. (1969). *Bhartṛhhari: A study of the Vākypadīya in the Light of the Ancient Commentaries.* Poona: Deccan College.

Jain, B.D. (1926). 'A Phonology of Panjabi as Spoken about Ludhiana'. Ph.D. thesis University of London.

Joos, M. (1957) (ed.) *Readings in Linguistics I.* Chicago: University of Chicago Press.

Kachru, Y. (1980). *Aspects of Hindi Grammar.* New Delhi: Manohar Publications.

Kazanas, N. (2015). *Vedic and Indo-European Studies.* Delhi: Aditya Prakashan.

Kellogg, S.H. (1875). *A Grammar of the Hindi Language.* Second edition of 1893 reprinted by Munshiran Manoharlal, New Delhi in 1972.

Kielhorn, F. (1962). *The Vyākaraṇa Mahābhaṣya of Patañjali*, Vol 1. (3rd Edition). Poona: Bhandarkar Oriental Research Institute.

Klein, W. (1994). *Time in Language.* London: Routledge.

Ladefoged, P. and Maddieson, I. (1996). *The Sounds of the World's Languages.* Oxford: Blackwell Publishing.

Lakoff, G. and Johnson, M. (1980). *Metaphors We Live By.* Chicago: University of Chicago Press.

___ (1999). *Philosophy in the Flesh.* New York: Basic Books.

Lal, Beehari (1867). ਪੰਜਾਬੀ ਬਿਆਕਰਣ **Panjābi Biākaraṇ**. Lahore.

Langacker, R.W. (2008). *Cognitive Grammar: A Basic Introduction.* Oxford: Oxford University Press.

Larsen-Freemen, D, and Cameron, L. (2008). *Complex Systems and Applied Linguistics.* Oxford: Oxford University Press.

Leech, G.N. (2006). *A Glossary of English Grammar.* Edinburgh: Edinburgh University Press.

Levins, R. and Lewontin, R. (1985). *The Dialectical Biologist.* Cambridge MA: Harvard University Press.

Lyons, J. (1967). 'A Note on Possessive, Existential, and Locative Sentences'. *Foundation of Language 3:* 390-96.

Mahal, I. (1998). ਸੁਰਾਂ ਦੇ ਸੁਦਾਗਰ **surā̃ de sudāgar**. Delhi: Navyug Publishers.

___ (2000). سُراں دے سوداگر **surā̃ de sudāgar.** Lahore: Chetar Publishers.

Masica, C.P. (1976). *Defining a Linguistic Area: South Asia.* Chicago: University of Chicago Press.

___ (1993). *The Indo-Aryan Languages.* Cambridge: Cambridge University Press.

Matthews, D. and Dalvi, M.K. (2014). *Complete Urdu.* London: Hodder Education.

Matthews, P.H. (2007). *Oxford Concise Dictionary of Linguistics.* (2nd Edition). Oxford: Oxford University Press.

Nabha, Kahn Singh (1930). ਗੁਰੁਸ਼ਬਦ ਰਤਨਾਕਰ ਮਹਾਨ ਕੋਸ਼ **guruśabad ratnākar mahān koś**. Reprinted by National Bookshop, Delhi in 1990.

Nesfield, J.C. (2013 (1898)). *Manual of English Grammar and Composition.* London: Read books.

Newton, E.P. (1898). *Punjabi Grammar with Exercises and Vocabulary.* Ludhiana.

Padam, P.S. (1954). ਪੰਜਾਬੀ ਬੋਲੀ ਦਾ ਇਤਿਹਾਸ **panjābī bolī dā itihās**. Patiala.

Pāṇini. See Vasu.

Pannikkar (1976). 'Time and History in the Tradition of India: Kala and Karma' in Gardet, L., Gurevich, A.J., Kagme, A. Lloyd, G.E.R., Neher, A., Panikkar, R., Pàttaro, G., and Ricoeur, P. (eds). *Cultures and Time: At the Crossroads of Culture*. Paris: Unesco Press.

Patañjali. See Kielhorn.

Phillauri. S.R. (1866). ਸਿੱਖਾਂ ਦੇ ਰਾਜ ਦੀ ਵਿਥਿਆ **sikkhān de rāj dī vik^{h}iā**. Ludhiana.

___ (1868). ਪੰਜਾਬੀ ਬਾਤ ਚੀਤ **panjābī bāt cīt**. Ludhiana.

Puar, J.S. (1990). *The Panjabi Verb Form and Function.* Patiala: Punjabi University.

Punjabi University, Patiala (1973). *Linguistic Atlas of the Punjab*. Patiala.

Punjabi University, Patiala (1994). *English-Punjabi Dictionary.* Patiala.

Punjabi University, Patiala (1994). *Punjabi-English Dictionary.* Patiala.

Quirk, R., Greenbaum, S., Leech, G., and Svartvik, J. (1985). *A Comprehensive Grammar of the English Language*. London: Longman.

Rao, V.S. (1969). *The Philosophy of the Sentence and its Parts.* New Delhi: Munshiram Manoharlal.

Ryding, K.C. (2005). *A Reference Grammar of Modern Standard Arabic.* Cambridge: Cambridge University Press.

Seely, J. (1977). 'An Ergative Historiography'. *Historiographia Linguistica 4:* 191-206.

Sekhon, S.S. (1961). ਪੰਜਾਬੀ ਬੋਲੀ ਦਾ ਇਤਿਹਾਸ **panjābī bolī dā itihās**. Patiala: Language Department.

Sidhu, G.S. (2004). *Panjab and Panjabi.* London: Guru Nanak Charitable Trust.

Singh, G.B. (1950). ਗੁਰਮੁਖੀ ਲਿਪੀ ਦਾ ਜਨਮ ਤੇ ਵਿਕਾਸ **gurmukʰī lipī dā janam te vikās**. Chandigarh: Panjab University Publication Bureau.

Singh, Harkirat (1988) (ed.) ਪੰਜਾਬੀ ਸ਼ਬਦ-ਰੂਪ ਤੇ ਸ਼ਬਦ-ਜੋੜ ਕੋਸ਼ **panjābī śabad-rūp te śabad-joṛ koś**. Patiala: Punjabi University.

___ (2011). ਗੁਰਬਾਣੀ ਦੀ ਭਾਸ਼ਾ ਤੇ ਵਿਆਕਰਨ **gurbāṇī dī bʰāśā te viākaran**. Patiala: Punjabi University.

Singh, J.D. (1971). 'Pāṇini's Theory of Language' in Ghatge, A.M., Bhat, M.M., Kulkarni, E.D., and Pandit, P.B. (eds) *Proceedings of the First All- India Conference of Linguists 1970.* Poona: Linguistic Society of India.

Singh, Jawahir (1930). *A Guide to Panjabi.* Reprinted by Asian Educational Services, Delhi.

Singh, Jodh (1959). Preface to Duni Chandra 1959.

Singh, Karam (1929). ਨਵੀਨ ਪੰਜਾਬੀ ਵਿਆਕਰਣ ਭਾਗ 3 **navīn panjābī viakaraṇ bhāg 3.** Amritsar.

Singh, Kirpal (ed) (1969). ਜਨਮ ਸਾਖੀ ਪਰੰਪਰਾ **janam sākʰī paramparā**. Patiala: Punjabi University.

Singh, Ram (1924). ਵੱਡਾ ਪੰਜਾਬੀ ਵਿਆਕਰਣ **vaḍḍā panjābī viakaraṇ**. Amritsar.

Singh, Randhir (1954). ਗੁਰਬਾਣੀ ਲਗਾਂ ਮਾਤ੍ਰਾਂ ਦੀ ਵਿਲੱਖਣਤਾ **gurbāṇī lagā̃ mātrā̃ dā villakʰaṇtā**. Ludhiana.

Singh, Sahib (1935). ਗੁਰਬਾਣੀ ਵਿਆਕਰਣ **gurbāṇī viākaraṇ.** Amritsar.

Slobin, D. (1987). 'Thinking for Speaking' in *Proceedings of the Thirteenth Annual Meeting of the Berkeley Linguistics Society* (1987 pp. 435–445).

___ (1996). 'From "Thought and Language" to "Thinking for Speaking"' in Gumperz, J.J. and Levinson, S.C. (eds) *Rethinking Linguistic Relativity.* Cambridge: Cambridge University Press.

Stcherbatsky. T. (1923). *The Central Conception of Buddhism.* London Royal Asiatic Society.

Taylor, J.R. (2002). *Cognitive Grammar.* Oxford: Oxford University Press.

Thomas, E.J. (1951). *The History of Buddhist Thought.* (2nd Edition). London: Routledge and Kegan Paul.

Tolstaya, N.I. (1981). *The Panjabi Language: A Descriptive Grammar.* London: Routledge and Kegan Paul.

Tomasello (2005). *Constructing a Language: A Usage-based Theory of Language Acquisition.* Cambridge MA: Harvard University Press.

___ (2009). 'Universal Grammar is Dead' comments (pp. 470-471) in Evans and Levinson 2009.

Varma, S. (1961 (1929)). *Critical Studies in the Phonetic Observations of Indian Grammarians.* Reprinted in 1961 by Mushi Ram Manohar Lal, Delhi.

Vasu, S.C. (1891). *The Aṣṭādhyāyī of Pāṇini*. Reprinted by Motilal Banarsidas, New Delhi in 1980.

Whitney, W.D. (1972 (1893)). 'On Recent Studies in Hindu Grammar'. Reprinted in J.F. Stall (ed.) 1972. *A Reader on Sanskrit Grammarians.* Cambridge MA: MIT Press.

Wittgenstein, L. (2009 (1953)). *Philosophical Investigations*. 4th Edition 2009. Chichester: Wiley-Blackwell.

Index of Grammatical Words

This index lists (in the order of a Gurmukhi Panjabi dictionary) the grammatical words used in the book. The page numbers indicate where the particular word is first introduced and/or explained in detail. Page references printed in *italics* indicate tables. The **adjectival** words are given in the **masculine singular** form only.

1. Pronouns and related words

Personal pronouns

ਅਸਾਂ	**asā̃**	117
ਅਸੀਂ	**asī̃**	117
ਤੁਸਾਂ	**tusā̃**	117
ਤੁਸੀਂ	**tusī̃**	117
ਤੂੰ	**tū̃**	*117,119*
ਮੈਂ	**mã^{i}**	*117,119*

Personal pronominal adjectives

ਅਸਾਂ ਦਾ	**asā̃ dā**	*119*
ਸਾਡਾ	**sāḍā**	*119*
ਤੇਰਾ	**merā**	*119*
ਤੁਸਾਂ ਦਾ	**tusā̃ dā**	*119*
ਤੁਹਾਡਾ	**tuhāḍā**	*119*
ਮੇਰਾ	**merā**	*119*

Personal pronouns with postpositions ਤੋਂ **tõ** and ਨੂੰ **nū̃**

ਅਸਾਂ ਤੋਂ	**asā̃ tõ**	117
ਅਸਾਂ ਨੂੰ	**asā̃ nū̃**	117
ਸਾਥੋਂ	**sāt^{h}õ**	*117*
ਸਾਨੂੰ	**sānū̃**	*117*
ਤੁਸਾਂ ਤੋਂ	**tusā̃ tō̃**	*117*
ਤੁਸਾਂ ਨੂੰ	**tusā̃ nū̃**	*117*
ਤੁਹਾਥੋਂ	**tuhāt^{h}ō̃**	*117*
ਤੁਹਾਨੂੰ	**tuhānū̃**	*117*
ਤੈਥੋਂ	**ta^{i}t^{h}ō̃**	*117*
ਤੈਨੂੰ	**ta^{i}nū̃**	*117*
ਤੈਂ	**tã^{i}**	117
ਮੈਥੋਂ	**ma^{i}t^{h}ō̃**	*117*

ਹੋ	**ho**	*183*
ਸਕ	**sak**	*183*
ਚਲ	**cal**	*183*
ਚੁਕ	**cuk**	*183*
ਛੱਡ	**c^{h}aḍḍ**	*182*
ਜਾ	**jā**	*182*
ਦੇ	**de**	*182*
ਨਿਕਲ਼	**nikal**	*183*
ਪੈ	**pa^{i}**	*182,* 260, 261
ਬੈਠ	**ba^{i}ṭ^{h}**	*182*
ਮਾਰ	**mār**	*182*
ਰਹਿ	**ra^{i}h**	160, *182,* 261
ਰੱਖ	**rakk^{h}**	*182*
ਲੈ	**la^{i}**	*182*

6. Co-ordinators

Ø		309
ਉੱਤੋਂ	**uttõ**	310, 311
ਅਤੇ (ਤੇ)	**ate (te)**	309
ਇਸ ਕਰਕੇ	**is karke**	312
ਇਸ ਲਈ	**is laī**	312
ਸਗੋਂ	**sagõ**	311
ਸਿਰਫ਼ ਹੀ ਨਹੀਂ. . . ਸਗੋਂ ਵੀ **sirf hī nahī̃... sagõ**		310
ਸੋ	**so**	312
ਕਾਹਦਾ	**kāhdā**	314
ਚਾਹੇ. . . ਚਾਹੇ	**cahe...cahe**	311
ਜਾਂ. . . ਜਾਂ	**jā̃...jā̃**	311
ਜਾਂ . . . ਜਾਂ ਫਿਰ	**jā̃...jā̃ p^{h}ir**	311
ਥੋੜੇ	**t^{h}oṛe**	
ਸਿਰਫ਼ ਨਹੀਂ. . . ਸਗੋਂ **sirf nahī̃...sagõ**		314
ਨਾ. . . ਨਾ	**nā ...nā**	311
ਨਾਲ਼ੇ. . . ਨਾਲ਼ੇ	**nāḷe ...nāḷe**	312
ਨਿਰਾ ਨਹੀਂ. . . ਸਗੋਂ **nirā nahī sagõ**		310
ਪਰ **par**		311

7. Subordinators

ਹਾਲਾਂਕਿ	**hālā̃ki**	324
ਕਿ	**ki**	311, 323
ਕਿਉਂਕਿ	**kiũki**	323
ਜਿਵੇਂ	**jivẽ**	324
ਜਿਵੇਂ ਕਿ	**jive ki**	324
ਤਾਂਕਿ	**tā̃ki**	323
ਤਾਂ ਜੁ	**tā̃ ju**	323
ਜੇ	**je**	324

The **J-words** listed above are often used to introduce **adjectival (relative) clauses** and **adverbial clauses.**

Subject Index

This index of grammatical categories and subjects is intended to be used in conjunction with the Table of Contents, where the reader can find a clearer view of how the material is arranged, particularly the topics covered extensively. Many of the terms that appear in this index are also defined in the Glossary. Panjabi grammatical words are listed separately in the Index of Grammatical Words. Page references printed in **bold** type below indicate major topics. The page references printed in *italics* indicate the groups of words also included in the Index of Grammatical Words, and the page references in ***bold italics*** indicate diagrams or maps.

A